OUR SYSTEM FOR SUCCESS IS EXPAN

NO SYSTEM OFFERS MORE OPTIONS

GLEIM/DELANEY
CPA EXAMINATION REVIEW:
MICROCOMPUTER DIAGNOSTICS
FOR THE IBM-pc

- Designed to be used with and enhance the Gleim/Delaney books.
- The program allows you to switch back and forth between a STUDY and EXAM mode, and create the type of study environment that's correct for you.
- In STUDY mode, the program provides instant feedback and rationale for correct and incorrect answers.
- In EXAM mode, the program builds a record of grade analysis, assessment of knowledge by topic, a report card, and an evaluation of important time considerations.

DELANEY/GLEIM
CPA EXAMINATION REVIEW:
AUDIO CASSETTE PROGRAM

- Now you can study wherever there is a tape player (in the car, the yard, or while exercising).
- Organized around the same modular format as our 2 and 3 volume books.
- Written and recorded especially for CPA Exam candidates – this is **not** a "re-hash" of old materials or lectures.
- 48 cassettes in all – Auditing (12 cassettes), Theory and Practice (24 cassettes), and Business Law (12 cassettes).
- Cassette modules prepared by Kurt Pany, Arizona State University; Harold Wright and John R. Simon, Northern Illinois University; David Buehlmann, University of Nebraska; Edward C. Foth, DePaul University.
- Sampler cassette available upon request.

See order form on preceding page.

IF FOUND, please notify and arrange return to owner. This text is important for the owner's preparation for the Uniform Certified Public Accountant Examination.

Name of CPA Candidate ______________________________

Address ______________________________

City, State, Zip ______________________________

Telephone ( ) ______________________________

Additional texts are available at your local bookstore

or directly from John Wiley and Sons, Inc.

Order information and order forms can be found at the back of the book

—————— †† ——————

The Authors invite readers to correspond directly with them.

A form for this purpose is provided inside the back cover.

Special Insert for
DELANEY/GLEIM AUDIO CASSETTE
Users

The following questions are discussed on Introductory Tape B of the *Delaney/Gleim CPA Examination Review: Audio Cassettes,* 1985 Edition. These questions are included in this volume, but are identified by a different number than is indicated on the audio locator and cross-reference sheet. The table below provides the cross-reference to these questions in this volume.

Module	*Question*	*Question number in Business Law 1986 Edition*
	Multiple Choice	
13	Business Law 584,L1,4	3
	Essay and Problems	
12	Business Law 1183,L3b	Problem 1

CPA

EXAMINATION REVIEW

BUSINESS LAW

1986 EDITION

Patrick R. Delaney, Ph.D., CPA
Northern Illinois University
DeKalb, Illinois

&

Irvin N. Gleim, Ph.D., CPA
University of Florida
Gainesville, Florida

JOHN WILEY & SONS
New York Chichester Brisbane Toronto Singapore

Permissions

The following items copyright © by the American Institute of Certified Public Accountants, Inc. are reprinted with permission:

1. *Uniform CPA Examination Questions and Answers,* 1974, 1975, 1976, 1977, 1978, 1979, 1980, 1981, 1982, 1983, 1984, and 1985. Those which have been adapted are so identified.
2. *Content Specification Outlines for the Uniform Certified Public Accountant Examination,* Board of Examiners.

ISBN 0–471–82928–5

10 9 8 7 6 5 4 3 2 1

PREFACE

The objectives of this review text are to provide study outlines of business law as it is tested on the Uniform CPA Examination, to provide CPA candidates with recent examination questions organized by topic, and to explain the AICPA unofficial answers to the questions included in this text.

This review manual is organized into 16 manageable study units (modules) to assist candidates in organizing their study programs. The clear, concise phraseology of the study outlines is supplemented by brief examples and illustrations designed to help candidates quickly understand and retain the material. The multiple choice questions in this book are an effective means of studying the material tested on past exams; however, it is also necessary to work with essay questions to develop the solutions approach (the ability to solve CPA essay questions efficiently). To assist candidates in developing a solutions approach and to assist them in reviewing the material tested, outlines of the unofficial answers published by the AICPA are provided. A significant feature of this book concerns the tables summarizing the frequency and extent to which topical areas have been tested on each of the last nine exams. Our classification of the coverage of these exams is based on the AICPA's Revised Content Specification Outlines for the Uniform Certified Public Accountant Examination (effective for the May 1986 exam). A Sample Examination for Business Law is included in Appendix A at the end of this book. The content of this exam is based on an analysis of the last six exams.

This book has been updated and revised to include new authoritative pronouncements through November 15, 1985. All of the multiple choice questions from the November 1985 examination have been added to the modules to which they pertain. The schedule below lists the essay questions from the May 1985 exam which have been added to the problem material appearing in *CPA Examination Review*, Volume II, Twelfth Edition (June 1985).

Module	*Module number*	*Added to this Business Law manual*
Contracts (CONT)	7	585,L2
Accountant's Legal Liability (ACCO)	18	585,L4

New questions illustrate the type and format of questions being used on the examination. Changes in the Board of Examiners, their philosophy, and most important, the AICPA examination staff, result in changing types and formats of questions.

A major feature of this text is the grouping of the multiple choice questions into topical categories. These categories correspond to the sequencing of the text material as it appears within each of the corresponding modules in this manual. Another feature is the inclusion of **Mini Outlines** of each module to be used as a "final review."

The authors are indebted to the American Institute of Certified Public Accountants for permission to reproduce and adapt examination materials from past certification examinations.

The authors deeply appreciate the enthusiastic and dedicated attitude of the many CPA candidates with whom the authors have had the pleasure to work. As always, the authors welcome any comments concerning materials contained in or omitted from this text. A form for this purpose is provided inside the back cover.

Please read Chapter 1 carefully, especially "Attributes of Examination Success" and "Purpose and Organization of This Review Textbook."

Good Luck on the Exam,

Patrick R. Delaney
Irvin N. Gleim
November 15, 1985

ABOUT THE AUTHORS

Patrick R. Delaney is Professor of Accountancy at Northern Illinois University. He received his PhD in Accountancy from the University of Illinois. He is past president of the Rockford Chapter, National Association of Accountants; is Vice Chairman of the Illinois CPA Society's Accounting Principles Committee; and has served on numerous other professional committees. He is a member of the American Accounting Association, American Institute of Certified Public Accountants, and National Association of Accountants. Professor Delaney has published in *The Accounting Review* and is a recipient of NIU's Excellence in Teaching Award and Lewis University's Distinguished Alumnus Award. He has been involved in NIU's CPA Review Course as director and instructor and has served as an instructor of NASBA's Critique Program.

Irvin N. Gleim is Professor of Accounting at the University of Florida and is a CPA, CIA and CMA. He received his PhD in Accountancy from the University of Illinois. He is a member of the American Institute of Certified Public Accountants, Florida Institute of Certified Public Accountants, American Accounting Association, American Business Law Association, Institute of Internal Auditors, Institute of Management Accounting, and National Association of Accountants. He has published professional articles in the *Journal of Accountancy, The Accounting Review,* and *The American Business Law Journal.* He has developed and taught both proprietary and university CPA review courses. He is author of *CIA Examination Review* and *CMA Examination Review*, both published by Accounting Publications, Inc.

ABOUT THE CONTRIBUTORS

Martin A. Bubley, JD, MBA, CPA, prepared some revisions in several modules.

Duane R. Lambert, JD, MBA, CPA, is an Associate Professor of Business Administration at California State University, Hayward where he teaches courses in Business Law and Accounting. He also has been a Visiting Lecturer and a Visiting Associate Professor at the University of California, Berkeley. He is a member of the American Bar Association, the American Accounting Association, the American Business Law Association, the Western Regional Business Law Association, the Utah Bar Association and the Section of Corporation, Banking and Business Law in the American Bar Association. Professor Lambert has "Big Eight" experience and has taught CPA review courses for the past several CPA examinations. He wrote new material and revised modules to reflect current treatment for the CPA examination.

Harold O. Wright, JD, is Coordinator and Assistant Professor of Business Law at Northern Illinois University. He has taught in NIU's CPA Review Course for the past eleven years, has served as an instructor of NASBA's Critique Program, and is a recipient of NIU's Excellence in Teaching Award. Professor Wright prepared new material and the multiple choice answer explanations, updated questions in need of change to reflect the most recent law, selected the problem material, and prepared the index.

TABLE OF CONTENTS

As explained in Chapter 1, this book is organized into 16 modules (manageable study units). For easy reference, numbered index tabs appear on the first page of each module. The numbering of the modules commences with number 7 to correspond with the numbering system used in our two-volume set.

Acknowledgements

Writing an annualized text is always a publishing event and a rejuvenating human experience. The authors are most grateful to the many users of previous editions, both instructors and students who have so generously shared with us their satisfaction with our work and their suggestions for changes and improvements. We hope that this will continue for we have benefited from those communications.

This work continues to be a "community effort." In addition to those colleagues cited as contributors above, we would like to acknowledge and thank those many friends who gave us so many devoted hours to bring this edition to you so quickly after the November 1985 Examination: Mary Ann Benson, Jill Coerver, Sandy Donnelly, Joyce Dvorak, Lee Gampfer, Penelope Le Few, Fran Miller, Pam Miller, Denise Smith, and Eileen Thorsen.

OTHER CONTRIBUTORS AND REVIEWERS

The following individuals assisted in the preparation of this manual by reviewing revisions of the outlines and drafting and reviewing explanations of the multiple choice answers.

Michael Baker, MBA, CPA, is employed by Price Waterhouse.

William R. Hartig, MBA, CPA, is an accountant with Allstate Insurance Company.

Edward Oehler, BS, CPA, CMA, is a candidate for the MIS degree and a Graduate Teaching Assistant at Northern Illinois University.

Douglas M. Stein, BS (Accountancy and Computer Science), CMA, CPA, is a candidate for the MAS degree at Northern Illinois University.

CHAPTER ONE

BEGINNING YOUR CPA REVIEW PROGRAM

To maximize the efficiency of your review program, begin by studying (not merely reading) this chapter and the next three chapters of this volume. They have been carefully organized and written to provide you with important information to assist you in successfully completing the business law part of the CPA exam. Beyond providing a comprehensive outline to help you organize the material tested on the business law exam, Chapter 1 will assist you in organizing a study program to prepare for the business law exam (self-discipline is essential).

GENERAL COMMENTS ON THE EXAMINATION

Successful completion of the Uniform CPA Examination in Business Law is an attainable goal. Keep this point foremost in your mind as you study the first four chapters in this volume and develop your study plan.

Purpose of the Examination[1]

The CPA examination is designed to measure basic technical competence including

1. Technical knowledge and application of such knowledge
2. Exercise of good judgment
3. Understanding of professional responsibilities

The CPA examination is one of many screening devices to assure the competence of those licensed to perform the attest function and to render professional accounting services. Other screening devices are educational requirements, ethics examinations, etc.

The examination appears to test the material covered in accounting programs of the better business schools. It also appears to be based upon the body of knowledge essential for the practice of public accounting and perhaps specifically the audit of a medium-sized client. Since the examination is primarily a textbook or academic examination, you should plan on taking it as soon as possible after completing your undergraduate accounting education.

The difficulty of the examination is undoubtedly increasing. This phenomenon is directly related to the rapid expansion of accounting as a body of knowledge. The Institute has suggested that the level of the examination will proceed to the body of knowledge attainable from a five-year college accounting program.

Examination Content

Guidance concerning topical content of the CPA examination in business law can be found in a document prepared by the Board of Examiners of the AICPA entitled Content Specification Outlines for the Uniform Certified Public Accountant Examination.

The Board's objective in preparing this detailed listing of topics tested on the exam is to help "in assuring the continuing validity and reliability of the Uniform CPA Examination." These outlines are an excellent source of guidance concerning the areas and emphasis to be given each area on future exams.

---

[1]The following general comments are largely adapted from Information for CPA Candidates published by the American Institute of Certified Public Accountants. Information for CPA Candidates is usually sent to CPA candidates by their state board of accountancy as they apply to sit for the CPA examination. If you will not be immediately applying to your state board of accountancy to sit for the exam, you may wish to request a complimentary copy from your state board or the AICPA. (Write to AICPA, Examination Division, 1211 Avenue of the Americas, New York, New York 10036.)

We have included the content outline for business law at the beginning of Chapter 5. Additionally, we have used the outline as the basis for our frequency analysis of the last nine exams (Nov. 1981 - Nov. 1985). The outline/frequency analysis should be used as an indication of the topics' relative importance on past exams. The Board of Examiners has issued a revision of the Content Specification Outlines which is effective beginning with the May 1986 Exam. Any changes from the previous coverage are noted in the affected outlines/frequency analyses and study modules in this volume.

The AICPA does not test new law until approximately 12 months after it is enacted. It is quite likely, however, that recent law (within 12 months) will be germane to some questions, because the AICPA frequently develops questions dealing with current issues and controversies in the accounting profession (the areas in which new law is likely). When a question appears on a topic on which a law has been enacted in the previous 12 months, the graders give credit for the old law as well as the new law.

Schedule of Examinations

The Uniform Certified Public Accountant Examination is given twice a year, usually the first consecutive Wednesday-Thursday-Friday in May and November. The subject and time schedules are

CPA EXAM SCHEDULE AND EXPECTED FORMAT

	Wednesday	Thursday	Friday
A.M.		Auditing 8:30 a.m. – 12 noon 5 Questions: 1 Question of 60 M/C 4 Essays	Business Law 8:30 a.m. – 12 noon 5 Questions: 1 Question of 60 M/C 4 Essays
P.M.	Practice I 1:30 – 6:00 p.m. 5 Questions: 3 Questions of 20 M/C each 2 Problems	Practice II 1:30 – 6:00 p.m. 5 Questions: 3 Questions of 20 M/C each 2 Problems	Theory 1:30 – 5:00 p.m. 5 Questions: 1 Question of 60 M/C 4 Essays

Recent exams have followed the format presented in the schedule above. Currently, the exam consists of 60% multiple choice (M/C) in all parts, but the time allocations within each part are different. For example, the 3 multiple choice questions on the Practice I exam were given 45-55 minutes each, for an average of about 2 1/2 minutes per individual multiple choice item. The 60 multiple choice items in Business Law were assigned a time range of 110-130 minutes, or about 2 minutes per question. You should note the suggested time limits for each question as you begin working the exam.

You receive four scores; accounting practice is considered one section. Seventy-five is considered passing. Rules for partial credit on the examination vary from state to state (see "State Boards of Accountancy" below.)

The dates for future CPA examinations are

1986	May 7, 8, 9	1987	May 6, 7, 8
	November 5, 6, 7		November 4, 5, 6

State Boards of Accountancy

The right to practice public accounting as a CPA is governed by individual state statutes. While some rules regarding the practice of public accounting vary from state to state, all State Boards of Accountancy use the Uniform CPA Examination and AICPA advisory grading service as one of the requirements to practice public accounting. Every candidate should inquire of his/her State Board of Accountancy to determine the requirements to sit for the exam, e.g., education, filing dates, references, and fees. A frequent problem candidates encounter is failure to apply by the deadline. APPLY TO SIT FOR THE EXAMINATION EARLY. ALSO, YOU SHOULD USE EXTREME CARE IN FILLING OUT APPLICATION AND MAILING REQUIRED MATERIALS TO YOUR STATE BOARD OF ACCOUNTANCY. If possible, have some friend review your completed application before mailing with check, photos, etc. Too many candidates are turned down for sitting for a particular CPA examination simply because of minor technical details overlooked (photos not signed on back, check not enclosed, question not answered on application, etc.). BECAUSE OF VERY HIGH VOLUME OF APPLICATIONS RECEIVED IN THE MORE POPULOUS STATES, THE ADMINISTRATIVE STAFF DOES NOT HAVE TIME TO CALL OR WRITE TO CORRECT MINOR DETAILS AND WILL SIMPLY REJECT YOUR APPLICATION. This can be extremely disappointing particularly after spending many hours in preparing to sit for a particular exam.

The various state requirements to take the CPA exam are listed on the following page. The data are based on the CCH Accountancy Law Reporter, AICPA Legislative Reference Service, and a survey of state boards. Note that the presentation is condensed and generalized; there are numerous "alternatives," etc. Be sure to inquire of your state board for specified and current requirements.

It is possible for candidates to sit for the examination in another state as an out-of-state candidate. Candidates desiring to do so should contact the State Board of Accountancy in their home state. Addresses of all 54 Boards of Accountancy appear on the next page.

INDIVIDUAL STATE CPA REQUIREMENTS

Compiled May 1, 1985

	State Board address	Educ.[1]	Application deadline First time	Re-exam	Exam[2] fee	Cond. requirements[3]	Life of[4] condition	Yrs. exp.	Cont. ed. requirements hrs./yrs.
AL	20 Commerce Row, 529 S. Perry St., Montgomery 36104	4	2-28,8-31	3-31,9-30	$125	2 or P	4NE	2-3	40 1
AK	Pouch D, Juneau 99811	2-4	60 days	same	$ 50	2 or P	5Y	2-4	60 2
AZ	3110 N. 19th Ave., Suite 140, Phoenix 85015	4	2-28,8-31	same	$100	2 or P	3Y	2	80 2
AR	1515 W. Seventh St., Ste. 320, Little Rock 72201	4	60 days	30 days	$100	2 or P,50	5NE	1-2	40 1 120 3
CA	2135 Butano Dr., Ste. 112, Sacramento 95825	0-4	3-1,9-1	same	$ 75	2 or P	3Y	2-4	80 2
CO	617 State Services Bldg., Denver 80203	4	3-1,9-1	same	varies	2 or P	5NE	0-1	80 2
CT	165 Capitol Ave., Hartford 06106	4	60 days	same	$100	2 or P,50	3Y	3	40 1
DE	P.O. Box 1401, Dover 19901	2	3-1,9-1	same	$125	2 or P,75	5NE	2-4	Yes[5]
DC	614 H St., NW, Rm. 923, Washington 20001	4	90 days	60 days	$100	2 or P	5NE	2	Yes
FL	4001 NW 43rd St., Ste. 16, Gainesville 32606	4[5]	2-1,8-1	3-1,9-1	$125	2 or P,50	5NE	0-1	16-64 2[5]
GA	166 Pryor St., SW, Atlanta 30303	4	2-1,8-1	3-1,9-1	$125	2,40[5]	5NE	2-5	60 2
GU	P.O. Box P, Agana 96910	4	60 days	same	$ 35	2 or P,50	6NE	1-2	
HI	P.O. Box 3469, Honolulu 96801	5	3-1,9-1	same	$100	2 or P,50	6NE	2	80 2
ID	700 W. State St., 2nd Fl., Boise 83720	4	3-1,9-1	same	$ 75	2 or P,50	6NE	1-2	80 2
IL	10 Administration Bldg., 506 S. Wright, Urbana 61801	4	2-27,8-28	same	$125	2 or P,50	3 of N6E	0	
IN	1021 State Office Bldg., Indianapolis 46204	4	3-1,9-1	same	$125	2,50	6NE	2-6	80 2
IA	Executive Hills, West, 1209 Court Ave., Des Moines 50319	4	2-28,8-31	same	$ 90	2 or P,50	5NE	1-3	120 3
KS	503 Kansas, Rm. 236, Topeka 66603	4-5	3-15,9-15	same	$100	2,50	4 of N6E	2[5]	40 1
KY	332 W. Broadway, Ste. 310, Louisville 40202	4	3-1,9-1	same	$ 75	2 or P,50	6NE	2-4	20 1
LA	1515 ITM Bldg., 2 Canal St., New Orleans 70130	4[5]	3-1,9-1	same	$ 75	2,50	1 of N4E	2-6	120 3
ME	84 Harlow St., Bangor 04401	4	4-15,10-1	same	$ 80	2 or P	3Y	1-2	12 1
MD	501 St. Paul Place, Rm. 902, Baltimore 21202	4	60 days	same	$ 70	2 or P,50	5NE	0	40 1
MA	100 Cambridge St., Rm. 1524, Boston 02202	4	42 days	same	$115	2 or P,50	6NE	2-9	80 2
MI	P.O. Box 30018, Lansing 48909	4	60 days	same	$100	2 or P,50	6NE	2	40 1
MN	Metro Square Bldg., 5th Fl., St. Paul 55101	4[5]	60 days	same	$100	2,50	5NE	1-6	120 3
MS	P.O. Box 55447, Jackson 39216	4	3-15,9-15	same	$ 92	2 or P,45	8NE	1-3	120 3
MO	P.O. Box 613, Jefferson City 65102	4[5]	3-1,9-1	same	$100	2 or P,50	6NE	0	–[5]
MT	1424 9th Ave., Helena 59620-0407	4	3-15,9-15	same	$100	2 or P,50	5NE	1-2	120 3
NE	P.O. Box 94725, Lincoln 68509	0-4	3-31,9-30	same	$ 90	2 or P,50	5NE	2-4	120 3
NV	One East Liberty St., Suite 614, Reno 89501	4	3-1,9-1	same	$ 75	2 or P,35	6NE	2-4	80 2[5]
NH	Two and One-Half Beacon St., Concord 03301-4447	4	4-1,10-1	same	$125	2,50	5Y	1-2	80 2[5]
NJ	1100 Raymond Blvd., Rm. 507-A, Newark 07102	4	2-1,8-1	same	$100	2 or P,50[5]	6NE	2-4	
NM	P.O. Drawer 8770, Albuquerque 87198	4	3-1,9-1	same	$ 60	2	3Y	1	120 3
NY	Cultural Education Center, Albany 12230	4	90 days	60 days	$245	2 or P	6NE	1-2	
NC	P.O. Box 12827, Raleigh 27605	2	2-28,8-31	same	$125	2 or P	5NE	1-5	Yes[5]
ND	Box 8104, Univ. Sta., Grand Forks 58202	0	3-15,9-15	same	$100	2 or P	5NE	0-4	120 3
OH	65 S. Front St., Ste. 222, Columbus 43215	4	3-1,9-1	4-1,10-1	$100	1	8Y	1-4	120 3
OK	265 West Ct., 4545 Lincoln Blvd., Oklahoma City 73105	0-4[5]	60 days	same	$100	2 or P	1 of 3 N6E	0-3	24 1
OR	403 Labor & Industries Bldg., Salem 97310	0-4	3-1,9-1	same	$ 75	2 or P,50	6NE	1-2	80 2
PA	P.O. Box 2649, Harrisburg 17105-2649	4	2-15,8-15	3-1,9-1	$ 80	1,20	Unlimited	1-2	80 2
PR	Box 3271, San Juan 00904	0-4[5]	60 days	same	$ 50	2	Unlimited	0-6	
RI	100 N. Main St., Providence 02903	4	45 days	same	$100	2 or P	Unlimited	1-2	120 3
SC	P.O. Box 11376, Columbia 29211	4	5 weeks or 35 days	same	$100	2 or P,40	3NE	2	60 2
SD	1509 S. Minnesota Ave., Ste. 1, Sioux Falls 57105	2-4	50 days	same	$165	2 or P,50	4Y	2	120 3
TN	408 Doctors Building, 706 Church St., Nashville 37219	4	3-1,9-1	same	$ 75	2 or P,50	6NE or 3Y	2-3	120 3
TX	1033 LaPosada, Ste. 340, Austin 78752-3892	2	2-28,8-31	same	$100	2	5Y	1-6	
UT	Heber M. Wells Bldg., 160 E. 300 S., Box 45802, Salt Lake City 84145	4	60 days	same	$ 75	2 or P,50	6NE	1-2	80 2
VT	109 State St., Montpelier 05602	0	4-1,10-1	same	$100	2 or P	6NE	2	80 2
VI	Royal Strand Bldg., Christiansted, St. Croix 00820	0	3-15,9-15	same	$100	2	Unlimited	2-6	
VA	3600 West Broad St., Richmond 23230	4	60 days	same	$ 85	2 or P,50	5NE	2,3&4	
WA	210 E. Union, Ste. H, EP-21, Box 9131, Olympia 98504	4	3-1,9-1	same	$ 75	2 or P,50	6NE	1	80 2
WV	825 Charleston National Plaza, Charleston 25301	4	3-1,9-1	same	$ 40[5]	1	3Y	0	
WI	P.O. Box 8936, Madison 53708	4	3-1,9-1	same	$ 50	2,50	2 of N4E	1½	
WY	Barrett Bldg., 3rd Fl., Cheyenne 82002	4	3-15,9-15	same	$125	2 or P	3Y	2	120 3

[1] *Years of higher education*

[2] *First-time fee*

[3] *Number of parts, specific parts, and minimum scores on parts failed*

[4] *Y = years; NE = next exams*

[5] *Check with your local State Board for specific requirements*

ATTRIBUTES OF EXAMINATION SUCCESS

Your objective in preparing for the CPA exam in business law is to pass. Other objectives such as learning new and reviewing old material should be secondary. The five attributes of examination success discussed below are <u>essential</u>. You should study the attributes and work toward achieving/developing each of them <u>before</u> the next examination.

1. Knowledge of Material

Two points are relevant to "knowledge of material" as an attribute of examination success. <u>First</u>, there is a distinct difference between being familiar with material and knowing the material. Frequently we (you) confuse familiarity with knowledge. Can you remember when you just could not answer an examination question or did poorly on an examination, but maintained to yourself or your instructor that you knew the material? You probably were only familiar with the material. On the CPA examination, familiarity is insufficient; you must know the material. Discussion of the material (knowledge) is required on the CPA examination. This text contains outlines of the topical areas in business law. Return to the original material, e.g., your business law textbook, UCC Code Sections, etc., when the outlines less than reinforce material you already know. <u>Second</u>, The Uniform Certified Public Accountant Examination in Business Law tests a literally overwhelming amount of material at a rigorous level. <u>Furthermore</u>, as noted earlier, the CPA exam tests new material. In other words, you are not only responsible for material you <u>should</u> have learned in your business law course(s), but also for all new developments in business law.

2. Solutions Approach

The solutions approach is a systematic approach to solving the questions found on the CPA examination. Many candidates know the material fairly well when they sit for the CPA exam, but they do not know how to take the examination. Candidates generally neither work nor answer questions efficiently in terms of time or grades.

The solutions approach permits you to avoid drawing "blanks" on CPA exam questions; using the solutions approach coupled with grader orientation (see the next side heading) allows you to pick up a sizable number of points on questions testing material with which you are not familiar.

Chapter 3 outlines the solutions approach for essay questions and multiple choice questions. Example questions are worked as well as explained.

3. Grader Orientation

Your score on each section of the exam is determined by the sum of points assigned to individual questions. Thus, you must attempt to maximize your points on each individual question. The name of the game is satisfy the grader, as s/he is the one who awards you points. Your answer and the grading guide (which conforms closely to the unofficial answer) are the basis for the assignment of points.

This text helps you develop grader orientation by analyzing AICPA grading procedures and grading guides (this is explained further in Chapter 2). The authors believe that the solutions approach and grader orientation, properly developed, are worth at least 10 to 15 points on each section to most candidates.

4. Examination Strategy

Prior to sitting for the examination, it is important to develop an examination strategy, i.e., a preliminary inventory of the questions, the order of working questions, etc.

Your ability to cope successfully with 3 1/2 hours of examination can be improved by

a. Recognizing the importance and usefulness of an examination strategy
b. Using Chapter 4 "Taking the Examination" and previous examination experience to develop a "personal strategy" for the exam
c. Testing your "personal strategy" on recent CPA questions under examination conditions (using no reference material and with a time limit)

5. Examination Confidence

You need confidence to endure the physical and mental demands of 3 1/2 hours of test-taking under tremendous pressure. Examination confidence develops from proper preparation for the exam including mastery of the first four attributes of examination success. Examination confidence is also necessary to be able to overcome the initial frustration with questions for which you may not be specifically prepared.

This study manual, properly used, should contribute to your examination confidence. The systematic outlines herein will provide you with a sense of organization such that as you sit for the examination, you will feel reasonably prepared (it is impossible to be completely prepared).

Reasons for Failure

The Uniform Certified Public Accountant Examination is a formidable hurdle in your accounting career. Candidates, generally with a college degree and an accounting major, face about a 30% pass rate nationally on each section of the exam. About 20% of all candidates (first time and re-exam) sitting for each examination successfully complete that examination. The cumulative pass rate on the exam is about 70-75%; that is, the percentage of first-time candidates who eventually pass the exam. It is even higher for serious candidates (80%-90%) because a significant number of candidates "drop out" after failing the exam the first time.

Attempt to identify and to correct your weaknesses before you sit for the examination based on your experience with undergraduate and previous CPA examinations. Also, analyze the contributing factors to incomplete or incorrect solutions to CPA problems prepared during your study program. The most common reasons for failure are

1. Failure to understand the requirements
2. Misunderstanding the text of the problem
3. Lack of knowledge of material tested
4. Inability to apply the solutions approach
5. Lack of an exam strategy, e.g., time budgeting
6. Sloppiness, computational errors, etc.
7. Failure to proofread and edit

The above are not mutually exclusive categories. Some candidates get in such a hurry that they misread the requirements and the text of the question, fail to use a solutions approach, and omit proofreading and editing.

PURPOSE AND ORGANIZATION OF THIS REVIEW TEXTBOOK

This book is designed to help you prepare adequately for the business law examination. Unfortunately (or fortunately, depending on your point of view), there is no easy approach (that is also effective) to prepare for successful completion of the business law exam.

The objective of this book is to provide study materials supportive to CPA candidates. While no guarantees are made concerning the success of those using this text, this book promotes efficient preparation by

1. Explaining how to "satisfy the grader" through analysis of examination grading and illustration of the solutions approach
2. Defining areas tested previously through the use of the content specification outlines/frequency analyses described earlier. Note that predictions of future exams are not made. You should prepare yourself for all possible topics rather than gambling on the appearance of certain questions.
3. Organizing your study program by comprehensively outlining all of the subject matter tested on the examination in 15 easy-to-use study modules. Each study module is a manageable task which facilitates your exam preparation. Turn to the TABLE OF CONTENTS and peruse it to get a feel for the organization of this book.
4. Providing CPA candidates with recent examination questions organized by topic, e.g., contracts, negotiable instruments, etc.

5. Explaining the AICPA unofficial answers to the examination questions included in this text. The AICPA publishes unofficial answers to all past CPA examinations; however, no explanation is made of the approach that should have been applied to the examination questions to obtain these unofficial answers. Relatedly, the AICPA unofficial answers to multiple choice questions provide no justification and/or explanation.

A significant feature of this review text is the grouping of multiple choice questions into topical categories. These categories correspond to the sequencing of material as it appears within the text portion of each module. In the answer explanations for the multiple choice questions in each module, we have included headings which provide cross-references to the text material. For example, in Module 9, Negotiable Instruments, a heading appears above the answers to questions dealing with a holder in due course. This heading is identified by the letter "F." To find the topical coverage of a holder in due course in the text, the candidate would refer to the Table of Contents for Business Law modules (Chapter 5) and look under the module title (Negotiable Instruments) for the letter "F." At the right on the line marked "F." would be the appropriate page number in Negotiable Instruments related to a holder in due course.

As you read the next few paragraphs which describe the contents of this book, flip through the chapters to gain a general familiarity with the book's organization and contents.

Chapters 2, 3, and 4 are to help you "satisfy the grader."

Chapter 2 Examination Grading and Grader Orientation
Chapter 3 The Solutions Approach
Chapter 4 Taking the Examination

Chapters 2, 3, and 4 contain material that should be kept in mind throughout your study program. Refer back to them frequently. Reread them for a final time just before you sit for the exam.

Chapter 5 (Business Law Modules) contains

1. AICPA Content Specification Outlines combined with the authors' frequency analysis thereof
2. Outlines of material tested on the business law examination
3. Multiple choice questions
4. Essay questions
5. AICPA unofficial answers with the authors' explanations for the multiple choice questions
6. AICPA unofficial answers prefaced by the authors' answer outlines for the essay questions

Also included at the end of this text is a complete Sample Business Law CPA Examination. The selection of multiple choice items and essays was based on a statistical analysis of recent exams. The sample exam is included to enable candidates to gain experience in taking a "realistic" exam. While studying the modules, the candidate can become accustomed to concentrating on fairly narrow topics. By working through the sample examination near the end of their study program, candidates will be better prepared for taking the actual examination.

Other Textbooks

Since this text is a compilation of study guides and outlines, it may be necessary to supplement it with textbooks and other materials. You probably already have a business law textbook. In such a case, you must make the decision whether to replace it and trade familiarity (including notes therein, etc.), with the cost and inconvenience of obtaining the newer text containing a more updated presentation.

Before spending time and money acquiring a new book, begin your study program with CPA EXAMINATION REVIEW: BUSINESS LAW to determine your need for a supplemental text.

Ordering Other Textual Materials

The pervasive need of candidates will be AICPA materials. Candidates should locate an AICPA member to order their materials, since members are entitled to a 20% discount (educators obtain a 40% discount) and may place telephone orders. The backlog at the order department is substantial; telephone orders decrease delivery time from a month or more to about a week.

AICPA
Telephone: (212) 575-6426 Address: 1211 Avenue of the Americas
New York, New York 10036

You may request shipment by first class, which is billed separately.

Working CPA Questions

The content outlines/frequency analyses, study outlines, etc., will be used to acquire and assimilate the knowledge tested on the examination. This, however, should be only one-half of your preparation program. The other half should be spent practicing how to work questions.

Most candidates probably spend over 90% of their time reviewing material tested on the CPA exam. Much more time should be allocated to working old examination questions under exam conditions.

Working old examination questions serves two functions. First, it helps you develop a solutions approach as well as solutions that will satisfy the grader. Second, it provides the best test of your knowledge of the material.

The multiple choice questions and answer explanations can be used in many ways. First, they may be used as a diagnostic evaluation of your knowledge. For example, before beginning to review negotiable instruments you may wish to answer 10 to 15 multiple choice questions to determine your ability to answer CPA examination questions on negotiable instruments. The apparent difficulty of the questions and the correctness of your answers will allow you to determine the necessary breadth and depth of your review. Additionally, exposure to examination questions prior to review and study of the material should provide motivation. You will develop a feel for your level of proficiency and an understanding of the scope and difficulty of past examination questions. Moreover, your review materials will explain concepts encountered in the diagnostic multiple choice questions.

Second, the multiple choice questions can be used as a post-study or post-review evaluation. You should attempt to understand all concepts mentioned (even in incorrect answers) as you answer the questions. Refer to the explanation of the answer for discussion of the alternatives even though you selected the correct response. Thus, you should read the explanation of the unofficial answer unless you completely understand the question and all of the alternative answers.

Third, you may wish to use the multiple choice questions as a primary study vehicle. This is probably the quickest, but least thorough approach in preparing for the exam. Make a sincere effort to understand the question and to select the correct response before referring to the unofficial answer and explanation. In many cases, the explanations will appear inadequate because of your unfamiliarity with the topic. Always refer back to an appropriate study source, such as the outlines and text in this volume, your business law textbook, UCC Code Sections, etc.

The multiple choice questions outnumber the essay questions by greater than 10 to 1 in this book. This is similar to a typical CPA exam. The May 1985 exam contained:

	Multiple Choice	Essay
Business Law	60	4

The numbers are somewhat misleading in that most essay questions contain multiple (and often unrelated) parts.

One problem with so many multiple choice questions is that you may overemphasize them. Candidates generally prefer to work multiple choice questions because they are

1. Shorter and less time consuming
2. Solvable with less effort
3. Less frustrating than essay questions

Multiple choice questions from the most recent exam appear at the end of each module. Questions labeled REPEAT QUESTIONS are either identical to or have been changed only slightly from the question to which it is referred.

Essay questions require the ability to organize and compose a solution, as well as knowledge of the subject matter. Remember, working essay questions from start to finish is just as important as, if not more important than, working multiple choice questions.

Another problem with the large number of multiple choice questions is that you may tend to become overly familiar with the questions. The result may be that you begin reading the facts and assumptions of previously studied questions into the questions on your examination. Guard against this potential problem by reading each multiple choice question with extra care.

The essay questions and unofficial answers may also be used for study purposes without preparation of answers. Before turning to the unofficial answers, study the question and outline the solution (either mentally or in the margin of the book). Look at our answer outline preceding the unofficial answer for each question and compare it to your own. Next, read the unofficial answer, underlining keywords and phrases. The underlining should reinforce your study of the answer's content and also assist you in learning how to structure your solutions. Answer outlines, representing the major concepts found in the unofficial answer, are provided for each business law question. These will facilitate your study of essay questions.

REMEMBER! The AICPA does not accept solutions in outline form. THE AICPA EXPECTS THE GRADING CONCEPTS TO BE EXPLAINED IN CLEAR, CONCISE, WELL-ORGANIZED SENTENCES. However, your answer may be organized in outline form in the same sequence as the requirements.

The questions and solutions in this volume provide you with an opportunity to diagnose and correct any exam-taking weaknesses prior to sitting for the examination. Continually analyze your incorrect solutions to determine the cause of the error(s) during your preparation for the exam. Treat each incorrect solution as a mistake that will not be repeated (especially on the examination). Also attempt to generalize your weaknesses so that you may change, reinforce, or develop new approaches to exam preparation and exam taking.

SELF-STUDY PROGRAM

The following suggestions will assist you in developing a systematic, comprehensive, and successful self-study program to help you complete the business law exam.

CPA candidates generally find it difficult to organize and to complete their own self-study program. A major problem is determining what and how to study. Another major problem is developing the self-discipline to stick to a study program.

Relatedly, it is often difficult for CPA candidates to determine how much to study, i.e., determining when they are sufficiently prepared. The following self-study suggestions will address these and other problems that you face in preparing for the business law exam. Remember that these are only suggestions. You should modify them to suit your personality, available study time, and other constraints. Some of the suggestions may appear trivial, but CPA candidates generally need all the assistance they can get to systemize their study program.

Study Facilities and Available Time

Locate study facilities that will be conducive to concentrated study. Factors which you should consider include

1. Noise distraction
2. Interruptions
3. Lighting
4. Availability, e.g., a local library is not available at 5:00 A.M.
5. Accessibility, e.g., your kitchen table vs. your local library
6. Desk or table space

You will probably find different study facilities optimal for different times, e.g., your kitchen table during early morning hours and local libraries during early evening hours.

Next review your personal and professional commitments from now until the exam to determine regularly available study time. Formalize a schedule to which you can reasonably commit yourself. In the appendix to this chapter you will find a detailed approach to managing your time available for the exam preparation program.

Self-Evaluation

The CPA EXAMINATION REVIEW: BUSINESS LAW self-study program is partitioned into 15 topics or modules. Since each module is clearly defined and should be studied separately, you have the task of preparing for the CPA business law exam partitioned into 15 manageable tasks. Partitioning the overall project into 15 modules makes preparation psychologically easier, since you sense yourself completing one small step at a time rather than seemingly never completing one or a few large steps.

By completing the "Preliminary Estimate of Your Present Knowledge of Subject" inventory on the next page, organized by the 16 modules in this program, you will have a tabulation of your strong and weak areas at the beginning of your study program. This will help you budget your limited study time. Note that you should begin studying the material in each module by answering up to 1/4 of the total multiple choice questions covering that module's topics (see instruction "4.A." in the next section). This "mini-exam" should constitute a diagnostic evaluation as to the amount of review and study you need.

PRELIMINARY ESTIMATE OF YOUR PRESENT KNOWLEDGE OF SUBJECT*

No.	Module	Proficient	Fairly Proficient	Generally Familiar	Not Familiar
	BUSINESS LAW				
7	Contracts				
8	Sales				
9	Negotiable Instruments				
10	Secured Transactions				
11	Bankruptcy				
12	Suretyship				
13	Agency				
14	Partnership Law				
15	Corporations				
16	Antitrust and Gov. Regulation				
17	Federal Securities Law				
18	Accountant's Legal Liability				
19	Employer-Employee Relationships				
20	Property				
21	Insurance				
22	Trusts and Estates				

*Note: The numbering of modules in this text commences with number 7 to correspond with the numbering system used in our two-volume set.

Time Allocation

The study program below entails an average of 72 hours (Step "5." below) of study time. The breakdown of total hours is indicated in the left margin.

[2 1/2 hrs.] 1. Study Chapters 2-4 in this volume. These chapters are essential to your efficient preparation program.

Time estimate includes candidate's review of the examples of the solutions approach in Chapters 2 and 3.

[1/2 hr.] 2. Begin by studying the introductory material at the beginning of Chapter 5.

3. Study one module at a time. The modules are listed above in the self-evaluation section.

4. For each module

[12 hrs.] A. Work 1/4 of the multiple choice questions (e.g., if there are 40 multiple choice questions in a module, you should work every 4th question). Score yourself.

This diagnostic routine will provide you with an index of your proficiency and familiarity with the type and difficulty of questions.

Time estimate: 3 minutes each, not to exceed 1 hour total.

[25 hrs.] B. Study the outlines and illustrations. Where necessary, refer to your business law textbook and original authoritative pronouncements, e.g., UCC code sections. (This will occur more frequently for topics in which you have a weak background.)

Time estimate: 1 hour minimum per module with more time devoted to topics less familiar to you.

[15 hrs.] C. Work the remaining multiple choice questions. Study the explanations of the multiple choice questions you missed or had trouble answering.

Time estimate: 3 minutes to answer each question and 2 minutes to study the answer explanation of each question missed.

[12 hrs.] D. Under exam conditions, work at least 2 essay questions. Work additional questions as time permits.

Time estimate: 20 minutes for each essay question and 10 minutes to review the answer outline and unofficial answer for each question worked.

[5 hrs.] E. Work through the sample CPA examination presented at the end of this text. The exam should be taken in one sitting.

Take the examination under simulated exam conditions, i.e., in a strange place with other people present (your local municipal library). Apply your solutions approach to each question and your exam strategy to the overall exam.

You should limit yourself to the allotted exam time, and spend time afterwards grading your work and reviewing your effort. It might be helpful to do this with other CPA candidates. Another person looking over your exam might be more objective and notice things such as clarity of essays, etc.

Time estimate: To take the exam and review it later, approximately 5 hours.

5. The total suggested time of 72 hours is only an average. Allocation of time will vary candidate by candidate. Time requirements vary due to the diverse backgrounds and abilities of CPA candidates.

Allocate your time so you gain the most proficiency in the least time. Remember that while 72 hours will be required, you should break the overall project down into 16 more manageable tasks. Do not study more than one module during each study session.

Using Notecards

On the following page are one candidate's notecards on business law topics which illustrate how key definitions, lists, etc. can be summarized on index cards for quick review. Since candidates can take these anywhere they go, they are a very efficient review tool.

NEGOTIABLE INSTRUMENT

- in writing
  Semi permeable movable form
- signed by appropriate person
- unconditional promise to pay sum certain in money
- Words of negotiability
- No 2nd promise (Collateral-OK)
- payable on demand or at definite date.

ELEMENTS OF A BINDING AGREEMENT

1) Manifestation of Mutual Assent
   a) offer
   b) acceptance
2) Reality of consent
3) Consideration
4) capacity of Parties
5) Legality of object
6) compliance w/ Statute of Frauds

Prepared by Cindy Johnson, former student, Northern Illinois University

Level of Proficiency Required

What level of proficiency do you have to develop with respect to each of the topics to pass the exam? You should work toward a minimum correct rate on the multiple choice questions of 70 to 75%.

As explained in Chapter 2, recent exams in business law have been graded by adding "difficulty points" to the candidates' raw scores.

Warning: Disproportional study time devoted to multiple choice questions (relative to essay questions) can be disastrous on the exam. You should work a substantial number of essay questions under exam conditions, even though multiple choice questions are easier to work and are used to gauge your proficiency. The authors believe that a serious effort on essay questions will also improve your proficiency on the multiple choice questions.

Conditional Candidates

Once you have a "leg on the exam" (received partial credit for passing 2 or more sections), you have to bear down on the remaining section(s). Unfortunately, many candidates let up after conditioning the exam, relying on luck to get them through the remaining section(s). As a result many candidates lose their conditional status (as their time to complete the exam expires).

PLANNING FOR THE EXAMINATION

Overall Strategy

An overriding concern should be an orderly, systematic approach toward both your preparation program and your examination strategy. A major objective should be to avoid any surprises or anything else that would rattle you as you take the examination. In other words, you want to be in complete control as much as possible. "Control" is of paramount importance from both positive and negative viewpoints. The presence of "control" on your part will add to your confidence and your ability to prepare for and take the exam. Moreover, the presence of "control" will make your preparation program more enjoyable (or at least less distasteful). On the other hand, a lack of organization will result in inefficiency in preparing and taking the examination, with a highly predictable outcome. Likewise, distractions during the examination (e.g., inadequate lodging, long drive) are generally disastrous.

In summary, your establishment of a systematic, orderly approach to the examination is of paramount importance.

1. Develop an overall strategy at the beginning of your preparation program (see below)
2. Supplement your overall strategy with outlines of material tested on the business law exam
3. Supplement your overall strategy with an explicitly stated set of question solving procedures--the solutions approach
4. Supplement your overall strategy with an explicitly stated approach to each examination session (see Chapter 4)
5. Evaluate your preparation progress on a regular basis and prepare lists of things "to do." (See Weekly Review of Preparation Program Progress on following page.)
6. RELAX: You can pass the exam. About 10,000 candidates successfully complete the exam each sitting. You will be one of them if you complete an efficient preparation program and execute well (i.e., solutions approach and exam strategy) while writing the exam.

The following outline is designed to provide you with a general framework of the tasks before you. You should tailor the outline to your needs by adding specific items and comments.

A. Preparation Program (refer to Self-Study Program discussed previously)

   1. Obtain and organize study materials
   2. Locate facilities conducive for studying and block out study time
   3. Develop your solutions approach (including solving essay questions as well as multiple choice questions)
   4. Prepare an examination strategy

5. Study the material tested recently and prepare answers to actual exam questions on these topics under examination conditions
6. Periodically evaluate your progress

B. Physical Arrangements

1. Apply to and obtain acceptance from your State Board
2. Reserve lodging for examination night(s)

C. Taking the Examination (covered in detail in Chapter 4)

1. Become familiar with exam facilities and procedures
2. Implement examination strategies and the solutions approach

Weekly Review of Preparation Program Progress

The next two pages contain a hypothetical weekly review of Program progress. You should prepare a similar review report. This procedure, taking only five minutes per week, will help you proceed through a more efficient, complete preparation program.

Make notes of materials and topics

1. That you have studied
2. That you have completed
3. That need additional study

Weeks to go	Comments on progress, to do items, etc
8	1. Read CONT and SALES → take notecards 2. Work some MC and Essays in these areas
7	1. Read NEGO and SECU → take notecards 2. Work some MC and Essays in these areas 3. Review Remedies for Breach
6	1. Read BANK, SURE, AGEN → take notecards 2. Work some MC and Essays in these areas 3. Review Firm Offer Examples and Battle of Forms
5	1. Read PLAW. CORP. FEDE. ACCO → take notecards 2. Work some MC and Essays in these areas 3. Requirements of Negotiability needs work

4	1. Review Requirements of Negotiability → take notecards 2. Work essays from various mods
3	1. Read ERLE, PROP, INSU, TRUS → take notecards 2. Work some MC and some Essays in these areas 3. Still need work on CORP, AGEN, FEDE
2	1. Review strong areas — Contracts, NEGO, SECU, etc. 2. Work through Essays in strong areas 3. Work MC in strong areas
1	1. Review weak areas - CORP. law, Trusts and Estates, Federal Securities Regulations 2. Work through Essays in weak areas 3. Work MC in weak areas
0	1. Took sample exam in Bus. law 2. Review exam policies and procedures 3. Review notecards

APPENDIX

TIME MANAGEMENT FOR CPA CANDIDATES

Twice a year, candidates begin preparing for the CPA exam. They buy CPA review manuals, notebooks, dividers, pens, pencils, erasers, and even books that say to "keep a positive mental attitude toward this new and difficult assignment." All this is important to you as you begin studying for the exam. However, let us raise a note of caution--do not charge into your studies with such enthusiasm that you neglect to consider the magnitude of the task.

We know you have heard "war stories" from previous CPA candidates about the number of hours that you will have to spend during the next three to four months working problems and reading official pronouncements. We know that all too often candidates do not realize the extent to which their time will be committed to studying for the exam. Common sense should tell you that finding those hours for study will not be a simple task.

In this section of your CPA review program, we will help you to identify the hours you have available for studying for the CPA exam. We ask that you complete a short exercise using the "Time Analysis Matrix." After completing this exercise, you will have identified the "time blocks" that are currently available to you for study. This is an important exercise for you, whether you are a full-time student or a full-time practitioner.

Time Analysis Matrix. The "Time Analysis Matrix" (last page of this appendix) covers one complete week (i.e. seven days, twenty-four hours per day). The days of the week move across the matrix, while the hours of the day are listed down the left-hand side of the matrix. Each box represents a one-hour time block that is available to you. You have 168 (7 days x 24 hours) one-hour time blocks to work with every week.

Analyzing Your Fixed Time. Fixed time is the time you have allocated for SPECIFIC PURPOSES throughout your CURRENT WEEKLY SCHEDULE. For example, if you are a full-time student, your CURRENT CLASS SCHEDULE should represent fixed time. When you are in class, you cannot be in the library or the coffee shop. You are committed to using this time in a specific way. If you are working full-time, your normal working hours should be considered fixed time. Additionally, hours allotted to normal sleep time should be considered fixed time. IN SHORT, ANY HOURS YOU HAVE

SPECIFICALLY COMMITTED TO USING REGULARLY DURING THE WEEK SHOULD BE CONSIDERED FIXED TIME.

Take a few moments and examine the TIME ANALYSIS MATRIX. Use a colored pencil or pen and shade in the time blocks that represent FIXED TIME in your CURRENT WEEKLY SCHEDULE. After you have finished shading in the time blocks, COUNT the shaded blocks and complete the following equations:

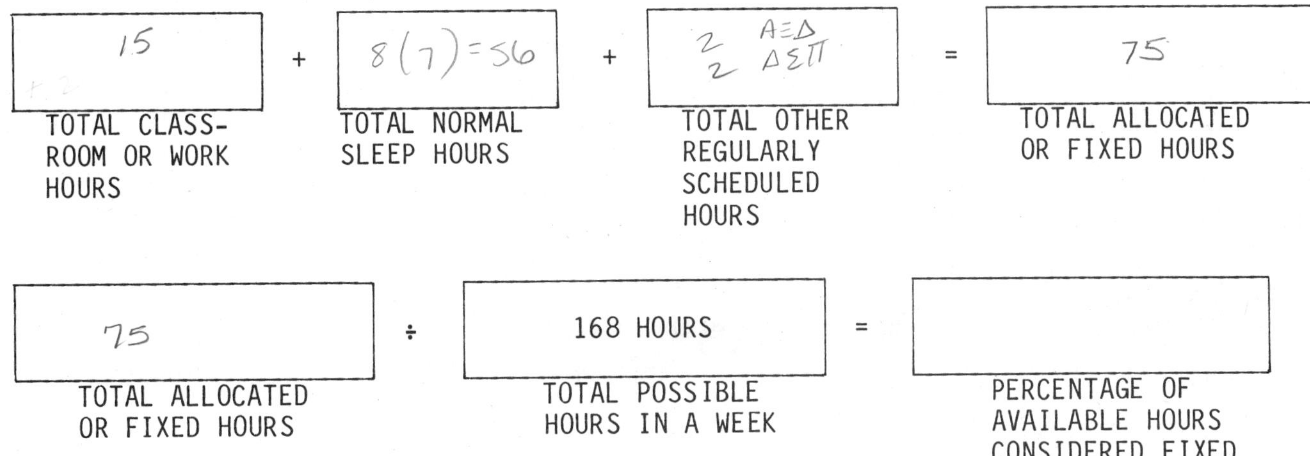

75	÷	168 HOURS	=	
TOTAL ALLOCATED OR FIXED HOURS		TOTAL POSSIBLE HOURS IN A WEEK		PERCENTAGE OF AVAILABLE HOURS CONSIDERED FIXED

<u>Now For The Moment of Truth</u>. If you are like most <u>undergraduate students</u>, your percentage of fixed hours should be around 46%. If this is true, you probably have approximately 54% or 91 hours per week that can be used in a DISCRETIONARY manner. It is with these DISCRETIONARY HOURS that PERSONAL TIME MANAGEMENT techniques can really be of help to you. If you can make the discretionary hours productive, you will find there is more than enough time to adequately prepare for the CPA exam.

If you are <u>working full-time</u> and studying for the exam through a review course or on your own, you will probably find that approximately 70% of your time will be fixed. Therefore, you have approximately 30% or 50 hours per week to use at your DISCRETION. You will have to work even harder at making the discretionary hours productive hours.

<u>Approaching Your Discretionary Hours</u>. CPA CANDIDATES DO NOT LIVE BY SOLVING PROBLEMS ALONE! Believe it or not, even CPA candidates need time to relax and refresh their minds. However, you must carefully limit and properly sequence the discretionary time you spend relaxing and refreshing your mind.

Each hour on the TIME ANALYSIS MATRIX that is not shaded is considered discretionary. For each of these time blocks, you have to make an important decision. HOW DO YOU WANT TO USE EACH DISCRETIONARY HOUR? Take a few moments and shade in the discretionary time blocks. (Use a light-colored pencil which is a different color than the one used for FIXED TIME.) This will make them stand out so you can see the impact of this free time and where it is located on the matrix.

How do you make a discretionary hour become a PRODUCTIVE HOUR? As you look at the discretionary hours on the time analysis matrix, where do you need both a PHYSICAL and a MENTAL break? Think about your personal needs, since no two people work, study, or rest in exactly the same way. Where you need BOTH the PHYSICAL and MENTAL break period, WRITE THE LETTER "B" in the time block. Now the discretionary time period has become a PRODUCTIVE-FIXED time period.

Review the time analysis matrix. At this point, you have allocated time blocks to "fixed hours" and to "break hours". The REMAINING hours are what you have to work with as you begin to set the remainder of your schedule.

Now--What Time Do You Have Left? At this point, any time blocks that are shaded as DISCRETIONARY and do not contain the letter "B" are available for scheduling. LOOK FOR TIME PERIODS THAT ARE AVAILABLE CONSISTENTLY FROM DAY TO DAY. For example, you might find that 7-9 P.M. is open Monday through Friday. This would be a perfect time slot for allocating to STUDY TIME. It is a reasonable length of study time, and it is available every day. REASONABLENESS OF THE STUDY PERIOD AND CONSISTENCY OF AVAILABILITY ARE "CRUCIAL" TO USING THE TIME BLOCKS AS PRODUCTIVE STUDY PERIODS. Take a few moments and mark the time blocks you want to designate as STUDY PERIODS. WRITE THE LETTER "S" in these time blocks.

The Final Analysis. Review the time analysis matrix and count the number of hours you have designated as being FIXED. Next, count the number of hours you originally designated as DISCRETIONARY, but which have now been marked as being DISCRETIONARY-USED FOR BREAKS (i.e. the letter "B"). Finally, count the number of hours you have marked as being DISCRETIONARY-USED FOR STUDY (i.e., the letter "S"). Complete the following equation and see how you have allocated your time. ARE YOU GETTING THE MOST OUT OF YOUR TIME? IF NOT, STEP BACK AND REWORK YOUR SCHEDULE.

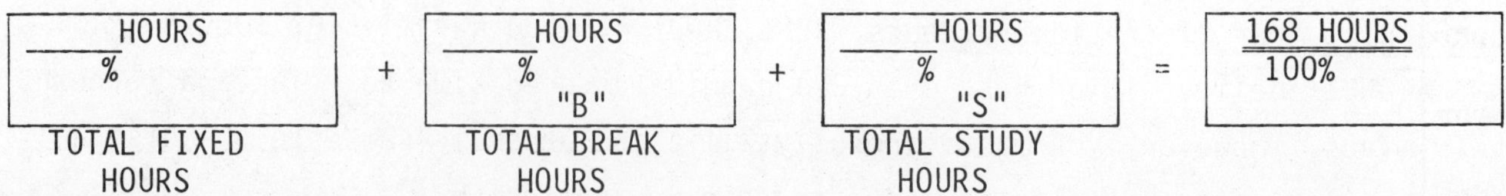

NOTE: For the FINAL ANALYSIS, consider time designated as neither FIXED nor DISCRETIONARY-USED FOR STUDY, to be DISCRETIONARY-USED FOR BREAKS. Therefore, "Break Time" will be used for both relaxation and for time not otherwise assigned for a specific purpose.

TIME ANALYSIS MATRIX

	MON	TUES	WED	THURS	FRI	SAT	SUN
1 am							
2 am							
3 am							
4 am							
5 am							
6 am							
7 am							
8 am							
9 am							
10 am							
11 am							
12 pm							
1 pm							
2 pm							
3 pm							
4 pm							
5 pm							
6 pm							
7 pm							
8 pm							
9 pm							
10 pm							
11 pm							
12 am							

CHAPTER TWO

EXAMINATION GRADING AND GRADER ORIENTATION

All State Boards of Accountancy use the AICPA advisory grading service. As your grade is to be determined by this process, it is very important that you understand the AICPA grading process and its implications for your preparation program and for the solution techniques you will use during the examination.

The AICPA has a full-time staff of CPA examination personnel whose responsibilities include:

1. Preparing questions for the examination
2. Working with outside consultants who prepare questions
3. Preparation of grading guides and unofficial answers
4. Supervising and reviewing the work of examination graders

The AICPA examination staff is under the supervision of the AICPA Board of Examiners which has responsibility for the CPA examination.

This chapter contains a description of the AICPA grading process based on the description of AICPA grading in Information for CPA Candidates, AICPA grading guides, etc.

The AICPA Grading Process

The AICPA exercises very tight control over all of the examination papers during the grading process and prior to their return to the individual State Boards of Accountancy. Upon receipt from the exam sites, papers are assigned to control groups, reviewed for candidate numbers, and checked against state board records of examination papers submitted.

Multiple choice questions are graded electronically. Essay questions are graded individually on the basis of grading guides. Grading guides consist of grading concepts, which are ideas, constructs, principles, etc., that can be clearly defined.

While tentative grading guides (answers) are prepared prior to the examination, the final grading guides are based upon two test gradings of samples of actual examinations. Once grading guides are developed, "production graders" perform the first grading of the examination. The "production graders" are practicing CPAs, university professors, attorneys, etc., retained by the AICPA on a per diem basis to grade the examination. These graders specialize in a single essay question and grade answers to that question for about six weeks. About 200 graders, some full-time, some part-time, are required for each examination.

After the multiple choice questions are machine-graded and returned to their respective examinations, the first grading of essay questions begins. The control group of papers moves from grader to grader. Attached to each examination is a grading guide similar to the "Hypothetical Grading Guide" on page 29. The purpose of the first grading is to separate examinations as to pass, fail, and marginal.

The second grading is performed by reviewers who generally inspect the work of the "production graders" but emphasize review of the marginal examinations, i.e., papers with grades of 70 to 74. Papers with grades of 70 to 74 are regraded to grades of 69 or 75. One of the major reasons for this procedure is to relieve State Boards of Accountancy of requests for regrading failing papers "very near" 75. Most 72s, 73s, and 74s are regraded to 75. All of the questions on papers selected for regrading are reevaluated. Grade changes (when made) are made to the essay questions. An analysis is undertaken of all essay questions to differentiate sophisticated grading concepts (those included by most candidates passing the exam) from rudimentary grading concepts (those included by candidates both passing and failing the exam). Answers which include sophisticated grading concepts are generally graded up and papers with only rudimentary grading concepts are generally graded down. Note this procedure is only applied to papers in the 70 through 74 range. In all cases, as throughout the grading procedure, the candidate is given the benefit of the doubt.

The third grading is administered to papers that have several passing parts but have a failing score on a particular part. A fourth and final grading may be performed on papers that continue to have inconsistent grades after the third grading, e.g., 88, 84, 68, 89.

Note that the first grading is directed to individual questions while the second grading is directed to individual sections, e.g., Theory, Law, etc. The third grading is a review of failing parts written by candidates who have done well on other remaining parts (or for example, conditional candidates with one part to go). The fourth and final grading is directed to any remaining inconsistencies. It should be emphasized that answer format, presentation, logic, etc., are given more consideration on the regradings than on the first grading.

An adding machine tape totaling the grade on individual questions for each section is then prepared. The examination papers, grades, and grading tapes are returned to the individual state boards several weeks prior to the official grade release date. The grade release date is usually at the end of January for the November exam, and at the end of July for the May exam.

What Graders are Looking For

Based on Information for CPA Candidates, the examination instructions, examination questions, unofficial answers, etc., the examiners appear to be looking for

1. Knowledge of the academic content of the typical undergraduate accounting major (including business law)
2. Ability to apply this knowledge to specific situations with good judgment
3. Precise and concise use of the English language
4. Examination, evaluation, and classification of data in complex situations
5. Organization and presentation of accounting data
6. Application of business law principles and concepts to specific situations
7. Reasonable facility with disciplines relatively close to accounting, e.g., quantitative methods, statistics, finance, economics, etc.

Multiple Choice Grading

Conversion tables are developed for each overall question which consists of a number of individual multiple choice questions. These tables assign one point for each correct response on the business law section of the examination. Grades on this part have been modified by "difficulty points" whereby candidates are "spotted" points for attempting the multiple choice questions (note that this is a means of "curving" the grades on the entire section).

The May 1985 multiple choice point allocation and grading were typical of recent exams. The Business Law exam's 60 multiple choice questions comprised Problem 1. Each correct response was worth 1 point. "Difficulty points" awarded on the May 1985 Business Law exam are indicated in the following table.

	No. of MC	% of Section Grade	"Difficulty Points"	No. of Correct Responses for a 75	Correct Response Rate Req.
Business Law	60	60%	8	37	62%

Implications: Since grading is on a relative basis, do your best regardless of the difficulty of the questions. Perfect and use a "multiple choice question solutions approach" which is discussed in Chapter 3. If you are unsure about a particular question, you should guess, i.e., pick the "best" answer. This assumes that "your grade will be based on your total correct answers," i.e., no penalty for incorrect answers. The grading procedure for multiple choice questions is explained in the instructions at the beginning of each section of the exam. The importance of carefully reading and following these, and all other, instructions cannot be overemphasized.

Essay Grading

To illustrate the grading of essay questions, we have included question Number 5b from the November 1981 Business Law Examination in this section. Each essay question on the business law examination normally consists of two unrelated parts with equal point value. Following the question are the AICPA Unofficial Answer and a hypothetical grading guide.

Number 5b

Part b. Maxwell was window shopping one day when she noticed an advertisement at Ultraclear Electronics for the sale of a shortwave radio for $495. Beneath the large caption indicating the sale and the price were the following:

- Never sold before below $550.
- Listen to the BBC, Radio Moscow, Radio Tokyo, and other international radio stations.
- Easy tuning, great reception, and made of the highest quality material.
- Don't hesitate, this is a limited offer on the buy of a lifetime.

Maxwell entered the store and proceeded to the place where the shortwave radio featured in the window was displayed with a similar although smaller sign extolling the virtues of the radio. Maxwell was examining the radio when Golden, an Ultraclear salesman, approached her. Maxwell told Golden that she was a great music lover and that she had long wished to listen to the Moscow symphony, the Moscow opera, and the music of the Bolshoi Ballet. Golden merely nodded his head and smiled knowingly. Golden said that at this price the company could not afford to give any implied warranties of quality beyond the replacement of defective parts for ninety days.

When Maxwell got home and used the radio she found it to be in proper working order and that the shortwave reception was satisfactory for much of the world, but that it was not capable of picking up Moscow without severe static and at an exceptionally low audio level. Maxwell returned to Ultraclear and demanded that the radio be put in proper working order. The complaint department told her there was nothng they could do about it, that the set was in proper working order and the fact that reception of Radio Moscow was poor was something she would just have to live with. Maxwell asserted that there has been a breach of warranty and demanded her money back. This was refused. Ultraclear's agent then informed Maxwell that she had no warranty protection. The company never "guaranteed" or "warranted" anything. In fact, the only thing stated with respect to warranties at all was Golden's remark clearly disclaiming any and all warranties.

Required: Answer the following, setting forth reasons for any conclusions stated.

In the subsequent suit brought by Maxwell against Ultraclear to rescind the sale, who will prevail?

UNOFFICIAL ANSWER

Part b.

Maxwell will prevail. As a result of advertising placed in the window and at the display counter, she may rely upon an express warranty of fitness of the radio's capability of receiving adequate reception of radio broadcasts. This would be characterized as a written express warranty, as many recent cases have held written advertising statements about the product in question to be. Next, Maxwell could claim that an oral express warranty was given by Golden, although this would appear to be a rather weak argument in regard to both the facts and the law. Maxwell's recovery also can be based upon the implied warranty protection of the Uniform Commercial Code. First, she could assert that a shortwave radio intended to receive transmissions from throughout the world was not of merchantable quality (fair and average) if it were incapable of receiving clear transmissions from the Soviet Union. Although this may be a plausible argument, it is obvious that the implied warranty of fitness for the purpose indicated is a better theory upon which to proceed. She clearly made her needs or purposes known to Golden, who nodded and smiled in apparent agreement. Thus, Maxwell has a wide variety of warranties to which she may resort in seeking recovery.

There are two arguments that Ultraclear would make in defense and that are alluded to in the final paragraph of the facts. First, they made no warranty as a result of the advertising. This they would claim to be merely opinion or puffing. They would couple this with the fact that they didn't use the term *warrant* or *guarantee*. However, the UCC does not require the use of such words to create a warranty, and the statement "Listen to Radio Moscow" is a statement of fact or promise and not mere puffing or opinion.

Next, Ultraclear would rely upon its oral disclaimer as a defense. Although Ultraclear purported to negate any implied warranty protection, this argument would fail because it is inapplicable insofar as the express warranties discussed above are concerned. The oral disclaimer is also ineffective with repect to the implied warranty of merchantability, since the code requires that any such disclaimer specifically mention the word merchantability. To exclude the warranty of fitness, the code also requires that the exclusion be in writing and be conspicuous.

Since there are several warranties that have been made or implied and that have been breached by Ultraclear, and since its defenses will be of no avail, Maxwell should win her case for rescission.

Essay questions are generally graded based on the number of grading concepts in the candidate's solution. The grading guide is a list of the grading concepts and raw point(s) assigned to each concept. The total raw points listed are usually in excess of the maximum points which a candidate may earn on the question. A hypothetical grading guide for the preceding business law essay question appears below. Note that while question 5b has 9 available grading points, a maximum of 5 points can be earned on this part. The maximum for the entire question (parts "a" and "b") is 10 points. (Part "a" is not included in this hypothetical grading guide.)

NOVEMBER 1981 BUSINESS LAW, NUMBER 5b

HYPOTHETICAL GRADING GUIDE*

		Grading Points
b.	Maxwell will prevail against Ultraclear	1
	Express warranty created by Ultraclear advertising radio's capabilities	1
	Seller's affirmations become part of the basis of the bargain	1
	This was not simply opinion or "puffing" of seller; nor is it necessary for seller to use formal words for creation of express warranty	1
	Ultraclear's oral disclaimer of any implied warranty is ineffective against express warranties	1
	Implied warranty of merchantability created since seller is merchant	1
	Ultraclear's oral disclaimer is ineffective because to disclaim this warranty, the language of the disclaimer must mention "merchantability"	1
	Implied warranty of fitness for particular purpose created since seller knows of Maxwell's needs	1
	Ultraclear's oral disclaimer is ineffective because to disclaim this warranty, the disclaimer must be in writing and be conspicuous	1
	Grading points possible	9

The conversion scale below converts the "raw" grading points shown above to the grade earned on this question.

CONVERSION SCALE—Part b

Grading Points Earned	9-7	6	5-4	3	2-1
Grade	5	4	3	2	1

Total Grade: Number 5 ____

Part "a" grade ____

Part "b" grade ____

Demerit for form, etc. ____

*The AICPA Board of Examiners does not release the grading guides used for scoring essay questions. The grading guide above was prepared by the authors to illustrate to candidates the manner in which points are allocated to grading concepts.

In the above grading guide, note that each grading concept is summarized by several keywords. Graders undoubtedly scan for these keywords during the first grading.

Another consideration is "cross-grading." Often candidates answer one requirement elsewhere than required; i.e., the answer to requirement "a" may be written as part of the answer to requirement "b." Frequently, the grading guides permit "cross-grading," i.e., giving credit in one part of the answer for a correct response in another part of the answer. To assure full credit, however, candidates should be very careful to organize their answers to meet the question requirements, i.e., you should answer requirement "a" in answer "a," answer requirement "b" in answer "b," etc. Additionally, the efficient use of time is of the utmost importance. If you have included grading concepts in one part of a question that are applicable to another part of the same question, do not repeat them. Simply refer the grader to your previous answer.

Two common misconceptions about the AICPA grading of essay questions have cost candidates points in recent years. First, answers should not consist of a listing (or outline) of keywords. Answers should be set forth in short, concise sentences, organized per the requirements of the question. Second, a candidate should not answer only one or two parts of a question very thoroughly and leave the remaining parts blank. Even though the grading guide may contain 3 times as many grading concepts as there are points available, each part of a question will usually have a limited number of attainable points.

Notice that the last grading concept in the example grading guide is "Demerit for form, etc." Grading guides may provide a penalty for sloppiness, inadequate form, etc. Alternatively, they may provide a bonus for good form and appearance. A closely related matter is the examiner's consideration of the candidates' ability to express themselves in acceptable written language. Recent examinations have contained the following paragraph in the instructions for each section of the exam:

> A CPA is continually confronted with the necessity of expressing opinions and conclusions in written reports in clear, unequivocal language. Although the primary purpose of the examination is to test the candidate's knowledge and application of the subject matter, the ability to organize and present such knowledge in acceptable written language will be considered by the examiners.

The grading guide might be thought of as a brief outline of the unofficial answer. Note the similarities between the grading guide and the unofficial answer.

Allocation of Points to Questions

Information for CPA Candidates states that the "maximum point values for each question are approximately proportional to the minutes allotted to the question in the suggested time budget printed in the examination booklet." Candidates should be concerned with point allocations for the purpose of allocating their time on the exam.

Grading Implications for CPA Candidates

Analysis of the grading process helps you understand what graders are looking for and how you can present solutions to "satisfy the grader." Before turning to Chapter 3 for a discussion of how to prepare solutions, consider the following conclusions derived from the foregoing grading analysis.

1. Your solutions should be neat and orderly to avoid demerits and to obtain bonuses
2. Allocate your time based on AICPA minimum suggested times
3. Do your best on every question, no matter how difficult
    a. Remember the test is graded on a relative basis
    b. If a question is difficult for you, it probably is difficult for others also
    c. Develop a "solutions approach" to assist you
4. No supporting notes or computations are required for the multiple choice questions; however, you may use scratch paper for related notes, computations, etc. The multiple choice answers are machine-graded and any related work on scratch paper is ignored.
5. Essay solutions should be numbered and organized according to the problem requirements, e.g., a, b1, b2, c1, c2, c3, d1, d2
    a. Label your solutions parallel to the requirements
    b. Emphasize keywords
    c. Separate grading concepts into individual sentences or short paragraphs
        1) Do not bury grading concepts in lengthy paragraphs that might be missed by the grader. Include as many sensible grading concepts as possible.
        2) Use short, uncomplicated sentence structure
        3) DO NOT PRESENT YOUR ANSWER IN OUTLINE FORMAT
    d. Do not omit any requirements

In summary, SATISFY THE GRADER. You need neat, readable solutions organized according to the requirements, which will also be the organization of the grading guides. Remember that a legible, well-organized, grammatically correct answer gives a professional appearance. Additionally, recognize the plight of the grader having to decipher one mess after another, day after day. Give him/her a break with a neat, orderly solution. The "halo" effect will be rewarded by additional consideration (and hopefully points!).

NOW IS THE TIME
TO MAKE A COMMITMENT

CHAPTER THREE

THE SOLUTIONS APPROACH

The solutions approach is a systematic problem-solving methodology. The purpose is to assure efficient, complete solutions to CPA exam questions.

Essay Question Solutions Approach Algorithm

The steps outlined below are only one of many possible series of solution steps. Admittedly, the procedures suggested are *very* structured; thus, you should adapt the suggestions to your needs. You may find that some steps are occasionally unnecessary, or that certain additional procedures increase your problem-solving efficiency. Whatever the case, substantial time should be allocated to developing an efficient solutions approach before taking the examination. You should develop your solutions approach by working old CPA questions.

Note that the steps below relate to a specific question; overall examination strategies are discussed in Chapter 4.

1. *Glance over the question.* Only scan the question. Get a feel for the type or category of question. Do not read it. Until you understand the requirements, you cannot discriminate important data from irrelevant data.

2. *Study the requirements.* "Study" as differentiated from "read." Candidates continually lose points due to misunderstanding the requirements. Underline key phrases and words.

2a. *Visualize the solution format.* Determine the expected format of the required solution. Often a single requirement will require two or more responses. A common example is a question followed by "why" or "explain." Explicitly recognize multiple requirements by numbering or lettering them on your examination booklet, expanding on the letters already assigned to question parts.

3. *Outline the required procedures mentally.* Interrelate the data in the text of the question to the expected solution format, mentally noting a "to do" list. Determine what it is you are going to do before you get started doing it.

3a. Review applicable principles, knowledge. Before immersing yourself in the details of the question, quickly (30-60 seconds) review and organize the principles and your knowledge applicable to the question. Jot down any acronyms, formulas, or other memory aids relevant to the topic of the question. Otherwise, the details of the question may confuse and overshadow your previous knowledge of the applicable principles.

4. Study the text of the question. Read the question carefully. With the requirements in mind, you now can begin to sort out relevant from irrelevant data. Underline and circle important data. The data necessary for answering each requirement may be scattered throughout the question. As you study the text, use arrows, etc. to connect data pertaining to a common requirement. List the requirements (a, b, etc.) in the margin alongside the data to which they pertain. Use a wild colored pen to mark up the question. Heavy colored underlining and comments are attention getting and give you confidence.

4a. Write down keywords (concepts). Jot down a list of keywords (grading concepts) in the margin of the examination. The proximity of the keywords to the text of the question will be more efficient than making notes on a separate sheet of paper which may be misplaced.

4b. Organize the keywords into a solution outline. After you have noted all of the grading concepts which bear on the requirements, reorganize the outline for the entire answer. Make sure that you respond to each requirement and do not preempt answers to other requirements.

5. Prepare the solution. You now are in a position to write a neat, complete, organized, labeled solution. Remember that a legible, well-organized, grammatically correct answer gives a professional appearance.

6. Proofread and edit. Do not underestimate the utility of this step. Just recall all of the "silly" mistakes you made on undergraduate examinations. Corrections of errors and completion of oversights during this step can easily be the difference between passing and failing.

7. Review the requirements. Assure yourself that you have answered them all.

Essay Question Solutions Approach Example

To illustrate the use of the solutions approach in answering essay questions, we have included Question 5b from the November 1981 Examination in Business Law (same question that was used to illustrate grading in Chapter 2). The illustration begins on page 36.

Highlights of the Solutions Approach to Essay Questions

After studying the requirements and visualizing the format of the unofficial answer, study the text of the question making notes and also preparing a keyword outline. Next, organize the outline for the entire answer. Make sure that you answer each requirement (and only that requirement) completely. Be careful not to preempt an answer to another requirement. The keyword outline for the example question should be similar to the grading guide in Chapter 2. Next, write your solution and edit as needed. If you have time later, review your solution again.

Revisions may be made in the margin of your answer sheet. Or, you might use only 3/4 of every page to write up your solution. The remaining 1/4 can then be used to add material and to make revisions which can be keyed to the text with asterisks. Alternatively, write on every other line. The solution will thus be easier for the grader to read. It will also be easier for you to proofread and edit. Remember, there is no limit on the number of answer sheets you may use.

Note: You must write out the answers to the essay questions. Keyword outlines are not sufficient. The AICPA requires you to show an understanding of the grading concepts, not merely a listing of grading concepts.

Prepare brief paragraphs consisting of several concise sentences about each grading concept. The paragraphs may be numbered in an outline format similar to that of the unofficial answers.

Multiple Choice Question Solutions Approach Algorithm

1. Work individual questions in order
    a. If a question appears lengthy or difficult, skip it until you can determine that extra time is available. Put a big question mark in the margin to remind you to return to questions you have skipped or need to review.
2. Cover the choices before reading each question
    a. The answers are frequently ambiguous and may cause you to misread or misinterpret the question
3. Read each question carefully to determine the topical area
    a. Study the requirements first so you know which data are important
    b. Underline keywords and important data
    c. Identify pertinent information with notations in the margin of the exam
    d. Be especially careful to note when the requirement is an exception, e.g., "Which of the following is not an effective disclaimer of the implied warranty of merchantability?"
    e. If a set of data is the basis for two or more questions, read the requirements of each of the questions before beginning to work the first question (sometimes it is more efficient to work the questions out of order or simultaneously)
4. Anticipate the answer before looking at the alternative answers
    a. Recall the applicable principle (e.g., offer and acceptance, requisites of negotiability, etc.) and the respective applications thereof
5. Read the answers and select the best alternative
6. Mark the correct (or best guess) answer on the examination booklet itself

Number 5b

Part b. Maxwell was window shopping one day when she noticed an advertisement at Ultraclear Electronics for the sale of a shortwave radio for $495. Beneath the large caption indicating the sale and the price were the following:

- Never sold before below $550.
- Listen to the BBC, Radio Moscow, Radio Tokyo, and other international radio stations.
- Easy tuning, great reception, and made of the highest quality material.
- Don't hesitate, this is a limited offer on the buy of a lifetime.

Maxwell entered the store and proceeded to the place where the shortwave radio featured in the window was displayed with a similar although smaller sign extolling the virtues of the radio. Maxwell was examining the radio when Golden, an Ultraclear salesman, approached her. Maxwell told Golden that she was a great music lover and that she had long wished to listen to the Moscow symphony, the Moscow opera, and the music of the Bolshoi Ballet. Golden merely nodded his head and smiled knowingly. Golden said that at this price the company could not afford to give any implied warranties of quality beyond the replacement of defective parts for ninety days.

When Maxwell got home and used the radio she found it to be in proper working order and that the shortwave reception was satisfactory for much of the world, but that it was not capable of picking up Moscow without severe static and at an exceptionally low audio level. Maxwell returned to Ultraclear and demanded that the radio be put in proper working order. The complaint department told her there was nothing that they could do about it, that the set was in proper working order and the fact that reception of Radio Moscow was poor was something she would just have to live with. Maxwell asserted that there has been a breach of warranty and demanded her money back. This was refused. Ultraclear's agent then informed Maxwell that she had no warranty protection. The company never "guaranteed" or "warranted" anything. In fact, the only thing stated with respect to warranties at all was Golden's remark clearly disclaiming any and all warranties.

Required:

Answer the following, setting forth reasons for any conclusions stated.

In the subsequent suit brought by Maxwell against Ultraclear to rescind the sale, who will prevail?

KEYWORD OUTLINE

ULTRACLEAR IS MERCHANT CREATES IMPLIED WARRANTY OF MERCHANTABILITY

AFFIRMATION OF FACT FORMS BASIS OF THE BARGAIN

CREATES EXPRESS WARRANTY

FURTHER EVIDENCE OF EXPRESS WARRANTY

SELLER KNOWS OF MAXWELL'S NEEDS

CREATES IMPLIED WARRANTY OF FITNESS FOR PARTICULAR PURPOSE

IMPROPER DISCLAIMER OF IMPLIED WARRANTIES

DOES NOT CONFORM TO SELLER'S AFFIRMATION

NOT OF MERCHANTABLE QUALITY; NOT FIT FOR MAXWELL'S PARTICULAR PURPOSE

BREACH OF EXPRESS AND IMPLIED WARRANTIES

FORMAL WORDS NOT NECESSARY

ORAL DISCLAIMER INEFFECTIVE

STEP 1:
Glance over quickly

STEP 2:
Study requirements

STEP 2A:
Visualize solution format

Solution will be in paragraph format reciting requisite legal analysis for determination of which party will ultimately prevail based upon warranty liability

STEP 3:
Outline the required procedures mentally

Read problem carefully to develop an understanding of the facts to determine basis for deciding resultant rights and obligations of each party based upon warranty liability

STEP 3A:
Review applicable principles

1. Purchaser of product may sue seller based upon warranties made
2. Express warranties created when seller makes affirmation of fact to buyer which becomes part of basis of the bargain
    Not necessary that the seller use formal words ("warrant" or "guarantee")
3. Implied warranty of merchantability created when seller is merchant
    Seller has duty to provide goods that meet certain quality standards
4. Implied warranty of fitness for particular purpose created when seller has reason to know particular purpose for which purchaser needs goods
    Seller has duty to provide goods that shall be fit for such purpose
5. Warranty liability may be modified by disclaimers
    a. To disclaim implied warranty of merchantability language must mention "merchantability"
    b. To disclaim implied warranty of fitness for particular purpose disclaimer must be in writing and conspicuous

STEP 4:
Study the text

STEP 4A:
Keyword outline

STEP 4B:
Organize into solution outline

1. Maxwell will prevail against Ultraclear
    a. Warranties created and subsequently breached
    b. Maxwell entitled to rescind sale
2. Express warranty created by advertising radio's capabilities
    a. Seller's affirmations become part of basis of the bargain
    b. Formal words not necessary to create warranty
    c. Ultraclear's oral disclaimer is ineffective against express warranty
3. Implied warranty of merchantability created
    a. Goods shall be merchantable implied in sales by merchants
    b. To disclaim implied warranty of merchantability language must mention "merchantability"
        Ultraclear's oral disclaimer is ineffective
4. Implied warranty of fitness for particular purpose created
    a. Ultraclear had knowledge of Maxwell's particular needs
    b. To disclaim implied warranty of fitness for particular purpose disclaimer must be in writing and be conspicuous
        Ultraclear's oral disclaimer is ineffective

***STEP 5:**
Prepare solution

***STEP 6:**
Proofread and edit

***STEP 7:**
Review

* See Unofficial Answer in Chapter 2

7. After completing all of the individual questions in an overall question, transfer the answers to the machine gradeable answer sheet with extreme care
   a. Be very careful not to fall out of sequence with the answer sheet. A mistake would cause most of your answers to be wrong. SINCE THE AICPA USES ANSWER SHEETS WITH VARYING FORMATS, IT WOULD BE VERY EASY TO GO ACROSS THE SHEET INSTEAD OF DOWN OR VICE VERSA. Read the instructions carefully!
   b. Review to check that you have transferred the answers correctly
   c. Do not leave this step until the end of the exam as you may find yourself with too little time to transfer your answers to the answer sheet. The exam proctors are not permitted to give you extra time to transfer your answers.

Multiple Choice Question Solutions Approach Example

A good example of the multiple choice solutions approach is provided, using multiple choice question number 13 from the May 1982 Examination in Business Law.

13. Foster offered to sell Lebow his garage for $27,000. The offer was in writing and signed by Foster. Foster gave Lebow five days to decide. On the fourth day Foster accepted a better offer from Dilby, who was unaware of the offer to Lebow. Foster subsequently conveyed the property to Dilby. Unaware of the sale to Dilby, Lebow telephoned Foster on the fifth day and unconditionally accepted the offer. Under the circumstances, Lebow

a. Is entitled to specific performance by Foster.
b. Has no rights against Foster.
c. Is entitled to damages.
d. Can obtain specific performance by Dilby upon depositing in court the $27,000 he agreed to pay.

NOT SALE OF GOODS
FIRM OFFER RULE DOES NOT APPLY
NO OPTION CREATED
GOOD FAITH PURCHASER

STEP 3:

Topical area? Contracts/Revocation of offer

STEP 4:

Principle? Offeror has power to revoke offer; but revocation is effective only when communicated to offeree

STEP 5:

A. Wrong -Normally a remedy, but property was already sold to good faith purchaser, Dilby
B. Wrong } Lebow is entitled to damages; his acceptance created a contract because offer had not been effectively revoked by Foster
C. Right }
D. Wrong -Dilby is a good faith purchaser

Currently, all multiple choice questions are scored based on the number correct, i.e., there is no penalty for guessing. The rationale is that a "good guess" indicates knowledge. Thus, you should answer all multiple choice questions.

Time Requirements for the Solutions Approach

Many candidates bypass the solutions approach, because they feel it is too time consuming. Actually, the solutions approach is a time saver, and more importantly, it helps you prepare better solutions to all essays.

Without committing yourself to using the solutions approach, try it step-by-step on several essay questions. After you conscientiously go through the step-by-step routine a few times, you will begin to adopt and modify aspects of the technique which will benefit you. Subsequent usage will become subconscious and painless. The important point is that you have to try the solutions approach several times to accrue any benefits.

Antithesis of a Solutions Approach

The mark of an inefficient solution is one wherein the candidate immediately begins to write an essay solution. Remember, the final solution is one of the last steps in the solutions approach. You should have the solution under complete control (with the keyword outline) before you begin your final solution.

Efficiency of the Solutions Approach

While the large amount of intermediary work in the solutions approach may appear burdensome and time-consuming, the technique results in more complete solutions in less time than with haphazard approaches. Moreover, the solutions approach really allows you to work out essays that you feel unfamiliar with at first reading. The solutions approach, however, must be mastered prior to sitting for the CPA examination. In other words, the candidate must be willing to invest a reasonable amount of time toward perfecting his/her own solutions approach.

In summary, the solutions approach may appear foreign and somewhat cumbersome. At the same time, if you have worked through the material in this chapter, you should have some appreciation for it. Develop the solutions approach by writing down the steps in the solutions approach algorithm at the beginning of this chapter, and keep them before you as you work recent CPA exam questions. Remember that even though the suggested procedures appear very structured and time-consuming, integration of these procedures into your own style of problem solving will help improve your solutions approach. The next chapter discusses strategies for the overall examination.

**NOW IS THE TIME
TO MAKE A COMMITMENT**

CHAPTER FOUR

TAKING THE EXAMINATION

This chapter is concerned with developing an examination strategy, e.g., how to cope with the environment at the examination site, what order to work questions, etc.

EXAMINATION STRATEGIES

Your performance during the examination is final and not subject to revision. While you may sit for the examination again if you are unsuccessful, the majority of your preparation will have to be repeated, requiring substantial, additional amounts of time. Thus, examination strategies (discussed in this chapter) which maximize your exam-taking efficiency are very important.

Getting "Psyched Up"

The CPA exam is quite challenging and worthy of your best effort. Explicitly develop your own psychological strategy to get yourself "up" for the exam. Pace your study program such that you will be able to operate at peak performance when you are actually taking the exam. Many candidates "give up" because they have a bad day or encounter a rough problem. Do the best you can; the other candidates are probably no better prepared than you.

Examination Supplies

The AICPA recommends that candidates prepare their solutions in pencil. As you practice your solutions approach, experiment with pencils, lead types, erasers, etc., that are comfortable to use and also result in good copy for the grader. In preparing the essay solutions, a hard lead pencil is recommended for better erasability and neatness (remember that a soft lead pencil is needed to fill out the multiple choice answer grid on the exam).

In addition to an adequate supply of pencils and erasers, it is very important to take a watch to the examination. Also, take refreshments (as permitted) which are conducive to your exam efficiency. Finally, dress to assure your comfort during the exam. Layered clothing is recommended for possible variations in temperature at the examination site.

Do not take study materials to the examination room. You will not be able to use them. They will only act to muddle your mind and get you "up tight." Finally, DO NOT carry notes or crib sheets upon your person: This can only result in the gravest of problems.

Lodging, Meals, Exercise

Make advance reservations for comfortable lodging convenient to the examination facilities. Do not stay with friends, relatives, etc. Both uninterrupted sleep and total concentration on the exam are a must. Consider the following in making your lodging plans:

1. Proximity to exam facilities
2. Lodging and exam parking facilities
3. Availability of meals and snacks
4. Recreational facilities

Plan your meal schedule prior to and during the exam to provide maximum energy and alertness during the day and maximum rest at night.

Do not experiment with new foods, drinks, etc., during the examination time period. Within reasonable limits, observe your normal eating and drinking habits. Recognize that overconsumption of coffee during the exam could lead to a hyperactive state and disaster. Likewise, overindulgence in alcohol to overcome nervousness and to induce sleep the night before might contribute to other difficulties the following morning.

Tenseness should be expected before and during the examination. Rely on a regular exercise program to unwind yourself at the end of the day. As you select your lodging for the examination, try to accommodate your exercise pleasure, e.g., running, swimming, etc. Continue to indulge in your exercise program on the days of the examination.

To relieve tension or stress while studying, try breathing or stretching exercises. Use these exercises before and during the examination to start and to keep your adrenaline flowing. Do not hesitate to attract attention by doing pushups, jumping jacks, etc., in a lobby outside of the examination room if it will improve your exam efficiency. Remain determined not to go through another examination to obtain your certificate.

A problem you will likely experience during the exam related to general fatigue and tenseness is writer's cramp. Experiment with alternative methods of holding your pencil, rubbing your hand, etc., during your preparation program.

In summary, the examination is likely to be both rigorous and fatiguing. Expect it and prepare for it by getting in shape, planning methods of relaxation during the exam and exam evenings, and finally building the courage and competence to complete the exam (successfully).

Examination Facilities and Procedures

Visit the examination facilities at least the evening before the examination to assure knowledge of the location. Remember: no surprises. Having a general familiarity with the facilities will lessen anxiety prior to the examination.

Talking to a recent veteran of the examination will give you background for the general examination procedures, such as

1. Procedure for distributing exam booklets, papers, etc.
2. Accessibility of restrooms
3. Availability of coffee and snacks at exam location
4. Admissibility of coffee and snacks in the exam room
5. Peculiar problems of exam facilities, e.g., noise, lighting, temperature, etc.
6. Permissibility of early departure from exam
7. A copy of his/her exam booklet
8. His/her experience in taking the exam
9. Any other suggestions s/he might make

As you can see, it is important to talk with someone who recently sat for the examination at the same location where you intend to sit. The objective is to reduce your anxiety just prior to the examination and to minimize any possible distractions. Finally, if you have any remaining questions regarding examination procedure, call or write your state board.

On a related point, do not be distracted by other candidates who show up at the examination completely relaxed and greet others with confidence. These are most likely candidates who have been there before. Probably the only thing they are confident of is a few days' vacation from work. Also, do not become distracted when they leave early: some candidates may leave after signing in for that session.

Arrive at the Examination Early

On the day of the exam, be sure to get to the examination site at least 30 minutes early to reduce tension and to get yourself situated. It is probably wise to sit away from the door and the administration table to avoid being distracted by candidates who arrive late, leave early, ask questions, etc., and proctors who occasionally converse. AVOID ALL POSSIBLE DISTRACTIONS. Stay away from friends.

Find a seat that will be comfortable: consider sunlight, interior lighting, heating/air conditioning, pedestrian traffic, etc. Most states have assigned seating. If this is the case, you will be seated by your candidate ID number.

Usually the proctors open the sealed boxes of exams and distribute the booklets to candidates 10 minutes before the scheduled beginning of the examination. You are not permitted to open the booklet, but you should study the instructions printed on the front cover. The instructions generally explain

1. How to turn in examination papers
2. Handling of
   a. Multiple choice answer sheets
   b. Scratch sheets
   c. Columnar work sheets
3. Examiners' consideration of the candidate's ability to express him/herself in acceptable written language

You will be given a supply of answer paper as you enter the exam room or as the test booklets are passed out. You will not be permitted to write anything except the headings on an adequate supply of columnar and lined answer paper. The heading is:

Candidate's No. ______________________________

Date ______________________________

State ______________________________

Subject ______________________________

Problem _______________ Page _______________

Do not use your name; write only your candidate number, which will be assigned to you at the beginning of the exam. If a problem requires a name signature, e.g., on an audit report, do not use your own name or initials.

You probably will not work the examination questions in order. There is a possibility of confusion since you cannot number your answer sheets consecutively until the end of the exam. To alleviate this problem, take 10 or 15 paper clips to the exam room to keep the answer sheets of each question separate and in order, while you answer other questions. At the end of the exam, put the packets of answer sheets in proper order and number them consecutively.

Inventory of the Examination Content

When you receive your examination booklet, carefully read the instructions. The objective is to review the standard instructions and to note any new or special instructions. After reviewing the instructions on the front of your examination booklet, make note of the number of questions and the time allocated to each.

Immediately after receiving permission to open the examination booklet, glance over each of the questions sufficiently and jot down the topics on the time schedule on the front of the exam booklet. This will give you an overview of the ensuing 3 1/2 hours of work.

Allocation of Time

Budget your time. Time should be carefully allocated in your attempt to maximize your points. Remember the maximum points available on each question are proportional to the suggested time allotments on the front of each exam booklet. Theoretically, time should be allocated so that you maximize points per minute.

While you have to develop your own strategy with respect to time allocation, some suggestions may be useful. Allocate 5 minutes to reading the instructions and to taking an inventory, jotting the topics tested by question on the front cover. Write the topic next to the time allotment. Assuming 60 individual multiple choice and 4 essay questions, you should spend about 5-10 minutes keyword outlining each of the 4 essay questions. Then, plan on spending about 1 3/4 minutes working each of the individual multiple choice questions. (You will probably be adding grading concepts to your keyword outlines as you read the multiple choice questions.)

After completing these tasks, you now have spent 2 1/4 hours and have substantially completed both the multiple choice questions and essay questions. Revise the keyword outline and prepare the final solutions of the essay questions one at a time. Allocate about 15 minutes to each solution. Recognize that you can write all the grader will care to read in 15 minutes from a well-developed outline. Next, complete the multiple choice answer sheet by CAREFULLY transferring your answers from the exam booklet to the machine gradable form. This should take about five minutes. The answers must be transferred before the exam session ends. THE PROCTORS ARE NOT ALLOWED TO GIVE YOU EXTRA TIME TO DO THIS.

Finally, you have 10 minutes to proofread and to edit. Remember that this is a hypothetical time allocation for illustrative purposes only.

Hypothetical Time Budget
Business Law Exam
(60 individual multiple choice, 4 essay questions)

	Minutes
Inventory of exam	5
Keyword outline of 4 essay questions	25
Answer 60 multiple choice questions	105
Completion of multiple choice answer sheet	5
Final solution of 4 essay questions	60
Extra time	10
Total	210

Order of Working Questions

Select the question that you are going to work first from the notes you made on the front of your examination. Some will select the question that appears easiest to get started and build confidence. Others will begin with the question they feel is most difficult to get it out of the way. Multiple choice questions generally should not be worked first on the business law exam, since each question may contain 4 or 5 grading concepts (for possible inclusion in your essay solutions) as alternate answers. You should, therefore, work through the multiple choice questions only after you have keyword outlined all of the essay questions (but before you write up your final solution).

Once you select a question, you should apply the solutions approach. Essay questions should be worked only through the keyword outline prior to moving on to the next question. Recall that essay questions are generally graded with an open-ended grading guide. Thus, you want to include as many grading concepts as possible in your solution. Waiting to write your essay solution until after all other questions have been dealt with will force you to take a fresh look at the question. As a result, additional grading concepts are often found. As you recognize grading concepts applicable to other questions, turn to the respective question and jot down the keywords (remember that the keyword outlines should be prepared in the margin of your exam booklet).

Note that the AICPA grading curves generally reflect decreasing returns to scale. That is to say, candidates get more credit for the first correct answer than for the last correct answer. This comes about through the use of base points, i.e., a relatively large amount of credit is given to the initial stages of the solution.

The existence of decreasing returns to scale in the AICPA grading curves implies that candidates should allocate more time to the questions which are troublesome. The natural tendency is to write on and on for questions with which you are conversant. Remember to do the opposite: spend more time where more points are available, i.e., you may already have earned the maximum allowable on the question familiar to you.

Never, but never, leave a question blank, as this almost certainly precludes a passing grade on that section. Some candidates talk about "giving certain types of questions to the AICPA", i.e., no answer. The only thing being given to the AICPA is grading time since the grader will not have to read a solution. Expect a couple of "far out" or seemingly "insurmountable" questions. Apply the solutions approach - imagine yourself having to make a similar decision, explanation, etc., in an actual situation and come up with as much as possible.

Page Numbering

Carefully follow the instructions on the front of each exam booklet with regard to turning in papers. Remember a lost answer is a zero. The typical instructions include

1. Arrange your answers in numerical order and number them consecutively, e.g., if you have 15 sheets answering Business Law, number them 1 through 15
2. Write "continued" on the bottom of sheets where another answer sheet for the same problem follows
3. Printed answer sheets for multiple choice questions should be the first answers turned in, i.e., on top, and numbered 1

Postmortem of Your Performance

DON'T DO IT and especially don't do it until Friday evening. Do not speak to other candidates about the exam after completing sections on Wednesday evening, Thursday noon, Thursday evening, and Friday noon. Exam postmortem will only upset, confuse, and frustrate you. Besides, the other candidates probably will not be as well prepared as you, and they certainly cannot influence your grade. Often, those candidates who seem very confident have overlooked an important requirement(s) or fact(s). As you leave the exam room after each session, think only ahead to achieve the best possible performance on each of the remaining sections.

AICPA GENERAL RULES GOVERNING EXAMINATION

1. The only aids you are allowed to take to the examination tables are pens, pencils, and erasers. Rulers, slides rules and calculators are prohibited.
2. You will be furnished an identification card containing your candidate identification number. **Make a note of the identification number for future reference.** Use this identification number on all of your papers. The importance of remembering this number and recording it on your examination papers correctly cannot be overemphasized. If a question calls for an answer involving a signature, do not sign your own name or initials. The required form of identification must be available for inspection by the proctors throughout the examination.
3. Any reference during the examination to books or other matters or the exchange of information with other persons shall be considered misconduct sufficient to bar you from further participation in the examination.
4. Answers must be written on paper furnished by the Board. Heading up answer papers is allowed prior to the start of the examination. **Extra time is not allowed for this at the end of the session.** All unused paper must be returned to the Board at the end of each examination session.
5. You must observe the fixed time for each session which will start and end promptly. It is your responsibility to be ready at the start of the period and to stop writing when told to do so.
6. Question booklets will be distributed shortly before each session begins. You are not permitted to look at the booklet until the starting signal is given.
7. All answers (including the blackening of spaces on the multiple choice answer sheets) should be written in pencil, preferably with No. 2 lead.

8. Identify your answers by using the proper question number. Begin your answer to each question on a separate page and number pages **in accordance with the instructions on the printed examination booklets.** Use only one side of each sheet. Arrange your answers in the order of the questions.

9. The estimated minimum and maximum time that you may need for giving adequate answers to each question is printed in the examination booklet. These estimates should be used as a guide to allot your time. It is recommended that you not spend more than the estimated maximum time on any one question until the others have been completed except to the extent that the maximum time has not been used on prior questions. No point values are shown for the individual questions. Points will be approximately proportionate to the time required. The following is an example of time estimates as they might appear in a printed examination booklet:

All questions are required:

	Estimated Minutes	
	Minimum	*Maximum*
No. 1	90	110
No. 2	15	25
No. 3	15	25
No. 4	15	25
No. 5	15	25
Total	150	210

10. All amounts given in a question are to be considered material unless otherwise stated.

11. Answer sheets for the multiple choice items may vary for each part of the examination. It is important to pay strict attention to the manner in which your answer sheet is structured. As you proceed with the examination, be absolutely certain that the space in which you have indicated your answer corresponds directly in number with the item in your question booklet. **If you mark your answers on the examination booklet, be certain you transfer them to the multiple choice answer sheet before the session ends.**

12. You should attempt to answer all multiple choice items. There is no penalty for incorrect responses. Since objective items are computer-graded, your comments and calculations associated with them are not considered and should not be submitted.

13. Attach all computations to the papers containing your answers for Accounting Practice I and Accounting Practice II. Identify them as to the questions to which they relate. The rough calculations and notes may assist the graders in understanding your answers.

14. The CPA is continually confronted with the necessity of expressing opinions and conclusions in written reports in clear, unequivocal language. Although the primary purpose of the examination is to test your knowledge and application of the subject matter, the ability to organize and present such knowledge in acceptable written language will be considered by the graders. Neatness and orderly presentation of work are also very important. Credit cannot be given for answers that are illegible.

15. Formal journal entries should not be prepared unless specifically required. Time may be saved by entering adjustments, reclassifications, etc., directly on working papers. Elaborate working papers should not be prepared unless they are of assistance in meeting the stated requirements. If both working papers and formal statements are required and time is not adequate to complete both, the working papers should be completed.

16. You should avoid explaining how to answer a question instead of actually attempting a solution. If time grows short, a brief statement to the point is permissible, but full credit cannot be obtained by doing this. A partial answer is better than none and will be awarded appropriate credit.

17. Due consideration and credit, if appropriate, will be given to alternative answers which can arise because there are slight variations in practical accounting procedures or techniques and there are different schools of thought on certain accounting matters.

18. You may retain your examination booklet providing you do not leave the examination room **before one-half hour prior to scheduled completion time.** You are not permitted to take the question booklet or examination papers when you leave your table temporarily. You are responsible for protecting your papers at all times and should turn them face down when temporarily leaving for any reason.

19. Penalties will be imposed on any candidate who is caught cheating before or during an examination. These penalties may include expulsion from this and future examination sessions.

In addition to the above general rules, oral instructions will be given by the examination supervisor shortly before the start of each session. They should include the location and/or rules concerning

a. Storage of briefcases, handbags, books, personal belongings, etc.
b. Food and beverages
c. Smoking
d. Rest rooms
e. Telephone calls and messages
f. Requirements (if any) that candidates must take all parts not previously passed each time they sit for the examination. Minimum grades (if any) needed on parts failed to get credit on parts passed.
g. Official clock, if any
h. Additional supplies
i. Assembly, turn-in, inspection, and stapling of solutions

The next section is a detailed listing (mind jogger) of things to do for your last-minute preparation. It also contains a list of strategies for the exam.

CPA EXAM CHECKLIST

One week before exam

1. Review law notecards, **mini outlines** (Appendix B), and other law notes for important terms, lists, and key phrases.
2. If time permits, work through a few questions in your weakest areas so that applicable law principles and concepts are fresh in your mind.
3. Assemble materials listed under "1." above into a manageable "last review" notebook to be taken with you to exam.

What to bring

1. **Registration material** for the CPA exam.
2. **Hotel confirmation.**
3. **Cash** — payment for anything by personal check is rarely accepted.
4. **Major credit card** — American Express, MasterCard, etc.
5. **Alarm clock** — this is too important an event to trust to a hotel wake-up call that might be overlooked.
6. **Food** — candidates may wish to pack a sack lunch for Thursday and Friday as time is often limited between the conclusion of the morning session and returning to the afternoon session in plenty of time to check in, since it is suggested that candidates arrive no later than 30 minutes prior to each session's starting time. Bring snack foods that will provide energy and sustenance, such as fruit and cheese.
7. **Clothing** that is comfortable and that can be layered to suit the temperature range over the three-day period and the examination room conditions.
8. **Watch** — it is imperative that you be aware of the time remaining for each session.
9. **Other** — "last review" materials, pencils, erasers, leads, sharpeners, pens, etc.

While waiting for the exam to begin

1. Put ID card on table for ready reference to your number. Fill out attendance form that proctor will pick up prior to distributing exam booklet.
2. Fill out all page headings (except for questions and page number) and divide papers on table into computational forms, essay sheets (use every other line when using this form), and columnar workpaper. Make sure your ID number is CORRECT on each answer sheet. Fill in ID number on M/C answer form, filling in circles that correspond to your ID number.
3. Realize that proctors will be constantly circulating throughout each exam session. You need only raise your hand to receive more paper at any time or paper will be available at nearby tables.
4. Take a few deep breaths and compose yourself. Resolve to do your very best and to go after every point you can get!

Before leaving for exam each day

1. Put ID card in wallet, purse, or on person for entry to take the exam. This is your official entrance permit that allows you to participate in all sections of the exam.
2. Remember your hotel room key.
3. Pack snack items and lunch (optional).
4. Limit consumption of liquids.
5. Realize that on Friday A.M. you must check out and arrange for storage of your luggage (most hotels have such a service) PRIOR TO departing for the Law and Theory sections in order to prevent late charges on your hotel bill.

Evenings before exams

1. Reviewing the evenings before the exams could earn you the extra points needed to pass a section. Just keep this last-minute effort in perspective and do NOT panic yourself into staying up all night trying to cover every possible point. This could lead to disaster by sapping your body of the endurance needed to attack questions creatively during the next day.
2. Reread law mini outlines and/or notecards on Thursday evening, reviewing important terms, key phrases, and lists (i.e., essential elements for a contract, requirements for a holder in due course, etc.) so that they will be fresh in your mind Friday a.m.
3. Go over mnemonics you have developed as study aids. Test yourself by writing out the letters on paper while verbally giving a brief explanation of what the letters stand for.

4. Avoid postmortems during the examination period. Nothing you can do will affect your grade on sections of the exam you have already completed. Concentrate only on the work ahead in remaining sections.
5. GET A GOOD NIGHT'S REST! Being well rested will permit you to meet each day's challenge with a fresh burst of creative energy.

Exam Taking Strategy

1. Check exam booklet for completeness as you note number of M/C questions (you can expect 60), and read "required" sections of essay questions, noting the time allotted to each question.
2. Reconcile the question numbers with the questions listed on the front of the exam booklet and check consecutive page numbers in your booklet.
3. Use the solutions approach to briefly outline key concepts that apply to each requirement. These are fresh in your mind now and can be supplemented later after answering M/C questions. Your subconscious will also be working on added ideas.
4. You will need the maximum time available for the law essay questions because they usually consist of 8 unrelated yet involved fact situations that you **must** address. Thus, you must use the minimum time allotted in answering the law M/C.
5. The crucial technique to use for business law M/C is to read through each fact situation CAREFULLY, underlining keywords such as "oral, without disclosing, subject to mortgage," etc. Then read EACH CHOICE carefully before you start eliminating inappropriate answers. In business law, often the 1st or 2nd answer may sound correct, but a later answer may be MORE CORRECT. Be discriminating! Reread the question and choose the right response.
6. Law essay fact situations are often lengthy and involved. Read carefully and decide which areas of law apply.
7. The most important technique to use for ALL essay questions is to constantly remind yourself that the grader assumes you know nothing (s/he cannot read your mind) and you, as a candidate for a professional designation, must convince him/her of your knowledge of the subject matter under question. NEVER OMIT THE OBVIOUS! Explain each answer as if you were explaining the concept to a beginning business student.
8. Tell the grader that you are applying the UCC or Common Law, or the Act of 1933 or 1934, etc.
9. State the issue involved or the requirements that you are testing for (i.e., all six elements of a contract are present).
10. State the rule of law that applies to the issue.
11. Tell the grader how this affects the parties involved.
12. Limit discussion to relevant issues. Too often, candidates spend more time than allotted on a question they are sure of, only to sacrifice points on another question where those extra minutes are crucial.
13. Remember that on the law section you have a maximum of about 10 minutes per fact situation.
14. If you draw a blank as to a conclusion, telling the grader all the points of law that you know about the fact situation may salvage the question.
15. As each question is completed, quickly reread the "required" section to make sure you have responded to each requirement.
16. Double check to make certain you have answered ALL parts of EVERY question to the best of your ability.
17. Transfer M/C answers to the form provided. Be especially careful to follow the numbers exactly, because number patterns differ on each answer form. Don't wait until too late. The proctors are not authorized to give you extra time for this.
18. Remember: A legible, well-organized, grammatically correct answer gives a professional appearance.

CHAPTER FIVE

BUSINESS LAW MODULES

BUSINESS LAW INDEX

Introduction

Module 7/Contracts (CONT)

Outlines and Study Guides

Problems and Solutions*

Module 8/Sales (SALE)

Outlines and Study Guides

**Each question is coded as to month, year, exam section, problem number, and multiple choice question number. For example (583,L1,37) indicates May 1983, law problem 1 and question number 37.*

Problems and Solutions

	Exam reference	No. of minutes	Page no. Problem	Page no. Answer
36 Multiple Choice			134	142
4 Essays:				
1. Sale of Goods by Nonowner; Entrusting	1184,L4c	15–25	140	148
2. Option Contract; Risk of Loss	1178,L5a&b	12–15	140	148
3. Consignments	580,L4a	7–10	141	149
4. Breach of Warranty; Breach of Sales Contract	582,L5	15–20	141	149

Module 9/Negotiable Instruments (NEGO)

Outlines and Study Guides

Problems and Solutions

	Exam reference	No. of minutes	Page no. Problem	Page no. Answer
54 Multiple Choice			171	183
3 Essays:				
1. Trade Acceptance; Nonnegotiable Instrument; Holder in Due Course	1183,L2b	7–10	181	192
2. Rights of Holder in Due Course; Unauthorized Signatures; Liability of Drawee Bank	581,L2	15–20	181	192
3. Shelter Rule; Secondary Liability	583,L5a	7–10	182	194

Module 10/Secured Transactions (SECU)

Outlines and Study Guides

Problems and Solutions

	Exam reference	No. of minutes	Page no. Problem	Page no. Answer
31 Multiple Choice			207	215
3 Essays:				
1. Purchase Money Security Interest in Consumer Goods; Equipment	1183,L2a	7–10	213	221
2. Perfection of True Consignment; Priority of Conflicting Security Interests	583,L3	15–20	213	221
3. Attachment; Perfection; Good Faith Purchaser of Consumer Goods	1184,L4a&b	15–25	214	223

Module 11/Bankruptcy (BANK)

Outlines and Study Guides

Problems and Solutions

Module 12/Suretyship (SURE)

Outlines and Study Guides

Problems and Solutions

Module 13/Agency (AGEN)

Outlines and Study Guides

Problems and Solutions

	Exam reference	*No. of minutes*	*Page no. Problem*	*Page no. Answer*
29 Multiple Choice			287	294
2 Essays:				
1. Ratification; Agency Coupled With an Interest	580,L5a&b	10–15	292	300
2. Vicarious Liability	1178,L3a&b	10–15	292	300

Module 14/Partnership Law (PLAW)

Outlines and Study Guides

Problems and Solutions

	Exam reference	*No. of minutes*	*Page no. Problem*	*Page no. Answer*
32 Multiple Choice			307	315
4 Essays:				
1. Creation of Partnership; Limited Partnership	581,L5	15–20	313	320
2. Assumed Name Statute; Fiduciary Responsibility; Dissolution; Assignment of Partnership Interest	579,L4	20–25	313	321
3. Partnership Property Rights of Individual Partner's Spouse and Creditors	1182,L3b	12–15	314	322
4. Withdrawal and Admission of Partner	584,L5a	7–10	314	323

Module 15/Corporations (CORP)

Outlines and Study Guides

Problems and Solutions

	Exam reference	No. of minutes	Page no. Problem	Page no. Answer
35 Multiple Choice			341	349
3 Essays:				
1. Dividends; Contracts with Director; Director Fiduciary Responsibility	579,L3	25–30	347	355
2. Promoter's Preincorporation Contracts; Cash Dividends; Director's Liability	1184,L5	15–25	348	356
3. Proxy Solicitation	1182,L4b	8–12	348	357

Module 16/Antitrust and Government Regulation

(This module was deleted because the AICPA has discontinued coverage effective 5/86.)

Module 17/Federal Securities Law (FEDE)

Outlines and Study Guides

Problems and Solutions

	Exam reference	No. of minutes	Page no. Problem	Page no. Answer
24 Multiple Choice			369	373
2 Essays:				
1. Legal Implications of Merger; Securities Implications in Employee Stock Purchase Plan	1181,L2	15–20	371	375
2. Registration Requirements Under 1933 Act	582,L2	15–20	371	376

Module 18/Accountant's Legal Liability (ACCO)

Outlines and Study Guides

Problems and Solutions

Module 19/Employer–Employee Relationships (EREE)

Outlines and Study Guides

Problems and Solutions

Module 20/Property (PROP)

Outlines and Study Guides

Problems and Solutions

Module 21/Insurance (INSU)

Outlines and Study Guides

Problems and Solutions

Module 22/Trusts and Estates (TRUS)

Outlines and Study Guides

Problems and Solutions

Mini Outlines

INTRODUCTION

The business law section of the CPA examination tests the candidate's:

1. Ability to recognize legal problems
2. Knowledge of legal principles with respect to the topics listed above
3. Ability to apply the legal principles to the problem situation in order to derive the textbook solution

Refer to "Self-Study Program" in Chapter 1 for detailed suggestions on how to study the business law outlines and business law questions. The basic procedure for each of the 15 business law modules is:

1. Work 10 to 15 multiple choice questions to indicate your proficiency and familiarity with the type and difficulty of questions
2. Study the outlines in this volume
3. Work the remaining multiple choice questions. Study the answer explanations of those you missed or had trouble with.
4. Work the essay questions

Answering Business Law Questions

Law essay questions frequently require a conclusion, e.g.,

Is the instrument in question negotiable commercial paper?

Assuming the instrument is negotiable, does Meglo qualify as a holder in due course entitled to collect the full $3,000?

In many cases, you will be asked to begin your answer with an unequivocal yes or no followed by a period. Recognize that you are not used to this type of situation. Follow the solutions approach for essay questions as outlined in Chapter 3.

Virtually all of these questions requiring conclusions also require the reasons for the conclusions. Clearly, an unsupported yes or no will be worth little more than a blank answer. Always explain the legal principle(s) involved, and justify your application of the principle(s). Do not wander into other areas or deal with legal principles not specifically required by the question. Once again, "what will appear on the unofficial solution?"

The AICPA Content Specification Outline of the coverage of business law, including the authors' frequency analysis thereof (last nine exams), appears on the following pages.

Sources of the Law

Law comes from two sources: statutes and common law. Common law is that which has evolved through court decisions. Decisions of higher courts are binding on lower courts in the same jurisdiction. Common law is applied where there is no statute covering the issue and also to help interpret statutes.

Most business law is regulated by the individual states and therefore may differ from state to state. The Uniform Commercial Code (UCC) has been adopted (sometimes with small changes) by all states except Louisiana, and also is law in the District of Columbia. The CPA exam tests the content of the 1972 Uniform Commercial Code (as amended). The UCC has caused both modernization of business law and uniformity among the states. Wherever applicable, the UCC is to be used on the CPA Examination. The UCC covers the following areas on the CPA Examination.

1. Contracts - for Sales of Goods only
2. Negotiable Instruments
3. Secured Transactions
4. Documents of Title
5. Investment Securities

Most other areas are governed by individual state statutes and common law. Nevertheless, general rules of law can be stated for these areas and the rules provided herein are to be used on the CPA Examination. For some subjects, there are uniform acts, e.g., Uniform Partnership Act. These are not to be confused with federal law. They are uniform in that most states have enacted them as statutes either in their entirety or with small changes and therefore can be used as the general law in that area.

The areas covered by federal law are:

1. Accountant's Legal Liability (as provided in the Securities Acts)
2. Federal Securities Law
3. Bankruptcy
4. Employer-Employee Relationships (except for Worker's Compensation)

Mini Outlines/Final Review

At the end of this chapter we have provided Mini Outlines of the modules in this chapter. These outlines are to be used as a final review tool and not as a primary study source.

AICPA CONTENT SPECIFICATION OUTLINE/FREQUENCY ANALYSIS*
BUSINESS LAW

	Nov. 1981	May 1982	Nov. 1982	May 1983	Nov. 1983	May 1984	Nov. 1984	May 1985	Nov. 1985
I. The CPA and the Law									
A. Common Law Liability to	-	-	-	-	4	-	5	-	-
Clients and Third Persons	[1]	[.50]	[.50]	[.25]		[1]		[.50]	[1]
B. Federal Statutory Liability									
1. Securities Acts	-	-	-	-	2	-	2	-	-
			[.50]	[.75]				[.50]	
2. Internal Revenue Code	-	-	-	-	2	-	2	-	-
C. Workpapers, Privileged Communication, and Confidentiality	-	-	-	-	2	-	1	-	-
		[.50]							
Total MC	-	-	-	-	10	-	10	-	-
Total Essays	1	1	1	1	-	1	-	1	1
Actual Percentage**(AICPA 10%)	10%	10%	10%	10%	10%	10%	10%	10%	10%
II. Business Organizations									
A. Agency									
1. Formation and Termination	3	-	1	-	1	1	1	3	-
									[.50]
2. Liabilities of Principal	1	1	-	1	1	1	-	-	-
3. Disclosed and Undisclosed Principals	-	1	-	-	1	1	-	-	-
4. Agency Authority and Liability	1	1	2	1	1	1	1	2	-
B. Partnerships and Joint Ventures									
1. Formation and Existence	1	2	-	1	2	-	-	2	-
2. Liabilities and Authority of Partners and Joint Owners	3	2	-	1	2	-	-	1	-
			[.25]						
3. Allocation of Profit or Loss	1	-	-	-	-	-	-	-	-
4. Transfer of Interest	1	-	-	1	1	-	1	2	-
			[.25]			[.50]			[.50]
5. Termination, Winding Up, and Dissolution	1	-	-	-	-	-	2	1	-
C. Corporations									
1. Formation, Purposes, and Powers	-	3	-	-	-	1	-	1	1
							[.33]		

*The classifications are the authors'.

**The Actual Percentage was calculated by adding the Total MC Questions to the 10 points for each essay (or portion of), relating to this area (i.e., I, II, etc.) and dividing by 100 (total points available for all Business Law areas).

AICPA CONTENT SPECIFICATION OUTLINE/FREQUENCY ANALYSIS (CONTINUED)
BUSINESS LAW

	Nov. 1981	May 1982	Nov. 1982	May 1983	Nov. 1983	May 1984	Nov. 1984	May 1985	Nov. 1985
2. Stockholders, Directors, and Officers	–	1	–	–	3	1	–	2	2
			[.25]	[.50]			[.33]		
3. Financial Structure, Capital, and Dividends	–	–	–	–	1	2	–	1	1
			[.25]	[.50]			[.33]		
4. Merger, Consolidation, and Dissolution	–	–	–	–	1	2	–	–	–
	[.25]			[.25]					
D. Estates and Trusts									
1. Formation and Purposes	3	1	–	–	–	–	–	1	1
					[.25]	[.50]			
2. Allocation Between Principal and Income	1	1	–	–	–	–	–	–	–
3. Fiduciary Responsibilities	–	1	–	–	–	–	–	–	–
					[.25]				
4. Distributions and Termination	–	–	–	–	–	–	–	–	–
Areas No Longer Tested	–	–	–	–	–	–	–	–	1
Total MC	16	14	3	5	14	10	5	16	6
Total Essays	.25	–	1	1.25	.5	1	1	–	1
Actual % (AICPA 20%; was 15% prior to 5/86)	18.5%	14%	13%	17.5%	19%	20%	15%	16%	16%

III. Contracts	Nov. 1981	May 1982	Nov. 1982	May 1983	Nov. 1983	May 1984	Nov. 1984	May 1985	Nov. 1985
A. Offer and Acceptance	5	2	3	2	3	2	4	4	3
						[.25]			
B. Consideration	–	1	2	1	2	1	–	–	1
		[.25]							
C. Capacity, Legality, and Public Policy	–	–	1	–	–	1	1	–	1
					[.25]		[.50]		
D. Statute of Frauds	–	–	–	3	–	–	2	1	1
					[.50]	[.25]		[.50]	
E. Statute of Limitations	1	–	–	–	–	–	–	1	–
F. Fraud, Duress, and Undue Influence	1	1	1	1	–	–	–	2	3
		[.50]				[.25]			
G. Mistake and Misrepresentation	1	–	1	1	–	1	–	–	1
					[.25]				
H. Parol Evidence Rule	–	–	1	2	–	–	1	1	1
I. Third-Party Rights	–	–	1	1	–	–	1	1	1
J. Assignments	1	–	2	1	–	–	–	1	1
K. Discharge, Breach, and Remedies	1	1	2	3	1	1	1	–	1
		[.25]				[.25]			
Areas No Longer Tested	1	–	–	1	–	–	–	1	1
Total MC	11	5	14	16	6	6	10	12	15
Total Essays	–	1	–	–	1	1	.50	.50	–
Actual Percentage (AICPA 15%)	11%	15%	14%	16%	16%	16%	15%	17%	15%

AICPA CONTENT SPECIFICATION OUTLINE/FREQUENCY ANALYSIS (CONTINUED)
BUSINESS LAW

	Nov. 1981	May 1982	Nov. 1982	May 1983	Nov. 1983	May 1984	Nov. 1984	May 1985	Nov. 1985
IV. Debtor-Creditor Relationships									
A. Suretyship									
1. Liabilities and Defenses	4	2	3	1	– [.50]	2	–	–	1
2. Release of Parties	1	2	1	1	–	1	– [.50]	–	1
3. Remedies of Parties	1	–	1	1	–	1	–	–	–
B. Bankruptcy									
1. Voluntary and Involuntary Bankruptcy	– [.50]	2	2	2	– [.50]	1	1	–	2
2. Effects of Bankruptcy on Debtor and Creditors	–	2	1	1	–	3	2	– [1]	2
3. Reorganizations	–	1	1	1	–	–	–	–	1
Areas No Longer Tested	– [.50]	1	1	3	–	2	2	–	3
Total MC	6	10	10	10	–	10	5	–	10
Total Essays	1	–	–	–	1	–	.50	1	–
Actual Percentage (AICPA 10%)	16%	10%	10%	10%	10%	10%	10%	10%	10%
V. Government Regulation of Business									
A. Regulation of Employment									
1. Federal Insurance Contributions Act	1	–	–	1	1	1	1	1	1
2. Federal Unemployment Tax Act	–	–	–	–	1	–	1	1	–
3. Worker's Compensation Acts	–	–	2	1	–	1	1	1	1
B. Federal Securities Acts									
1. Securities Registration	–	– [1]	1	–	–	2	1	–	–
2. Reporting Requirements	– [.75]	–	–	–	–	–	–	–	–
3. Exempt Securities and Transactions	–	–	1	–	–	1	–	2	– [.75]
4. Proxy Solicitations and Tender Offers*	–	–	– [.50]	– [.25]	–	–	–	–	–
Areas No Longer Tested	4	8	5 [.50]	3 [.50]	13	5 [.50]	11	– [1]	3 [.25]
Total MC	5	8	9	5	15	10	15	5	5
Total Essays	.75	1	1	.75	–	.50	–	1	1
Actual % (AICPA 10%; was 15% prior to 5/86)	12.5%	18%	19%	12.5%	15%	15%	15%	15%	15%

AICPA CONTENT SPECIFICATION OUTLINE/FREQUENCY ANALYSIS (CONTINUED)
BUSINESS LAW

	Nov. 1981	May 1982	Nov. 1982	May 1983	Nov. 1983	May 1984	Nov. 1984	May 1985	Nov. 1985
VI. Uniform Commercial Code									
A. Commercial Paper									
1. Types of Negotiable Instruments	–	1	3	–	– [.25]	3	3	2	1
2. Requisites for Negotiability	2	2	3	–	– [.25]	1	1	2	2
3. Transfer and Negotiation	2	2	2	–	–	2	1	1	2
4. Holders and Holders in Due Course	1	1	2	– [.25]	–	2	1	1	2
5. Liabilities, Defenses, and Rights	4	2	1	– [.25]	1	2	1	1	1
6. Discharge	–	1	–	–	–	–	–	–	1
B. Documents of Title and Investment Securities									
1. Warehouse Receipts	2	1	–	1	–	1	–	1	–
2. Bills of Lading	–	–	1	1	–	–	–	–	–
3. Issuance, Transfer, and Registration of Securities	–	2	–	2	1	–	–	–	–
C. Sales									
1. Contracts Covering Goods	1	–	2	1	3	1	2	1 [.50]	1
2. Warranties	– [.50]	– [.50]	1	2	2	3	1	1	–
3. Product Liability	–	–	–	–	2	–	–	–	– [1]
4. Risk of Loss	–	–	1	– [.50]	3	2	–	–	2
5. Performance and Obligations	–	– [.25]	–	–	1	2	–	–	1
6. Remedies and Defenses	–	2 [.25]	1	1	2	1	1	1	–
D. Secured Transactions									
1. Attachment of Security Agreements	2	–	1	1	–	1	–	1	–
2. Perfection of Security Interests	2	2	4	2	–	1	1 [.33]	1	–
3. Priorities	–	–	–	1	– [.50]	1	1 [.67]	3	1
4. Rights of Debtors, Creditors, and Third Parties	1	–	2	2	–	1	2	2	1
Total MC	17	16	24	14	15	24	15	18	15
Total Essays	.50	1	–	1	1	–	1	.50	1
Actual Percentage (AICPA 25%)	22%	26%	24%	24%	25%	24%	25%	23%	25%

AICPA CONTENT SPECIFICATION OUTLINE/FREQUENCY ANALYSIS (CONTINUED)
BUSINESS LAW

	Nov. 1981	May 1982	Nov. 1982	May 1983	Nov. 1983	May 1984	Nov. 1984	May 1985	Nov. 1985
VII. Property									
A. Real and Personal Property									
1. Distinctions Between Realty and Personalty	-	-	- [.50]	1	-	-	-	1	1
2. Types of Ownership	-	-	-	-	-	- [.50]	-	-	1
3. Lessor-Lessee	-	-	-	-	-	-	- [.50]	-	1
4. Deeds, Recording, Title Defects, and Title Insurance	-	2	-	2	-	-	-	2	1
B. Mortgages									
1. Characteristics	-	1	-	1	-	-	- [.50]	-	1
2. Recording Requirements	-	-	-	1	-	-	-	1	1
3. Priorities	- [.50]	1	-	1	-	-	-	1	1
4. Foreclosure	-	-	-	1	-	-	-	1	-
C. Fire and Casualty Insurance									
1. Coinsurance	1	1	- [.25]	1	-	-	-	1	1
2. Multiple Insurance Coverage	-	-	- [.25]	-	-	-	-	-	-
3. Insurable Interest	3	2	-	1	-	-	-	1	1
Areas No Longer Tested	1	-	-	1	- [.50]	-	-	1	-
Total MC	5	7	-	10	-	-	-	9	9
Total Essays	.50	-	1	-	.5	.5	1	-	-
Actual Percentage (AICPA 10%)	10%	7%	10%	10%	5%	5%	10%	9%	9%

CONTRACTS

Overview

The area of contracts is very heavily tested on the CPA Examination. A large portion of the contract rules serves as a basis for many other law topics; consequently, a good understanding of the material in this module will aid you in comprehending the material in other modules.

It is important that you realize that there are two sets of contract rules to learn. The first set is the common law contract rules which govern transactions involving real property, insurance, and employment. The second set is the contract rules contained in Article Two of the Uniform Commercial Code (UCC). The UCC governs transactions involving the sale of goods, i.e., tangible personal property. Hence, if the contract is for the sale or purchase of tangible personal property, the provisions of the UCC will apply, and not the common law. For every contract question, it is important that you determine which set of rules to apply. Fortunately many of the rules under the two sets are the same. The best way for you to master this area is to first study the common law rules for a topic. Then review the rules that are different under the UCC. Since the common law and the UCC rules have much in common, you will be learning contract law in the most understandable and efficient manner.

Contract law is tested by both essay and multiple choice questions. You need to know the essential elements of a contract because the CPA Examination tests heavily on offer and acceptance. Also, understand that an option is an offer supported by consideration. Distinguish between an option and a firm offer and understand how these are affected by revocations and rejections. You need to comprehend what consideration is and that it must be bargained for to be valid. The exam also requires that you understand that "past consideration" and moral obligations are not really consideration at all. You should have a solid understanding of the Statute of Frauds.

A. Essential Elements of a Contract

1. Offer
2. Acceptance
    a. When offer and acceptance have occurred, an agreement is said to have been made
3. Consideration
4. Legal capacity
5. Legality (legal purpose)
6. Reality of consent
    a. Technically not a true element, but important to consider
7. Statute of Frauds
    a. Not a true element, but each factual situation should be examined to determine whether it applies

B. Discussion of Essential Elements of a Contract

1. Offer
    a. May be either written or oral
    b. Based on intent of offeror
        1) Courts use objective test to determine intent

a) Would reasonable person think that offer had been intended

2) Subjective intent (what offeror actually intended or meant) is not considered

3) Promises made in apparent jest are not offers

EXAMPLE: S says, "I offer to sell to you, B, my car for $5,000." This is an offer, even though S may be actually joking, as long as given the way it was said, a reasonable person would think that S did intend to make the offer to sell his/her car.

4) Statements of opinion or of intent are not offers

EXAMPLE: A doctor tells a patient that he will fully recover in a couple of days, but it actually takes two weeks. This is a statement of opinion, not an offer.

EXAMPLE: "I am going to sell my car for $400." This is a statement of intent, not an offer.

5) Invitations to negotiate (preliminary negotiations) are not offers, e.g., price tags or lists, auctions, inquiries, advertisements

a) But an ad for a limited quantity sold on first-come basis may be an offer

7

c. Offer must be definite and certain as to what will be agreed upon in contract

1) Essential terms are parties, price, time for performance, subject matter (quantity and type)

2) If unclear or open terms are clarified in subsequent negotiations, contract will become valid

3) See UCC Rules - UCC will regard communications as offers if there is clear intent, even if all terms are not present

d. Must be communicated to offeree by offeror or his/her agent

1) Offeree may learn of a public offer, e.g., reward in any way; s/he merely needs knowledge of it

e. Unilateral offer is one which expects acceptance by action rather than with promise

EXAMPLE: M says he will pay J $5 if she will mow his lawn. M has made a unilateral offer which is accepted when J mows the lawn. If J never mows the lawn, there is no contract and therefore no breach of contract.

1) Unilateral contract contains one promise (offer by offeror) and acceptance by action

f. Bilateral offer is one which expects acceptance by a promise from offeree

1) Bilateral contract is formed when offeree accepts with a promise

EXAMPLE: R says to E, "Will you agree to work for me for 3 months at $5,000 per month?" This is a bilateral offer.

2) Bilateral contract contains two promises

g. Mistakes in transmission of offer are deemed to be offeror's fault (risk) because s/he chose method

1) Offeree is less likely to realize error

2) Offeror can recover from transmitter if performance was negligent

h. Mistaken offers. These involve errors in facts such as submitting a bid based on erroneous computations, errors in words or symbols such as typing mistakes, and errors in transmission such as by a telegraph operator.

1) If offeree knows or should know it is a mistake, then s/he cannot accept and form a valid contract

a) E.g., offeror's bid is unduly lower than the others

2) If offeree does not know or should not know it is a mistake, then acceptance forms a valid contract

a) Offeror may be able to rescind by notifying offeree before offeree changes his/her position in reliance on the contract

EXAMPLE: A construction company submits an erroneous bid to replace an old wing in X's building. Even if S accepts the bid, the construction company may be able to rescind the contract if it notifies X of the error before X takes further action. However, if X demolishes the old wing in reliance on the bid, the contract cannot be rescinded.

i. An auction is an invitation to negotiate. A bid is an offer. Falling of hammer is acceptance.

1) Offeror may revoke his offer prior to falling of hammer
2) Offeree may reject highest bid unless auction is "without reserve," then highest bid must be accepted

j. Termination of offer

1) Rejection by offeree

a) Must be communicated to offeror to be effective
b) Rejection is effective when received by offeror

1] Exception: if offeree sends a rejection and then an acceptance, the first received by offeror is effective

2) Revocation by offeror

a) Generally, offeror may revoke offer at any time prior to acceptance by offeree

1] Revocation is effective when received

EXAMPLE: X offers to sell his car to Y stating that the offer will remain open for 10 days. However, on the 5th day Y receives a revocation of the offer from X. The offer would be terminated on the 5th day even though X stated that it would remain open for 10 days.

b) If offeree learns by reliable means that offeror has already sold subject of offer, it is revoked
c) Public offers must be revoked by same amount of publicity used in making offer

EXAMPLE: Offer of reward for apprehension of arsonist in a newspaper makes headlines. It cannot be revoked by a small notice in the back of the newspaper.

d) An <u>option</u> is an offer that is supported by consideration and cannot be revoked before stated time (See C.3. for types and examples of consideration)

1] Option is actually a separate contract to keep offer open

a] Also called an option contract

2] Also, rejection does not terminate option

EXAMPLE: O offers to sell her car to P and states that she will keep the offer open for 10 days if P will pay her $50. P pays the $50 and six days later O attempts to revoke the offer. P then accepts the offer by the seventh day. An agreement has been formed because the offer was an option and could not be revoked before the 10 days. Note that there were actually two contracts between O and P. The first one was the option to keep the offer open. The second was the actual sale of the car.

EXAMPLE: Same example as above except that O asked P to promise to pay $50 within 10 days to keep the offer open. The result is the same because a promise to pay money is also consideration (see C.3.a.).

e) Part performance of unilateral offer removes offeror's right to revoke for a reasonable time. See UCC Rules for firm offers by merchants concerning sale of goods

3) Counteroffer is a rejection coupled with new offer

a) Must be in form of an offer

EXAMPLE: An offer is made to sell a car for $3,000 and a counteroffer is, "I'll give you $2,500."

b) A mere inquiry or request for additional or different terms is not a counteroffer and does not terminate offer

EXAMPLE: An offer is made to sell a car for $3,000 and an inquiry is, "Will you sell for $2,500?"

4) Lapse of time

a) Offeror may specify period of time, e.g., one week
b) If no time is specified, after reasonable time
c) Offeror may specify happening of an event

1] The offeree need not be informed of occurrence of event

5) Death or insanity of offeror terminates offer

a) Does not affect option contract since it is already binding
b) Death or insanity of offeree also terminates private (personal) offers since only offeree can accept

6) Illegality

a) The offer terminates if after making offer and before it is accepted, it becomes illegal

EXAMPLE: X offers to rent to Y an upstairs floor for a cabaret. Before Y accepts, the city adopts a fire code making use of the premises illegal without substantial rebuilding.

7) Bankruptcy or insolvency of either offeror or offeree
8) Impossibility

a) The offer terminates if after making offer and before it is accepted, performance becomes impossible

EXAMPLE: X offers his car to Y for $500, but before Y agrees to the purchase, X's car is destroyed by fire.

2. Acceptance

a. May be written or oral
b. Offer may be accepted only by person to whom it was directed

1) Use objective test--to whom would a reasonable person believe it to be directed?
2) Rewards can usually be accepted by anyone who knows of them

c. Offeree must have knowledge of offer in order to accept

EXAMPLE: D advertises a reward of $100 for the return of his pet dog. G, unaware of the offer, returns D's dog. G cannot require that D pay the $100 (if he later hears of the offer) because he was unaware of the offer when he returned the dog. He could not "accept" an offer he did not know existed.

d. Intent to accept is required

1) Use objective test

e. Acceptance must generally be in form specified by offer

1) By a promise in a bilateral contract
2) By performance of requested act in a unilateral contract

a) Starting performance removes offeror's right to revoke offer, but offeree must fully perform to accept

f. Acceptance must be unequivocal and unconditional

1) An acceptance which attempts to change terms of offer is not acceptance, but both a rejection and a counteroffer

a) This is important--called the mirror image rule
b) Mere inquiry is not a counteroffer

2) A condition which does not change or add to terms of contract is not a counteroffer, i.e., a condition that is already part of contract because of law, even though not expressed in previous negotiations

3) See UCC Rules below for different rules when sale of goods involved

g. Silence is not acceptance unless

1) Offer indicated silence would constitute acceptance, e.g., offer states "your silence is acceptance," and offeree intended his/her silence as acceptance

a) If offeree does not intend to accept, such language has no effect

1] Offeree is under no duty to reply

2) Offeree has taken benefit of services or goods and exercised control over them when s/he had opportunity to reject them

a) However, statutes usually override common law rule by providing that unsolicited merchandise may be treated as a gift

3) Through course of dealings or course of performance between parties, silence can be mode of acceptance

h. Time of acceptance under common law

1) If acceptance is made by method specified in offer or by same method used by offeror, acceptance is effective when sent (i.e., when out of offeree's possession and into possession of independent agency for transmission--constructive communication); e.g., when placed in mail or when telegram is sent

EXAMPLE: Offeror mails a written offer without stating the mode of acceptance. Offeree mails acceptance. Offeror, before receipt, calls offeree to revoke the offer. The contract exists because acceptance was effective when mailed and revocation of offer came too late.

2) Other methods of acceptance are considered effective when actually received by offeror
3) Late acceptance is not valid--it is a counteroffer and a valid contract is formed only if original offeror then accepts
4) If acceptance is valid when sent, a lost or delayed acceptance does not destroy validity

EXAMPLE: R wires an offer to E asking her to accept by mail. The acceptance is correctly mailed but never arrives. There is a valid agreement.

5) Offeror can change above rules by stating other rule(s) in offer

EXAMPLE: Offeror mails a written offer to offeree stating that acceptance is valid only if received by the offeror within 10 days. Offeree mails back the acceptance within 10 days but it arrives late. Acceptance has not occurred even though the offeree used the same method.

6) See UCC Rules below for different rules when sale of goods is involved

i. Once there is an offer and acceptance, a contract is formed

1) Minor details, e.g., closing details, can be worked out later
2) Formalization often occurs later

j. Offers, revocations, rejections, and counteroffers are valid when received (under both common law and UCC)

1) Compare with rules for acceptances

k. Uniform Commercial Code Rules (Important differences from common law rules above for offers and acceptances)

1) The UCC applies to sale of goods (in area of contracts), i.e., tangible personal property, not real property, services, or insurance contracts
2) A written and signed offer for sale of goods, by a merchant, giving assurance that it will be held open for specified time is irrevocable for that period

a) Called firm offer
b) Unlike an option, no consideration needed
c) If no time is specified, reasonable time is inferred

1] In no case is period to exceed three months

EXAMPLE: Herb, an automobile dealer, offers to sell a car to Ike stating, "I promise to keep this offer open for 45 days." Since the offer is not written and signed by Herb, the firm offer rule does not apply and Herb may revoke the offer at any time prior to Ike's acceptance.

EXAMPLE: Same facts as above except that the offer is written and signed by Herb. In this case, the firm offer rule applies and Herb cannot revoke the offer for the stated period.

d) If assurance is given on form supplied by offeree, it must be separately signed by offeror

e) Compare:

1] Firm offer rule does not work under common law
2] Options are valid under UCC as well as common law and do not require a merchant

EXAMPLE: C (not a merchant) agrees to sell an automobile to B, with the offer to remain open for four months. This is not a firm offer so C may revoke this offer at any time by communicating the revocation to B.

EXAMPLE: Same facts as above except that B pays C to keep the offer open for four months. C cannot revoke this offer for four months because although it is not a firm offer, it is an option.

3) Unless otherwise indicated, an offer for sale of goods shall be construed as inviting acceptance in any manner and be any medium reasonable under circumstances

4) Time of acceptance under UCC

a) Acceptance valid when sent if reasonable method used
b) Above rule does not apply if another rule is stated in offer

EXAMPLE: A wires an offer to B without specifying when acceptance is valid but does state the offer will remain open for 5 days. Within the five days, B mails back the acceptance which arrives after 5 days. If the subject matter is a sale of goods, there is a contract because the acceptance was good when sent. Under common law, however, the acceptance takes effect under these facts when received, so no contract would result.

5) Offer to buy goods for prompt shipment which is ambiguous as to intent is construed to invite acceptance, either by prompt promise to ship or prompt shipment

a) Blurs distinction between unilateral and bilateral contracts
b) With respect to a unilateral offer, beginning of performance by offeree (i.e., part performance) will bind offeror if followed within a reasonable time by notice of acceptance

6) Unequivocal acceptance of offer for sale of goods is not necessary under UCC

a) An acceptance containing additional terms is valid acceptance (unless acceptance is expressly conditional upon additional terms)

1] Recall, under common law, this would be a rejection and counteroffer

b) The additional terms are considered proposals to offeror for additions to contract

c) Between merchants, these additional terms become part of contract unless

1] Original offer precludes such
2] New terms materially alter original offer
3] The original offeror gives notice of his objection within a reasonable time

7) Even if terms are left open, a contract for sale of goods will not fail for indefiniteness if there was intent to contract and a reasonable basis for establishing a remedy is available

a) Open price term--construed as reasonable price at time of delivery

1] Or parties can agree to allow third party to set price

b) Open place of delivery term--seller's place of business, if any

1] Otherwise, seller's residence or if identified goods are someplace else, known to both parties at time of contracting, then at that place

c) Open time of shipment or delivery--becomes a reasonable time

d) Open time for payment--due at time and place of receipt of goods or at time and place of delivery of documents of title, if any

1] If on credit, credit period begins running at time of shipment

8) Even if writings do not establish a contract, conduct by parties recognizing a contract will establish one

a) The terms will be those on which writings agree and those provided for in UCC where not agreed on, e.g., reasonable price, place of delivery

b) Often occurs when merchants send preprinted forms to each other with conflicting terms and forms are not read for more than quantity and price

3. Consideration--an act, promise, or forbearance which is offered by one party and accepted by other as inducement to enter into agreement

a. A party binds him/herself to do (or actually does) something s/he is not legally obligated to do, or when s/he surrenders legal right

EXAMPLE: A hits and injures P with his car. P agrees not to sue A when A agrees to settle out of court for $10,000. A's promise to pay the money is consideration. P's promise to refrain from bringing a lawsuit is consideration on his/her side.

EXAMPLE: Using the fact pattern above, further assume that it is not clear whether A is at fault. The settlement (contract) is still enforceable if made in good faith because of possible liability.

b. Legal detriment does not have to be economic, e.g., giving up drinking, smoking, and swearing

c. Forbearance to sue on claim is valid consideration

d. Consideration must be bargained for

   1) Acceptance of a gift or service does not mean one intends to return gift or service

e. Adequacy of consideration--courts generally do not look into amount of exchange

   1) An exchange of unequal amounts of money or fungible goods is not enforceable
   2) Negligible consideration may not be adequate, e.g., nominal consideration such as $1

f. Preexisting legal duty generally is not sufficient as consideration as no new legal detriment is suffered by performing prior obligation

   1) Agreement to pay lesser sum than already owed is unenforceable, but if debtor incurs a detriment in addition to paying, creditor's promise to accept lesser sum will be binding.

      EXAMPLE: X owes Y $1,000. Y agrees to accept $500 and X will also install Y's new furnace at no additional cost.

   2) Agreement to pay more to finish a job, such as building a house, is unenforceable unless unforeseen difficulties are encountered, e.g., underground stream or marshy land under a house
   3) Agreement to pay police officer to recover stolen goods is unenforceable
   4) Preexisting duty to third party gets same results as preexisting duty to contracting party

      EXAMPLE: X promises to pay Y, a jockey, $50 to ride as hard as he can in the race. Y already owes his employer, Z, that duty so there is no consideration to enforce the agreement.

g. Past consideration (consideration for a prior act, forbearance, or agreement) is not sufficient for new contract

h. Moral obligation is generally not consideration except

   1) Promise to pay or ratification of voidable antecedent debt or promise to perform voidable antecedent duty (e.g., ratification by infant upon reaching maturity)
   2) Promise to pay debt barred by Statute of Limitations. Acknowledgment or part payment coupled with intent to pay implies promise. Statutes may require writing.
   3) Promise to pay debt barred by bankruptcy. Promise must adhere to strict rules stated in Bankruptcy Reform Act of 1978 concerning reaffirmations of dischargeable debts.

i. Mutuality of obligation--means both parties must be bound or neither is bound

   1) Both parties must give consideration

j. Promissory estoppel acts as substitute for consideration and renders promise enforceable--promisor is estopped from asserting lack of consideration

   1) Necessary elements

a) Detrimental reliance on promise
b) Reliance is reasonable and foreseeable
c) Damage results (injustice) if promise is not enforced

2) Usually applied to gratuitous promises but trend is to apply to commercial transactions. At least recovery of expenses is allowed.

EXAMPLE: A wealthy man in the community promises to pay for a new church if it is built. The church committee reasonably (and in good faith) relies on the promise and incurs the expenses.

EXAMPLE: Uncle promises his nephew, who feels that college is too expensive, that he will pay for his education if the nephew obtains a degree. Nephew reasonably (and in good faith) relies on the promise and incurs the expenses.

k. Modifying existing contracts

1) Modification of contract needs new consideration on both sides to be legally binding

EXAMPLE: S agrees in a written contract to sell a piece of land to P for $40,000. S later changes his mind and demands $50,000 for the same piece of land. The original contract is enforceable (at $40,000) even if P agrees to the increased price because although P has agreed to give more consideration, S has not.

2) Under UCC, a contract (for sale of goods) may be modified orally or in writing without consideration if in good faith

EXAMPLE: S agrees to sell P 300 pairs of socks for $1.00 each. Due to rapid price increases in S's costs, he asks P if he will modify the price to $1.20 each. P agrees. The contract as modified is enforceable because it is covered under the UCC and does not need new consideration on both sides.

a) Statute of Frauds is applicable if contract as modified is within Statute (see B.7.)

EXAMPLE: X and Y enter into an oral agreement whereby X agrees to pay $450 for a dryer. Due to a price increase experienced by Y, X subsequently agrees to pay $500 for the same dryer. This modification must be in writing to be enforceable because the contract as modified is within the Statute of Frauds. If as modified the sale price would have been $480, the oral modification would be enforceable because it is less than $500.

b) Parties can, in signed writing, exclude future oral modifications

l. Requirements contracts

1) If one party agrees to supply what other party requires, agreement is supported by consideration

a) Reason: supplying party gives up right to sell those to another; purchasing party gives up right to buy from another

m. Output contract

1) One party agrees to sell all of output to another--is supported by consideration

a) However, illusory contracts are not supported by consideration

EXAMPLE: P agrees to buy from S all that he may want for the next month. This is not supported by consideration because P has not actually agreed to be bound.

4. Legal Capacity
   a. An agreement between parties in which one or both lack the capacity to contract is void or in some cases voidable
   b. Minors (persons under age 18 or 21)
      1) A minor may contract, but agreement is voidable by minor only
         a) Adult is held to contract unless minor disaffirms
      2) Minor who disaffirms, in the case of non-necessaries, normally must return what is left of consideration received and may recover all of consideration given
      3) Minor is liable for reasonable value of necessaries furnished to him on a quasi-contract theory
         a) Minor may disaffirm contract if it is executory, i.e., not completed
         b) Necessaries include food, clothing, shelter, education, etc., considering his age and position in life
      4) Minor may disaffirm contract at any time until a reasonable time after reaching majority
         a) Failure to disaffirm within reasonable time after reaching majority acts as ratification; e.g., one year is too long
      5) A minor may ratify within a reasonable time after reaching age of majority. Ratification prior to majority is not effective.
      6) Unless s/he dies or becomes insane, disaffirmance must be by minor
      7) If minor misrepresents his/her age, many jurisdictions will not allow minor to disaffirm contract; some allow other party to sue for fraud
      8) A minor usually is liable for own torts (civil wrongs), but this may depend on his age (above 14 commonly liable). Parents are not liable for torts of minors unless they direct or condone certain conduct or were negligent themselves
   c. Incompetent persons
      1) Agreement by person adjudicated insane is void from beginning
         a) Insane person need not return consideration
      2) If contract is made before adjudication of insanity, it may be voidable
         a) It will be valid provided there was no knowledge of insanity, the agreement is reasonable, and no advantage is taken of disabled party's condition
         b) Where courts hold such agreements voidable, restitution is condition precedent to disaffirmance
   d. Drunkard's legal capacity is determined by his/her ability to understand and by degree of intoxication
   e. Corporations contract through agents and are limited by their charters
   f. Aliens generally have no disabilities

5. Legality

a. Agreement is unenforceable if it is illegal or violates public policy
b. When both parties are guilty (in pari delicto), neither will be aided; i.e., if one party had already given some consideration, he will not get it back

   1) But if one party repudiates (repents) prior to performance, he may recover his consideration

      EXAMPLE: X contracts to buy stolen goods from Y. If X pays Y but then repents and refuses to accept the stolen goods, X may recover the money he paid Y.

c. When one party is innocent, s/he will usually be given relief

   1) A member of a class of people designed to be protected by a statute is considered innocent; e.g., purchaser of stock issued in violation of blue-sky laws

d. Types of illegal contracts

   1) Agreement to commit crime or tort
   2) Wagering contracts
   3) Usury (contract for greater than legal interest rate)
   4) Agreements to interfere with justice
   5) Illegal restraints of trade

      a) A sale of business between buyer and seller containing a covenant which prohibits seller from owning or operating similar business is legal and enforceable provided the time and geographical restrictions are reasonable

         1] Reasonable time is what is fair under the circumstances to protect buyer, e.g., 1 year or even 5 years sometimes, but not forever
         2] Reasonable area would be where the business is conducted, e.g., neighborhood. If business is statewide, then restriction can be for whole state.

         EXAMPLE: Seller of a bakery covenants not to compete in the immediate locality for five years. This is a reasonable area and length of time.

   6) Services rendered without a license when statute requires a license

      a) Two types of licensing statutes

         1] Regulatory licensing statute--one that seeks to protect public from incapable, unskilled, or dishonest persons

            a] Contract is unenforceable by either party
            b] Even if work done, other need not pay because not a contract

         2] Revenue-seeking statute--purpose is to raise revenue for government

            a] Contract is enforceable

7) Exculpatory clauses (party tries to relieve self of liability for own negligence) are against public policy

a) However, usually enforced if parties have relatively equal bargaining power

6. Reality of Consent--Mutual assent is essential to every agreement. If one of the following concepts is present, a contract may be void (i.e., no contract) or voidable (i.e., enforceable until party having right decides to pull out).

a. Fraud--must include following elements

1) Misrepresentation of a material fact

a) Can be total falsehood, series of truths not true together, or concealment of physical defect

b) Silence is not misrepresentation unless there is duty to speak, e.g.,

1] Fiduciary relationship between parties

2] Seller of property knows there is a dangerous latent (hidden) defect

c) Must be statement of past or present fact

1] Opinion, e.g., of value, is not fact unless from expert

2] Prophecy is not fact; e.g., "Next year you will make twice as much"

3] Dealers' talk, i.e., puffing, is not fact

4] Presently existing intention in mind of the speaker is fact

2) Intent to mislead--"scienter"

a) Need knowledge of falsity with intent to mislead, or

b) Reckless mistake or utter disregard for truth can be substitute (constructive fraud)

3) Reasonable reliance by injured party

a) One who knows the truth or might have learned it by a reasonable inquiry may not recover

4) Resulting in injury to others

a) Giving rise to an action for damages by injured party

5) Remedies for fraud

a) If contract is voidable

1] Defrauded party may affirm agreement and sue for damages under tort of deceit, or if party is sued on contract, then s/he may set up fraud in reduction of damages

2] Defrauded party may rescind contract

3] Once defrauded party affirms agreement, party cannot rescind contract

b) If contract is void

1] Defrauded party may sue for fraud and seek damages in tort

6) Fraud may occur

a) In the inducement

1] The misrepresentation occurs during contract negotiations
2] Creates voidable contract at option of defrauded party

EXAMPLE: A represents to B that A's car has been driven 50,000 miles when in fact it has been driven for 150,000 miles. If B purchases A's car in reliance on this misrepresentation, fraud in the inducement is present, creating a voidable contract at B's option.

b) In the execution

1] Misrepresentation occurs in actual form of agreement
2] Creates void contract

EXAMPLE: Larry Lawyer represents to Danny Dumb that Danny is signing his will, when in fact he is signing a promissory note payable to Larry. This promissory note is void because fraud in the execution is present.

b. Innocent misrepresentation

1) An innocent misstatement made in good faith, i.e., no scienter
2) All other elements same as fraud
3) Creates right of rescission (cancellation) in other party--to return both parties to their precontract positions

a) All benefits must be returned by both parties

c. Mistake--an act done under an erroneous conviction

1) Unilateral mistake generally is not grounds to rescind contract unless

a) Mistaken party is free of negligence
b) Other party knew of mistake
c) Failure to read provisions of contract before signing is generally no excuse
d) As to mistakes in computations, general rule is that contract is voidable if mistaken party was not negligent and amount of error was so great that other party should have known mistake had been made

2) Mutual mistake (by both parties) generally makes a contract voidable

a) Also called bilateral mistake
b) A contract may be reformed to comply with intent of parties if mistake was made in reducing agreement to writing
c) Where parties are merely ignorant as to value of subject matter, damaged party is not permitted to rescind

d. Duress--a contract entered into because of duress can be voided because of invalid consent

1) Any acts or threats of violence or extreme pressure against party or member of party's family, which in fact deprives party of free will and causes him to agree, is duress

EXAMPLE: X threatens to criminally prosecute Y unless he signs contract. This contract is made under duress.

2) Economic duress: contract is only voidable if one party puts other in desperate economic condition

e. Undue influence--the mental coercion of one person over another which prevents understanding or voluntary action

 1) Usually occurs when very dominant person has extreme influence over weaker person
 2) Also occurs through abuse of fiduciary relationship, e.g., CPA, attorney, guardian, trustee, etc.

f. Unconscionable contract--an oppressive contract in which one party has taken severe, unfair advantage of the other, usually because of latter's absence of choice or poor education

 1) Under these circumstances court may void contract or reform terms so as to be fair to both parties

  a) E.g., exclude unconscionable clause or limit it

g. Hardship, bad economic conditions, or a "bad deal" are <u>not</u> conditions creating voidable contracts

 1) These are assumed to have been contemplated

h. Infancy, incompetency, and noncompliance with Statute of Frauds may also create voidable contract

i. Adhesion contract--offeror is in position to say "take it or leave it" because of superior bargaining power

 1) Usually occurs when large business entity requires its customers to use their standard form contract without allowing modification

7. Conformity with the Statute of Frauds

 a. Contracts required to be in writing and signed by party to be charged--these are said to be within the Statute

  1) An agreement to sell land or any interest in land

   a) Includes buildings, easements, leases longer than 1 year, mortgages, and contracts to sell real estate

   b) Part performance typically satisfies Statute but this requires

    1] Possession of the land and
    2] Either part payment or making of improvements

  2) An agreement that cannot be performed within one year from the making of agreement

   a) Contract that can be performed in exactly one year may be oral

    1] Time is measured from date of making contract, not counting first day

   b) Concerned with when completion can be, not how long performance actually takes

EXAMPLE: W agrees to hire X for ten months starting in four months. This contract must be in writing because it will not be performed until 14 months after the agreement is made.

EXAMPLE: A agrees to paint B's portrait for $400. It actually is not completed until over a year later. This contract did not have to be in writing because it was possible to complete it within one year.

c) If performance is contingent on something which could take place in less than one year, agreement may be oral

EXAMPLE: "I will employ you as long as you live." Promisor could possibly die in less than one year.

d) But if its terms call for more than one year, it must be written even if there is possibility of taking place in less than one year

EXAMPLE: "I will employ you for 5 years." Death could shorten, but the terms control for the writing requirement under the Statute of Frauds.

e) Acceleration of payment of debt does not eliminate writing requirement

f) Generally, if one side of performance is complete but other side cannot be performed within year, it is not within Statue, i.e., may be oral. This is especially true if performance has been accepted and all that remains is the payment of money (e.g., sale with payments spread over two years).

3) An agreement to answer for debt or default of another (contract of guaranty)

a) A secondary promise is within this section of the Statute of Frauds (required to be in writing)

EXAMPLE: "If Jack doesn't pay, I will."

b) A primary promise is not within this section of the Statute of Frauds

EXAMPLE: "Let Jack have it, and I will pay."

c) Promise for benefit of promisor may be oral

EXAMPLE: Promisor agrees to answer for default of X, because X is promisor's supplier and he needs X to stay in business to keep himself in business.

d) Promise of indemnity (will pay no matter whose fault, e.g., insurance) is not within Statute

e) Assignor's promise to assignee, guaranteeing obligor's performance is not within Statute

f) Guarantee of del credere agent (see AGENCY) is not subject to the Statute of Frauds

4) An agreement by an executor or administrator to answer for debt of decedent out of assets of the executor, i.e., not out of estate of decedent

5) Agreement for sale of goods for $500 or more is required to be in writing under UCC

a) Exceptions to writing requirement (these are important)

1] Part performance makes contract enforceable to extent of performance (must be receipt or acceptance)

2] Specially manufactured goods not suitable for sale in ordinary course of seller's business if seller had made a substantial start in their manufacture before attempted repudiation of such agreement

3] Contract is enforceable against party who admits the contract in court. Enforceable to extent admitted.

4] Between merchants, if one party sends written confirmation to another stating terms of oral agreement, the other party must object within ten days to retain protection of this section of Statute of Frauds

b) Agreement creating in creditor nonpossessory security interest in goods. See SECURED TRANSACTIONS.
c) Agreement for sale of intangibles over $5,000; e.g., patents, copyrights, or contract rights
d) Also, agreement for sale of securities of any amount

b. No formal writing is required except that there must be some written note or memorandum signed by party sought to be charged

1) Any form will do, e.g., letter, telegram, receipt
2) Need not be single document, e.g., two telegrams
3) Need not be made at same time as contract

a) Must be made before suit is brought
b) Need not exist at time of suit, i.e., may have been destroyed

4) Should include such matters as

a) Identity of parties
b) Description of subject matter
c) Terms and conditions
d) Consideration
e) Signature

1] Only needs signature or authenticating mark of party sought to be bound
2] Signature need not be at end nor be in a special form so long as intent to authenticate existed, e.g., initials, stamp, printed letterhead, etc.

5) Under UCC a writing is adequate if it indicates contract has been made between parties and is signed by one to be bound

a) May omit material terms (e.g., price, delivery, time for performance) so long as quantity is stated. Reasonable terms will be inferred.

c. Noncompliance with Statute of Frauds, i.e., failure to make a writing, will make contract unenforceable
d. Promissory estoppel will prevent a party from asserting Statute of Frauds as a defense if he has promised not to and other party has relied on promise to his detriment
e. Parol evidence rule. A written agreement intended by parties to be final and complete (i.e., an integration) may not be contradicted by prior or contemporaneous oral evidence

1) Applies to written contracts even when not required under Statute of Frauds
2) Evidence of integration often shown by a merger clause such as "This agreement is the complete agreement between the parties; no other representations have been made."

EXAMPLE: A and B enter into a home purchase agreement which is intended as a complete contract. B wishes to introduce oral evidence into court that the price of $150,000 that was in the home purchase agreement was put in to get a larger loan from a bank. B claims that they orally agreed the price would be $130,000. The oral evidence is not allowed to contradict the written contract under the parol evidence rule.

3) Exceptions (party may present oral proof)

a) To show invalidity of contract between parties, e.g., fraud, forgery, duress, mistake, failure of consideration

b) To show terms not inconsistent with writing that parties would not be expected to have included

EXAMPLE: Builder promises to use reasonable care not to damage nearby trees when building a house.

c) To explain intended meaning of an ambiguity (proof cannot contradict terms in contract but can explain them)

d) To show condition precedent--oral proof can be presented to show a fact or event must occur before agreement is valid

e) Under UCC, written terms may be supplemented or explained by course of dealing, usage of trade, or course of performance

4) Does not apply to subsequent transactions, e.g., oral promises made after original agreement, or separate and distinct oral agreement made at same time as written contract

EXAMPLE: M and N have a complete written employment contract. Later, M and N orally modify the contract with M agreeing to pay more and N agreeing to take on more duties. The oral evidence is allowed because it arose subsequent to the written contract.

C. Assignment and Delegation

1. Assignment is the transfer by one person to another of a right under a contract

2. Delegation is the transfer of duties under a contract

3. Generally, a party's rights in a contract are assignable and duties are delegable

a. No consideration is needed for valid assignment

1) Gratuitous assignments are revocable

EXAMPLE: A owes B a debt for services B performed for A, but B has been unable to collect because A has been in financial difficulty. B may gratuitously assign this debt to X if X can collect it. If A's financial position improves, B may revoke the assignment to X and collect the debt himself or assign it to another for consideration.

b. Rights may be assigned without delegating duties, or duties may be delegated without assigning rights

c. Partial assignments may be made, e.g., only assign part of one's rights such as right to receive money

d. A delegation of duties is not an anticipatory breach

EXAMPLE: X Company contracted to deliver certain goods to Y. If X Company is low on these goods, it may delegate this duty to S Company, its subsidiary. It is not an anticipatory breach because X has not indicated that performance will not occur.

e. An assignment of a contract is taken to mean both assignment of rights and delegation of duties

f. Exceptions

1) Contract involving personal services, credit, trust, or confidence, e.g., an artist cannot delegate his duty to paint a portrait

a) But a contractor building a house according to a blueprint can delegate his duty to someone qualified because no special skill is involved, just following a set of directions

b) With permission, personal duties can be delegated

2) Provision of contract or statute prohibits assignment or delegation

a) Trend is to look with disfavor on prohibitions against assignments where only a right to money is concerned

b) The UCC makes prohibition against assignment of monetary rights ineffective

3) The assignment would materially change risk or obligations of other party

a) E.g., insurance contracts, requirement and output contracts, and contracts where personal credit is involved

4. An assignment generally extinguishes any rights of assignor but a delegation does not relieve delegant of his duties

a. The assignee acquires assignor's rights against obligor and has exclusive right to performance

b. If obligor has notice of assignment, he may not pay assignor without risk of also having to pay assignee. If obligor has no notice, he may pay assignor and assignee can recover from assignor.

c. Unless there is a novation, the delegating party is still liable if delegatee does not perform

1) Novation occurs when one of original parties to contract is released and new party is substituted in his/her place

a) Requires consent of all three parties

EXAMPLE: A sells a car to B and accepts payments over time. B sells the car to C who agrees to take over the payments. No novation has occurred unless A agrees to accept C and release B.

5. A party taking an assignment generally steps into shoes of assignor. S/he gets no better rights than assignor had.

a. Assignee is subject to any defenses obligor could assert against assignor

b. Assignee may recover from assignor if assignor causes obligor not to perform; e.g., assignor does not perform his duties and obligor asserts that as a defense

6. If assignor makes more than one assignment of same right, there are two rules to be applied depending upon the state

   a. Either first assignee to give notice to obligor prevails, or
   b. First to obtain assignment prevails
   c. Under the UCC, assignee can perfect his assignment by filing a financing statement (see SECURED TRANSACTIONS)

      1) First to file prevails

D. Third-Party Beneficiary Contracts

1. Contracting parties enter into agreement intended to benefit third party(ies).

   a. Creditor beneficiary--one party (the promisor) contracts with debtor (the promisee) to pay a debt owed to creditor (third-party beneficiary)

      EXAMPLE: X owes C $100. X contracts with Y to paint Y's house if Y will pay C $100. C is a creditor beneficiary.

      EXAMPLE: Buyer assumes the seller's mortgage. Mortgagee is a creditor beneficiary.

   b. Donee beneficiary--almost the same as creditor beneficiary except promisee's intent is to confer a gift upon third party through promisor's performance

      EXAMPLE: X contracts to buy Y's car if Y will deliver it to D, X's son. D is a donee beneficiary.

   c. Incidental beneficiary--third party who receives an unintended benefit from a contract. He obtains <u>no</u> rights.

      EXAMPLE: X and Y contract to build an apartment building. A, a nearby store owner, would benefit from increased business and is an incidental beneficiary.

2. Only intended beneficiary (creditor or donee) can maintain an action against contracting parties for nonperformance

   a. Intent of the promisee controls
   b. Creditor beneficiary can proceed against either contracting party

      EXAMPLE: X owes C $100. X contracts with M to paint M's house if M will pay C $100. If X does not paint M's house, C may sue X because X still owes C $100. C may also sue M, because M now owes C $100 under the contract. C is a creditor beneficiary and can sue either party.

   c. Donee beneficiary can proceed against the promisor only

      EXAMPLE: X contracts to buy Y's car if Y will deliver it to D. If Y does not deliver the car, D may sue Y. However, D may not sue X because it was a gift from X, not an obligation.

3. Until a third party has accepted the benefits of the contract, the parties may rescind and defeat his rights

   EXAMPLE: X owes C $100. X contracts with Y to paint Y's house if Y will pay C $100. X and Y may rescind the contract before Y pays C $100. Then there is no contract for C to enforce; however, C may still sue X for the $100 owed.

4. The promisor can assert any defenses against third-party beneficiary that s/he has against promisee

E. Discharge of Contracts

1. By performance. (See next section.)

2. By agreement: consideration is necessary, but often it is supplied by a promise for a promise, e.g., both parties agreeing to release other party of contractual obligation

   a. A novation is an agreement among all parties whereby initial agreement is discharged by creation of a new agreement

      1) May involve substitution of creditors, debtors or of obligations

      EXAMPLE: A party purchases land and assumes a mortgage. The original mortgagor is still liable unless a novation has occurred.

   b. Under UCC, no consideration is needed to modify a contract for sale of goods

   c. Mutual rescission involves dissolution of the contract and placing parties, so far as possible, in position they were in prior to making contract

   d. Mutual release is a subsequent agreement that contract is no longer binding

   e. Accord and satisfaction. The accord is a substituted agreement giving, usually, easier terms. The satisfaction is performance. The claim may be disputed or not. Until satisfaction is begun, promisee may recover on old contract.

      EXAMPLE: X sells a boat to Y who promises to pay in 30 days. Y fails. X and Y agree that Y will fix X's roof as satisfaction. Y is liable until he starts the roof repair.

3. By Release or Covenant not to sue

   a. Release of one joint obligor releases other(s) unless express reservation of rights against other(s) is made

      1) Reservation of rights is made by wording so in release, e.g., "I release X but reserve all rights against Y."

      2) Joint obligation--two or more parties promise to perform obligation together. It must be enforced against both (all) of them together.

         EXAMPLE: A and B enter into a contract with P in which they "jointly" promise to build a house for P. If A and B do not finish the house, P must sue both A and B in one lawsuit in order to recover damages.

      3) Joint and several obligation--two or more parties promise to perform obligation and any one of them will accept liability for entire performance. All or any one may be sued for entire amount.

         EXAMPLE: A and B enter into a contract with P in which each promises individually to build a house for P. If A and B do not finish the house, P may sue either A or B (or both) for the full amount of damage damages.

   b. Covenant not to sue one joint obligor does not affect other(s)

      EXAMPLE: X and Y are jointly liable to A. If A promises not to sue X, A may still sue Y. However, if A had released X from the obligation, Y would also be released.

4. By performance becoming objectively impossible
   a. Performance becomes illegal
   b. Death of party where personal service is necessary
   c. Destruction of subject matter without fault of promisor
   d. Bankruptcy of party
   e. Unanticipated and extreme difficulty will rarely excuse
      1) UCC provides for discharge on basis of commercial frustration in sale of goods where performance is "made impracticable by the occurrence of a contingency the nonoccurrence of which was a basic assumption on which the contract was made"

         EXAMPLE: The sole source of supply for the object of the contract disappears. Both buyer and seller assumed the source would be available.

      2) Discharge if other party prevents performance (a breach of contract)

5. By breach of contract (failure to carry out terms of contract)
   a. Partial breach (minor breach). Injured party is not discharged but may sue.
   b. Total breach. Injured party discharged and may sue or rescind.
      1) Material breach. Failure to perform a term so essential that purpose of parties is defeated.
   c. Anticipatory breach. Renunciation before performance is due.
      1) May sue at once, or
      2) Wait until time performance is due or for a reasonable time and then sue
      3) If other party has not changed position in reliance upon the repudiation, repudiating party can retract repudiation and perform at appointed time, thereby discharging his/her contractual obligation

         EXAMPLE: X agrees to convey and Y agrees to pay for land on April 1. On February 1, Y learns that X has sold to Z. Y may sue before April 1, or he may wait and sue on April 1.

F. Performance

1. Duty to perform is absolute under a covenant to perform; e.g., "I will pay you $100 when you deliver the goods."

2. Duty to perform may depend upon a condition, which is a fact or event, the occurrence or nonoccurrence of which creates or removes duty to perform
   a. Condition precedent is one which must occur before there is duty to perform; e.g., "I will lend you $1,000 if your credit checks out."
   b. Condition subsequent is one which removes preexisting duty to perform; e.g., "I will pay you for these goods unless I decide to return them."
   c. Conditions concurrent are mutually dependent upon performance at nearly the same time, e.g., delivery and payment for goods

d. Satisfaction as a condition. Normally when a contract guarantees satisfaction, this means agreement is performed when a reasonable person would be satisfied. However, if agreement is expressly conditioned upon personal satisfaction of one of contracting parties, then performance does not occur until that party is actually satisfied.

   1) Objective satisfaction. Satisfaction of a reasonable person is enough, e.g., constructing a sidewalk.

   2) Personal satisfaction. Contracts involving personal tastes or judgment; e.g., painting a portrait.

3. Tender of performance is an offer to perform; e.g., offer to pay debt

   a. Necessary to put other party in breach if concurrent conditions

      EXAMPLE: X has contracted to buy goods from Y with delivery and payment to take place concurrently. X must offer the money to Y before Y has breached the contract for failure to deliver.

   b. Must comply with contract as to time, place, and manner (amount and kind)
   c. If tender of payment is refused, tender has effect of

      1) Stopping the running of interest
      2) Discharging any security

   d. If tender of performance other than payment is refused, it is breach of contract and promisor is excused from performance

4. Under the doctrine of substantial performance (very important), performance is satisfied if

   a. There has been substantial performance (i.e., deviations are minor) and
   b. There has been good faith effort to comply with contract
   c. Damages for deviations are deducted from price if above are met

5. Part payment when debtor owes more than one debt to creditor

   a. Debtor may specify which debt payment applies to

      1) Otherwise, creditor can apply to either
      2) If neither specifies, law presumes application in order of maturity (oldest first). However, all unsecured debts are considered paid before secured debts, even if secured debts are older.

6. Executory contract--has not yet been performed; only promises have been given

   a. Wholly executory when there has been no performance, e.g., each party has merely promised
   b. Partially executory when only part of contract is still unperformed, e.g., one party has performed and the other has not

7. Executed contract--all parties have completely performed and no obligation remains

G. Remedies

1. Rescission--annulment of contract whereby parties are placed in position they held before contract was formed
   a. Often remedy for voidable contract
2. Restitution--return of consideration to injured party
   a. Not available if debt is owed or for severable part of contract which is complete
3. Specific performance--compels performance promised. Used only when money damages will not suffice; e.g., when subject matter is unique, or rare, as in contract for sale of land.
4. Injunction--compels an act by the party (positive injunction), or restrains an act (negative injunction)
5. Damages--payment of money
   a. Purpose is to place injured party in as good a position as he would have occupied if contract had been performed
   b. Actual or compensatory damages are equal to amount caused by breach
      1) Lost profits are difference between contract price and market price
         a) If market value is zero because of breach, then damages are full contract price
      2) Consequential and incidental damages are those reasonably foreseeable as result of breach, e.g., spoilage of goods and expenses incurred in expectation of fulfillment of contract such as traveling expenses
         a) These are recoverable
      3) Damages that are not foreseeable are not recoverable
   c. Punitive damages are generally not allowed
   d. Liquidated damages are damages that are known or certain in amount (fixed). Often determined by estimate and agreement beforehand and provided for in the contract.
      1) Excessive liquidated damages are penalties and not enforceable in court
      2) Reasonableness judged as of time contract was made
   e. Mitigation of damages. Party injured by breach must use reasonable care to minimize loss.

      EXAMPLE: One who receives perishables which are not the goods bargained for must take reasonable steps to prevent loss from spoilage.

      EXAMPLE: X contracts to fix Y's car. After X begins work, Y breaches and says "Stop." X cannot continue to work and incur more costs, i.e., put in more parts and labor.
6. Quasi-contract--a type of implied contract. It provides a remedy where one person has been unjustly enriched to detriment of another.

   EXAMPLE: D falsely claims to be a pauper and obtains care at a home for the aged. A large estate is discovered at his death. The home may sue for the reasonable value of services rendered.
7. Arbitration--resolution of dispute, outside of judicial system, by a party agreed to by disputing parties

H. Statute of Limitations

1. Bars suit if not brought within statutory period
   a. Periods vary for different types of cases
   b. Periods vary from state to state
2. Statute begins to run from time cause of action accrues, e.g., breach
3. Running of statute may be stopped (tolled) by
   a. Disability of plaintiff to sue, e.g., insanity
   b. Defendant's absence from jurisdiction

Multiple Choice Questions (1–69)

1. In determining whether a bilateral contract has been created, the courts look primarily at
   a. The fairness to the parties.
   b. The objective intent of the parties.
   c. The subjective intent of the parties.
   d. The subjective intent of the offeror.

2. The following conversation took place between Mary and Ed. Mary: "Ed, if you wanted to sell your table, what would you ask for it?" Ed: "I suppose $400 would be a fair price." Mary: "I'll take it, if you will have it refinished." Ed: "Sold." Thus
   a. Ed's statement: "I suppose $400 would be a fair price" constituted an offer.
   b. Mary's reply: "I'll take it, if you will have it refinished" was a conditional acceptance, terminating Ed's offer.
   c. No contract resulted since Ed never stated he would actually sell the table for $400.
   d. A contract was formed when Ed said: "Sold."

3. Harris wrote Douglas a letter which might be construed alternatively as an offer to sell land, an invitation to commence negotiations, or merely an invitation to Douglas to make an offer. Douglas claims that the communication was a bona fide offer which he has unequivocally accepted according to the terms set forth therein. In deciding the dispute in question, the court will
   a. Look to the subjective intent of Harris.
   b. Use an objective standard based on how a reasonably prudent businessman would have interpreted the letter to Douglas.
   c. Decide that an offer had **not** been made if any of the usual terms were omitted.
   d. Decide on the basis of what Douglas considered the writing to be.

4. The president of Smith, Inc., wrote to Johnson offering to sell the Smith warehouse for $190,000. The offer was sent by Smith on May 1 and was received by Johnson on May 5. The offer stated that it would remain open until November 15. The offer
   a. Is a firm offer under the UCC since it is in writing.
   b. Is a firm offer under the UCC but will be irrevocable for only three months.
   c. May be revoked by Smith any time prior to Johnson's acceptance.
   d. Constitutes an enforceable option.

5. On January 1, Lemon wrote Martin offering to sell Martin his ranch for $80,000 cash. Lemon's letter indicated that the offer would remain open until February 15 if Martin mailed $100 by January 10. On January 5, Martin mailed $100 to Lemon. On January 30, Martin telephoned Lemon stating that he would be willing to pay $60,000 for the ranch. Lemon refused to sell at that price and immediately placed the ranch on the open market. On February 6, Martin mailed Lemon a letter accepting the original offer to buy the ranch at $80,000. The following day, Lemon received Martin's acceptance. At that time the ranch was on the market for $100,000. Which of the following is correct?
   a. Martin's mailing of $100 to Lemon on January 5 failed to create an option.
   b. Martin's communication of January 30 automatically terminated Lemon's offer of January 1.
   c. The placing of the ranch on the market by Lemon constituted an effective revocation of his offer of January 1.
   d. Martin's letter of February 6 formed a binding contract based on the original terms of Lemon's January 1 letter.

6. West sent a letter to Baker on October 18, 1983, offering to sell a tract of land for $70,000. The offer stated that it would expire on November 1, 1983. Baker sent a letter on October 25, indicating the price was too high and that he would be willing to pay $62,500. On the morning of October 26, upon learning that a comparable property had sold for $72,500, Baker telephoned West and made an unconditional acceptance of the offer at $70,000. West indicated that the price was now $73,000. Baker's letter offering $62,500 arrived the afternoon of October 26. Under the circumstances
   a. West's letter was a firm offer as defined under the Uniform Commercial Code. No
   b. Baker validly accepted on the morning of October 26.
   c. There is **no** contract since Baker's acceptance was not in a signed writing.
   d. The parol evidence rule will preclude Baker from contradicting his written statements with oral testimony contra to his letter of October 25. No

7. Dustin received a telephone call on Monday from his oil supplier. The supplier offered him 1,000 barrels of heating oil at $48 a barrel, the current price in a rapidly changing market. Dustin said he would take the offer under advisement. The next day, the market price

rose to $50 a barrel and Dustin sent the supplier a letter late that afternoon accepting the offer at $48 a barrel. The letter arrived in the usual course on Thursday morning, by which time the market price had moved to $56 a barrel. The supplier called Dustin and said it would not accept his order. Dustin insisted that he had a contract. Which of the following is correct?

a. Acceptance took place on dispatch of Dustin's letter.
b. Acceptance did **not** take place upon dispatch as the offer had already expired.
c. Acceptance did **not** take place because the only means of acceptance Dustin could use was the phone.
d. Acceptance could only be made by a signed writing.

8. Fine Tuning, Inc., sent Watson a letter offering to sell Watson a custom made automobile for $75,000. Watson immediately sent a telegram to Fine purporting to accept the offer. However, the telegraph company erroneously delivered the telegram to Pine Tuna, Inc. Three days later, Fine mailed a letter of revocation to Watson which was received by Watson. Fine refused to sell Watson the automobile. Watson sued Fine for breach of contract. Fine

a. Will be liable for breach of contract.
b. Will avoid liability due to the telegraph company's error.
c. Will avoid liability since it revoked its offer prior to receiving Watson's acceptance.
d. Would have been liable under the deposited acceptance rule only if Watson had accepted by mail.

9. Justin made an offer to pay Benson $1,000 if Benson would perform a certain act. Acceptance of Justin's offer occurs when Benson

a. Promises to complete the act.
b. Prepares to perform the act.
c. Promises to perform and begins preliminary performance.
d. Completes the act.

10. Luxor wrote Harmon offering to sell Harmon Luxor's real estate business for $200,000. Harmon sent a telegram accepting the offer at $190,000. Later, learning that several other parties were interested in purchasing the business, Harmon telephoned Luxor and made an unqualified acceptance on Luxor's terms. The telegram arrived an hour after the phone call. Under the circumstances

a. Harmon's telegram effectively terminated the offer.
b. Harmon's oral acceptance is voidable, because real estate is involved.
c. The offer was revoked as a result of Harmon's learning that others were interested in purchasing the business.
d. Harmon has made a valid contract at $200,000.

11. Water Works had a long-standing policy of offering employees $100 for suggestions actually used. Due to inflation and a decline in the level and quality of suggestions received, Water Works decided to increase the award to $500. Several suggestions were under consideration at that time. Two days prior to the public announcement of the increase to $500, a suggestion by Farber was accepted and put into use. Farber is seeking to collect $500. Farber is entitled to

a. $500 because Water Works had decided to pay that amount.
b. $500 because the suggestion submitted will be used during the period that Water Works indicated it would pay $500.
c. $100 in accordance with the original offer.
d. Nothing if Water Works chooses **not** to pay since the offer was gratuitous.

12. Marglow Supplies Inc., mailed a letter to Wilson Distributors on September 15, 1981, offering a three-year franchise dealership. The offer stated the terms in detail and at the bottom stated that the offer would not be withdrawn prior to October 1, 1981. Which of the following is correct?

a. The statute of frauds would **not** apply to the proposed contract.
b. The offer is an irrevocable option which can **not** be withdrawn prior to October 1, 1981.
c. The offer can **not** be assigned to another party by Wilson if Wilson chooses **not** to accept.
d. A letter of acceptance from Wilson to Marglow sent on October 1, 1981, but **not** received until October 2, 1981, would **not** create a valid contract.

13. Wilcox mailed Norriss an unsigned contract for the purchase of a tract of real property. The contract represented the oral understanding of the parties as to the purchase price, closing date, type of deed, and other details. It called for payment in full in cash or certified check at the closing. Norriss signed the contract, but added above his signature the following:

> This contract is subject to my (Norriss) being able to obtain conventional mortgage

financing of $100,000 at 13% or less interest for a period of not less than 25 years.

Which of the following is correct?

a. The parties had already made an enforceable contract prior to Wilcox's mailing of the formalized contract.

b. Norriss would **not** be liable on the contract under the circumstances even if he had **not** added the "conventional mortgage" language since Wilcox had **not** signed it.

c. By adding the "conventional mortgage" language above his signature, Norriss created a condition precedent to his contractual obligation and made a counteroffer.

d. The addition of the "conventional mortgage" language has **no** legal effect upon the contractual relationship of the parties since it was an implied condition in any event.

14. Lally sent Queen Supply Company, Inc., a telegram ordering $700 of general merchandise. Lally's telegram indicated that immediate shipment was necessary. That same day Queen delivered the goods to the Red Freight Company. The shipment was delayed due to a breakdown of the truck which was transporting the goods. When the merchandise did not arrive as promptly as expected, Lally notified Queen that it revoked the offer and was purchasing the goods elsewhere. Queen indicated to Lally that the merchandise had been shipped the same day Lally had ordered it and Lally's revocation was not good. Which of the following statements best describes the transaction?

a. The statute of frauds will be a defense on any action by Queen to enforce the contract.

b. Prompt shipment of the merchandise by Queen constituted an acceptance.

c. Lally's revocation of the offer was effective since Lally had not received a notice of acceptance.

d. Lally's order was an offer to Queen to enter into a bilateral contract which could be accepted only by a promise.

15. Which of the following statements is correct with regard to an auction of goods?

a. The auctioneer may withdraw the goods at any time prior to completion of the sale unless the goods are put up without reserve.

b. A bidder may retract his bid before the completion of the sale only if the auction is without reserve.

c. A bidder's retraction of his bid will revive the prior bid if the sale is with reserve.

d. In a sale with reserve, a bid made while the hammer is falling automatically reopens the bidding.

16. Which of the following requires consideration in order to be binding on the parties?

a. Material modification of a sale of goods contract under the UCC.

b. Ratification of a contract by a person after reaching the age of majority.

c. Material modification of a contract involving the sale of real estate.

d. A written promise signed by a merchant to keep an offer to sell goods open for 10 days.

17. Dougal is seeking to avoid performing a promise to pay Clark $500. Dougal is relying upon lack of consideration on Clark's part sufficient to support his promise. Dougal will prevail if he can establish that

a. The contract is executory.

b. Clark's asserted consideration is worth only $100.

c. Prior to Dougal's promise, Clark had already performed the requested act. past consideration

d. Clark's only claim of consideration was the relinquishment of a legal right.

18. Williams purchased a heating system from Radiant Heating, Inc., for his factory. Williams insisted that a clause be included in the contract calling for service on the heating system to begin not later than the next business day after Williams informed Radiant of a problem. This service was to be rendered free of charge during the first year of the contract and for a flat fee of $200 per year for the next two years thereafter. During the winter of the second year, the heating system broke down and Williams promptly notified Radiant of the situation. Due to other commitments, Radiant did not send a man over the next day. Williams phoned Radiant and was told that the $200 per year service charge was uneconomical and they could not get a man over there for several days. Williams in desperation promised to pay an additional $100 if Radiant would send a man over that day. Radiant did so and sent a bill for $100 to Williams. Is Williams legally required to pay this bill and why?

a. No, because the pre-existing legal duty rule applies to this situation.

b. No, because the statute of frauds will defeat Radiant's claim.

c. Yes, because Williams made the offer to pay the additional amount.

d. Yes, because the fact that it was uneconomical for Radiant to perform constitutes economic duress which freed Radiant from its obligation to provide the agreed-upon service.

19. Aqua, Inc., a Florida corporation, entered into a contract for $30,000 with Sing, Inc., to perform plumbing services in a complex owned by Sing in Virginia. After the work was satisfactorily completed, Sing discovered that Aqua violated Virginia's licensing law by failing to obtain a plumbing license. Virginia's licensing statute was regulatory in nature, serving to protect the public against unskilled and dishonest plumbers. Upon Sing's request, independent appraisals of Aqua's work were performed, which indicated that the complex was benefited to the extent of $25,000. Sing refuses to pay Aqua. If Aqua brings suit it may recover

a. $30,000.
b. $25,000.
c. Nothing.
d. An amount sufficient to cover its out of pocket costs.

20. Mix entered into a contract with Small which provided that Small would receive $10,000 if he stole trade secrets from Mix's competition. Small performed his part of the contract by delivering the trade secrets to Mix. Mix refuses to pay Small for his services. Under what theory may Small recover?

a. Quasi contract, in order to prevent the unjust enrichment of Mix.
b. Promissory estoppel, since Small has changed his position to his detriment.
c. None, due to the illegal nature of the contract.
d. Express contract, since both parties bargained for and exchanged promises in forming the contract.

21. An oral contract to sell land will be enforceable if the

a. Contract is capable of full performance within one year.
b. Total sales price is less than $500.
c. Buyer has made a part payment. + possession
d. Parties have fully performed the contract.

22. Jim entered into an oral agency agreement with Sally whereby he authorized Sally to sell his interest in a parcel of real estate, Blueacre. Within seven days Sally sold Blueacre to Dan, signing the real estate contract on behalf of Jim. Dan failed to record the real estate contract within a reasonable time. Which of the following is correct?

a. Dan may enforce the real estate contract against Jim since it satisfied the statute of frauds.
b. Dan may enforce the real estate contract against Jim since Sally signed the contract as Jim's agent.
c. The real estate contract is unenforceable against Jim since Sally's authority to sell Blueacre was oral.
d. The real estate contract is unenforceable against Jim since Dan failed to record the contract within a reasonable time.

23. Glass Co. telephoned Hourly Company and ordered 2,000 watches at $2 each. Glass agreed to pay 10% immediately and the balance within ten days after receipt of the entire shipment. Glass forwarded a check for $400 and Hourly shipped 1,000 watches the next day, intending to ship the balance by the end of the week. Glass decided that the contract was a bad bargain and repudiated it, asserting the Statute of Frauds. Hourly sued Glass. Which of the following will allow Hourly to enforce the contract in its entirety despite the Statute of Frauds?

a. Glass admitted in court that it made the contract in question.
b. Hourly shipped 1,000 watches.
c. Glass paid 10% down.
d. The contract is **not** within the requirements of the Statute.

24. Certain oral contracts fall outside the Statute of Frauds. An example would be a contract between

a. A creditor and a friend of the debtor, providing for the friend's guaranty of the debt in exchange for the creditor's binding extension of time for payment of the debt.
b. A landlord and a tenant for the lease of land for ten years.
c. A school board and a teacher entered into on January 1, for nine months of service to begin on September 1.
d. A retail seller of television sets and a buyer for the sale of a TV set for $399 C.O.D.

25. A salesman for A & C Company called upon the purchasing agent for Major Enterprises, Inc., and offered to sell Major 1,500 screwdriver sets at $1.60 each. Major's purchasing agent accepted and the following day sent A & C a purchase order which bore Major's name and address at the top and also had the

purchasing agent's name and title stamped at the bottom with his initials. The purchase order recited the agreement reached orally the prior day. Subsequently, Major decided it did not want the screwdriver sets since it was overstocked in that item. Major thereupon repudiated the contract and asserted the statute of frauds as a defense. Under the circumstances, which of the following is correct?

a. The statute of frauds does not apply to this transaction since performance is to be completed within one year from the date of the making of the contract.
b. Major will lose but only if its purchasing agent's authority to make the contract was in writing.
c. The fact that an authorized agent of A & C did not sign the purchase order prevents its use by A & C against Major to satisfy the statute of frauds.
d. The purchase order is sufficient to satisfy the statute of frauds even though the purchasing agent never signed it in full.

26. Fred entered into a written contract with Joe to purchase a car. The written contract was intended to be the final and complete agreement of the parties. Fred is unhappy with the performance of the car and has commenced an action for breach of contract based on an oral representation made at the time the written contract was executed. Fred may introduce evidence of the representation if it

a. Completely modifies the written contract.
b. Contradicts the written agreement.
c. Serves to clarify an ambiguous term in the written contract.
d. Falls within the provisions of the statute of frauds.

27. Pam orally agreed to sell Jack her used car for $400. At the time the contract was entered into, the car had been stolen and its whereabouts were unknown. Neither party was aware of these facts at the time the contract was formed. Jack sues Pam for her failure to deliver the car in accordance with their agreement. Pam's best defense would be that the

a. Agreement was unenforceable because it was **not** evidenced by a writing.
b. Risk of loss for the car was on Jack.
c. Agreement is unconscionable.
d. Parties were under a mutual mistake of a material fact at the time the contract was entered into.

28. Smith, an executive of Apex Corporation, became emotionally involved with Jones. At the urging of Jones, and fearing that Jones would sever their relationship, Smith reluctantly signed a contract which was grossly unfair to Apex. Apex's best basis to rescind the contract would be

a. Lack of express authority.
b. Duress.
c. Undue influence.
d. Lack of consideration.

29. In order to establish a common law action for fraud, the aggrieved party must establish that

a. Although the defendant did **not** in fact know that his statements were false, he made the false statements with a reckless disregard for the truth.
b. The contract entered into is within the Statute of Frauds.
c. There was a written misrepresentation of fact by the defendant.
d. The plaintiff acted as a reasonably prudent businessman in relying upon the misrepresentation.

30. Paul filed a $20,000 fire loss claim with the Williams Fire Insurance Company. Dickerson, Williams' adjuster, called Paul on the phone and invited him to come to his hotel room to settle the claim. Upon Paul's entry to the room, Dickerson locked the door and placed the key in his pocket. He then accused Paul of having set the building on fire and of having been involved in several previous suspicious fire claims. Dickerson concluded by telling Paul that unless he signed a release in exchange for $500, he would personally see to it that Paul was prosecuted by the company for arson. Visibly shaken by all this, Paul signed the release. Paul has subsequently repudiated the release. The release is **not** binding because of

a. Fraud.
b. Lack of consideration.
c. Undue influence.
d. Duress.

31. Which of the following is **not** required in order for the plaintiff to prevail in an action for innocent misrepresentation?

a. That the misrepresentation was intended to induce reliance.
b. That the misrepresentation amounted to gross negligence.
c. That the plaintiff acted promptly and offered to restore what was received.
d. That the plaintiff relied upon the misrepresentation.

32. The assignment of a contract right
   a. Will **not** be enforceable if it materially varies the obligor's promise.
   b. Is invalid unless supported by consideration.
   c. Gives the assignee better rights against the obligor than the assignor had.
   d. Does not create any rights in the assignee against the assignor until notice is given to the obligor.

33. Walton owed $10,000 to Grant. Grant assigned his claim against Walton to the Line Finance Company for value on October 15, 1982. On October 25, 1982, Hayes assigned his matured claim for $2,000 against Grant to Walton for value. On October 30, 1982, Line notified Walton of the assignment to them of the $10,000 debt owed by Walton to Grant. Line has demanded payment in full. Insofar as the rights of the various parties are concerned
   a. Walton has the right of a $2,000 set-off against the debt which he owed Grant.
   b. Walton must pay Line in full, but has the right to obtain a $2,000 reimbursement from Grant.
   c. Line is a creditor beneficiary of the debt owed by Walton.
   d. The claimed set-off of the Hayes claim for $2,000 is invalid since it is for an amount which is less than the principal debt.

34. Conrad is seeking to avoid liability on a contract with Fuld. Conrad can avoid liability on the contract if
   a. A third party has agreed to perform his duty and has for a valuable consideration promised to hold Conrad harmless on the obligation to Fuld.
   b. The entire contract has been assigned.
   c. There has been a subsequent unexecuted accord between Fuld and himself.
   d. He has been discharged by a novation.

35. Fennell and McLeod entered into a binding contract whereby McLeod was to perform routine construction services according to Fennell's blueprints. McLeod assigned the contract to Conerly. After the assignment
   a. Fennell can bring suit under the doctrine of anticipatory breach.
   b. McLeod extinguishes all his rights and duties under the contract.
   c. McLeod extinguishes all his rights but is **not** relieved of his duties under the contract.
   d. McLeod still has all his rights but is relieved of his duties under the contract.

36. Monroe purchased a ten-acre land site from Acme Land Developers, Inc. He paid 10% at the closing and gave his note for the balance secured by a 20-year mortgage. Three years later, Monroe found it increasingly difficult to make payments on the note and finally defaulted. Acme Land threatened to accelerate the loan and foreclose if he continued in default. It told him either to get the money or obtain an acceptable third party to assume the obligation. Monroe offered the land to Thompson for $1,000 less than the equity he had in the property. This was acceptable to Acme and at the closing Thompson paid the arrearage, executed a new mortgage and note, and had title transferred to his name. Acme surrendered Monroe's note and mortgage to him. The transaction in question is a (an)
   a. Assignment and delegation.
   b. Third party beneficiary contract.
   c. Novation.
   d. Purchase of land subject to a mortgage.

37. Red purchased a life insurance policy from Ace Insurance Co. naming his wife Bertha as the sole beneficiary. In order for Bertha to qualify as a donee beneficiary she must
   a. Have had knowledge of the insurance contract at the time the contract was entered into.
   b. Be in privity of contract with Ace.
   c. Have provided consideration.
   d. Have been the person intended to be benefitted from the life insurance contract.

38. Wilson sold his factory to Glenn. As part of the contract, Glenn assumed the existing mortgage on the property which was held by Security Bank. Regarding the rights and duties of the parties, which of the following is correct?
   a. The promise by Glenn need **not** be in writing to be enforceable by Security.
   b. Security is a creditor beneficiary of Glenn's promise and can recover against him personally in the event of default.
   c. Security is a mere incidental beneficiary since it was **not** a party to the assignment.
   d. Wilson has **no** further liability to Security.

39. Stone engaged Parker to perform personal services for $1,000 a month for a period of three months. The contract was entered into orally on August 1, 1983, and performance was to commence January 1, 1984. On September 15, Parker anticipatorily repudiated the contract. As a result, Stone can

a. Obtain specific performance.
b. Not assign her rights to damages under the contract to a third party.
c. Immediately sue for breach of contract.
d. Not enforce the contract against Parker since the contract is oral.

40. Kent Construction Company contracted to construct four garages for Magnum, Inc., according to specifications provided by Magnum. Kent deliberately substituted 2 x 4s for the more expensive 2 x 6s called for in the contract in all places where the 2 x 4s would not be readily detected. Magnum's inspection revealed the variance and Magnum is now withholding the final payment on the contract. The contract was for $100,000, and the final payment would be $25,000. Damages were estimated to be $15,000. In a lawsuit for the balance due, Kent will

a. Prevail on the contract, less damages of $15,000, because it has substantially performed.
b. Prevail because the damages in question were not substantial in relation to the contract amount.
c. Lose because the law unqualifiedly requires literal performance of such contracts.
d. Lose all rights under the contract because it has intentionally breached it.

41. Smith contracted to perform for $500 certain services for Jones. Jones claimed that the services had been performed poorly. Because of this, Jones sent Smith a check for only $425. Marked clearly on the check was "payment in full". Smith crossed out the words "payment in full" and cashed the check. Assuming that there was a bona fide dispute as to whether Smith had in fact performed the services poorly, the majority of courts would hold that

a. The debt is liquidated, and Smith can collect the remaining $75.
b. The debt is liquidated, but Jones by adding the words "payment in full" cancelled the balance of the debt owed.
c. The debt is unliquidated and the cashing of the check by Smith completely discharged the debt.
d. The debt is unliquidated, but the crossing out of the words "payment in full" by Smith revives the balance of $75 owed.

42. Marblehead Manufacturing, Inc., contracted with Wellfleet Oil Company in June to provide its regular supply of fuel oil from November 1 through March 31. The written contract required Marblehead to take all of its oil requirements exclusively from Wellfleet at a fixed price subject to an additional amount not to exceed 10% of the contract price and only if the market price increases during the term of the contract. By the time performance was due on the contract, the market price had already risen 20%. Wellfleet seeks to avoid performance. Which of the following will be Wellfleet's best argument?

a. There is no contract since Marblehead was not required to take any oil.
b. The contract fails because of lack of definiteness and certainty.
c. The contract is unconscionable.
d. Marblehead has ordered amounts of oil unreasonably disproportionate to its normal requirements.

43. The Johnson Corporation sent its only pump to the manufacturer to be repaired. It engaged Travis, a local trucking company, both to deliver the equipment to the manufacturer and to redeliver it to Johnson promptly upon completion of the repair. Johnson's entire plant was inoperative without this pump, but the trucking company did not know this. The trucking company delayed several days in its delivery of the repaired pump to Johnson. During the time it expected to be without the pump, Johnson incurred $5,000 in lost profits. At the end of that time Johnson rented a replacement pump at a cost of $200 per day. As a result of these facts, what is Johnson entitled to recover from Travis?

a. The $200 a day cost incurred in renting the pump.
b. The $200 a day cost incurred in renting the pump plus the lost profits.
c. Actual damages plus punitive damages.
d. Nothing because Travis is not liable for damages.

44. Myers entered into a contract to purchase a valuable rare coin from Eisen. Myers tendered payment which was refused by Eisen. Upon Eisen's breach, Myers brought suit to obtain the coin. The court will grant Myers

a. Compensatory damages.
b. Specific performance.
c. Reformation.
d. Restitution.

45. The Balboa Custom Furniture Company sells fine custom furniture. It has been encountering difficulties lately with some customers who have breached their contracts after the furniture they have selected has been customized to their order or the fabric they have selected has been cut or actually installed on the piece of furniture purchased. The company therefore

wishes to resort to a liquidated damages clause in its sales contract to encourage performance or provide an acceptable amount of damages. Regarding Balboa's contemplated resort to a liquidated damages clause, which of the following is correct?

a. Balboa may not use a liquidated damages clause since it is a merchant and is the preparer of the contract.
b. Balboa can simply take a very large deposit which will be forfeited if performance by a customer is not made for any reason.
c. The amount of the liquidated damages stipulated in the contract must be reasonable in light of the anticipated or actual harm caused by the breach.
d. Even if Balboa uses a liquidated damages clause in its sales contract, it will nevertheless have to establish that the liquidated damages claimed did not exceed actual damages by more than 10%.

46. When a lengthy delay has occurred between the breach of a contract and the commencement of the lawsuit, the statute of limitations defense may be raised. The statute

a. Is three years irrespective of the type of legal action the plaintiff is bringing.
b. Does **not** apply to an action brought in a court of equity.
c. Is a defense to recovery if the requisite period of time has elapsed.
d. Fixes a period of time in which the plaintiff must commence the action or be barred from recovery, regardless of the defendant's conduct during the period.

May 1985 Questions

47. Race entered into a written agreement to sell a parcel of land to Lark for $50,000. At the time the agreement was executed, Race had consumed a large amount of alcoholic beverages which significantly impaired Race's ability to understand the nature and terms of the contract. Lark knew Race was very intoxicated and that the land had been appraised at $95,000. Race wishes to avoid the contract. The contract is

a. Voidable at Race's option.
b. Voidable at Race's option only if the intoxication was involuntary.
c. Void.
d. Legally binding on both parties in the absence of fraud or undue influence.

48. Mix offered to sell a parcel of land to Simon for $90,000. The offer was made by Mix in a signed writing and provided that it would not be revoked for five months if Simon promised to pay Mix $250 within 10 days. Simon agreed to do so. Which of the following is correct?

a. Simon's agreement to pay $250 is insufficient consideration to form an option contract.
b. Mix may withdraw the offer any time prior to Simon's payment of the $250.
c. An option contract is formed.
d. Although an option contract is formed, the duration of such a contract is limited to three months.

49. Fuller sent Blue a written offer to sell his tract of land located in Capetown for $75,000. The parties were engaged in a separate dispute. The offer stated that it would be irrevocable for 60 days if Blue would promise to refrain from suing Fuller during this time. Blue promptly delivered a promise not to sue during the term of the offer and to forego suit if she accepted the offer. Fuller subsequently decided that the possible suit by Blue was groundless and therefore phoned Blue and revoked the offer 15 days after making it. Blue mailed an acceptance on the 20th day. Fuller did not reply. Under the circumstances

a. Fuller's revocation, **not** being in writing, was invalid.
b. Fuller's offer was supported by consideration and was irrevocable when accepted.
c. Fuller's written offer would be irrevocable even without consideration.
d. Blue's promise was accepted by Fuller by his silence.

50. The primary distinction between an action based on innocent misrepresentation and an action based on common law fraud is that, in the former, a party need **not** allege and prove

a. That there has been a false representation.
b. The materiality of the misrepresentation.
c. Reasonable reliance on the misrepresentation.
d. That the party making the misrepresentation had actual or constructive knowledge that it was false.

Items 51 through 53 are based on the following information:

After substantial oral negotiations, Ida Frost wrote Jim Lane on May 1 offering to pay Lane $160,000 to build a warehouse. The writing contained the terms essential to form a binding contract. It also provided that the offer would remain open until June 1 and that acceptance must be received to be effective. On May 20, Lane mailed a signed acceptance. This was received by Frost on May 22. Lane completed the warehouse on July 15. On July 30, Lane assigned his right to receive payment to Reid Bank which did not notify Frost of the assignment. Two weeks later, Frost paid Lane $155,000 after deducting $5,000 in satisfaction of a dispute between them unrelated to the construction contract.

51. The agreement between Frost and Lane resulted in the formation of a(an)

a. Bilateral contract.
b. Unilateral contract.
c. Quasi contract.
d. Implied in fact contract.

52. Frost's offer

a. Was accepted and a contract duly formed on May 20.
b. Was irrevocable until June 1.
c. Constituted a firm offer under the UCC despite the lack of consideration.
d. Could have been revoked any time prior to the receipt of Lane's acceptance on May 22.

53. If Reid sues Frost on the contract, Reid will be entitled to recover

a. The full $160,000.
b. $160,000, less the $5,000 setoff.
c. Nothing, because notice of the assignment was **not** given to Frost.
d. Nothing, because it was **not** the primary beneficiary of the construction contract.

54. John Dash, an accountant, entered into a written contract with Kay Reese to perform certain tax services for Reese. Shortly thereafter, Reese was assessed additional taxes and she wanted to appeal the assessment. Reese was required to appeal immediately and the workpapers held by Dash were necessary to appeal. Dash refused to furnish Reese with the workpapers unless he was paid a substantially higher fee than was set forth in the contract. Reese reluctantly agreed in order to meet the filing deadline. The contract as revised is

a. Voidable at Reese's option based on undue influence.
b. Voidable at Reese's option based on duress.
c. Void on the ground of undue influence.
d. Void on the ground of duress.

55. Diel entered into a written contract to sell a building to Stone. The contract was properly recorded. Stone breached the contract and Diel has brought an action for breach of contract. Stone pleads the statute of limitations as a defense. The

a. Time period fixed by the statute of limitations is uniform throughout the states.
b. Recording of the contract stops the running of the statute of limitations.
c. Time period fixed by the statute of limitations begins when the contract is recorded.
d. Remedy sought by Diel will be barred when the period of time provided by the statute of limitations has expired.

56. Where the parties have entered into a written contract intended as the final expression of their agreement, the parol evidence rule generally prevents the admission into evidence of any

a. Other written agreement which is referred to in the contract.
b. Contemporaneous oral agreement which explains an ambiguity in the written contract.
c. Prior oral or written agreement and any contemporaneous oral agreement which contradict the terms of the written contract.
d. Subsequent oral modification of the contract.

57. Fink is the owner of a parcel of land which is encumbered by a mortgage securing Fink's note to State Bank. Fink sold the land to Bloom who assumed the mortgage note. State Bank

a. Is a donee beneficiary.
b. Is an incidental beneficiary.
c. Is a creditor beneficiary.
d. Can **not** collect from Fink if Bloom defaults.

Repeat Question

(585,L1,27) Identical to item 39 above

November 1985 Questions

58. On May 1, Apple mailed a signed offer to sell an office building to Fein for $90,000. The offer indicated that it would remain open until May 10. On May 5, Fein assigned the offer to Boyd for $5,000. On May 8, Boyd orally accepted Apple's offer. Apple refused to sell the building to Boyd. Which of the following statements is correct?

   a. Fein's assignment to Boyd was effective because an option contract was formed between Apple and Fein on May 1.
   b. Fein's assignment to Boyd was effective against Apple because valid consideration was given.
   c. Boyd's acceptance was ineffective because the offer could **not** be assigned.
   d. Boyd's acceptance was ineffective against Apple because it was oral.

59. Fenster Corp. requested Wein & Co., CPAs, to perform accounting services for it. Wein agreed to perform the services. Fenster and Wein had not discussed the amount of the fees. Which of the following is correct?

   a. No contract was formed since the amount of the fees was **not** agreed upon.
   b. A quasi contract was formed at the time Wein agreed to perform the services.
   c. A unilateral contract was formed at the time of Fenster's request.
   d. A bilateral contract was formed at the time of Wein's agreement to perform.

60. In order for an offer to confer the power to form a contract by acceptance, it must have all of the following elements **except**

   a. Be sufficiently definite and certain.
   b. Manifest an intent to enter into a contract.
   c. Be communicated by words to the offeree by the offeror.
   d. Be communicated to the offeree and the communication must be made or authorized by the offeror.

61. The statute of frauds

   a. Requires the formalization of a contract in a single writing.
   b. Applies to all contracts having a consideration valued at $500 or more.
   c. Applies to the sale of real estate but **not** to any leases.
   d. Does **not** require that the contract be signed by all parties.

62. On April 1, Knox signed and mailed a letter containing an offer to sell Wax a warehouse for $75,000. The letter also indicated that the offer would expire on May 3. Which of the following is correct?

   a. The offer is a firm offer under the UCC and can **not** be withdrawn by Knox prior to May 3.
   b. Wax can benefit from the early acceptance rule **no** matter what means of communication he uses as long as the acceptance is sent on or before May 3.
   c. If Wax purports to accept the offer on April 15 at $50,000 and Knox refuses to sell at that price, Wax nevertheless has the right to accept at $75,000 by May 3.
   d. A telephone call by Wax to Knox on May 3, accepting the offer at $75,000, will effectively bind Knox.

63. Ted King, a building subcontractor, submitted a bid for construction of a portion of a high-rise office building. The bid contained material errors in computation. Lago Corp., the general contractor, accepted the bid with knowledge of King's errors. King

   a. Must perform the contract unless he can show that Lago acted fraudulently.
   b. Must perform the contract according to the stated terms since his errors were unilateral.
   c. Will avoid liability on the contract only if his errors were **not** due to his negligence.
   d. Will avoid liability on the contract since Lago knew of King's errors.

64. In determining whether the consideration requirement has been satisfied to form a contract, the courts will be required to decide whether the consideration

   a. Was bargained for.
   b. Was fair and adequate.
   c. Has sufficient economic value.
   d. Conforms to the subjective intent of the parties.

65. Ruehl purchased a service station business from Lull. The purchase price included payment for Lull's goodwill. The agreement contained a covenant prohibiting Lull from competing with Ruehl in the service station business. Which of the following statements regarding the covenant is **incorrect**?

   a. The value to be assigned to it is the excess of the price paid over the seller's cost of all tangible assets.

b. The time period for which it is to be effective must be reasonable.
c. The restraint must be **no** more extensive than is reasonably necessary to protect the goodwill purchased by Ruehl.
d. The geographic area to which it applies must be reasonable.

66. John Tuck entered into a contract with Jack Doe. Doe asserts that he entered into the contract under duress. Which of the following best describes a necessary element of duress?
a. There must have been a confidential or fiduciary relationship between Tuck and Doe.
b. The contract entered into between Tuck and Doe was unconscionable.
c. Doe entered into the contract with Tuck because of Tuck's improper threats.
d. Tuck must have intended that Doe be influenced by the improper threats.

67. Sand sold a warehouse he owned to Quick Corp. The warehouse was encumbered by an outstanding mortgage securing Sand's note to Security Bank. Quick assumed Sand's note and mortgage at the time it purchased the warehouse from Sand. Within three months, Quick defaulted on the note and Security Bank commenced a mortgage foreclosure action. The proceeds of the resulting foreclosure sale were less than the outstanding balance on the note.

As to the contract between Sand and Quick, Security is
a. A third party creditor beneficiary.
b. A third party donee beneficiary.
c. A third party incidental beneficiary.
d. Not a beneficiary.

68. Fiore owed Lutz $5,000. As the result of an unrelated transaction, Lutz owed Bing that same amount. The three parties signed an agreement that Fiore would pay Bing instead of Lutz and Lutz would be discharged from all liability. The agreement among the parties is
a. Unenforceable for lack of consideration.
b. Voidable at Bing's option.
c. An executed accord and satisfaction.
d. A novation.

69. Kemp entered into a contract to sell Ward a parcel of land. Kemp was aware that Ward was purchasing the land with the intention of building a high-rise office building. Kemp was also aware of the fact that a subsurface soil condition would prevent such construction. The condition was extremely unusual and not readily discoverable in the course of normal inspections or soil evaluations. Kemp did not disclose the existence of the condition to Ward, nor did Ward make any inquiry of Kemp as to the suitability of the land for his intended development. Kemp's silence as to the soil condition
a. Renders the contract voidable at Ward's option.
b. Renders the contract void.
c. Will **not** affect the validity of the contract.
d. Entitles Ward only to money damages.

Repeat Questions

(1185,L1,10) Identical to item 29 above

(1185,L1,16) Identical to item 56 above

(1185,L1,18) Identical to item 28 above

Problems

Problem 1 (1184,L3)

(15 to 20 minutes)

Beach, a 17-year old minor, entered into an installment contract to purchase a travel agency from Reid. The purchase price included the fair market value of the tangible assets and an agreed upon value for goodwill. At the time the contract was entered into, Beach misrepresented his age to Reid, claiming that he was 19. The age of majority in their jurisdiction was 18. Since Reid was unsure of Beach's financial position, Reid requested that Beach obtain a surety. Therefore, Beach entered into an agreement for Abel to act as a surety on the installment contract. Beach knowingly induced Abel to become a surety by supplying Abel with false financial statements.

The contract also provided that Reid was to receive a substantial payment in consideration of his agreement not to operate a travel agency within a one mile radius of Beach's travel agency for a period of two years. After 19 months, Reid opened a new travel agency across the street from Beach's business. Within one month thereafter, Beach lost nearly all of his clients to Reid and Beach defaulted on the installment payments, causing the entire amount owed to Reid to become due. Reid has brought an action against Beach and Abel to recover all monies due him.

Beach claims he is not liable on the contract since:

- He was only 17 years old at the time the contract with Reid was signed.
- The clause prohibiting Reid from competing with him is legally valid and therefore Reid's violation of such clause constitutes a breach of the sale contract.

Abel claims that he is not liable to Reid since:

- He was induced into becoming a surety by Beach's fraud.
- Beach was 17 years old at the time the contract with Reid was entered into.
- Reid breached the sale contract by failing to comply with the express clause prohibiting competition with Beach.

Required:

Answer the following, setting forth reasons for any conclusions stated.

Assuming the contract is not divisible, discuss in separate paragraphs the assertions of Beach and Abel, indicating first whether such claims are correct.

Problem 2 (582,L4)

(15 to 20 minutes)

Part a. Craig Manufacturing Company needed an additional supply of water for its plant. Consequently, Craig advertised for bids. Shaw Drilling Company submitted the lowest bid and was engaged to drill a well. After a contract had been executed and drilling begun, Shaw discovered that the consistency of the soil was much harder than had been previously encountered in the surrounding countryside. In addition, there was an unexpected layer of bedrock. These facts, unknown to both Craig and Shaw when the contract was signed, significantly increased the cost of performing the contract. Therefore, Shaw announced its intention to abandon performance unless it was assured of recovering its cost. Craig agreed in writing to pay the amount of additional cost if Shaw would continue to drill and complete the contract. Shaw, on the strength of this written promise, completed the job. The additional cost amounted to $10,000 which Shaw now seeks to recover. Craig refuses to pay and asserts that the additional burden was a part of the risk assumed and that the only reason it agreed to pay the additional amount was that it needed the additional water supply on time as agreed.

Shaw has commenced legal action to recover the $10,000 in dispute. Craig denies liability.

Required:

Answer the following, setting forth reasons for any conclusions stated.

1. What is the legal liability of Craig as a result of the facts described above?
2. Suppose the contract had been for the purchase of computer parts and the manufacturer had encountered a significant increase in labor cost which it wished to pass on to the purchaser. Would the purchaser's subsequent written promise to make an additional payment have been binding?

Part b. Ogilvie is a wealthy, prominent citizen of Clarion County. Most of his activities and his properties are located in Vista City, the county seat. Among his holdings are large tracts of farmland located in the outlying parts of Clarion. He has not personally examined large portions of his holdings due to the distance factor and the time it would take. One of his agents told him that 95% of the land was fertile and could be used for general farming. Farber, a recent college graduate who inherited a modest amount of money decided to invest in farmland and raise avacados. He had read certain advertising literature extolling the virtues of avocado farming as an investment. He called upon Ogilvie and discussed the purchase of his land. In the process, Ogilvie praised his land as a great investment for the future. He stated that the land was virtually all splendid farmland and that it would be suitable for avocado growing. Farber entered into a contract of purchase and made a deposit of 10% on the purchase price.

On the eve of the closing, Farber learned of the presence of extensive rock formations at or near the surface of the land. These rock formations make avocado growing virtually impossible but still permit limited use for some other types of farming. These rock formations are partially visible and could have been seen if Farber had examined the property. They cover approximately 25% of the land.

Accordingly, Farber refused to perform the original contract and demanded that the unsuitable 25% of the land be severed from the contract and the price diminished accordingly.

Ogilvie asserted that "a contract is a contract" and that the doctrine of caveat emptor is applicable in the sale of land. Specifically, he stated that he committed no fraud because:

1. Nothing he said was a statement of fact. It was opinion or puffing.
2. His statements were not material since most of the land is okay, and the balance can be used for some types of farming.
3. He had not lied since he had no knowledge of the falsity of his statements.
4. Farber could have and should have inspected and by failing to do so he was negligent and cannot recover.

Farber then commenced legal proceedings against Ogilvie based on fraud.

Required:

Answer the following, setting forth reasons for any conclusions stated.

In separate paragraphs, discuss the validity of each of Ogilvie's four assertions that he committed no fraud.

Problem 3 (580,L3a&b)

(15 to 20 minutes)

Part a. Smithers contracted with the Silverwater Construction Corporation to build a home. The contract contained a detailed set of specifications including the type, quality, and manufacturers' names of the building materials that were to be used. After construction was completed, a rigid inspection was made of the house and the following defects were discovered.

1. Some of the roofing shingles were improperly laid.
2. The ceramic tile in the kitchen and three bathrooms was not manufactured by Disco Tile Company as called for in the specifications. The price of the alternate tile was $325 less than the Disco but was of approximately equal quality.
3. The sewerage pipes that were imbedded in concrete in the basement were also not manufactured by the specified manufacturer. It could not be shown that there was any difference in quality and the price was the same.
4. Various minor defects such as improperly hung doors.

Silverwater has corrected defects 1 and 4 but has refused to correct defects 2 and 3 because the cost would be substantial. Silverwater claims it is entitled to recover under the contract and demands full payment. Smithers is adamant and is demanding literal performance of the contract or he will not pay.

Required:

Answer the following, setting forth reasons for any conclusions stated.

1. If the dispute goes to court, who will prevail, assuming Silverwater's breach of contract was intentional?
2. If the dispute goes to court, who will prevail, assuming Silverwater's breach of contract was unintentional?

Part b. Jane Anderson offered to sell Richard Heinz a ten acre tract of commercial property. Anderson's letter indicated the offer would expire on March 1, 1980, at 3:00 p.m. and that any acceptance must be received in her office by that time. On February 29, 1980, Heinz decided to accept the offer and posted an acceptance at 4:00 p.m. Heinz indicated that in the event the acceptance did not arrive on time, he would assume there was a contract if he did not hear anything from Anderson in five days. The letter arrived on March 2, 1980. Anderson never responded to Heinz's letter. Heinz claims a contract was entered into and is suing thereon.

Required:

Answer the following, setting forth reasons for any conclusions stated.

Is there a contract?

Problem 4 (585,L2)

(15 to 20 minutes)

Reed, a manufacturer, entered into an oral contract with Rocco, a retailer, to deliver 10 leather jackets to Rocco's place of business within 15 days. The total sales price was $450. Prior to the delivery of the jackets the market price of leather increased drastically. Reed knew Rocco needed the jackets within the 15 days and telephoned Rocco stating that he would be unable to deliver the jackets unless the sales price was increased by $100. Rocco agreed to the new price. The following morning Reed sent Rocco a signed letter indicating the new sales price and that the sale was for 10 leather jackets. Rocco received the letter the next day and has taken no further action.

Reed entered into an oral contract to purchase Smith's vacant building for $50,000, giving $5,000 as a deposit. The parties intended to reduce their agreement to writing at a later date. Pursuant to the oral contract, Reed took possession of the building with Smith's permission and made permanent and substantial improvements. Due to a rise in the price of similar real estate, Smith serves notice on Reed to vacate the premises, contending that the sales contract was unenforceable.

Required:

Answer the following, setting forth reasons for any conclusions stated.

a. Discuss whether the original sales contract and the subsequent change in price by Reed are enforceable under the UCC Sales Article.

b. May Smith require Reed to vacate the building?

Multiple Choice Answers

1.	b	15.	a	29.	a	43.	a	57.	c
2.	d	16.	c	30.	d	44.	b	58.	c
3.	b	17.	c	31.	b	45.	c	59.	d
4.	c	18.	a	32.	a	46.	c	60.	c
5.	d	19.	c	33.	a	47.	a	61.	d
6.	b	20.	c	34.	d	48.	c	62.	d
7.	b	21.	d	35.	c	49.	b	63.	d
8.	a	22.	c	36.	c	50.	d	64.	a
9.	d	23.	a	37.	d	51.	a	65.	a
10.	d	24.	d	38.	b	52.	d	66.	c
11.	c	25.	d	39.	c	53.	c	67.	a
12.	c	26.	c	40.	d	54.	b	68.	d
13.	c	27.	d	41.	c	55.	d	69.	a
14.	b	28.	c	42.	d	56.	c		

Multiple Choice Answer Explanations

B.1. Offer

1. (583,L1,6) (b) In determining whether a contract has been created, the courts look primarily at the objective intent of the parties. The courts look to see what a reasonable person in the respective positions of each of the parties would be led to believe by the words and conduct of the other party, disregarding the parties' secret thoughts and subjective intent. Therefore, answers (c) and (d) are incorrect. Answer (a) is incorrect because while the courts do consider the fairness to the parties in examining a contract, this is not the primary factor in deciding whether a contract has been created.

2. (1184,L1,18) (d) Mary's statement, "I'll take it if you will have it refinished," constituted a valid offer. An offer must contain a serious proposal, be definite and complete, and be communicated to the offeree. Ed's statement, "Sold," is a valid acceptance in absolute accord with Mary's offer. A contract was formed at the moment Ed communicated his acceptance to Mary's offer. Answer (a) is incorrect because Ed's statement fails to communicate a serious intent to be legally bound, constituting merely an invitation to make an offer. Answer (b) is incorrect since Ed did not make an offer to Mary; therefore, she did not have the power to accept. Answer (c) is incorrect because Ed did not have to specify the price since prior negotiations would be incorporated into Mary's offer.

3. (1182,L1,2) (b) In determining whether a communication qualifies as an offer, the law uses an objective standard based on how a reasonably prudent businessman would have interpreted the communication. The subjective intent of Harris would be immaterial, as would Douglas' opinion, in deciding whether this letter constituted an offer. Therefore, answers (a) and (d) are incorrect. Answer (c) is incorrect because only the essential terms must be present in the communication, and even if some of these are missing, the needed terms can be added in later negotiations.

B.1.j. Termination of an Offer

4. (1184,L1,17) (c) In this fact situation, the common law is applicable since the contract does not involve the sale of tangible personal property. Under common law, an offer may be revoked at any time prior to acceptance even if the offeror states that the offer will be held open for a specified period of time. An exception to this rule exists in the case where consideration is received by the offeror in exchange for a promise to keep the offer open. This is known as an "option" and cannot be revoked since it constitutes a separate contract. Answer (d) is incorrect because Smith receives no consideration for their promise to keep the offer open in this case and thus may revoke the offer any time prior to Johnson's acceptance. Answers (a) and (b) are incorrect because the UCC "firm offer rule" is not applicable in this case. While it is true that a firm offer must be in writing, it must also be made by a merchant-offeror for the sale or purchase of tangible personal property, and the offer in this case does not involve the sale of goods.

5. (1184,L1,19) (d) In this fact situation, the common law is applicable since the contract does not involve the sale of tangible personal property. Under common law, the general rule is that the offeror can revoke the offer at any time prior to acceptance even if it is stated that the offer will remain open for a specified period. An exception to this rule exists when the offeror receives consideration in exchange for a promise to keep the offer open. This is known as an "option" and represents a separate legal agreement. Therefore, answer (a) is incorrect. In an option situation, the offeree forms a contract by unconditionally accepting the offer within the option period. However, since the offeror is legally bound to keep the offer open regardless of the actions of the offeree, the offeree may first reject the offer (or, as in this case, make a counter-offer) and subsequently accept the offer, thus forming a binding contract. Therefore, Martin's letter of February 6 formed a binding contract based on the original terms of Lemon's January 1 letter even though Martin's communication of January 30 constituted a rejection and counteroffer. If Lemon's offer had not been irrevocable (option or firm offer), communication of Martin's counteroffer would have terminated the offer

prior to acceptance. Thus, answer (b) is incorrect. Answer (c) is incorrect because when an option exists the offer cannot be revoked before the specified period elapses.

6. (1183,L1,29) (b) A rejection is never effective until communicated to the offeror. Consequently, Baker's letter of rejection was not effective until received by West. Thus, Baker's acceptance by phone on October 26 creates a contract. Answer (a) is incorrect because the Uniform Commercial Code only applies to contracts for the sale of goods. This contract involves the sale of real property. A firm offer is only present when a merchant offeror makes a written offer concerning the sale of goods stating that the offer will not be withdrawn. Answer (c) is incorrect because the Statute of Frauds would demand a writing signed only by the party to be charged, not both parties. Even if the agreement did not comply with the Statute of Frauds, there would still be a contract although it would be an unenforceable agreement. Answer (d) is incorrect because the parol evidence rule only applies if the two parties intend the written agreement to be the complete final expression of their contract. Obviously, Baker's written statements were not intended as the final expression of the agreement. Also, the parol evidence rule would not exclude evidence that occurred subsequent to the writing.

7. (1181,L1,1) (b) The offeree's opportunity to accept may be terminated by a lapse of time. If no time is stated in the offer, acceptance must be within a reasonable period of time given the surrounding facts, circumstances and subject matter of the contract. The barrels of heating oil are characterized by a rapidly fluctuating price market; therefore, a reasonable time for acceptance had elapsed and the offer had already expired. Answers (c) and (d) are incorrect because the U.C.C. states that unless otherwise indicated by the language or circumstances, an offer to make a contract shall be construed as inviting acceptance in any manner and by any medium reasonable in the circumstances.

B.2. Acceptance

8. (1184,L1,16) (a) In a contract for the sale of goods, acceptance is effective upon dispatch as long as it is communicated using the specified means, or any other reasonable means. A "reasonable means" is generally construed to imply any means as fast or faster than the means used to communicate the offer. In this case, a contract is formed as soon as Watson dispatches the telegram. Therefore, answer (c) is incorrect because Fine's revocation occurs after the contract is formed. Answer (d) is incorrect because the deposited acceptance rule does not demand that the acceptance be communicated by the same means as that of the offer. Rather, in a contract for the sale of goods, any reasonable means is acceptable. Answer (b) is incorrect because a lost or delayed acceptance is still valid. Note, however, that the offeror can protect against such a mishap by specifying that the acceptance will be valid only upon receipt.

9. (583,L1,8) (d) Acceptance of an offer for a unilateral contract can only occur by full performance of the act demanded, in exchange for the promise made by the offeror. Therefore, answer (a) is incorrect since a promise to perform the act does not constitute a valid acceptance of an offer for a unilateral contract. Answer (b) is incorrect because the preparation to perform the act is not a valid acceptance. Answer (c) is incorrect because the act must be completely performed in order for acceptance to occur in a unilateral contract.

10. (583,L1,9) (d) Harmon's telegram accepting the offer at $190,000 was a counteroffer that constituted a rejection of Luxor's original offer. However, a rejection is never effective until communicated to the offeror, and prior to Luxor receiving Harmon's telegram, Harmon telephoned an acceptance of the original terms. Therefore, the telephone acceptance was effective, resulting in a valid contract at $200,000. Consequently, answer (a) is incorrect. Answer (b) is incorrect because the sale of a real estate business does not constitute the sale of an interest in land, and therefore, does not need to be in writing under the section of the Statute of Frauds concerning real property. Answer (c) is incorrect because knowledge by the offeree that others were interested in the offer does not constitute a revocation of the offer. If Harmon had learned of the sale of the business to another party, this would have constituted a revocation of the offer.

11. (1181,L1,7) (c) An offeree cannot accept an offer unless the offeree knows of the existence of the offer; otherwise there is no objective meeting of the minds. Farber does not know of the increase of the monetary award to $500, and submitted his suggestion as an acceptance to the terms of the offer of which he knew, i.e., the $100. Even though Water Works later raised the amount and will use the suggestion in the later period, Farber only has a right to receive $100. Thus answers (a) and (b) are incorrect. Answer (d) is incorrect because Water Works' offer was not gratuitous; it was a manifestation of an intent to enter a contract. The offer was definite and certain and possessed the requisite essentials to make it operative; therefore,

Water Works must perform its promise of remuneration for Farber's accepted and used suggestion.

12. (1181,L1,10) (c) Offers to contract may only be accepted by the person to whom they were made. Offers are not assignable to others unless the offeror consents to such assignment. Answer (a) is incorrect because this proposed contract falls within the provisions of the Statute of Frauds, since by its terms it is not capable of being performed within one year. Answer (b) is incorrect because an option is only created when the offeree gives something of value to keep the offer open for a stated period of time. Therefore, no option was created, and Marglow can revoke its offer any time prior to acceptance by Wilson. Answer (d) is incorrect because acceptance is effective when it leaves the hands of the offeree if sent by a reasonable means of communication. In this problem mail would be considered a proper means; therefore, a valid contract would be created.

13. (581,L1,13) (c) The acceptance of an offer must conform exactly to the terms of the offer. If a party intends to accept an offer, but includes additional or different terms which are intended to become part of the contract, this constitutes a counteroffer and not an acceptance (a possible exception to this exists with contracts made between two merchants concerning the sale of goods). Norriss' additional term is a condition precedent and constitutes a counteroffer. Answer (a) is incorrect because a contract for the sale of real property must be in writing (under the Statute of Frauds) to be enforceable unless the doctrine of partial performance applies. Answer (b) is incorrect since a valid contract need only be signed by the party to be charged with performance. Answer (d) is untrue because the addition of a condition precedent has a significant effect on the contractual relationship since it prevents a contract from being formed unless Wilcox accepts the new term.

14. (1179,L1,9) (b) An offer which is ambiguous as to whether or not the offeror is bargaining for shipment of merchandise or the promise to ship can be accepted by the offeree doing either. Thus, the prompt shipment of the merchandise by Queen constitutes an acceptance and also passes the risk of loss (or delay as here) to the buyer, Lally. Answer (a) is incorrect because the statute of frauds has been satisfied by the telegram and by the fact that due to ambiguity the nature of the contract is unilateral requiring only that Queen ship the goods. Answer (c) is incorrect because Lally's revocation was not effective because it was received after acceptance. The absence of a notice of acceptance was a risk that Lally assumed in making a unilateral offer. Answer (d) is incorrect because Lally's order was an offer to enter into a unilateral contract since a reasonable reading of Lally's telegram was that they were bargaining for the act of immediate shipment and not a promise to ship.

15. (584,L1,50) (a) In an auction with reserve, the auctioneer may withdraw the goods at any time until he announces completion of the sale. If the auction is without reserve, the article cannot be withdrawn once the auctioneer calls for bids unless no bid is made within a reasonable time. Under the UCC, unless otherwise specified, auctions are presumed to be held with reserve. Answer (d) is incorrect because when a bid is made at the moment the hammer is falling, the auctioneer may, at his discretion, either reopen the bidding or close the sale on the bid on which the hammer was falling. Regardless of whether the auction is with or without reserve, a bidder may retract his bid until the auctioneer announces completion of the sale. A bidder's retraction does not revive any previous bid. Accordingly, answers (b) and (c) are incorrect.

B.3. Consideration

16. (584,L1,14) (c) At common law, which applies to the sale of real property, the modification of an existing contract must be supported by consideration. Under the UCC, however, a contract for the sale of goods may be modified either orally or in writing without consideration. Furthermore, a merchant's firm offer under the UCC does not require consideration. Accordingly, answers (a) and (d) are incorrect. A contract entered into by a minor is voidable by that minor. The minor may ratify the contract within a reasonable time after reaching the age of majority, and no consideration is required to support such a ratification. Answer (b) is, therefore, incorrect.

17. (583,L1,7) (c) Past consideration is not valid consideration. Past consideration is present when something done in the past is given for a present promise. This type of consideration lacks the bargained for element. Thus, if Clark had performed the act prior to Dougal's promise to pay, Dougal's promise was made in exchange for past consideration and Dougal will prevail. Answer (a) is incorrect because the fact that a contract is executory does not allow a party to avoid performance of the agreement; an executory contract is still a binding agreement. Answer (b) is incorrect because the value of the consideration is not considered by the court in determining whether the agreement has sufficient consideration. The court looks

merely for the presence of consideration and not for its adequacy. Answer (d) is incorrect because the relinquishment of a legal right is sufficient to act as consideration. Consideration is legally sufficient if it is either a legal benefit to the promisor or a legal detriment to the promisee. The promisee suffers a legal detriment if s/he promises to refrain from doing something s/he has a legal right to do.

18. (579,L1,9) (a) As part of the original contract Radiant agreed to service the heating system purchased by Williams for a flat rate of $200 per year. Thus, Radiant was under a pre-existing legal duty to perform the maintenance work and any subsequent promise to pay for such services is without consideration and unenforceable. Answer (b) is incorrect because the Statute of Frauds is not applicable to this problem. The dispute is over a service arrangement and not the sale of goods. Answer (c) is incorrect because the offer to pay the additional amount makes no difference with respect to the requirement of consideration. Answer (d) is incorrect because an uneconomical contract does not free a party from a contract unless significant unforeseen difficulties are encountered.

B.5. Legality

19. (1184,L1,20) (c) If a contract violates a regulatory licensing statute, it will be unenforceable by either party. The main function of a regulatory licensing statute is to protect the public against unskilled or dishonest persons. Another type of licensing statute is a revenue-seeking statute. The purpose of these types of statutes generally is to gain revenue for the governmental unit issuing the license. A contract that violates a revenue-seeking statute is enforceable. In this case, the facts stipulate that a regulatory licensing statute is violated. Consequently, Aqua may not enforce the agreement. Answers (a), (b), and (d) are incorrect because Aqua will recover nothing.

20. (584,L1,11) (c) The agreement to steal trade secrets is illegal and, therefore, unenforceable. Because both parties are guilty (pari delicto), the courts will not aid either Mix or Small in recovering the consideration exchanged. Consequently, Small will not be permitted to recover the $10,000 under any theory. Answers (a), (b), and (d) are, therefore, incorrect.

B.7. Conformity with the Statute of Frauds

21. (1184,L1,21) (d) The Statute of Frauds does not invalidate an oral contract relating to land if full performance or even sufficient part performance has been made. The Statute of Frauds seeks to guard against fraud and perjury. In the case of a fully executed agreement, the purpose of the Statute has been served. A fully performed oral contract for land is enforceable. Answers (a) and (b) are incorrect because a contract for the sale of an interest in land must be in writing regardless of the time of performance or the stipulated price. Answer (c) is incorrect because part payment by the buyer does not constitute sufficient part performance to eliminate the writing requirement of the Statute of Frauds. The buyer must take possession of the property, in addition to making part payment, before the doctrine of part performance allows the enforcement of an oral sale of real property.

22. (1184,L1,22) (c) An agency agreement must be in writing if it authorizes the agent to enter into a contract for the sale of the principal's real property. Since Sally's agency agreement was oral she did not possess the authority to bind Jim in a contract for the sale of Blueacre. The real estate contract is unenforceable against Jim. Answers (a) and (b) are incorrect because the real estate contract is unenforceable; the agreement was entered into by Sally who did not have the authority to bind Jim. Answer (d) is incorrect because it is irrelevant whether the contract was recorded. Recording the contract protects the buyer against subsequent sales of the property by the seller to good faith purchasers.

23. (583,L1,11) (a) Even though a contract for the sale of goods for greater than, or equal to, $500 must be in writing under the Statute of Frauds; a contract which is oral, but has been acknowledged in court by the defendant, is legally binding to the extent of the admission. Thus, since Glass admitted in court the contract with Hourly, this agreement will be enforced in its entirety. Answer (b) is incorrect because the shipment of 1,000 watches would not cause the contract to be enforceable in its entirety, but merely to the extent that goods have been delivered and accepted, in this case to the extent of the 1,000 watches. Answer (c) is incorrect since a down payment will only cause the contract to be enforceable to the extent of the payment made and accepted by Hourly, and not in the contract's entirety. Answer (d) is incorrect because the amount of the contract is $4,000, and any contract involving the sale of goods for $500 or more is within the requirements of the Statute of Frauds.

24. (583,L1,13) (d) Contracts involving the sale of goods for less than $500 fall outside the Statute of Frauds. Answer (a) is incorrect because it constitutes the promise to pay the debt of another, which falls

within the Statute of Frauds. Answer (b) is incorrect because, although a lease is not considered to be the sale of an interest in real property, a ten-year lease is within the Statute of Frauds because it is not capable of being performed within one year. Answer (c) is incorrect because although the duration of the services to be performed under the contract will only be nine months, when determining whether a contract is capable of being performed within one year, the time period starts the day the contract was formed. Therefore, this agreement falls within the Statute of Frauds because it cannot be performed within one year from January 1. It will not be completed until May 31 of the following year.

25. (1179,L1,8) (d) The purchase order which recited the oral agreement of the prior day is known under the UCC as a confirmation. For UCC cases, written confirmations satisfy the provision of the statute of frauds. The stamped name, title, and initials of the agent at the bottom of the purchase order would constitute a sufficient "signature" and therefore would indicate that Major Corporation's agent intended to authenticate the document. Answer (a) is incorrect because the statute of frauds does apply to this transaction since it involves the sale of goods in excess of $500. Answer (b) is incorrect because the purchasing agent's authority to make this particular contract need not be in writing but may be considered to be implied or apparent from his position. In general, there is no requirement that the authority of agents be in writing. Answer (c) is incorrect because the statute of frauds is satisfied if the party against whom the action is brought has signed. Thus, the absence of a signature by A & C is of no importance in so far as enforcement against Major is concerned. In any event, a confirmation which is binding on the sender is also binding on the receiver unless objected to by the receiver. Hence the confirmation satisfies the statute of frauds for both parties.

B.7.e. Parol Evidence Rule

26. (1184,L1,23) (c) When two parties reduce their agreement to writing, intending the written contract to represent a fully integrated and final expression of their agreement, the parol evidence rule prohibits any proof of prior or contemporaneous oral or written evidence that would contradict or modify the terms of this writing. Therefore, answers (a) and (b) are incorrect. An exception exists when the evidence merely serves to clarify an ambiguous term in the written agreement. The parol evidence rule does not prohibit this type of evidence. Answer (d) is incorrect because it would not matter whether the evidence falls within the provisions of the Statute of Frauds. Fred may introduce evidence of the contemporaneous oral representations **only** if it does not contradict or modify the written agreement.

B.6. Reality of Consent

27. (584,L1,12) (d) Because both parties were unaware of the fact that the car had been stolen, Pam and Jack entered the contract under a mutual mistake of a material fact. Consequently, the contract is voidable at the option of either party. Answer (a) is incorrect because the Statute of Frauds under the UCC requires written evidence of the contract only for the sale of goods for $500 or more. Answer (b) is incorrect because under the UCC, absent any breach, the risk of loss passes from a nonmerchant seller to the buyer on tender of delivery. Answer (c) is incorrect because there is no evidence to support the theory that Jack has a superior bargaining position or has otherwise taken unfair advantage of Pam.

28. (583,L1,15) (c) Undue influence occurs when a party entering into a contract is so greatly influenced by the second party because of their relationship with that party, that the party does not exercise free will in entering into the contract. In this case, Smith was unduly influenced by Jones because of their close personal relationship. Even though Smith, as an executive, is only an agent of Apex, it is as if the undue influence were exerted over Apex, the principal. Thus, Apex will be able to avoid the contract. Answer (a) is incorrect because even if express authority to enter into the contract had not been given to Smith, as an executive he would have either implied or apparent authority to do so, and accordingly, Apex would be bound to the contract. Answer (b) is incorrect because duress does not apply to the situation in which one party influences another by using the relationship existing between the two parties. Duress involves the use of a threat to overcome a party's free will and force the individual into a contract. Answer (d) is incorrect because there is no indication that a lack of consideration is present. Even though the contract is grossly unfair to Apex, the court is not primarily concerned with the adequacy of consideration. However, the fact that the contract was grossly unfair to Apex will help prove undue influence is present.

29. (1182,L1,9) (a) In order to establish a common law action for fraud, the plaintiff must prove either the defendant knew the falsity of his statements or the false statements were made with a reckless disregard for the truth. Answer (b) is incorrect because

the Statute of Frauds stipulates what contracts must be in writing to be enforceable and has no relevance in establishing an action for fraud. Answer (c) is incorrect because an oral misrepresentation of fact, as well as a written misrepresentation, can be the basis of fraud. Answer (d) is incorrect because in order to establish fraud there must be proof of justifiable reliance upon the misrepresentation by the plaintiff.

30. (582,L1,14) (d) Duress is the threat of harm to a party or to a member of the party's family, which deprives the party of free will and causes him to enter into a contract. Duress is present when one party uses the threat of criminal prosecution to force the second party to enter into an agreement. Dickenson's threat to prosecute Paul for arson would create a voidable contract at Paul's option due to duress. Consequently, answer (d) is correct while answers (a), (b), and (c) are incorrect.

B.6.b. Innocent Misrepresentation

31. (1182,L1,10) (b) An innocent misrepresentation is a misstatement of fact made with an honest and justifiable belief (in good faith), without intent to defraud (scienter). Therefore, a plaintiff is not required to prove that the misrepresentation amounted to gross negligence to prevail in an action for innocent misrepresentation. Answer (a) is incorrect because the misrepresentation, although innocent, must have been a substantial factor in inducing the plantiff to enter into the contract. Answer (c) is incorrect because in an action for innocent misrepresentation, any benefits received by the parties must be returned in order to restore each party to his/her precontractual position. Answer (d) is incorrect because the plaintiff must show that there was justifiable reliance upon a representation made with an intent to be relied upon.

C. Assignment and Delegation

32. (583,L1,18) (a) A contract right cannot be assigned if the assignment materially varies the obligor's promise. It would be unjust to enforce a contract against an obligor who, after agreeing to the terms of one contract, becomes subject to materially different terms merely because the other party assigned the rights to the contract. The obligor never really assented to the terms of the contract as changed by the assignment, thus the contract as assigned would be unenforceable against the obligor. Answer (b) is incorrect because the assignment of rights to a contract need not be supported by consideration. An assignment can be made with the intent of conferring a gift upon the assignee. Answer (c) is incorrect because an assignee generally steps into the shoes of the assignor and will have no better rights than the assignor had in the contract. Answer (d) is incorrect because knowledge by the obligor need not be present for a valid assignment to occur. However, if an obligor has no knowledge of the assignment, he can perform the contract by rendering performance to the assignor without suffering any liability to the assignee. In any case, the assignee will always have rights against the assignor provided that the assignment was valid and was not gratuitous in nature, in which case the assignment may be revoked.

33. (1182,L1,13) (a) Assignee takes the assignment subject to not only defenses or counterclaims which existed between the original parties at the time of the assignment, but also subject to additional defenses and counterclaims that arise subsequent to the assignment but before the obligor has knowledge of such assignment. Therefore, since Walton acquired the $2,000 claim against Grant prior to having notice of the assignment (from Grant to Line), Walton has the right to assert this counterclaim as a set-off against Line. Answer (b) is incorrect because since Walton's claim arose before he had knowledge of the assignment he acquires the right to set-off. If the counterclaim arose after notice of the assignment, then Walton must pay Line in full, but would have the right to obtain a $2,000 reimbursement from Grant. Answer (c) is incorrect because a third party beneficiary contract is an agreement whereby the two contracting parties intend to benefit a third party. Line is not a creditor beneficiary, since at the time of contracting, Walton and Grant did not intend to benefit Line. Walton's debt to Line arose out of the assignment by Grant. Answer (d) is incorrect because the fact that the set-off amount of $2,000 is less than the assigned principal debt does not make the set-off claim invalid.

34. (1182,L1,14) (d) A novation substitutes a new party and discharges one of the original parties to the contract. Consequently, a new contract is created with the same terms as the original one, wherein only the parties are changed. Therefore, Conrad can avoid liability on the contract if he has been discharged by a novation. Answer (a) is incorrect because the fact that the third party has agreed to hold Conrad harmless does not discharge Conrad from his contractual liability to Fuld, in the event that the third party does not perform. Answer (b) is incorrect because even though Conrad assigned the entire contract, he still remains liable for any default in the performance of his original contractual duties. Answer (c) is incorrect because since the accord is unexecuted (executory), the new substituted rights and duties have not yet come into being, and Conrad's liability under the old contract still exists.

35. (1181,L1,5) (c) An assignment of a contract is taken to mean both assignment of the rights and delegation of the duties. There can be a delegation without the other party's consent as long as a special skill is not needed to perform the duty or a materially different performance would result. McLeod can delegate his duty to Conerly, if qualified, since no special skill, other than following a set of blueprints, is involved. This assignment extinguishes McLeod's rights, but the delegation does not eliminate McLeod's obligation under the contract, unless there is a novation. Thus answers (b) and (d) are incorrect. Answer (a) is incorrect because a delegation of duties is not an anticipatory breach.

36. (1181,L1,6) (c) A novation substitutes a new party and discharges one of the original parties to the contract. Consequently a new contract is created with the same terms as the original one wherein only the parties are changed. In order to constitute a novation, there must be an agreement on the part of the creditor to substitute the new debtor in place of the original debtor and an agreement to release and discharge the original debtor. Therefore, this transaction constitutes a novation with Thompson being substituted for Monroe and a new contract being created. Answer (a) is incorrect because under an assignment and delegation, Monroe would still be liable under the mortgage contract. But in this case, Monroe is released and discharged of his obligation. Answer (b) is incorrect because a third party beneficiary contract is created when the two parties enter a contract that benefits a third person who is not a party to the agreement. But in this case, Thompson is a party to the contract with Acme. Answer (d) is incorrect because the novation releases Monroe from liability on the mortgage, making Thompson the party liable for payment of the obligation. Whereas, if this had been a purchase subject to the mortgage, Monroe, not Thompson, would have personal liability on the mortgage.

D. Third-Party Beneficiary Contracts

37. (1184,L1,25) (d) An essential requirement of a donee beneficiary contract is that the parties to the agreement intend to confer a gift on a third party. This is contrasted with a creditor beneficiary contract where one of the parties' primary purpose is to discharge an obligation owed to a third party. Red's purchase of life insurance shows an intent to confer a benefit on Bertha. Answer (a) is incorrect because to qualify as a donee beneficiary Bertha need not have knowledge of the insurance contract at the time the contract was entered into. Answer (b) is incorrect because the third party need not have a contractual relationship with the promissor, which is why it is called a third-party beneficiary contract. Answer (c) is incorrect because a donee beneficiary contract does not require consideration on the part of the third-party beneficiary. However, consideration must be present between the two contracting parties.

38. (1182,L1,12) (b) Wilson intended to discharge his debt owed to Security by the agreement he entered into with Glenn. Since Wilson and Glenn obviously intended Security to benefit from their agreement, Security is a creditor beneficiary with the right to recover against Glenn personally in the event of a default. Answer (a) is incorrect because the Statute of Frauds would apply since the agreement involves the sale of an interest in land and also because Glenn's promise would constitute a promise to answer for the debt of another. Consequently, Glenn's promise must be in writing. Answer (c) is incorrect because an incidental beneficiary is a third party whom the contract was not intended to benefit. Wilson and Glenn did intend to benefit Security; therefore, Security is not an incidental beneficiary. Answer (d) is incorrect because the fact the buyer assumes personal liability on the mortgage does not release the seller, the original mortgagor. An assumption of the mortgage creates a surety relationship, with the buyer being the principal debtor and the seller acting as the surety. Wilson's liability is terminated only when Security, the mortgagee, specifically releases Wilson.

E. Discharge of Contracts

39. (1183,L1,30) (c) When Parker anticipatorily repudiated a contract, Stone could immediately sue for breach of contract or wait for performance on the appointed date, and then sue for breach if performance was not rendered. Answer (a) is incorrect because specific performance is not available as a remedy for breach of personal service contract. It would violate the constitutional amendment prohibiting involuntary servitude. Answer (b) is incorrect because it is not illegal to assign your damages under a contract to a third party. However, it is illegal when one party pays another's costs and expenses in bringing a case to court with the understanding that if the case is successful, the party putting up the money will share in the proceeds (champerty). Answer (d) is incorrect because the oral agreement is enforceable since the agreement is capable of being performed within one year.

40. (583,L1,19) (d) Under the doctrine of substantial performance, a contract obligation may be discharged even though the performance tendered was not in complete conformity with the terms of the

agreement. Under this doctrine, if it can be shown that the defect in performance was only minor in nature, that a good faith effort was made to conform completely with the terms of the agreement, and if the performing party is willing to accept a decrease in compensation equivalent to the amount of the minor defect in performance, the contractual obligation will be discharged. Since Kent did not make a good faith effort to conform to the terms of the agreement, but in fact intentionally breached it, their obligation will not be discharged and they will lose all rights under the contract. Therefore, answers (a) and (b) are incorrect. Answer (c) is incorrect because the law does not demand literal performance of contracts, but will allow the discharge of an obligation to a contract when it has been substantially performed as described above under the doctrine of substantial performance.

41. (581,L1,7) (c) At the time the contract was made, the debt was liquidated since the amount was certain ($500). However, the bona fide dispute changed the debt to an unliquidated debt. Payment of a lesser sum to discharge an unliquidated debt will be effective if accepted as payment in full since each party gives consideration in the form of forfeiting a claim to dispute the amount of the debt. Smith's cashing of the check was acceptance of a settlement for the full amount of the debt. Answers (a) and (b) are incorrect since they refer to liquidated debts and this debt is unliquidated. Answer (d) is incorrect since the fact that Smith crossed out the words "paid in full" has no effect. The check must be accepted in the manner offered and Smith's cashing of the check discharges the entire unliquidated debt.

42. (580,L1,29) (d) The agreement involved is a requirements contract; thus Marblehead's ordering of unreasonably disproportionate amounts of oil would be a breach by them. A requirements contract is considered definite and both parties are viewed as having provided consideration, thus answers (a), (b), and (c) are incorrect.

43. (578,L1,22) (a) The trucking company was engaged to redeliver the pump promptly upon completion of the repair. The delay in returning the pump was a breach of contract. The $200/day pump rental is Johnson Corporation's actual damages which are recoverable. Answer (b) is incorrect because the lost profits are not recoverable. The lost profits were not foreseeable, i.e., the trucking company did not know the special circumstances of Johnson's plant. Answer (c) is incorrect because punitive damages are not normally allowed for breach of contract. Answer (d) is incorrect because in any breach of contract, the nonbreaching party is liable for a minimum of nominal damages.

G. Remedies

44. (583,L1,20) (b) The court will grant specific performance of a contract as a remedy if money damages will not be adequate to compensate the nonbreaching party. Since the coin is rare (unique) and cannot be readily purchased in the market, the court will grant specific performance to Myers. Thus, answer (a) is incorrect. Answer (c) is incorrect because reformation applies to written contracts containing ambiguities and would not be an appropriate remedy in this fact situation. Answer (d) is also incorrect because restitution involves both parties to a contract returning whatever they have received under the agreement. In this question, neither party rendered any performance, therefore restitution would be an inappropriate remedy.

45. (1180,L1,13) (c) A liquidated damage provision is a contractual provision which states the amount of damages that will occur if either party breaches the contract. If the amount is reasonable in light of the anticipated or actual harm caused by the breach, it is enforceable. Answer (c) is correct. Answer (a) is incorrect because the fact that the preparer of the contract is a merchant has no bearing on the use of a liquidated damage clause. Answer (b) is incorrect because retaining a large deposit could be considered unconscionable and unenforceable. The reasonableness of a liquidated damage clause is judged in light of anticipated harm, not by a set percentage by which the liquidated damages exceed the actual damages.

H. Statute of Limitations

46. (1181,L1,2) (c) The statute of limitations prescribes the time period in which a plaintiff must initiate the lawsuit, declaring that no suit shall be maintained on such causes of action unless brought within a specified period of time after the right accrued. The statute constitutes a defense to recovery once the requisite period of time has lapsed. Answer (a) is incorrect because there is no standard prescribed period of time for all cases. The time period fluctuates according to type of case involved (i.e., contracts, tort). Answer (b) is incorrect because the statute of limitations is equally applicable to actions brought in courts of equity as in courts of law. Answer (d) is incorrect because the running of the statutory period may be stopped if the defendent becomes absent from the court's jurisdiction during the period, effectively making it impossible for the plaintiff to institute a lawsuit.

May 1985 Answers

47. (585,L1,16) (a) Contracts are enforceable against a drunkard unless the drunkard was so intoxicated at the time of contracting that s/he lacked the ability to understand the nature and terms of the contract. A drunkard who lacked such ability has the option of voiding any contract entered into during the period of drunkeness, provided that s/he returns any item received under the terms of the contract in the same or similar condition. In this question since it states that Race's ability to understand was significantly impaired by his drunkeness, Race may void the contract at his option. Answer (b) is incorrect because it makes no difference whether the intoxication was involuntary or voluntary. Answer (c) is incorrect because the contract created is voidable, not void. The contract is enforceable if Race chooses not to void it. Answer (d) is incorrect because as discussed above, the contract is voidable due to Race's intoxication.

48. (585,L1,17) (c) An option contract is an irrevocable offer that is actually a contract if supported by sufficient consideration. In this case Mix's offer was an offer to form an option contract. Since the wording of the offer was such that Mix offered to hold the offer open in return for a promise to pay the $250, Simon's agreement to do so was a valid acceptance of the option contract offer. Thus, in this case an option contract has been formed. Therefore, answer (a) is incorrect. Answer (b) is incorrect because the formation of an option contract results in an irrevocable offer to enter into another contract for the term agreed upon (five months in this case). Answer (d) is incorrect because an option contract may be formed for any agreed upon period. A firm offer, which is a written offer to sell goods by a merchant, is limited to a maximum period of three months by the UCC. However, this limitation does not apply to option contracts.

49. (585,L1,18) (b) Sufferance of a legal detriment by the performing party is sufficient to act as consideration. In this case Blue suffered a legal detriment by agreeing not to sue during the term of the offer and to forego suit if she accepted the offer. Thus Fuller's offer to enter into an option contract was accepted by Blue when she agreed to forego suit, and an option contract resulted which would be irrevocable for 60 days. The fact that the possible suit by Blue may be groundless is irrelevant since Blue has the legal right to sue regardless of whether the outcome would be favorable or not and her giving up this right constituted a legal detriment on her part. Answer (a) is incorrect because Fuller's revocation was invalid since an option contract results in an irrevocable offer for the term of the option contract. Whether Fuller's revocation was in writing or was oral is irrelevant due to the existence of the option contract. Answer (c) is incorrect since consideration is required for an option contract to exist. No consideration is required for a firm offer. However, this type of offer only occurs when a merchant offeror engages in a written offer to sell goods, giving assurances that the offer will remain open. Since Fuller's offer concerns the sale of land, the common law would apply and thus, in order for the offer to be irrevocable, it must be supported by consideration (option contract). Answer (d) is incorrect because Blue's communication on the 20th day constituted the acceptance since the offer could not be revoked.

50. (585,L1,19) (d) Under innocent misrepresentation a contract is voidable by one party if the other party has misrepresented a material fact. The party voiding the contract need only prove that a misrepresentation has been made. There is no need to prove scienter on the part of the other party. Under common law fraud the party voiding the contract must prove that the misrepresentation was made with actual or constructive knowledge that it was false (scienter). Answer (a) is incorrect since an action based on either innocent misrepresentation or common law fraud requires proof that a false representation has been made. Answer (b) is incorrect because both actions require that the misrepresentation be of a material fact. Answer (c) is incorrect because both actions require the party to prove that there was reasonable reliance on the misstatement. One who knows the truth or who may have learned it by reasonable inquiry may not recover under either action.

51. (585,L1,20) (a) By definition a bilateral contract is a contract, whereby, a promise is exchanged for another promise. In this case Frost exchanged a promise to pay $160,000 in exchange for Lane's promise to build a warehouse. Thus, answer (b) is incorrect since a unilateral contract is an exchange of a promise for an act. Answer (c) is incorrect because a quasi contract is an implied in law contract. It is a means of providing a remedy when one person has been unjustly enriched by another. Since neither Lane nor Frost were unjustly enriched in this situation, and since the contract is an express contract as is evidenced by the written offer and acceptance, this contract is not a quasi contract. Answer (d) is incorrect because the contract presented in the case is an express contract, as noted above, rather than an implied in fact contract.

52. (585,L1,21) (d) An offeror may stipulate in his/her offer that an acceptance must be received in order to be valid. Such a stipulation effectively negates the rule whereby acceptance may take place upon dispatch. Thus, despite Lane's use of the same means of

communication, acceptance is not effective until receipt by Frost on May 22. Thus, Frost could have revoked the offer at any time up until May 22, since she had not yet received the acceptance. Answer (a) is therefore incorrect. Answer (b) is incorrect since under common law, absent any consideration, a promise to hold an offer open until a specified date is not binding on the offeror. Answer (c) is incorrect since the firm offer rule under the UCC deals only with the sale of goods and does not govern the sale of services such as the building of the warehouse.

53. (585,L1,22) (c) Even though an assignee is not required to give the obligor notice of assignment, his/her failure to do so may affect his/her recovery on the contract right. If an obligor has no knowledge of an assignment, s/he may discharge the obligation by paying the assignor rather than the assignee. In addition, if under a separate dispute or contract the assignor owes the obligor a debt, the obligor may set off this separate debt, if it was incurred prior to the obligor receiving notice of the assignment. Therefore Frost has the right to set off the $5,000 against the $160,000 owed Lane. In this case, since Frost had no knowledge of the assignment, he fully discharged his obligation when he paid Lane $155,000, and he has no liability to Reid Bank. Thus answers (a) and (b) are incorrect. Answer (d) is incorrect since the case involves an assignment of rights under a contract rather than a third-party beneficiary contract. Reid is an assignee, not a third-party beneficiary.

54. (585,L1,23) (b) Ordinary duress is the actual or threatened causing of an action or inaction which, contrary to a party's free will and judgment, forces him/her to enter into a contract. In this case, Dash's retention of workpapers caused Reese to pay the higher-than-contracted price against her free will; thus the contract is voidable at Rees's option based on ordinary duress. Answer (a) is incorrect because undue influence involves the forcing of a party to enter into a contract by taking unfair advantage of a relationship of trust between the two parties or by taking unfair advantage of another party's weakness of mind. Since Dash merely threatened Reese with the retention of working papers, undue influence is not present. Answers (c) and (d) are incorrect because contracts entered into because of an undue influence being imposed, or because of ordinary duress, are voidable not void.

55. (585,L1,24) (d) The statute of limitations bars actions at law on contracts unless they are brought within prescribed periods of time. In this case if Diel did not bring an action against Stone before the statute of limitations had expired, then the court will rule in favor of Stone and will not allow Diel to pursue the action any further. Answer (a) is incorrect because the time period fixed under the statute of limitations varies from state to state. Answer (b) is incorrect because the recording of a contract has no impact on the running of the statute of limitations. Answer (c) is incorrect because the time period covered by the statute of limitations begins to run from the date on which the cause of action occurred, not from the date of recording.

56. (585,L1,25) (c) The parol evidence rule states that a written agreement intended by the parties to be final and complete may not be contradicted by any prior or contemporaneous oral or written agreements. Answer (a) is incorrect because another written agreement may be incorporated as part of the integrated contract by reference to that agreement in the contract. Thus, evidence of this second agreement is admissable under the parol evidence rule. Answer (b) is incorrect because the parol evidence rule does not bar evidence which will clarify an ambiguous point in the written contract. Answer (d) is incorrect because the parol evidence rule applies only to evidence arising prior to or at the time of the formation of the contract; evidence of a subsequent oral modification of the contract is admissable.

57. (585,L1,26) (c) When the buyer of mortgaged property assumes the mortgage, the buyer becomes personally liable on the mortgage and a third-party beneficiary contract is formed. Specifically, a creditor-beneficiary contract is formed since this occurs when one party (the buyer) contracts with the debtor (seller/mortgagor) to pay a debt owed to the creditor (mortgagee). Answer (a) is incorrect because Fink's intent in selling the property to Bloom was not to confer a gift upon State Bank which is required for this to be a donee beneficiary contract. Answer (b) is incorrect because State Bank is not a third party who receives an unintended benefit from the contract governing the sale of the land as is the case with an incidental beneficiary. Fink's and Bloom's intent in entering into the contract was specifically for Bloom to pay the mortgage owed to State Bank. Answer (d) is incorrect because when a mortgage is assumed by a buyer of property, the seller remains primarily liable to the mortgagee unless released by the mortgagee through a novation. Since in this case there is no mention of a novation, State Bank will be able to collect from Fink if Bloom defaults. Fink, in turn, will have cause for legal action against Bloom. An assumption of a mortgage creates a suretyship relationship, with the seller acting as the surety and the buyer being the principal debtor.

November 1985 Answers

58. (1185,L1,6) (c) Contractual offers are not assignable, thus Feil's assignment of the offer to Boyd was invalid, and Boyd's acceptance is ineffective. Answer (a) is incorrect because there was no option contract formed between Apple and Boyd since Boyd did not give consideration in exchange for a promise by Apple to keep the offer open. Answer (b) is incorrect because the right to accept an offer is a nonassignable right. It makes no difference that Fein received consideration from Boyd. Answer (d) is incorrect since the fact that Boyd's acceptance was oral is not, by itself, enough to render it ineffective. This is true since Boyd is trying to enforce the contract against Apple. Apple's signed offer would be a sufficient writing to satisfy the Statute of Frauds.

59. (1185,L1,7) (d) A bilateral contract is defined as a promise given in exchange for another promise. In this case Fenster promised to pay Wein and Wein promised to perform the service. Thus, a bilateral contract was formed since both parties gave consideration in the form of a promise to do something that they would not otherwise be legally bound to do. Answer (a) is incorrect because under common law, certain terms of the contract—such as the amount of the fees—can be left open without destroying the validity of the agreement. Answer (b) is incorrect because a quasi-contract is a type of implied contract, which provides a remedy where one person has been unjustly enriched to the detriment of another. In this fact situation there is no unjust enrichment since Fenster implictly promised to pay. The issue is the amount of the fees. Answer (c) is incorrect because a unilateral contract is defined as a promise given in exchange for an act. In this case, a promise is being exchanged for a second promise.

60. (1185,L1,8) (c) In order for an offer to confer the power to form a contract by acceptance, it must be sufficiently definite and certain, it must manifest an intent to enter into a contract, it must be communicated to the offeree, and the communication must be made or authorized by the offeror. Therefore, answers (a), (b), and (d) are all incorrect. It is not necessary that the offer be communicated in words to the offeree. Any actions that manifest an intent to enter into a contract would be sufficient to constitute an offer. Answer (c) is therefore correct.

61. (1185,L1,9) (d) The Statute of Frauds requires only that the written contract be signed by the party to be charged, not by all parties to the contract. Answer (a) is incorrect because it is not required that the contract be formalized in a single writing. Two or more documents can be combined to create a sufficient writing to satisfy the Statute of Frauds if one of the documents refers to the others. Answer (b) is incorrect because the Statute of Frauds does not apply to all contracts having a consideration valued at $500 or more. The sale of services for $500 is not required to be in writing. Answer (c) is incorrect because the Statute of Frauds applies to leases that are not capable of being performed in one year.

62. (1185,L1,11) (d) Since Wax's acceptance is received by Knox before the offer has expired, a valid contract is formed. It is not necessary that Wax accept in writing to satisfy the Statute of Frauds because Knox's written offer is sufficient to meet the Statute of Frauds requirements. It states all material terms and is signed by the party to be charged. Answer (a) is incorrect because under the provisions of the UCC, a firm offer is a written offer by a merchant offeror for the purchase or sale of goods, not real property. Answer (b) is incorrect because Wax can benefit from the early acceptance rule—meaning that acceptance is effective upon dispatch—only if he uses the specified means of communication, or absent any such specification, the same means used to communicate the offer. Answer (c) is incorrect because such an action by Wax would constitute a rejection and counteroffer. In the absence of any consideration paid by Wax to keep the offer open (i.e., option contract), a rejection or counteroffer automatically terminates the original offer and thereby ends the right of the offeree to accept the original offer.

63. (1185,L1,12) (d) Normally, a unilateral mistake by one of the contracting parties will not destroy the validity of the agreement. However, where the second party knows, or has reason to know of the mistake, the mistaken party will be able to avoid liability on the contract, because the essential element of mutual assent is not present. Answer (a) is incorrect because it is not necessary that King show that Lago acted fraudulently, only that Lago knew of the unilateral mistake. Answer (b) is incorrect because King will not have to perform the contract according to the stated terms since Lago knew of the error. Answer (c) is incorrect because even when the mistake is due to the mistaken party's negligence, that party will still avoid liability if it can be shown that the other party knows, or has reason to know, of the mistake.

64. (1185,L1,13) (a) Consideration consists of two elements: a legal detriment must be incurred by

the promisee and the party must have bargained for what the party received in exchange. Thus, courts will decide if the consideration was bargained for. Answer (b) is incorrect because when deciding whether consideration is present the courts generally do not look to the fairness of the exchange. Answer (c) is incorrect because any legal detriment suffered, regardless of the economic value, is legally sufficient to act as consideration. Answer (d) is incorrect because the courts will look to the objective intent of the parties or, in other words, what a reasonable person viewing the agreement would have perceived to be the intent of the parties.

65. (1185,L1,14) (a) The covenant prohibiting Lull from competing with Ruehl is a restraint of trade covenant. The value to be assigned to the goodwill protected by the covenant would be the excess of the purchase price over the fair market value of the seller's net tangible assets. Answers (b), (c), and (d) are all incorrect because they are correct statements. In order for a restraint of trade covenant to be legal, it must be reasonable with regard to time period, extent of protection provided, and geographic area.

66. (1185,L1,15) (c) Duress exists when one of the contracting parties induces the other party into the agreement by acting or threatening to act in such a manner so as to deprive the second party of his free will in making the decision to enter the contract. Doe can therefore claim duress if improper threats are made by Tuck which deprive Doe of his free will and cause Doe to agree. Answer (a) is incorrect because although a confidential or fiduciary relationship must be present in order for undue influence to occur, there is no such requirement for duress. Answer (b) is incorrect because whereas duress occurs when there are improper acts or threats, an unconscionable contract is an oppressive contract wherein one party takes unfair advantage of the other, usually because of the latter's absence of choice or poor education. Answer (d) is incorrect because for duress to be present there is no requirement that the threatening party must have intended that the second party be influenced by the threats.

67. (1185,L1,17) (a) A third party beneficiary contract is present when the contracting parties enter into an agreement intended to benefit a third party. Security Bank is a third party creditor beneficiary because Quick is contracting with Sand, the debtor, to pay a debt owed to Security, the creditor. Answer (b) is incorrect because a donee beneficiary is one upon whom the contracting parties intended to confer a gift, not one, such as Security, to whom a debt is owed. Answer (c) is incorrect because an incidental beneficiary obtains no rights, but merely an unintended benefit from the two contracting parties. Answer (d) is incorrect because Security is a creditor beneficiary.

68. (1185,L1,19) (d) A novation is a three-party agreement between the contracting parties and a third party, whereby one of the contracting parties is discharged from his/her duty and the third party is substituted in the discharged party's place. In this case, all three parties agree to discharge the old contracts between Fiore and Lutz, and Lutz and Bing, by the creation of a new contract between Fiore and Bing. The new contract is a novation. Answer (a) is incorrect because Fiore gives consideration in the form of a promise to pay Bing, and Bing gives consideration by promising to forego his legal right to proceed against Lutz. Answer (b) is incorrect because Bing is bound by Fiore's promise to pay and does not, therefore, have the option to void the agreement. Answer (c) is incorrect because an accord and satisfaction is an agreement by two parties to terminate an existing contract between them by substituting a new agreement. It does not involve substitution of parties as does a novation.

69. (1185,L1,20) (a) As the seller of real property, Kemp has the duty to disclose all known material defects whether or not they are readily observable. Kemp's silence concerning the latent defect constitutes fraud in the inducement since it is a misrepresentation of a material fact upon which there was reasonable reliance by Ward, the injured party. Fraud in the inducement renders a contract voidable, not void, at the option of the injured party. Answer (b) is therefore incorrect. Answer (c) is incorrect because Kemp's silence affects the validity of the contract since it constitutes fraud in the inducement. Answer (d) is incorrect because in addition to entitling Ward to the right to sue for money damages under the tort of deceit, Kemp's fraud in the inducement gives Ward the option to void the agreement.

Answer Outline

Problem 1 Wrongful Interference with Contractual Relationship; Illegal Agreement (1184,L3)

Beach's minority defense is invalid
- Misrepresentation of age does not invalidate defense
- However, failure to disaffirm within reasonable time after reaching majority constitutes implied ratification

Beach's assertion that Reid's violation of noncompetition covenant constitutes breach is valid
- Noncompetition clause is reasonable in light of circumstances present

Abel's defense based on Beach's fraud is invalid
- Since Reid knew nothing of Beach's fraud he has no duty to inform Abel

Abel's defense based on Beach's minority is invalid
- Surety cannot use minority of principal debtor as defense to payment

Abel's defense based on Reid's violation of noncompetition covenant is valid
- Surety may use material breach of underlying contract by creditor as defense to payment
- Reid's violation of noncompetition clause constitutes breach

Unofficial Answer

Problem 1 Wrongful Interference with Contractual Relationship; Illegal Agreement (1184,L3)

Beach's minority at the time the contract with Reid was entered into will not be a valid defense. Despite Beach's misrepresentation of his age, the agreement with Reid was voidable at Beach's option while Beach was a minor. However, Beach's use and operation of the travel agency for at least seven months after reaching majority constituted an implied ratification of the contract. Some states may construe Beach's mere failure to disaffirm the contract within a reasonable time after reaching majority to be a ratification of the contract. Furthermore, a small number of states provide that minority is not a defense where the minor has entered into a business contract.

Beach's assertion that he is not liable due to Reid's violation of the contract clause prohibiting Reid from competing with Beach is correct because violation of the noncompetition covenant is a material breach of the contract. Since the case at issue involves the sale of a business including its goodwill, the legal validity of a clause prohibiting competition by the seller is determined by its reasonableness regarding the time and geographic area covered. Each case must be considered on its own facts, with a determination of what is reasonable under the particular circumstances. It appears that, according to the facts of this case, the prohibition against Reid's operating a competing travel agency within a one mile radius of Beach's travel agency for two years is reasonable.

Abel's claim that he is not liable to Reid because of Beach's fraud in supplying him with false financial statements is incorrect. Although a creditor has a duty to disclose to the surety all material facts that would increase the surety's risk, the breach of such duty is not a valid defense of the surety if the creditor lacks knowledge of such facts. Therefore, unless Abel can show that Reid knew or had reason to know of the fraud committed by Beach, Abel will not be relieved of his surety undertaking.

Abel's claim that he is not liable to Reid because of Beach's minority is without merit. Beach's minority is a personal defense that in a proper case may be exercised only at Beach's option. Therefore, whether Beach has the power to disaffirm his contract with Reid will have no effect on Abel's surety obligations to Reid.

Abel's assertion that his liability to Reid will be discharged because of Reid's failure to comply with the express promise not to compete with Beach is correct. Unlike the defense of the principal debtor's minority, a material breach of the underlying contract between the principal debtor and creditor may be properly asserted by the surety. The creditor's failure to perform in accordance with the material terms of the underlying contract without justification will discharge the principal debtor's obligation to perform, thereby increasing the risk of the principal debtor's nonperformance. Thus, the surety will also be discharged from liability due to his own increased risk of loss on the surety contract. It seems clear that Reid's opening of a travel agency across the street from Beach's business after only 19 months constituted a material breach of the sale contract. Therefore, Abel will be discharged from his surety obligation.

Answer Outline

Problem 2 Preexisting Contractual Duty; Elements of Fraud (582,L4)

Part a.

1. Modification of preexisting contract under common law
   - Normally, if no new consideration

Modification is not binding
Shaw gave no additional consideration
Because he has preexisting legal duty
Some courts recognize exception concerning construction contracts
Where one party encounters unforeseen substantial difficulty not in the parties' contemplation at time of contracting

2. Modification of preexisting contract for sale of goods
Apply the Uniform Commercial Code
No new consideration needed to make modification binding
Complies with Statute of Frauds
Modification in writing
Signed by party charged

Part b.

Fraud in the inducement
Statement of fact vs. opinion
Ogilvie engaged in a statement of fact concerning suitability of land for avocado growing
Materiality of misrepresentation was significant
Reason Farber purchased the land
Ogilvie made the representations negligently
With reckless disregard for the truth
Negligent as well as intentional misrepresentation
Qualifies as proper basis for fraud in the inducement
Justifiable reliance will not demand inspection of this property
Considering seller's inability to engage in such inspection
Due to vast holdings, distance factor, and time needed

Unofficial Answer

(Author Modified)

Problem 2 Preexisting Contractual Duty; Elements of Fraud (582,L4)

Part a.

1. The described fact situation deals with the sale of services, not the sale of goods. Consequently, the common law, not the Uniform Commercial Code applies. The general rule under common law is that a modification of an existing contract needs new consideration before it is binding. Shaw gave no additional consideration for Craig's promise to bear the additional cost. Thus, normally Craig would not be liable for the additional $10,000 because Shaw is merely promising to complete the well in the modification which he was already obligated to do under the original contract (i.e. a preexisting legal duty).

However, recently, several courts have recognized an exception to this rule, with regard to construction contracts, even under common law. The exception relates to the situation where one party upon beginning performance discovers a substantial difficulty which is unforseen and not in the contemplation of the parties at the time of contracting. If this situation is present, these courts allow enforcement of the modification even though there is no new consideration. This exception would apply in the given fact situation, since Shaw Drilling Company discovered a substantially harder soil consistency than was expected and initially contemplated by both Shaw and Craig at the time of contracting. Therefore, Craig's promise to pay the additional money to Shaw falls within the exception and would be enforceable in courts that recognize this exception, thusly resulting in Craig's liability for the additional cost of $10,000.

2. Yes. If the purchase of computer parts were involved in the agreement, it would constitute a contract for the sale of goods. Instead of applying common law, as we did in the above question, the Uniform Commercial Code would now govern. Under the Uniform Commercial Code, a modification of a pre-existing contract for the sale of goods does not require new consideration to be binding. Thus, even though the manufacturer is merely promising to perform what it was already obligated to do under the original contract, the modification would be binding.

Another issue would be whether the Statute of Frauds applies to the modification. It appears the modification would involve the sale of goods for $500 or more. Consequently, the Statute of Frauds would require the modification to be in writing. Since the question states the purchaser engaged in a subsequent written promise, this would satisfy the Statute of Frauds requirement, in that the writing is signed by the party to be charged (the purchaser).

Part b.

Ogilvie's first assertion is invalid. Since Ogilvie is the seller of real property, many of his statements could be construed to be opinion and "puffing" in an attempt to promote the sale of his land. But Ogilvie did engage in a statement of fact when he stated that the land was suitable for avocado growing. This is a representation which is definite, objective and verifiable. Since the land was not suitable for avocado growing, Ogilvie's statement was false. Therefore, the first requirement for establishing fraud, a misstatement of fact, has been met.

Ogilvie's second assertion that his statements were not material is also invalid. In determining the materiality of a representation, courts look to the impression made upon the mind of the party to whom it was made. The representation must relate to something of sufficient substance to induce reliance. Since Farber purchased the land for the exclusive use of growing avocados, Ogilvie's representation that the land was suitable for avocado growing was material in nature.

Ogilvie's third assertion that he had not lied is invalid. Ogilvie had not personally examined the farmland in question, so he apparently had little basis for making the representations he made. But this lack of knowledge of the facts does not excuse Ogilvie. A party has imputed knowlege (thereby satisfying the knowledge requirement necessary to establish fraud) if s/he makes the representations negligently, with a reckless disregard and indifference as to their truthfulness. Many courts have imputed such knowledge to a party, such as Ogilvie, and have held him responsible where the means of his knowledge was such as to make it his duty to know the truth or falsity of his representations. Ogilvie who represents something as being true based on his own knowledge, but who is in fact completely ignorant of the subject, is treated in the law as knowingly making a false statement, thereby satisfying the scienter (knowledge) requirement of establishing fraud.

The final assertion deals with the reliance requirement necessary to establish fraud. Ogilvie asserts that Farber cannot justifiably rely on Ogilvie's representations since if Farber would have inspected the land he would have discovered the rock formations. Normally, where the accuracy of the seller's statements can be verified, and it would be feasible to do so, justifiable reliance requires such verification. But in this fact situation, the seller was unable to personally examine the land due to the distance factor and the time it would take. Therefore, the buyer can not be expected to do something which the seller did not do. To allow Ogilvie's assertion to be a valid defense would result in the promotion of engaging in fraud, because a person who makes a misrepresentation with intent to induce action could simply state that the buyer should have looked for himself/herself.

Answer Outline

Problem 3 Substantial Performance; Effectiveness of Acceptance (580,L3a&b)

a. Result if dispute goes to court
   Common-law requires literal performance; anything less is a breach releasing either party from duty to perform
   Courts have developed doctrine of substantial performance as an exception concerning construction contracts
   If breach is immaterial; party who breached may recover, less damages. Party who breached must prove
      1. Defect was not structural in nature
      2. Breach was minor relative to total job (95% is a guide courts use)
      3. Breach was not intentional
   Elements 1 and 2 appear to be met in this case
   Satisfaction of element 3 is not determinable from facts given
      Would be met if substitutions were due to mistake or mere negligence, and Silverwater would prevail
      If substitution was willful, no recovery by Silverwater

b. No contract for sale of real property
   Offer is governed by common law of contracts
   Offer stipulations stated that acceptance must be received before effective
      Negated possibility of acceptance being effective even though sent by same means
   Purported acceptance was counteroffer
      Had to be accepted to create contract
      Silence does not constitute acceptance unless
         1. Parties intended silence as acceptance
         2. Prior dealing indicates silence is acceptable
         3. Custom of industry recognizes silence as acceptance
   Above exceptions do not apply, and there is no contract

Unofficial Answer

Problem 3 Substantial Performance; Effectiveness of Acceptance (580,L3a&b)

Parts a1. and a2.

The general common-law rules require literal performance by a party to a contract. Failure to literally perform constitutes a breach. Since promises are construed to be dependent upon each other, the failure by one party to perform releases the other. However, a strict and literal application of this type of implied condition often results in unfairness and hardship, particularly in cases such as this. Therefore, the courts developed some important exceptions to the literal performance doctrine. The applicable rule is known as the substantial performance doctrine, which applies to construction contracts and is a more specific statement of the material performance rule that applies to contracts other than construction contracts. The general rule holds that if the breach is immaterial, the party who breached may nevertheless recover under the contract, less damages caused by the breach. The substantial performance doctrine requires the builder (party breaching) to prove the following facts.

a. The defect was not a structural defect.
b. The breach was relatively minor in relation to the overall performance of the contract. The courts and texts sometimes talk in terms of a 95 percent or better performance.
c. The breach must be unintentional or, to state it another way, the party breaching must have been acting in good faith.

It would appear that requirements a and b are clearly satisfied on the basis of the facts. Requirement c cannot be determined on the facts given. If Silverwater deliberately (with knowledge) substituted the improper and cheaper tile or sewerage pipes, then it may not be entitled to the benefit of the substantial performance exception. On the other hand, if these breaches were the result of an innocent oversight or mere negligence on its part, recovery should be granted. The recovery must be decreased by the amount of the damages caused by the breach. The substitute of sewer pipe of like quality and value would be considered substantial performance.

Part b.

No. The offer for the sale of real property is governed by the common law of contracts.

Anderson's letter constituted an offer that stated it would expire at a given time. In addition to stating the time, the letter indicated that acceptance "must be received in her (Anderson's) office" by said time. This language is clear and unambiguous and effectively negated the rule whereby acceptance may take place upon dispatch. Thus, despite use of the same means of communication, acceptance was not effective until receipt by Anderson on March 2, 1980. This was too late. Thus, the purported acceptance was a mere counteroffer by Heinz and had to be accepted in order to create a contract. Silence does not usually constitute acceptance. In fact, the common-law exceptions to this rule are limited in nature and narrowly construed. The law clearly will not permit a party to unilaterally impose silence upon the other as acceptance. The narrow exceptions are the following:

1. The parties intended silence as acceptance.
2. Prior dealing indicates that silence is an acceptable method of acceptance.
3. The custom of the trade or industry recognizes silence as acceptance.

It is clear that our case is not within any of the exceptions; hence, silence does not constitute acceptance, and there is no contract.

Answer Outline

Problem 4 Modification of a Contract For the Sale of Goods; Doctrine of Part Performance (585,L2)

a. Original contract is sale of goods less than $500
    No writing required
  Good faith modification needs no consideration
  Contract as modified falls within Statute of Frauds (sale of goods $500 or more)
    Must be in writing or supported by a confirmation
  Reed's letter acts as a confirmation because:
    It is a signed writing
    It states the quantity
    Rocco and Reed are merchants
    Rocco did not refute it within 10 days after receipt

b. Normally contract for sale of land must be in writing
  However, if buyer engages in part performance and reasonable reliance, oral contract is enforceable
  Reed's part payment, taking possession, and making substantial improvements constitutes part performance

Unofficial Answer

Problem 4 Modification of a Contract For the Sale of Goods; Doctrine of Part Performance (585,L2)

a. The sale of leather jackets is governed by the Uniform Commercial Code Sales Article which applies to transactions in goods. Under the Uniform Commercial Code, an oral contract for the sale of goods under $500 does not fall within the provisions of the statute of frauds. Thus, the contract between Reed and Rocco is enforceable by either party without the necessity of a signed writing since the sales price is $450. The UCC provides that an agreement to modify a contract for the sale of goods needs no consideration to be binding. However, the modification made must meet the test of good faith. The modification must also satisfy the requirements of the statute of frauds if the contract, as modified, falls within its provisions. Whether Reed acted in good faith is determined by an examination of the facts. Here, the shift in the market may satisfy the requirement of good faith if Reed can show that he would have suffered a loss had he sold the jackets at $450. However, if Reed refused to sell the jackets at $450 merely to derive a greater profit, with knowledge that Rocco was in immediate need of the goods, the modification may not meet the test of good faith.

Since the sales price increased from $450 to $550, the contract must satisfy the statute of frauds in order to be enforceable. The UCC statute of frauds may be satisfied by a confirmation if

- Both parties are merchants.
- It is in writing.
- The writing is signed by the sender.
- The writing states the quantity.
- The writing is received by the recipient within a reasonable time.
- The recipient has reason to know the contents of the writing.
- The recipient fails to give written notice of objection to its contents within 10 days after receipt.

As the facts clearly indicate, the mailing of the signed letter by Reed to Rocco the day after the contract was orally modified, coupled with Rocco's failure to object within ten days after receipt will satisfy the requirements of the statute of frauds.

b. No. As a general rule, a contract for the sale of real property must be supported by a written memo signed by the party to be charged. However, an oral contract to sell real property may be removed from the statute of frauds where there has been part performance and reasonable reliance on the oral contract. The part payment of the sales price by Reed, in addition to Reed's taking possession of the building with Smith's consent and making permanent and substantial improvements, generally will prevent Smith from setting the contract aside or requiring Reed to vacate the building.

SALES

Overview

The law of sales is simply the rules governing a contract for the sale of goods. Since a sale of goods is involved, it is important for you to recognize that Article 2 of the Uniform Commercial Code (UCC) applies. A sale of goods under the UCC is the sale of tangible, moveable property.

The single most tested area in sales is product liability. When studying this area, you should pay particular attention to the legal theories under which an injured party may recover. Realize that an injured party may recover under the legal theories of breach of warranty, negligence, and strict liability. It is important that you know the circumstances under which these theories may be used. Other areas which are heavily tested are warranties and disclaimers; the concept of identification; risk of loss and remedies, rights, and duties of the buyer and seller.

You should understand that a binding contract may be present under the UCC, if the parties had intended to be bound, even though certain elements of a contract may be missing. These open terms will be filled by specific provisions of the UCC. The parties to a sale need not be merchants for the UCC to apply; however, some rules vary if merchants are involved in the sales contract.

A. Contracts for Sale of Goods

1. Article 2 of the Uniform Commercial Code controls contracts for the sale of goods in almost all state jurisdictions
   a. In general, "goods" include tangible property
      1) Does not include sale of investment securities, accounts receivable, or contract rights

         EXAMPLE: S sells to B a stereo. The UCC applies whether S normally sells stereos or not.

         EXAMPLE: S sells a home to B. The common law rules apply to this contract since it involves the sale of real property.

   b. The tendency of the UCC is to find a contract obligation in cases where it is plainly the intent of the parties, even though some technical element of a contract may be missing. The intent of the UCC is to facilitate and expedite commercial transactions.
   c. The express elements necessary for a sales contract are
      1) Parties
      2) Price - can be omitted and contract will be enforced at a reasonable price
      3) Time for performance
         a) If not present, reasonable time is implied
         b) If agreement states time is of essence, then delay in performance is a material breach and nonbreaching party can terminate performance and sue for damages

4) Subject matter

a) Normally, quantity must be included before agreement is considered enforceable

d. Open terms will not cause a contract for the sale of goods to fail for indefiniteness if there was an intent to contract and a reasonable basis for establishing a remedy is available. If the place of delivery is left open, the UCC provides that the seller's place of business shall be the proper place of delivery.

2. Definitions

a. Merchant--one who deals in the kind of goods being sold, or one who holds self out as having superior knowledge and skills as to the goods involved, or one who employs another who qualifies as a merchant

b. Goods--all things which are moveable at the time of identification to the contract for sale

1) To be distinguished from investment securities and things in action, e.g., contracts, documents of title, commercial paper

2) The goods must be both existing and identified for an interest to pass to the buyer

3) Moveable distinguishes goods from real property

a) A contract for the sale of oil, minerals, etc. is a sale of goods if they are to be severed by the seller or standing timber to be cut by either party

4) Fungible goods--so similar that one unit is considered the equivalent of any other, e.g., bushel of U.S. No. 1 wheat or corn

c. Firm offer--a written signed offer, by a merchant, giving assurance that it will be held open for a specified time is irrevocable for that period, not to exceed three months

d. Battle of forms--between merchants, additional terms included in the acceptance become part of the contract unless

1) Original offer precludes such, or
2) New terms materially alter the original offer, or
3) The original offeror gives notice of his objection within a reasonable time

e. Bailment--Bailor (usually owner of property) transfers temporary possession of personal property to bailee without transferring title

EXAMPLE: Herb borrows Ike's law notes to prepare for CPA exam. A bailment is created with Ike the bailor and Herb the bailee.

f. Consignment--arrangement in which agent (consignee) is appointed by consignor to sell goods if all of the following conditions are met:

1) Consignor keeps title to goods
2) Consignee is not obligated to buy or pay for goods
3) Consignee receives a commission upon sale and
4) Consignor receives proceeds of sale

8

g. Shipment terms

1) C.O.D. shipments--collect on delivery
2) F.O.B.--free on board. Means the seller will pay the freight and bear the risk of loss to the place named

a) It will be a shipping contract if the place of shipment is named, i.e., buyer pays freight

Example: Seller is in Dallas, buyer is in Chicago: F.O.B. Dallas.

b) It will be a destination contract if the place of destination is named, i.e., seller pays freight

Example: Seller is in Dallas, buyer is in Chicago: F.O.B. Chicago.

3) F.A.S. vessel--free along side

a) Seller must deliver goods along side the named vessel at his own risk and expense

4) C.I.F.--cost, insurance, and freight included in price

a) Seller puts goods in hands of a carrier and obtains insurance in buyer's name, who then has risk of loss

h. No arrival, no sale--seller ships but if goods do not arrive, contract fails and neither party is liable

i. Sale on approval--goods may be returned even if they conform to the contract

1) Goods bought for use, e.g., consumer purchaser
2) Seller retains title and risk of loss until acceptance
3) Creditors of buyer cannot reach goods until buyer accepts

j. Sale or return--goods may be returned even if they conform to the contract

1) Goods bought for resale, e.g., merchant buyer
2) Seller retains title but buyer has risk of loss
3) Creditors of buyer can reach the goods, unless notice of seller's interest is posted or filed as required

k. Document of title--any document which in the regular course of business is accepted as adequate evidence that the person in possession of the document is entitled to receive, hold and dispose of the document and the goods it covers

l. Bill of lading--a document of title which is issued by a private or common carrier in exchange for goods delivered to it for shipment. It may be negotiable or nonnegotiable.

m. Warehouse receipt--a document of title issued by a person engaged in the business of storing goods, i.e., a warehouseman. It acknowledges receipt of the goods, describes the goods stored, and contains the terms of the storage contract. It may be negotiable or nonnegotiable.

3. Passage of title

a. Once goods are identified to the contract, the parties may agree as to when title passes

   b. Otherwise, title generally passes when the seller completes his performance with respect to physical delivery
      1) If a destination contract, title passes on tender at destination, i.e., buyer's place of business
      2) If a shipping contract, title passes upon the seller putting the goods in the possession of the carrier
   c. If seller has no duty to move the goods:
      1) Title passes upon delivery of documents of title
      2) If no document of title exists, title passes at the time and place of contracting if the goods are identifiable
      3) If goods not identified, there is only a contract to sell; no title passes
   d. Rejection of goods or a justified revocation of acceptance by buyer revests title in seller

4. Sale of goods by nonowner
   a. If seller has a void title (no title) to goods then bona fide purchaser acquires no title
   b. If seller has a voidable title to goods (i.e., seller obtained goods through fraud inducement) then bona fide purchaser receives good title
   c. Entrusting--transferring possession of goods to a merchant who deals in such goods gives the merchant the power to transfer all rights of the entruster to a good faith purchaser in ordinary course of business

   Example: A leaves a ring with B, a jeweler, to be cleaned. B sells the ring to C. C has good title to the ring and A would have to sue B for the loss.

5. Identification--occurs when the goods that are going to be used to perform the contract are shipped, marked or otherwise designated as such
   a. Identification creates a special property interest in the goods on behalf of buyer. This means buyer has:
      1) An insurable interest in the goods
      2) Right to inspect goods at reasonable time and at buyer's expense
      3) Right to sue for damages caused by any third party who wrongfully destroys or damages goods
      4) If within 10 days of buyer's first payment seller is insolvent, the right to demand goods upon offering full contract price

6. Risk of loss (unlike common law, does not depend on title under the UCC)
   a. Parties may agree as to who bears the risk, otherwise UCC rules apply
   b. If a breach of contract, the party in breach has the risk of loss unless the party not in breach has the goods fully insured
   c. If the goods are to be shipped by a carrier:
      1) And the seller must deliver the goods to a specified destination (destination contract), seller has risk of loss until duly tendered by carrier at destination
      2) And the seller is not required to deliver the goods to specified destination (shipping contract), buyer has risk of loss once goods are delivered to an appropriate carrier

d. If the goods are in possession of a bailee (e.g., public warehouse) and seller does not have to move them, risk of loss passes to buyer when

   1) Buyer receives a negotiable document of title, or
   2) Bailee acknowledges buyer's right to possession, or
   3) Buyer receives a non-negotiable document of title or written direction to the bailee to deliver the goods. Buyer has reasonable time to present to bailee.

e. In a case not within "c." or "d.," risk passes to buyer on receipt if seller is a merchant. If he is not, risk passes on tender of delivery.

f. Sale on approval keeps the risk with the seller until goods are accepted by buyer

g. Sale or return puts the risk on the buyer until he returns the goods

h. Risk of loss can be covered by insurance. In general, party has an insurable interest whenever he can suffer damage

   1) Buyer usually allowed an insurable interest when goods are identified to the contract
   2) Seller usually has an insurable interest so long as he has title or a security interest

7. Product liability--a manufacturer or seller may be responsible when a product is defective and causes injury or damage to a person or property. There are three theories under which manufacturers and sellers may be held liable.

   a. Negligence--the injured party must prove the defendant failed to exercise reasonable care (common law remedy)

      Example: Negligent design, negligent packaging or inadequate instructions for use of product.

      Example: A car manufacturer is negligent in a structural design and as a result, a driver of a car is severely injured. The driver may sue the manufacturer even though he did not contract with the manufacturer.

      1) It is generally difficult to prove this type of negligence
      2) Privity of contract (contractual connection between parties, e.g., buyer-seller) is not needed because the suit is not based on a contract
      3) The negligence theory is being replaced in some states by strict liability

   b. Strict liability--a manufacturer or seller may be held liable for injuries caused by a product because of its inherent danger without proving negligence. (Generally based on statutes.)

      1) Injured party generally must show

         a) Product was defective when it left hands of seller, and
         b) The defect caused the injury, and
         c) The defect caused the product to be unreasonably dangerous

      2) Neither bad intent nor fault of the retailer or wholesaler need be found. They are liable merely for selling it in the defective condition received from the manufacturer. They may in turn sue the manufacturer.

      3) Privity of contract is not needed because the suit is not based on a contract

a) Any user or consumer of the product who is injured may sue. In some instances, they can also recover for property damages.

c. Warranty liability--purchaser of a product may sue based on the warranties made

1) Warranty of title

a) Seller warrants good title, rightful transfer and freedom from any security interest or lien that the buyer has no knowledge of

Example: A seller of stolen goods would be liable to a buyer for damages.

b) Merchant warrants goods to be free of any rightful claim of infringement, e.g., patent or trademark, unless buyer furnished specifications to seller for manufacture of the goods

c) Can only be disclaimed by specific language or circumstances which give buyer reason to know he is receiving less than full title

1] Cannot be disclaimed by language such as "as is"

2) Express warranties

a) Any affirmation of fact or promise made by the seller to the buyer which relates to the goods and becomes part of the basis of the bargain creates an express warranty that the goods shall conform to the affirmation or promise

1] Sales talk, puffing, or a statement purporting to be merely the seller's opinion does not create a warranty

2] No reliance is necessary (need not be proven) on part of buyer
3] Must form part of the basis of bargain

a] Would include advertisements read by buyer
b] Normally would not include warranties given after the sale or contract was made

4] No intent to create warranty is needed on the part of the seller

b) Any description of the goods which is made part of the basis of the bargain creates an express warranty that the goods shall conform to the description
c) Any sample or model which is made part of the basis of the bargain creates an express warranty that the goods shall conform to the sample or model
d) It is not necessary to the creation of an express warranty that the seller use formal words such as "warranty" or "guarantee"

3) Implied warranties (a promise arising by operation of law)

a) Merchantability--goods are fit for the ordinary purpose for which goods of this type are used and will pass without objection in the trade. This warranty also guarantees that the goods are properly packaged and labeled. This warranty is implied if

1] The seller is a merchant with respect to goods of the kind being sold
2] Warranty is not modified or excluded

b) Fitness for a particular purpose

1] This warranty is created when the seller knows of the particular use for which the goods are required and further knows that the buyer is relying on the skill and judgment of the seller to select and furnish suitable goods for this particular use

EXAMPLE: A buyer relying upon a paint salesman to select a particular exterior house paint that will effectively cover existing siding.

2] Buyer must actually rely on seller and cannot have superior knowledge

3] The product is then warranted for the particular expressed purpose and the seller may be liable if the product fails to so perform

4] Applicable both to merchants and nonmerchants

4) UCC, being consumer oriented, allows these warranties to extend to parties other than the purchaser even without privity of contract

a) Extends to a buyer's family and also to guests in the home who may reasonably be expected to use and/or be affected by the goods and who are injured

EXAMPLE: A dinner guest breaks a tooth on a small piece of metal in the food. Note that in food, the substance causing injury must be foreign, not something customarily found in it (bone in fish).

5) Disclaimers. Warranty liability may be escaped or modified by disclaimers (also available at common law without rules defining limits of disclaimers).

a) A disclaimer inconsistent with an express warranty is not effective, i.e., a description of a warranty in a contract cannot be disclaimed

b) Disclaimers must be clear and conspicuous

c) A disclaimer of merchantability must use the word "merchantability" unless all implied warranties are disclaimed as in "e." below

d) To disclaim the implied warranty of fitness for a particular purpose, the disclaimer must be in writing and conspicuous

e) All implied warranties (including merchantability) can be disclaimed by language such as "as is" or "with all faults" which makes plain that there is no implied warranty

f) If the buyer has had ample opportunity to inspect the goods or sample, there is no implied warranty as to any defects which ought reasonably to have been discovered

g) Implied warranties may be excluded or modified by course of dealing, course of performance, or usage of trade

B. Remedies for breach of contract for sale of goods

1. In general, either party may, upon breach by the other, cancel the contract and terminate executory obligations. Unlike common law rescission, however, cancellation does not discharge a claim for damages.
2. A seller's duty to perform under a contract for sale is excused if performance as agreed has been made impracticable by the occurrence of a contingency, non-occurrence of which was a basic assumption on which the contract was made
3. Either party may demand adequate assurance of performance when reasonable grounds for insecurity arise with respect to performance of the other party
   a. E.g., buyer falls behind in payments or seller delivers defective goods to other buyers
   b. Party may suspend performance while waiting for assurance
   c. Failure to provide assurance within a reasonable time, not to exceed 30 days, is repudiation of the contract
   d. Provision in contract, that seller may accelerate payment when he has a good faith belief that makes him insecure, is valid
4. Seller's remedies
   a. Seller has right to "cure" nonconformity, i.e., tender conforming goods
      1) Within original time of contract or
      2) Within reasonable time if seller thought nonconforming tender would be acceptable
      3) Seller must notify buyer of his intention to cure
   b. A seller may resell the goods if buyer breaches in acceptance
      1) May be a public or private sale
         a) If private, must give notice to buyer who breached, otherwise losses cannot be recovered
         b) In any event, good faith purchasers take free of original buyer's claims
      2) If seller resells in a commercially reasonable manner, he may recover any loss on the sale from the buyer who breached, but he is not responsible to the buyer who breached for profits made on the resale
   c. A seller may stop a shipment of any size in the hands of a carrier if the buyer is insolvent
      1) He may stop only carloads, truckloads, or larger lots for repudiation or failure to pay by buyer
      2) Seller must notify carrier in time so carrier can reasonably stop before delivery
      3) Seller is liable to carrier for any damages
      4) If the goods have negotiable documents of title, carrier (bailee) can demand surrender of them before returning goods
         a) Bailee is under a duty to turn goods over to the holder of negotiable documents of title regardless of insolvency
      5) If carrier has acknowledged buyer's right to goods, carrier has no right to stop

d. A seller may recover goods received by an insolvent buyer if demand is made within 10 days of receipt

   1) However, if the buyer has made a written misrepresentation of solvency within 3 months before delivery, this 10-day limitation does not apply

   2) If buyer is insolvent, seller may demand cash to make delivery

e. Seller may recover damages

   1) If buyer repudiates agreement or refuses goods, seller may recover the difference between market price at time of tender and contract price, plus incidental damages, minus expenses saved due to buyer's breach

   2) If the measure of damages stated above in "1)" is inadequate to place the seller in as good a position as performance would have, then the seller can sue for the lost profits, plus incidental damages, less expenses saved due to the buyer's breach

   3) The seller can recover the full contract price when

      a) The buyer has already accepted the goods
      b) Conforming goods have been destroyed after the risk of loss has transferred to buyer
      c) The seller is unable to resell the identified goods

f. Remedies for anticipatory breach (see Breach of Contract) apply here, i.e., sue at once or wait until time for performance

   1) If breach by buyer comes during manufacture of goods, seller may

      a) Complete goods and identify to contract, or
      b) Cease and sell for scrap, or
      c) Proceed in other reasonable manner

   2) Any of the above must be done while exercising reasonable commercial judgment
   3) Buyer who breaches is then liable for damages measured by whatever course of action seller takes

5. Buyer's remedies

   a. Buyer may reject nonconforming goods, either in entirety or any commercial unit, e.g., bale, carload, etc.

      1) Must do so in reasonable time and give notice to seller (failure may operate as acceptance)

         a) Buyer must have reasonable time to inspect even after physical acceptance

      2) Buyer must care for goods until returned
      3) If buyer is a merchant, he must follow reasonable instructions of seller, e.g., ship, sell

         a) Right to indemnity for costs

      4) If goods are perishable or threatened with decline in value, buyer must make reasonable effort to sell
      5) Buyer has a security interest in any goods in his possession to the extent of any payments made to seller and any expenses incurred

         a) He may sell the goods as a seller may in "3.b." above

b. Buyer may accept nonconforming goods

   1) Buyer must pay at contract price but may still recover damages, i.e., deduct damages from price if he gives seller notice

   2) Buyer may revoke acceptance in a reasonable time if

      a) Accepted expecting nonconformity to be cured
      b) Accepted because of difficulty of discovering defect
      c) Accepted because seller assured conformity

c. Buyer may recover damages measured by the difference between the contract price and the market value of the goods at the time buyer learns of the breach, plus any incidental damages and consequential damages

   1) Consequential damages are damages resulting from buyer's needs which the seller was aware of at the time of contracting

d. Buyer has the right of cover

   1) Buyer can buy substitute goods from another seller. The buyer will still have the right to damages after engaging in "cover."

      a) Damages are difference between cost of cover and contract price, plus incidental and consequential damages
      b) Failure to cover does not bar other remedies

6. Statute of Limitations for sale of goods is 4 years

   a. An action for breach must be commenced within this period
   b. Parties may agree to reduce to not less than one year but may not extend it
   c. Statute of Limitations begins running when the contract is breached
   d. Breach of warranty occurs upon tender of delivery
   e. If warranty expressly extends to future performance, statute runs from time breach occurs or should have been discovered

Multiple Choice Questions (1–36)

1. Where an oral agreement pertaining to goods is entered into without any consideration, the agreement will be binding if it
   a. Relates to a requirements contract.
   b. Is a firm offer made by a merchant promising to hold the offer open for two months.
   c. Modifies the price on an existing sales contract from $600 to $450.
   d. Disclaims the implied warranty of fitness for a particular purpose.

2. The UCC Sales Article applies
   a. Exclusively to the sale of goods between merchants.
   b. To the sale of real estate between merchants.
   c. To the sale of specially manufactured goods.
   d. To the sale of investment securities.

3. In order to have an irrevocable offer under the Uniform Commercial Code, the offer must
   a. Be made by a merchant to a merchant.
   b. Be contained in a signed writing which gives assurance that the offer will be held open.
   c. States the period of time for which it is irrevocable.
   d. Not be contained in a form supplied by the offeror.

4. A claim has been made by Donnegal to certain goods in your client's possession. Donnegal will be entitled to the goods if it can be shown that Variance, the party from whom your client purchased the goods, obtained them by
   a. Deceiving Donnegal as to his identity at the time of the purchase.
   b. Giving Donnegal his check which was later dishonored.
   c. Obtaining the goods from Donnegal by fraud, punishable as larceny under criminal law.
   d. Purchasing goods which had been previously stolen from Donnegal.

5. Wilson Corporation entered into a contract to sell goods to Marvin who has a place of business in the same town as Wilson. The contract was clear with respect to price and quantity, but failed to designate the place of delivery. Which of the following statements is correct?
   a. The contract is unenforceable because of indefiniteness.
   b. The place for delivery must be designated by the parties within five days or the contract is voidable.
   c. The seller's place of business is the proper place for delivery.
   d. The buyer's place of business is the proper place for delivery.

6. Bizzy Corp. wrote Wang ordering 100 Wang radios for $2,500. Wang unequivocably accepted Bizzy's offer but in doing so Wang added a clause providing for interest on any overdue invoices pertaining to the sale, a practice which is common in the industry. If Wang and Bizzy are both merchants and there are **no** further communications between the parties, relating to the terms, then
   a. Wang has made a counteroffer.
   b. A contract can **not** be formed unless Bizzy expressly accepts the term added by Wang.
   c. A contract is formed incorporating only the terms of Bizzy's offer.
   d. A contract is formed with Wang's additional term becoming a part of the agreement.

7. On October 1, Baker, a wholesaler, sent Clark, a retailer, a written signed offer to sell 200 pinking shears at $9 each. The terms were F.O.B. Baker's warehouse, net 30, late payment subject to a 15% per annum interest charge. The offer indicated that it must be accepted no later than October 10, that acceptance would be effective upon receipt, and that the terms were not to be varied by the offeree. Clark sent a telegram which arrived on October 6, and accepted the offer expressly subject to a change of the payment terms to 2/10, net/30. Baker phoned Clark on October 7, rejecting the change of payment terms. Clark then indicated it would accept the October 1 offer in all respects, and expected delivery within 10 days. Baker did not accept Clark's oral acceptance of the original offer. Which of the following is a correct statement?
   a. Baker's original offer is a firm offer, hence irrevocable.
   b. There is **no** contract since Clark's modifications effectively rejected the October 1 offer, and Baker never accepted either of Clark's proposals.
   c. Clark actually created a contract on October 6, since the modifications were merely proposals and did **not** preclude acceptance.
   d. The statute of frauds would preclude the formation of a contract in any event.

8. Darrow purchased 100 sets of bookends from Benson Manufacturing, Inc. Darrow made substantial prepayments of the purchase price. Benson is insolvent

nd the goods have not been delivered as promised. Darrow wants the bookends. Under the circumstances, which of the following will prevent Darrow from obtaining the bookends?

a. The fact that he did **not** pay the full price at the time of the purchase even though he has made a tender of the balance and holds it available to Benson upon delivery.

b. The fact that he can obtain a judgment for damages.

c. The fact that he was **not** aware of Benson's insolvency at the time he purchased the bookends.

d. The fact that the goods have **not** been identified to his contract.

9. Wexford Furniture, Inc., is in the retail furniture business and has stores located in principal cities in the United States. Its designers created a unique cocktail table. After obtaining prices and schedules, Wexford ordered 2,000 tables to be made to its design and specifications for sale as a part of its annual spring sales promotion campaign. Which of the following represents the earliest time Wexford will have an insurable interest in the tables?

a. At the time the goods are in Wexford's possession.

b. Upon shipment of conforming goods by the seller.

c. When the goods are marked or otherwise designated by the seller as the goods to which the contract refers.

d. At the time the contract is made.

10. Nat purchased a typewriter from Rob. Rob is not in the business of selling typewriters. Rob tendered delivery of the typewriter after receiving payment in full from Nat. Nat informed Rob that he was unable to take possession of the typewriter at that time, but would return later that day. Before Nat returned, the typewriter was destroyed by a fire. The risk of loss

a. Passed to Nat upon Rob's tender of delivery.

b. Remained with Rob, since Nat had **not** yet received the typewriter.

c. Passed to Nat at the time the contract was formed and payment was made.

d. Remained with Rob, since title had **not** yet passed to Nat.

11. Hack Company owned 100 tires which it deposited in a public warehouse on April 25, receiving a negotiable warehouse receipt in its name. Hack sold the tires to Fast Freight Co. On which of the following dates did the risk of loss transfer from Hack to Fast?

a. May 1—Fast signed a contract to buy the tires from Hack for $15,000. Delivery was to be at the warehouse.

b. May 2—Fast paid for the tires.

c. May 3—Hack negotiated the warehouse receipt to Fast.

d. May 4—Fast received delivery of the tires at the warehouse.

12. In deciding a controversy involving the question of who has the risk of loss, the court will look primarily to

a. The intent of the parties manifested in the contract.

b. The shipping terms used by the parties.

c. Whether title has passed.

d. The insurance coverage of the parties.

13. Falcon, by telegram to Southern Wool, Inc., ordered 30 bolts of cloth, first quality, 60% wool and 40% dacron. The shipping terms were F.O.B. Falcon's factory in Norwalk, Connecticut. Southern accepted the order and packed the bolts of cloth for shipment. In the process it discovered that one half of the bolts packed had been commingled with cloth which was 50% wool and 50% dacron. Since Southern did not have any additional 60% wool cloth, it decided to send the shipment to Falcon as an accommodation. The goods were shipped and later the same day Southern wired Falcon its apology informing Falcon of the facts and indicating that the 15 bolts of 50% wool would be priced at $15 a bolt less. The carrier delivering the goods was hijacked on the way to Norwalk. Under the circumstances, who bears the risk of loss?

a. Southern, since they shipped goods which failed to conform to the contract.

b. Falcon, since the shipping terms were F.O.B. Falcon's place of business.

c. Southern, because the order was **not** a signed writing.

d. Falcon, since Falcon has title to the goods.

14. Hall is suing the manufacturer, the wholesaler, and the retailer for bodily injuries caused by a lawnmower Hall purchased. Under the theory of strict liability

a. Privity will be a bar insofar as the wholesaler is concerned if the wholesaler did **not** have a reasonable opportunity to inspect.

b. Contributory negligence on Hall's part will always be a bar to recovery.

c. The manufacturer will avoid liability if it can show it followed the custom of the industry.

d. Hall may recover despite the fact that he can **not** show that any negligence was involved.

15. Under the UCC, the warranty of title for the sale of goods

a. May **not** be excluded by the seller.
b. May be excluded by the phrase "as is."
c. Will vest title absolutely in a bona fide purchaser for value provided that the seller is a merchant.
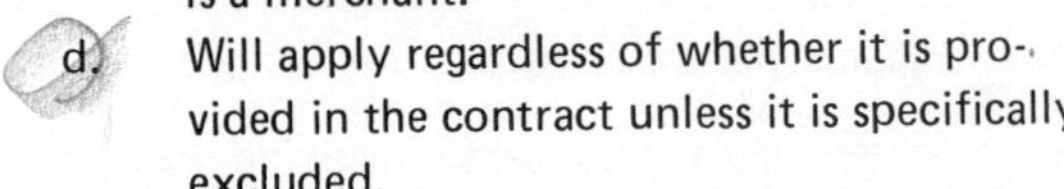
d. Will apply regardless of whether it is provided in the contract unless it is specifically excluded.

16. The Uniform Commercial Code provides for a warranty against infringement. Its primary purpose is to protect the buyer of goods from infringement of the rights of third parties. This warranty

a. Only applies if the sale is between merchants.
b. Must be expressly stated in the contract or the Statute of Frauds will prevent its enforceability.
c. Protects the seller if the buyer furnishes specifications which result in an infringement.
d. Can **not** be disclaimed.

17. Which of the following factors will be most important in determining if an express warranty has been created?

a. Whether the promises made by the seller became part of the basis of the bargain.
b. Whether the seller intended to create a warranty.
c. Whether the statements made by the seller were in writing.
d. Whether the sale was made by a merchant in the regular course of business.

18. Wally, a CPA and a neighbor of Rita's, offered to sell Rita his power chain saw for $400. Rita stated that she knew nothing about chain saws but would buy the saw if it were capable of cutting down the trees in her backyard, which had an average diameter of five feet. Wally assured Rita that the saw "would do the job." Relying on Wally's assurance, Rita purchased the saw. Wally has created a warranty that

a. The saw is of an average fair quality.
b. The saw is fit for the ordinary purposes for which it is used.
c. The saw is capable of cutting the trees in Rita's backyard.
d. Is unenforceable because it is **not** in writing.

19. The Uniform Commercial Code implies a warranty of merchantability to protect buyers of goods. To be subject to this warranty the goods need **not** be

a. Fit for all of the purposes for which the buyer intends to use the goods.
b. Adequately packaged and labeled.
c. Sold by a merchant.
d. In conformity with any promises or affirmations of fact made on the container or label.

20. The Uniform Commercial Code's position on privity of warranty as to personal injuries

a. Resulted in a single uniform rule being adopted throughout most of the United States.
b. Prohibits the exclusion on privity grounds of third parties from the warranty protection it has granted.
c. Applies exclusively to manufacturers.
d. Allows the buyer's family the right to sue only the party from whom the buyer purchased the product.

21. Webster purchased a drill press for $475 from Martinson Hardware, Inc. The press has proved to be defective and Webster wishes to rescind the purchase based upon a breach of implied warranty. Which of the following will preclude Webster's recovery from Martinson?

a. The press sold to Webster was a demonstration model and sold at a substantial discount; hence, Webster received no implied warranties.
b. Webster examined the press carefully, but as regards the defects, they were hidden defects which a reasonable examination would **not** have revealed.
c. Martinson informed Webster that they were closing out the model at a loss due to certain deficiencies and that it was sold "with all faults."
d. The fact that it was the negligence of the manufacturer which caused the trouble and that the defect could **not** have been discovered by Martinson without actually taking the press apart.

22. Marvin contracted to purchase goods from Ling. Subsequently, Marvin breached the contract and Ling is seeking to recover the contract price. Ling can recover the price if

a. Ling does **not** seek to recover any damages in addition to the price.
b. The goods have been destroyed and Ling's insurance coverage is inadequate, regardless of risk of loss.

c. Ling has identified the goods to the contract and the circumstances indicate that a reasonable effort to resell the goods at a reasonable price would be to no avail.

d. Marvin anticipatorily repudiated the contract and specific performance is **not** available.

23. Sanders Hardware Company received an order for $900 of assorted hardware from Richards & Company. The shipping terms were F.O.B. Lester Freight Line, seller's place of business, 2/10, net/30. Sanders packed and crated the hardware for shipment and it was loaded upon Lester's truck. While the goods were in transit to Richards, Sanders learned that Richards was insolvent in the equity sense (unable to pay its debts in the ordinary course of business). Sanders promptly wired Lester's office in Denver, Colorado, and instructed them to stop shipment of the goods to Richards and to store them until further instructions. Lester complied with these instructions. Regarding the rights, duties, and liabilities of the parties, which of the following is correct?

a. Sanders' stoppage in transit was improper if Richards' assets exceeded its liabilities.

b. Richards is entitled to the hardware if it pays cash.

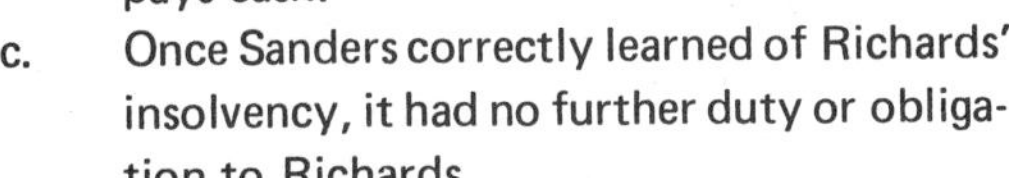

c. Once Sanders correctly learned of Richards' insolvency, it had no further duty or obligation to Richards.

d. The fact that Richards became insolvent in no way affects the rights, duties, and obligations of the parties.

24. Kent, a wholesale distributor of cameras, entered into a contract with Williams. Williams agreed to purchase 100 cameras with certain optional attachments. The contract was made on October 1, 1976, for delivery by October 15, 1976; terms: 2/10, net 30. Kent shipped the cameras on October 6, and they were delivered on October 10. The shipment did not conform to the contract, in that one of the attachments was not included. Williams immediately notified Kent that he was rejecting the goods. For maximum legal advantage Kent's most appropriate action is to

a. Bring an action for the price less an allowance for the missing attachment.

b. Notify Williams promptly of his intention to cure the defect and make a conforming delivery by October 15.

c. Terminate his contract with Williams and recover for breach of contract.

d. Sue Williams for specific performance.

25. On February 1, 1983, Nugent Manufacturing, Inc. contracted with Costello Wholesalers to supply Costello with 1,000 integrated circuits. Delivery was called for on May 1, 1983. On March 15, 1983, Nugent notified Costello that it would not perform and that Costello should look elsewhere. Nugent had received a larger and more lucrative contract on February 27, 1983, and its capacity was such that it could not fulfill both orders. The facts

a. Are **not** sufficient to clearly establish an anticipatory repudiation.

b. Will prevent Nugent from retracting its repudiation of the Costello contract.

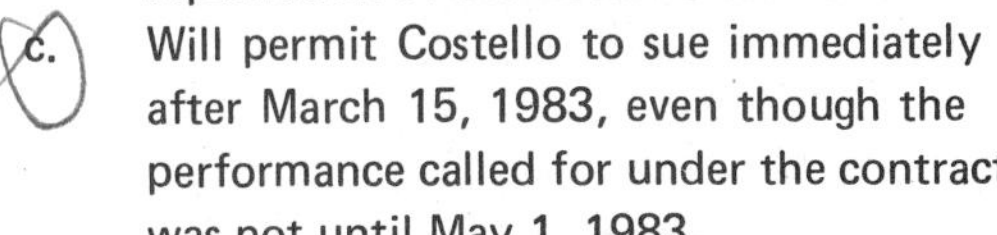

c. Will permit Costello to sue immediately after March 15, 1983, even though the performance called for under the contract was not until May 1, 1983.

d. Will permit Costello to sue only after May 1, 1983, the latest performance date.

26. Brown ordered 100 cases of Delicious Brand peas at list price from Smith Wholesaler. Immediately upon receipt of Brown's order, Smith sent Brown an acceptance which was received by Brown. The acceptance indicated that shipment would be made within ten days. On the tenth day Smith discovered that all of its supply of Delicious Brand peas had been sold. Instead it shipped 100 cases of Lovely Brand peas, stating clearly on the invoice that the shipment was sent only as an accommodation. Which of the following is correct?

a. Smith's shipment of Lovely Brand peas is a counteroffer, thus **no** contract exists between Brown and Smith.

b. Smith's note of accommodation cancels the contract between Smith and Brown.

c. Brown's order is a unilateral offer, and can only be accepted by Smith's shipment of the goods ordered.

d. Smith's shipment of Lovely Brand peas constitutes a breach of contract.

27. Gibbeon Manufacturing shipped 300 designer navy blue blazers to Custom Clothing Emporeum. The blazers arrived on Friday, earlier than Custom had anticipated and on an exceptionally busy day for its receiving department. They were perfunctorily examined and sent to a nearby warehouse for storage until needed. On Monday of the following week, upon closer examination, it was discovered that the quality of the linings of the blazers was inferior to that specified in the sales contract. Which of the following is correct insofar as Custom's rights are concerned?

a. Custom can reject the blazers upon subsequent discovery of the defects.
b. Custom must retain the blazers since it accepted them and had an opportunity to inspect them upon delivery.
c. Custom's only course of action is rescission.
d. Custom had no rights if the linings were of merchantable quality.

28. Cox Manufacturing repudiated its contract to sell 300 televisions to Ruddy Stores, Inc. What recourse does Ruddy Stores have?
a. It can obtain specific performance by the seller.
b. It can recover punitive damages.
c. It must await the seller's performance for a commercially reasonable time after repudiation if it wishes to recover anything.
d. It can "cover," that is, procure the goods elsewhere and recover any damages.

29. Devold Manufacturing, Inc., entered into a contract for the sale to Hillary Company of 2,000 solid-state CB radios at $27.50 each, terms 2/10, N/30, FOB Hillary's loading platform. After delivery of the first 500 radios, a minor defect was discovered. Although the defect was minor, Hillary incurred costs to correct the defect. Hillary sent Devold a signed memorandum indicating that it would relinquish its right to recover the costs to correct the defect, provided that the balance of the radios were in conformity with the terms of the contract and the delivery dates were strictly adhered to. Devold met these conditions. Shortly before the last shipment of radios arrived, a dispute between the parties arose over an unrelated matter. Hillary notified Devold that it was not bound by the prior generous agreement and would sue Devold for damages unless Devold promptly reimbursed Hillary. In the event of litigation, what would be the result and the basis upon which the litigation would be decided?
a. Devold will lose in that Hillary's relinquishment of its rights was not supported by a consideration.
b. Devold will win in that the defect was minor and the substantial performance doctrine applies.
c. Hillary will lose in that the communication constituted a waiver of Hillary's rights.
d. Hillary will win in that there was a failure to perform the contract, and Hillary suffered damages as a result.

30. Park purchased from Derek Truck Sales a truck which had serious mechanical problems. Park learned of the defects six months after the date of sale. Five years after the date of sale Park commenced an action for breach of warranty against Derek. Derek asserts the statute of limitations as a defense. Which of the following statements made by Derek is correct?
a. A clause in the original contract reducing the statute of limitations to nine months is enforceable.
b. Park was required to bring the action within the statute of limitation as measured from Derek's tender of delivery.
c. Park was required to bring the action within the statute of limitation as measured from the time the breach was discovered or should have been discovered.
d. Park is precluded from asserting under any circumstances that the statute of limitations stopped running.

31. *Deleted by AICPA; effective 5/86*

May 1985 Questions

32. Taylor signed and mailed a letter to Peel which stated: "Ship promptly 600 dozen grade A eggs." Taylor's offer
a. May be accepted by Peel only by a prompt shipment.
b. May be accepted by Peel either by a prompt promise to ship or prompt shipment with notice.
c. Is invalid since the price terms were omitted.
d. Is invalid since the shipping terms were omitted.

33. Flax telephoned Sky Corp. and ordered a specially manufactured air conditioner for $1,900. Subsequently, Flax realized that he miscalculated the area which was to be cooled and concluded that the air conditioner would not be acceptable. Sky had already completed work on the air conditioner, demanded payment, and was unable to resell the unit at a reasonable price. If Flax refuses to pay and Sky brings an action seeking as damages the price plus reasonable storage charges of $50, Sky will recover
a. Nothing, because of the Statute of Frauds.
b. Only its lost profit.
c. The full $1,950.
d. Only $1,900.

Repeat Question

(585,L1,42) Identical to item 20 above

November 1985 Questions

34. Which of the following terms generally must be included in a writing which would otherwise satisfy the UCC statute of frauds regarding the sale of goods?

a. The warranties to be granted.
b. The price of the goods.
c. The designation of the parties as buyer and seller.
d. The quantity of the goods.

35. Dill purchased a computer from Park, who regularly sells computers to the general public. After receiving payment in full, Park tendered delivery of the computer to Dill. Rather than take immediate delivery, Dill stated that he would return later that day to pick up the computer. Before Dill returned, thieves entered Park's store and stole Dill's computer. The risk of loss

a. Remained with Park since title had **not** yet passed to Dill.
b. Remained with Park since Dill had **not** yet received the computer.
c. Passed to Dill upon Park's tender of delivery.
d. Passed to Dill at the time the contract was formed and payment was made.

36. Kirk Corp. sold Nix an Ajax freezer, Model 24, for $490. The contract required delivery to be made by June 23. On June 12, Kirk delivered an Ajax freezer, Model 52, to Nix. Nix immediately notified Kirk that the wrong freezer had been delivered and indicated that the delivery of a correct freezer would not be acceptable. Kirk wishes to deliver an Ajax freezer, Model 24 on June 23. Which of the following statements is correct?

a. Kirk may deliver the freezer on June 23 without further notice to Nix.
b. Kirk may deliver the freezer on June 23 if it first seasonably notifies Nix of its intent to do so.
c. Nix must accept the nonconforming freezer but may recover damages.
d. Nix always may reject the nonconforming freezer and refuse delivery of a conforming freezer on June 23.

Repeat Question

(1185,L1,45) Identical to item 11 above

(1185,L1,33) *

(1185,L1,34) *

(1185,L1,35) *

**These questions were deleted because the AICPA has discontinued coverage effective May 1986.*

Problems

Problem 1 (1184,L4c)

(15 to 25 minutes)

Tom Sauer purchased a computer and a stereo from Zen Sounds, Inc., for personal use. With regard to the computer, Sauer signed an installment purchase note and a security agreement. Under the terms of the note Sauer was to pay $100 down and $50 a month for 20 months. The security agreement included a description of the computer. However, Zen did not file a financing statement. Sauer paid $800 cash for the stereo.

Two months later, Sauer sold the computer to Ralph for $600 cash. Ralph purchased the computer for personal use without knowledge of Zen's security interest.

Three months later, Sauer brought the stereo back to Zen for repair. Inadvertently, one of Zen's sales persons sold the stereo to Ned, a buyer in the ordinary course of business.

Required:

Answer the following, setting forth reasons for any conclusions stated.

As between Sauer and Ned, who has title to the stereo?

Problem 2 (1178,L5a&b)

(12 to 15 minutes)

Part a. Clauson Enterprises, Inc., was considering adding a new product line to its existing lines. The decision was contingent upon its being assured of a supply of an electronic component for the product at a certain price and a positive market study which clearly justified the investment in the venture.

Clauson's president approached Migrane Electronics and explained the situation to Migrane's president. After much negotiation, Migrane agreed to grant Clauson an option to purchase 12,000 of the necessary electronic components at $1.75 each or at the prevailing market price, whichever was lower. Clauson prepared the option below incorporating their understanding.

Option Agreement
Clauson Enterprises/Migrane Electronics

Migrane Electronics hereby offers to sell Clauson Enterprises 12,000 miniature solid state electronic breakers at $1.75 each or at the existing market price at the time of delivery, whichever is lower, delivery to be made in 12 equal monthly installments beginning one month after the exercise of this option. This option is irrevocable for six months from January 1, 1978.

Clauson Enterprises agrees to deliver to Migrane its market survey for the product line in which the component would be used if it elects not to exercise the option.

Both parties signed the option agreement and Migrane's president signed Migrane's corporate name alongside the last sentence of the first paragraph. On May 1, 1978, Migrane notified Clauson that it was revoking its offer. The market price for the component had increased to $1.85. On May 15, 1978, Clauson notified Migrane that it accepted the offer and that if Migrane did not perform, it would be sued and held liable for damages. Migrane replied that the offer was not binding and was revoked before Clauson accepted. Furthermore, even if it were binding, it was good for only three months as a matter of law.

Upon receipt of Migrane's reply, Clauson instituted suit for damages.

Required:

Answer for following, setting forth reasons for any conclusions stated.

Who will prevail? Discuss all the issues and arguments raised by the fact situation.

Part b. On May 30, 1978, Hargrove ordered 1,000 spools of nylon yarn from Flowers, Inc., of Norfolk, Virginia. The shipping terms were "F.O.B., Norfolk & Western RR at Norfolk." The transaction was to be a cash sale with payment to be simultaneously exchanged for the negotiable bill of lading covering the goods. Title to the goods was expressly reserved in Flowers. The yarn ordered by Hargrove was delivered to the railroad and loaded in a boxcar on June 1, 1978. Flowers obtained a negotiable bill of lading made out to its own order. The boxcar was destroyed the next day while the goods were in transit. Hargrove refused to pay for the yarn and Flowers sued Hargrove for the purchase price.

Required:

Answer the following, setting forth reasons for any conclusions stated.

Who will prevail?

Problem 3 (580,L4a)

(7 to 10 minutes)

Part a. After much study and deliberation, the marketing division of Majestic Enterprise, Inc., has recommended to the board of directors that the corporation market its products almost exclusively via consignment arrangements instead of other alternate merchandising-security arrangements. The board moved favorably upon this proposal.

Required:

Answer the following, setting forth reasons for any conclusions stated.

What are the key legal characteristics of a consignment?

Problem 4 (582,L5)

(15 to 20 minutes)

Part a. Sure Rain Apparel, Inc., manufactures expensive, exclusive rain apparel. One model is very popular and sold widely throughout the United States. About six months after their initial sale to distributors, Sure started receiving complaints that there was a noticeable fading of the color of the material. Many of the distributors seek to return the goods, recover damages, or both. Sure denies liability on the following bases: (1) there was an "Act of God," (2) there was no breach of warranty since the fading was to be expected in any event, and (3) any and all warranty protection was disclaimed unless expressly stated in the contract.

The contract contained the following provisions relating to warranty protection:

First: The manufacturer warrants that the material used to make the raincoats is 100% Egyptian long fiber cotton.

Second: The manufacturer guarantees the waterproofing of the raincoat for one year if the directions as to dry cleaning are followed.

Third: There are no other express warranties granted by the seller, except those indicated above. This writing is intended as a complete statement and integration of all express warranty protection.

Fourth: The manufacturer does not purport to give any implied warranty of merchantability in connection with this sale. The express warranties above enumerated are granted in lieu thereof.

Fifth: There are no warranties which extend beyond the description above.

The fourth and fifth provisions were conspicuous and initialed by the buyers.

Several buyers have commenced legal actions against Sure based upon implied warranties and express oral warranties made prior to the execution of the contract.

Required:

Answer the following, setting forth reasons for any conclusions stated.

Is Sure liable for breach of warranty?

Part b. Nielson Wholesalers, Inc., ordered 1,000 scissors at $2.50 a pair from Wilmot, Inc., on February 1, 1982. Delivery was to be made not later than March 10. Wilmot accepted the order in writing on February 4. The terms were 2/10, net/30, F.O.B. seller's loading platform in Baltimore. Due to unexpected additional orders and a miscalculation of the backlog of orders, Wilmot subsequently determined that it could not perform by March 10. On February 15, Wilmot notified Nielson that it would not be able to perform, and cancelled the contract. Wilmot pleaded a reasonable mistake and impossibility of performance as its justification for cancelling. At the time the notice of cancellation was received, identical scissors were available from other manufacturers at $2.70. Nielson chose not to purchase the 1,000 scissors elsewhere, but instead notified Wilmot that it rejected the purported cancellation and would await delivery as agreed. Wilmot did not deliver on March 10, by which time the price of the scissors had risen to $3.00 a pair. Nielson is seeking to recover damages from Wilmot for breach of contract.

Required:

Answer the following, setting forth reasons for any conclusions stated.

1. Will Nielson prevail and, if so, how much will it recover?

2. Would Nielson be entitled to specific performance under the circumstances?

3. Assuming that Wilmot discovers that Nielson was insolvent, will this excuse performance?

Multiple Choice Answers

1.	c	9.	c	16.	c	23.	b	30.	b
2.	c	10.	a	17.	a	24.	b	31.	*
3.	b	11.	c	18.	c	25.	c	32.	b
4.	d	12.	a	19.	a	26.	d	33.	c
5.	c	13.	a	20.	b	27.	a	34.	d
6.	d	14.	d	21.	c	28.	d	35.	b
7.	b	15.	d	22.	c	29.	c	36.	b
8.	d								

Deleted by AICPA; effective 5/86

Multiple Choice Answer Explanations

A. Contracts for Sale of Goods

1. (1184,L1,55) (c) A subsequent agreement modifying an existing contract for the sale of goods needs no consideration to be binding. Also, if the contract, as modified, is the sale of goods for a price less than $500, the Statute of Frauds does not apply, and the oral modification is enforceable. Answer (a) is incorrect because requirements contracts must have consideration. Answer (b) is incorrect because a firm offer is only present when a merchant-offeror engages in a written offer. Answer (d) is incorrect because the implied warranty of fitness for a particular purpose can only be disclaimed in writing.

2. (584,L1,55) (c) The Sales Article of the UCC applies to the sale of goods, specially manufactured or otherwise. Although certain provisions apply only to transactions between merchants, the general scope of the Article extends to sales by nonmerchants as well. By UCC definition, the term "goods" does not include investment securities. Goods is defined as all things (including specially manufactured goods) which are moveable at the time of identification to the contract, except money, investment securities, intangible property, contract rights, or accounts receivable. Goods include the unborn young of animals, growing crops, and standing timber to be cut. The sale of investment securities is, therefore, covered by a separate Article. The sale of real estate is governed by common law, not Article 2 of the UCC. Answers (a), (b), and (d) are, therefore, incorrect.

3. (1183,L1,51) (b) In order to have an irrevocable offer (firm offer) under the UCC, the offer must be made by a merchant offeror in a signed writing which gives assurances that the offer will be held open. There is no requirement that the offeree also be a merchant. A firm offer does not need to state the period of time for which it is irrevocable. If no time period is stated it is irrevocable for a reasonable period of time. Normally, a firm offer would be contained in a form provided by the offeror; however, it could be contained in a form provided by the offeree if the merchant offeror signs outside the paragraph that contains the firm offer. Therefore, answers (a), (c), and (d) are incorrect.

4. (582,L1,47) (d) Donnegal will be entitled to return of the goods if the goods have been stolen from him. A thief has no power to transfer a good title in goods to a good faith purchaser. However, a person with a voidable title may transfer good title in the goods to a good faith purchaser. A person has a voidable title when the goods have been delivered under a transaction of purchase and (1) the transferor was deceived as to the identity of the purchaser, or (2) the delivery was in exchange for a check which is later dishonored, or (3) the delivery was procured through fraud punishable as larceny under criminal law. Therefore, answers (a), (b), and (c) are incorrect.

5. (578,L1,43) (c) Open terms will not cause a contract for the sale of goods to fail for indefiniteness if there was an intent to contract and a reasonable basis for establishing a remedy is available. If the place of delivery is left open, the UCC provides that the seller's place of business shall be the proper place of delivery. Answer (a) is incorrect because the Code supplies the omitted delivery terms. Answer (b) is incorrect because no rule requires the parties to designate place of delivery within 5 days. Nor is the buyer's place of business [answer (d)] the proper place of delivery unless so stated in the contract.

A.2.d. Battle of Forms

6. (1184,L1,53) (d) Since Bizzy Corp. and Wang are both merchants, the battle of forms rule allows Wang to include an additional term in its acceptance without this additional term constituting a counteroffer. In fact, this additional term is a part of the contract unless: the offer states Wang may only accept the terms stated; or the additional term materially alters the offer; or the Bizzy Corp. refuses the term within a reasonable time. Since none of these three factors are present, a contract is formed with Wang's additional term becoming a part of the agreement. Therefore, answers (a), (b), and (c) are incorrect.

7. (1183,L1,53) (b) Clark's telegram of October 6 does not operate as an effective acceptance of Baker's offer because Clark's acceptance was expressly conditioned on the change in payment terms. Consequently, the battle of the forms exception does not apply. This telegram is actually a counteroffer which Baker expressly rejected in the October 7 telephone conversation. Clark's subsequent offer to honor the terms as originally expressed on October 1 was never

cepted by Baker and, therefore, there is no contract between the parties. Answer (c) is incorrect because Clark expressly conditioned his acceptance on the modifications. If, in fact, Clark's changes were mere proposals, the modifications would still not have become part of the contract since this transaction was between merchants, and Baker expressly stated that the terms in his offer were not to be varied. Answer (d) is incorrect because under the Uniform Commercial Code a writing will satisfy the Statute of Frauds as long as it indicates a contract has been made, is signed by the party to be bound, and states the quantity. Assuming Clark is seeking to enforce the contract against Baker, Baker's written signed offer of October 1 stating a quantity of 200 pinking shears complies with the Statute of Frauds. Answer (a) is incorrect because Baker's original offer does not satisfy the requirements for a firm offer. Under the Uniform Commercial Code a merchant cannot revoke a written signed offer to buy or sell goods if he gives assurances that the offer will be held open. Such an offer is irrevocable for the stated time, up to a maximum of 3 months. If no period is specified, then a reasonable time is implied. Baker's offer is not a firm offer because it does not contain assurances that it will be held en. The statement that the offer "must be accepted later than October 10" only establishes the expiration date of the offer. Baker has determined when the offer will lapse without expressly committing himself to keeping the offer open until October 10.

A.5. Identification

8. (581,L1,20) (d) Upon identification of the goods that relate to a contract, several specific rights are granted to the buyer of these goods. Among these is the right to take delivery of goods upon insolvency of the seller if full or partial payment was made at the time of the purchase and any balance due is tendered to the seller. Since the question asks which condition will prevent recovery of the goods, lack of identification is correct because identification must occur before any rights of repossession accrue to the buyer. It is not necessary that the full price be paid at the time of purchase (a) as long as tender of the balance due is made to the seller. Answers (b) and (c) are incorrect since the fact that a buyer may obtain a judgment for damages to the goods by third parties or that a buyer is not aware of a seller's insolvency will not prevent the buyer from gaining possession of the goods.

(578,L1,14) (c) Under the UCC, the buyer tains an insurable interest in goods when they are identified to the contract. In the case of future goods, identification occurs when the goods are shipped, marked, or otherwise designated by the seller as the goods to which the contract refers. Answer (d) is incorrect because the insurable interest is not obtained at the time the contract is made. Answer (a) is incorrect because an insurable interest can arise before the goods are in the buyer's possession. Answer (b) is incorrect because an insurable interest will be obtained before shipment when the goods are identified for shipment.

A.6. Risk of Loss

10. (584,L1,48) (a) The risk of loss rules under the UCC operate independently of any transfer of title. Specifically, the UCC states that absent any breach, the risk of loss passes from a nonmerchant seller to the buyer on tender of delivery. Accordingly, answers (b), (c), and (d) are incorrect.

11. (1183,L1,46) (c) Provided there is no agreement to the contrary and neither party is in breach, risk of loss to goods, which are held in a warehouse for delivery without being moved, will pass at the time the document of title is properly negotiated to the buyer. If the document of title is nonnegotiable, then the risk of loss passes a reasonable time after the buyer receives the document. Where there is no document of title representing the goods, risk of loss will pass once the warehouseman acknowledges the buyer's right to the goods. Answers (a), (b), and (d) are incorrect since Hack Company has a negotiable document of title which is properly negotiated to Fast Freight Company on May 3.

12. (1183,L1,56) (a) The UCC rules concerning risk of loss only apply if the parties have not allocated risk of loss in their contract. Consequently, shipping terms used and insurance coverage of the parties would not be relevant in allocating risk of loss if the parties had manifested their intent in the contract. Therefore, answers (b) and (d) are incorrect. Answer (c) is incorrect because the fact that title of the goods has passed to the buyer does not mean that risk of loss has also passed, and vice versa. The UCC allocates risk of loss irrespective of title. One party may have title to the goods, while the other party has risk of loss.

13. (1182,L1,48) (a) The UCC places risk of loss on the breaching party. Since Southern shipped nonconforming goods, they breached the contract and would have risk of loss until the nonconforming goods were accepted by the buyer. Answer (b) is incorrect because the shipping term FOB would only control passage of risk of loss if conforming goods had been shipped. However, even if conforming goods had been ship-

ped under "FOB Falcon's factory," risk of loss would not have shifted to Falcon until the goods arrived at the factory. Answer (c) is incorrect because Falcon's telegram would act as a signed writing. Answer (d) is incorrect because Falcon does not have title to the goods. However, even if title had passed, Southern would still have risk of loss because title to the goods has no relevance in allocating risk of loss.

A.7. Product Liability

14. (1183,L1,60) (d) Under strict liability a seller engaged in the business of selling a product is held liable for injuries caused by that product, provided he sold it in a defective and unreasonably dangerous condition. A seller is, therefore, liable regardless of whether he was negligent or at fault for the defective condition of the product. Finally, a seller engaged in the business of selling the product is defined to include not only the buyer's immediate seller, but also the prior sellers in the distribution chain such as the wholesaler and manufacturer. Answers (a), (b), and (c) are incorrect because the only defenses available in strict liability are misuse and assumption of the risk. An individual misuses a product when he uses it for some purpose other than for which the product was originally intended. Assumption of the risk exists when an individual proceeds to use a product in disregard of a known danger associated with that product. Contributory negligence, compliance with industry standards or custom, and lack of privity of contract are not defenses to strict liability. Although the fact that the wholesaler did not have a reasonable opportunity to inspect the goods may be of importance under the negligence theory of product liability, it is irrelevant in strict liability since the showing of fault is not required to impose liability on a seller.

A.7.c.1) Warranty of Title

15. (584,L1,52) (d) Under the UCC every seller warrants good title, rightful transfer, and freedom from any security interest or lien of which the buyer has no actual knowledge. This warranty of title may only be disclaimed by specific language or such circumstances which give the buyer reason to know that he is not receiving full title. A general disclaimer of all warranties or such language as "as is" is insufficient. A breach of the warranty of title does not vest good title in a bona fide puchaser but, instead, allows the purchaser to sue for breach of warranty. Answers (a), (b), and (c) are, therefore, incorrect.

16. (581,L1,14) (c) In a sale by a merchant, the merchant warrants that the goods are free from a rightful claim of infringement of patent or trademark by third parties. (A seller will be protected against liability under a warranty against infringement if the buyer furnishes the specifications used to manufacture the product that infringes upon another party's patent or trademark rights.) Answer (a) is incorrect because only the seller need be a merchant. Answer (b) is incorrect because a warranty against infringment is granted along with the warranty of title and thus, does not need to be expressly stated in the contract to be enforceable. Like the warranty of title, a warranty against infringement can be disclaimed by specific language or circumstances that indicate that this warranty is not extended. Therefore, answer (d) is incorrect.

A.7.c.2) Express Warranties

17. (584,L1,56) (a) Any seller, not only a merchant seller, may create an express warranty by making any affirmation of fact or promise which forms part of the basis of the bargain. Such a warranty may be made either orally or in writing and will exist regardless of the seller's intent. Answers (b), (c) and (d) are, therefore, incorrect.

A.7.c.3) Implied Warranties

18. (1184,L1,54) (c) Under the stated facts, Wally is creating the implied warranty of fitness for a particular purpose. This warranty is created when the seller (merchant or nonmerchant) has reason to know the buyer's particular purpose and knows the buyer is relying on the seller's judgment to provide appropriate goods. This warranty guarantees the goods are fit for the buyer's particular purpose. It is the implied warranty of merchantability that guarantees the goods are of an average fair quality and are fit for ordinary purposes, but Wally did not create this warranty since he is not a merchant-seller. Since the warranty of fitness for a particular purpose is an implied warranty, there is no requirement that it be in writing. Therefore, answers (a), (b), and (d) are incorrect.

19. (1183,L1,54) (a) Every merchant seller of goods impliedly warrants that the goods sold are fit for the ordinary purposes for which such goods are used, are adequately packaged and labeled, and conform to promises or affirmations of fact made on the package or label. This implied warranty of merchantability does not guarantee that the goods are fit for all possible purposes for which the buyer might use the goods. Accordingly, answers (b), (c), and (d) are incorrect.

20. (583,L1,40) (b) The Uniform Commercial Code, being consumer oriented, has broadened the basis of liability and modified the concept of privity of contract, thereby allowing warranties to extend to

parties other than the purchaser. The UCC prohibits the exclusion on privity grounds of third parties from the warranty protection it has granted. Answer (a) is incorrect because there is no single uniform rule, rather there is disagreement over how far warranty liability should extend. In order to satisfy opposing views of the various states, the drafters of the UCC proposed three alternatives for warranty liability to third parties. Answer (c) is incorrect because the UCC's position on privity of warranty also applies to retail sellers and the ultimate purchaser or consumer. Answer (d) is incorrect because the buyer's family could sue the manufacturer as well as the retail seller from whom the buyer purchased the product. Most courts have abolished the requirement of vertical privity in actions for breach of warranty.

21. (1182,L1,47) (c) When goods are sold "as is" or "with all faults", all implied warranties are disclaimed including the implied warranty of merchantability. Normally, a disclaimer of the implied warranty of merchantability must contain some form of the word "merchantability" to be effective. However, goods sold "with all faults" is an exception to that rule. Answer (a) is incorrect because selling a demonstration model at a substantial discount would not disclaim the implied warranties. Answer (b) is incorrect because offering an inspection of the goods to a buyer only disclaims the implied warranties concerning patent defects, not concerning latent (hidden) defects in the goods. Answer (d) is incorrect because a merchant seller of goods gives an implied warranty that the goods are fit for ordinary purposes, regardless of which party caused the defect in the goods. The breach of warranty theory is not based on negligence.

B.4. Seller's Remedies

22. (1183,L1,58) (c) The seller can recover the full contract price if the buyer has accepted the goods before breaching the contract, the goods have already been identified to the contract and the seller is unable to resell them at a reasonable price, or the goods are lost or destroyed after the risk of loss has passed to the buyer. Accordingly, answer (b) is incorrect. Answer (a) is incorrect because the seller is entitled to seek incidental damages in addition to the full contract price. Answer (d) is incorrect because, even if one assumes that Marvin anticipatorily repudiated the contract, the seller has the choice of either suing at once or waiting until the time for performance. In any event, the seller is entitled to the usual contract remedies. However, Ling could only sue for the full contract price if one of the above mentioned three situtations is present.

23. (1182,L1,50) (b) Even though Sanders, the seller, learns of Richards' insolvency before the goods are delivered, Richards, the buyer, is entitled to performance if it pays cash. Therefore, answer (c) is incorrect. Answer (a) is incorrect because the seller's right to stoppage in transit is available if the buyer is insolvent in the equity sense (unable to pay its debts when due) even though the buyer is still solvent in the bankruptcy sense (assets exceed liabilities). Answer (d) is incorrect because the insolvency of the buyer allows the seller to refuse to perform under the terms of the agreement (2/10, net/30), and instead, demand cash upon delivery of the goods.

24. (1176,L1,9) (b) Under the UCC, a seller has the right to cure nonconforming goods within the original time of the contract if he notifies the buyer. This would put Kent in the position of having fulfilled the contract and having complied with the UCC. Then Wiliams would be the one in breach of the contract if he does not pay on time.

If on the other hand, Kent does not cure the defect and brings an action for the price less an allowance, Williams would have the defense that the goods were nonconforming and he had the right to reject them. Then Kent could not recover for breach of contract, because it was he who breached it by tendering non-conforming goods. In the case of duplicatable cameras, specific performance would not be available to either party.

B.5. Buyer's Remedies

25. (583,L1,42) (c) Anticipatory repudiation occurs when a party renounces the duty to perform the contract before the party's obligation to perform arises. Therefore, because Nugent Manufacturing notified Costello of its intent not to perform, it has engaged in anticipatory repudiation. Anticipatory repudiation discharges the nonrepudiating party (Costello) from the contract and allows this party to sue for breach immediately. However, if commercially reasonable, the nonrepudiating party can ignore the repudiation and await performance at the appointed time. If the nonrepudiating party chooses this latter course of action, the repudiating party may retract the renunciation and perform as promised. Therefore, answers (a), (b), and (d) are incorrect.

26. (581,L1,15) (d) Shipment of a different brand of peas, even as an accommodation, constitutes a breach of contract because the terms of the contract have not been complied with. Answer (a) is incorrect

because the shipment cannot be considered a counter-offer since there was already a contract in existence between Brown and Smith. Answer (b) is untrue because only the promised performance will discharge Smith, unless Brown accepts the accommodation. Answer (c) is incorrect since Brown's offer to Smith constitutes a bilateral offer which was accepted by Smith's communication to Brown. This bilateral offer could have been accepted by delivery of the specified goods as well.

27. (1180,L1,12) (a) Answer (a) is correct since the buyer has a reasonable time in which to reject defective goods. Discovering the defect on Monday would be considered within a reasonable time, considering the goods had been delivered on Friday. Answer (d) is incorrect since the specification concerning the linings in the sales contract would be an express warranty which was breached when the linings were found to be inferior to what had been stated. Thus, the merchantable quality of the linings would be irrelevant.

28. (1179,L1,1) (d) The nonbreaching party under a contract for sale can attempt to mitigate damages by "cover," that is, by procuring the goods elsewhere and recovering as damages the difference between the contract price and the price of cover. Answer (a) is incorrect because specific performance is available only upon the damaged party showing that money damages are inadequate or other unique conditions exist which require actual performance. There is nothing here to indicate that the televisions are unavailable in the market or other unique conditions exist. Answer (b) is incorrect because punitive damages are never recoverable for breach of contract. Answer (c) is incorrect since a nonbreaching party need not wait after a breach occurs to begin proceedings to recover.

29. (578,L1,41) (c) The communication constituted a waiver of Hillary's rights which is not retractable if it would be unjust because Devold relied on it. Waivers of claims arising out of an alleged breach of contract require no consideration to be valid under the UCC. Thus answer (a) is incorrect under the Code, although it would be correct under common law. Answer (b) is incorrect because the doctrine of substantial performance provides that performance is satisfied if deviations have been minor. However, damages would still be available except that Hillary waived his right to them. Answer (d) is incorrect because Hillary would win had he not, under the rules of the Code, waived his claim to damages.

B.6. Statute of Limitations

30. (584,L1,54) (b) When a warranty explicitly extends to the future performance of the goods, a cause of action for breach of that warranty must be brought within the Statute of Limitations period as measured from the time the breach was discovered or should have been discovered. If the warranty does not explicitly extend to future performance, a cause of action for breach accrues at tender of delivery. Derek Truck Sales, a merchant, has sold a truck with serious mechanical problems, thereby breaching the implied warranty of merchantability—such a defective truck is not fit for its ordinary purposes. An implied warranty, by definition, is not explicit; and, therefore, Park's cause of action for breach of the implied warranty of merchantability accrued when delivery of the truck was tendered. Since the parties did not agree to otherwise reduce the statutory period, the four-year limitations period established by the UCC controls; and Park must, therefore, file his lawsuit within four years of tender of delivery. Accordingly, answer (c) is incorrect. Answer (a) is incorrect because the parties may, in their original contract, agree to reduce the UCC statutory period of four years to a period of not less than one year. Under no circumstances, however, may the parties extend the Statute of Limitations. Answer (d) is incorrect because a plaintiff may, in proper circumstances (i.e., disability of plaintiff to sue or defendant's absence from the jurisdiction), claim that the running of the Statute of Limitations has been tolled (stopped).

C. Bulk Transfers

31. *Deleted by AICPA; effective 5/86*

May 1985 Answers

32. (585,L1,41) (b) Under the common law, an acceptance must be unequivocal and unqualified, in the precise terms in which the offer specified. The Uniform Commercial Code alters this general rule as far as the sale of goods is concerned. An offer to buy goods for prompt shipment is construed to invite acceptance, either by a prompt promise to ship or prompt shipment unless the language of the offer specifically stipulates otherwise. Peel may accept Taylor's offer by promptly promising to ship the goods or by prompt shipment. Answer (a) is correct under common law, but not under the UCC. The sale of eggs would constitute a sale of goods that would be governed by the UCC. Answers (c) and (d) are incorrect because both price and shipping terms can be omitted without destroying an acceptance under the UCC. If no price stated, a reasonable price at the time of delivery will be imposed, and if shipment terms are omitted, the seller's place of business is the place of delivery.

33. (585,L1,43) (c) When a buyer fails to pay the price as it becomes due, the seller may recover the purchase price of the goods identified to the contract plus incidental damages if the seller is unable to resell them at a reasonable price after making a reasonable effort. Sky Corporation will be able to recover the purchase price of $1,900 plus the incidental costs of $50 for storage for a total of $1,950 from Flax. Answer (a) is incorrect because Flax will not be able to use the Statute of Frauds as a defense in this case. Where a seller has manufactured special goods for the buyer and made a substantial beginning, no writing is needed to support the promise to buy and pay for the goods. Flax must pay for the goods even though no writing evidences the agreement. Answer (b) is incorrect because Sky is not limited to recovering only his lost profits since the goods could not be sold. Answer (d) is incorrect because Sky may recover purchase price plus incidental damages.

November 1985 Answers

34. (1185,L1,46) (d) Under common law a writing, in order to be legally sufficient to satisfy the Statute of Frauds, must identify the parties, subject matter, the essential terms and the consideration, as well as being signed by the party to be charged. However, under the UCC the writing only has to include the quantity term and be signed by the party to be charged. Therefore, answers (a), (b), and (c) are incorrect.

35. (1185,L1,47) (b) Provided there is no agreement to the contrary and neither party is in breach, risk of loss will ordinarily pass upon tender of delivery. However, because Park is a **merchant seller** the risk of loss does not pass until the buyer takes receipt of the goods. Answer (a) is incorrect because unlike common law, the passage of risk of loss does not depend upon the passsage of title under the UCC. Answer (c) is incorrect because Park is a merchant seller. Answer (d) is incorrect because the time of the formation of a contract and payment do not affect the transfer of risk of loss.

36. (1185,L1,48) (b) A seller has the right to "cure" nonconforming performance when there is still time left for performance under the contract. To do so a seller must seasonably notify the buyer of his intention to cure, and must tender conforming goods within the original time specified by the contract. Answer (a) is incorrect because the seller must give notice of his intent to cure. Answer (c) is incorrect because Nix is not required to accept the nonconforming goods. A buyer may accept the nonconforming goods and recover damages. Answer (d) is incorrect because to refuse delivery of conforming goods on June 23 would be considered a breach of contract if the seller has seasonably notified the buyer of his intent to "cure."

Answer Outline

Problem 1 Sale of Goods by Nonowner; Entrusting (1184,L4c)

Ned Sauer's delivery constituted an entrusting
Gives merchant power to transfer rights to good faith purchaser
Ned qualifies as good faith purchaser

Unofficial Answer

Problem 1 Sale of Goods by Nonowner; Entrusting (1184,L4c)

Ned. The UCC sales provisions state that any entrusting of possession of goods to a merchant who deals in goods of that kind gives such merchant the power to transfer all rights of the entruster to a buyer in the ordinary course of business. Furthermore, the entruster, in delivering and acquiescing in the merchant's retention of possession of the goods, must be the rightful owner in order for the merchant to acquire the power to transfer complete ownership and title. Since Sauer's delivery of the stereo to Zen constituted an entrusting, Zen acquired the power to transfer title and ownership to Ned. Thus, upon Ned's purchase of the stereo in good faith and without knowledge of Sauer's true ownership interests, Ned acquired title to the stereo.

Answer Outline

Problem 2 Option Contract, Risk of Loss (1178,L5a&b)

a. Clauson will prevail. If no consideration, firm offer rule of UCC Article 3 applies
Offer by merchant
Signed writing
Assurance that offer is not revocable
Limited in all cases to three months
Three-month limit not applicable due to consideration
I.e., a binding contract exists
Clauson's acceptance was lawful and timely
Clauson is entitled to recover damages

b. Flowers will prevail
Risk of loss on Hargrove per shipping terms
Terms specified FOB N&W RR at Norfolk
I.e., specified shipper and FOB shipping point
Risk of loss passed to Hargrove when delivered to N&W
Reservation of title has no effect on risk of loss

Unofficial Answer

Problem 2 Option Contract, Risk of Loss (1178,L5a&b)

Part a.

Clauson Enterprises will prevail. The option in question is supported by consideration and consequently is a binding contract. The offer is definite and certain despite the fact that the pricing terms are not presently determinable. The Uniform Commercial Code is extremely liberal regarding satisfaction of the pricing terms.

Except for the presence of consideration in the form of the promise by Clauson to deliver the market survey to Migrane, the option would not have been binding beyond three months and Migrane would have prevailed. Section 2-205 of the Uniform Commercial Code provides as follows:

> An offer by a merchant to buy or sell goods in a signed writing which by its terms gives assurance that it will be held open is not revocable, for lack of consideration, during the time stated or if no time is stated for a reasonable time, but in no event may such period of irrevocability exceed three months; but any such term of assurance on a form supplied by the offeree must be separately signed by the offeror.

It is apparent from the wording of this section that the option was valid without consideration, but only for three months. It was an offer by a merchant contained in a signed writing and clearly stated its irrevocability. Furthermore, the separately signed requirement where the form is supplied by the offeree was satisfied. But the section is inapplicable to the facts of this case since bargained-for consideration was present. The Uniform Commercial Code's three-month limitation does not apply to options where consideration is present. Hence, Clauson's acceptance was valid, and if Migrane refuses to perform, Clauson will be entitled to damages.

Part b.

Flowers will prevail because Hargrove has the risk of loss. The shipping terms determine who had the risk of loss. Section 2-509(1) of the Uniform Commercial Code provides that "Where the contract requires or authorizes the seller to ship the goods by carrier, (a) if it does not require him to deliver at a particular destination, the risk of loss passes to the buyer when the goods are duly delivered to the arrier, even though the shipment is under reservation . . ."

The facts that title was reserved by Flowers and that Flowers retained the negotiable bill of lading do not affect the determination of who is to bear the risk of loss. The code makes it clear that title is irrelevant in determining the risk of loss.

Answer Outline

Problem 3 Consignments (580,L4a)

a. Key legal characteristics of consignments
   Consignor — owner of goods
   Consignee — agent who is to sell goods
   Characteristics
   1. Title stays with consignor
   2. Consignee has no obligation to purchase or pay for goods
   3. Consignee is paid a commission for goods sold
   4. Proceeds are consignor's

Unofficial Answer

Problem 3 Consignments (580,L4a)

Part a.

A consignment is a selling arrangement between the owner, called the *consignor*, and the party who is to sell the goods, called the *consignee*. The consignee is appointed the agent to sell the owner's merchandise. The following are the key characteristics.

1. Title to the goods remains at all times with the consignor.
2. The consignee is at no time obligated to buy or pay for the goods.
3. The consignee receives a commission for the goods sold.
4. The proceeds belong to the consignor.

Answer Outline

Problem 4 Breach of Warranty; Breach of Sales Contract (582,L5)

Part a.

No. Sure not liable for breach of warranty
   Sure did not give any implied warranties
      Disclaimed implied warranty of merchantability
         Disclaimer mentioned "merchantability"
      Disclaimed implied warranty of fitness of purpose
         Disclaimer was in writing and was conspicuous
   Contract was considered final expression of agreement
      Parol evidence rule negates prior express warranties

Part b.

1. Yes. Wilmot's defenses for nonperformance are without merit
   Wilmot engaged in anticipatory repudiation
      Buyer can sue for difference between contract price and market value at time learned of breach
2. No. Monetary damages are adequate
   Puts Nielson in same position as if performance had occurred
3. No. Upon seller's learning of buyer's insolvency
   Seller need only perform if buyer pays with cash
   Seller also has right to demand written assurances

Unofficial Answer
(Author Modified)

Problem 4 Breach of Warranty; Breach of Sales Contract (582,L5)

Part a.

No. Both implied and express warranties may be present in a sale of goods. In the described fact situation, it appears that the fading of the coats could be considered a breach of both the implied warranty of merchantability and the implied warranty of fitness of purpose. However, due to the disclaimers contained in provisions four and five of the sales contract, Sure did not extend these warranties in this sale of goods. For the seller to disclaim the implied warranty of merchantability, the disclaimer, if in writing, must be conspicuous and contain some form of the word "merchantability". Provision four meets both of these requirements, and consequently would operate to disclaim the implied warranty of merchantability.

To disclaim the implied warranty of fitness of purpose, the seller need not use the exact language (i.e., fitness of purpose). The seller must use a conspicuous written statement that would alert the reasonable buyer to the fact that this warranty is being disclaimed. Provision five would meet this requirement. Consequently, in this sale of goods, neither implied warranty has been granted by Sure.

In deciding whether Sure breached the oral express warranties, the parol evidence rule must be applied, since Sure and its distributors intended the written contract as a complete and final expression of their agreement. The parol evidence rule states that a final writing intended by the parties as their complete agreement may not be changed, modified, altered or varied by any oral or written evidence occuring prior to, or contemporaneously with the signing of the agreement. Consequently, any express oral warranties made by Sure prior to the execution of this contract would have no legal effect.

Thus, the only warranties granted by Sure would be those contained in the first and second provisions of the written contract, and neither of these have been breached. Therefore, Sure would not be liable for breach of warranty.

Part b.

1. Yes. It appears that Wilmot is attempting to assert the defense of mistake of an existing fact which, if present, would destroy the reality of consent needed for a binding agreement and create an unenforceable contract. However, in the described situation, there is no mistake of an existing fact, only poor business judgement which would not discharge Wilmot's contractual obligation.

Wilmot is also claiming impossibility as a defense. Objective impossibility, if present, does discharge a party's contractual duty to perform. Objective impossibility occurs when: (1) needed subject matter is destroyed, (2) subsequent statute makes activity involved in contract illegal, (3) incapacitation of individual whose services are needed. None of these three situations are present in the described facts. Wilmot's impossibility would be subjective impossibility, which does not discharge the party's duty to perform. Thus, Wilmot breached the contract when he attempted to cancel on February 15.

Wilmot's cancellation constituted anticipatory repudiation. Upon such repudiation by the seller, the buyer may immediately terminate the contract and sue for the appropriate remedy (in this problem—monetary damages). However, if commercially reasonable, the buyer also has the option of ignoring the seller's repudiation, and waiting for the seller to perform at the appointed time (by March 10). If seller's performance does not occur at that time, then the buyer is able to sue for breach.

Nielson engaged in this latter course of action. This presents an issue as to which market value of the goods should be used in computing the buyer's damages, market value at time of cancellation ($2.70) or market value at date for performance ($3.00). The rule states that the market value at the time the buyer learned of the breach should be used in computing the buyer's damages. However, the Uniform Commercial Code is not exactly clear on what this means with regard to anticipatory repudiation. Section 2-723 of the Uniform Commercial Code states that if the action based on anticipatory repudiation comes to trial before time for performance, the market price used to compute the buyer's damages is the price prevailing at the time the buyer learned of the repudiation. However, the Uniform Commercial Code states nothing concerning an action coming to court after the date for performance (March 15). Thus, one could argue that if the buyer was adhering to the duty to mitigate one's damages by awaiting the contract time for performance, the court should use the market value at the time of performance to compute the buyer's damages. If this situation existed in the stated problem, Nielson would then collect $.50 per pair of scissors [the difference between the contract price ($2.50) and the market value at time of performance ($3.00)] plus incidental and consequential damages minus any expenses saved due to the seller's breach. However, if it was not commercially reasonable to await performance, then Nielson could only collect $.20 per pair [the difference between the contract price ($2.50) and the market value at time Nielson learned of breach ($2.70)].

2. No. Specific performance is only available in a breach of contract action when monetary damages would be inadequate to redress the injury that the nonbreaching party suffered. In this problem, monetary damages would be adequate to put Nielson in the same position it would have occupied if Wilmot had performed as promised.

3. No. When the seller discovers that the buyer is insolvent before delivering the goods, the seller must still perform if the insolvent buyer is willing to pay cash. Also, when Wilmot learned of Nielson's insolvency, it could have demanded written assurances of performance. The Uniform Commercial Code states that when reasonable grounds for insecurity concerning the other party's performance are learned, the aggrieved party can suspend their performance and demand adequate assurances of performance from the other party. If Nielson does not provide these assurances within a reasonable period of time, Wilmot may consider the agreement breached.

NEGOTIABLE INSTRUMENTS
(COMMERCIAL PAPER)

Overview

Commercial paper is heavily tested on the CPA exam. Coverage includes the types of negotiable instruments, the requirements of negotiability, negotiation, the holder in due course concept, defenses, and the rights of parties to a negotiable instrument. The function of commercial paper is to provide a medium of exchange which is readily transferable like money and yet does not require present payment. In effect it creates credit, yet it is easier to transfer than contract rights and not subject to as many defenses as contracts are. To be negotiable, an instrument must

a. Be a writing signed by the maker or drawer;
b. Contain an unconditional promise or order to pay a sum certain in money;
c. Be payable on demand or at definite time;
d. Be payable to order or bearer;
e. Contain no other promise except the payment of money.

These requirements must be present on the face of the instrument. Instruments which do not comply with these provisions are non-negotiable and are transferable only by assignment. The assignee of a non-negotiable instrument takes it subject to all defenses.

The central theme of exam questions on negotiable instruments is the liability of the primary parties and of secondarily liable parties under various fact situations. Similar questions in different form emphasize the rights that a holder of a negotiable instrument has against primary and secondary parties. Your review of this area should emphasize the legal liability arising upon execution of negotiable commercial paper, the legal liability arising upon various types of indorsements, and the warranty liabilities of various parties upon transfer or presentment for payment. A solid understanding of the distinction between real and personal defenses is required. Also frequently tested is the relationship between a bank and its customers.

A. Negotiable Instrument

1. A contractual obligation which calls for the payment of money but at the same time provides a medium of exchange in lieu of money by allowing the exchange of funds in the form of a note, check, draft, etc.

   a. Most important concept is that a subsequent holder, by meeting certain requirements, can take an instrument free of most contractual claims or defenses on it

      1) Normally an assignee of a contract right is subject to defenses on the contract, e.g., nonperformance

         EXAMPLE: X Company entered into a contract to sell goods to Y Company. X Company assigned its contract right to payment for the goods to Z Company in payment of a debt. If the goods do not conform to the contract, Y Company can refuse to pay Z Company by asserting its defenses on the contract.

      2) But a holder in due course of a negotiable instrument would be free of most claims of the maker or promisor of a note against the payee

         EXAMPLE: X Company entered into a contract to sell goods to Y Company, but Y Company gave X Company a negotiable note before receiving the goods. X Company transferred the note to Z Company (who qualified as a HDC). Y Company must now pay on the note regardless of any contractual defenses against X Company.

   b. A nonnegotiable instrument can still be assigned as in a contract but the taker or holder is subject to all the defenses of prior parties

9

B. Types of Negotiable Instruments

1. A promissory note is a promise to pay a sum of money
   a. It is a two-party instrument: maker and payee
   b. The person promising to pay is the maker, and the person to be paid is the payee
   c. May be payable on demand or on a date
   d. May include provisions for collection fees, attorney's fees, interest, etc.

   EXAMPLE: "I promise to pay to bearer $1,000 on July 4, 1980."

2. A draft is an order from one person directing another to pay a third person
   a. It is a three-party instrument: drawer, drawee and payee
   b. The person ordering payment is the "drawer"
   c. The person to whom the order is directed is the "drawee"
   d. The person to receive payment is the "payee"
   e. Drafts may be payable on sight (on demand) or within a certain time

   EXAMPLE: "Bank, pay to bearer $1,000 in 30 days."

3. Checks are an order by the drawer directing a bank to pay money to the payee
   a. A type of draft
   b. Must be drawn on a bank
   c. Must be payable on demand (holder can ask for payment any time)

4. Certificates of deposit are written acknowledgments by a bank of receipt of money with a promise to repay
   a. A type of note

5. Trade acceptance is an order by a buyer directing some payor (bank) to pay seller
   a. Given to seller for a sale of goods
   b. Buyer must accept it by signing
   c. A type of draft

6. Other instruments which may be negotiable and have consequences similar to those of notes and drafts but which are not governed by this section (Articles 3 and 4 of UCC) and do not have holders in due course
   a. Letter of credit is an engagement by a bank in behalf of a customer (buyer) to honor demands for payment of seller upon compliance with specified conditions
   b. Bill of lading (document of title) is a receipt for the delivery of goods to a carrier. Goods are only released on surrender of it.
      1) Use same basic rules to determine who is a holder in due course and whether one exists (although called "holder to whom duly negotiated")
      2) Major difference is documents of title are not payable in money but rather in delivery of identified goods
   c. Investment security evidences an interest in property, an enterprise (stock), or an obligation, e.g., bond
      1) All are negotiable
      2) Issued in bearer form or registered, i.e., specific holder is registered
      3) "Bona fide purchaser" is the term used similar to a holder in due course

. Requirements of Negotiability (all are required)

a) Written and signed by the maker (note) or the drawer (draft)
b) Unconditional promise or order to pay a sum certain in money
c) Payable at a definite time or on demand
d) Payable to order or to bearer
e) Contains no other promise or obligation

1. Must be written and signed by the maker or drawer

   a. Writing is satisfied by handwriting, printing, typing, or any other reduction to physical form
   b. Signing is satisfied by any symbol intended to represent a signature

      1) Intent is the important factor
      2) May use own name or assumed name
      3) Rubber stamp, printing, or initials are accepted

   c. See AGENCY for signature by agent and liability thereon

2. Must contain an unconditional promise or order to pay a sum certain in money

   a. Unconditional means not subject to any conditions

      1) If payment depends upon (subject to) another agreement or transaction, then it is conditional and nonnegotiable

         a) It may state the consideration given for the underlying transaction, or that it arose out of a separate agreement

         b) If provision requires one to refer to something not within four corners of instrument to determine his rights, it is conditional and nonnegotiable

         EXAMPLE: "I promise to pay $100 to bearer if X completes his contract," is conditional and nonnegotiable.

      2) If payment is only to be from a certain source, then it is conditional and nonnegotiable. However, instrument is still unconditional if:

         a) It indicates a particular account that is to be debited (for bookkeeping purposes)
         b) By government, it can be limited to payment from a particular fund or source
         c) It is limited to entire assets of a partnership, association, trust, or estate

         EXAMPLE: "I promise to pay $100 to bearer only out of my account in Bank X," is conditional and nonnegotiable.

      3) If there are other promises or agreements, but payment is not dependent upon them, then it is still unconditional

         a) May state that it is secured
         b) May promise to maintain or protect collateral

   b. Promise or order is more than an acknowledgment or request

      1) A promise is an undertaking to pay
      2) An order is a direction to pay

   c. It is a sum certain even if it includes installments, possible discounts, interest rates, collection fees, and attorney's fees

1) If not stated, interest runs from date of issue
2) Even if no interest on note, judgment rate (specified by state statute) of interest runs from time of demand of payment
3) Sum certain if, at any time of payment, holder can determine the amount payable

d. Money is any accepted medium of exchange

1) Foreign currency is acceptable
2) Option to be paid in money or in consideration other than money destroys negotiability because of possibility that payment will not be in money

3. Must be payable at a definite time or on demand

a. It is a definite time if payable:

1) On a certain date, or
2) X days after a certain date, or
3) Within a certain time, or
4) On a certain date subject to acceleration

a) E.g., where a payment is missed, total balance may become due at once

5) On a certain date subject to an extension of time, if:

a) At the option of the holder
b) At the option of the maker or drawer only if extension is limited to a definite amount of time

b. It is not definite if payable on an act or event that is not certain as to time of occurrence, e.g., death
c. On demand includes:

1) Payable on sight
2) Payable on presentation
3) No time for payment stated

4. Document must be payable to order or to bearer. These are the magic words of negotiability.

a. The instrument is payable to order if made payable to the order of:

1) Any person, including the maker, drawer, drawee, or payee
2) Two persons together or alternatively
3) Any entity

b. The instrument is also payable to order if it is payable to a person and his "assigns"
c. The instrument is not payable to order if it is only payable to a person, e.g., "pay John Doe"

1) Not negotiable
2) It should be "pay to the order of John Doe" to be negotiable

d. The instrument is payable to bearer if it is payable to:

1) "Bearer"
2) "Cash"
3) "A person or bearer"

a) But not to a person only, e.g., "pay to John Doe"

4) "Order of bearer" or "order of cash"

e. If payable both to order and to bearer, it is payable to order unless bearer words are typed or handwritten (not part of preprinted form)

f. The instrument cannot be made payable to persons consecutively, e.g., the maker cannot specify subsequent holders

g. Distinction between "order" or "bearer" is important for negotiation. See Negotiation.

D. Interpretation of Ambiguities in Negotiable Instruments

1. Contradictory terms

a. Words control over figures
b. Handwritten terms control over typewritten and printed terms
c. Typewritten terms control over printed (typeset) terms
d. If ambiguity exists as to whether a note or a draft, it can be treated as either
e. An instrument containing "I promise to pay" and signed by two persons results in joint and several liability for both

2. Omissions

a. Uncompleted instrument at time of signing is not enforceable until completed

1) Holder may complete as authorized
2) If completed without authority, it is treated as a material alteration. See Rights of a Holder in Due Course.
3) Omits an essential date

a) Essential if payment refers to it

EXAMPLE: "Pay X days after date."

b) If not essential, then enforceable and negotiable as a demand instrument

EXAMPLE: "Pay to bearer."

b. Omission of statement of consideration does not affect negotiability (presumed)
c. Omission of where instrument is drawn or payable does not affect negotiability
d. If rate of interest is omitted when interest is provided for, use statutory judgment rate from the date of the instrument or the date of issue if undated
e. Seal is not needed

3. Others

a. Instrument may be postdated or antedated
b. Instrument may provide that by indorsing or cashing it, the payee acknowledges full satisfaction of debt
c. If an instrument is payable to order of more than one person:

1) Either payee may negotiate or enforce it if payable to him in the alternative

EXAMPLE: "Pay $100 to the order of X or Y." Either X or Y may indorse it.

2) All payees must negotiate or enforce it if not payable to them in the alternative

EXAMPLE: "Pay $100 to the order of X and Y." Both X and Y must indorse it to obtain payment.

d. Where instrument contains an extension of time provision

1) The extension is limited to a period of time not longer than the original period if the provision does not specify otherwise
2) A consent to extension embodied in the instrument binds those who sign it
3) Holder may not extend time if maker or acceptor objects and tenders full payment

e. Transferor and transferee may modify terms of a negotiable instrument as between them by a written agreement executed as part of the same transaction

1) Affects subsequent transferees, except
2) HDC not affected if he takes without notice

E. Negotiation

1. Mere "transfer" of an instrument is the transfer without the requirements of negotiation

a. Transferee obtains only the rights the transferor had, i.e., any defenses against the transferor are good against the transferee

b. Transferee may subsequently have the requirements fulfilled, i.e., indorsement, and become a holder of a negotiated instrument at that date

1) If order instrument transferred for value without indorsement, transferee has right to require transferor's indorsement

2. "Negotiation" is the transfer of an instrument by the proper means so the transferee becomes a holder (necessary to be a holder in due course)

a. Bearer paper is negotiated by mere delivery
b. Order paper requires the party negotiating to indorse and deliver the instrument
c. Indorsement must convey entire instrument or it is a partial assignment and not effective for negotiation

3. Indorsements

a. Blank indorsement is the transferor's signature alone, and converts order paper to bearer paper, e.g., indorse a check by signing it

1) Holder may write above the indorsement and convert it to a special indorsement

b. Special indorsement is made to a specific person called an indorsee, e.g., on a check indorsed "payable to Smith, signed Jones"

1) May only be further negotiated by payee's (Smith's) indorsement
2) Notice that negotiability is not destroyed by an indorsement. The words "order" or "bearer" only need to be on the face of the instrument.

EXAMPLE: A check that is payable to the order of Clark on its face has the following indorsements on its back:

Herb Clark
Pay to the order of P. White
Ike Smithers

On its face this instrument is order paper, thus Clark's indorsement is needed for proper negotiation. When Clark signs blank indorsement this changes the instrument to bearer paper in Smithers' hands. Smithers can properly negotiate the check by mere delivery. When Smithers engages in a special indorsement this changes the check back to order paper in the hands of White.

c. Restrictive indorsement restricts payment, e.g., "for deposit only" or "pay if X work is done"

   1) Subsequent transferees must comply with the indorsement or be sure it has been done
   2) Restrictions prohibiting further transfer are of no effect

d. Qualified indorsement disclaims (contract but not warranty) liability if the instrument is dishonored, e.g., "without recourse"

   1) This has the effect of reducing the warranty of "no defense" to "no knowledge of any defense." (See Liability.)

4. Negotiation is effective even if it may be rescinded, e.g., made by a minor or obtained by fraud or duress

5. If a prior party reacquires an instrument, he may cancel any indorsement not necessary to his title, e.g., all those after his earlier indorsement

   a. He may further negotiate the instrument
   b. A party whose indorsement is stricken is discharged against all (has no further liability), even against a subsequent HDC
   c. If he renegotiates it without cancelling parties, the parties between his two indorsements are discharged to all except subsequent HDC

6. Use of another's name

   a. Indorsement is effective if payee named is not intended to have an interest in the instrument

   EXAMPLE: Agent has authority to sign checks. He makes one out to a non-existent payee, indorses, and cashes it himself (fictitious payee exception).

   EXAMPLE: Employee submits time card of nonexistent employee and drawer, in good faith, signs the check. Employee indorses and cashes it himself (fictitious payee exception).

   EXAMPLE: Imposter represents himself as another. Drawer makes check out to this other person and imposter indorses and cashes it (imposter exception).

b. If the named payee was intended to have the instrument, then indorsement by another is forgery and not effective

EXAMPLE: Payroll check is delivered to a rightful employee. The employee loses the check and the finder of the check indorses the employee's name on it.

c. Not fraudulent to use a name other than one's own if not for a fraudulent purpose
d. If payee's name is misspelled, he may indorse in proper spelling or in misspelling, but a taker for value may require both

F. Holder in Due Course

1. In general, a holder in due course (HDC) is a designation for a person who is entitled to payment on a negotiable instrument regardless of the payor's contractual claims
2. To be a holder in due course, a taker must:

   a. Be a holder (explained in Negotiation, just above)
   b. Take the instrument for value

      1) A holder gives value if he:

         a) Pays or performs the agreed consideration
         b) Acquires a security interest in the instrument, e.g., the holder takes possession of the instrument as collateral for another debt
         c) Gives another negotiable instrument
         d) Takes as a satisfaction of a previous existing debt

      2) A bank takes for value (has a security interest) to the extent that credit has been given for a deposit and withdrawn

         a) FIFO method is used to determine whether it has been withdrawn

         EXAMPLE: Y opens an account in X bank for $500 cash. Later Y deposits a $500 check. If Y withdraws $500, X bank has not yet given value for the check because the original $500 cash has been withdrawn under FIFO. However, if Y withdraws $1,000, X bank has given value for the check.

      3) An executory promise is not value unless it is irrevocable, e.g., contract
      4) Value does not have to be for full amount of instrument

         a) If less, HDC only to extent value given
         b) Purchase at discount is value for full face amount of instrument provided HDC took in good faith, as long as not too large a discount

      EXAMPLE: Purchase of a $1,000 instrument in good faith for $950 is considered full value, but purchase of the same instrument for $500 is not considered full value due to the grossly excessive discount.

   c. Take in good faith

      1) Adopts a subjective test of good faith ("empty head, pure heart theory"), rather than an objective test based on what might be commercially reasonable under the circumstances

d. Take without notice that it is overdue, has been dishonored, or that any person has a defense or claim to it

1) Holder has notice when he knows or has reason to know
2) Overdue

a) Domestic checks presumed overdue in 30 days
b) Acceleration of an instrument is notice

3) Defense or claim

a) So incomplete, irregular, or obvious signs of forgery
b) If purchaser has notice that any party's claim is voidable or that all parties have been discharged

4) There is no notice of a defense or claim if

a) It is antedated or postdated
b) He knows that there has been a default in payment or interest

5) But one may acquire notice <u>after</u> becoming a holder and giving value

a) I.e., once one is a HDC, acquiring notice does not end HDC status

G. <u>Rights of a Holder in Due Course (HDC)</u>

1. HDC takes free of any personal defenses

a. Personal defenses--defenses or claims arising between original parties (other than real defenses) such as absence or failure of consideration, fraud in the inducement (see "G.3.c."), breach of contract, and breach of warranty

2. Important exceptions

a. HDC takes subject to all personal defenses of person with whom HDC dealt
b. HDC takes subject to all real defenses (see "G.3.")
c. Federal Trade Commission has abolished the HDC rule (i.e., HDC will take subject to all defenses) in consumer credit sales where

1) Third party takes consumer's note or installment contract in a retail sale
2) It only applies to consumer credit transactions
3) It does not apply where no credit is given, i.e., where consumer pays with a check
4) Purpose is to prevent a consumer from being required to pay on a negotiable instrument when he has a contractual claim against the seller

3. Real defenses generally exist when the instrument lacks legal validity at its inception. Real defenses that a HDC takes subject to are

a. Forgery

1) Applies to signatures of makers, drawers, and indorsers
2) May be ratified and thereby not a defense
3) Includes authorized agents exceeding their authority
4) A forged signature creates no liability against the person whose signature it purports to be, but instead operates as the signature of the unauthorized signer
5) Exceptions

a) Fictitious payee rule - If the person signing the instrument on behalf of the maker or drawer, or supplying the name of the payee to the maker or drawer, intends the payee to have no interest in the instrument, then such person has the power to indorse the instrument in the payee's name and transfer good title to a holder in due course. This would not create a real defense on the instrument.

EXAMPLE: Hawkins, the assistant to the controller of a general partnership, told the controller that the firm owed Samuel $500. The alleged Samuel represented by Hawkins to be a creditor was a fictitious person. Relying upon Hawkins' statement, the controller signed the firm name to the check. Hawkins indorsed the check on its back, signing the name "Henry Samuel," and cashed it at a liquor store. The drawee bank can charge the firm's account since the partnership has no real defense because of the fictitious payee exception. Anyone could indorse this instrument with "Henry Samuel" and transfer good title to the check because Hawkins never intended that the payee have an interest in the check. (Fact situation found in Question 43 of November 1977 CPA Exam.)

b) Imposter exception - This exception occurs when an imposter induces the maker or drawer to issue the instrument to the imposter in the name of the person the imposter is representing himself to be. The indorsement of the imposter does not constitute a forgery.

EXAMPLE: Davidson bears a remarkable physical resemblance to Ford, one of the town's most prominent citizens. He presented himself one day at the Friendly Finance Company, represented himself as Ford, and requested a loan of $500. Accordingly, being anxious to please so prominent a citizen, the manager at Friendly delivered to Davidson a $500 check payable to Ford. When Davidson signs Ford's name on the back of the check this does not create the real defense of forgery because of the imposter rule. A holder in due course could enforce this instrument against Friendly. (Fact situation found in Question 47 of November 1978 CPA Exam.)

c) If person's negligence substantially contributes to the forgery that person is prevented from raising the defense of forgery.

EXAMPLE: Drawer has a signature stamp and leaves it lying around.

b. Material alterations of instrument

1) Alteration of amount, date, parties, etc.

a) If fraudulent, it discharges any party whose contract is thereby changed as against any other party other than a subsequent HDC

EXAMPLE: X makes a check payable to Y for $100. Y manages to change it to $1,000. X is no longer liable on the check to Y.

b) A subsequent HDC may enforce it according to its original tenor

EXAMPLE: If Y in the above example negotiates the $1,000 check to a HDC, the HDC may still enforce it against X for $100.

2) Also unauthorized completion

a) If fraudulent, it discharges any party whose contract is thereby changed as against any party other than a subsequent HDC

EXAMPLE: X writes a check for $100 but does not fill in to whom it is to be paid. Y steals this check and completes it as payable to Y. X is not liable on the check to Y.

b) A subsequent HDC may enforce it as completed

EXAMPLE: Y in the above example negotiates the check, which he made payable to himself, to a HDC. The HDC may enforce the check against X.

3) No defense if the drawer's or maker's negligence substantially contributed to the alteration or completion

EXAMPLE: Drawer leaves signed but uncompleted checks in his desk.

c. Fraud

1) Applies to the instrument itself

a) E.g., misrepresentation as to the character of or terms of the instrument

EXAMPLE: X writes a note payable to himself and induces Y, who cannot read, to sign it by telling Y that it is a receipt needed to win a prize.

2) Fraud as to the underlying consideration or inducement to give the instrument is a personal defense, i.e., it is not a real defense, and it cannot be asserted against a HDC

d. Void transaction (not voidable)

1) Caused by duress, illegality (e.g., usury), incapacity
2) Determined by state law, not UCC

e. Infancy unless for necessities
f. Discharge in bankruptcy or another discharge that the holder has notice of when he takes the instrument

EXAMPLE: Crossed out indorsements are notice that the parties crossed out are discharged. These crossed out parties have a real defense against a HDC.

4. A person who takes through a holder in due course acquires the same rights as a holder in due course due to <u>Shelter Provision</u>

a. A holder in due course (HDC) has the effect of "washing" the instrument

EXAMPLE: A HDC transfers a note to X who knows that the payee violated the terms of the contract under which the note was issued. X is not a HDC because he has notice of a defense on the note. However, X has the rights of a HDC because he took it after a HDC. The defense is personal and X may recover on the note from the maker.

b. Does not apply to holders who also held subject to the defense prior to the HDC, i.e., person who reacquires instrument

c. Does not apply to defenses arising by holders subsequent to the HDC

5. A person who is not a HDC and who has not taken through a HDC takes the instrument subject to all defenses and any party's claim

H. Liability of Parties

1. Maker of a note and acceptor of an instrument have primary liability, i.e., they promise to pay the instrument according to its tenor

   a. Acceptance is the drawee's signed engagement to honor it when presented

      1) By writing on the instrument; signature alone is good
      2) By certification (bank unconditionally promises to pay a check)

         a) Where a holder obtains certification of an instrument, the drawer and all prior indorsers are discharged
         b) Where a drawer obtains certification of an instrument, all prior indorsers are discharged but the drawer is not
         c) Bank has no obligation to certify

   b. Drawee is not liable at all until acceptance

      1) Holder cannot require a drawee to accept

         a) Refusal to accept is dishonor of the instrument

      2) Drawee is liable only to drawer if he does not accept

   c. Co-makers have joint and several liability, i.e., either one can be held liable for full amount
   d. No party is ever (contractually) liable until he signs the instrument in some manner

2. Drawer and indorsers are secondarily liable, i.e., they promise to pay only upon dishonor of the instrument and notice of the dishonor

   a. Either may sign "without recourse" and avoid this liability (but it may be difficult to transfer as such)
   b. Indorsers are liable in the order in which they signed, i.e., from bottom up

      1) Parties are only liable to subsequent holders or the payor
      2) May agree otherwise
      3) Practical effect is that the first solvent indorser will be held liable and he will in turn have to proceed against a prior indorser

      EXAMPLE: Maker of a note is insolvent and indorsers signed in the following order, from top to bottom: A, B, C, D. The holder of the note seeks payment. D is liable first, then C, then B, then A. If C and D are insolvent, B will be liable as the first solvent indorser.

   c. Any indorser makes the following warranties upon transfer and receipt of consideration

      1) Has good title or is authorized to receive payment by one who does
      2) All signatures are good
      3) No material alterations
      4) No defense of any party is good against him

         a) A transferor indorsing "without recourse" warrants only that he has no knowledge of any defense of any party that is good against him

      5) No knowledge of any insolvency proceeding against maker or drawer
      6) Transferor makes these warranties only to his transferee if he does not indorse. If he does he also makes them to all subsequent holders who take in good faith.

Note: These warranties are one reason why an indorser who is held liable on the note can proceed against a prior indorser.

d. Any unauthorized signature operates as signature of the unauthorized party and he may be held liable in the capacity in which he signed

3. Any person who obtains payment or acceptance and any prior transferor warrants to the payor, e.g., maker, drawee, that:

   a. He has good title or is authorized to receive payment by one who does
   b. He has no knowledge of forgery of maker's or drawer's signature

      1) HDC does not so warrant to maker or drawer with respect to maker's or drawer's own signature
      2) HDC does not so warrant to drawee if acting in good faith

   c. No material alterations

      1) HDC does not so warrant to maker or drawer

4. Accommodation party is liable in the capacity in which he has signed even if taker knows of his accommodation status

   a. Accommodation party is one who signs to lend his name to other party

      EXAMPLE: Father-in-law indorses a note for son-in-law so creditor will accept it.

   b. Accommodating maker is liable as a maker would be
   c. Accommodating indorser is liable as an indorser would be
   d. Indorsement that shows it is not in chain of title is notice of its accommodation character

      EXAMPLE: A check is payable to P. P indorses on the back, "Pay to the order of X, signed P." However X requires Y to sign as an accommodation indorser for P before X will take the check. If Y signs after P, it is out of order since X would normally sign after P. Therefore subsequent holders have notice that Y is an accommodation indorser.

      1) Notice of default need not be given to accommodation party

   e. The accommodation party has right of recourse against accommodated party if the accommodation party is held liable

      1) In effect, a surety

5. Guarantor adds words of guarantee to signature

   a. Payment guaranteed--if instrument not paid when due, he will pay

      1) Holder need not resort to any other party

   b. Collection guaranteed--if instrument not paid when due, he will pay only after a judgment is obtained and it cannot be collected, or if the acceptor is insolvent
   c. Presentment (defined in "2.a" on next page) and notice of dishonor not necessary

6. Agent is liable if:

   a. He signs in his name only (principal is not liable)

b. He signs in his name and names the principal but does not show he signed in a representative capacity (principal is also liable)

EXAMPLE: Signed, "ABC company, John Doe."

c. He signs in his name showing a representative capacity but does not name the principal (principal is not liable)

EXAMPLE: Signed, "John Doe, Agent."

d. Agent should sign "John Doe as agent for ABC Company" or similarly

I. Holding Parties Liable

1. Due presentment and due notice of dishonor are necessary to hold parties liable

   a. Delay of either one will discharge all indorsers

   b. Delay will only discharge drawer, acceptor, or maker if:

      1) Instrument is payable at a bank, and
      2) Bank becomes insolvent, and
      3) The drawer, acceptor, or maker assigns holder his right against the insolvent bank

   c. Protest may also be needed for foreign drafts (drawn or payable outside the U.S.)

      1) A formal attestation of dishonor by a U.S. consul
      2) Only limited use any more

2. Presentment

   a. A demand for acceptance or payment to maker, acceptor, drawee, or other payor
   b. May be made in person, by mail, or through a clearing house
   c. Must be made on or before the date it is payable or within a reasonable time if a demand instrument

      1) For drawer reasonable time is 30 days after date or issue, whichever is later
      2) For indorser reasonable time is 7 days after indorsement
      3) Must be at a reasonable hour--at bank during banking hours

   d. Payment or acceptance is due by the end of the business day following presentment but may be deferred by the person who is to pay (maker, acceptor, or drawee) for one business day

      1) Effect is that payment or acceptance must be made by the end of the next business day or there is dishonor

3. Notice of dishonor--dishonor occurs when acceptance or payment is refused after presentment

   a. Must be given to secondarily liable parties to hold them liable
   b. Must be given to each party one wishes to hold liable

      1) One notice operates for all who have rights against party notified

         EXAMPLE: Maker dishonors a note. The holder gives timely notice of the dishonor to all indorsers; A, B, and C who signed in order from top to bottom. If holder holds C liable, C may hold B liable. Holder's notice to B was effective for C also.

c. May be written, oral, or in any other reasonable manner. Effective if sent to last known address.
d. Notice must be given by:
   1) Banks before midnight of the next banking day following receipt of item or receipt of notice of dishonor, whichever is later
   2) Others before midnight of the third business day following dishonor or receipt of notice of dishonor
e. Notice to one partner is notice to all partners even if partnership is dissolved
f. Written notice is deemed to be received when sent (even though lost and never received)

EXAMPLE: A and B have indorsed a note. C presents it to maker for payment. Maker refuses to pay (dishonor). C notifies B of the dishonor within three days, but A is not notified for a week. C holds B liable. A cannot be held liable because he was not given timely notice of dishonor. B must resort to the maker.

4. Excused presentment and notice of dishonor
   a. Delay of presentment and notice of dishonor is excused when party has no notice that instrument is due, e.g., acceleration without knowledge
   b. Failure of presentment and notice of dishonor are excused when party to be charged (e.g., indorser) waives it
      1) Waiver may be express or implied; either before or after presentment or notice is due
         a) Waiver is express, if party to be charged writes, "I waive holder's failure to make presentment or to give notice of dishonor"
         b) Waiver is implied if party to be charged pays
   c. Failure of notice of dishonor is excused when party to be charged has dishonored it himself
   d. Presentment is excused when obligor is dead or insolvent, or appears futile for other reasons
   e. Waiver is often embodied in instrument itself and is binding on all parties
      1) If only written above indorser's signature, it is only binding on that one indorser
5. Discharge of parties from liability
   a. Upon discharge, a party is released from liability except:
      1) A discharge is not effective against a subsequent HDC who does not have notice of the discharge when he takes the instrument
   b. Discharge has already been stated with respect to:
      1) Reacquisition and renegotiation--see <u>Negotiation</u>
      2) Fraudulent and material alteration--see <u>Rights of a Holder in Due Course</u>
      3) Certification--see <u>Liability of Parties</u>
      4) Delay in presentment and notice--see above
   c. Discharge is also obtained
      1) To the extent of payment or satisfaction to the holder

a) Cannot be made in bad faith, e.g., knowledge of theft of instrument

EXAMPLE: Maker knows the instrument has been stolen from payee and payee's name forged. Maker is not discharged on the note if he pays a holder because payee may still collect from maker.

b) Cannot be made in violation of restrictive indorsement

2) By making tender of full payment

a) Discharged to extent of subsequent liability for interest, costs and attorney's fees
b) Holder's refusal to accept tender discharges any party with recourse against party making tender

1] E.g., accommodation party of one making tender
2] E.g., indorsers are discharged from liability when maker tenders to holder

3) By cancellation, e.g., striking out another party's signature discharges the party whose signature is struck out

a) Holder may strike out any prior party's signature
b) No consideration needed

4) By renunciation, i.e., holder renounces rights against a particular party

a) Must be by a writing signed and delivered, or by surrendering the instrument to the party

5) Any person in position of a surety is discharged as in SURETYSHIP to the extent the holder releases, agrees not to sue, extends time, or impairs collateral, unless:

a) Holder preserves his rights against surety and surety's rights to recourse against others
b) Accommodation party and indorsers are in the same positions as sureties

6) Drawer and indorsers are discharged if holder assents to drawee's acceptance which varies the terms of the instrument
7) Any party may be discharged by an act or agreement with another party that would discharge a contract

a) Discharge is between those parties only

EXAMPLE: A, B, C, and D have signed as indorsers. A may pay D $10 not to ever hold A liable. However B and C may still hold A liable if they are held liable first.

J. Banks

1. Relationship between bank and depositor is debtor-creditor

a. Even though the depositor has funds in the bank, a payee cannot force a drawee to make payment. Banks are only liable to the drawer.
b. Only a drawer has an action against the bank-drawee for wrongfully dishonoring a check

2. Checks
   a. Banks are not obligated to pay on a check presented more than 6 months after date
      1) But they may pay in good faith and charge customer's account
   b. Even if a check creates an overdraft, a bank may charge customer's account
      1) In effect it is a loan
   c. Bank is liable to drawer for wrongful dishonor of a check
      1) Wrongful dishonor may occur if the bank in error believes funds are insufficient when they are sufficient
      2) Damages include consequential damages, e.g., damages resulting from nonpayment of the check
   d. Payment of bad checks, e.g., forged, altered, etc.
      1) Bank is liable to drawer for payment on bad checks unless drawer's negligence contributed
      2) Bank cannot recover from an innocent holder in due course to whom the bank paid on a bad check
      3) Drawer must inspect cancelled checks and inform bank promptly of any bad checks which were paid
   e. Oral stop payment is good for 14 days; written is good for six months and is renewable
      1) Stop-payment order must be given so as to afford the bank a reasonable opportunity to act on it
      2) Bank is liable to drawer if it pays after effective stop-payment order when drawer can prove that the bank's failure to obey the order caused drawer's loss. If drawer has no valid defense to justify dishonoring instrument then bank has no liability for failure to obey stop-payment order.

         EXAMPLE: Smith buys a T.V. set from the ABC Appliance Store and pays for the set with a check. Later in the day Smith finds a better model for the same price at another store. Smith telephones his bank and orders the bank to stop payment on the check. If the bank mistakenly pays Smith's check two days after receiving the stop order, the bank will not be liable since Smith could not rightfully rescind his agreement with ABC. Thus, Smith suffered no damages due to the bank's mistake. (Fact situation found in Question No. 5, November 1980 CPA Exam.)

      3) If drawer stops payment on the check, he is still liable to holder of check unless he has a valid defense (e.g., if holder qualifies as a holder in due course then drawer must be able to assert a real defense to free himself of liability)
   f. If depositor dies or becomes incompetent, bank may pay checks until it knows and then has a reasonable time to act
      1) May pay for 10 days after death even with knowledge, unless ordered to stop by an interested party, e.g., executor

g. Bank is entitled to a depositor's indorsement on checks deposited with the bank

   1) If missing, bank may supply

K. Transfer of Negotiable Documents of Title

1. The transfer of documents of title is governed by Article 7 of the UCC. The transfer of such documents is very similar to the transfer of negotiable instruments under Article 3 of the UCC.

2. Types of documents of title

   a. Bill of lading is a document issued by a carrier (a person engaged in the business of transporting or forwarding goods) evidencing receipt of the goods for transfer

   b. A warehouse receipt is a document issued as evidence of receipt of goods by a person engaged in the business of storing goods for hire

3. Form

   a. Negotiable. The document of title is negotiable if the face of the document contains the words of negotiability (order or bearer).

      1) Order document -- a document of title containing a promise to deliver the goods to the order of a named person. The person may be named on the face of the document or, if there are indorsements on the back of the document and the last indorsement is a special indorsement.

         a) Proper negotiation requires delivery of the document and indorsement by the named individual(s)

      2) Bearer document -- a document of title containing a promise to deliver the goods to bearer. "Bearer" may be stated on the face of the document or, if there are indorsements on the back of the document and the last indorsement is a blank indorsement.

         a) Proper negotiation merely requires delivery of the document

   b. Nonnegotiable (straight) documents of title are assigned, not negotiated. The assignee will never receive any better rights than the assignor had in the document.

      1) Indorsement of a nonnegotiable document neither makes it negotiable nor adds to the transferee's rights

4. Due negotiation. A document of title is "duly negotiated" when it is negotiated to a holder who takes it in good faith in the ordinary course of business without notice of a defense and pays value.

   a. Value does not include payment of a preexisting (antecedent) debt. This is an important difference from the value concept required to create a holder in due course under Article 3 of the UCC.

5. Rights acquired by due negotiation. A holder by due negotiation acquires rights very similar to those acquired by a holder in due course.

   a. These rights include:

1) Title to the document
2) Title to the goods
3) All rights accruing under the law of agency or estoppel, including rights to goods delivered to the bailee after the document was issued, and
4) The direct obligation of the issuer to hold or deliver the goods according to the terms of the document

b. A holder by due negotiation defeats similar defenses to those defeated by a holder in due course under Article 3 of the UCC (personal but not real defenses)

c. A document of title procurred by a thief upon placing stolen goods in a warehouse confers no rights in the underlying goods. This defense is valid against a subsequent holder to whom the document of title has been duly negotiated. Therefore, the original owner of the goods can assert better title to the goods than a holder who has received the document through due negotiation.

6. Rights acquired in the absence of due negotiation

   a. A transferee of a document, whether negotiable or nonnegotiable, to whom the document has been delivered, but not duly negotiated, acquires the title and rights which his transferor had or had actual authority to convey

7. Warranties transferred upon negotiation. A transferor for value warrants:

   a. That the document is genuine
   b. That he has no knowledge of any fact that would impair its validity or worth, and
   c. That his negotiation or transfer is rightful and fully effective with respect to the document of title and the goods it represents

L. <u>Transfer of Investment Securities</u>

1. The transfer of investment securities (stocks and bonds) are governed by Article 8 of the UCC. This Article states that investment securities are negotiable instruments. Consequently, the rules applicable to the transfer of investment securities are very similar to the rules contained in Article 3 of the UCC which governs the transfer of promissory notes, drafts, etc.

2. Proper negotiation of investment securities

   a. If no indorsements on the back of the certificate look to the face of the security

      1) If a registered security (names person entitled to the security) specified person must deliver and indorse
      2) If a bearer security only delivery of the security is needed

   b. If there are indorsements on the back of the certificate proper negotiation would be:

      1) Delivery if the last indorsement is a blank indorsement
      2) Delivery and indorsement by specified person if the last indorsement is a special indorsement

3. A bona fide purchaser (BFP) of an investment security is someone who:

a. Receives the security through proper negotiation (delivery of a bearer security or delivery and indorsement of a registered security), and
b. Gives value, and
c. Takes in good faith and without notice of any adverse claim

4. A bona fide purchaser acquires the security free of most adverse claims such as fraud, duress, failure of consideration, theft of a bearer security, etc. This status is comparable to a holder in due course under Article 3 of the UCC.

5. A bona fide purchaser does not take the security free of theft of a registered security which would result in the claim of a forged indorsement. However, if the issuer (normally a corporation) transfers the registration of the security to the BFP based upon the unauthorized indorsement, the BFP has title to the security. The original owner of the security (the party the thief stole the instrument from) is also entitled to receive a new certificate from the issuer evidencing the security that was stolen.

EXAMPLE: Herb stole from Ike an unindorsed registered certificate of stock (an order certificate). Ike gave the issuing corporation notice of loss within a reasonable period of time. Herb, the thief, forges Ike's name to the certificate and then delivers it to Danny, a bona fide purchaser who pays value and takes the certificate without knowledge of the theft or forgery. Ike is still the owner of the shares, and Herb is liable to Ike for their value. If Danny surrenders the certificate to the issuing corporation which cancels it and issues a new one in Danny's name, Danny is now owner of the shares represented by the certificate registered in his name. However, Ike is entitled to receive from the corporation a new certificate for the same number of shares.

6. A purchaser who does not qualify as a bona fide purchaser receives the rights of his/her transferor unless the purchaser took part in creating the defense present or is trying to better his/her position by passing the security through the BFP (similar to the shelter provision under Article 3 of the UCC).

7. A transferor of a security for value

   a. Extends the following warranties:

      1) Transfer is effective and rightful, and
      2) The security is genuine and has not been materially altered, and
      3) S/he knows of no fact that might impair the validity of the security

   b. Is entitled to a reissued certificate of stock without giving further compensation to the issuer, if bona fide purchaser originally received a stock certificate containing an unauthorized signature of an employee of the issuer, who had been entrusted with the responsible handling of stock certificates.

Multiple Choice Questions (1–54)

Items 1 through 2 involve commercial paper under Article 3 of the Uniform Commercial Code.

1. Assuming each of the following instruments is negotiable, which qualifies as commercial paper?
   a. Bearer documents of title.
   b. Investment securities endorsed in blank.
   c. Foreign currency.
   d. A foreign draft.

2. Assuming each of the following is negotiable, which qualifies as a draft?
   a. A bearer bond.
   b. A trade acceptance.
   c. A certificate of deposit.
   d. A demand promissory note.

3. Which of the following on the face of an otherwise negotiable instrument will affect the instrument's negotiability?
   a. The instrument contains a promise to provide additional collateral if there is a decrease in value of the existing collateral.
   b. The instrument is payable six months after the death of the maker.
   c. The instrument is payable at a definite time subject to an acceleration clause in the event of a default.
   d. The instrument is postdated.

4. The requirements in order for an instrument to qualify as negotiable commercial paper
   a. Are the same as the requirements for a bill of lading.
   b. Permit some substitution or variance from the literal language of the UCC.
   c. May be satisfied by a statement in the instrument that it is to be considered negotiable despite its omission of one or more requirements.
   d. May be waived by the parties in a signed writing.

5. Your client has in its possession the following instrument:

$700.00 Provo, Utah June 1, 1983

Thirty days after date I promise to pay to the order of

Cash

Seven hundred Dollars

at Boise, Idaho

Value received with interest at the rate of ten percent per annum.

This instrument is secured by a conditional sales contract.

No. 20 Due July 1, 1983 Ann Bowie

This instrument is
   a. A negotiable time draft.
   b. A nonnegotiable note since it states that it is secured by a conditional sales contract.
   c. Not negotiable until July 1, 1983.
   d. A negotiable bearer note.

6. Ash Company has in its possession the following note:

October 15, 1982

I, Joseph Gorman, promise to pay or deliver to Harold Smalley or to his order ONE THOUSAND DOLLARS ($1,000) or at his option to deliver an amount of stock in the Sunrise Corporation which, on the due date of this instrument, is worth not less than ONE THOUSAND DOLLARS ($1,000). This note is due and payable on the 1st of November, 1982.

Joseph Gorman

Joseph Gorman

This note is
   a. Not commercial paper, but instead a negotiable investment security.
   b. A negotiable promissory note since it is payable to Smalley's order and contains an unconditional promise to pay $1,000 if the holder so elects.
   c. Nonnegotiable since it gives Smalley the option to take stock instead of cash.
   d. Nontransferable.

7. The following instrument has been received by your client:

> October 15, 1981
>
> To: Bill Souther
> Rural Route 1
> Waverly, Iowa
>
> Pay to the order of James Olson six hundred dollars.
>
> Robert Smythe
> Robert Smythe

Which of the following is correct?

a. The instrument is payable on demand.
b. The instrument is a negotiable note.
c. As Bill Souther is the drawer, he is primarily liable on the instrument.
d. As Bill Souther is the drawee, he is secondarily liable on the instrument.

8. Which of the following provisions contained in an otherwise negotiable instrument will cause it to be nonnegotiable?

a. It is payable in Mexican pesos.
b. It contains an unrestricted acceleration clause.
c. It grants to the holder an option to purchase land.
d. It is limited to payment out of the entire assets of a partnership.

9. In order to be a holder of a bearer negotiable instrument, the transferee must

a. Give value for the instrument.
b. Have physical possession of the instrument.
c. Take the instrument before receipt of notice of a defense.
d. Take in good faith.

10. Drummond broke into the Apex Drug Store and took all of the cash and checks which were in the cash register. The checks reflect payments made to Apex for goods sold. Drummond disposed of the checks and has disappeared. Apex is worried about its ability to recover the checks from those now in possession of them. Which of the following is correct?

a. Apex will prevail as long as its signature was necessary to negotiate the checks in question.
b. Since there was no valid transfer by Apex to Drummond, subsequent parties have no better rights than the thief had.
c. Apex will prevail only if the checks were payable to cash.
d. Apex will not prevail on any of the checks since it was the only party that could have prevented the theft.

11. Hoover is a holder in due course of a check which was originally payable to the order of Nelson or bearer and has the following indorsements on its back:

> Nelson
> Pay to the order of Maxwell
> Duffy
> Without Recourse
> Maxwell
> Howard

Which of the following statements about the check is correct?

a. It was originally order paper.
b. It was order paper in Howard's hands.
c. Maxwell's signature was **not** necessary for it to be negotiated.
d. Presentment for payment must be made within seven days after indorsement to hold an indorser liable.

12. Balquist sold a negotiable instrument payable to her order to Farley. In transferring the instrument to Farley, she forgot to indorse it. Accordingly

a. Farley qualifies as a holder in due course.
b. Farley has a specifically enforceable right to obtain Balquist's unqualified indorsement.
c. Farley obtains a better right to payment of the instrument than Balquist had.
d. Once the signature of Balquist is obtained, Farley's rights as a holder in due course relate back to the time of transfer.

13. Filmore had a negotiable instrument in its possession which it had received in payment of certain equipment it had sold to Marker Merchandising. The instrument was originally payable to the order of Charles Danforth or bearer. It was indorsed specially by Danforth to Marker which in turn negotiated it to Filmore via a blank indorsement. The instrument in question, along with some cash and other negotiable instruments, was stolen from Filmore on October 1, 1981. Which of the following is correct?

a. A holder in due course will prevail against Filmore's claim to the instrument.

b. Filmore's signature was necessary in order to further negotiate the instrument.
c. The theft constitutes a common law conversion which prevents anyone from obtaining a better title to the instrument than the owner.
d. Once an instrument is bearer paper it is always bearer paper.

14. Johnson lost a check that he had received for professional services rendered. The instrument on its face was payable to Johnson's order. He had indorsed it on the back by signing his name and printing "for deposit only" above his name. Assuming the check is found by Alcatraz, a dishonest person who attempts to cash it, which of the following is correct?

a. Any transferee of the instrument must pay or apply any value given by him for the instrument consistent with the indorsement.
b. The indorsement is a blank indorsement and a holder in due course who cashed it for Alcatraz would prevail.
c. The indorsement prevents further transfer or negotiation by anyone.
d. If Alcatraz simply signs his name beneath Johnson's indorsement, he can convert it into bearer paper and a holder in due course would take free of the restriction.

15. Sample has in his possession a negotiable instrument which was originally payable to the order of Block. It was transferred to Sample by a mere delivery by Cox, who took it from Block in good faith in satisfaction of an antecedent debt. The back of the instrument read as follows, "Pay to the order of Cox in satisfaction of my prior purchase of a desk, signed Block." Which of the following is correct?

a. Sample has the right to assert Cox's rights, including his standing as a holder in due course and also has the right to obtain Cox's signature.
b. Block's endorsement was a special endorsement, thus Cox's signature was **not** required in order to negotiate it.
c. Sample is a holder in due course.
d. Cox's taking the instrument for an antecedent debt prevents him from qualifying as a holder in due course.

16. Which of the following will **not** constitute value in determining whether a person is a holder in due course?

a. The taking of a negotiable instrument for a future consideration.
b. The taking of a negotiable instrument as security for a loan.
c. The giving of one's own negotiable instrument in connection with the purchase of another negotiable instrument.
d. The performance of services rendered the payee of a negotiable instrument who endorses it in payment for services.

17. Who among the following can personally qualify as a holder in due course?

a. A payee.
b. A reacquirer who was not initially a holder in due course.
c. A holder to whom the instrument was negotiated as a gift.
d. A holder who had notice of a defect but who took from a prior holder in due course.

18. Barber has in his possession a negotiable instrument which he purchased in good faith and for value. The drawer of the instrument stopped payment on it and has asserted that Barber does not qualify as a holder in due course since the instrument is overdue. In determining whether the instrument is overdue, which of the following is incorrect?

a. A reasonable time for a check drawn and payable in the United States is presumed to be 30 days after issue.
b. A reasonable time for a check drawn and payable in the United States is presumed to be 20 days after the last negotiation.
c. All demand instruments, other than checks, are not overdue until a reasonable time after their issue has elapsed.
d. The instrument will be deemed to be overdue if a demand for payment had been made and Barber knew this.

19. Ajax, Inc., sold a refrigerator to Broadway Bill's Restaurant and accepted Broadway's negotiable promissory note for $600 as payment. The note was payable to Ajax's order one year after the date of issue. Thirty days after receiving the note, Ajax indorsed the note with a blank indorsement and sold it to National Bank for $550. National credited Ajax's checking account with $550, which brought Ajax's balance to $725. Ajax drew checks for a total of $675 which National honored. National then learned that the refrigerator had not been delivered by Ajax. The note is now due and unpaid. When National brings suit, Broadway pleads lack of consideration on the note. Which of the following is a valid statement with respect to the above facts?

a. The discount on the note is so great as to impugn National's taking in good faith.
b. In ascertaining the extent to which value had been given by National, the FIFO rule will apply to checks or notes deposited and the proceeds withdrawn.
c. Broadway has no liability on the note since it never received the refrigerator.
d. Broadway has only secondary liability on the note in question.

20. Which of the following is a valid defense against a holder in due course of a negotiable instrument?
a. Execution of the instrument by one without authority to sign the instrument.
b. Fraudulent statements made to the drawer as to the value of the consideration given for the instrument.
c. Duress on the drawer which renders the instrument voidable at the drawer's option.
d. Delivery of the instrument subject to a condition precedent which has yet to be performed.

21. Which of the following defenses may be successfully asserted by the maker against a holder in due course?
a. Wrongful filling in of an incomplete instrument by a prior holder.
b. Total failure to perform the contractual undertaking for which the instrument was given.
c. Fraudulent misrepresentations as to the consideration given by a prior holder in exchange for the negotiable instrument.
d. Discharge of the maker of the instrument in bankruptcy proceedings.

22. Dodger fraudulently induced Tell to issue a check to his order for $900 in payment for some nearly worthless securities. Dodger took the check and artfully raised the amount from $900 to $1,900. He promptly negotiated the check to Bay who took in good faith and for value. Tell, upon learning of the fraud, issued a stop order to its bank. Which of the following is correct?
a. Dodger has a real defense which will prevent any of the parties from collecting anything.
b. The stop order was ineffective against Bay since it was issued after the negotiation to Bay.
c. Bay as a holder in due course will prevail against Tell but only to the extent of $900.
d. Had there been no raising of the amount by Dodger, the bank would be obligated to pay Bay despite the stop order.

23. Dilworth, an employee of Excelsior Super Markets, Inc., stole his payroll check from the cashier before it was completed. The check was properly made out to his order but the amount payable had not been filled in because Dilworth's final time sheet had not yet been received. Dilworth filled in an amount which was $300 in excess of his proper pay and cashed it at the Good Luck Tavern. Good Luck took the check in good faith and without suspecting that the instrument had been improperly completed. Excelsior's bank paid the instrument in due course. Excelsior is demanding that the bank credit its account for the $300 or that it be paid by Good Luck. Which of the following is correct?
a. Good Luck has **no** liability for the return of the $300.
b. Excelsior's bank must credit Excelsior's account for the $300.
c. A theft defense would be good against all parties including Good Luck.
d. Only in the event that negligence on Excelsior's part can be shown will Excelsior bear the loss.

24. Ed Moss has a negotiable draft in his possession. The draft was originally payable to the order of John Davis. The instrument was endorsed as follows:

(1) Carl Bass
(2) John Davis
(3) Pay to the order of Nix & Co.
(4) Pay to Ed Moss, without recourse, Nix & Co. per Jane Kirk, President
(5) For deposit, Ed Moss

Which of the following is correct regarding the above endorsements?
a. Number 1 prevents further negotiation since Bass is not the payee.
b. Number 2 does **not** change the instrument to bearer paper since it was originally payable to the order of Davis.
c. Number 4 eliminates all the contractual liability of the endorser.
d. Number 5 prevents any further negotiation.

25. Regarding certification of a check,
a. Certification by a bank constitutes an acceptance of the check.

b. Certification of a check obtained by the drawer releases the drawer.
c. A bank is obligated to certify a customer's check if a holder demands certification and there are sufficient funds in the drawer's account.
d. If a holder obtains certification of a check, all prior endorsers are discharged, but the drawer remains liable.

26. Kirk made a check payable to Haskin's order for a debt she owed on open account. Haskin negotiated the check by a blank indorsement to Carlson who deposited it in his checking account. The bank returned the check with the notation that payment was refused due to insufficient funds. Kirk is insolvent. Under the circumstances

a. Kirk has a real defense assertable against all parties including Carlson, a holder in due course.
b. If Kirk files for bankruptcy, Haskin or Carlson could successfully assert that there had been an assignment of whatever funds were in Kirk's checking account.
c. If there is a proper presentment, and notice is properly given by Carlson to Haskin, Carlson may recover the amount of the check from Haskin.
d. Haskin or Carlson can correctly assert the standing of a secured creditor.

27. Your client, Ensign Factors Corporation, has purchased the trade acceptance shown below from Mason Art Productions, Inc. It has been properly indorsed in blank on the back by Mason.

October 15, 1981

Adams Wholesalers, Inc.
49 Buena Vista Avenue
Santa Monica, California

Pay to the order of Mason Art Productions, Inc., ten thousand and 00/100 dollars ($10,000.00).

Gilda Loucksi, Pres.
Gilda Loucksi, President
Mason Art Productions, Inc.

Accepted October 24, 1981
Adams Wholesalers, Inc.

By Charles Lurch, President

As to the rights of Ensign, which of the following is correct?

a. The instrument is nonnegotiable, hence Ensign is an assignee.
b. Until acceptance, Mason had primary liability on the instrument.
c. After acceptance by Adams Wholesalers, Adams is primarily liable and Mason is secondarily liable.
d. After acceptance by Adams, Mason is primarily liable, and Adams is secondarily liable.

28. Smith buys a TV set from the ABC Appliance Store and pays for the set with a check. Later in the day Smith finds a better model for the same price at another store. Smith immediately calls ABC trying to cancel the sale. ABC tells Smith that they are holding him to the sale and have negotiated the check to their wholesaler, Glenn Company, as a partial payment on inventory purchases. Smith telephones his bank, the Union Trust Bank, and orders the bank to stop payment on the check. Which of the following statements is correct?

a. If Glenn can prove it is a holder in due course, the drawee bank, Union Trust, must honor Smith's check.
b. Union Trust is **not** bound or liable for Smith's stop payment order unless the order is placed in writing.
c. If Union Trust mistakenly pays Smith's check two days after receiving the stop order, the bank will **not** be liable.
d. Glenn can **not** hold Smith liable on the check.

29. Gomer developed a fraudulent system whereby he could obtain checks payable to the order of certain repairmen who serviced various large corporations. Gomer observed the delivery trucks of repairmen who did business with the corporations, and then he submitted bills on the bogus letterhead of the repairmen to the selected large corporations. The return envelope for payment indicated a local post office box. When the checks arrived, Gomer would forge the payees' signatures and cash the checks. The parties cashing the checks are holders in due course. Who will bear the loss assuming the amount cannot be recovered from Gomer?

a. The defrauded corporations.
b. The drawee banks.
c. Intermediate parties who indorsed the instruments for collection.
d. The ultimate recipients of the proceeds of the checks even though they are holders in due course.

30. An otherwise valid negotiable bearer note is signed with the forged signature of Darby. Archer, who believed he knew Darby's signature, bought the note in good faith from Harding, the forger. Archer transferred the note without indorsement to Barker, in partial payment of a debt. Barker then sold the note to Chase for 80% of its face amount and delivered it without indorsement. When Chase presented the note for payment at maturity, Darby refused to honor it, pleading forgery. Chase gave proper notice of dishonor to Barker and to Archer. Which of the following statements best describes the situation from Chase's standpoint?

a. Chase can **not** qualify as a holder in due course for the reason that he did **not** pay face value for the note.
b. Chase can hold Barker liable on the ground that Barker warranted to Chase that neither Darby nor Archer had any defense valid against Barker.
c. Chase can hold Archer liable on the ground that Archer warranted to Chase that Darby's signature was genuine.
d. Chase can **not** hold Harding, the forger, liable on the note because his signature does **not** appear on it and thus, he made no warranties to Chase.

31. Mask stole one of Bloom's checks. The check was already signed by Bloom and made payable to Duval. The check was drawn on United Trust Company. Mask forged Duval's signature on the back of the check and cashed the check at the Corner Check Cashing Company which in turn deposited it with its bank, Town National Bank of Toka. Town National proceeded to collect on the check from United. None of the parties mentioned was negligent. Who will bear the loss assuming the amount cannot be recovered from Mask?

a. Bloom.
b. Duval.
c. United Trust Company.
d. Corner Check Cashing Company.

32. Robb stole one of Markum's blank checks, made it payable to himself, and forged Markum's signature to it. The check was drawn on the Unity Trust Company. Robb cashed the check at the Friendly Check Cashing Company which in turn deposited it with its bank, the Farmer's National. Farmer's National proceeded to collect on the check from Unity Trust. The theft and forgery were quickly discovered by Markum who promptly notified Unity. None of the parties mentioned was negligent. Who will bear the loss, assuming the amount cannot be recovered from Robb?

a. Markum.
b. Unity Trust Company.
c. Friendly Check Cashing Company.
d. Farmer's National.

33. Woody Pyle, a public warehouseman, issued Merlin a negotiable warehouse receipt for fungible goods stored. Pyle

a. May **not** limit the amount of his liability for his own negligence.
b. Will be absolutely liable for any damages in the absence of a statute or a provision on the warehouse receipt to the contrary.
c. May commingle Merlin's goods with similar fungible goods of other bailors.
d. Is obligated to deliver the goods to Merlin despite Merlin's improper refusal to pay the storage charges due.

34. Thieves broke into the warehouse of Monogram Airways and stole a shipment of computer parts belonging to Valley Instruments. Valley had in its possession a negotiable bill of lading covering the shipment. The thieves transported the stolen parts to another state and placed the parts in a bonded warehouse. The thieves received a negotiable warehouse receipt which they used to secure a loan of $20,000 from Reliable Finance. These facts were revealed upon apprehension of the thieves. Regarding the rights of the parties

a. Reliable is entitled to a $20,000 payment before relinquishment of the parts.
b. Monogram will be the ultimate loser of the $20,000.
c. Valley is entitled to recover the parts free of Reliable's $20,000 claim.
d. Valley is **not** entitled to the parts but may obtain damages from Monogram.

35. The Uniform Commercial Code deals differently with negotiable documents of title than with commercial paper. Which of the following will prevent a due negotiation of a negotiable document of title?

a. The transfer by delivery alone of a title document which has been endorsed in blank.
b. The receipt of the instrument in payment of an antecedent money obligation.
c. The taking of a bearer document of title from one who lacks title thereto.
d. The fact that the document of title is more than one month old.

36. In order to qualify as an investment security under the Uniform Commercial Code, an instrument must be

a. Issued in registered form, and **not** bearer form.
b. Of a long-term nature not intended to be disposed of within one year.
c. Only an equity security or debenture security, and **not** a secured obligation.
d. In a form that evidences a share, participation or other interest in property or in an enterprise, or evidences an obligation of the issuer.

37. Dwight Corporation purchased the following instrument in good faith from John Q. Billings:

> No. 7200 ●●●REGISTERED●●● $10,000
> Magnum Cum Laude Corporation
>
> Ten year 14% Debenture, Due May 15, 1990
>
> Magnum Cum Laude Corporation, a Delaware Corporation, for value received, hereby promises to pay the sum of TEN THOUSAND DOLLARS ($10,000) to JOHN Q. BILLINGS, or registered assigns, at the principal office or agency of the Corporation in Wilmington, Delaware.

On the reverse side of the instrument, the following appeared:

"For value received, the undersigned sells, assigns, and transfers unto DWIGHT CORPORATION, (signed) JOHN Q. BILLINGS." Billings' signature was guaranteed by Capital Trust Company.

Magnum's 14% debentures are listed on the Pacific Coast Exchange. The instrument is

a. A registered negotiable investment security which Dwight took free of adverse title claims.
b. Nonnegotiable since the instrument must be registered with Magnum to be validly transferred.
c. Negotiable commercial paper.
d. A nonnegotiable investment security since the instrument lacks the words of negotiability, "to the order of or bearer."

38. While auditing the common stock ledger of Sims Corporation a CPA uncovers the following situation. An investor has purchased a certificate representing 500 shares of common stock of the Sims Corporation from a former clerk of the corporation. It was the duty of the clerk to prepare stock certificates from a supply of blanks for signature of the corporate secretary. The clerk forged the corporate secretary's signature on a bearer certificate and delivered the certificate for value to the investor who did not have notice of the forgery and who now demands a reissued certificate in the investor's name from the corporation. The corporation asserts that it has no liability to reissue a certificate in the name of the investor and that the investor's bearer certificate is null and void. Which of the following is correct?

a. The certificate is valid and the investor is entitled to a reissued certificate.
b. The certificate issued is invalid and the corporation has **no** liability to reissue.
c. An appropriate recourse of the investor is to sue the corporation and clerk for dollar damages and to sue the clerk for the crime of forgery.
d. The corporation is required to reissue a certificate only if appropriately compensated by the investor.

39. Wilberforce & Company has in its possession certain securities which it took in good faith and for value from Dunlop. An adverse claim or defense has been asserted against the securities. Which of the following warranties may Wilberforce validly assert against Dunlop, its prior transferor?

a. There is **no** defect in the prior chain of title.
b. The securities are genuine and have **not** been materially altered.
c. There is **no** defect which might impair the validity of the securities.
d. Dunlop will defend the purchasers' title from adverse claim or defects which would impair the validity of the securities.

May 1985 Questions

40. The following instrument was received by Kerr:

> Madison, Wisconsin April 5, 1985
>
> Sixty days after date pay to the order of Donald Kerr, one hundred and fifty dollars ($150). Value received and charge the trade account of Olympia Sales Corp., N.Y.
>
> Olympia Sales Corp.
>
> To: New City Bank, by Carl Starr
> U.N. Plaza, President
> New York, N.Y.

The instrument is a

a. Negotiable time draft.
b. Check.
c. Promissory note.
d. Trade acceptance.

41. Jason contracted to sell his business to Farr. Upon execution of the contract by Farr, he delivered a note in lieu of earnest money which recited the nature of the transaction and indicated that it was payable on the date of the closing which was to be determined by the mutual consent of the parties. The note is

a. Nonnegotiable because **no** consideration is given.
b. Nonnegotiable because of the recitation of the transaction which gave rise to it.
c. Nonnegotiable since it is **not** payable at a definite time.
d. Negotiable.

42. A holder in due course will take free of which of the following defenses?

a. A wrongful filling-in of the amount payable which was omitted from the instrument.
b. Duress of a nature which renders the obligation of the party a nullity.
c. Infancy to the extent that it is a defense to a simple contract.
d. Discharge of the maker in bankruptcy.

43. Your client, MDS Discount Services, Inc., purchased the following instrument from John Cross on February 15, 1985. Cross had received it in connection with the sale to Dann Corp. of real property he owned located in Utah. Cross endorsed it in blank and received $24,000 from MDS.

> $26,000.00 Boston, Massachusetts
> February 2, 1985
>
> Sixty days after date, I promise to pay to the order of John Cross Twenty Six Thousand & 00/100 Dollars at the Second National Bank of Provo, Utah.
>
> Value received with interest at the rate of 14% per annum. This instrument arises out of the sale of real estate located in the state of Utah. It is further agreed that this instrument is:
>
> 1. Subject to all implied and constructive conditions.
> 2. Secured by a first mortgage given as per the sale of the real estate mentioned above.
> 3. To be paid out of funds deposited in the City Bank of Wabash, Illinois.
>
> Dann Corp.
>
> by Joan Dann
> President

The instrument is

a. Nonnegotiable due to the language contained in clause number 1.
b. Nonnegotiable since it incorporates by reference the terms of the mortgage indicated in clause number 2.
c. Negotiable since it contains the words "value received" and specifies the required recitation of the transaction out of which it arose.

d. Negotiable despite the language contained in clauses numbered 1, 2, and 3.

44. Bond fraudulently induced Kent to make a note payable to Baker to whom Bond was indebted. Bond delivered the note to Baker. Baker negotiated the instrument to Monk who purchased it with knowledge of the fraud and after it was overdue. If Baker qualifies as a holder in due course, which of the following is correct?

a. Monk can personally qualify as a holder in due course.
b. Monk has the standing of a holder in due course through Baker.

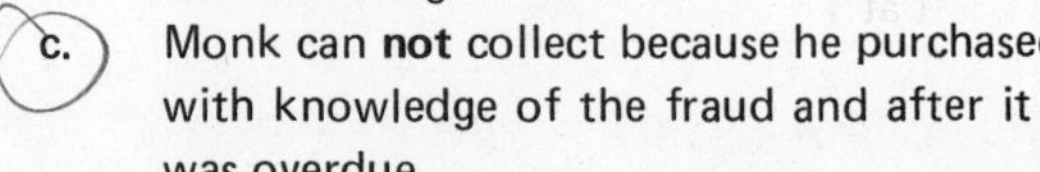

c. Monk can **not** collect because he purchased with knowledge of the fraud and after it was overdue.
d. Kent can successfully assert the defense of fraud against Monk.

45. In connection with a check and a promissory note, which of the following is correct?

a. A promissory note may only be made payable to the order of a named payee.
b. A promissory note may only be payable at a stated time in order to meet the requirements for negotiability.
c. A check may be made payable upon the happening of an event uncertain as to the time of occurrence without affecting its negotiability.
d. A check may be made payable to the order of the drawer or to bearer.

46. A person who endorsed a check "without recourse"

a. Has the same liability as an accommodation endorser.
b. Only negates his liability insofar as prior parties are concerned.
c. Gives the same warranty protection to his transferee as does a special or blank endorser.
d. Does **not** promise or guarantee payment of the instrument upon dishonor even if there has been a proper presentment and proper notice has been given.

47. Unless otherwise agreed, which of the following warranties will **not** be conferred by a person negotiating a negotiable warehouse receipt for value to his immediate purchaser?

a. The document is genuine.
b. The transferor is without knowledge of any fact which would impair its validity or worth.
c. The goods represented by the warehouse receipt are of merchantable quality.
d. Negotiation by the transferor is rightful and fully effective with respect to the title to the document.

November 1985 Questions

48. An instrument complies with the requirements for negotiability contained in the UCC Article on Commercial Paper. The instrument contains language expressly acknowledging the receipt of $40,000 by Mint Bank and an agreement to repay principal with interest at 11% six months from date. The instrument is

a. A banker's acceptance.
b. A banker's draft.
c. A negotiable certificate of deposit.
d. Nonnegotiable because of the additional language.

49. Jane Lane, a sole proprietor, has in her possession several checks which she received from her customers. Lane is concerned about the safety of the checks since she believes that many of them are bearer paper which may be cashed without endorsement. The checks in Lane's possession will be considered order paper rather than bearer paper if they were made payable (in the drawer's handwriting) to the order of

a. Cash.
b. Ted Tint, and endorsed by Ted Tint in blank.
c. Bearer, and endorsed by Ken Kent making them payable to Jane Lane.
d. Bearer, and endorsed by Sam Sole in blank.

50. John Daly received a check which was originally made payable to the order of one of his customers, Al Pine. The following endorsement was written on the back of the check:

Al Pine, without recourse, for collection only

The endorsement on this check would be classified as

a. Blank, unqualified, and nonrestrictive.
b. Blank, qualified, and restrictive.
c. Special, unqualified, and restrictive.
d. Special, qualified, and nonrestrictive.

51. Below is a note which your client Best Realtors obtained from Green in connection with Green's purchase of land located in Rye, NY. The note was given for the balance due on the purchase and was secured by a first mortgage on the land.

$90,000.00 Rye, NY
May 1, 1985

For value received, six years after date, I promise to pay to the order of Best Realtors NINETY THOUSAND and 00/100 DOLLARS with interest at 16% compounded annually until fully paid. This instrument arises out of the sale of land located in NY and the law of NY is to be applied to any question which may arise. It is secured by a first mortgage on the land conveyed. It is further agreed that:

1. Purchaser will pay the costs of collection including attorney's fees upon default.
2. Purchaser may repay the amount outstanding on any anniversary date of this note.

Ted Green
Ted Green

This note is a

a. Negotiable promissory note.
b. Negotiable investment security under the UCC.
c. Nonnegotiable promissory note since it is secured by a first mortgage.
d. Nonnegotiable promissory note since it permits prepayment and requires the maker's payment of the costs of collection and attorney's fees.

52. Frey paid Holt $2,500 by check pursuant to an agreement between them whereby Holt promised to perform in Frey's theater within the next year. Holt endorsed the check, making it payable to Len Able. Holt's status with regard to the check was one of a(n)

a. Assignee since a payee may **not** also be a holder in due course.
b. Holder since Holt's promise failed to satisfy the value requirement necessary to become a holder in due course.
c. Holder in due course under the shelter rule since Able's rights as a holder in due course revert to Holt.
d. Holder in due course since all the requirements have been satisfied.

53. Blue is a holder of a check which was originally drawn by Rush and made payable to Silk. Silk properly endorsed the check to Field. Field had the check certified by the drawee bank and then endorsed the check to Blue. As a result

a. Field is discharged from liability.
b. Rush alone is discharged from liability.
c. The drawee bank becomes primarily liable and both Silk and Rush are discharged.
d. Rush is secondarily liable.

54. Ore Corp. sold 10 tons of steel to Bay Corp. with payment to be by Bay's check. Since the price of steel was fluctuating daily, Ore requested that the amount of Bay's check be left blank and it would fill in the current market price. Bay complied with Ore's request. Within two days Ore received Bay's check. Although the market price of 10 tons of steel at the time Ore received Bay's check was $40,000, Ore filled in the check for $50,000 and negotiated it to Cam Corp. Cam took the check in good faith, without notice of Ore's act or any other defense, and in payment of an antecedent debt. Bay will

a. Be liable to Cam for $50,000.
b. Be liable to Cam but only for $40,000.
c. Not be liable to Cam since the check was materially altered by Ore.
d. Not be liable to Cam since Cam failed to give value when it acquired the check from Ore.

Repeat Questions

(1185,L1,38) Identical to item 4 above

(1185,L1,41) Identical to item 15 above

Problems

Problem 1 (1183,L2b)

(7 to 10 minutes)

Part b. Hardy & Company was encountering financial difficulties. Melba, a persistent creditor whose account was overdue, demanded a check for the amount owed to him. Hardy's president said that this was impossible since the checking account was already overdrawn. However, he indicated he would be willing to draw on funds owed by one of the company's customers. He drafted and presented to Melba the following instrument.

> October 1, 1983
>
> TO:
> Stitch Fabrications, Inc.
> 2272 University Avenue
> Pueblo, Colorado 81001
>
> Pay Hardy & Company, ONE THOUSAND and no/100 dollars ($1,000.00) 30 days after acceptance, for value received in connection with our shipment of August 11, 1983.
>
> Hardy & Company
>
> by Charles Hardy, President
>
> 242 Oak Lane Drive
> Hinsdale, Illinois 60521
>
> Accepted by: ______________

Hardy endorsed the instrument on the back as follows:

> Pay to the order of Walter Melba
>
> Hardy & Company
>
> Charles Hardy, President

Melba asserts that he is a holder in due course.

Required:

Answer the following, setting forth reasons for any conclusions stated.

1. What type of instrument is the above? How and in what circumstances is it used?
2. Is it negotiable?
3. Assume that the instrument is negotiable and accepted by Stitch, but prior to payment, Stitch discovers the goods are defective. May Stitch successfully assert this defense against Melba to avoid payment of the instrument?

Problem 2 (581,L2)

(15 to 20 minutes)

Part a. Oliver gave Morton his 90-day negotiable promissory note for $10,000 as a partial payment for the purchase of Morton's business. Morton had submitted materially false unaudited financial statements to Oliver in the course of establishing the purchase price of the business. Morton also made various false statements about the business' value. For example, he materially misstated the size of the backlog of orders. Morton promptly negotiated the note to Harrison who purchased it in good faith for $9,500, giving Morton $5,000 in cash, a check for $3,500 payable to him which he indorsed in blank and an oral promise to pay the balance within 5 days. Before making the final payment to Morton, Harrison learned of the fraudulent circumstances under which the negotiable promissory note for $10,000 had been obtained. Morton has disappeared and the balance due him was never paid. Oliver refuses to pay the note.

Required:

Answer the following, setting forth reasons for any conclusions stated.

In the subsequent suit brought by Harrison against Oliver, who will prevail?

Part b. McCarthy, a holder in due course, presented a check to the First National Bank, the drawee bank named on the face of the instrument. The signature of the drawer, Williams, was forged by Nash who took the check from the bottom of Williams' check book along with a cancelled check in the course of burglarizing Williams' apartment. The bank examined the signature of the drawer carefully, but the signature was such an artful forgery of the drawer's signature that only a handwriting expert could have detected a difference. The bank therefore paid the check. The check was promptly returned to Williams, but he did not discover the forgery until thirteen months after the check was returned to him.

Required:

Answer the following, setting forth reasons for any conclusions stated.

1. Williams seeks to compel the bank to credit his account for the loss. Will he prevail?
2. The facts are the same as above, but you are to assume that the bank discovered the forgery before returning the check to Williams and credited his account. Can the bank in turn collect from McCarthy the $1,000 paid to McCarthy?
3. Would your answers to 1 and 2 above be modified if the forged signature was that of the payee or an indorser rather than the signature of the drawer?

Problem 3 (583,L5a)

(7 to 10 minutes)

Part a. Dunhill fraudulently obtained a negotiable promissory note from Beeler by misrepresentation of a material fact. Dunhill subsequently negotiated the note to Gordon, a holder in due course. Pine, a business associate of Dunhill, was aware of the fraud perpetrated by Dunhill. Pine purchased the note for value from Gordon. Upon presentment, Beeler has defaulted on the note.

Required:

Answer the following, setting forth reasons for any conclusions stated.

1. What are the rights of Pine against Beeler?
2. What are the rights of Pine against Dunhill?

Multiple Choice Answers

1.	d	12.	b	23.	a	34.	c	45.	d
2.	b	13.	a	24.	c	35.	b	46.	d
3.	b	14.	a	25.	a	36.	d	47.	c
4.	b	15.	a	26.	c	37.	a	48.	c
5.	d	16.	a	27.	c	38.	a	49.	c
6.	c	17.	a	28.	c	39.	b	50.	b
7.	a	18.	b	29.	a	40.	a	51.	a
8.	c	19.	b	30.	b	41.	c	52.	b
9.	b	20.	a	31.	d	42.	a	53.	c
10.	a	21.	d	32.	b	43.	d	54.	a
11.	d	22.	c	33.	c	44.	b		

Multiple Choice Answer Explanations

B. Types of Negotiable Instruments

1. (584,L1,36) (d) A foreign draft is merely a draft which on its face is either drawn or payable outside the United States. Four types of negotiable instruments are included in the term "commercial paper"—drafts, checks, certificates of deposit, and notes—and are accordingly governed by Article 3 of the UCC. Answers (a) and (b) are incorrect because documents of title and investment securities, even though sometimes negotiable, do not qualify as commercial paper and are not governed by Article 3 of the UCC. Answer (c) is incorrect because foreign currency is money and, therefore, does not qualify as commercial paper. Commercial paper provides a medium of exchange in lieu of money.

2. (584,L1,37) (b) A draft is an instrument where the drawer orders the drawee to pay a stated sum of money to the payee. Thus, the draft has three parties present and contains an order. A trade acceptance is a draft drawn by the seller of goods on the buyer and is made payable to the seller. A bond is a two-party instrument that contains a promise. The same would be true of a demand promissory note. A certificate of deposit is an acknowledgement by a bank of receipt of money with a promise to repay. It is a specialized form of a note. Therefore, answers (a), (c), and (d) are incorrect.

C. Requirements of Negotiability

3. (1184,L1,50) (b) In order to be a negotiable instrument, it must be payable at a definite time. If an instrument is payable six months after the death of the drawer, it is not payble at a definite time and hence is not a negotiable instrument. Answer (a) is incorrect because the instrument's negotiability will not be destroyed by a promise to provide additional collateral if there is a decrease in value of the existing collateral. Answer (c) is incorrect because an acceleration clause will not destroy the instrument's negotiability as long as there is a definite time for payment. Answer (d) is incorrect because an instrument may be postdated and still be negotiable as long as it is payable at a definite time.

4. (584,L1,38) (b) The requirements in order for an instrument to qualify as negotiable commercial paper permit some substitution or variance from the literal language of the UCC. Answer (a) is incorrect because the requirements in order for an instrument to qualify as negotiable commercial paper are much more extensive than the requirements for a bill of lading (Article 7 of the UCC). Answer (c) is incorrect because the face of the instrument must contain the nine requirements of negotiability as listed by Article 3 of the UCC, regardless of any provision on the instrument stating that it is to be considered negotiable. A statement to this effect has no impact whatsoever on the negotiability of the instrument. Answer (d) is incorrect because the requirements for negotiability cannot be waived by the parties to the instrument.

5. (584,L1,39) (d) The instrument meets all of the requirements needed for a negotiable instrument. It is a two-party instrument containing an unconditional promise to pay a stated sum and consequently, is a negotiable promissory note. It is a bearer note because it is payable to the order of cash. The designation of the place of payment does not affect the negotiability of an instrument. The negotiable aspect of an instrument is not affected by a provision on the face of the instrument that states security is given for the instrument. Therefore, answers (a) and (b) are incorrect. Answer (c) is incorrect because a negotiable instrument is negotiable immediately after it has been issued.

6. (1182,L1,41) (c) This instrument is nonnegotiable since it gives Smalley the option to take stock instead of cash. A negotiable promissory note must be payable only in money. The provision granting the payee the option to select stock as a second medium of payment would destroy the negotiable aspect of the instrument since it is possible to pay this instrument in something besides money. Therefore, answer (b) is incorrect. Answer (a) is incorrect because an investment security would not contain a promise to pay a sum certain in money. Answer (d) is incorrect because even though the instrument is nonnegotiable, Smalley could assign the instrument. Such a transfer would be governed by the law of assignments, not Article 3 of the UCC.

7. (582,L1,35) (a) The negotiable instrument in question is a draft payable on demand. If an instrument has no stated time for payment it is payable on demand. Answer (b) is incorrect because the instrument is a three-party instrument containing an order (a draft). A note is a two-party instrument that contains a promise. Answer (c) is incorrect because Souther is the drawee, not the drawer. Also, a drawer is secondarily liable on the instrument. This means the holder must first present the instrument to the drawee, the instrument must be dishonored and notice of dishonor must be given to the drawer before his secondary liability comes into effect. Answer (d) is incorrect because Souther, as the drawee, would have no liability on the instrument until he accepted the draft and then he would have primary liability.

8. (582,L1,43) (c) Generally, if an instrument contains a promise to do any act in addition to the payment of money, it is nonnegotiable. An exception to this rule occurs when the additional promise concerns providing security for the instrument. Granting to the holder an option to purchase land is an additional promise that does not concern the providing of security. Consequently, this second promise would destroy the negotiable aspect of the instrument. Answer (a) is incorrect because an instrument that is payable in foreign currency is considered to be a sum certain in money even though the exchange rate might fluctuate from day to day. Answer (b) is incorrect because a negotiable instrument may be made payable at a definite time subject to acceleration at the option of the holder. Answer (d) is incorrect because a negotiable instrument must contain an unconditional promise or order. Normally a promise or order is conditional if the instrument states that it is to be paid only out of a particular fund. However, there is an exception to the particular fund rule that allows a partnership to issue a negotiable instrument that limits payment to the entire assets of the partnership.

E. Negotiation

9. (584,L1,42) (b) In order for someone in possession of a negotiable instrument to qualify as a holder, it is necessary that he receive the instrument through proper negotiation. Proper negotiation of bearer paper requires nothing more than the mere delivery of the instrument to the holder. Thus, in order to qualify as a holder of bearer paper, all that is necessary is that the transferee must have physical possession of the instrument. Answers (a), (c), and (d) are all incorrect because the requirements that the transferee give value for the instrument, take the instrument before receipt of notice of a defense, and take the instrument in good faith are all requirements in attaining holder in due course status. None of these are necessary requirements in order to be merely a holder of a bearer instrument.

10. (1182,L1,60) (a) If the checks are order instruments, then Apex's indorsement is necessary for proper negotiation. Theft of order paper creates the real defense of forgery, the unauthorized signing of a necessary signature. Consequently, if the checks stolen by Drummond were order instruments, he would have to forge Apex's name to properly negotiate the check, creating the real defense of forgery which would be good against all subsequent holders, including holders in due course. Answer (b) is incorrect because theft of a bearer negotiable instrument creates only a personal defense on the instrument which a holder in due course will defeat. Answer (c) would be incorrect because checks payable to cash would be bearer instruments and theft of such checks creates only a personal defense. Answer (d) is incorrect because the fact Apex was the only party that could have prevented the theft would have no bearing on Apex's right to recover the checks.

11. (582,L1,40) (d) A check must be presented for payment within seven days after indorsement to hold an indorser liable. Answer (a) is incorrect because an instrument is bearer paper if it states it is payable to a named person or bearer and there are no indorsements on the back. Answer (b) is incorrect because Maxwell's blank indorsement converts the instrument from order paper to bearer paper in Howard's possession. A blank indorsement is present when the indorser does not name a specified person in the indorsement as the indorsee. Answer (c) is incorrect because Duffy's indorsement is an example of a special indorsement which creates order paper in Maxwell's possession. Proper negotiation of order paper demands delivery and indorsement. Consequently, Maxwell's signature was necessary for negotiation of the check.

12. (582,L1,42) (b) When an order instrument is transferred for value without indorsement, the transferee has a specifically enforceable right to obtain the transferor's unqualified indorsement. Although the transferee may compel an indorsement, negotiation occurs only when the indorsement is given. Thus Farley's rights as a holder in due course relate to the time the indorsement is made and do not relate back to the time of transfer. If Farley learns of a defense before acquiring the indorsement, she will not qualify as a holder in due course. Therefore, answer (d) is incorrect. Answers (a) and (c) are incorrect because

to be a holder in due course, a person must receive the instrument by negotiation. Since this instrument was an order instrument, proper negotiation would demand delivery and indorsement. Until Farley receives Balquist's indorsement, she is unable to qualify as a holder in due course, instead she is merely an assignee with no better right to payment of the instrument than Balquist.

13. (1181,L1,39) (a) An instrument payable to order and indorsed in blank becomes payable to bearer, i.e., bearer paper. Theft of bearer paper constitutes a personal defense and a holder in due course takes free of all personal defense of any party to the instrument with whom he has not dealt. Therefore, a holder in due course will defeat Filmore's claim to the instrument. In contrast, theft of order paper would constitute a real defense, which a holder in due course would take subject to, since proper negotiation of order paper requires delivery and indorsement, which would necessitate a forgery by the thief. Answer (b) is incorrect because since the instrument is bearer paper, delivery alone would constitute proper negotiation. Answer (c) is incorrect because a holder in due course can acquire better rights than the owner. Answer (d) is incorrect because bearer paper can be converted to order paper by a special indorsement. A holder may convert a blank indorsement into a special indorsement by writing above the signature of the indorser any contract consistent with the character of the indorsement (e.g., "pay to the order of . . .").

14. (579,L1,28) (a) If an order instrument is indorsed with a restrictive indorsement, such as "for deposit only," and signed by the payee, then any transferee of the instrument must pay or apply any value given by them for the instrument consistent with the restrictive indorsement. Answer (b) is incorrect because a subsequent holder in due course who cashes the check for Alcatraz would not be acting in a manner consistent with the restrictive indorsement and would therefore not prevail against Johnson. Answer (c) is incorrect because restrictive indorsements that attempt to prevent further transfer or negotiation are of no effect. Answer (d) is incorrect because when a restrictive indorsement is placed on an instrument, all subsequent transferees must comply with the restriction in paying value for the instrument. Alcatraz would have notice that the indorsement was not complied with if the check was not held by a bank.

F. Holder in Due Course

15. (1184,L1,51) (a) Transfer of an instrument vests in the transferee such rights as the transferor has in the instrument. Therefore, Sample has the right to assert Cox's rights and his standing as a holder in due course. Also, any transfer for value of an order instrument gives the transferee the right to obtain an unqualified endorsement of the transferor. Thus, Sample may demand Cox's signature. Answer (b) is incorrect since Block's endorsement was a special endorsement; it created order paper, and Cox's signature was necessary for proper negotiation. Answer (c) is incorrect because Sample is not a holder of the instrument, much less a holder in due course, until he receives Cox's signature. Answer (d) is incorrect because Cox taking the instrument for an antecedent debt constitutes taking the instrument for value, which is a requirement for qualifying as a holder in due course.

16. (584,L1,43) (a) According to Article 3 of the UCC, in order for a holder to achieve holder in due course status, he must give executed value in exchange for the negotiable instrument. Future consideration is not considered to be adequate value in determining whether a person is a holder in due course. The consideration must be performed to qualify as executed value. Answer (b) is incorrect because the taking of a negotiable instrument as security for a loan will constitute executed value in determining whether a holder is a holder in due course. In this situation the holder will be deemed to have given value to the extent of the debt being secured. Answer (c) is incorrect because the exchange of one negotiable instrument for another constitutes the giving of executed value in determining whether a person is a holder in due course. Answer (d) is incorrect since the negotiable instrument is being given in exchange for services which have already been performed; thus, executed value in the form of completed services has been given in exchange for the instrument.

17. (1180,L1,1) (a) The correct answer is (a) since the payee is the only holder who can meet the requirements of a holder in due course. A holder in due course must be a holder who gives executed value for the instrument (cannot be a gift). The holder in due course may have no knowledge of the fact that the instrument (principal only) is overdue nor knowledge of any defense on the instrument when he or she receives it. A holder in due course must also take the instrument in good faith. Answer (b) is incorrect since a holder who does not qualify as a holder in due course cannot better his rights by transferring the instrument through a HIDC. Answer (c) is incorrect because the holder failed to give value. The holder in answer (d) cannot qualify as HIDC since he has knowledge of a defense, but the holder does receive the rights of a HIDC since he acquired the instrument through a HIDC.

18. (580,L1,22) (b) Under the law of commercial paper to qualify as a holder in due course, the holder must have no knowledge that the instrument is overdue. A check is considered overdue if outstanding more than 30 days after issue. All other demand instruments are overdue after a reasonable time has elapsed, or if the holder is aware demand has been made for payment. Consequently, the only incorrect statement among the four answers is (b). Therefore, answers (a), (c), and (d) are incorrect.

19. (1177,L3,37) (b) In ascertaining value given by a bank, FIFO is used. In this case the bank has given value of $500. While the bank credited Ajax's account for $550, Ajax only spent $500. Answer (a) is incorrect because a $50 discount is not so great to affect good faith on a one-year note. Answer (c) is incorrect because Broadway has liability to the extent the bank is a holder in due course because nondelivery is a personal defense. Answer (d) is incorrect because as maker of a note, Broadway has primary liability.

G. Rights of a Holder in Due Course

20. (1184,L1,52) (a) Execution of the instrument by one without authority to sign constitutes forgery, which is a real defense and valid against a holder in due course. Answers (b), (c), and (d) are incorrect because fraud in the inducement, ordinary duress, and failure of a condition precedent are all personal defenses which are not valid against a holder in due course.

21. (584,L1,44) (d) A holder in due course takes a negotiable instrument subject only to the real defenses of that instrument. The assertion of any personal defense against a holder in due course will be unsuccessful. Since the discharge of the maker of an instrument in bankruptcy proceedings is a real defense, this defense can be successfully asserted against a holder in due course, thereby destroying the holder's right to collect on the instrument. The unauthorized completion of an incomplete instrument, the breach of a contractual obligation, and fraudulent misrepresentations are all merely personal defenses which could not be successfully asserted against a holder in due course. Consequently, answers (a), (b), and (c) are all incorrect.

G.3.b. Material Alterations of Instrument

22. (1182,L1,43) (c) Bay, as a holder in due course, took the instrument free of all personal defenses but would be unable to defeat real defenses present on the instrument. Fraud in the inducement is a personal defense which would not be good against Bay. However, Dodger materially altered the check which creates a personal defense to the extent of the original tenor of the check ($900) and a real defense to the extent the instrument was altered ($1000). Consequently, Bay will prevail against Tell to the extent of $900. Answer (a) is incorrect because Dodger, being the party who materially altered the check, would have no defense to payment of this instrument. Answer (b) is incorrect because a customer (i.e., drawer) has the right to order his/her bank to stop payment of an item if the order is received at such time and in such manner as to afford the bank a reasonable opportunity to act on it prior to payment. Therefore, it would not matter that Tell's stop payment order was issued after the negotiation to Bay. Answer (d) is incorrect because normally a holder has no right to compel payment of a check by the drawee bank. This is true even though a stop payment order has not been issued by the drawer. Only when the bank has certified the check can the holder compel payment by the drawee bank.

23. (1181,L1,42) (a) Unauthorized completion of an incomplete instrument and lack of delivery are personal defenses. Thus, Good Luck, a holder in due course, takes the instrument free of these personal defenses and may enforce it as completed. Answer (b) is incorrect because a payor bank which pays an instrument which was completed in an unauthorized manner may charge the drawer's account for the face value of the instrument, except where the bank knows that the completion was improper. Answer (c) is incorrect because lack of delivery is a personal defense. Forgery, a real defense, is not present because the party who stole the instrument was Dilworth, the named payee. Answer (d) is incorrect because Excelsior will bear the loss with regard to both Good Luck and the bank, regardless of Excelsior's negligence. The loss should fall upon the party whose conduct left the instrument incomplete and made the unauthorized completion possible.

H. Liability of Parties

24. (584,L1,41) (c) A qualified indorsement eliminates all contractual liability of the indorsing party. Thus, since Nix & Co. indorsed the instrument in a qualified manner (without recourse), they will have no contractual liability. Answer (a) is incorrect because when an indorsement appears on a negotiable instrument without apparent reason (i.e., indorsement which is not in the chain of title), it is assumed that the indorsing party is an accommodation party. The presence of an accommodation party does not prevent further negotiation of an instrument. Answer (b) is incorrect because the blank indorsement of order paper

changes the instrument from order paper to bearer paper. Answer (d) is incorrect because a restrictive indorsement does not prevent any further negotiation of the instrument.

25. (584,L1,45) (a) Certification by a bank constitutes an acceptance of the check. Upon the writing of a draft, no party to the draft has primary liability although the drawer and indorsers have secondary liability. Only after a draft has been accepted by the drawee does any party have primary liability with regard to the draft. Upon certification of a check, the bank has accepted the check and is, in effect, stating that it agrees to pay the check according to its terms. The bank's liability with regard to the check changes from no liability to primary liability upon certification. If any party other than the drawer requests certification of the check, the secondary liability of the drawer and all prior indorsers is destroyed. Therefore, answer (d) is incorrect. Answer (b) is incorrect because if certification is obtained by the drawer, the drawer's secondary liability remains intact. Only when certification is obtained by another party is the drawer's secondary liability destroyed. Answer (c) is incorrect because a bank is not obligated to certify a customer's check upon demand by the holder, even though sufficient funds are present in the drawer's account.

26. (1182,L1,38) (c) When Haskin negotiated the check with an unqualified indorsement, he extended contractual liability. Under the concept of contractual liability, the indorser guarantees payment of the instrument if the appropriate party for payment dishonors the instrument. Consequently, if there was proper presentment and notice given, Carlson may recover from Haskin when the bank dishonored the check. Answer (a) is incorrect because the fact that Kirk is insolvent does not create a real defense. If Kirk had been discharged from the debt in a bankruptcy proceeding, Kirk would then be able to assert a real defense that would be good against the holder in due course. The issuance of a check does not act as an assignment of the funds held in the bank, nor does it create a security interest on the part of the holder of the instrument. Therefore, answers (b) and (d) are incorrect.

27. (582,L1,41) (c) The instrument is a negotiable draft payable on demand and Ensign is a holder. Although Mason and Adams are the only parties to this instrument it qualifies as a draft (a three-party instrument) because Mason is both the drawer and the payee. The drawee on the instrument is Adams Wholesalers, who is primarily liable on the draft after accepting the instrument. Before acceptance, Adams had no liability on the draft. Mason, the payee and indorser, is secondarily liable on the instrument. No party would have primary liability until acceptance by the drawee. Therefore, answers (a), (b) and (d) are incorrect.

28. (1180,L1,5) (c) The correct answer is (c) since the bank is only liable to the drawer if failure to obey stop payment order caused the drawer a loss. Since Smith has no grounds for rescinding the sale, the Union Trust bank has no liability. Answer (a) is incorrect since a payee has no right to compel payment of a check by drawee bank. There is no privity of contract between the payee and drawee bank. Answer (b) is incorrect because the stop payment order can be oral or written. An oral order is effective for 14 days and a written order is effective for 6 months. A stop payment order does not destroy the drawer's liability on the instrument unless he has a valid defense, therefore, answer (d) is false.

29. (580,L1,19) (a) Normally forgeries of the payee's signature would be sufficient to relieve the defrauded corporations of any liability on these instruments. However, a drawer who voluntarily transfers payment to an imposter (Gomer) must bear the loss if a holder in due course subsequently tries to collect. Therefore, answer (a) is correct. Forgery is usually a real defense that would be good against all subsequent holders in due course but the imposter exception would allow the banks, intermediate parties, and the recipients to avoid the loss. The rationale for such a result is the fact that the defrauded corporations were in the best position to keep the defense (forgery) from occurring.

H.2.c. Warranties

30. (1180,L1,9) (b) Barker, having received value for the instrument, has warranty liability to Chase, the immediate holder. Barker grants five warranties, one of which is that no defense is good on the instrument. Answer (b) is correct since this warranty was breached. If a holder performs the full agreed upon consideration or value promised for the instrument, he is a holder in due course to the face value of the instrument. This makes answer (a) incorrect. Answer (c) is incorrect because Archer's failure to endorse the instrument only extends his warranty liability (including the warranty that states all signatures are genuine) to the immediate holder, Barker. Answer (d) is incorrect since Harding is liable for the forgery he placed on the instrument.

31. (580,L1,15) (d) Corner Check Cashing Company must bear the loss because as a holder obtaining payment, it warrants that it has good title to the instrument. However, it does not have good title because the forgery prevented good title from passing. Therefore answers (a) and (c) are incorrect because of Corner Check Cashing Company's warranty of good title. Answer (b) is incorrect because Duval has a real defense in that his indorsement was forged. Corner Check Cashing Company's only recourse is to recover from Mask.

32. (580,L1,30) (b) If the drawee bank (Unity Trust Company) pays a check on which the drawer's signature (Markum) was forged, the bank is bound by the acceptance and the drawee can only recover the money paid from the forger (Robb). Normally a person who presents an instrument for payment makes three warranties. These warranties are: warranty of title; warranty of no knowledge that the signature of the drawer is unauthorized; warranty of no material alterations. However, a holder in due course or someone with the rights of a holder in due course does not warrant to the drawee bank that the drawer's signature is genuine because the drawer bank is in a better position to determine the genuineness of the drawer's signature. Therefore, the drawee bank should bear the loss.

K. Transfer of Negotiable Documents of Title

33. (584,L1,46) (c) Normally a warehouseman is not allowed to commingle goods of one bailor with those of another. However, in the case of fungible goods, warehousemen may commingle similar fungible goods of different bailors. Answer (a) is incorrect because a bailee may limit his liability to a stipulated maximum. To do this the warehouseman must offer the customer a choice of full liability at one rate and limited liability at a lower rate. Answer (b) is incorrect because warehousemen are not absolutely liable for any damages. The warehouseman must exercise ordinary care and is only liable for damages that could have been avoided through the exercise of due care. Answer (d) is incorrect because in the event that a bailor refuses to pay any storage charges due, a warehouseman has a lien against the goods to the extent of storage charges due and, as a result, can refuse to deliver the goods to the bailee.

34. (1183,L1,47) (c) A document of title procured by a thief upon placing stolen goods in a warehouse confers no rights in the underlying goods. This defense is valid against a subsequent holder to whom the document of title has been duly negotiated. Therefore, Valley Instruments, the original owner of the goods, can assert better title to the goods than Reliable Finance. Accordingly, answers (a) and (d) are incorrect. Answer (b) is incorrect because Reliable Finance will be the ultimate loser, assuming Reliable is unable to collect from the thieves.

35. (583,L1,43) (b) Due negotiation of a negotiable document of title occurs when it is negotiated to a holder who takes in good faith, in the ordinary course of business, without notice of any defenses against the document, and pays value for the document. In the area of negotiable documents of title, which is governed by Article 7 of the UCC, value does not include payment of an antecedent debt. This is an important difference from the value concept required to create a holder in due course under Article 3. Answer (a) is incorrect because the transfer of a bearer contract (a document of title containing a blank endorsement is a bearer document) by delivery alone will not prevent due negotiation since a bearer document requires no endorsement for negotiation. Answer (c) is incorrect because delivery of a bearer document from one who lacks title will not prevent due negotiation. However, delivery of an order document from someone without title does prevent due negotiation. Answer (d) is incorrect because a document of title, unlike a check, is not considered overdue 30 days after issue.

L. Transfer of Investment Securities

36. (1183,L1,48) (d) The Uniform Commercial Code defines an investment security as written evidence of debt, ownership, or other legal interest in a business which is issued in bearer or registered form and traded in markets or on securities exchanges as a medium of investment. Answer (a) is, therefore, incorrect. Answer (b) is incorrect because an investment security does not have to be of a long-term nature. Answer (c) is incorrect because an investment security may be either a secured or unsecured obligation.

37. (583,L1,46) (a) The given instrument is a debenture bond that is a negotiable investment security. Dwight, as a bona fide purchaser (received through proper negotiation, gave value, took in good faith and without notice of any adverse claim), acquires the security free of adverse title claims. Answer (b) is incorrect because the registration requirement for transfer would not affect the negotiable nature of the security, nor the rights of a bona fide purchaser. Answer (c) is incorrect because the instrument is a negotiable investment security governed by Article 8 of the UCC, not a negotiable instrument governed by Article 3. Answer (d) is incorrect because the word " assigns" is an acceptable substitute for the words of negotiability.

38. (582,L1,44) (a) An unauthorized signature placed on a stock certificate is effective in favor of a purchaser for value of the certificated security, if the purchaser is without notice of the lack of authority of the signing party and the signing has been done by an employee of the issuer entrusted with the responsible handling of the stock certificate. Therefore, the certificate is valid and the investor is entitled to a reissued certificate without having to further compensate the issuer, Sims Corporation. Answer (c) is incorrect because the investor is not entitled to sue the clerk for a criminal action; the criminal prosecution for the crime of forgery must be brought by the appropriate governmental state or federal authority.

39. (582,L1,45) (b) A person, by transferring a certificated security to a purchaser for value, warrants only that: (1) his transfer is effective and rightful; (2) the security is genuine and has not been materially altered; and (3) he knows of no fact which might impair the validity of the security. Therefore, since Wilberforce took the securities for value, he is entitled to assert any one of these three warranties against his transferor, Dunlop. The distinction between answer (c) and the third aforementioned warranty is that Dunlop only warrants that he has no knowledge of a defect which might impair the securities' validity, not that there is no defect.

May 1985 Answers

40. (585,L1,33) (a) The instrument is a negotiable draft since it meets all of the requirements of a negotiable instrument and is a three-party instrument which contains an order on its face. Olympia Sales Corp. is the drawer, New City Bank is the drawee, and Donald Kerr is the payee. It is specifically a negotiable time draft since it is payable at some future, determinable time (60 days after date). Answer (b) is incorrect because a check is a form of a draft which is drawn on a bank and payable on demand. The instrument presented is not payable on demand but is payable 60 days after date. Answer (c) is incorrect because a promissory note involves only two parties, a maker and a payee, and contains a promise on its face. Answer (d) is incorrect because this instrument is not a trade acceptance since it is not drawn on and accepted by the buyer.

41. (585,L1,34) (c) One of the requirements for negotiability is that the instrument be payable on demand or at a definite time. An instrument which by its terms is payable only upon an act or event, uncertain as to time of occurrence, is not payable at a definite time. The instrument presented is not payable on demand, and its payment rests upon an event which is uncertain as to time of occurrence; therefore it is not negotiable. Answer (a) is incorrect since the instrument was given as part of the purchase price to be exchanged for Jason's business. Thus, the business is consideration for the instrument. Also there is no requirement that an instrument must be issued for consideration to be negotiable. Answer (b) is incorrect because a negotiable instrument may recite the transaction which gave rise to it without destroying its negotiability, so long as the payment of the instrument is not "subject to" or conditioned upon performance of the recited agreement. Answer (d) is incorrect since this instrument is nonnegotiable as discussed above.

42. (585,L1,35) (a) An unauthorized completion of an incomplete instrument is a personal defense, and as such, will not be good against a holder in due course. Answers (b), (c), and (d) are incorrect because extreme duress, infancy (unless instrument is exchanged for necessities), and the discharge of a maker in bankruptcy are all real defenses which will be good against a holder in due course.

43. (585,L1,36) (d) The instrument meets all of the requirements needed for negotiability. It is a two-party instrument that contains a promise and is consequently, a negotiable promissory note. The statements listed at the bottom of the note do not destroy its negotiability. The reference to all implied and constructive conditions does not affect the negotiability of the instrument; only when payment of an instrument is expressly conditioned on its face is the negotiability destroyed. The reference to the security provided by a first mortgage does not destroy the note's negotiability since a negotiable instrument may contain a second promise (another promise besides the unconditional promise to pay a sum certain in money) if the second promise provides security for the instrument. The third statement stating that the note is to be paid out of funds deposited in the City Bank of Wabash is merely a bookkeeping notation. Negotiability would only be destroyed in this type of situation if the language were stronger (e.g., "To be paid out of only those funds deposited in the City Bank of Wabash."). Thus answers (a) and (b) are incorrect. Answer (c) is incorrect since the words "value received" and a recitation of the underlying transaction are not requirements of negotiability.

44. (585,L1,37) (b) A person who takes a negotiable instrument from a holder in due course acquires the rights of a holder in due course under the Shelter Provision. Monk, because he knew of the fraud committed by Bond, could not qualify personally as a holder in due course. However under the Shelter Provision since Monk took the note from a holder in due course, s/he has the rights of a holder in due course. Answer (a) is incorrect because as discussed above, Monk cannot qualify as a holder in due course since s/he had knowledge of the fraud underlying the instrument. Answer (c) is incorrect since, as discussed above, Monk has the rights of a holder in due course. Answer (d) is incorrect because, since Monk has the rights of a holder in due course, a personal defense such as fraud in the inducement will not bar his/her recovery on the instrument.

45. (585,L1,38) (d) A check may be made payable to the order of the drawer or to bearer. Answer (a) is incorrect because a note may be made payable to bearer. Answer (b) is incorrect since a promissory note may be made payable on demand and still retain its negotiability. Answer (c) is incorrect because the negotiability of a check is destroyed if it is made payable upon the happening of an event uncertain as to the time of occurrence.

46. (585,L1,39) (d) A person who endorsed a negotiable instrument (without recourse) has engaged in a qualified endorsement. Such an endorsement destroys the endorser's contractual liability, (i.e., the endorser does not promise payment of the instrument upon dishonor). Answer (a) is incorrect because an accommodating party is liable in the position that the party signs the instrument. As an accommodating endorser, the person would have contractual liability, (i.e., guarantees payment upon dishonor). Answer (b) is incorrect because an endorser only has liability to subsequent holders and a qualified endorsement negates this liability. Answer (c) is incorrect because a qualified endorser receiving consideration only warrants that s/he has no knowledge of any defense good against the instrument, while a special or blank endorser for consideration warrants that no defense of any party is good against the instrument. All other warranties extended by a qualified endorser are the same as those extended by a blank or special endorser.

47. (585,L1,40) (c) A person who negotiates a negotiable document of title for value extends the following warranties to his immediate purchaser: (1) the document is genuine, (2) the transferor is without knowledge of any fact which would impair its validity or worth, (3) negotiation by the transferor is rightful and fully effective with respect to the title to the document. However, such a transferor does not necessarily guarantee that the goods represented by the document are of merchantable quality. A merchant seller of goods grants such an implied warranty under Article 2 of the UCC. Therefore answers (a), (b), and (d) are incorrect.

November 1985 Answers

48. (1185,L1,36) (c) The instrument in question is a certificate of deposit since it meets all of the requirements of a negotiable instrument (explicitly stated in the question) and is a written acknowledgement by a bank of receipt of money with a promise to repay. Answer (a) is incorrect because a banker's acceptance is a type of draft drawn by a party (creditor) against his or her bank (debtor). Answer (b) is incorrect because a banker's draft is a check drawn by a bank on another bank. Answer (d) is incorrect because the question explicitly states that the instrument is negotiable and the additional language would not affect the instrument's negotiability.

49. (1185,L1,37) (c) If the last endorsement on a negotiable instrument is a special endorsement, the instrument is order paper. A special endorsement specifies the person to whom or to whose order it makes the instrument payable. Answer (a) is incorrect because a check made payable to the order of cash is bearer paper. Answers (b) and (d) are incorrect because a check endorsed in blank is bearer paper.

50. (1185,L1,39) (b) The endorsement in question is a blank, qualified, restrictive endorsement. The endorsement is blank because it does not specify the person to whom the instrument is payable. The endorsement is qualified because the words "with recourse" are present, thus disclaiming contract liability if the instrument is dishonored. The endorsement is restrictive because it restricts payment to a specific condition. Answers (a), (c), and (d) are incorrect because they fail to correctly identify one or more of the endorsement characteristics.

51. (1185,L1,40) (a) The instrument in question is a promissory note that contains all the requirements of negotiability per Article 3 of the UCC. A promissory note is a two-party instrument in which the maker promises to pay a sum certain in money to the payee. Answer (b) is incorrect because a negotiable investment security is a median for investment that evidences a share or other interest in property per Article 8 of

the UCC. Answer (c) is incorrect because stating the security given for the note does not affect the promissory note's negotiability. Answer (d) is incorrect because provisions for prepayment by the purchaser and certain additions to the sum certain (such as costs of collection and attorney's fees) do not affect the promissory note's negotiability. The instrument is still payable at a definite time and contains a sum certain in money.

52. (1185,L1,42) (b) For a holder of a negotiable instrument to become a holder in due course (HIDC), the holder must take the instrument for executed value, in good faith, and without knowledge of any defense or claim on the instrument. Since Holt's promise to perform did not constitute executed value, Holt does not qualify as a HIDC. Holt can only be a holder. Answer (a) is incorrect because a payee can qualify as a HIDC. Answer (c) is incorrect because the shelter rule does not transfer the rights of a HIDC to prior holders, but to individuals who hold the instrument after it has been held by a HIDC. Answer (d) is incorrect because all of the requirements of a HIDC (specifically giving executed value) have not been met.

53. (1185,L1,43) (c) When a holder obtains certification of a check, the drawer and all prior endorsers are discharged from secondary liability and the bank alone becomes primarily liable. Since Field (a holder) had the bank certify the check, Silk (the payee) and Rush (the drawer) are discharged and the bank becomes primarily liable. Answer (a) is incorrect because the holder who had the check certified (Field) is not relieved of any liability. Answer (b) is incorrect because Silk, as the payee and a prior holder, is also discharged by the certification. Answer (d) is incorrect because certification of a check by a holder discharges the drawer (Rush) of secondary liability.

54. (1185,L1,44) (a) When a check is completed through the negligence of the drawer, the defense created on the instrument is the personal defense of unauthorized completion, not the real defense of material alteration. Since Bay was negligent to send an incomplete check to Ore, the personal defense created was unauthorized completion. Cam, as a holder in due course (HIDC) who took the check for executed value and without knowledge of the unauthorized completion, can defeat the personal defense and receive the full $50,000 from Bay. Therefore, answers (b) and (c) are incorrect. Answer (d) is incorrect because Cam gave value for the check acquired from Ore in the form of payment of an antecedent debt. Payment of an antecedent debt qualifies as executed value when determining HIDC status.

Answer Outline

Problem 1 Trade Acceptance; Nonnegotiable Instrument; Holder in Due Course (1183,L2b)

Part b.

1. Instrument is a trade acceptance
   - Used in sales transactions, allowing seller to draw upon buyer for payment of goods
   - Seller is both drawer and payee
2. No, instrument lacks words of negotiability
   - Endorsement does not cure defect on face of instrument
3. No, Melba will prevail since he is a holder in due course
   - Discharging antecedent debt constitutes giving value for instrument
   - Holder in due course takes free of personal defenses
     - I.e., breach of warranty and contractual defenses

Unofficial Answer

Problem 1 Trade Acceptance; Nonnegotiable Instrument; Holder in Due Course (1183,L2b)

Part b.

1. The instrument in question is a draft and is commonly known as a trade acceptance. Such an instrument arises out of a sales transaction, whereby the seller is authorized to draw upon the purchaser for payment of the goods. Normally, as is the case here, the seller is both the drawer and the payee. The instrument is then presented for the buyer's acceptance.

2. No. The instrument lacks the magic words of negotiability on its face. That is, it is not payable to order or bearer but instead payable solely to Hardy & Company. The endorsement on the back of the instrument neither cures the defect nor provides the requisite words of negotiability. Hence, the instrument is not negotiable. The "for value received . . ." does not in any way affect negotiability.

3. No. Melba would be a holder in due course. He took in good faith and gave value even though the value in question is an antecedent indebtedness. The Uniform Commercial Code specifically provides that an antecedent indebtedness is value. Therefore, Melba as a holder in due course takes free of the so-called personal defenses. Breach of warranty and contractual defenses are personal defenses and a holder in due course such as Melba is not subject to them.

Answer Outline

Problem 2 Rights of Holder in Due Course; Unauthorized Signatures; Liability of Drawee Bank (581,L2)

a. Harrison will prevail against Oliver
   - Harrison is a holder in due course
     - Instrument is negotiable
     - Harrison holder by negotiation
     - Harrison took in good faith and for value
     - Harrison took without notice of fraudulent procurement
   - Harrison is able to recover to extent of value given ($8,500)
     - Value given to extent agreed consideration has been performed
       - Includes the $5,000 cash given
       - Includes the $3,500 check (i.e., negotiable instrument) given
     - Unperformed promise of $1,000 is executory in nature
       - Does not constitute value given

b1. Williams will not prevail against the bank
   - Williams must exercise reasonable care to examine items returned by the bank
     - So as to discover unauthorized signature or alterations
   - Williams must notify bank promptly after discovery thereof
   - Williams must give notice within one year from the time such item is available to him
     - Or else his claim against the bank is absolutely barred
       - Regardless of negligence of either party

b2. The bank cannot collect the money paid to McCarthy
   - The bank is required to know the signatures of its customers
     - Bank is in superior position to detect forgery
       - Deemed to have such knowledge of drawer's signature
   - Bank is denied recovery from innocent holder, McCarthy, who has, in good faith, received proceeds of a forged instrument

b3. Answer to b1. would be changed to allow Williams to prevail over the bank
- A forged indorsement is ineffective to negotiate an order instrument
  - Bank not entitled to charge drawer's account for payment
- Williams is able to maintain claim against the bank
  - But must give notice of forged indorsement within three years from time item available to Williams
  - Williams precluded from asserting claim if his negligence contributed to the forgery
    - But bank must be free from negligence
- Answer to b2. would be changed to allow the bank to collect from McCarthy
- A forged indorsement is ineffective to negotiate an order instrument
  - Bank is permitted to recover from McCarthy who took under a forged indorsement
    - Bank is not deemed to know genuineness of indorser's signature
  - Bank is able to recover on "breach of warranty" theory
    - McCarthy breached warranty to the bank
      - That he has "good title" to the instrument.

Unofficial Answer

Problem 2 Rights of Holder in Due Course; Unauthorized Signatures; Liability of Drawee Bank (581,L2)

Part a.

Harrison will prevail, but only to the extent of "value," here $8,500, given for the negotiable promissory note. The primary issue in the case is the "value" requirement for holding in due course. The facts reveal that Harrison purchased the instrument in good faith, that it was not overdue, and, at the time the negotiation took place, Harrison had no knowledge of the fraudulent circumstances under which the instrument was originally obtained from Oliver. The facts indicate that the note was negotiable and that the negotiation requirement was satisfied.

The Uniform Commercial Code section dealing with "taking for value" provides that a holder, here Harrison, takes for value to the extent that the agreed consideration has been performed. Certainly the payment of the $5,000 in cash constitutes value. The code further provides that when a holder gives a negotiable instrument for the instrument received, he has given value. Although this provision is primarily concerned with the giving of one's own negotiable instrument, it is obvious that the negotiation of another's negotiable instrument as payment is value. However, the promise to pay an agreed consideration is not value even though it constitutes consideration.

Part b.

1. No. Williams will not prevail. The Uniform Commercial Code imposes upon the depositor the responsibility for reasonable care and promptness in discovering and reporting his unauthorized signature. In any case, the depositor must discover and report his unauthorized signature within one year from the time the items (checks) are made available to him. The latter rule applies irrespective of lack of care on the part of either the bank or depositor. This absolute rule is based in part upon the rationale that, after certain periods of time have elapsed in respect to commercial transactions, finality is the most important factor to be considered. Thus, after this amount of time has elapsed, existing expectations and relations are not to be altered.

2. No. The bank cannot collect from McCarthy. The Uniform Commercial Code places the burden upon the bank to know at its peril the signature of its drawer. Therefore, when the bank has paid on the forged signature of a depositor, it cannot recover the loss by seeking collection from a party who has received payment in good faith.

3. The first answer (b.1.) would be changed in that the law allows the depositor a three-year period in which to discover the forged signature of the payee or an indorser. Thus, if both the bank and depositor are not negligent (as it would appear from the excellence of the forgery), the loss rests with the bank. However, if it can be shown that the depositor was negligent (for example, he disregarded a notice from the proper party that he had not received payment), the bank will prevail if it was in no way negligent.

The restated circumstances also change the second answer (b.2.). A bank is not deemed to know the signatures of indorsers; therefore, the bank may recover its loss from McCarthy, the party collecting on the item. Section 3-417 of the Uniform Commercial Code provides that a party receiving payment on the instrument warrants to the payor that he has good title to the instrument.

Answer Outline

Problem 3 Shelter Rule; Secondary Liability (583,L5a)

Part a.

1. Pine would recover from Beeler
   - Fraud in inducement not valid against holder who has acquired the rights of holder in due course
     - This is shelter rule
2. Pine could recover against Dunhill if he gives notice of dishonor
   - Dunhill's indorsement makes him secondarily liable
     - I.e., he promises to pay if appropriate party does not

Unofficial Answer

Problem 3 Shelter Rule; Secondary Liability (583,L5a)

Part a.

1. Pine is not a holder in due course because he has knowledge of a defense against the note. However, Pine has the rights of a holder in due course because he acquired the note through Gordon, who was a holder in due course. The rule where a transferee not a holder in due course acquires the rights of one by taking from a holder in due course is known as the "shelter rule." Through these rights, Pine is entitled to recover the proceeds of the note from Beeler. The defense of fraud in the inducement is a personal defense and not valid against a holder in due course or one with the rights of a holder in due course.

2. As one with the rights of a holder in due course, Pine is entitled to proceed against any person whose signature appears on the note, provided he gives notice of dishonor. When Dunhill negotiated the note to Gordon, Dunhill's signature on the note made him secondarily liable. As a result, if Pine brings suit against Dunhill, Pine would prevail because of Dunhill's secondary liability.

SECURED TRANSACTIONS

Overview

The concept of secured transactions is important to modern business. A creditor often requires some security from the debtor beyond a mere promise to pay. In general, the creditor may require the debtor to provide some collateral to secure payment on the debt. If the debt is not paid, the creditor then can resort to the collateral. Under Article 9 of the UCC, the collateral is generally personal property or fixtures. You need to understand the concept of attachment. For attachment to occur (1) there must be a security agreement, (2) the secured party must give value, and (3) the debtor must have rights in the collateral used to secure payment.

You also need to understand the important concept of perfection discussed in this module which allows a secured party to obtain greater rights over many third parties. Be sure to understand the three methods by which perfection can be accomplished. The examination also covers rules of priorities when competing interests exist in the same collateral.

A. Scope of Secured Transactions

1. Comes from Article 9 of UCC
   a. CPA exam now tests the 1972 official text of UCC which is covered in this module
2. Applies to transactions in which creditor intends to obtain greater security in debt by taking a security interest in personal property or fixtures (which are used as collateral)
   a. Types of personal property
      1) Tangible personal property (goods)--there are four types
         a) Consumer goods are those for personal, family, or household use
         b) Inventory consists of goods for lease or sale in the ordinary course of business
         c) Equipment consists of goods used primarily in the business
         d) Farm products are livestock, crops, and supplies used in farming
         e) Use of collateral by debtor, not nature of collateral, determines type of tangible personal property

         EXAMPLE: B purchases a refrigerator from S, an appliance dealer, giving S a security interest. If B bought it for home use, it involves consumer goods. If B bought it for use in his restaurant, it is equipment.

         EXAMPLE: In the above example, assume that S borrows from a bank to buy the refrigerators to sell from the appliance store. S gives the bank a security interest in the refrigerators. In the hands of S, the refrigerators are inventory.

10

2) Quasi-tangible personal property (documentary collateral)

a) Represented by piece(s) of paper instead of property

EXAMPLE: Negotiable instruments, non-negotiable instruments, documents of title, bonds, and shares of stock are in this category.

EXAMPLE: One or more writings that together show a monetary obligation as well as a security interest can be used as collateral. These writings are referred to as chattel paper.

3) Intangible personal property

a) Accounts (accounts receivable) not evidenced by a writing

EXAMPLE: The sale of accounts receivable is covered under secured transactions.

b) General intangibles, e.g., copyrights, patents, goodwill

b. Fixtures

1) Former personal property that has been attached to real property in a relatively permanent manner

EXAMPLE: An air conditioning system installed in a home. It is now a fixture.

2) Detachable trade fixtures are considered personal property rather than part of the real property

3. Article 9 of the UCC does not apply

a. If collateral is real property (see Mortgages in PROPERTY)
b. To assignment of wage claims
c. To claims from court proceedings
d. To statutory liens

B. Attachment of Security Interests

1. Upon attachment, security interest is enforceable against debtor and the secured party

a. Has priority over third parties actually aware of security interest
b. Does not have priority over third parties unaware of security interest

2. Security interest is said to attach when all of the following occur in any order (these are important)

a. There is a security agreement
b. Secured party gives value
c. Debtor has rights in collateral

3. Security agreement

   a. Is a contract or agreement that creates a security interest

      1) Secured party is the one in whose favor the security interest exists

         EXAMPLE: A bank makes a loan to D using D's personal jewelry as collateral. The bank is the secured party.

         EXAMPLE: B buys a stereo on credit from S allowing the stereo to be used as collateral for the credit purchase. S, the seller, is the secured party.

   b. May be oral if collateral is in possession of secured party or some other third party by arrangement

      1) Pledge is used to mean debtor gives possession of collateral to other party to secure obligation

         EXAMPLE: D pledges his shares of stock as collateral for a bank loan The bank holds the stock until the loan is paid. This security agreement need not be in writing.

   c. If collateral in possession of debtor, security agreement must

      1) Be in writing
      2) Be signed by debtor
      3) Contain a reasonable description of collateral

4. Value given by secured party

   a. Includes any consideration that supports a contract (see CONTRACTS)
   b. Preexisting claim (although not consideration) is value

      EXAMPLE: D already owes S $5,000 on a previous debt. Subsequently, D signs a security agreement giving S an interest in some furniture owned by D. Value has been given by S based on the previous debt.

      EXAMPLE: A bank grants a loan to allow B to purchase a washer and dryer. This extension of credit is a typical type of value.

5. Debtor must have rights in collateral

   a. Ownership interest or
   b. Some right to possession
   c. Need not have title

      EXAMPLE: M obtains a loan from a bank to purchase a sofa. She signs a security agreement granting the credit union a security interest in any sofa that she will buy with this loan. Attachment cannot occur until she buys a sofa.

C. Perfecting a Security Interest

1. Entails steps in addition to attachment (with one exception, see "C.2.c.") to give secured party priority over many other parties that may claim collateral

a. Attachment focuses primarily on rights between creditor and debtor
b. However, perfection focuses on rights between various other parties that may claim an interest in same collateral

   1) Generally, perfecting a security interest gives (constructive) notice to other parties that perfecting party claims an interest (security interest) in certain collateral

2. Three methods of perfection (know these)

   a. Filing a financing statement

      1) Written notice filed in public records

   b. Secured party (creditor) taking possession of collateral
   c. Perfection on attachment

      1) Under some conditions, once attachment takes place, perfection is automatic with no further steps

3. Filing a financing statement

   a. For all collateral except money and instruments (they must be possessed, see "C.4.")

      1) Only method for contract rights, accounts, and other intangibles (because there is nothing to possess)

   b. Financing statement must

      1) Give names of debtor and creditor
      2) Contain addresses of both
      3) Identify type of or describe collateral

         a) Unlike description in security agreement, it need not identify the specific collateral. It must merely identify the type of collateral.

      4) Be signed by the debtor (secured party need not sign)
      5) The security agreement may suffice as financing if it complies with the above

         a) But a copy of it must be filed as below

   c. Filing

      1) By statute, usually in county recorder's office, Secretary of State, or both

         a) Financing statement covering fixtures or minerals must also be filed in real estate records

      2) Has functional purpose of giving notice to the public of creditor's security interest in the collateral
      3) Lasts for five years and may be continued for another five years (by a continuation statement)
      4) Upon full payment to the creditor, debtor may request a release from the creditor, which the debtor can then file (termination statement)

   d. Filing may be done anytime, even before the security agreement is made. But perfection does not occur until all requirements (of attachment plus filing) are met.

EXAMPLE: Bank is going to finance the inventory of a car dealer who is beginning business. They immediately file a financing statement. When the inventory arrives, they sign a security agreement. Perfection occurs when the security agreement is signed in this case because then all requirements of attachment plus filing have taken place.

EXAMPLE: Same example as above except that the bank obtains the security agreement first, then the inventory arrives, and afterwards the bank files a financing statement. Attachment is effective when the inventory arrives. (Note that the dealer has rights in the inventory at that time.) Perfection in this case is accomplished at the time of filing.

e. Perfection is ineffective if financing statement is improper or if it is filed in wrong place

4. Perfection by possession

   a. Secured party takes possession of collateral
   b. For negotiable instruments, securities, and money, possession is only method allowed for perfection

      1) For other collateral capable of possession, possession may also be used for perfection but of course debtor may not desire losing use during creditor's possession

         EXAMPLE: P wishes to borrow money from a bank using several shares of stock that she owns. In addition to completing the three steps needed for attachment, the bank must possess the shares in order to perfect. Filing is not effective in this case.

   c. Cross reference: When creditor has possession of collateral, an oral security agreement suffices. Furthermore, possession also accomplishes perfection.
   d. Perfection is effective as long as creditor retains possession
   e. While in possession, the secured party

      1) Must use reasonable care to preserve the property
      2) May keep stock dividends, newborn calf, etc. as additional collateral

         a) Dividends, interest, etc. belong to debtor

   f. The debtor (owner)

      1) Must bear any accidental loss to the collateral provided the secured party has used reasonable care

         a) Each party has an insurable interest in the collateral

      2) Is liable for reasonable expenses, e.g., taxes, insurance of the collateral

5. Perfection by attachment (automatic perfection)

   a. Under certain conditions only, perfection is accomplished by completing attachment with no further steps

      1) Purchase money security interest in consumer goods

         a) Purchase money security interest occurs in two important cases

            1] Seller retains a security interest in same item sold on credit to secure payment

            2] Another party such as bank provides loan for and retains security interest in same item purchased by debtor

         b) "In consumer goods" means that goods are bought primarily for personal, family, or household purposes

            EXAMPLE: B buys a refrigerator for his home from Friendly Appliance Dealer on credit. Friendly has B sign a written security agreement. Because all three elements needed for attachment took place, this is automatic perfection. This is true because the refrigerator is a purchase money security interest in consumer goods.

            EXAMPLE: Same as previous example except that Second Intercity Bank provides the loan having B sign a security agreement. This is also a purchase money security interest in consumer goods. Perfection takes place when all three elements of attachment occur.

            EXAMPLE: In the two examples above, if B had purchased the refrigerator for use in a restaurant, the collateral would be equipment. Therefore, automatic perfection would not occur. However, the secured party could file a financing statement to perfect the security interest in both cases.

         c) Perfection by attachment does not occur for motor vehicles--perfected by a lien on certificate of title filed with state

         d) Automatic perfection is not effective against bona fide purchaser for value who buys goods from consumer for consumer use

            1] Is effective, however, if secured party had filed

               EXAMPLE: B purchases a washer and dryer from Dear Appliances for use in his home giving Dear a security interest then sells the washer and dryer to C for a fair price for C's household use. C is unaware of the security interest that Dear has in the washer and dryer. Dear's perfection on attachment is not effective against C.

               EXAMPLE: Same example as above except that Dear had filed a financing statement. Dear wins because filing is effective even against a subsequent bona fide purchaser such as C even if he buys for consumer use.

EXAMPLE: In the two examples above, if C had purchased the items from B for other than consumer use, C is not free of Dear's security interest. This is so because the rule only applies to bona fide purchasers for consumer use. The extra step of filing had no effect in this case.

2] Is effective if subsequent purchaser knows of security interest before buying

EXAMPLE: An appliance dealer sells a freezer to Jack for family use. Assume attachment has occurred. Jack then sells it to Cindy who is aware of the security interest that the dealer still has in the freezer. Even if Cindy is buying this for household use, she takes subject to the security interest.

D. Other Issues under Secured Transactions

1. After-acquired property and future goods may also become part of collateral if agreement so states

EXAMPLE: An agreement states that the collateral consists of all of debtor's furniture now located in his office as well as all office furniture subsequently acquired. The security interest in the new furniture cannot attach until the debtor acquires rights in the other office furniture.

a. Typically used for inventory and accounts receivable when debtor also has rights to sell inventory and collect accounts, i.e., a floating lien

EXAMPLE: A, an automobile dealer, to obtain a loan, grants a bank a security interest covering "all automobiles now possessed and hereafter acquired." As the dealer obtains rights in the new inventory of automobiles, the security interest attaches as to those newly acquired automobiles.

b. Certain restrictions exist if debtor buys consumer goods to protect consumer

2. Security interest continues in identifiable proceeds from sale of secured goods unless security agreement states otherwise

EXAMPLE: Undeposited checks, cash that has not been deposited or commingled, accounts receivable, or new property received in exchange for the collateral are automatically covered by a security agreement.

3. Field warehousing

a. A device used to perfect a security interest in inventory by (in essence) possession

1) The inventory is kept on debtor's premises but under the control of a bonded warehouseman or employee of secured party

2) It is less expensive than renting an outside warehouse and makes the goods more accessible to debtor when it is in effect a floating lien on the inventory

b. Warehouseman (on behalf of secured party) must have dominion and control over the security

1) A separate room or warehouse is used or an area is fenced off on the debtor's premises

2) Locks are changed

        3) It is posted showing the secured party's possession
        4) Temporary relinquishment of control is permissible to allow for exchange of collateral (a revolving type of collateral arrangement)

    c. Secured party can file a financing statement as to the goods rather than rely on field warehousing device

4. Consignments

    a. Amendments to the UCC set forth procedures a consignor must follow in order to prevail against his/her consignee's creditors

    b. A consignment is a type of agreement

        1) If it is a "true consignment," consignee is simply a sales agent who does not own the goods but sells them for consignor

            a) "True consignment" exists when

                1] Consignor retains title to goods
                2] Consignee has no obligation to buy goods
                3] Consignor has right to all proceeds (pays consignee commission)

                EXAMPLE: Manufacturer (consignor) gives possession of goods to a marketing representative (consignee) to sell those goods on commission.

            b) To perfect his/her interest, a consignor must

                1] Comply with applicable local law by posting a sign on the consignee's premises disclosing the consignor's interest in the goods, or
                2] Establish that the consignee is generally known as selling goods owned by other individuals, or
                3] File a financing statement under secured transactions law and give notice to the consignee's creditors who have perfected security interests in the same type of goods

                    a] Notice must contain description of the goods to be delivered and be given before the consignee receives possession of goods

                    EXAMPLE: P delivers goods to A on consignment. The consignment is a "true consignment" in that P has title to the goods and pays A a commission for selling the goods. Any goods that are unsold, are returned by A to P. A does not pay for any unsold goods. Creditors of A can assert claims against the goods that A possesses unless P has given notice to the creditors. The general way to accomplish this is by filing under the secured transactions law.

        2) If it is not a true consignment because it is actually a <u>sale</u> from creditor to debtor in which debtor then owns the goods, look for a security agreement

            a) Attachment and perfection occur as in typical secured transaction

5. Temporary perfection for

   a. Proceeds of collateral for 10 days where interest in original collateral was perfected and proceeds are of type that cannot be perfected by filing or by filing in same place as original collateral

      1) If proceeds are of same type as original collateral, they are automatically perfected if original collateral was perfected

         EXAMPLE: Debtor sells equipment for a promissory note. Secured creditor has temporary perfection for ten days in the note.

         EXAMPLE: Debtor trades equipment in on new equipment. New equipment is perfected if old equipment was. No temporary perfection is needed.

   b. Instruments and negotiable documents for 21 days to the extent new value is given under an existing written security agreement

E. Priorities

1. If more than one party claims a security interest in same collateral, rules of priority should be examined

2. Although the rules on priorities are complex with many exceptions the following will give the general, important rules to prepare you for the exam

3. General rules of priorities

   a. If both parties perfect by filing then first to file has priority

      1) This is true even if filing takes place before attachment

         EXAMPLE: K obtains a written security agreement on day 1 on collateral that D owns and possesses. On day 2, K files a financing statement but does not loan the money (give value) until day 10. L obtains a written security agreement on the same collateral on day 3 and gives value on day 4 and files on day 6. Since both perfected by filing, K has priority because he filed first even though attachment and perfection did not occur until later (day 10). To test your understanding, note that for L, attachment took place on day 4 and perfection on day 6.

   b. If both do not perfect by filing, then priority is by order of perfection

      1) This is true regardless of order of attachment

   c. Perfected security interests win over unperfected ones
   d. If neither is perfected, then the first to attach prevails
   e. General creditors (unsecured creditors) lose to secured creditors (perfected or unperfected)

4. Other principles on priorities

   a. Buyers in the ordinary course of business take free of any security interest whether perfected or not (be sure to know this one)

      1) In general, buying in the ordinary course of business means buying from inventory of a person or company that normally deals in those goods

2) Buyer has priority even if knows that security agreement exists

a) Unless actually knows that sale is in direct violation of security agreement (this is rare)

3) Purpose is to allow purchasers to buy from merchants without fear of security agreements between merchants and other parties

EXAMPLE: S, a dealer in stereos, obtained financing from L by securing the loan with her inventory in stereos. B purchases one of the stereos from that inventory. B takes free of the security interest that L has in the inventory of S whether it is perfected or not.

b. Distinguish between buyers in the ordinary course of business (see "E.4.a." above) and the subsequent bona fide purchasers from consumers [see "C.5.a.1)d)"]

1) The latter defeats only a purchase money security interest in consumer goods (perfection on attachment) unless filing takes place--applies to sale by consumer to consumer
2) The former applies whether buyer is consumer or not but seller is dealer in those goods

EXAMPLE: See previous example. The result is the same whether or not B was a consumer when he bought in the ordinary course of business from S.

EXAMPLE: Refer again to the same example using S, L, and B. Now let's add on one more security interest in that B is buying the stereo on credit from S and for his own personal use. Attachment has occurred. There is perfection by attachment because between B and S, it is a purchase money security interest in consumer goods. If B sells the stereo to N, his neighbor, for consumer use, then N takes free of the perfected security interest (unless S had filed or N had notice of the security interest).

c. In the case of a purchase money security interest, if the secured party files within 10 days after the debtor receives the collateral, then this defeats other security interests by use of a 10-day grace period

EXAMPLE: On August 1, B purchased some equipment from S on credit. All elements of attachment are satisfied on this date. On August 3, B borrows money from a bank using equipment purchased from S as collateral. Attachment is accomplished and a financing statement is correctly filed by the bank on August 3. On August 7, S then files a financing statement. Because of the 10-day grace period, S has priority over the bank.

EXAMPLE: Same as above except that S files after the 10-day grace period or not at all. The bank has priority.

1) If inventory, no 10-day leeway is allowed for perfection to have priority

a) Party with purchase money security interest must give notice to other secured party
b) Party with purchase money security interest must perfect prior to debtor's taking possession

2) Knowledge of preexisting security interest has no effect

d. Holder in due course of negotiable instruments wins over perfected or unperfected security interest
e. Security interest, perfected or unperfected, wins over subsequent perfected security interest if latter party knew of previous security interest
f. Possessor of negotiable document of title has priority over others
g. Lien creditor, e.g., repairman or contractor
    1) Has priority over an unperfected security interest
        a) Knowledge of security interest is immaterial
    2) Has priority over a security interest perfected after attachment of the lien
    3) A security interest perfected before the lien usually has priority
    4) Lien by statute (not by judgment or court order) has priority over a prior perfected security interest unless state statute expressly provides otherwise

    EXAMPLE: A person such as a repairman, in the ordinary course of business, furnishes services or materials with respect to goods subject to a security interest. The repairman (artisan lien) has priority.

h. Trustee in bankruptcy as a lien creditor (see BANKRUPTCY, Mod 11)
    1) Trustee has the rights of a lien creditor from the date of filing of petition in bankruptcy
        a) So has priority over a security interest perfected after date of filing petition
    2) Trustee also takes the position of any existing lien creditor

F. Rights of Parties Upon Default

1. If collateral consists of claims, e.g., receivables, the secured party has the right of collection from third parties
    a. Secured party may notify third party to pay secured party directly
    b. Secured party must account for any surplus and debtor is liable for any deficiency
    c. Secured party may deduct his reasonable expenses
2. Secured party may retain collateral already in his possession or may take possession from debtor
    a. May do so himself if can without breach of the peace
    b. Otherwise, s/he must use judicial process
    c. Secured party has duty to take reasonable care of collateral in his/her possession
        1) Expenses to protect collateral are responsibility of debtor
3. If secured party proposes to satisfy obligation by retaining the collateral, s/he must
    a. Send written notice to debtor
    b. Must notify other secured parties, unless consumer goods
    c. Can only retain consumer goods if debtor has paid less than 60 percent of the purchase price or obligation

   1) If 60 percent or more has been paid, secured party must sell collateral within 90 days after taking possession or be liable to the debtor unless debtor waives this right to sale <u>after</u> the default

4. Secured party may sell collateral
   a. May be a public or a private sale
   b. Must use commercially reasonable practices
   c. Must sell within a commercially reasonable time
   d. Must notify debtor before sale unless collateral is perishable, threatens to decline in value, or is type sold on a recognized market
      1) Must also notify other secured parties (who have sent written notice of their interest) unless collateral consists of consumer goods
   e. Secured party may buy at any public sale and also at a private sale if rights of debtor protected
   f. Debtor is entitled to any surplus and is liable for any deficiency
5. Debtor has right to redeem collateral before secured party disposes of it by paying
   a. Entire debt, and
   b. Secured party's reasonable expenses
6. Most remedies can be varied by agreement if reasonable
   a. Provision that secured party must account for any surplus to debtor cannot be varied by agreement
7. Good faith purchaser for value of collateral with no knowledge of defects in the sale takes free of debtor's rights or any secured interest
   a. If sale was improper, remedy of debtor is money damages against secured party who sold collateral, not against good faith purchaser
8. Termination of security interest
   a. If security was perfected by filing a financial statement, when debt is paid
      1) Secured party files termination statement at same place financing statement was filed
      2) If financing statement covers consumer goods, termination statement must be filed within one month after debt is paid
      3) If debtor requests termination statement in writing, it must be filed within ten days after debt is paid
      4) Failure by secured party to comply makes party liable for $100 and loss caused by failure to provide termination statement

Multiple Choice Questions (1–31)

1. Which of the following is included within the scope of the Secured Transactions Article of the Code?

a. The outright sale of accounts receivable.
b. A landlord's lien.
c. The assignment of a claim for wages.
d. The sale of chattel paper as a part of the sale of a business out of which it arose.

2. Donaldson, Inc., loaned Watson Enterprises $50,000 secured by a real estate mortgage which included the land, buildings, and "all other property which is added to the real property or which is considered as real property as a matter of law." Star Company also loaned Watson $25,000 and obtained a security interest in all of Watson's "inventory, accounts receivable, fixtures, and other tangible personal property." There is insufficient property to satisfy the two creditors. Consequently, Donaldson is attempting to include all property possible under the terms and scope of its real property mortgage. If Donaldson is successful in this regard, then Star will receive a lesser amount in satisfaction of its claim. What is the probable outcome of Donaldson's action?

a. Donaldson will not prevail if the property in question is detachable trade fixtures.
b. Donaldson will prevail if Star failed to file a financing statement.
c. Donaldson will prevail if it was the first lender and duly filed its real property mortgage.
d. The problem will be decided by taking all of Watson's property (real and personal) subject to the two secured creditors' claims and dividing it in proportion to the respective debts.

3. Which of the following is necessary in order to have a security interest attach?

a. The debtor must have rights in the collateral.
b. The creditor must take possession of the collateral.
c. There must be a proper filing.
d. The debtor must sign a security agreement which describes the collateral.

may be oral if possession

4. Unless otherwise agreed, when collateral, covered under the Secured Transactions Article of the UCC, is in the secured party's possession

a. The risk of accidental loss is on the debtor to the extent of any deficiency in any effective insurance coverage.
b. The secured party will lose his security interest if he commingles fungible collateral.
c. Reasonable expenses incurred to preserve the collateral are chargeable to the secured party.
d. Any repledge of the collateral by the secured party will be unenforceable.

5. Attachment and perfection will occur simultaneously when

a. The security agreement so provides.
b. There is a purchase money security interest taken in inventory.
c. Attachment is by possession.
d. The goods are sold on consignment.

6. Tawney Manufacturing approached Worldwide Lenders for a loan of $50,000 to purchase vital components it used in its manufacturing process. Worldwide decided to grant the loan but only if Tawney would agree to a field warehousing arrangement. Pursuant to their understanding, Worldwide paid for the purchase of the components, took a negotiable bill of lading for them, and surrendered the bill of lading in exchange for negotiable warehouse receipts issued by the bonded warehouse company that had established a field warehouse in Tawney's storage facility. Worldwide did not file a financing statement. Under the circumstances, Worldwide

a. Has a security interest in the goods which has attached and is perfected.
b. Does **not** have a security interest which has attached since Tawney has not signed a security agreement.
c. Must file an executed financing statement in order to perfect its security interest.
d. Must **not** relinquish control over any of the components to Tawney for whatever purpose, unless it is paid in cash for those released.

7. The Town Bank makes collateralized loans to its customers at 1% above prime on securities owned by the customer, subject to existing margin requirements. In doing so, which of the following is correct?

a. Notification of the issuer is necessary in order to perfect a security interest.
b. Filing is a permissible method of perfecting a security interest in the securities if the circumstances dictate.
c. Any dividend or interest distributions during the term of the loan belong to the bank.
d. A perfected security interest in the securities can only be obtained by possession.

8. On October 1, 1982, Winslow Corporation obtained a loan commitment of $250,000 from Liberty National Bank. Liberty filed a financing statement on October 2, 1982. On October 5, 1982, the $250,000 loan was consummated and Winslow signed a security agreement granting the bank a security interest in inventory, accounts receivable, and proceeds from the sale of the inventory and collection of the accounts receivable. Liberty's security interest was perfected

a. On October 1.
b. On October 2.
c. On October 5.
d. By attachment.

9. Vista Motor Sales, a corporation engaged in selling motor vehicles at retail, borrowed money from Sunshine Finance Company and gave Sunshine a properly executed security agreement in its present and future inventory and in the proceeds therefrom to secure the loan. Sunshine's security interest was duly perfected under the laws of the state where Vista does business and maintains its entire inventory. Thereafter, Vista sold a new pickup truck from its inventory to Archer and received Archer's certified check in payment of the full price. Under the circumstances, which of the following is correct?

a. Sunshine must file an amendment to the financing statement every time Vista receives a substantial number of additional vehicles from the manufacturer if Sunshine is to obtain a valid security interest in subsequently delivered inventory.
b. Sunshine's security interest in the certified check Vista received is perfected against Vista's other creditors.
c. Unless Sunshine specifically included proceeds in the financing statement it filed, it has no rights to them.
d. The term "proceeds" does not include used cars received by Vista since they will be resold.

10. Milo Manufacturing Corp. sells baseball equipment to distributors, who in turn sell the equipment to various retailers throughout the U.S. The retailers then sell the equipment to consumers who use the equipment for their own personal use. In all cases, the equipment is sold on credit with a security interest taken in the equipment by each of the respective sellers. Which of the following is correct?

a. The security interests of all of the sellers remain valid and will take priority even against good faith purchasers for value, despite the fact that resales were contemplated.
b. The baseball equipment is inventory in the hands of all the parties concerned.
c. Milo's security interest is automatically perfected since Milo qualifies as a purchase money secured party.
d. Milo and the distributors must file a financing statement or take possession of the baseball equipment in order to perfect their security interests.

11. Clearview Manufacturing, Inc., sells golf equipment to wholesale distributors, who sell to retailers, who in turn sell to golfers. In most instances, the golf equipment is sold on credit with a security interest in the goods taken by each of the respective sellers. With respect to the above described transactions

a. The only parties who qualify as purchase money secured parties are the retailers.
b. The security interests of all of the parties remain valid even against good faith purchasers despite the fact that resale was contemplated.
c. Except for the retailers, all of the sellers must file or have possession of the goods in order to perfect their security interests.
d. The golf equipment is inventory in the hands of all the parties involved.

12. Bass, an automobile dealer, had an inventory of 40 cars and ten trucks. He financed the purchase of this inventory with County Bank under an agreement dated January 5 that gave the bank a security interest in all vehicles on Bass' premises, all future acquired vehicles, and the proceeds from their sale. On January 10, County Bank properly filed a financing statement that identified the collateral in the same way that it was identified in the agreement. On April 1, Bass sold a passenger car to Dodd for family use and a truck to Diamond Company for its hardware business. Which of the following is correct?

a. The security agreement may **not** provide for a security interest in after-acquired property even if the parties so agree.
b. County Bank's security interest is perfected as of January 5.
c. The passenger car sold by Bass to Dodd continues to be subject to the security interest of County Bank.
d. The security interest of County Bank does **not** include the proceeds from the sale of the truck to Diamond Company.

13. Field warehousing is a well-established means of securing a loan. As such, it resembles a pledge in many legal respects. Which of the following is correct?

a. The field warehouseman must maintain physical control of and dominion over the property.
b. A filing is required in order to perfect such a financing arrangement.
c. Temporary relinquishment of control for any purpose will suspend the validity of the arrangement insofar as other creditors are concerned.
d. The property in question must be physically moved to a new location although it may be a part of the borrower's facilities.

14. Sax purchased from Bosch Tools a new saw for his home workshop for cash. One week later, Sax was called by Cary Finance. Cary explained to Sax that it had been financing Bosch's purchases from the manufacturers and that to protect its interest it had obtained a perfected security interest in Bosch's entire inventory of hardware and power tools, including the saw which Sax bought. Cary further explained that Bosch had defaulted on a payment due to Cary, and Cary intended to assert its security interest in the saw and repossess it unless Sax was willing to make payment of $100 for a release of Cary's security interest. If Sax refuses to make the payment, which of the following statements is correct?

a. Even if Sax had both actual notice and constructive notice via recordation of Cary's interest, he will prevail if Cary seeks to repossess the saw.
b. Cary's security interest in the saw in question is invalid against all parties unless its filing specifically described and designated the particular saw Sax purchased.
c. Sax must pay the $100 or the saw can be validly repossessed and sold to satisfy the amount Bosch owes Cary and any excess paid to Sax.
d. Sax will **not** take free of Cary's security interest if he was aware of said interest at the time he purchased the saw.

15. On January 5, Wine purchased and received delivery of new machinery from Toto Corp. for $50,000. The machinery was to be used in Wine's production process. Wine paid 30% down and executed a security agreement for the balance. On January 9, Wine obtained a $150,000 loan from Safe Bank. Wine signed a security agreement which gave Safe a security interest in Wine's existing and after-acquired machinery. The security agreement was duly filed by Safe that same day. On January 10, Toto properly filed its security agreement. If Wine defaults on both loans and there are insufficient funds to pay Toto and Safe, which party will have a superior security interest in the machinery purchased from Toto?

a. Safe, since it was the first in time to file and perfect its security interest.
b. Safe, since Toto perfected its security interest by filing after Wine took possession.
c. Toto, since it filed its security agreement within the permissible time limits.
d. Toto, since it acquired a perfected purchase money security interest without filing.

16. Fogel purchased a TV set for $900 from Hamilton Appliance Store. Hamilton took a promissory note signed by Fogel and a security interest for the $800 balance due on the set. It was Hamilton's policy not to file a financing statement until the purchaser defaulted. Fogel obtained a loan of $500 from Reliable Finance which took and recorded a security interest in the set. A month later, Fogel defaulted on several loans outstanding and one of his creditors, Harp, obtained a judgment against Fogel which was properly recorded. After making several payments, Fogel defaulted on a payment due to Hamilton, who then recorded a financing statement subsequent to Reliable's filing and the entry of the Harp judgment. Subsequently, at a garage sale, Fogel sold the set for $300 to Mobray. Which of the parties has the priority claim to the set?

a. Reliable.
b. Hamilton.
c. Harp.
d. Mobray.

17. An insolvent debtor made transfers of approximately 70% of inventory to secured creditors in satisfaction of debts. The debts were secured by the inventory. Under the circumstances

a. Secured creditors must give notice to the other creditors of the debtor.
b. Transfers in settlement of the security interest are excepted from the bulk sales provisions.
c. Inventory must be held for one month to enable the creditors to file their claims for any surplus which may arise from its sale.
d. Failure of the secured creditors to demand and obtain a list of the other creditors of the debtor will invalidate the transfer.

18. Thrush, a wholesaler of television sets, contracted to sell 100 sets to Kelly, a retailer. Kelly signed a security agreement with the 100 sets as collateral. The security agreement provided that Thrush's security interest extended to the inventory, to any proceeds therefrom, and to the after-acquired inventory of Kelly. Thrush filed his security interest centrally. Later, Kelly sold one of the sets to Haynes who purchased with knowledge of Thrush's perfected security interest. Haynes gave a note for the purchase price and signed a security agreement using the set as collateral. Kelly is now in default. Thrush can

a. Not repossess the set from Haynes, but is entitled to any payments Haynes makes to Kelly on his note.
b. Repossess the set from Haynes as he has a purchase money security interest.
c. Repossess the set as his perfection is first, and first in time is first in right.
d. Repossess the set in Haynes' possession because Haynes knew of Thrush's perfected security interest at the time of purchase.

19. Robert Cunningham owns a shop in which he repairs electrical appliances. Three months ago Electrical Supply Company sold Cunningham, on credit, a machine for testing electrical appliances and obtained a perfected security interest at the time as security for payment of the unpaid balance. Cunningham's creditors have now filed an involuntary petition in bankruptcy against him. What is the status of Electrical in the bankruptcy proceeding?

a. Electrical is a secured creditor and has the right against the trustee if not paid to assert a claim to the electrical testing machine it sold to Cunningham.
b. Electrical must surrender its perfected security interest to the trustee in bankruptcy and share as a general creditor of the bankrupt's estate.
c. Electrical's perfected security interest constitutes a preference and is voidable.
d. Electrical must elect to resort exclusively to its secured interest or to relinquish it and obtain the same share as a general creditor.

20. Pine has a security interest in certain goods purchased by Byron on an installment contract. Byron has defaulted on the payments resulting in Pine's taking possession of the collateral. Which of the following is correct?

a. Byron may waive his right of redemption at the time he executes the security agreement.
b. Pine must sell the collateral if Byron has paid more than 60% of the cash price on a purchase money security interest in business equipment.
c. The collateral may be sold by Pine at a private sale and, if the collateral is consumer goods, without notice to other secured parties.
d. Unless otherwise agreed, Pine must pay Byron for any increase in value of the collateral while the collateral is in Pine's possession.

21. Under the UCC, which of the following is correct regarding the disposition of collateral by a secured creditor after the debtor's default?

a. The collateral must be disposed of at a public sale.
b. It is improper for the secured creditor to purchase the collateral at a public sale.
c. Secured creditors with subordinate claims retain the right to redeem the collateral after the disposition of the collateral to a third party.
d. A good faith purchaser for value and without knowledge of any defects in the sale takes free of any subordinate liens or security interests.

22. Gilbert borrowed $10,000 from Merchant National Bank and signed a negotiable promissory note which contained an acceleration clause. In addition, securities valued at $11,000 at the time of the loan were pledged as collateral. Gilbert has defaulted on the loan repayments. At the time of default, $9,250, plus interest of $450, was due, and the securities had a value of $8,000. Merchant

a. Must first proceed against the collateral before proceeding against Gilbert personally on the note.
b. Can **not** invoke the acceleration clause in the note until ten days after the notice of default is given to Gilbert.
c. Must give Gilbert 30 days after default in which to refinance the loan.
d. Is entitled to proceed against Gilbert on either the note or the collateral or both.

May 1985 Questions

Items 23 and 24 are based on the following information:

On June 3, Muni Finance loaned Page Corp. $20,000 to purchase four computers for use in Page's trucking business. Page contemporaneously executed a promissory note and security agreement. On June 7, Page purchased the computers with the $20,000, obtaining possession that same day. On June 10, Mort, a judgment creditor of Page, levied on the computers.

23. Which of the following statements is correct?
   a. Muni failed to qualify as a purchase money secured lender.
   b. Muni's security interest attached on June 3.
   c. Muni's security interest attached on June 7.
   d. Muni's security interest did **not** attach.

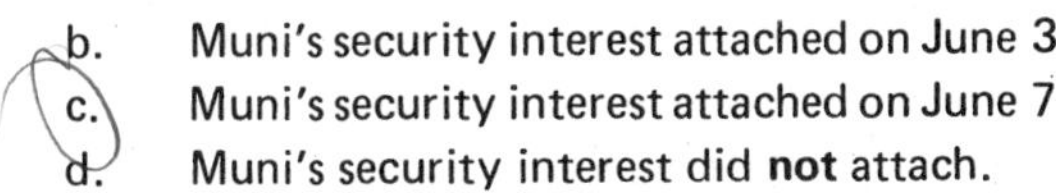

24. If Muni files a financing statement on June 11, which of the parties will have a priority security interest in the computers?
   a. Mort, since he lacked notice of Muni's security interest.
   b. Mort, since Muni failed to file before Mort levied on the computers.
   c. Muni, since its security interest was perfected within the permissible time limits.
   d. Muni, since its security interest was automatically perfected upon attachment.

25. Perfection of a security interest under the UCC by a creditor provides added protection against other parties in the event the debtor does not pay his debts. Which of the following is **not** affected by perfection of a security interest?
   a. The trustee in a bankruptcy proceeding.
   b. A buyer in the ordinary course of business.
   c. A subsequent personal injury judgment creditor.
   d. Other prospective creditors of the debtor.

Items 26 and 27 are based on the following information:

Foxx purchased a stereo for personal use from Dix Audio, a retail seller of appliances. Foxx paid 30% of the $600 sales price and agreed to pay the balance in 12 equal principal payments plus interest. Foxx executed a security agreement giving Dix a security interest in the stereo. Dix properly filed a financing statement immediately. After making six payments Foxx defaulted.

26. If Dix takes possession of the stereo, it
   a. Must dispose of the stereo at a public sale.
   b. Must dispose of the stereo within 90 days after taking possession or be liable to the debtor.
   c. May retain possession of the stereo, thereby discharging Foxx of any deficiency.

   d. May retain possession of the stereo and collect any deficiency plus costs from Foxx.

27. If after making the third installment payment, Foxx sold the stereo to Lutz for personal use, who would have a superior interest in the stereo assuming Lutz lacked knowledge of Dix's security interest?
   a. Dix, since it filed a financing statement.
   b. Dix, since more than 30% of the purchase price had been paid.
   c. Lutz, since title passed from Foxx to Lutz.
   d. Lutz, since he purchased without knowledge of Dix's security interest and for personal use.

28. Cole purchased furniture for her home from Thrift Furniture. The contract required Cole to pay 10% cash and the balance in equal installments over 36 months. Cole signed a security agreement with the furniture listed as collateral. Thrift properly filed a financing statement. If Cole makes the final payment due on the contract, Thrift
   a. Must file a termination statement **no** later than one month after final payment in order to avoid liability unless Cole demands earlier filing.
   b. Must file a termination statement in order to avoid liability only if Cole makes a written demand.
   c. Does **not** have to file a termination statement since the collateral is consumer goods.
   d. Does **not** have to file a termination statement since the term of the financing statement is less than five years and will automatically terminate.

29. Minor Corp. manufactures exercise equipment for sale to health clubs and to retailers. Minor also sells directly to consumers in its wholly-owned retail outlets. Minor has created a subsidiary, Minor Finance Corp., for the purpose of financing the purchase of its products by the various customers. In which of the following situations does Minor Finance **not** have to file a financing statement to perfect its security interest against competing creditors in the equipment sold by Minor?
   a. Sales made to retailers who in turn sell to buyers in the ordinary course of business.
   b. Sales made to any buyer when the equipment becomes a fixture.
   c. Sales made to health clubs.
   d. Sales made to consumers who purchase for their own personal use.

November 1985 Questions

30. A typewriter, which was subject to a prior UCC security interest, was delivered to Ed Fogel for repair. Fogel is engaged in the business of repairing typewriters. Fogel repaired the typewriter. However, the owner of the typewriter now refuses to pay for the services performed by Fogel. The state in which Fogel operates his business has a statute which gives Fogel a mechanics lien on the typewriter. Fogel's mechanics lien

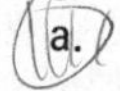

a. Takes priority over a prior perfected security interest under all circumstances.

b. Is subject to a prior perfected purchase money security interest under all circumstances.

c. Is subject to a prior unperfected security interest where the statute is silent as to priority.

d. Takes priority over a prior perfected security interest unless the statute expressly provides otherwise.

31. Under the UCC, collateral which has been sold in a private sale by a secured party to a good faith purchaser for value after the debtor's default

a. May be redeemed by the debtor within 10 days after the disposition.

b. May be redeemed by creditors with subordinate claims.

c. Remains subject to the security interests of subordinate lien creditors in all cases where the collateral is disposed of at a private sale.

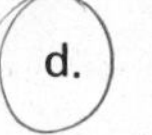

d. Discharges the security interest pursuant to which such sale was made and any security interest or lien subordinate thereto.

Problems

Problem 1 (1183,L2a)

(7 to 10 minutes)

Part a. Despard Finance Company is a diverse, full-line lending institution. Its "Problems & Potential Litigation" file revealed the following disputes involving loans extended during the year of examination.

- Despard loaned Fish $4,500 to purchase a $5,000 video recording system for his personal use. A note, security agreement, and financing statement, which was promptly filed, were all executed by Fish. Unknown to Despard, Fish had already purchased the system from Zeals Department Stores the previous day for $5,000. The terms were 10% down, the balance monthly, payable in three years, and a written security interest granted to Zeals. Zeals did not file a financing statement until default.
- Despard loaned Moderne Furniture Co. $13,000 to purchase certain woodworking equipment. Moderne did so. A note, security agreement, and financing statement were executed by Moderne. As a result of an oversight the financing statement was not filed until 30 days after the loan-purchase by Moderne. In the interim Moderne borrowed $11,000 from Apache National Bank using the newly purchased machinery as collateral for the loan. A financing statement was filed by Apache five days prior to Despard's filing.

Required:

Answer the following, setting forth reasons for any conclusions stated.

What are the priorities among the conflicting security interests in the same collateral claimed by Despard and the other lenders?

Problem 2 (581,L3)

(15 to 20 minutes)

Part a. Walpole Electric Products, Inc., manufactures a wide variety of electrical applicances. Walpole uses the consignment as an integral part of its marketing plan. The consignments are "true" consignments rather than consignments intended as security interests. Unsold goods may be returned to the owner-consignor. Walpole contracted with Petty Distributors, Inc., an electrical applicance wholesaler, to market its products under this consignment arrangement. Subsequently, Petty became insolvent and made a general assignment for the benefit of creditors. Klinger, the assignee, took possession of all of Petty's inventory, including all the Walpole electrical products. Walpole has demanded return of its appliances asserting that the relationship created by the consignment between itself and Petty was one of agency and that Petty never owned the appliances. Furthermore, Walpole argues that under the consignment arrangement there is no obligation owing by Petty at any time, thus there is nothing to secure under the secured transactions provisions of the Uniform Commercial Code. Klinger has denied the validity of these assertions claiming that the consignment is subject to the Code's filing provisions unless the Code has otherwise been satisfied. Walpole sues to repossess the goods.

Required:

Answer the following, setting forth reasons for any conclusions stated.

1. What are the requirements, if any, to perfect a true consignment such as discussed above?
2. Will Walpole prevail?

Part b. Lebow Woolens, Inc., sold several thousand bolts of Australian wool on credit to Fashion Plate Exclusives, Inc., a clothing manufacturer, obtaining a duly executed security agreement and a financing statement. Fashion Plate became delinquent in meeting its payments. Lebow subsequently discovered that a miscaptioned financing statement for a $12,500 sale had been filed under the name of Fashion Styles Limited, another customer. Lebow took the following actions. First, on August 11, 1980, it repossessed the bolts of wool which were not already altered by Fashion Plate. This amounted to some 65% of the invoice in question. Next on August 20, 1980, it filed a corrected financing statement covering the sale in question. Dunbar, another creditor of Fashion Plate's, levied against Fashion Plate's inventory, work in process, and raw materials on August 13th and obtained a judgment of $14,000 against Fashion Plate, an amount in excess of the value of the Lebow bolts of wool. The judgment was obtained and entered on August 18, 1980. Dunbar asserts its rights as a lien judgment creditor.

Required:

Answer the following, setting forth reasons for any conclusions stated.

Problem 3 (1184,L4a & b)

(15 to 25 minutes)

Tom Sauer purchased a computer and a stereo from Zen Sounds, Inc., for personal use. With regard to the computer, Sauer signed an installment purchase note and a security agreement. Under the terms of the note Sauer was to pay $100 down and $50 a month for 20 months. The security agreement included a description of the computer. However, Zen did not file a financing statement. Sauer paid $800 cash for the stereo.

Two months later, Sauer sold the computer to Ralph for $600 cash. Ralph purchased the computer for personal use without knowledge of Zen's security interest.

Three months later, Sauer brought the stereo back to Zen for repair. Inadvertently, one of Zen's sales persons sold the stereo to Ned, a buyer in the ordinary course of business.

Required:

Answer the following, setting forth reasons for any conclusions stated.

a. Did Zen fulfill the requirements necessary for the attachment and perfection of its security interest in the computer?

b. Will Ralph take the computer free of Zen's security interest?

Multiple Choice Answers

1. a	8. c	14. a	20. c	26. b
2. a	9. b	15. c	21. d	27. a
3. a	10. d	16. b	22. d	28. a
4. a	11. c	17. b	23. c	29. d
5. c	12. b	18. a	24. c	30. d
6. a	13. a	19. a	25. b	31. d
7. d				

Multiple Choice Answer Explanations

A.1. Article 9 of UCC

1. (1180,L1,38) (a) The only item listed that is within the scope of article 9 (secured transactions) is the outright sale of accounts receivable.

A.2. Types of Collateral

2. (578,L1,29) (a) Detachable trade fixtures are considered personal property, not real property. Therefore, a real estate mortgagee will not obtain a security interest in property classified as a detachable trade fixture. Answer (b) is incorrect because Donaldson's mortgage does not cover any personal property which is the issue here. Answer (c) is incorrect because the mortgage attaches only to real property. Thus property which is classified as personal will not be included whether the mortgage is recorded or not. Answer (d) is incorrect because the court's job is to distinguish between real and personal property and it lacks authority to divide disputed property in proportion to respective claims.

B. Attachment of Security Interests

3. (584,L1,60) (a) A security interest attaches when the following occur, in any order: secured creditor gives value, debtor has rights in the collateral, and a security agreement exists. Possession of the collateral and filing a financing statement are two methods of perfecting a security interest; they are not steps essential to the creation or attachment of a security interest. Accordingly, answers (b) and (c) are incorrect. Answer (d) is incorrect because if the secured creditor takes possession of the collateral, the security agreement between the parties may be oral. In all other instances, the security agreement must be in writing, demonstrate the debtor's intent to create a security interest, describe the collateral, and be signed by the debtor.

C.4. Perfection by Possession

4. (1184,L1,60) (a) The risk of accidental loss is on the debtor to the extent of any deficiency in any effective insurance coverage. However, the secured party must exercise reasonable care while possessing the collateral. The secured party has liability when the collateral is damaged through the negligence of the secured party. Answer (b) is incorrect because the secured party may commingle fungible collateral without destroying his security interest. Answer (c) is incorrect because reasonable expenses to preserve the collateral (such as insurance and taxes) are chargeable to the debtor, not the secured party. Answer (d) is incorrect because the secured party may repledge the collateral upon terms which do not impair the debtor's right to redeem it.

5. (583,L1,47) (c) Since possession is a method of perfecting a security interest, attachment and perfection will occur simultaneously when attachment is by possession. Answer (a) is incorrect because a statement in a security agreement specifying that attachment and perfection will occur simultaneously will have no legal effect. The secured party must still engage in one of the three methods of perfection before the security interest will be perfected. Answer (b) is incorrect because attachment and perfection will occur simultaneously if there is a purchase money security interest taken in consumer goods, but this does not occur when the collateral is inventory. Answer (d) is incorrect because a security interest in goods sold on consignment is not automatically perfected upon attachment. These goods qualify as inventory in the debtor's possession and, consequently, perfection would occur only when the secured party files a proper financing statement.

6. (1182,L1,55) (a) Since documents of title, i.e., the negotiable warehouse receipts, merely represent the goods, a perfected security interest in the warehouse receipts (by taking possession of the documents) is also a perfected security interest in the goods covered by the documents. Answer (b) is incorrect because the debtor, Tawny, does not have to sign the security agreement if the collateral is in the possession of the secured party, Worldwide, pursuant to agreement. When a secured party is taking a possessory security interest, an oral security agreement is sufficient to create such an interest. Answer (c) is incorrect because Worldwide does not have to file a financing statement to perfect its security interest, since Worldwide has already perfected its security interest by taking possession of the negotiable warehouse receipts. Worldwide could have perfected its security interest by filing a financing statement, but this filing would not protect Worldwide against a good faith purchaser to whom the warehouse receipts have been duly negotiated. Answer (d) is incorrect because temporary and limited relinquishment of control of the goods to the debtor is acceptable. The

Uniform Commercial Code provides for a 21 day continuation of the perfected security interest in the collateral from the date of release to the debtor.

7. (1180,L1,34) (d) A perfected security interest in securities can only be obtained by possession. An exception to this rule is when the creditor temporarily returns the security to the debtor (for sale, exchange, etc.). In such situations, the creditor's security interest remains perfected for 21 days. However, a bona fide purchaser of the security will defeat the creditor's security interest. Thus, answer (d) is correct. To perfect a security interest in securities there is no need to notify the issuer. Dividends and interest earned during the secured transaction are the property of the debtor.

C.3. Perfection by Filing

8. (1182,L1,56) (c) Perfection of a security interest may be accomplished by the filing of a financing statement. Filing may be done anytime, even before the security agreement is made. But perfection does not occur until all the requirements for attachment of a security interest are met. The requisite acts of perfection are not a substitute for the attachment of a security interest, but are additional steps. Therefore, because a financing statement has already been filed, Liberty's security interest was perfected on October 5, when all three elements for attachment existed. Answers (a) and (b) are incorrect because attachment of the security interest has not yet occurred. Answer (d) is incorrect because a security interest will automatically be perfected upon attachment only when creditor takes a purchase money security interest in consumer goods.

9. (1179,L1,26) (b) Under the facts given, Sunshine's security interest in the certified check that Vista received is perfected against Vista's other creditors. Answer (c) is incorrect because the security interest attaches to proceeds automatically without special mention in the financing statement. Answer (d) is incorrect because the term "proceeds" is broad enough to include anything received in exchange for the collateral including used motor vehicles, i.e., "trade-ins." Answer (a) is incorrect because Sunshine covered itself in the executed security agreement by stating that the security agreement covered both present and future inventory. Therefore, an amendment is unnecessary every time Vista receives a substantial number of vehicles from the manufacturer.

C.5. Perfection by Attachment Alone

10. (1184,L1,58) (d) Since the collateral is inventory in the hands of both the distributors and retailers, there is no automatic perfection by attachment even though purchase money security interests are present. Automatic perfection by attachment only occurs when a purchase money security interest is taken in consumer goods. The use of the debtor determines the type of collateral present. Consequently, Milo and the distributors must file a financing statement or take possession in order to perfect their security interest. Therefore, answer (c) is incorrect. Answer (a) is incorrect because a purchaser in the ordinary course of business would defeat a prior perfected secured party in inventory. Also, a good faith purchaser would defeat a secured party who perfected his security interest by attachment alone (the retailers with regard to the sale of the baseball equipment to the consumers). Answer (b) is incorrect because the baseball equipment is consumer goods in the hands of the consumers.

11. (1182,L1,58) (c) Perfection of a security interest may occur in three ways: by attachment of a security interest; by possession of the collateral; or by the filing of a financing statement. When a creditor takes a purchase money security interest in consumer goods, such interest is automatically perfected upon attachment. The retailers are the only secured parties taking a security interest in collateral that would qualify as consumer goods. Therefore, all of the sellers, except for the retailers, must file or have possession of the goods in order to perfect their security interests. Answer (a) is incorrect because a security interest is a "purchase money security interest" when taken or retained by the seller of the collateral to secure all or part of the purchase price. Therefore, both the wholesalers and the retailers qualify as purchase money secured parties. Answer (b) is incorrect because a perfected security interest in inventory is defeated by a purchaser in the ordinary course of business. Also, even though the retailer's security interest was perfected upon attachment and is good against the buyer's creditors, the perfected security interest is not valid against a subsequent bona fide purchaser from the consumer. Answer (d) is incorrect because the golf equipment is consumer goods in the hands of the golfers who purchased from the retailers, since it was bought primarily for personal, family, or household purposes.

12. (1181,L1,45) (b) Even though filing did not occur until January 10, County Bank's security interest is perfected as of January 5 upon attachment of the security interest. Answer (a) is incorrect because an after-acquired property clause is very typical of a security agreement that creates a security interest (floating lien) in inventory. Answer (c) is incorrect because a purchase in the ordinary course of business

by Dodd defeats a prior perfected security interest in inventory. This is true even if Dodd had knowledge of County Bank's security interest prior to purchasing the car. Answer (d) is incorrect because proceeds include what is received upon sale of the collateral. County Bank does have a perfected security interest in the proceeds from the sale of a truck because the security agreement states proceeds are covered. The general rule states that security interest in proceeds is automatically perfected for a 10-day period if the security interest in the original collateral was perfected. However, if the security agreement states that the security interest is to cover proceeds, the perfected security interest will continue beyond the 10-day period without any additional filing.

D.3. Field Warehousing

13. (1177,L2,24) (a) A pledge is possession of the debtor's property by the creditor to secure a debt. This is the same as possessing collateral to perfect a security interest, i.e., the creditor must possess the collateral. This is done by the field warehouseman or his agent, by maintaining physical control and dominion over the property. Answer (b) is incorrect because filing is not required where there is possession. Answer (c) is incorrect because temporary relinquishment of control is acceptable to allow for an exchange of collateral, to allow the debtor to temporarily use or work on the goods. However, a holder in due course or bona fide purchaser who suffers legal detriment, i.e., purchases, lends money on, etc., during such interval will prevail. Answer (d) is incorrect because the collateral need not be moved to a new location; rather, it must be segregated and controlled.

E. Priorities

14. (1184,L1,59) (a) A purchaser in the ordinary course of business will prevail against a perfected secured party in inventory even if the purchaser had both actual and constructive notice of the perfected security interest. There is no requirement that the purchaser buy in good faith. Thus, Sax, a purchaser in the ordinary course of business, will prevail if Cary seeks to repossess the saw. Therefore, answers (c) and (d) are incorrect. Answer (b) is incorrect because Cary's filing need only describe the collateral as "inventory" and that would be sufficient to perfect his security interest in the particular saw.

15. (584,L1,58) (c) A purchase money security interest in collateral other than inventory has priority over all other security interests if it is perfected when the debtor receives possession of the collateral or within ten days thereafter. Because Toto perfected its purchase money security interest in equipment by filing within ten days of January 5, Toto has priority over Safe Bank. Answer (d) is incorrect because a security interest in equipment must be perfected either by possession or filing. Answer (b) is incorrect because Toto, a purchase money secured creditor with collateral other than inventory, had a ten-day grace period to perfect its interest. Answer (a) is incorrect because the "first to file or perfect" rule does not apply to purchase money security interests.

16. (583,L1,51) (b) Hamilton took a purchase money security interest in the TV set which would be considered consumer goods in Fogel's possession. Consequently, Hamilton's security interest was perfected automatically upon attachment. Therefore, Hamilton can defeat Reliable because Hamilton's security interest was perfected prior to the time Reliable perfected its security interest by filing. Hamilton can also defeat Harp because Harp's judgment was subsequent to Hamilton's perfection. Normally Mobray, as a good faith purchaser for personal use, would defeat a prior perfected secured party who gained his/her perfection through automatic perfection by attachment. However, Hamilton engaged in a second method of perfection (filing a financing statement) prior to the sale of the TV set to Mobray, allowing Hamilton to defeat the good faith purchaser for personal use. Therefore, answers (a), (c), and (d) are incorrect.

17. (1182,L1,23) (b) Transfers in settlement of a security interest are excepted from the bulk sales provisions of Article 6 of the UCC. Consequently, the secured creditors would not need to obtain a list of the debtor's other creditors, nor would they have to give notice to these creditors. Therefore, answers (a) and (d) are incorrect. Answer (c) is incorrect because there is no requirement that the inventory must be held for one month to enable the creditors to file their claims for any surplus which may arise from its sale.

18. (1182,L1,57) (a) Proceeds include whatever is received upon the sale of the collateral. The secured party, Thrush, has the ability to assert rights against the proceeds received by the debtor, Kelly, upon sale of the collateral. Thrush has a perfected security interest in the proceeds from the sale of the television sets because the security agreement states proceeds are covered. Therefore, Thrush is entitled to any payments Haynes makes to Kelly on the note. Normally, access to the proceeds upon default by the debtor is an integral part of an inventory financing agreement. Haynes, as a purchaser in the ordinary course of business, takes free of Thrush's perfected security interest in inventory.

Answers (b), (c) and (d) are incorrect because since Haynes is a buyer in the ordinary course of business, he will defeat the rights of the secured creditor, Thrush, even if he were aware of Thrush's security interest at the time of purchase. Therefore, Thrush will not be able to repossess the television set. Haynes would take subject to Thrush's security interest **only** when he **knows** that the sale of the inventory is in violation of some term in the security agreement.

19. (579,L1,22) (a) Electrical, as a secured creditor, may assert a reclamation claim against the trustee in bankruptcy for the testing machine. Answer (b) is incorrect because the secured party may enforce its perfected security interest and then proceed as a general creditor against the bankrupt's estate to the extent the collateral does not satisfy the debt. Electrical's perfected security interest does not constitute a voidable preference as stated in answer (c) since the simultaneous sale and creation of the security interest is considered a fair exchange. Answer (d) is incorrect because a secured party is not forced to make an exclusive choice of remedy but may proceed against the security until it is exhausted and may then proceed in the bankruptcy action as a general creditor for any deficiency.

F. Rights of Parties on Default

20. (1184,L1,57) (c) If the collateral is consumer goods, Pine may sell the collateral at a private sale without notice to other secured parties. However, Pine must notify the debtor before the sale unless the collateral is perishable or threatens to decline in value. Answer (a) is incorrect because the debtor may not waive his right of redemption at the time the debtor executes the security agreement. The debtor has the right to reclaim the collateral if the debtor tenders payment of the entire debt and the secured party's reasonable expenses. Answer (b) is incorrect because Pine only has the option of selling the collateral if the debtor has paid 60% of the cash price on a purchase money security interest in consumer goods, not business equipment. Since the collateral is equipment, Pine would still have the option of keeping the collateral as full payment of the obligation if, after giving written notice to Byron of this desire, Byron did not object within 21 days. Answer (d) is incorrect because Pine may keep the increase in value of the collateral as additional security unless actual money is received by Pine, in which case the secured party must give it to the debtor or apply the amount to the obligation.

21. (584,L1,59) (d) A purchaser for value at a public sale who is without knowledge of any defects in that sale and who is not in collusion with the secured creditor will take the property free of the debtor's rights and any security interests. A purchaser for value at a private sale will take free of the debtor's rights and any security interests if he acts in good faith. The debtor's remedy for an improperly conducted sale is a cause of action for money damages against the secured party. The debtor and any secondarily secured party have an absolute right to redeem the collateral at anytime **prior** to the sale of the collateral by tendering all amounts due the secured party. Answers (a) and (b) are incorrect because a secured creditor may dispose of the collateral at either a public or private sale. The secured party may buy at any public sale and may also buy at a private sale if the collateral is either widely distributed at a standard price or is customarily sold in a recognized market. Answer(c) is incorrect because secured parties with subordinate claims do not have the right to redeem the collateral after disposition to a third party has been made. Subordinate secured parties, however, do have a right to the proceeds from the disposition after payment of the secured party's reasonable expenses and the debt secured by the collateral.

22. (583,L1,52) (d) Merchant is entitled to proceed against Gilbert on either the note or the collateral or both. The reason a creditor desires collateral for an obligation is to provide another source of payment besides the debtor's personal promise. Merchant, the creditor, need not first proceed against the collateral before proceeding against Gilbert personally. Therefore, answer (a) is incorrect. Answer (b) is incorrect because Merchant is not required to wait until 10 days after notice of default is given Gilbert before invoking the acceleration clause. The clause can be invoked as stipulated on the face of the note. Answer (c) is incorrect because there is no requirement that states a debtor must be given 30 days after default in which to refinance a loan. Upon default Merchant may immediately proceed against Gilbert and the collateral.

May 1985 Answers

23. (585,L1,44) (c) Attachment of a security interest in personal property occurs when the following three requirements have been fulfilled; the debtor executes a security agreement, the secured party gives value and the debtor acquires rights in the collateral. The secured party gave value and the security agreement was executed on June 3, but the debtor did not acquire any rights in the collateral until June 7, the day of the purchase. Answer (a) is incorrect because Muni is a

purchase money secured lender (i.e., the value given by Muni was used to obtain the collateral). Answers (b) and (d) are incorrect because the security interest did attach but not until June 7.

24. (585,L1,45) (c) A purchase money security interest in collateral other than inventory (such as equipment) will have priority if the secured party perfects his interest no later than 10 days after the debtor takes possession of the collateral. Muni perfected his security interest by filing within 10 days of Page's obtaining possession and therefore will have superior rights in the collateral upon default. Answer (a) is incorrect because the fact Mort lacked notice of Muni's security interest would not allow Mort to defeat Muni's interest. Answer (b) is incorrect because perfection of Muni's security interest will relate back to the date of attachment for purposes of determining priority. Answer (d) is incorrect because Muni's security interest in the computers (business equipment) did not automatically perfect upon attachment. Automatic perfection by attachment occurs only when the secured party takes a purchase money security interest in consumer goods of the debtor.

25. (585,L1,46) (b) Even perfection will not protect a secured party when a purchaser buys goods in the ordinary course of business from a seller who deals in goods of that kind. The purchaser will take free of any existing security interest (perfected or unperfected) even if the buyer knows of the secured party's security interest at the time of the sale. Therefore, a buyer in the ordinary course of the debtor's business will be unaffected by a prior perfected security interest. Answers (a) and (c) are incorrect because a trustee in bankruptcy and a judgment creditor will have subordinate claims to a prior perfected security interest (i.e., secured party must have a **perfected** security interest). Answer (d) is incorrect because other creditors whether secured or unsecured will be affected by a prior perfected security interest.

26. (585,L1,47) (b) A secured party cannot retain the collateral if a purchase money security interest has been taken in consumer goods, and the consumer has paid 60% of the purchase price before default. The secured party must sell the collateral within 90 days of obtaining possession or be held liable for the tort of conversion. Since Foxx paid in excess of 60% of the cash price, Dix will have to sell the collateral in a commercially reasonable manner, applying the proceeds to any expenses incurred and the outstanding balance. Answer (a) is incorrect because Dix may sell the collateral at a private or public sale as long as every aspect of the sale is conducted in a commercially reasonable manner. Answers (c) and (d) are incorrect because Dix must sell the collateral as required under the Uniform Commercial Code.

27. (585,L1,48) (a) A subsequent consumer buyer who purchases goods from a debtor without knowledge of a prior security interest will take them free of a prior perfected security interest where perfection occurred automatically upon attachment (i.e., a purchase money security interest in consumer goods). However, if the prior perfected secured party, which gained perfection automatically upon attachment, also files a financing statement, then this secured party has a superior interest in the collateral over the good faith consumer purchaser. Since Dix has filed a financing statement, Lutz has constructive notice of the prior security interest and will not take free of Dix's interest. Answers (b) and (c) are incorrect because payment of 30% of the purchase price and passage of title have no bearing on the issue of priority in the collateral. A creditor's security interest will continue despite a sale of the collateral subject to some exceptions (i.e., buyer in ordinary course of business). Answer (d) is incorrect because even though Lutz did not have actual knowledge of the prior security interest, he had constructive knowledge due to the filed financing statement.

28. (585,L1,49) (a) When a debtor has fully paid a creditor, and the financing statement covered consumer goods, a termination statement must be filed within one month after the debt has been paid by the secured party. If the debtor requests a termination statement in writing, the creditor must file one no later than ten days after the debt is paid. Therefore, Thrift must file a termination within one month of Cole's final payment. Answers (b), (c), and (d) are incorrect because in all cases where the collateral is consumer goods, the secured party must file a termination statement whether or not the debtor makes a written request or the financing statement lapses.

29. (585,L1,50) (d) Generally, when a purchase money security interest is acquired in consumer goods, the secured party's security interest automatically perfects upon attachment. As long as the goods are to be used for personal or household use, Minor Finance, the secured party, need not file a financing statement to perfect its interest. Answer (a) is incorrect because a secured party is not automatically perfected where goods are sold to a retailer as inventory. The secured party must file a financing statement to perfect his/her interest in inventory. However, if the retailer sells to a buyer in the ordinary course of business, the purchaser

will take the collateral free of any security interest (perfected or unperfected) even if the buyer has notice of the prior security interest. Answer (b) is incorrect because a security interest in a fixture will not be perfected until the secured party makes a fixture filing at the time the collateral is affixed to the real property or a regular filing if movable factory or office machines are involved. Answer (c) is incorrect because in that situation the collateral would be equipment and the secured party would have to file a financing statement to perfect its security interest.

November 1985 Answers

30. (1185,L1,49) (d) The UCC states that when a person in the ordinary course of business furnishes services or materials for goods subject to a security interest, a mechanics lien on such goods, which arises under state law, takes priority over prior perfected security interests unless the statute expressly provides otherwise. Therefore, answers (a), (b), and (c) are incorrect.

31. (1185,L1,50) (d) Upon the default of a debtor, a secured party may sell the collateral in a private sale to a good faith purchaser for value. The proceeds of such a sale are applied in the following order: (1) secured part's reasonable expenses, (2) debt secured by the collateral, (3) other secured debts of subordinate third parties. Answer (a) is incorrect because although the debtor has the right to redeem the collateral before the secured party disposes of it by tendering the entire debt and the secured party's reasonable expenses, the debtor may not redeem the collateral once it is sold to a good faith purchaser after the debtor's default. Answer (b) is incorrect because creditors with subordinate claims may not redeem the collateral after it is disposed by the secured party. Rather, the proceeds from the sale are applied to the subordinate claims after the secured party's reasonable expenses and secured debt have been satisfied. Answer (c) is incorrect because once the collateral has been sold, the subordinate creditors have no further claims to it, and must look to the remaining assets of the debtor for satisfaction of their claims.

Answer Outline

Problem 1 Purchase Money Security Interest in Consumer Goods; Equipment (1183,L2a)

Part a.

Zeals will prevail over Despard
Zeals' interest is purchase money security interest in consumer goods that is automatically perfected upon attachment
Despard's interest is not protected until filed, which is subsequent to Zeals' perfection
Filing is necessary to protect purchase money security interest in equipment
Despard as a purchase money lender has a ten-day grace period for filing
Despard did not file for 30 days
Despard's interest was not perfected until filed
Apache will prevail since the interest was perfected before Despard's

Unofficial Answer

Problem 1 Purchase Money Security Interest in Consumer Goods; Equipment (1183,L2a)

Part a.

- Zeals has priority over Despard regarding the competing security interests of the parties. Zeals is a purchase money secured party involving the sale of consumer goods. As such, the security interest is enforceable against other creditors of the buyer without the necessity of a filing. Despard would also attempt to assert a purchase money security interest in the goods, but this is questionable at best since the money advanced was obviously not used for the purchase of the goods. Even if Despard qualified as a purchase money secured party, Despard was second in point of time. The fact that it filed does not change the priority since filing was not required to perfect the interest in the consumer goods (the video system).
- Apache has priority over Despard in this instance. Although Despard was the first to advance credit and qualified as a purchase money lender, it was second in time to perfect its security interest. The subject matter of the sale was equipment and filing is required to perfect Despard's security interest. The purchase money lender has the benefit of a 10-day grace period for filing. Despard's security interest was not perfected until it filed, which was after the grace period and five days after Apache's filing.

Answer Outline

Problem 2 Perfection of True Consignment; Priority of Conflicting Security Interests (581,L3)

a1. A true consignment in a commercial sense implies an agency relationship
Perfection of true consignment enables consignor, Walpole, to prevail agains Petty's creditors
Walpole must comply with applicable law providing for consignor's interest to be evidenced by posted sign, or Walpole must establish that Petty is generally known by his creditors to be engaged in selling goods of others, or Walpole must comply with filing provision of Article 9 of UCC
Consignor must give written notification to Petty's creditors who have security interest in same type of goods
But only if the creditors perfected their security interest before date of filing made by Walpole
Notice must be received by creditors within five years before consignee receives possession of the goods
Notification states consignor expects to deliver goods on consignment to the consignee
Describing the goods by item or type

a2. Walpole will not prevail aginst Klinger
Walpole was unable to perfect a true consignment as outlined in a1.
Article 2 of UCC provides that where goods are delivered under a consignment agreement for sale
The goods are deemed to be on "sale or return" with respect to claims of consignee's creditors
Walpole is subject to claims of Petty's creditors

b. Conflicting security interests rank according to priority in time of filing or perfection
Lebow will prevail over Dunbar with regard to the bolts it repossessed (65% of the invoice)
Lebow's repossession of goods constituted a perfection of security interest
Security interest perfected before Dunbar's lien attaches has priority over the lien
Lebow's filing of the miscaptioned statement is ineffective to create any interests or rights in Lebow
Financing statement not relevant with regard to priority time frame
Dunbar will prevail over Lebow with regard to goods not repossessed by Lebow

Dunbar's levy and judicial lien occurs prior in time to Lebow's filing of corrected financing statement

Applies to the remaining goods

Unofficial Answer

Problem 2 Perfection of True Consignment; Priority of Conflicting Security Interests (581,L3)

Part a.

1. In order to prevail against the creditors of a party to whom goods have been consigned, the consignor may do one of three things according to the Uniform Commercial Code (section 2-326):

a. Comply with applicable state law providing for a consignor's interest to be evidenced by a posted sign. Most states do not have such statutes.

b. Establish that the person conducting the business is generally known by his creditors to be substantially engaged in selling the goods of others. This is either not the case or is difficult to prove.

c. Comply with the filing provisions of Article 9: Secured Transactions. From a practical standpoint, this last course of action appears to be the most logical, if not the only, choice.

Article 9 (section 9-114) requires that a consignor comply with the general filing requirements of the code (section 9-302) and also give notice in writing to the creditors of the consignee who have a perfected security interest covering the same type of goods. The written notice must be given before the date of filing by the consignor and received within five years before the consignee takes possession of the goods. The notice must state that the consignor expects to deliver goods on consignment to the consignee and must contain a description of the goods.

2. No. Walpole will not prevail. Whether a consignment is a "true" consignment (an agency relationship) or is intended as a security interest, the Uniform Commercial Code requires that notice be given to creditors of the consignee.

A consignment is governed by sections from two articles of the code: Article 2: Sales and Article 9: Secured Transactions. Section 2-326 treats a consignment as a "sale or return" because "the goods are delivered primarily for resale." Section 2-326(3) provides the following:

> Where goods are delivered to a person for sale and such person maintains a place of business at which he deals in goods of the kind involved, under a name other than the name of the person making delivery, then with respect to claims of creditors of the person conducting the business the goods are deemed to be on sale or return. The provisions of this subsection are applicable even though an agreement purports to reserve title to the person making delivery until payment or resale or uses such words as "on consignment" or "on memorandum."

It is obvious from the facts, that Walpole's marketing arrangement is covered by the above language. The code further provides that the creditors of the consignee will be able to assert claims against goods sold on a sale or return basis unless some form of notice is given.

Part b.

Lebow will prevail to the extent of the 65 percent of the bolts of wool that it repossessed on August 11, 1980. Since Lebow obtained possession of 65 percent of the shipment prior to attachment or judgment by Dunbar, Lebow's security interest with respect to those goods had been perfected as of August 11. The original erroneous filing is invalid against the creditors of Fashion Plate. Lebow's security interest was not perfected by filing initially, and, therefore, Lebow will not prevail over the rights of Dunbar, a subsequent lien creditor of Fashion Plate. The facts of the case indicate that the security interest was not perfected by filing until August 20, 1980. However, prior to that time Dunbar levied against the goods on August 13 and obtained a judgment against Fashion Plate on August 18, 1980. Both dates are prior to the August 20 filing by Lebow; thus, the lien creditor would have priority over Lebow's claim based exclusively on perfection by filing. Perfection can also be accomplished by possession, but if perfection by either method precedes the time that the lien creditor obtains rights against the property, it prevails.

Answer Outline

Problem 3 Attachment; Perfection; Good Faith Purchaser of Consumer Goods (1184,L4a & b)

a. Yes. Attachment of security interest requires
   - Valid security agreement
   - Secured party gives value
   - Debtor has rights in collateral

   Transaction involves purchase money security interest in consumer goods
   - Automatic perfection by attachment occurs

b. Yes. Secured party with perfected security interest generally takes priority
   - Exception in case of consumer goods
   - Subsequent good faith purchaser takes free of prior perfected security interests if he purchases before financing statement is filed

Unofficial Answer

Problem 3 Attachment; Perfection; Good Faith Purchaser of Consumer Goods (1184,L4a & b)

a. Yes. In order for a security interest in collateral to attach, the following three requirements must be met: 1. the collateral is in the possession of the secured party pursuant to agreement, or the debtor has signed a security agreement that contains a description of the collateral; 2. value has been given by the secured party; and 3. the debtor has rights in the collateral.

Zen, under the stated facts has fulfilled all three requirements, thereby creating an enforceable security interest that has attached to the computer. Since the transaction involves a purchase money security interest in consumer goods—that is, goods used or bought primarily for personal, family, or household purposes—it is not necessary for the secured party to file a financing statement or take possession of the collateral in order to perfect its interest. The security interest is perfected when the three requirements set forth have been fulfilled.

b. Yes. Generally, a secured party with a perfected security interest has priority over all subsequent claims to the same collateral. However, in the case of consumer goods, where perfection is achieved solely by attachment, a subsequent buyer will take free of such prior perfected security interests if he buys without knowledge of the security interest, for value, for his own personal, family, or household use and before a financing statement is filed by the secured party. Since Ralph has complied with those qualifications, he will take the computer free of Zen's perfected security interest.

BANKRUPTCY

Overview

The overall objective of bankruptcy law is to allow honest insolvent debtors to surrender most of their assets and obtain release from their debts. A secondary purpose is to give creditors fair opportunity to share in the debtor's limited assets in proportion to their claims.

Bankruptcy is typically tested by either a few multiple choice questions or a portion of an essay question. These questions normally emphasize when involuntary and voluntary proceedings can be conducted, the federal exemptions, the role of the trustee in bankruptcy, preferential transfers (very important), priorities, and conditions under which debts may be discharged in bankruptcy. Although bankruptcy under Chapter 7 is emphasized, you should also be familiar with the other portions of this module.

A. Alternatives to Bankruptcy Proceedings

1. Creditors may choose to do nothing
   a. Expense of collection may exceed what creditors could recover if
      1) Much property is secured or mortgaged
      2) Exemptions may be high, i.e., amount the debtor may keep after bankruptcy proceedings
   b. Creditors may expect debtor to pull through
   c. Tax deduction is available for bad debts if uncollectibility of debt established
   d. Creditors may simply extend the time when payment is due
2. Grab law
   a. Creditors may rush to satisfy their claims individually through legal proceedings
   b. Methods
      1) Obtain legal judgments against debtor
      2) Seize and sell property
      3) Attach liens to property
      4) Garnish debts owed to debtor
      5) Recover property fraudulently conveyed to a third person, e.g., given to relative to put beyond creditors' reach
   c. May result in bankruptcy proceedings
      1) Especially if some creditors do not fare well and are dissatisfied
      2) Liens, preferential transfers, and fraudulent conveyances may be set aside

3. Assignment for the benefit of creditors
   a. Provided for the benefit of creditors
   b. Debtor voluntarily transfers all of his assets to an assignee (or trustee) to be sold for the benefit of creditors
   c. Assignee takes legal title
      1) Debtor must cease all control of assets
      2) Assignment is irrevocable
   d. No agreement between creditors is necessary
   e. Dissatisfied creditors may file a timely petition in bankruptcy and assignments may be set aside
4. Creditors' committee
   a. Submission of business and financial affairs by the debtor to the control of a committee of creditors
   b. Creditors' committee is given management of assets or business but not necessarily title
   c. Not as severe as assignment because assets not liquidated
   d. Nevertheless, it is similar to assignment for benefit of creditors
5. Composition with creditors
   a. Creditors agree to accept less than is due, i.e., a percentage of their claims, in full satisfaction of the debt
   b. Must have consideration
      1) The creditors' mutual promises to accept less than full amount
         a) Must have more than one creditor because one creditor is not bound by promise to accept less, but if more than one creditor, their mutual promises bind them
         b) All the creditors need not agree unless the agreement so states
      2) Debtor pays (pro rata) creditors
   c. Debts are not discharged until debtor performs agreement
   d. Creditors who do not agree are not bound
   e. Dissatisfied creditors may be able to force debtor into bankruptcy
6. Receiverships
   a. This provides for the general administration of a debtor's assets by a court appointee for the benefit of all parties

B. <u>Bankruptcy in General</u>

1. Bankruptcy is based on federal law
2. Bankruptcy Reform Act of 1978 made several important changes over prior law
   a. Recent federal legislation (Bankruptcy Amendments and Federal Judgeship Act of 1984) created a new Bankruptcy Court arrangement with the purpose of replacing certain Bankruptcy Act provisions that were found unconstitutional in a recent Supreme Court decision

1) Based on constitutional provision that judicial power should be placed with judges having life tenure and having protection against salary decreases

3. Bankruptcy provides a method of protecting creditors' rights and granting the debtor relief from his/her indebtedness

   a. Debtor is permitted to have a fresh start
   b. Creditors are treated more fairly according to the priorities stated in bankruptcy laws to effect an equitable distribution of debtor's property

C. Chapter 7 Voluntary Bankruptcy Petitions

1. A voluntary bankruptcy petition is a formal request by the debtor for an order of relief

   a. The petition is filed with the court along with a list of the debtor's assets and liabilities
   b. Debtor need not be insolvent--merely needs to state that s/he has debts
   c. The debtor is automatically given an order of relief upon filing of petition

2. Any person, partnerships, or corporation may file a bankruptcy petition with the exception of a

   a. Governmental unit--may file under Chapter 9
   b. Railroad
   c. Insurance company
   d. Banking corporation
   e. Building and loan association
   f. Credit union

D. Chapter 7 Involuntary Bankruptcy Petitions

1. An involuntary bankruptcy petition may be filed with the bankruptcy court by the creditors requesting an order for relief

2. Requirements to file petition

   a. If there are fewer than twelve creditors, a single creditor may file the petition as long as his claim aggregates $5,000 in excess of any security he may hold

      1) Claims must not be contingent as to liability

   b. If there are twelve or more creditors, then at least three must sign the petition and they must have claims which aggregate $5,000 in excess of any security held by them

      1) Claims must not be contingent as to liability
      2) Claims subject to bona fide dispute are not counted in above $5,000 tests

   c. Creditors who file in bad faith may be assessed damages (actual and punitive) by the court

3. Exempt from involuntary bankruptcy are
   a. Persons (individuals, partnerships, or corporations) owing less than $5,000
   b. Farmers--if 80% of their income comes from farming operations
   c. Governmental units, railroads, insurance companies, banks, savings and loan associations, and credit unions
   d. Charitable organizations
4. Bankruptcy not available (voluntarily or involuntarily) for deceased person's estate
   a. But once bankruptcy has begun, it is not stopped if bankrupt (debtor) dies
5. An order of relief will be granted if the requirements for filing are met, and
   a. The petition is uncontested; or
   b. The petition is contested; and
      1) The debtor is generally not paying his/her debts as they become due; or
      2) During the 120 days preceding the filing of the petition, a custodian was appointed or took possession of substantially all of the property of the debtor

         EXAMPLE: Debtor assigns his property for the benefit of his creditor.
   c. Note that the above rules involve a modified insolvency in the "equity sense" (i.e., debtor not paying debts as they become due). The rest of the Bankruptcy Act uses insolvency in the "bankrupt sense" (i.e., liabilities exceed fair market value of all assets). The use of insolvency in the equity sense for involuntary proceedings is an important change that the Bankruptcy Reform Act of 1978 made.
6. Creditors may be required to file a bond to indemnify debtor for losses in contesting to defer frivolous involuntary petitions
   a. Court may award attorneys' fees and court costs to debtor if successfully challenges petition
   b. Punitive damages possible for bad faith petitions

E. Chapter 7 Bankruptcy Proceedings

1. Take place under federal law
   a. An order of relief must be granted
   b. Court appoints interim trustee
   c. Filing petition automatically stays (suspends) other legal proceeding against debtor's estate until bankruptcy case is over or until court orders otherwise

      EXAMPLE: Mortgage foreclosure by savings and loan will be suspended against debtor.
2. First creditors' meeting
   a. Debtor furnishes a schedule of assets, their locations, and a list of creditors

1) Claims of omitted creditors who do not obtain actual notice of the bankruptcy proceedings within the 6-month period in which creditors must file claims are not discharged

b. Creditors must be given 20 days notice
c. Called within 25-45 days after order for relief
d. Claims are deemed allowed unless objected to, in which case the court will determine their validity

 1) Contingent and unliquidated claims are estimated

e. Trustee may be elected in Chapter 7 proceeding. If no election requested by creditors, interim trustee appointed by Court continues in office.

 1) Creditor voting for election of trustee requires a majority as to the amount of claims being voted and the voting creditors must represent 20% of all claims entitled to vote

  a) Secured creditor can only vote to extent claim exceeds collateral
  b) Creditors who are not allowed to vote include

   1] Relatives (of an individual debtor)
   2] Officers, directors, and stockholders (of a corporate debtor)

3. Trustee--the representative of the estate

 a. Court appoints an interim trustee until creditors elect one
 b. Permanent trustee may be elected at first creditors' meeting

  1) Often creditors do not find it worthwhile to attend the creditors' meeting and the interim trustee will remain as trustee

 c. Trustee has right to receive compensation for services rendered
 d. Duties--to collect, liquidate, and distribute the estate, keeping accurate records of all transactions

  1) Creditors have six months to file claims in Chapter 7 case

 e. The Estate which the trustee represents consists of any property presently owned (or received) by the debtor within six months after petition for bankruptcy--by bequest, devise, inheritance, property settlement with spouse, divorce decree, or life insurance

  1) Property acquired, other than by methods listed above, by debtor after filing is "new estate" and not subject to creditors' claims in bankruptcy proceeding
  2) Exemptions--debtor is entitled

   a) To keep any interests in joint tenancy property if those interests are exempt under other nonbankruptcy law, and

   b) The option of choosing <u>either</u> certain necessaries permitted by the state law where the petition is filed (state exemptions) <u>or</u> the federal exemptions (unless the particular state involved has enacted legislation to eliminate federal exemptions)

    1] Typical state exemptions (limited in monetary value) include

     a] Small amount of money
     b] Residence
     c] Clothing
     d] Tools of trade
     e] Insurance

2] Allowable federal exemptions include

a] $7,500 equity in principal residence
b] $1,200 equity in one motor vehicle
c] $750 in books and tools of one's trade
d] $200 per item qualifying for personal, family, or home use (has an aggregate ceiling of $4,000)
e] $500 in jewelry
f] Social security and alimony
g] Prescribed health aids
h] Interest in any property not to exceed $400 plus $3,750 of any unused portion of the homestead exemption (item a]); can be used to protect any type of property including cash

f. Powers of trustee

1) Trustee may take any legal action necessary to carry out duties

a) Trustee may utilize any defense available to the debtor against third parties
b) Trustee may continue or cease any legal action started by the debtor for the benefit of the estate

2) Trustee, with court approval, may employ professionals, e.g., accountants and lawyers, to assist trustee in carrying out duties which require professional expertise

a) Employed professional must not hold any interest adverse to that of debtor
b) Employed professional has right to receive compensation for reasonable value of services performed
c) Trustee, with court approval, may act in professional capacity and be compensated for professional services rendered

3) Trustee must within 60 days of the order for relief assume or reject any executory contract, including leases, made by the debtor

a) Any not assumed are deemed rejected
b) Trustee must perform all obligations on lease of nonresidential property until lease is either assumed or rejected

c) Rejection of a contract is a breach of contract and the injured party may become an unsecured creditor

d) Trustee may assign leases if good for bankrupt's estate

4) Trustee may set aside liens (those which arise automatically under law)

a) Becomes effective when bankruptcy petition is filed or when debtor becomes insolvent
b) Is not enforceable against a bona fide purchaser when the petition is filed
c) Is enforceable against landlord for rent

5) Trustee may set aside transfers made within one year prior to the filing of the bankruptcy petition if

a) The transfer was made with intent to hinder, delay, or defraud any creditor. The debtor need not be insolvent at time of transfer.

b) Debtor received less than a reasonably equivalent value in exchange for such transfer or obligation and the debtor

1] Was insolvent at the time, or became insolvent as a result of the transfer
2] Was engaged in business, or was about to engage in a transaction, for which debtor's property was unreasonably small capital
3] Intended or believed it would incur debts beyond its ability to pay them as they matured

c) If the fact that the transfer was a fraudulent conveyance was the only grounds for avoiding the transfer; once avoided by trustee, transferee that gave value in good faith has a lien on property transferred to the extent of value given

6) Trustee may also set aside preferential transfers of property to a creditor made within the previous 90 days while insolvent in the "bankruptcy sense"

a) Preferential transfers are those made for antecedent debts which enable the creditor to receive more than he would have otherwise under a Chapter 7 liquidation proceeding

b) The Bankruptcy Act presumes that the debtor is insolvent during the 90 days prior to the date the petition was filed

1] Does not require that transferee have knowledge of insolvency

c) Preferential transfers made to insiders within the previous 12 months may be set aside

1] Insiders are relatives, officers, directors, controlling stockholders of corporations, or general partners of partnerships

2] If preference occurred within the period between 90 days prior to the filing of the petition and 1 year before the filing, under earlier law the trustee had the burden of proving that debtor was insolvent in "bankruptcy sense" and that insider/creditor had reason to believe the debtor was insolvent at the time of the transfer. However, the trustee is no longer required to show that insider had reasonable cause to believe that debtor was insolvent.

EXAMPLE: One year ago Herb purchased a car on credit from Ike. Thirty days before filing for bankruptcy, Herb, while insolvent, makes a payment to Ike concerning the auto. This is a preference. If Ike were Herb's brother, this payment would have been a preference if it had occurred, for example, 120 days before the filing of the petition while Herb was insolvent (insider preference).

d) Exceptions to trustee's power to avoid preferential transfers

1] A substantially contemporaneous exchange between creditor and debtor whereby debtor receives new value

EXAMPLE: Herb while insolvent purchases a car for cash from Ike within 90 days of filing a petition in bankruptcy. The trustee could not avoid this transaction because Herb, the debtor, received present (i.e., new) value, the car, for the cash transferred to Ike, the creditor. This is not a voidable preference.

2] A payment made by debtor in the ordinary course of business is not a preference (45 day limit under prior law was eliminated)

3] A security interest given by debtor to acquire property that is perfected within 10 days after such security interest attaches

g. Trustee may sue or be sued
h. Trustee makes interim reports to the court and makes a final accounting of the administration of the estate

F. <u>Claims</u>

1. Property rights -- where claimant has a property right, property is turned over to claimant, because not considered part of debtor's estate

   a. Reclamation is a claim against specific property by a person claiming it to be his

      EXAMPLE: A person rented a truck for a week and in the meantime he becomes bankrupt. The lessor will make a reclamation.

   b. Trust claim is made by beneficiary for trust property when the trustee is bankrupt

      EXAMPLE: Trustee maintains a trust account for beneficiary under a trust set up in a will. Trustee becomes bankrupt. The trust account is not part of trustee's estate. The beneficiary may claim the trust account as his property.

   c. Secured claim when debtor has a security interest, e.g., mortgage, in property or security interest under Article 9 of UCC

      1) As long as trustee does not successfully attack the security--basically, security interest must be without defects to prevail against trustee (i.e., perfected security interests)

      2) Secured status may be achieved by subrogation, e.g., surety is subrogated to creditor's collateral

   d. Set-offs are allowed to the extent the bankrupt and creditor have mutual debts whether unsecured or not

2. Filing of claims

   a. All claims must be filed within six months after the first creditors' meeting
   b. Claims must

      1) State consideration for claim
      2) Be signed by creditor
      3) Be under oath
      4) State security held
      5) List payments on claim
      6) State that claim is just

3. Proof of Claims

   a. Claims are deemed allowed unless an objection is made

      1) Contingent and unliquidated claims may be estimated

   b. Claims below are not allowed if an objection is made

1) Unenforceable claims (by law or agreement)
2) Unmatured interest as of date of filing bankruptcy petition
3) Claims which may be offset
4) Property tax claim in excess of the property value
5) Insider or attorney claims in excess of reasonable value of services
6) Alimony, maintenance, and support claims for amounts due after bankruptcy petition is filed (they are not dischargeable)
7) Landlord's damages for lease termination in excess of any unpaid rent and the greater of
   a) One year's rent, or
   b) 15% of the remaining lease not to exceed 3 years rent
8) Damages for termination of an employment contract in excess of one year's wages
9) Certain employment tax claims

4. Priority of claims (be sure to know)
   a. Property rights, e.g., secured debts
      1) Technically, they are not a part of the priorities because they never become part of the bankrupt estate. But practically, the validity of the property right must be determined and they are the first claims to be satisfied. (Any amount owed to the creditor in excess of the secured debt claim is settled as unsecured, see "c.7)" below.)
   b. Unsecured claims are paid to each level of priority before any lower level is paid
      1) If there are insufficient assets to pay any given level then assets are prorated at that level (the next levels get $0)
   c. Levels of priority
      1) Administration costs
         a) Includes fees to attorneys, accountants, trustees and appraisers as well as expenses incurred in recovering or discovering property that should be included in bankrupt's estate
      2) Claims arising in ordinary course of debtor's business after bankruptcy petition is filed
      3) Wages of bankrupt's employees ($2,000 maximum each) accrued within 3 months before the petition in bankruptcy was filed
      4) Contributions to employee reduced benefit plans within the prior 180 days, limited to $2,000 per employee, reduced by amount received as wage preference
      5) Consumer deposits for undelivered goods or services limited to $900 per individual
      6) Taxes (federal, state, and local)
      7) General (unsecured) creditors

G. <u>Discharge of a Bankrupt</u>

1. A discharge is the release of a debtor from all his debts not paid in bankruptcy except those not dischargeable
   a. Granting an order of relief to an individual is an automatic application for discharge

b. Corporations and partnerships cannot receive a discharge

2. A debtor must be adjudged an "honest debtor" to be discharged

3. Acts that bar discharge of all debts

   a. Improper actions during bankruptcy proceeding

      1) Making false claims against the estate
      2) Making any false entry in or on any document of account relating to bankrupt's affairs
      3) Concealing property
      4) Transfer of property after filing with intent to defeat the law
      5) Received money for acting or not acting in bankruptcy proceedings
      6) These acts are also punishable by fines and imprisonment

   b. Failed to satisfactorily explain any loss of assets
   c. Refused to obey court orders
   d. Removed or destroyed property within twelve months prior to the filing of the petition
   e. Destroyed, falsified, concealed, or failed to keep books of account or records unless such act was justified under the circumstances
   f. Been discharged in bankruptcy proceedings within the past six years
   g. "Substantial abuse" of bankruptcy (under Chapter 7) by individual debtor with primarily consumer debts

4. Employers (both governmental and private) cannot fire employee for having declared bankruptcy

H. Debts Not Discharged by Bankruptcy (even though general discharge allowed)

1. Taxes within three years of filing bankruptcy petition
2. Liability for obtaining money or property by false pretenses
3. Willful and malicious injuries to a person or property of another
4. Debts incurred by driving while legally intoxicated
5. Alimony, separate maintenance, or child support
6. Unscheduled debts unless creditor had actual notice of proceedings, i.e., where bankrupt failed to list creditor and debt
7. Those created by fraud (e.g., embezzlement) while acting in a fiduciary capacity
8. Governmental fines or penalties imposed within prior 3 years
9. Educational loans of a governmental unit or nonprofit institution which became due within prior 5 years unless liability would impose "undue hardship" on debtor or debtor's dependents
10. Those from a prior bankruptcy proceeding in which the debtor waived discharge or was denied discharge
11. To avoid the practice of "loading up on luxury goods" before bankruptcy, there is a presumption of nondischargeability for

    a. Consumer debts to a single debtor of $500 or more for luxury goods or services
    b. Certain cash advances based on consumer credit exceeding $1,000

I. Revocation of Discharge

1. Discharge may be revoked if bankrupt committed fraud during bankruptcy proceedings

   EXAMPLE: A bankrupt conceals assets in order to defraud creditors.

2. Must be applied for by an interested party within one year of discharge

   a. Interested party is someone affected, e.g., creditor who never received payment

J. Reaffirmation

1. Debtor promises to pay a debt that will be or has been discharged. The code makes it difficult to reaffirm a dischargeable debt.

   a. Reaffirmation of a dischargeable debt to be enforceable must satisfy the following conditions

      1) New agreement must be enforceable under appropriate state contract law
      2) New agreement must have been made before the granting of a discharge
      3) Debtor has 60 days after the date the agreement becomes enforceable to rescind the agreement
      4) If debtor is an individual

         a) Debtor must have received appropriate warnings from the court or attorney on effects of reaffirmation

         b) And if also involves consumer debt not secured by real property, court must approve new agreement as being in best interests of debtor and not imposing undue hardship on debtor

K. Debts Adjustment Plans - Chapter 13

1. To be eligible debtor must

   a. Have regular income, and
   b. Owe unsecured debts of less than $100,000, and
   c. Owe secured debts of less than $350,000

2. Initiated when debtor files voluntary petition in bankruptcy court

   a. Creditors may not file involuntary petition under Chapter 13
   b. Petition normally includes composition or extension plan

      1) Composition--see "A.5."
      2) Extension--provides debtor up to three years (five years if court approves) for payments to creditors

   c. Filing of petition stays all collection and straight bankruptcy proceedings against debtor
   d. Debtor has exclusive right to propose plan

      1) If debtor does not file plan, creditors may force debtor into involuntary proceeding under Chapter 7

e. Plan will be confirmed or denied by court without approval of creditors

   1) However, unsecured creditors must receive as much as they would get under Chapter 7

f. Court must appoint trustee in Chapter 13 cases
g. Debtor engaged in business may continue to operate that business subject to limitations imposed by court
h. Completion of plan discharges debtor from debts covered
i. If composition were involved, then discharge bars another discharge for six years unless debtor paid 70% of debts covered

L. Business Reorganization - Chapter 11

1. Goal is to keep financially troubled firm in business. It is an alternative to liquidation under Chapter 7 (straight bankruptcy).
2. Can be initiated by debtor (voluntary) or creditors (involuntary)
3. Available to individuals, partnerships, or corporations including railroads. All other entities ineligible to be debtors under Chapter 7 are ineligible under Chapter 11.
4. If involuntary, same requirements must be met as needed to initiate a Chapter 7 involuntary proceeding. (See "D.2.")
5. Creditors' committee is selected from unsecured creditors after court accepts petition and grants order for relief

   a. Duties include

      1) Determine if business should continue to operate
      2) Determine if court should be asked to appoint a trustee or examiner
      3) Conduct an investigation of the debtor's financial affairs
      4) Generally consult with the debtor or trustee in the administration of the case

6. A trustee may be appointed "for cause" or "in the interest of creditors"

   a. Cause shall include fraud, dishonesty, incompetence, or gross mismanagement
   b. Trustee may be appointed only upon request of a party of interest and after notice and hearing

7. Unless the court orders otherwise, the debtor may continue to operate the business
8. If debtor does not submit plan within 120 days of order of relief, creditor may then file reorganization plan
9. Once confirmed plan is a binding contract between debtor and creditor concerning financial rehabilitation of the firm

Multiple Choice Questions (1–22)

1. A client has joined other creditors of the Ajax Demolition Company in a composition agreement seeking to avoid the necessity of a bankruptcy proceeding against Ajax. Which statement describes the composition agreement?
   a. It provides for the appointment of a receiver to take over and operate the debtor's business.
   b. It must be approved by all creditors.
   c. It does not discharge any of the debts included until performance by the debtor has taken place.
   d. It provides a temporary delay, not to exceed six months, insofar as the debtor's obligation to repay the debts included in the composition.

2. A voluntary bankruptcy proceeding is available to
   a. All debtors provided they are insolvent.
   b. Debtors only if the overwhelming preponderance of creditors have **not** petitioned for and obtained a receivership pursuant to state law.
   c. Corporations only if a reorganization has been attempted and failed.
   d. Most debtors even if they are **not** insolvent.

3. Bar, a creditor of Sy, has filed an involuntary petition in bankruptcy against Sy. Sy is indebted to six unsecured creditors including Bar for $6,000 each. If Sy opposes the petition, which of the following is correct?
   a. Bar must be joined by at least two other creditors in filing the petition.
   b. The court must appoint a trustee within ten days after the filing of the petition.
   c. Bar may be required to file a bond indemnifying Sy for any losses which Sy may incur.
   d. The court may **not** award attorney's fees to Sy due to its limited authority under the Bankruptcy Code.

4. An involuntary petition in bankruptcy
   a. Will be denied if a majority of creditors in amount and in number have agreed to a common law composition agreement.
   b. Can be filed by creditors only once in a seven-year period.
   c. May be successfully opposed by the debtor by proof that the debtor is solvent in the bankruptcy sense.
   d. If **not** contested will result in the entry of an order for relief by the bankruptcy judge.

5. The trustee in bankruptcy of a landlord-debtor under a Chapter 7 liquidation
   a. Must be elected by the creditors immediately after a bankruptcy petition is filed.
   b. May **not** be appointed by the court after the order for relief has been entered.
   c. Must reject the executory contracts of the debtor.
   d. May assign the leases of the debtor.

6. A bankrupt who has voluntarily filed for and received a discharge in bankruptcy
   a. Will receive a discharge of any and all debts owed by him as long as he has **not** committed a bankruptcy offense.
   b. Can obtain another voluntary discharge in bankruptcy after five years have elapsed from the date of the prior discharge.
   c. Must surrender for distribution to the creditors amounts received as an inheritance if the receipt occurs within 180 days after filing of the petition.
   d. Is precluded from owning or operating a similar business for two years.

7. Haplow engaged Turnbow as his attorney when threatened by several creditors with a bankruptcy proceeding. Haplow's assets consisted of $85,000 and his debts were $125,000. A petition was subsequently filed and was uncontested. Several of the creditors are concerned that the suspected large legal fees charged by Turnbow will diminish the size of the distributable estate. What are the rules or limitations which apply to such fees?
   a. None, since it is within the attorney-client privileged relationship.
   b. The fee is presumptively valid as long as arrived at in an arm's-length negotiation.
   c. Turnbow must file with the court a statement of compensation paid or agreed to for review as to its reasonableness.
   d. The trustee must approve the fee.

8. Under the Bankruptcy Code, one of the elements that must be established in order for the trustee in bankruptcy to void a preferential transfer to a creditor who is not an insider is that

a. The transferee-creditor received more than he would have received in a liquidation proceeding under the Bankruptcy Code.
b. Permission was received from the bankruptcy judge prior to the trustee's signing an order avoiding the transfer.
c. The transfer was in fact a contemporaneous exchange for new value given to the debtor.
d. The transferee-creditor knew or had reason to know that the debtor was insolvent.

9. The federal bankruptcy act contains several important terms. One such term is "insider." The term is used in connection with preferences and preferential transfers. Which among the following is not an "insider?"

a. A secured creditor having a security interest in at least 25% or more of the debtor's property.
b. A partnership in which the debtor is a general partner.
c. A corporation of which the debtor is a director.
d. A close blood relative of the debtor.

Items 10 and 11 are based on the following information:

Frank has been involuntarily petitioned into bankruptcy under the liquidation provisions of the Bankruptcy Code. After reducing Frank's nonexempt property to cash, the following expenses and unsecured claims of creditors remain:

Expenses:	
Fees incurred to recover property belonging in the bankrupt's estate	$ 9,000
Costs necessary to sell the property of the estate	$ 6,000
Unsecured claims:	
Wage claims of John Doe, earned as an employee of Frank within 61 days of the filing of the bankruptcy petition	$ 3,000
Income taxes for the two years immediately preceding the filing of the bankruptcy petition	$80,000

10. If the cash available for distribution is $12,000, what amount(s) will be distributed for expenses?

	Fees to recover property of the estate	*Costs to sell property of the estate*
a.	$0	$0
b.	$6,000	$6,000
c.	$7,200	$4,800
d.	$9,000	$3,000

11. If the cash available for distribution is $25,000, what amount will be distributed for the income tax claims?

a. $ 7,000
b. $ 8,000
c. $10,000
d. $25,000

12. The Bankruptcy Reform Act of 1978 provides that certain allowed expenses and claims are entitled to a priority. Which of the following is **not** entitled to such a priority?

a. Claims of governmental units for taxes.
b. Wage claims, but to a limited extent.
c. Rents payable within the four months preceding bankruptcy, but to a limited extent.
d. Unsecured claims for contributions to employee benefit plans, but to a limited extent.

13. A debtor will be denied a discharge in bankruptcy if the debtor

a. Failed to timely list a portion of his debts.
b. Unjustifiably failed to preserve his books and records which could have been used to ascertain the debtor's financial condition.
c. Has negligently made preferential transfers to favored creditors within 90 days of the filing of the bankruptcy petition.
d. Has committed several willful and malicious acts which resulted in bodily injury to others.

14. White is a general creditor of Ned. Ned filed a petition in bankruptcy under the liquidation provisions of the Bankruptcy Code. White wishes to have the bankruptcy court either deny Ned a general discharge or not have his debt discharged. The discharge will be granted, and it will include White's debt even if

a. Ned has unjustifiably failed to preserve the records from which Ned's financial condition might be ascertained.

b. Ned had received a previous discharge in bankruptcy under the liquidation provisions within six years.
c. White's debt is unscheduled.
d. White was a secured creditor who was **not** fully satisfied from the proceeds obtained upon disposition of the collateral.

15. Hapless is a bankrupt. In connection with a debt owed to the Suburban Finance Company, he used a false financial statement to induce it to loan him $500. Hapless is seeking a discharge in bankruptcy. Which of the following is a correct statement?
a. Hapless will be denied a discharge of any of his debts.
b. Even if it can be proved that Suburban did not rely upon the financial statement, Hapless will be denied a discharge either in whole or part.
c. Hapless will be denied a discharge of the Suburban debt.
d. Hapless will be totally discharged despite the false financial statement.

16. Hard Times, Inc., is insolvent. Its liabilities exceed its assets by $13 million. Hard Times is owned by its president, Waters, and members of his family. Waters, whose assets are estimated at less than a million dollars, guaranteed the loans of the corporation. A consortium of banks is the principal creditor of Hard Times having loaned it $8 million, the bulk of which is unsecured. The banks decided to seek reorganization of Hard Times and Waters has agreed to cooperate. Regarding the proposed reorganization
a. Waters' cooperation is necessary since he must sign the petition for a reorganization.
b. If a petition in bankruptcy is filed against Hard Times, Waters will also have his personal bankruptcy status resolved and relief granted.
c. Only a duly constituted creditors committee may file a plan of reorganization of Hard Times.
d. Hard Times will remain in possession unless a request is made to the court for the appointment of a trustee.

17. Which of the following was a significant reform made in the reorganization provisions of the Bankruptcy Reform Act of 1978?
a. Separate treatment of publicly-held corporations under its provisions.
b. Elimination of the separate and competing procedures contained in the various chapters of the prior Bankruptcy Act.
c. Elimination of participation in bankruptcy reorganizations by the Securities and Exchange Commission.
d. The exclusion from its jurisdiction of partnerships and other noncorporate entities.

18. Skipper was for several years the principal stockholder, director, and chief executive officer of the Canarsie Grocery Corporation. Canarsie had financial difficulties and an order of relief was filed against it, and subsequently discharged. Several creditors are seeking to hold Skipper personally liable as a result of his stock ownership and as a result of his being an officer-director. Skipper in turn filed with the bankruptcy judge a claim for $1,400 salary due him. Which of the following is correct?
a. Skipper's salary claim will be allowed and he will be entitled to a priority.
b. Skipper has **no** personal liability to the creditors as long as Canarsie is recognized as a separate legal entity.
c. Skipper can **not** personally file a petition in bankruptcy for seven years.
d. Skipper is personally liable to the creditors for Canarsie's losses.

November 1985 Questions

19. Lux Corp. has been suffering large losses for the past two years. Because of its inability to meet current obligations, Lux has filed a petition for reorganization under Chapter 11 of the Bankruptcy Code. The reorganization provisions under the Bankruptcy Code
a. Require that the court appoint a trustee in all cases.
b. Permit Lux to remain in possession of its assets.
c. Apply only to involuntary bankruptcy.
d. Will apply to Lux only if Lux is required to register pursuant to the federal securities laws.

20. Fox, a sole proprietor, has been involuntarily petitioned into bankruptcy under the liquidation provisions of the Bankruptcy Code. Sax, CPA, has been appointed trustee of the debtor's estate. If Sax also wishes to act as the tax return preparer for the estate, which of the following statements is correct?
a. Sax may employ himself to prepare tax returns if authorized by the court and may receive a separate fee for services rendered in each capacity.

b. Sax is prohibited from serving as both trustee and preparer under any circumstances since serving in that dual capacity would be a conflict of interest.

c. Although Sax may serve as both trustee and preparer, he is entitled to receive a fee only for the services rendered as a preparer.

d. Although Sax may serve as both trustee and preparer, his fee for services rendered in each capacity will be determined solely by the size of the estate.

21. Sly has serious financial problems and is unable to meet current unsecured obligations of $30,000 to 19 creditors who are demanding immediate payment. Sly owes Kane $6,500 and Kane has decided to file an involuntary petition in bankruptcy against Sly. Which of the following is necessary in order for Kane to validly petition Sly into bankruptcy?

a. Kane must allege and establish that Sly's liabilities exceed the fair market value of Sly's assets.

b. Kane must be joined by at least two other creditors.

c. Sly must have committed an act of bankruptcy within 120 days of the filing.

d. Kane must be a secured creditor.

22. Which of the following will **not** be discharged in a bankruptcy proceeding?

a. Claims resulting out of an extension of credit based upon false representations.

b. Claims of secured creditors which remain unsatisfied after their receipt of the proceeds from the disposition of the collateral.

c. Claims for unintentional torts which resulted in bodily injury to the claimant.

d. Claims arising out of the breach of a contract by the debtor.

Repeat Question

(1185,L1,29) Identical to item 6 above

Problems

Problem 1 (1183,L3a)

(7 to 10 minutes)

Part a. Skidmore, doing business as Frock & Fashions, is hopelessly insolvent. Several of his aggressive creditors are threatening to attach his property or force him to make preferential payments of their debts. In fairness to himself and to all his creditors, Skidmore has filed a voluntary petition in bankruptcy on behalf of himself and Frock & Fashions. An order for relief has been entered.

Skidmore's bankruptcy is fairly straightforward with the following exceptions:

- Skidmore claims exemptions for his summer cottage and for his home.
- Morse, a business creditor, asserts that commercial creditors have a first claim to all Skidmore's property, business and personal.
- Walton seeks a denial of Skidmore's discharge since Skidmore obtained credit from him by use of a fraudulent financial statement.
- Harper claims a priority for the amount owed him which was not satisfied as a result of his resorting to the collateral securing his loan.

Required:

Answer the following, setting forth reasons for any conclusions stated.

1. What are the principal avoiding powers of the trustee in bankruptcy?
2. Discuss in separate paragraphs each of the various claims and assertions stated above.

Problem 2 (1181,L4a)

(10 to 15 minutes)

Part a. A small business client, John Barry, doing business as John Barry Fashions, is worried about an involuntary bankruptcy proceeding being filed by his creditors. His net worth using a balance-sheet approach is $8,000 ($108,000 assets – $100,000 liabilities). However, his cash flow is negative and he has been hard pressed to meet current obligations as they mature. He is, in fact, some $12,500 in arrears in payments to his creditors on bills submitted during the past two months.

Required:

Answer the following, setting forth reasons for any conclusions stated.

1. What are the current requirements for a creditor or creditors filing an involuntary petition in bankruptcy and could they be satisfied in this situation?
2. Will the fact that Barry is solvent in the bankruptcy sense result in the court's dismissing the creditors' petition if Barry contests the propriety of the filing of a petition?

Problem 3 (1180,L3b)

(7 to 10 minutes)

Part b. In connection with the audit of One-Up, Inc., a question has arisen regarding the validity of a $10,000 purchase money security interest in certain machinery sold to Essex Company on March 2nd. Essex was petitioned into bankruptcy on May 1st by its creditors. The trustee is seeking to avoid One-Up's security interest on the grounds that it is a preferential transfer, hence voidable. The machinery in question was sold to Essex on the following terms: $1,000 down and the balance plus interest at nine percent (9%) to be paid over a three-year period. One-Up obtained a signed security agreement which created a security interest in the property on March 2nd, the date of the sale. A financing statement was filed on March 10th.

Required:

Answer the following, setting forth reasons for any conclusions stated.

1. Would One-Up's security interest in the machinery be a voidable preference?
2. In general, what are the requirements necessary to permit the trustee to successfully assert a preferential transfer and thereby set aside a creditor's security interest?

Multiple Choice Answers

1. c	6. c	11. b	15. c	19. b
2. d	7. c	12. c	16. d	20. a
3. c	8. a	13. b	17. b	21. b
4. d	9. a	14. d	18. b	22. a
5. d	10. c			

Multiple Choice Answer Explanations

A. Alternatives to Bankruptcy Proceedings

1. (578,L1,24) (c) A composition with creditors is an agreement made between a debtor and creditors whereby the creditors agree with one another and the debtor to accept less than the full amount due. The composition does not discharge any of the debts until performance by the debtor has taken place. However, the agreement is valid from the time made. Answer (a) is incorrect because a composition does not provide for an appointment of receiver which is called a receivership. Answer (b) is incorrect because it need not be approved by all creditors, only those who wish to participate. Answer (d) is incorrect because a valid composition discharges the unpaid portion of the debts and does not merely provide a temporary delay.

C. Voluntary Bankruptcy Petitions

2. (583,L1,21) (d) A voluntary bankruptcy proceeding is available to all debtors who owe debts, irrespective of whether the debtor is insolvent, except for municipalities, railroads, banks, insurance companies, and savings and loan associations. Whether the debtor's creditors have petitioned and obtained a receivership would not effect the debtor's rights to initiate a voluntary proceeding under Chapter 7 of the Bankruptcy Reform Act. Corporations do not need to first attempt a reorganization under Chapter 11 before filing a voluntary petition. Therefore, answers (a), (b) and (c) are incorrect.

D. Involuntary Bankruptcy Petitions

3. (584,L1,19) (c) Creditors filing an involuntary petition in bankruptcy may be required to file a bond indemnifying the debtors for any losses which are incurred by the debtor in resisting the petition. This is to deter the filing of any frivolous petitions. Answer (a) is incorrect because, according to the Bankruptcy Code, when a debtor has less than 12 creditors, a petition need only be filed by one or more creditors who are owed unsecured debts of at least $5,000. Only when there are 12 or more creditors is it necessary for at least 3 creditors (whom claim aggregate at least $5,000 over any security held by the creditors) to join in filing a petition. Answer (b) is incorrect because there is no requirement under the Bankruptcy Code which states that a trustee must be appointed by the court within 10 days after filing the petition. Only after an order for relief has been granted, will the court appoint an interim trustee until the permanent trustee can be elected at the first creditors' meeting. Answer (d) is incorrect since, in the event that a petition is rejected, the bankruptcy court has the authority to award the debtor attorneys' fees and other costs incurred by the debtor in refuting the petition. If the petition was filed in bad faith, punitive damages may also be awarded the debtor.

4. (583,L1,22) (d) An involuntary petition in bankruptcy, if not contested will automatically result in the entry of an order for relief by the bankruptcy court. Only if the petition is contested will the creditor(s) be required to prove either that the debtor is not paying her/his debts as they mature, or that during the 120 days preceeding the filing of a petition, a custodian was appointed or took possession of the debtors property. Answer (a) is incorrect because the presence of a composition agreement will not cause denial of an involuntary petition. In many cases a creditor who is left out of such a composition agreement may wish to file an involuntary petition in order to protect her/his interest before the debtor uses a major portion of her/his assets in settling the debts owed to only the creditors involved in the composition agreement. Answer (b) is incorrect because a petition may be filed only once in a six year period, not a seven year period. Answer (c) is incorrect because a debtor need only prove that s/he is solvent in the equity sense (i.e., that s/he is paying her/his debts as they mature) and that a custodian was not appointed or did not take possession of the debtors property within 120 days before the filing of the petition. The debtor need not prove that her/his assets exceed her/his liabilities (solvency in the bankruptcy sense).

E. Bankruptcy Proceedings

5. (1184,L1,28) (d) The trustee may assign the leases of the landlord-debtor if that is considered to be in the best interest of the debtor's estate. The trustee's duty is to acquire as many assets as possible for distribution to the creditors who filed claims in the bankruptcy proceeding. Answer (a) is incorrect because the creditors do not have the opportunity to elect a trustee until the first creditors' meeting. An interim trustee, who is appointed by the court, serves prior to the election of the trustee. Answer (b) is incorrect

because as soon as the order for relief has been entered, the court appoints an interim trustee to serve until the first creditors' meeting. If the creditors are unable to agree on the selection of a trustee, the court will then appoint a permanent trustee. Answer (c) is incorrect because the trustee has the option of performing or rejecting the executory contracts of the debtor. The best interests of the debtor's estate will dictate what course of action the trustee chooses.

6. (583,L1,23) (c) The estate which the trustee represents, consists of any property presently owned or received by the debtor within 180 days after filing of the petition by inheritance, as a result of a property settlement with a spouse, or as a beneficiary of a life insurance policy. Answer (a) is incorrect because it refers to the commission of "bankruptcy offenses" which is a term associated with the prior bankruptcy act and which is not present in the current bankruptcy law as established in the Bankruptcy Reform Act of 1978. Answer (b) is incorrect because bankruptcy can only be filed once in every 6 year period, not once in every five year period. Answer (d) is incorrect because bankruptcy law does not preclude a bankrupt who received a discharge in bankruptcy from owning or operating a similar business in the future.

7. (581,L1,42) (c) According to the Rules of Bankruptcy Procedure, it is necessary to file a proof of claims against the debtor's estate. The filing must be timely (within a six-month period) or the claim will be barred. A claim that is filed on time is given prima facie validity and is approved unless there is an objection by one of the creditors. Answer (a) is incorrect since all claims are subject to filing and review. Answer (b) is also false because a fee may result from an arms-length negotiation and still be disallowed by Bankruptcy Procedure. Claims for services by an attorney of the debtor, to the extent a fee exceeds a reasonable value for services rendered, are disallowed. The court must approve the reasonableness of the claim even if the transaction is an arms-length negotiation. Answer (d) is false because it is the courts, not the trustee, which approve the fees.

E.3.c.5) Preferential Transfers

8. (584,L1,18) (a) Under the Bankruptcy Code, one of the elements which must be established in proving that a preferential transfer was made is that the transferee-creditor received more than he would have received in a liquidation proceeding. Answer (b) is incorrect because a trustee need not obtain the permission from the bankruptcy judge prior to avoiding a preferential transfer. Answer (c) is incorrect because one of the elements which must be present to prove that a preferential transfer has been made is that the transfer involved an antecedent debt. Since the transfer described in answer (c) was a contemporaneous exchange for new value given, no antecedent debt was involved; thus, no preferential transfer can exist. Answer (d) is incorrect because the question asks what element is necessary to prove that a preferential transfer to a creditor who is not an insider exists. Although the element described in answer (d) is necessary when proving that an insider preference has occurred within one year of the filing of the bankruptcy petition, it is not a necessary element needed to prove that a general preference has occurred within 90 days of the filing of the bankruptcy petition.

9. (580,L1,3) (a) Answer (a) is correct because a secured creditor is not an "insider" for the purposes of a preferential transfer. However, a partner is an insider with regard to the partnership, a director is an insider concerning the corporation, and a close relative is an insider to the debtor.

F. Claims

10. (1184,L1,26) (c) Under the liquidation provision of the Bankruptcy Code, administrative expenses are in the category of first priority claims. Fees and costs incurred to recover and sell the property of the bankrupt's estate qualify as administrative expenses. All creditors entitled to first priority have the right to be paid before any creditors entitled to lower priorities are paid. If there are not sufficient assets to pay all creditors at a given priority, then the distribution is made on a pro rata basis. Thus, $7,200 of the fees to recover the property and $4,800 of the cost to sell the property will be paid. Therefore, answers (a), (b), and (d) are incorrect.

11. (1184,L1,27) (b) If $25,000 is available for distribution, the $15,000 of administrative expenses will be paid in full since administrative expenses are first priority claims. The next highest priority among the listed claims is wages owed to John Doe earned within 90 days before the date of the filing of the petition. However, this priority has a maximum of $2,000 per claimant. Thus, John Doe will only receive $2,000. The remaining $8,000 will be distributed for the income tax claims. Therefore, answers (a), (c), and (d) are incorrect.

12. (582,L1,20) (c) Under the Bankruptcy Reform Act of 1978 rent claims are no longer entitled to a priority concerning the distribution of the assets in the debtor's estate. Rent claims are considered claims

of general creditors and these claims would be the last debts satisfied in the bankruptcy proceeding (on a pro rata basis with claims of other general creditors). Answers (a), (b), and (d) are incorrect because the new Act does retain priorities for taxes, wages earned within 90 days of the filing of the petition to a maximum of $2,000 or contributions to employee benefit plans arising from services rendered within 180 days of the filing.

G. Discharge of a Bankrupt

13. (584,L1,16) (b) A debtor will be denied a general discharge if that debtor destroyed, falsified, concealed, or failed to keep books of account or record unless such act was justified under the circumstances. Answer (a) is incorrect because the failure to list a portion of the debts will result only in the denial of discharge of those specific debts not listed. Answer (c) is incorrect because a negligent preferential transfer to favored creditors within 90 days of the filing will merely result in the setting aside of the transfer by the trustee; a general discharge will not be denied. However, had the transfer been a fraudulent conveyance, i.e., a transfer made with the intent to hinder, delay, or defraud any creditor, the court would have sufficient grounds to deny a general discharge. Answer (d) is incorrect since only those debts which were directly caused by the commission of willful and malicious acts will be nondischargeable. A general discharge may still be granted.

14. (584,L1,17) (d) The fact that the debt of a secured party was not fully satisfied from the proceeds obtained from disposition of the collateral will not result in a denial of a general discharge, nor will the remaining portion of the secured debt be nondischargeable. In such situations the secured party has the same priority as a general unsecured creditor (lowest priority) concerning the unpaid portion of the debt. Answer (a) is incorrect because a debtor who fails to keep books will be denied a general discharge. Answer (b) is incorrect because a debtor who has received a previous discharge in bankruptcy under the liquidation provisions within six years will be denied a general discharge. Answer (c) is incorrect because unscheduled debts are not discharged in a bankruptcy proceeding.

15. (580,L1,35) (c) If the debtor supplies false information to obtain credit, the debt incurred will not be discharged in a bankruptcy proceedings. Answer (a) is incorrect because only the debt involving the false information will not be discharged. All other dischargeable debts will be terminated at the end of the bankruptcy proceedings. Answer (b) is incorrect because the creditor must rely on the false information before the resulting debt becomes nondischargeable. Answer (d) is incorrect because Hapless will be denied a discharge of the Suburban debt.

L. Business Reorganization — Chapter 11

16. (583,L1,24) (d) Under a Chapter 11 reorganization, a debtor is allowed to remain in possession of its business unless the court upon request by a party in interest appoints a trustee to take over management of the debtor's business. The court will approve such a request when it appears gross mismanagement of the business has occurred, or that the takeover by a trustee would be in the best interest of the debtor's estate. Answer (a) is incorrect because a corporate reorganization can be voluntary or involuntary. Answer (b) is incorrect because Waters, as a separate entity from Hard Times, will not have his personal bankruptcy status resolved when a petition is filed against Hard Times. Waters may be forced into bankruptcy by a separate petition, but since the corporation is a separate entity from Waters, the filing of a petition for bankruptcy against Hard Times will not automatically cause Waters' bankruptcy status to be resolved. Answer (c) is incorrect because in a Chapter 11 reorganization only the debtor may file a plan within the first 120 days after the date of the order for relief. If the debtor does not meet the 120 day deadline, any party in interest can propose a plan, but at no time is a "duly constituted creditors committee" the only party able to file a plan.

17. (582,L1,21) (b) The Bankruptcy Reform Act of 1978 eliminated the separate and competing procedures concerning reorganizations contained in Chapters 10 and 11 of the prior Bankruptcy Act. Under the new Act only one chapter (Chapter 11) concerns reorganizations. Answers (a) and (d) are incorrect because the new Bankrutpcy Reform Act does not provide separate treatment of publicly-held corporations, nor does it exclude noncorporate entities from its reorganization provisions. Answer (c) is incorrect because the Act does limit the power of the SEC concerning the Commission's participation in reorganizations, but it does not completely eliminate the SEC's participation in bankruptcy reorganizations.

Other

18. (582,L1,17) (b) A corporation is considered a separate legal entity from its owners (the shareholders). Generally, the shareholders are not personally liable for the debts of the corporation. This is normally true even concerning a principal stockholder who is a

director and chief executive officer of the corporation. However, if the purpose of incorporation is to defraud the creditors, then the courts will "pierce the corporate veil" and hold the shareholders personally liable. Answer (c) is incorrect because due to the separate legal entity concept, the bankruptcy of the corporation would not affect Skipper's right to file bankruptcy in the future. Answer (a) is incorrect because claims for services rendered by insiders (a director is an insider) are only allowed to the extent the court decides the claims are reasonable. Even if the court decides the claim is reasonable, the priority given to wage claims in a bankruptcy proceeding does not include salary claims by officers of the corporation.

November 1985 Answers

19. (1185,L1,26) (b) Under a Chapter 11 reorganization normally a debtor is allowed to remain in possession of its assets. The purpose of a Chapter 11 reorganization is to keep the financially troubled firm in business. Answer (a) is incorrect because the courts aren't required to appoint a trustee. The court will only appoint a trustee if one is requested by a party in interest to take over the debtor's business. The court will approve such a request when there is evidence of fraudulent actions by the debtor, gross mismanagement of the business, or it appears that the takeover by the trustee would be in the best interest of the debtor's estate. Answer (c) is incorrect because Chapter 11 business reorganizations permits both voluntary and involuntary proceedings. Answer (d) is incorrect. There is no such relationship between the provisions of the Bankruptcy Code and the registration requirements of the Federal Securities Laws.

20. (1185,L1,27) (a) A trustee in bankruptcy has the power to employ court approved professionals, such as accountants and attorneys, to handle estate matters which require professional expertise. These professionals have the right to reimbursement for services rendered. A trustee is not deemed to have the appropriate expertise required to prepare tax returns; thus, a trustee may employ a CPA to perform this function. Sax, as trustee, has the power to employ himself to prepare tax returns if authorized by the court and may receive a separate fee for services rendered. Answer (b) is incorrect because Sax may serve as both trustee and preparer if authorized to do so by the court. Answer (c) is incorrect because Sax has the right to receive fees for services rendered as both a trustee and a preparer. Answer (d) is incorrect because the fee for services rendered in each capacity is determined on the basis of the value of the services rendered, not solely the size of the estate.

21. (1185,L1,28) (b) Under an involuntary bankruptcy petition, if there are twelve or more creditors, then at least three of the creditors must sign the bankruptcy petition and they must have combined claims of at least $5,000 in excess of any security held by the creditors. Since Kane's unsecured debt exceeds the $5,000 minimum, Kane must find two other creditors (all unsecured in this case) to join him in the bankruptcy petition. Answer (a) is incorrect because a debtor does not have to establish that the debtor's liabilities exceed the fair market value of the debtor's assets. Answer (c) is incorrect because there is no such thing as an "act of bankruptcy" under the Bankruptcy Reform Act. Answer (d) is incorrect because there is no requirement that the petitioning creditors be secured creditors.

22. (1185,L1,30) (a) If a debtor provides false information to obtain credit or an extension of credit, then the debt will not be discharged in a bankruptcy proceeding. Answer (b) is incorrect because the claims of secured creditors which remain unsatisfied after their receipt of the proceeds from the disposition of the collateral are discharged in a bankruptcy proceeding. Answer (c) is incorrect because claims arising from an unintentional tort which resulted in bodily injury to the claimant are discharged in a bankruptcy proceeding; however, claims which arise out of malicious torts are not discharged. Answer (d) is incorrect because claims arising out of a breach of a contract by the debtor are discharged in a bankruptcy proceeding.

Answer Outline

Problem 1 Trustee's Avoiding Powers; Exempt Property; Priority of Secured Creditor (1183,L3a)

Part a.

1. Trustee has avoiding powers to set aside
   Certain statutory liens
   Preferential transfers
   Fraudulent conveyances
   Post-petition transfers
2. Resolution of claims and assertions
   Claim for cottage disallowed
   Bankruptcy Code provides one exemption on principal residence not > $7,500
   Home qualifies
   No rule separates business assets from personal assets
   Skidmore and his business are one and the same
   All assets collected and shared among creditors regardless of source
   Bankruptcy Code states fraudulent FSs will not deny general discharge of bankrupt
   However, Code will exempt such debt from discharge in bankruptcy
   Walton's claim survives
   Secured creditor entitled to collateral or equivalent
   If collateral is insufficient, secured creditor has general creditor status for balance

Unofficial Answer

Problem 1 Trustee's Avoiding Powers; Exempt Property; Priority of Secured Creditor (1183,L3a)

Part a.

1. The principal avoiding powers of the trustee are

- The power to set aside certain statutory liens.
- The power to set aside preferential transfers.
- The power to set aside fraudulent conveyances.
- The power to set aside post-petition transfers.

2. The various claims and assertions would be resolved as follows:

- The claim for an exemption allowance for the cottage will be disallowed. The Bankruptcy Code provides for one exemption for one's principal residence, not to exceed $7,500. The home will qualify for this exemption.
- There is no such rule applicable to business assets as contrasted with personal assets. In fact, there is no distinction between Skidmore and his business, Frock & Fashions. They are one and the same and all assets will be collected and shared among the creditors without distinction as to the source.
- The Bankruptcy Code makes it clear that such conduct would not result in a denial of the discharge of the bankrupt. It will, however, result in the denial of that particular debt from discharge in bankruptcy. Thus, Walton's claim will survive the bankruptcy proceeding.
- A bona fide secured creditor is entitled to the collateral or its monetary equivalent. If this is insufficient to satisfy the loan, the secured creditor has the status of a general creditor for the balance. The priorities section of the Bankruptcy Code provides for no such priority as claimed by Harper.

Answer Outline

Problem 2 Involuntary Bankruptcy Petition (1181,L4a)

a1. Under Bankruptcy Reform Act of 1978, an involuntary petition may be filed by creditors
   If there are 12 or more creditors
   At least three must sign the petition
   If there are fewer than 12 creditors
   A single creditor may file the petition
   The creditor(s) must have claim or claims aggregating $5,000
   In excess of the value of any liens securing the claims
   Involuntary petition could be validly filed by creditors

a2. Barry's defense of being solvent in the bankruptcy sense will not persuade the court to dismiss creditors' petition
   Under the Bankruptcy Act, insolvency is measured in the equity sense
   A debtor is deemed insolvent if not able to meet currently maturing obligations
   Barry is unable to pay debts as they become due
   A debtor is deemed insolvent if within 120 days preceding the filing of the petition a custodian of the debtor's property is appointed
   Solvency in the equity sense would be a viable defense to the petition

Unofficial Answer

Problem 2 Involuntary Bankruptcy Petition (1181,L4a)

Part a.

1. Under the Bankruptcy Reform Act of 1978, an involuntary petition may be filed by three or more creditors having claims aggregating $5,000 more than the value of any liens securing the claims. In the event there are fewer than 12 creditors, one or more creditors with claims of $5,000 or more can file. The facts indicate that Barry has $12,500 in overdue debts. It would appear likely that these requirements could be met and an involuntary petition could be validly filed. The act permits the involuntary debtor to file an answer to the petition.

2. No. Under the 1978 act, the principal defense available to an involuntary debtor would still be solvency. However, the defense of solvency in the bankruptcy sense (essentially a balance sheet approach) has been rejected when an involuntary liquidation is sought. Instead, the act has adopted a modified or expanded version of insolvency in the equity sense. A debtor is insolvent if he is generally not paying debts as they become due. In addition, a debtor is insolvent if within 120 days before the date of the filing of the petition a custodian was appointed or took possession of the debtor's property. Barry, of course, appears to be squarely within the scope of the first part of this test. Realistically, he could not hope to have the petition dismissed on the grounds of solvency.

Answer Outline

Problem 3 Security Interest as a Voidable Preference (1180,L3b)

b1. No, security interest is not voidable preference
Purchase money security interest perfected within 10 days after attachment is exempted from preference states

b2. Trustee may avoid any transfer of property as preferential which is:
1. To or for benefit of a creditor
2. For antecedent debt owed by debtor before such transfer
3. Made while debtor insolvent in bankrupt sense
    a. Transfer was to "insider"
    b. Transferee had reasonable cause to believe debtor insolvent at time of transfer
4. Transfer that enables creditor to receive more than in straight liquidation proceeding

Unofficial Answer

Problem 3 Security Interest as a Voidable Preference (1180,L3b)

Part b.

1. No. The Bankruptcy Reform Act of 1978 has not only modified the requirements for establishing a voidable preference, it has also specified transactions that do not constitute preferences. One such transaction is the creditor's taking a security interest in property acquired by the debtor as a contemporaneous exchange for new value given to the debtor to enable him to acquire such property (a purchase money security interest). The security interest must be perfected (filed) within 10 days after attachment. The act is in harmony with the secured transactions provisions of the Uniform Commercial Code. Thus, One-Up has a valid security interest in the machinery it sold to Essex.

2. The Bankruptcy Reform Act of 1978 does not require that the creditor have knowledge or reasonable cause to believe the debtor is insolvent in the bankruptcy sense. Instead, under the act, where such insolvency exists on or within ninety days before the filing of the petition, knowledge of insolvency by the transferee need not be established. The act also assumes th[at] the debtor's insolvency is presumed if the transfer alleged to be preferential is made within 90 days. Finally, the time period in which transfers may be set aside is 90 days unless the transferee is an "insider." If the transfer is to an insider, the trustee may avoid transfers made within one year prior to the filing of the petition. Thus, the trustee may avoid as preferential any transfer of property of the debtor that is

- To or for the benefit of a creditor.
- For or on account of an antecedent debt owed by the debtor before such transfer was made.
- Made while the debtor was insolvent in the bankruptcy sense (however, if the transfer is made within 90 days, the debtor's insolvency is presumed).
- Made on or within 90 days of the filing of the petition (or if made after the 90 days but within one year prior to the date of the filing of the petition and the transfer was to an "insider," it may be set aside if the transferee had reasonable cause to believe the debtor was insolvent at the time of the transfer).
- Such that it enables the creditor to receive more than he would if it were a straight liquidation proceeding.

The bankruptcy act contains a lengthy definition of the term "insider" that includes common relationship[s] that the transferee has to the debtor, which, in case [of] an individual debtor, could be certain relatives, a partnership in which he is a general partner, his fellow general partners, or a corporation controlled by him.

SURETYSHIP

Overview

Suretyship is a broad legal term describing relationships where one person agrees to be answerable for the debt or default of another person. Suretyship is a form of security so that if the principal debtor is unable or unwilling to perform, the creditor has an immediate and direct remedy against a third party, called the surety, to satisfy the obligation of the debtor. Thus, suretyship allows creditors to protect themselves against the principal debtor's defenses of lack of capacity, death, bankruptcy, or inability to pay. However, the undertaking of a surety is not absolute. The surety may defend against payment of the debt or obligation by asserting any of its available defenses.

Suretyship is typically tested by a few multiple choice questions and sometimes by a portion of an essay question. The questions emphasize the rights, remedies, and liabilities of the three parties in a suretyship relationship. You should understand which defenses can be used in this relationship. Also, be sure to understand the rights of subrogation and contribution among co-sureties.

A. Nature of Suretyship

1. A suretyship contract is a relationship whereby one person agrees to answer for debt, default, or tort of another
    a. Surety agrees with creditor to satisfy obligation if principal debtor does not
    b. Purpose of a suretyship agreement is to protect creditor by providing creditor with added security for obligation and reduce creditor's risk of loss

    EXAMPLE: In order for X to obtain a loan from Bank, M (who has a good credit standing) promises to Bank that he will pay debt if X defaults.

2. Suretyship agreements involve three parties
    a. Creditor (Bank in above example)
    b. Principal debtor (X in above example)
        1) Has liability for debt owed to creditor
    c. Surety (M in above example)
        1) Promises to perform or pay debt on default of principal debtor
            a) Surety is primarily liable because promise is not conditional
                1] Creditor need not attempt collection from debtor first
                2] Creditor need not give notice of debtor's default
                3] Surety is liable if debtor does not perform

12

3. Examples of typical suretyship arrangements
   a. Seller of goods on credit requires buyer to obtain a surety to guarantee payment of goods purchased
   b. Bank requires owners or directors of closely held corporation to act as sureties for loan to corporation
   c. Indorser of negotiable instrument because agrees to pay if instrument not paid (unless indorses "without recourse"). (See NEGOTIABLE INSTRUMENTS.)
   d. In order to transfer a check or note, transferor may be required to obtain a surety (accommodation indorser) to guarantee payment. (See Liability of Parties in NEGOTIABLE INSTRUMENTS.)
   e. Purchaser of real property expressly assumes seller's mortgage on property (i.e., promises to pay mortgage debt). Seller becomes surety and purchaser is principal debtor.
4. Suretyship (guaranty) contracts should satisfy elements of contracts in general (See Essential Elements of a contract in CONTRACTS.)
   a. If surety's agreement arises at same time as the contract between creditor and debtor, no separate consideration is needed (consideration between creditor and debtor is sufficient)
      1) Where creditor has extended credit prior to surety's promise, independent consideration is required to support surety's promise
   b. Surety's agreement to answer for debt or default of another must be in writing. (See Statute of Frauds in CONTRACTS.)
      1) However, if surety's promise is primarily for his/her own benefit, it need not be in writing

         EXAMPLE: S agrees to pay D's debt to D's creditor if he defaults. The main purpose of S is to keep D in business to assure a steady supply of an essential component. S's agreement need not be in writing.

         EXAMPLE: A del credere agent is one who sells goods on credit to purchasers for the principal and agrees to pay the principal if the customers do not. Since his promise is primarily for his own benefit, it need not be in writing.

         EXAMPLE: Owners and officers of a closely held corporation agreed orally to act as sureties for a corporate loan. Because the loan is to benefit primarily the corporation, the suretyship agreement must be in writing. The indirect benefit the owners and officers receive does not take this agreement out of the Statute of Frauds.
5. Third-party beneficiary contract is not a suretyship contract
   a. Third-party beneficiary contract is one in which third party receives benefits from agreement made between promisor and promisee, although third person is not party to contract

      EXAMPLE: Father says: "Ship goods to my son and I will pay for them." This describes a third-party beneficiary contract, not a suretyship arrangement. Father is not promising to pay the debt of another, but rather engaging in an original promise to pay (i.e., a debtor) for goods creditor delivers to son.

6. Indemnity contract is not a suretyship contract

   a. An indemnity contract is between two parties (rather than three) whereby indemnitor makes a promise to a potential debtor, indemnitee, (not to creditor as in suretyship arrangement), to indemnify and reimburse debtor for payment of debt or for loss that may arise in future. Indemnitor pays because it has assumed risk of loss, not because of any default by principal debtor as in suretyship arrangement.

      EXAMPLE: Under terms of standard automobile collision insurance policy, insurance company agrees to indemnify automobile owner against damage to his/her car caused by collision.

7. Surety and guarantor are generally considered to be synonymous

   a. Unconditional guaranty is the standard suretyship relationship in which there are no further conditions required for guarantor to be asked to pay if debtor does not

      EXAMPLE: G agreed in writing to act as a surety when D took out a loan with C, the lender. If D does not pay, C may proceed directly against G. C need not try to collect from D first.

   b. Distinguish between unconditional guaranty and conditional guaranty

      1) In case of conditional guaranty, specified condition(s) must be met before creditor can resort to guarantor.

      2) Typical conditions require creditor to give guarantor notice and first exhaust remedies available against principal debtor before attempting to collect from guarantor

8. Capacity to act as surety

   a. In general, individuals that have capacity to contract
   b. Partnerships may act as sureties unless partnership agreement expressly prohibits it from entering into suretyship contracts
   c. Individual partner has no authority to bind partnership as surety 1) unless it is in furtherance of partnership business, 2) is expressly authorized in articles of copartnership, or 3) copartners expressly authorize such action
   d. Modern trend is that corporations can

B. <u>Creditor's Rights and Remedies</u>

1. Against principal debtor

   a. Creditor has right to receive payment or performance specified in contract
   b. Creditor may proceed immediately against debtor upon default, unless conditions state otherwise in contract
   c. When debtor has more than one debt outstanding with same creditor and makes a part payment, debtor may give instructions as to which debt the payment is to apply

      1) If debtor gives no instructions, creditor is free to apply part payment to whichever debt s/he chooses; fact that one debt is guaranteed by surety and other is not makes no difference in absence of instructions by debtor

2) Does not affect risk to surety and is not defense of surety

EXAMPLE: If debtor owes two debts to creditor and surety only guaranteed one, creditor may apply a payment from debtor to one not guaranteed (absent instructions by debtor) and surety is not released.

2. Against surety

a. Creditor may proceed immediately against surety upon principal debtor's default

1) Unless contract requires, it is not necessary to give surety notice of debtor's default
2) Since surety is immediately primarily liable, he can be sued without creditor first attempting to collect from debtor

3. Against guarantor of collection

a. A guarantor of collection's liability is conditioned on creditor notifying guarantor of debtor's default and creditor first attempting to collect from debtor
b. Creditor must exhaust remedies by reducing claim against debtor to judgment and showing judgment remains unsatisfied (unpaid) before guarantor of collection's liability arises

4. On security (collateral) held by surety or creditor

a. Upon principal debtor's default, creditor may resort to collateral to satisfy debt

1) If creditor does resort to collateral, any excess collateral or amount realized by its disposal over debt amount must be returned to principal debtor
2) If collateral is insufficient to satisfy debt, creditor may proceed against surety or debtor for balance due (deficiency)

b. Creditor is not required to use collateral; creditor may instead proceed immediately against surety or principal debtor

1) If surety pays, surety is subrogated (see "C.1.d." below) to creditor's rights in collateral and is therefore entitled to it
2) If principal debtor pays obligation, collateral must be returned to debtor along with any income earned thereon

C. <u>Surety's Rights and Remedies</u>

1. When the debt or obligation for which surety has given promise is due

a. Surety may request creditor to resort first to collateral if surety can show collateral is seriously depreciating in value, or if surety can show undue hardship will otherwise result

b. Exoneration

1) Surety may sue to compel debtor to pay obligation owed to creditor when debtor has sufficient assets and is wrongfully withholding payment
2) Exoneration is not available if creditor demands prompt performance from surety upon debtor's default

c. If surety pays, s/he is entitled to right of reimbursement from debtor

1) May recover only actual payments to creditor
2) Surety is entitled to resort to collateral as satisfaction of right of reimbursement
3) Surety's payment after having received notice of principal debtor's valid defense against creditor causes surety to lose right of reimbursement

d. Subrogation

1) If surety pays, surety obtains same rights that creditor had against debtor; therefore can recover from debtor as creditor could (surety steps into creditor's shoes)

a) Permits surety to obtain rights that did not have before surety's satisfaction of debtor's obligation

EXAMPLE: C, the creditor, required D, the debtor, to put up personal property as collateral on a loan and to also use S as a surety on the same loan. Upon D's default, C chooses to resort to S for payment. Upon payment, S may now sell the collateral under the right of subrogation because the creditor could have used the same right of sale of the collateral.

b) If debtor is bankrupt, surety is subrogated to rights of creditor's priority in bankruptcy proceeding

e. Right of contribution exists among co-sureties. (See "E.3." below.)

D. <u>Surety's Defenses</u>

1. Surety may generally exercise defenses on contract which would be available to debtor

a. Breach or failure of performance by <u>creditor</u>
b. Impossibility or illegality of performance
c. Failure of consideration
d. Creditor obtains debtor's promise by fraud, duress, or misrepresentation
e. Statute of Limitations
f. Except that surety may not use debtor's personal defenses. (See "D.4." below.)

2. Surety may take advantage of own contractual defenses

a. Fraud or duress

1) If creditor obtains surety's promise by fraud or duress, contract is voidable at surety's option

EXAMPLE: Creditor forces X to sign suretyship agreement at threat of great bodily harm.

2) Fraud by principal debtor on surety to induce a suretyship agreement will not release surety if creditor has extended credit in good faith

a) But if creditor had knowledge of debtor's fraudulent representations, then surety may avoid liability

EXAMPLE: Y asked Ace to act as surety on a loan from Bank. In order to induce Ace to act as surety, Y made fraudulent representations concerning its financial position to Ace. This fraud by Y will not release surety, Ace, if the creditor, Bank, had no knowledge of the fraud and extended credit in good faith. But if Bank had knowledge of Y's fraudulent representations, then Ace has a good defense and can avoid liability.

b. Suretyship contract itself is void due to illegality
c. Incapacity of surety (e.g., surety is a minor)
d. Failure of consideration for suretyship contract
    1) However, when surety's and principal debtor's obligations are incurred at same time, there is no need for any separate consideration beyond that supporting principal debtor's contract; if surety's undertaking is entered into subsequent to debtor's contract, it must be supported by separate consideration. (See "A.4.a." above.)
e. Suretyship agreement is not written as required per Statute of Frauds
f. Creditor fails to notify surety of any material facts within creditor's knowledge concerning debtor's ability to perform
    1) Material facts are those facts pertaining to risk assumed by surety such that surety may not have assumed obligation had s/he been aware of these facts because they cause an increase in surety's risk

EXAMPLE: Creditor's failure to report to surety that debtor has defaulted on several previous occasions.

EXAMPLE: Creditor's failure to report to surety that debtor submitted fraudulent financial statements to surety to induce suretyship agreement.

3. Acts of creditor or debtor materially affecting surety's performance
    a. Release of principal debtor from liability by creditor without consent of surety will also discharge surety's liability
        1) But surety is not released if creditor specifically reserves his/her rights against surety
    b. Release of surety by creditor
        1) Does <u>not</u> release principal debtor since his/her obligation is not affected by surety's release
    c. Release, surrender, destruction, or impairment of collateral by creditor before or after debtor's default will release surety to extent of value of collateral released, surrendered, or impaired
    d. Proper performance by debtor or satisfaction of creditor through collateral will discharge surety
    e. Tender of performance by debtor or surety and refusal by creditor will discharge surety
        1) However, tender of performance for obligation to pay money does not normally release principal debtor; stops accrual of interest on debt

f. A material alteration or variance in terms and conditions of contract subsequent to surety's undertaking is a defense for surety if it increases risk or surety's undertaking. (This is important.)

   1) Substitution of debtors (i.e., a change in identity of principal debtor or a delegation of principal debtor's obligation to another party)
   2) Change or modification in duties of principal debtor
   3) Extension of time, without surety's consent
      a) Compensated surety is normally not discharged, but is entitled to have his/her obligation reduced by extent of loss due to extension of time
   4) Variance in amount, place, time, or manner of principal debtor's payments
   5) Surety can consent to any alteration and thereby waive his defense
   6) In general, an accommodation (noncompensated) surety is completely discharged if creditor does anything that varies surety's risk. However, a compensated surety is discharged only if creditor actually causes a binding material increase in risk, and then surety is discharged only to extent of increased risk.
   7) Surety is not released if creditor modifies principal debtor's duties to be beneficial to surety (i.e., decreases surety's risk)

      EXAMPLE: Creditor reduces interest rate on loan to principal debtor from 12% to 10%.

   8) In order to release surety, there must be an actual alteration or variance in terms of contract and not an option or election that principal debtor can exercise under express terms of original agreement which surety has guaranteed

      EXAMPLE: Tenant and landlord entered into a two year leasing agreement which expressly contained an option for an additional year which could be exercised by tenant, with X acting as surety on lease contract. If tenant exercises this option, X still remains bound as surety.

4. Following are <u>not defenses of surety</u>. (Be sure to know these.)

   a. Personal defenses of principal debtor
      1) Death of debtor or debtor's lack of capacity, e.g., debtor is a minor
      2) Insolvency (or discharge in bankruptcy) of debtor
         a) Possibility of debtor's insolvency is a primary reason for engaging in a surety arrangement
      3) Personal debtor's set-offs
         a) Unless debtor assigns them to surety
   b. Creditor did not give notice to surety of debtor's default or creditor did not first proceed against principal debtor
      1) Unless a conditional guarantor
   c. Creditor does not resort to collateral

E. Co-sureties

1. Co-sureties exist when there is more than one surety for same obligation of principal debtor to same creditor
   a. It does not matter that co-sureties do not know of each other or that they become sureties at different times; they need only share same burden
   b. Co-sureties need not be bound for same amount; they can guarantee equal or unequal amounts of debt
      1) Collateral, if any, need not be held equally
2. Co-sureties are jointly and severally liable to creditor
   a. That is, creditor can proceed against both sureties jointly or against each one individually to extent surety has assumed liability
   b. If creditor sues both sureties, he may recover in any proportion from each, but may only recover total amount of debtor's obligation
3. Right of contribution exists among co-sureties
   a. Right of contribution arises when co-surety, in performance of debtor's obligation, pays more than his/her proportionate share of total liability, and thereby entitles co-surety to compel other co-sureties to compensate him/her for excess amount paid (i.e., contribution from other co-sureties for their pro rata share of liability)
4. Co-sureties are only liable in contribution for their proportionate share
   a. Co-surety's pro rata share is proportion that each surety's risk (i.e., amount each has personally guaranteed) bears to total amount of risk assumed by all sureties

$$\left(\frac{\text{Dollar amount individual co-surety personally guaranteed}}{\text{Total dollar amount of risk assumed by all co-sureties}}\right)$$

EXAMPLE: X and Y are co-sureties for $5,000 and $10,000, respectively, of a $10,000 debt. Each is liable in proportion to amount each has personally guaranteed. Since X guaranteed $5,000 of debt and Y guaranteed $10,000 of debt, then X is individually liable for 1/3 ($5,000/$15,000) of debt and Y is individually liable for 2/3 ($10,000/$15,000) of debt. Debtor defaults on $3,000 of debt. X is liable for $1,000 (1/3 x $3,000) and Y is liable for $2,000 (2/3 x $3,000). Although creditor may recover $3,000 from either, each co-surety has right of contribution from other co-surety.

EXAMPLE: Refer to the preceding example. If the creditor recovers all of the $3,000 debt from Y, then Y, under the right of contribution, can recover $1,000 from X so that each will end up paying his/her proportionate amount.

5. Each co-surety is entitled to share in any collateral pledged (either held by creditor or other co-surety) in proportion to co-surety's liability for debtor's default

EXAMPLE: If in above illustration, co-surety Y held collateral pledged by debtor worth $900, both co-sureties X and Y would be entitled to share in collateral in proportion to their respective liabilities. X would be entitled to 1/3 ($5,000/$15,000) of $900 collateral, or $300; and Y would be entitled to 2/3 ($10,000/$15,000) of $900 collateral, or $600.

6. Discharge or release of one co-surety by creditor results in a reduction of liability of remaining co-surety

    a. Remaining co-surety is released only to extent of released co-surety's pro rata share of debt liability (unless there is a reservation of rights by creditor against remaining co-surety)

    EXAMPLE: A and B are co-sureties for $4,000 and $12,000, respectively, on a $12,000 debt. If creditor releases co-surety A, co-surety B is released to extent of co-surety A's liability. Each is liable in proportion to amount each has personally guaranteed. Since A guaranteed $4,000 of debt and B guaranteed $12,000 of debt, then A is individually liable for 1/4 ($4,000/$16,000) of debt and B is individually liable for 3/4 ($12,000/$16,000) of debt, i.e., $9,000. Therefore, co-surety B is released of A's pro rata liability of $3,000 (1/4 X $12,000), and only remains a surety for $9,000 ($12,000 - $3,000) of debt.

7. A co-surety is not released from obligation to perform merely because another co-surety refuses to perform. However, upon payment of full obligation, co-surety can demand a pro rata contribution from his nonperforming co-surety.

F. Surety Bonds

1. An acknowledgment of an obligation to make good the performance by another of some act, duty, or responsibility

    a. Usually issued by companies which for a stated fee assume risk of performance by bonded party
    b. Performance of act, duty, or responsibility by bonded party discharges surety's obligation

2. Construction bonds (performance bonds) are given by surety to a landowner guaranteeing builder's obligation to perform construction

    a. If builder fails to perform, surety can be held liable for damages, but not specific performance

3. Fidelity bonds are form of insurance that protects an employer against losses sustained by dishonest employees (i.e., guarantees faithful performance of duties by employee)

    a. Any significant change in the employee's duties may serve to release surety bonding company from its obligation

4. Surety bonding company retains right of subrogation against bonded party

Multiple Choice Questions (1–27)

1. Which of the following transactions does **not** establish Samp as a surety?
   a. Samp says: "Ship goods to my son and I will pay for them."
   b. Samp signs commercial paper as an accommodation indorser for one of his suppliers.
   c. Samp guarantees a debt of a corporation he controls.
   d. Samp sells an office building to Park, and, as a part of the consideration, Park assumes Samp's mortgage on the property.

2. Which of the following transactions does not create a surety relationship?
   a. The assumption of a mortgage by the purchaser of a parcel of real estate.
   b. The blank indorsement of a check.
   c. Signing a nonnegotiable promissory note as an accommodation maker.
   d. Obtaining professional malpractice insurance by a CPA.

3. When the debtor has defaulted on its obligation, the creditor is entitled to recover from the surety, unless which of the following is present?
   a. The surety is in the process of exercising its right of exoneration against the debtor.
   b. The debtor has died or become insolvent.
   c. The creditor could collect the entire debt from the debtor's collateral in his possession.
   d. The surety is a guarantor of collection and the creditor failed to exercise due diligence in enforcing his remedies against the debtor.

4. Knott obtained a loan of $10,000 from Charles on January 1, 1982, payable on April 15, 1982. At the time of the loan, Beck became a noncompensated surety thereon by written agreement. On April 15, 1982, Knott was unable to pay and wrote to Charles requesting an extension of time. Charles made no reply, but did not take any immediate action to recover. On May 30, 1982, Charles demanded payment from Knott and, failing to collect from him, proceeded against Beck. Based upon the facts stated
   a. Charles was obligated to obtain a judgment against Knott returned unsatisfied before he could collect from Beck.
   b. Beck is released from his surety obligation because Charles granted Knott an extension of time.
   c. Charles may recover against Beck despite the fact Beck was a noncompensated surety.
   d. Beck is released because Charles delayed in proceeding against Knott.

5. The Martin Corporation was a small family-owned corporation whose owners were also the directors and officers. The corporation's bankers insisted that if any further credit were to be extended to the corporation the owners must guarantee payment by the corporation. This guaranty was agreed to by the owners in writing, and an additional $50,000 loan was granted to Martin Corporation. Which of the following best describes the legal significance of these events?
   a. The guaranty by the owners need not have been in writing since it was primarily for their own benefit.
   b. Once the owners agreed to the undertaking they automatically assumed responsibility for all of the corporation's prior debts.
   c. In the absence of specific provisions to the contrary, the owners are immediately liable on the debt in the event of the corporation's default.
   d. Since the owners each participated equally in the guaranty, each can be held liable by the bank, but only to the extent of his proportionate share in relation to the others.

6. Park owed Collins $1,000 and $2,000, respectively, on two separate unsecured obligations. Smythe had become a surety on the $2,000 debt at the request of Park when Park became indebted to Collins. Both debts matured on June 1. Park was able to pay only $600 at that time, and he forwarded that amount to Collins without instructions. Under these circumstances
   a. Collins must apply the funds pro rata in proportion to the two debts.
   b. Collins must apply the $600 to the $2,000 debt if there is no surety on the $1,000 debt.
   c. Smythe will be discharged to the extent of $400 if Collins on request of Smythe fails to apply $400 to the $2,000 debt.
   d. Collins is free to apply the $600 to the debts as he sees fit.

7. Hargrove borrowed $40,000 as additional working capital for her business from the Old Town Bank. Old Town required that the loan be collateralized to the extent of 60%, and an acceptable surety for the entire amount be obtained. Prudent Surety Company agreed to act as surety on the loan and Hargrove pledged $24,000 of bearer negotiable bonds, which belonged to her husband, with Old Town. Hargrove has defaulted. Which of the following is correct?

a. As a result of the default, Prudent and Hargrove's husband are cosureties.
b. Old Town must first proceed against Hargrove and obtain a judgment for payment before it can proceed against the collateral.
c. Old Town must first liquidate the collateral before it can proceed against Prudent.
d. Prudent is liable in full immediately upon default by Hargrove, but will upon satisfaction of the debt be entitled to the collateral.

8. Welch is a surety on Stanton's contract to build an office building for Brent. Stanton intentionally abandoned the project after it was 85% completed because of personal animosity which developed toward Brent. Which of the following is a correct statement concerning the rights or responsibilities of the various parties?

a. Any modification of the contract, however slight and even if beneficial to Welch, will release Welch.
b. Welch would be ordered to specifically perform the completion of the building if Brent sought this remedy.
c. Neither Stanton's failure to give Welch prior notice of its intention to abandon the project **nor** its actual abandonment of the project will release Welch.
d. Welch can **not** engage a contractor to finish the job and obtain from Brent the balance due on the contract.

9. Jane wishes to obtain a loan of $90,000 from Silver Corp. At the request of Silver, Jane has entered into an agreement with Bing, Piper, and Long to act as co-sureties on the loan. The agreement between Jane and the co-sureties stated that the maximum liability of each co-surety is: Bing $60,000, Piper $30,000, and Long $90,000. Based upon the surety relationship, Silver agreed to make the loan. After paying three installments totalling $30,000, Jane defaulted.

Prior to making payment, the co-sureties may seek the remedy of

a. Contribution.
b. Indemnification.
c. Subrogation.
d. Exoneration.

10. The right of subrogation

a. May permit the surety to assert rights he otherwise could **not** assert.
b. Is denied in bankruptcy.
c. Arises only to the extent that it is provided in the surety agreement.
d. Can **not** be asserted by a cosurety unless he includes all other cosureties.

11. Dependable Surety Company, Inc., issued a surety bond for value received which guaranteed: (1) completion of a construction contract Mason had made with Lund and (2) payment by Mason of his workmen. Mason defaulted and did not complete the contract. The workers were not paid for their last week's work. Mason had in fact become insolvent, and a petition in bankruptcy was filed two months after the issuance of the bond. What is the effect upon Dependable as a result of the above events?

a. If Dependable pays damages to Lund as a result of the default on the contract, Dependable is entitled to recover in the bankruptcy proceedings the entire amount it paid prior to the payment of the general creditors of Mason.
b. If Dependable pays the workers in full, it is entitled to the same priority in the bankruptcy proceedings that the workers would have had.
c. If Dependable has another separate claim against Lund, Dependable may **not** set it off against any rights Lund may have under this contract.
d. As a compensated surety, Dependable would be discharged from its surety obligation by Mason's bankruptcy.

12. Which of the following defenses will release a surety from liability?

a. Insanity of the principal debtor at the time the contract was entered into.
b. Failure by the creditor to promptly notify the surety of the principal debtor's default.
c. Refusal by the creditor, with knowledge of the surety relationship, to accept the principal debtor's unconditional tender of payment in full.
d. Release by the creditor of the principal debtor's obligation without the surety's

consent but with the creditor's reservation of his rights against the surety.

13. Allen was the surety for the payment of rent by Lear under a lease from Rosenthal Rentals. The lease was for two years. A clause in the lease stated that at the expiration of the lease, the lessee had the privilege to renew upon thirty days' prior written notice or, if the lessee remained in possession after its expiration, it was agreed that the lease was to continue for two years more. There was a default in the payment of rent during the extended term of the lease and Rosenthal is suing Allen for the rent due based upon the guarantee. Allen contends that he is liable only for the initial term of the lease and not for the extended term. Allen is

a. Not liable since it does **not** appear that a judgment against Lear has been returned unsatisfied.
b. Not liable because there has been a material alteration of the surety undertaking.
c. Not liable because there was a binding extension of time.
d. Liable on the surety undertaking which would include the additional two years.

14. Which of the following will release a surety from liability?

a. Release of the principal debtor from liability with the consent of the surety.
b. Delegation of the debtor's obligation to another party with the acquiescence of the creditor.
c. Lack of capacity because the debtor is a minor.
d. Discharge of the debtor in bankruptcy.

15. Dinsmore & Company was a compensated surety on the construction contract between Victor (the owner) and Gilmore Construction. Gilmore has defaulted and Victor has released Dinsmore for a partial payment and other consideration. The legal effect of the release of Dinsmore is

a. To release Gilmore as well.
b. Contingent on recovery from Gilmore.
c. Binding upon Victor.
d. To partially release Gilmore to the extent that Dinsmore's right of subrogation has been diminished.

16. Dustin is a very cautious lender. When approached by Lanier regarding a $2,000 loan, he not only demanded an acceptable surety but also collateral equal to 50% of the loan. Lanier obtained King Surety Company as his surety and pledged rare coins worth $1,000 with Dustin. Dustin was assured by Lanier one week before the due date of the loan that he would have no difficulty in making payment. He persuaded Dustin to return the coins since they had increased in value and he had a prospective buyer. What is the legal effect of the release of the collateral upon King Surety?

a. It totally releases King Surety.
b. It does **not** release King Surety if the collateral was obtained after its promise.
c. It releases King Surety to the extent of the value of the security.
d. It does **not** release King Surety unless the collateral was given to Dustin with the express understanding that it was for the benefit of King Surety as well as Dustin.

17. Cornwith agreed to serve as a surety on a loan by Super Credit Corporation to Fairfax, one of Cornwith's major customers. The relationship between Fairfax and Super deteriorated to a point of hatred as a result of several late payments on the loan. On the due date of the final payment, Fairfax appeared 15 minutes before closing and tendered payment of the entire amount owing to Super. The office manager of Super told Fairfax that he was too late and would have to pay the next day with additional interest and penalties. Fairfax again tendered the payment, which was again refused. It is now several months later and Super is seeking to collect from either Cornwith or Fairfax or both. What are Super's rights under the circumstances?

a. It cannot collect anything from either party.
b. The tender of performance released Cornwith from his obligation.
c. The tender of performance was too late and rightfully refused.
d. Cornwith is released only to the extent that the refusal to accept the tender harmed him.

18. Markum contacted the Variable Loan Company for a business loan. Variable refused to make the loan unless adequate security or an acceptable surety could be provided. Markum asked Duffy, one of his trade customers, to act as surety on the loan. In order to induce Duffy to sign, Markum made certain fraudulent representations and submitted a materially false financial statement. He also promised Duffy favorable treatment if Duffy would agree to act as surety for him. Markum is now insolvent and Variable seeks to hold Duffy liable. Duffy may avoid liability

a. Since the surety undertaking was void at the inception.
b. Based upon fraud if Duffy can show Variable was aware of the fraud.

c. Because Variable had a duty to warn Duffy about Markum's financial condition and did **not** do so.
d. Because the law of suretyship favors the surety where neither the surety nor the creditor is at fault.

19. Which of the following defenses by a surety will be effective to avoid liability?
a. Lack of consideration to support the surety undertaking.
b. Insolvency in the bankruptcy sense by the debtor.
c. Incompetency of the debtor to make the contract in question.
d. Fraudulent statements by the principal-debtor which induced the surety to assume the obligation and which were unknown to the creditor.

20. Don loaned $10,000 to Jon, and Robert agreed to act as surety. Robert's agreement to act as surety was induced by (1) fraudulent misrepresentations made by Don concerning Jon's financial status and (2) a bogus unaudited financial statement of which Don had no knowledge, and which was independently submitted by Jon to Robert. Which of the following is correct?
a. Don's fraudulent misrepresentations will **not** provide Robert with a valid defense unless they were contained in a signed writing.
b. Robert will be liable on his surety undertaking despite the facts since the defenses are personal defenses.
c. Robert's reliance upon Jon's financial statements makes Robert's surety undertaking voidable.
d. Don's fraudulent misrepresentations provide Robert with a defense which will prevent Don from enforcing the surety undertaking.

21. Maxwell was the head cashier of the Amalgamated Merchants Bank. The Excelsior Surety Company bonded Maxwell for $200,000. An internal audit revealed a $1,000 embezzlement by Maxwell. Maxwell persuaded the bank not to report him, and he promised to pay the money back within ten days. The bank acquiesced and neither the police nor Excelsior was informed of the theft. Maxwell shortly thereafter embezzled $75,000 and fled. Excelsior refuses to pay. Is Excelsior liable? Why?
a. Excelsior is liable since the combined total of the embezzlements is less than the face amount of the surety bond.
b. Excelsior is liable for $75,000, but not the $1,000 since a separate arrangement was agreed to by Amalgamated with Maxwell.
c. Excelsior is liable since it is a compensated surety and as such assumed the risk.
d. Excelsior is not liable since the failure to give notice of the first embezzlement is a valid defense.

22. Jane wishes to obtain a loan of $90,000 from Silver Corp. At the request of Silver, Jane has entered into an agreement with Bing, Piper, and Long to act as co-sureties on the loan. The agreement between Jane and the co-sureties stated that the maximum liability of each co-surety is: Bing $60,000, Piper $30,000, and Long $90,000. Based upon the surety relationship, Silver agreed to make the loan. After paying three installments totalling $30,000, Jane defaulted.

If Long properly paid the entire debt outstanding of $60,000, what amount may Long recover from the co-sureties?
a. $30,000 from Bing and $30,000 from Piper.
b. $20,000 from Bing and $20,000 from Piper.
c. $20,000 from Bing and $10,000 from Piper.
d. $15,000 from Bing and $15,000 from Piper.

23. A distinction between a surety and a co-surety is that only one is entitled to
a. Compensation.
b. Subrogation.
c. Contribution.
d. Notice upon default.

24. A release of a co-surety by the creditor
a. Will have **no** effect on the obligation of the other co-surety.
b. Will release the other co-surety entirely.
c. Will release the other co-surety to the extent that his right to contribution has been adversely affected.
d. Need **not** be a binding release in order to affect the rights of the parties.

25. In order to establish a co-surety relationship the two or more sureties must
a. Be aware of each other's existence at the time of their contract.
b. Sign the same contract creating the debt and the co-surety relationship.

c. Be bound to answer for the same debt or duty of the debtor.
d. Be bound for the same amount and share equally in the obligation to satisfy the creditor.

November 1985 Questions

26. Frost borrowed $120,000 as additional working capital for his business from Safe Bank. Safe required that the loan be collateralized to the extent of 50%, and an acceptable surety for the entire amount be obtained. Thrift Surety Co. agreed to act as surety on the loan and Frost pledged $60,000 of negotiable bearer bonds, which belonged to his wife, with Safe. Frost has defaulted. Which of the following is correct?

a. Safe must first proceed against Frost and obtain a judgment for payment before it can proceed against the collateral.
b. As a result of the default, Thrift and Frost's wife are co-sureties.
c. Thrift is liable in full immediately upon default by Frost, but will upon satisfaction of the debt be entitled to the collateral.
d. Safe must first liquidate the collateral before it can proceed against Thrift.

27. West promised to make Noll a loan of $180,000 if Noll obtained sureties to secure the loan. Noll entered into an agreement with Carr, Gray, and Pine to act as co-sureties on his loan from West. The agreement between Noll and the co-sureties provided for compensation to be paid to each of the co-sureties. It further indicated that the maximum liability of each co-surety would be as follows: Carr $180,000, Gray $60,000, and Pine $120,000. West accepted the commitment of the sureties and made the loan to Noll. After paying nine installments totaling $90,000, Noll defaulted. Gray's debts (including his surety obligation to West on the Noll loan) were discharged in bankruptcy. Subsequently, Carr properly paid the entire debt outstanding of $90,000. What amounts may Carr recover from the co-sureties?

	Gray	*Pine*
a.	$0	$30,000
b.	$0	$36,000
c.	$15,000	$30,000
d.	$30,000	$30,000

Problems

Problem 1 (1183,L3b)

(7 to 10 minutes)

Part b. Mars Finance Company was approached by Grant, the president of Hoover Corp., for a loan of $25,000 for Hoover. After careful evaluation of Hoover's financial condition, Mars decided it would not make the loan unless the loan was collateralized or guaranteed by one or more sureties for a total of $30,000. Hoover agreed to provide collateral in the form of a security interest in Hoover's equipment. The initial valuation of the equipment was $20,000 and Hoover obtained Victory Surety Company as a surety for the additional $10,000. Prior to the granting of the loan, the final valuation on the equipment was set at $15,000 and Mars insisted on additional surety protection of $5,000. Grant personally assumed this additional surety obligation. Hoover has defaulted and Mars first proceeded against the collateral, which was sold for $17,000. It then proceeded against Victory for the balance. Victory paid the $8,000 and now seeks a $4,000 contribution from Grant.

Grant asserts the following defenses and arguments in order to avoid or limit his liability:

- That he is not liable since Mars elected to proceed against the collateral.
- That Mars by suing Victory for the deficiency, released him.
- That he is not a cosurety because Victory did not know of his existence until after default and his surety obligation was not assumed at the same time nor was it equal in amount, hence, there is no right of contribution.
- That in no event is he liable for the full $4,000 sought by Victory.

Required:

Answer the following, setting forth reasons for any conclusions stated.

Discuss in separate paragraphs each of the above defenses asserted by Grant and indicate the amount of Grant's liability.

Problem 2 (1179,L4)

(20 to 25 minutes)

Part a. The King Surety Company, Inc., wrote a performance bond for Allie Stores, Inc., covering the construction of a department store. Rapid Construction Company, the department store contractor, is a general contractor and is simultaneously working on several buildings. Until the entire building is completed, the bond contained a provision that obligated Allie to withhold 20% of the progress payments to be made to Rapid at various stages of completion. After approximately two-thirds of the project had been satisfactorily completed, Rapid pleaded with Allie to release the 20% withheld to date. Rapid indicated that he was having a cash flow problem and unless funds were released to satisfy the demands of suppliers, workmen, and other creditors, there would be a significant delay in the completion date of the department store. Rapid claimed that if the 20% withheld were released, the project could be completed on schedule. Allie released the amounts withheld. Two weeks later Rapid abandoned the project, citing as its reason rising cost which made the contract unprofitable. Allie has notified King of the facts and demands that either King complete the project or respond in damages. King denies liability on the surety bond.

Required:

Answer the following, setting forth reasons for any conclusions stated.

Who will prevail?

Part b. Barclay Surety, Inc., is the surety on a construction contract that the Gilmore Construction Company made with Shadow Realty, Inc. By the terms of the surety obligation, Barclay is not only bound to Shadow, but also is bound to satisfy materialmen and laborers in connection with the contract. Gilmore defaulted, and Barclay elected to complete the project and pay all claims and obligations in connection with the contract, including all unpaid materialmen and laborers' claims against Gilmore. The total cost to complete exceeded the construction contract payments Barclay received from Shadow. Some of the materialmen who were satisfied had either liens or security interests against Gilmore. Gilmore has filed a voluntary bankruptcy petition.

Required:

Answer the following setting for reasons for any conclusions stated.

What rights does Barclay have as a result of the above facts?

Problem 3 (1180,L3a)

(7 to 10 minutes)

Part a. Hardaway Lending, Inc., had a 4-year $800,000 callable loan to Superior Metals, Inc., outstanding. The loan was callable at the end of each year upon Hardaway's giving 60 days written notice. Two and one-half years remained of the four years. Hardaway reviewed the loan and decided that Superior Metals was no longer a prime lending risk and it therefore decided to call the loan. The required written notice was sent to and received by Superior 60 days prior to the expiration of the second year. Merriweather, Superior's chief executive officer and principal shareholder, requested Hardaway to continue the loan at least for another year. Hardaway agreed, provided that an acceptable commercial surety would guarantee $400,000 of the loan and Merriweather would personally guarantee repayment in full. These conditions were satisfied and the loan was permitted to continue.

The following year the loan was called and Superior defaulted. Hardaway released the commercial surety but retained its rights against Merriweather and demanded that Merriweather pay the full amount of the loan. Merriweather refused, asserting the following:

- There was no consideration for his promise. The loan was already outstanding and he personally received nothing.
- Hardaway must first proceed against Superior before it can collect from Merriweather.
- Hardaway had released the commercial surety, thereby releasing Merriweather.

Required:

Answer the following, setting forth reasons for any conclusions stated.

Discuss the validity of each of Merriweather's assertions.

Multiple Choice Answers

1. a	7. d	13. d	18. b	23. c
2. d	8. c	14. b	19. a	24. c
3. d	9. d	15. c	20. d	25. c
4. c	10. a	16. c	21. d	26. c
5. c	11. b	17. b	22. c	27. b
6. d	12. c			

Multiple Choice Answer Explanations

A. Nature of Suretyship

1. (1182,L1,22) (a) A suretyship relationship exists where one person agrees to be answerable for the debt of another by assuring performance upon the debtor's default. A suretyship agreement involves three parties: the principal debtor, the creditor and the surety. Answer (a) is correct because it describes a third party beneficiary contract, not a suretyship arrangement. Samp is not promising to pay the debt of another, but rather engaging in an original promise, to pay for the goods the creditor delivers to Samp's son. Answer (b) is incorrect because an accommodation indorser is a surety since the indorser engages to pay if the negotiable instrument is not paid by the appropriate party after proper presentment and notice. Answer (c) is incorrect because Samp is entering into a suretyship arrangement whereby he promises to pay if the principal debtor (the corporation) does not pay. Answer (d) is incorrect because when Park, the purchaser, assumed the mortgage, a surety relationship was created in which Park, the buyer, was the principal debtor and Samp, the seller, was the surety.

2. (1177,L2,17) (d) A suretyship relationship exists when one person agrees to be answerable for the debt or default of another. Unlike a suretyship relation, insurance is the distribution of the cost of risk over a large number of individuals. Malpractice insurance is spreading the cost of possible professional liability over a large number of professionals. Answer (a) is incorrect because an assumption of a mortgage creates a suretyship relationship in which the buyer becomes the principal debtor and the seller becomes the surety. Answer (b) is incorrect because a person who endorses a check in blank is a surety in that he promises to pay if the check is dishonored (endorsement "without recourse" disclaims this liability). Answer (c) is incorrect because an accommodation maker of a nonnegotiable note is a surety in that he promises to pay if the maker does not.

B. Creditor's Rights

3. (1181,L1,25) (d) Normally, a creditor can immediately sue the surety upon the debtor's default. However, when a surety is a guarantor of collection, the creditor must exhaust his remedies against the principal debtor by reducing his claim against the debtor to judgment and showing the judgment remains unpaid before the guarantor's obligation arises. Answer (a) is incorrect because exoneration is when the surety seeks to compel the principal debtor to pay the creditor. But such relief is not available if the creditor demands prompt performance from the surety upon default. Answer (b) is incorrect because the death or insolvency of the principal debtor does not release the surety. The possibility of the debtor's insolvency is a primary reason for engaging in a surety arrangement. Answer (c) is incorrect because the creditor need not resort to the collateral pledged; instead, he may proceed immediately against the surety. But once the surety satisfies the obligation, s/he is subrogated to the creditor's rights in the collateral.

4. (1182,L1,24) (c) If the surety's undertaking arises at the time the creditor extends the loan to the principal debtor, the surety does not need to receive independent consideration to be bound. Consequently, Beck, even as a noncompensated surety, would be bound to pay Knott. Answer (a) is incorrect because since the surety is primarily liable, the creditor may proceed immediately against the surety upon debtor's default without demand first being made upon the debtor. However, when a surety is a guarantor of collection, the guarantor's liability will be conditioned on the creditor first attempting to collect from the debtor. The creditor must exhaust his remedies against the principal debtor by reducing his claim against the debtor to judgment and showing the judgment remains unpaid before the guarantor's obligation arises. Normally, an extension of time to debtor, without surety's consent, releases the surety due to a material increase in the surety's risk. However, answer (b) is incorrect because such a variance of terms must be legally enforceable and binding on the creditor in order for the surety to be released. In this case, the debtor only made a request for an extension of time, but the extension was not granted by the creditor. Answer (d) is incorrect because a delay in the creditor proceeding against the debtor does not discharge the surety, unless such time delay exceeds the statutory period within the Statute of Limitations.

5. (576,L1,11) (c) As sureties, the owners are immediately liable on the debts if the corporation defaults. No notice need be given them. If the guarantee

was primarily for the owners' benefit, the guarantee would not need to be in writing. But since the benefit only accrues to the owners indirectly (through the corporation), it is not considered to be primarily for their benefit. They only guaranteed one loan and did not assume responsibility for other debts. The bank can hold any one of them fully liable for the entire debt and the others may be required to contribute their proportionate share to the one held liable.

6. (574,L1,13) (d) When a debtor has more than one debt outstanding with the same creditor and makes a part payment, the debtor may give instructions as to which debt the part payment is to apply. If the debtor makes no instructions the creditor is free to apply the part payment to whichever debt he chooses. The fact that one debt is guaranteed by a surety makes no difference in the absence of instructions by the debtor. So Collins can apply the $600 to the debts as he sees fit.

7. **(1181,L1,28)** (d) The essence of a surety arrangement is that the surety promises to perform upon default of the principal debtor. Further action by the creditor versus the principal debtor is not necessary (unlike a guarantor of collection). The surety, upon satisfaction of the principal debtor's obligation to the creditor, is subrogated to the creditor's rights in the collateral. Answer (a) is incorrect because co-sureties exist when more than one surety is bound to answer for the same obligation of a debtor. Prudent is the only surety; Hargrove's husband provided only the collateral. Answer (b) is incorrect because the creditor (Old Town) is capable of resorting to the collateral pledged without reducing his claim against the debtor to judgment and execution having been returned unsatisfied. Answer (c) is incorrect because the creditor need not resort to the collateral pledged; instead, she/he may proceed against the surety as soon as the obligation is due.

8. (581,L1,37) (c) Unless the contract is a conditional guaranty, it is unnecessary for creditors to give notice of the debtor's default to the surety. With or without notice, upon default the surety is liable for the performance guaranteed under the agreement. Answer (a) is incorrect because any modifications of the contract that have the possibility of increasing the surety's risk would release the surety. Brent could sue the surety for compensatory damages, not specific performance; therefore, answer (b) is incorrect. Answer (d) is incorrect since if Welch, the surety, **did** satisfy the obligation by engaging a contractor to finish the job, Welch could collect the balance due on the agreement.

C. Surety's Rights

9. (584,L1,22) (d) Before paying the debt, the surety may seek the remedy of exoneration where the surety files a suit in equity to compel the debtor to pay the creditor. Indemnification, subrogation, and contribution are all remedies available to the surety after he has paid the creditor. Specifically, indemnification is the surety's right to reimbursement from the principal debtor in the amount paid. The rule of subrogation states that the surety, to the extent he has paid, succeeds to the creditor's rights against the principal debtor, including the right to any security interests the creditor might have in the debtor's property. The right of contribution arises when a co-surety has paid more than his proportionate share of the debt and is, therefore, entitled to compensation from the other co-sureties for the excess amount paid. Answers (a), (b), and (c) are, therefore, incorrect.

10. (583,L1,27) (a) The right of subrogation is where the surety pursuant to his contractual undertaking fully satisfies the obligation of the principal debtor to the creditor, and succeeds to the creditor's rights (i.e., "steps into the creditor's shoes") against the debtor. The surety acquires the identical claims or rights the creditor possessed against the principal debtor, permitting the surety to assert rights he otherwise could not assert. Answer (b) is incorrect because the right of subrogation is granted in bankruptcy. Since the surety is subrogated to the rights of the creditor, the surety is entitled to the same priority as the creditor would have in a bankruptcy proceeding. Answer (c) is incorrect because the right of subrogation exists regardless of whether it is explicitly provided for in the surety agreement. Answer (d) is incorrect because the right of subrogation can be asserted by a co-surety without including all other co-sureties. But the other co-sureties have the right to contribution.

11. **(1181,L1,26)** (b) When the surety pursuant to his contractual undertaking fully satisfies the obligation of the creditor, he is then subrogated to the rights of that creditor. Therefore, Dependable would be entitled to the same priority as the workers would have in the bankruptcy proceeding. Answer (a) is incorrect because since Lund is a general creditor, Dependable is subrogated to Lund's rights upon payment. Therefore, Dependable would have equal priority with other general creditors of Mason. Answer (c) is incorrect because the surety may set off any claims that s/he has against the creditor even if they do not arise out of the surety obligation. Answer (d) is incorrect because insolvency (bankruptcy) of the principal debtor does not release the surety.

D. Surety's Defenses

12. (584,L1,24) (c) The surety will be discharged by the creditor's refusal to accept the principal debtor's tender of full payment on a mature debt. However, the tender of full payment will not discharge the principal debtor but will merely stop the running of interest on the monetary obligation. Answer (a) is incorrect because a surety may not exercise the principal debtor's personal defenses (i.e., insanity). Answer (b) is incorrect because, unless the contract states otherwise, the creditor has no duty to notify the surety of the principal debtor's default. Although a release of the principal debtor without the surety's consent will usually discharge the surety, there is no discharge if the creditor expressly reserves his rights against the surety. Answer (d) is, therefore, incorrect.

13. (1181,L1,29) (d) The leasing arrangement, to which Allen is a surety, remained intact with no modifications. The lease, itself, expressed a holdover clause which went into existence when Lear remained in possession after the original leasing period. The essence of a surety arrangement is that the surety promises to perform upon default of the principal debtor. Therefore, Allen becomes liable when Lear defaults during the extended term of the lease. Answer (a) is incorrect because Allen is a surety, not a guarantor of collection; therefore, the creditor need not reduce his claim against the principal debtor to judgment and have execution be unsatisfied before proceeding against the surety on his promise. Answer (b) is incorrect because there was no alteration of the contract which materially affected the risks to the surety. Answer (c) is incorrect because a binding extension of time refers to a creditor granting additional time to the debtor to satisfy his obligation. The holdover provision was part of the original agreement and, consequently, would not be considered an alteration.

14. (1182,L1,25) (b) A material alteration of a suretyship contract by the debtor and creditor, thereby modifying the principal debtor's duty, is a defense for the surety since it changes the risk of his undertaking. A delegation of the debtor's obligation to another party is a significant variance in the surety agreement, such that the surety will be released from liability. However, if the surety had acquiesced to the alteration, then the surety would waive this defense. Answer (a) is incorrect because the surety would be released from his liability only when the debtor is released by the creditor **without** the consent of the surety. Answer (c) is incorrect because minority of the principal debtor does not release the surety from his/her obligation to pay. Answer (d) is incorrect because the discharge of the debtor in bankruptcy does not release the surety from liability. The possibility of the debtor's insolvency is a primary reason for engaging in a surety arrangement.

15. (582,L1,24) (c) Victor's release of Dinsmore, the surety, is binding because it is supported by consideration. When the debtor releases the surety, the release completely discharges the surety's obligation if the release is supported by consideration. However, a release of the surety does not also release Gilmore, the principal debtor. Gilmore's obligation would not be affected in any way by Victor's release of Dinsmore, the surety. Therefore, answers (a), (b), and (d) are incorrect.

16. (1181,L1,24) (c) Upon default, the creditor (Dustin) may resort to the collateral he holds or may proceed against the surety on his promise. But when the creditor surrenders the collateral before or after the debtor's default, the surety is released to the extent of the value of the collateral. Answers (b) and (d) are incorrect because it does not matter when the collateral was obtained by Dustin or if it was expressly understood that the collateral was to benefit King Surety. Once the collateral is returned, this reduces the surety obligation to the extent of the value of the collateral.

17. (580,L1,44) (b) The tender of performance by the principal debtor completely releases the surety from his obligation. However, such tender does not release the principal debtor if the contractual duty consists of the obligation to pay money. If the contractual duty consisted of anything but the obligation to pay money, then the tender of such performance would have also released Fairfax.

18. (1182,L1,15) (b) Fraud by the principal debtor on the surety to induce a suretyship agreement will not release the surety if the creditor has extended credit in good faith. But if the creditor (Variable) had knowledge of the debtor's (Markum's) fraudulent representations, then the surety (Duffy) may avoid liability. Answer (a) is incorrect because the surety undertaking was not void. Fraud in the inducement would create a voidable, not void, surety agreement. If the creditor fails to notify the surety of any material facts within the creditor's knowledge concerning the debtor and his ability to perform, the surety may assert this as a defense to avoid a liability. But answer (c) is incorrect because the creditor (Variable) did not have any knowledge that the debtor, Markum, made fraudulent representations to induce the surety agreement. Answer (d) is incorrect because the law of suretyship would not favor the surety where neither party is at

fault. Since the essence of a surety agreement is that the surety promises to perform upon default of the principal debtor, it is the creditor who would be favored.

19. (582,L1,23) (a) If the surety's undertaking is not supported by consideration, the surety will avoid liability. However, when the surety's and principal debtor's obligations are incurred at the same time, there is no need for any separate consideration beyond that supporting the principal debtor's contract. If the surety's undertaking is entered into subsequent to the debtor's contract, it must be supported by separate consideration. Answers (b) and (c) are incorrect because the debtor's insolvency in either sense (equity or bankruptcy) or the debtor's lack of contractual capacity will not release the surety. Answer (d) is incorrect because fraud by the principal debtor on the surety will not release the surety unless the creditor was aware of this fraud. Obviously, fraud by the creditor on the surety will release the surety.

20. (581,L1,36) (d) If the creditor obtains the surety's promise by fraud, the surety has a valid defense against the creditor. The fact that the creditor's fraud was not contained in a signed writing (answer a) will not invalidate the surety's defense. Answer (b) is incorrect because the fact that fraud in the inducement is a personal defense has relevance only under the law of negotiable instruments, not the law of suretyship. Fraud by the principal debtor on the surety will not permit the surety to avoid liability to the creditor (answer c).

21. (1178,L1,20) (d) The general rule is that a surety is released from liability for acts of the creditor which materially increase the surety's risk. In this case the failure of the creditor to give notice of the prior embezzlement materially increased the surety's risk. Answers (a) and (b) are incorrect because when the surety is released from liability it is immaterial that the embezzlements did not exceed the face value of the bond. Answer (c) is incorrect because Excelsior has not assumed the risk that the creditor would negligently and knowingly withhold material information from the surety.

E. Co-sureties

22. (584,L1,23) (c) Co-sureties are jointly and severally liable to the creditor. A co-surety who is held severally liable may proceed against the other co-sureties and seek contribution for their proportionate share. To calculate the proportionate share, divide the amount each surety has individually guaranteed by the total guaranty and then multiply by the total debt paid by the co-surety seeking contribution. In the instant case, the calculation is as follows:

$$\frac{\text{Individual guaranty}}{\text{Total guaranty}} \times \text{Total debt paid by co-surety}$$

$$\text{Bing:}\quad \frac{\$\ 60{,}000}{\$180{,}000} \times \$60{,}000 = \underline{\underline{\$20{,}000}}$$

$$\text{Piper:}\quad \frac{\$\ 30{,}000}{\$180{,}000} \times \$60{,}000 = \underline{\underline{\$10{,}000}}$$

23. (583,L1,25) (c) Co-sureties exist when more than one surety is bound to answer for the same debt or duty of a debtor, and who, as between themselves, should proportionately share the loss caused by the default of the debtor. The right of contribution arises when a co-surety, in performance of the debtor's obligation, pays more than his proportionate share, and thereby entitles the co-surety to compel the other co-sureties to compensate him for the excess amount paid. Answer (a) is incorrect because neither a surety nor a co-surety need to be compensated for acting as a surety. If the surety's or co-surety's undertaking arises at the time the creditor extends the loan to the principal debtor, the surety or co-surety does not need to receive independent consideration to be bound. But, if the surety's or co-surety's undertaking is subsequent to the debtor-creditor contract, it must be supported by separate consideration. Answer (b) is incorrect because both a surety and co-surety are entitled to subrogation. When the surety or co-surety pursuant to his contractual undertaking fully satisfies the principal debtor's obligation to the creditor, he is then subrogated to the rights of the creditor and can recover from the debtor in the same manner as the creditor. Answer (d) is incorrect because unless the contract so stipulates, (i.e., a conditional guaranty) it is unnecessary for the creditor to give the surety or co-surety notice of the debtor's default. The creditor can proceed immediately against the surety or co-surety upon the default of the debtor.

24. (583,L1,26) (c) Co-sureties exist when more than one surety is bound to answer for the same obligation or duty of a debtor, and who, as between themselves, should proportionately share the loss caused by the default of the debtor. Unless the creditor specifically reserves his rights, a release of a co-surety by the creditor will release the other co-surety to the extent of the released co-surety's liability (i.e., to the extent that the remaining co-surety's right to contribution has been adversely affected). Therefore, answers (a) and (b) are incorrect. Answer (d) is incorrect because in order for a release of one co-surety to affect the rights of the other co-surety, the release by the creditor must be binding.

25. (1176,L2,31) (c) Co-sureties are two or more sureties bound to answer for the same debt or duty of the debtor. They need not be aware of each other's existence either at the time of their contract or later. They need not sign the same contract. The only necessary connection is that they are both bound to answer for the same debt irrespective of the time they became bound. Co-sureties also need not be bound for the same amount, e.g., one could be bound for 60% and the other for 40%.

November 1985 Answers

26. (1185,L1,31) (c) Upon default by the principal debtor, the creditor has the option of either proceeding immediately against the surety or resorting to the collateral to satisfy the debt. If the creditor chooses to proceed immediately against the surety, then the surety is entitled to the right of reimbursement from the principal debtor and has a right to any collateral the principal debtor is holding as satisfaction of that right. Answer (a) is incorrect because the creditor, Safe, need not first proceed against the principal debtor, Frost, and obtain a judgment for payment before proceeding against the collateral. Answer (b) is incorrect because in order to be a co-surety, the party must agree to satisfy the same obligation that the other surety has guaranteed. Frost's wife, in this case, has made no such agreement but has merely provided the collateral for the loan as required by Safe Bank. Answer (d) is incorrect because upon Frost's default Safe has the option of either proceeding immediately against the surety or resorting to the collateral to satisfy the debt.

27. (1185,L1,32) (b) The right of contribution arises when one co-surety, in performance of debtor's obligation, pays more than his proportionate share of the total liability. The right of contribution entitles the performing co-surety to reimbursement from the other co-sureties for their pro rata shares of the liability. Since Gray's debts have been discharged in bankruptcy, Carr may only exercise his right of contribution against Pine, and may recover nothing from Gray. Pine's pro rata share of the remaining $90,000 would be determined as follows:

$$\frac{\text{(Dollar amount guaranteed by Pine)}}{\text{(Total amount of risk assumed by remaining co-sureties)}} \times \text{Remaining obligation}$$

$$\frac{120{,}000}{120{,}000 + 180{,}000} \times 90{,}000 = 36{,}000$$

Answers (a), (c), and (d) are therefore incorrect.

Answer Outline

Problem 1 Creditor Holding Collateral; Co-suretyship; Co-surety's Right of Contribution (1183,L3b)

Part b.

Grant incorrect in first three assertions, correct in fourth because
- Resort to collateral does not affect creditor's right to proceed against surety for balance
- Creditor has option of suing one or more sureties without impairing rights against those not sued
- Grant is cosurety because
  - He is answering same debt as Victory
  - Victory has right of contribution against him
- Grant had 1/3 of total surety undertakings
  - Liable for 1/3 of $8,000 (2,666.67), not full $4,000

Unofficial Answer

Problem 1 Creditor Holding Collateral; Co-suretyship; Co-surety's Right of Contribution (1183,L3b)

Part b.

Grant is incorrect in his first three assertions and correct in connection with his fourth assertion for the following reasons:

- The law is clear regarding the right to collateral and its effect as between the creditor and the surety. The creditor has the right to resort to any available collateral. Resort to the collateral by the creditor in no way affects the creditor's right to proceed against a surety or sureties for the balance.
- A creditor may choose to sue one or more of the sureties without impairing his rights against those not sued. Similarly, he has the right to sue one surety if he wishes, and such a choice does not release the surety who was not sued insofar as the rights of his fellow surety to seek contribution. Suing one but not all of the sureties does not constitute a release by the creditor.
- All of the defenses asserted in the fact situation are invalid. Grant is a cosurety since he is answering for the same debt as Victory and there is a right of contribution which Victory may assert against Grant.
- Since Grant's surtey undertaking was one-third of the combined surety undertakings, he is liable for $2,666.67 only and not the full $4,000.

Answer Outline

Problem 2 Modification of Surety's Contract; Surety's Right of Reimbursement (1179,L4)

a. King (Surety) will prevail
   - The creditor modified the surety contract
     - Without the surety's consent
   - Noncompensated surety is discharged on any modification
   - Compensated surety is discharged if change materially increases risk
     - If not material, surety's liability is decreased
   - Here the change materially increased the risk
     - The released monies were not committed to the project
     - The withheld monies induced builder to complete
     - The withheld monies reduced surety's exposure

b. Barclay is entitled to reimbursement from Gilmore
   - But since Gilmore is bankrupt
     - Normally Barclay would have same position as other creditors
     - Except Barclay is subrogated to materialmen and laborers' rights
       - Liens and security interests of materialmen
       - Limited priorities of wage earners

Unofficial Answer

Problem 2 Modification of Surety's Contract Surety's Right of Reimbursement (1179,L4)

Part a.

King Surety Company will prevail. The creditor (Allie), without King's consent, has modified the surety contract. Under these circumstances, a noncompensated surety would be discharged without question; however, a compensated surety is not discharged completely unless the modification materially increases the risk. If the risk is not materially increased, the obligation is decreased to the extent of the loss. In this case, there was a material increase in the risk. First, there is nothing to indicate that the monies released by Allie were committed by Rapid to the particular project (Allie's department store) because Rapid had several simultaneous projects. Moreover, it is clear that the monies withheld provided a strong inducement for a builder such as Rapid to complete the undertaking since the expected final payment would have been large in relation to the final outlays to complete construction. Finally, the withheld payments reduced the exposure of the surety to the extent of 20 percent.

Part b.

Barclay is, of course, entitled to reimbursement from Gilmore. However, since Gilmore is bankrupt, Barclay will receive the same percentage on the dollar as will all other general creditors of Gilmore's estate. However, Barclay is subrogated to the rights of the materialmen and laborers it has satisfied. Specifically, it would have the right to assert the liens and security interests of the materialmen. Furthermore, wage earners are entitled to a limited priority in a bankruptcy proceeding, which Barclay could assert.

Answer Outline

Problem 3 Surety's Consideration; Surety's Liability Upon Default (1180,L3a)

a. Hardaway's foregoing legal right to call the loan acts as adequate consideration
   Fact that loan is already outstanding is irrelevant
   There is no requirement that creditor first proceed against debtor
   Creditor may proceed against either debtor or surety
   Release of commercial surety partially released Merriweather
   Right of contribution has been impaired to the extent contribution could have been demanded from surety

Unofficial Answer

Problem 3 Surety's Consideration; Surety's Liability Upon Default (1180,L3a)

Part a.

The first two defenses asserted by Merriweather are invalid. The third defense is partially valid.

Consideration on Hardaway's part consisted of foregoing the right to call the Superior Metals loan. The fact that the loan was already outstanding is irrelevant. By permitting the loan to remain outstanding for an additional year instead of calling it, Hardaway relinquished a legal right, which is adequate consideration for Merriweather's surety promise. Consideration need not pass to the surety; in fact, it usually primarily benefits the principal debtor.

There is no requirement that the creditor first proceed against the debtor before it can proceed against the surety, unless the surety undertaking expressly provides such a condition. Basic to the usual surety undertaking is the right of the creditor to proceed immediately against the surety. Essentially, that is the reason for the surety.

Hardaway's release of the commercial surety from its $400,000 surety undertaking partially released Merriweather. The release had the legal effect of impairing Merriweather's right of contribution against its co-surety (the commercial surety). Thus, Merriweather is released to the extent of 1/3 ($400,000 (commercial surety's guarantee)/$1,200,000 (the aggregate of the co-sureties's guarantees) of the principal amount ($800,000), or $266,667.

AGENCY

Overview

Agency is a relationship in which one party (agent) voluntarily acts as a business representative of another (principal) for the purpose of entering into contracts with third parties. The law of agency is concerned with the rights, duties, and liabilities of these three parties that arise as a result of the agency relationship. Important to this relationship is the fact that the agent has a fiduciary duty to act in the best interest of the principal. A good understanding of this module is important because partnership law is a special application of agency law.

The CPA exam emphasizes the creation and termination of the **agency** relationship, the undisclosed principal relationship, unauthorized acts or torts committed by the agent within the course and scope of the agency relationship and principal's liability for agent's unauthorized contracts.

A. Characteristics

1. Agency is a relationship by consent (agreement) between two parties, whereby one party (agent) agrees to act on behalf of the other party (principal). A contract is not required.
   a. Agent is subject to the continuous control of the principal
   b. Agent is a fiduciary and he must act for the benefit of the principal
   c. An agent can be used for other purposes, e.g., to perform physical acts, but we are primarily concerned with agents that agree to act for the principal in business transactions with third parties
   d. Agent's specific authority is determined by the principal but generally an agent has authority:
      1) To perform legal acts for the principal
      2) More specifically, to bind the principal contractually with third parties
2. Servant distinguished from an agent
   a. Servant is a type of agent
   b. Servant is subject to control of his physical conduct by master
      1) Master is a type of principal and is called such when the agent is a servant
      2) Agent is subject to a lesser and a more general control, i.e., what to do and when to do it, but not control of physical conduct
      3) Servant is usually employed for manual service, e.g., sales clerk
      4) Master is generally liable for servant's torts if committed within course and scope of employment relationship

3. Independent contractor distinguished from an agent

   a. Not subject to control of employer
   b. Not subject to regular supervision as a servant (or employee)
   c. Employer seeks the results only and contractor controls the methods

      EXAMPLE: A builder of homes has only to produce the results.

   d. Generally, employer is not liable for torts committed by independent contractor

      1) Unless independent contractor is employed to do something imminently or inherently dangerous, e.g., blasting

   e. Independent contractor may also be an agent in certain cases

      EXAMPLE: A public accounting firm represents a client in tax court.

4. Types of agents

   a. General--one who has broad power to act for the principal in various types of transactions

      1) Principal may be liable for unauthorized acts which similar general agents are authorized for

   b. Special--appointed for a limited purpose or a specific task

      1) If s/he performs unauthorized acts, principal is less likely to be liable than if s/he were a general agent

   c. Gratuitous--agrees to act without expectation of compensation

      1) Is not bound to perform, but once started must perform duties in non-negligent manner
      2) Not subject to as high a degree of care as a compensated agent

   d. Subagent--one appointed by an authorized agent to perform for the agent

      EXAMPLE: P hires A to manage a branch office and tells A to hire anyone he needs. If A hires X as an assistant, X is a subagent of P.

      1) If first agent is authorized only to employ for principal, then second agent is an agent of the principal, not a subagent

         EXAMPLE: P asks A to hire 5 people to work in P's branch office. Those hired by A are agents of P, not agents of A.

      2) If first agent has no authority to employ, second agent will be an agent to first agent and not a subagent of principal

         EXAMPLE: P hires A to manage a branch office but tells A not to hire anyone, that P will supply anyone needed. If A hires X as an assistant, X is an agent of A's, not a subagent of P.

5. Examples of agents--usually special agents

   a. Agency coupled with an interest -- agent has an interest in the subject matter of the agency: either a property interest or a security interest

1) E.g., mortgagee with right to sell property on default of mortgagor
2) Principal cannot terminate the agency

b. Attorney--practices law for a number of persons
c. Auctioneer--agent for seller of property. Once property sells, s/he acts as agent for both buyer and seller.
d. Broker--special agent acting for either buyer or seller in business transactions, e.g., real estate broker
e. Del credere--a sales agent who, prior to the creation and as a condition of the agency, guarantees the accounts of the customers to his/her principal (if the customers fail to pay)

   1) Guarantee is not within the Statute of Frauds, i.e., it is not required to be in writing

f. Exclusive--only agent the principal may deal with for a certain purpose during life of the contract, e.g., real estate broker who has sole right to sell property except for personal sale by principal

g. Factor--commercial agent employed to sell goods

   1) Factor has possession of goods and may sell in the factor's own name

h. Promoter--commonly used to designate person who attempts to form a corporation

   1) Generally held personally liable for preincorporation contracts with third parties, even if corporation does come into being
   2) See CORPORATIONS for promoter's liability

6. Types of principals

   a. Disclosed--when the third party knows or should know the agent is acting for a principal and who the principal is

      1) Principal becomes a party to authorized contracts made by the agent in the principal's name

      EXAMPLE: Signed, "John Doe as agent for Tom Thumb, principal." Therefore, only Tom Thumb is liable on the contract.

   b. Partially disclosed--when the third party knows or should know the agent is acting for a principal but does not know who the principal is

      1) Both the agent and the principal become parties to the contract

      EXAMPLE: Signed, "John Doe as agent."

   c. Undisclosed--when the third party has no notice that the agent is acting for a principal

      1) Both agent and principal become parties to all authorized contracts if the agent so intended to act for principal

      EXAMPLE: Signed, "John Doe."

B. Methods of Creation

1. Appointment

   a. Express--by agreement between the principal and agent. No formalities necessary.

      1) Generally needs to be written for compensated agent to purchase or sell real estate

   b. Implied--created by conduct of principal showing the intention that the relationship exists

      1) This conduct is usually, but not necessarily, directed toward the agent and must cause the agent to reasonably believe it is the principal's intention

2. Estoppel--principal is not allowed to deny agency relationship when s/he causes third party to believe it exists

   a. Imposed by law rather than by agreement
   b. The third party must rely to his/her detriment on this appearance of agency before the principal is estopped from denying it

   EXAMPLE: A, not an agent of P, in P's presence, bargained with X to buy goods for P. If P remains silent, he will not be able to deny the agency.

3. Representation--principal represents to third party that someone is his/her agent.

   a. Creates apparent (ostensible) authority
   b. Does not require reliance by third party
   c. Directed toward third party causing third party to believe (as opposed to implied appointment when agent is led to believe)

   EXAMPLE: Principal writes to a third party that A is his agent and has authority. Even if A has no actual authority, he is an agent by representation.

4. Necessity--when a situation arises that makes it a matter of public policy to presume an agency relationship, e.g., in an emergency to contract for medical aid

5. Ratification--approval after the fact of an unauthorized act done by an agent or one not yet an agent

   a. By affirming the act or by accepting the benefits of the act
   b. Other party to the contract can withdraw before principal ratifies
   c. Ratification is effective retroactively back to time of agent's act
   d. Ratification is not retractable
   e. Requirements to be valid

      1) Act must be one that would have been valid if agent had been authorized, i.e., lawful and delegable

         a) Torts can be ratified, but not crimes

      2) Principal must have been in existence and competent when the act was done
      3) Principal must have capacity when he ratifies
      4) Agent must have purported to act on behalf of the one who later ratifies

5) Principal must be aware of all material facts
6) Act must be ratified in its entirety, i.e., cannot ratify the beneficial part and refuse the rest

EXAMPLE: Receptionist has no authority to contract for X Company but signs a service contract on behalf of X Company. Officers of X Company make use of service contract. The receptionist's act is ratified.

C. Authority

1. Actual authority
   a. Express--consists of all authority expressly given by the principal to his/her agent
   b. Implied--authority that can be reasonably implied from express authority and from the conduct of the principal. See Methods of Creation.
      1) E.g., agent drives principal's car. Principal acquiesces by not objecting, so agent has implied authority to do it again.
      2) E.g., principal ratifies unauthorized act. Depending on circumstances, agent may have implied authority to do similar act.
      3) Includes authority reasonably necessary or usual to carry out express authority; e.g., authority to drive car home when s/he has authority to buy it
2. Apparent (ostensible) authority -- third party(ies) must have reasonable belief based on principal's representations. Principal has clothed agent with apparent authority to do acts customary to one in the relationship of an agent to the principal.
   a. E.g., an agent insofar as third persons are concerned can do what the predecessor did or what agents in similar positions in the general business world are deemed authorized to do for their principals
   b. Secret limitations have no effect

   EXAMPLE: Principal makes agent manager of his store but tells him not to purchase goods on his own. Agent has apparent authority to purchase as similar managers would.

   c. Apparent authority exists only for those who know of principal's representations whether directly or indirectly
   d. Agent has apparent authority after termination of agency until those with whom the agent has dealt are given actual notice, others constructive notice
      1) Notice may come from any source
3. Estoppel--not true authority, but an equitable doctrine to protect a third party who has detrimentally relied, by estopping the principal from denying the existence of authority
   a. Often indistinguishable from effects of apparent authority or ratification
      1) Estoppel may be applied where other doctrines technically won't work

b. Only creates rights in the third party(ies)

EXAMPLE: A sells P's race horse to T in P's behalf. P did not give authority, but since the race horse continues to lose races, P does not object. When the horse begins to win races, P claims A never had authority to sell. If A does not have apparent authority and if P did not technically ratify, P can be estopped from denying the authority on equitable grounds.

D. Capacity To Be Agent or Principal

1. Principal must be able to give legal consent

   a. If act requires some legal capacity, e.g., legal age to sell land, then principal must meet this requirement or agent cannot legally perform even if s/he has capacity. Capacity cannot be increased by appointment of an agent.

   b. Infant (person under age of majority, i.e., 18 or 21) can, in most jurisdictions, appoint an agent

      1) If not to secure necessities, the appointment can be voided at the infant-principal's option

   c. Insane person's agreements are voidable if made before s/he is judicially found insane and void if made after the judicial determination
   d. Marriage is not a bar for either spouse to be a principal or agent for the other
   e. Partnerships have all the partners as agents who, in turn, may appoint other agents
   f. Corporations, being artificial persons, must act entirely through agents
   g. Unincorporated associations are not legal entities and therefore cannot appoint agents

      1) Individual members will be responsible as principals if they appoint an agent

2. An agent must merely have sufficient mental and physical ability to carry out instructions of his/her principal

   a. Can bind principal even if agent is a minor or legally unable to act for himself
   b. Corporations, unincorporated associations, and partnerships may act as agents
   c. A mental incompetent or an infant of tender years may not be an agent

E. Obligations and Rights

1. Principal's obligations to agent

   a. Compensate agent as per agreement, or, in the absence of an agreement, pay a reasonable amount for the agent's services
   b. Guarantee agents reasonable expenses and indemnify agent against loss or liability for duties performed at the principal's direction which are not patently illegal

   c. Not to discredit agent, nor interfere with his/her work
   d. Inform agent of risks, e.g., physical harm, pecuniary loss
   e. Only duty to subagent is indemnification. Agent has duties of principal to subagent.
   f. May have remedies of discharging agent, restitution, damages, and accounting, or an injunction

2. Agent's obligations to principal
   a. Agent is a fiduciary and must act in the best interest of the principal and with complete loyalty
   b. Carry out instructions of principal exercising reasonable care and skill
      1) Cannot appoint subagent or delegate nonmechanical duties unless authorized, necessary, or customary
   c. To account to the principal for profits and everything which rightfully belongs to the principal and not commingle funds
   d. To indemnify principal for any damage wrongfully caused principal, e.g., tort while in course of employment
   e. Give any information to principal which s/he would want or need to know
   f. Duty not to compete or act adversely to principal
      1) Includes not acting for oneself unless principal knows and acquiesces
   g. After termination, must cease acting as agent
      1) May still have duty not to reveal secrets of principal

3. Principal's liability to third parties
   a. Disclosed or partially disclosed principal is liable on contracts and conveyances
      1) Where agent has actual authority, implied authority, apparent authority, or contract is later ratified
      2) Also held liable for any representations made by agent with authority to make them
      3) Principal not liable where third party has any notice that agent is exceeding his actual authority
   b. Undisclosed principal is similarly liable unless
      1) Third party holds agent responsible (third party has choice)
      2) Agent has already fully performed contract
      3) Undisclosed principal is expressly excluded by contract
      4) Contract is a negotiable instrument
         a) Only fully disclosed (in instrument) principal is liable on a negotiable instrument
   c. If a writing is required under Statute of Frauds, principal will only be liable if agent signs
   d. Principal has his/her own personal defenses, e.g., lack of capacity, and defenses on the contract, e.g., nonperformance by the third party
      1) Principal does not have agent's personal defenses, e.g., right of setoff where third party owes agent debt

e. Notice to agent is considered notice to the principal except where notice was given to agent before the formation of the agency relationship

   1) If agent is acting against interest of principal, i.e., in collusion with third party, then this third party's notice to agent is not notice to principal

f. Principal is not liable for agent's crimes (violations of statutes) unless s/he was a party to the crime or acquiesced in commission

g. Principal is liable for servant's torts committed within course and scope of employment (Doctrine of Respondeat Superior)

   1) A tort is a personal or civil wrong. Not under contract and not criminally prosecuted, although some actions may be both torts and crimes.

      EXAMPLE: A breaks T's arm. This is a tort and T may sue A for damages. A may also be prosecuted for criminal negligence. T may also hold A's principal (P) liable for the damages if he can prove that A was acting for P (in furtherance of P's interest) when T was injured.

   2) Servant need not be following instructions

      a) Rule applies even if servant/agent violated principal's instructions in committing tort

   3) Principal is only liable for agent's (who is not a servant) torts if s/he is doing an act within his/her authority

      a) Very little difference from liability for servant. On exam, can use course of employment rule for agents

   4) Of course, agent is still liable to third parties if they choose to sue him/her rather than the principal
   5) Contributory negligence, i.e., third party's negligence, is generally a defense for both the agent and his/her principal

      a) Some jurisdictions have adopted comparative negligence which means that the amount of damages is determined by comparing each party's negligence

4. Agent's liability to third parties

   a. Agent is liable on contract when

      1) Principal is undisclosed or partially disclosed

         a) Agent is not relieved from liability until principal performs or third party elects to hold principal liable

      2) S/he contracts in his/her own name
      3) S/he guarantees principal's performance and principal fails
      4) S/he signs a negotiable instrument and does not sign in a representative capacity and does not include the principal's name (undisclosed principal)
      5) S/he knows principal does not exist or is incompetent

         a) Liable even if third party also knows

      6) S/he knowingly acts without authority

b. Agent is not liable when

1) Principal is disclosed and agent signs all documents in representative capacity
2) Principal ratifies unauthorized act
3) Third party elects to hold partially disclosed or undisclosed principal liable

c. Agent has his/her personal defenses, e.g., right of offset if third party owes him/her debt, and defenses on the contract, e.g., nonperformance by the third party

1) Agent does not have principal's personal defenses, e.g., lack of capacity

d. Agent is liable if s/he does not deliver property received from third party for principal
e. Agent is liable for his/her own crimes and torts

5. Third parties' liability to principal and agent

a. Third party has no contractual liability to agent unless:

1) Agent is a party to the contract, i.e., undisclosed or partially disclosed principal, or
2) Agent has an interest in the contract, e.g., agent invests in the contract

b. Third party is liable to disclosed, partially disclosed, and undisclosed principals

1) Third party has personal defenses against principal, e.g., lack of capacity, and defenses on the contract, e.g., nonperformance by principal
2) Against undisclosed principal, third party also has personal defenses against agent

F. Termination of Principal-Agent Relationship

1. Acts of the parties

a. By agreement

1) Time specified in original agreement, e.g., agency for one year
2) Mutual consent
3) Accomplishment of objective, e.g., agency to buy a piece of land

b. Principal may revoke or agent may renounce

1) Party that terminates may be liable to other for breach of contract
2) If either party violates duties, the other may terminate relationship without being in breach
3) If agency was gratuitous, no breach
4) Exception: Principal does not have power to revoke agency coupled with an interest [see "F.2.b.2)" below]

c. Notice of termination is required (see "F.3." below)

2. By operation of law
   a. If subject of agreement becomes illegal or impossible
   b. Death or insanity of either party
      1) Principal's estate is not liable to agent or for contracts made by agent after principal's death except as provided by statute
      2) Exception is an agency coupled with an interest

         EXAMPLE: If mortgagee has power to sell the property to recover his loan, this authority to sell as mortgagor's agent is not terminated by mortgagor's death.
   c. Bankruptcy of principal terminates the relationship
      1) Bankruptcy of agent does not affect unless agent's solvency is needed for performance
   d. If terminated by operation of law no notice need be given
3. Third parties must be given notice if terminated by acts of the parties
   a. Otherwise, agent may still be able to bind principal by apparent authority
   b. Constructive notice, e.g., publishing in a newspaper, is sufficient to third parties who have not previously dealt with agent
   c. Actual notice, e.g., orally informing or sending a letter, must be given to third parties who have previously dealt with agent unless third party learns of termination from another source

Multiple Choice Questions (1–29)

1. The key characteristic of a servant is that
   a. His physical conduct is controlled or subject to the right of control by the employer.
   b. He is paid at an hourly rate as contrasted with the payment of a salary.
   c. He is precluded from making contracts for and on behalf of his employer.
   d. He lacks apparent authority to bind his employer.

2. Winter is a sales agent for Magnum Enterprises. Winter has assumed an obligation to indemnify Magnum if any of Winter's customers fail to pay. Under these circumstances, which of the following is correct?
   a. Winter's engagement must be in writing regardless of its duration.
   b. Upon default, Magnum must first proceed against the delinquent purchaser-debtor.
   c. The above facts describe a del credere agency relationship and Winter will be liable in the event his customers fail to pay Magnum.
   d. There is no fiduciary relationship on either Winter's or Magnum's part.

3. Jim, an undisclosed principal, authorized Rick to act as his agent in securing a contract for the purchase of some plain white paper. Rick, without informing Sam that he was acting on behalf of a principal, entered into a contract with Sam to purchase the paper. If Jim repudiates the contract with Sam, which of the following is correct?
   a. Rick will be released from his contractual obligations to Sam if he discloses Jim's identity.
   b. Upon learning that Jim is the principal, Sam may elect to hold either Jim or Rick liable on the contract.
   c. Rick may **not** enforce the contract against Sam.
   d. Sam may obtain specific performance, compelling Jim to perform on the contract.

4. Steel has been engaged by Lux to act as the agent for Lux, an undisclosed principal. As a result of this relationship
   a. Steel has the same implied powers as an agent engaged by a disclosed principal.
   b. Lux can **not** be held liable for any torts committed by Steel in the course of carrying out the engagement.
   c. Steel will be free from personal liability on authorized contracts for Lux when it is revealed that Steel was acting as an agent.
   d. Lux must file the appropriate form in the proper state office under the fictitious business name statute.

5. Which of the following is **not** an essential element of an agency relationship?
   a. It must be created by contract.
   b. The agent must be subject to the principal's control.
   c. The agent is a fiduciary in respect to the principal.
   d. The agent acts on behalf of another and **not** himself.

6. Duval Manufacturing Industries, Inc., orally engaged Harris as one of its district sales managers for an 18-month period commencing April 1, 1980. Harris commenced work on that date and performed his duties in a highly competent manner for several months. On October 1, 1980, the company gave Harris a notice of termination as of November 1, 1980, citing a downturn in the market for its products. Harris sues seeking either specific performance or damages for breach of contract. Duval pleads the Statute of Frauds and/or a justified dismissal due to the economic situation. What is the probable outcome of the lawsuit?
   a. Harris will prevail because he has partially performed under the terms of the contract.
   b. Harris will lose because his termination was caused by economic factors beyond Duval's control.
   c. Harris will lose because such a contract must be in writing and signed by a proper agent of Duval.
   d. Harris will prevail because the Statute of Frauds does **not** apply to contracts such as his.

7. A power of attorney is a useful method of creation of an agency relationship. The power of attorney
   a. Must be signed by both the principal and the agent.
   b. Exclusively determines the purpose and powers of the agent.
   c. Is the written authorization of the agent to act on the principal's behalf.
   d. Is used primarily in the creation of the attorney-client relationship.

8. Gladstone has been engaged as sales agent for the Doremus Corporation. Under which of the following circumstances may Gladstone delegate his duties to another?

a. Where an emergency arises and the delegation is necessary to meet the emergency.
b. Where it is convenient for Gladstone to do so.
c. Only with the express consent of Doremus.
d. If Doremus sells its business to another.

9. Harp entered into a contract with Rex on behalf of Gold. By doing so, Harp acted outside the scope of his authority as Gold's agent. Gold may be held liable on the contract if

a. Gold retains the benefits of the contract.
b. Gold ratifies the entire contract after Rex withdraws from the contract.
c. Rex elects to hold Gold liable on the contract.
d. Rex was aware of the limitation on Harp's authority.

10. Davidson is the agent of Myers, a fuel dealer. Myers is an undisclosed principal. Davidson contracts with Wallop to purchase 30,000 tons of coal at $20 per ton. Which of the following is correct?

a. If Davidson acts outside the scope of his authority in entering into this contract, Myers can **not** ratify the contract.
b. Wallop is bound to this contract only if Davidson acts within the scope of his authority.
c. If Davidson acts within the scope of his authority, Wallop can **not** hold Davidson personally liable on the contract.
d. Should Davidson refuse to accept delivery of the coal, Wallop will become an agent of Myers by substitution.

11. Mathews is an agent for Sears with the express authority to solicit orders from customers in a geographic area assigned by Sears. Mathews has no authority to grant discounts nor to collect payment on orders solicited. Mathews secured an order from Davidson for $1,000 less a 10% discount if Davidson makes immediate payment. Davidson had previously done business with Sears through Mathews but this was the first time that a discount-payment offer had been made. Davidson gave Mathews a check for $900 and thereafter Mathews turned in both the check and the order to Sears. The order clearly indicated that a 10% discount had been given by Mathews. Sears shipped the order and cashed the check. Later Sears attempted to collect $100 as the balance owed on the order from Davidson. Which of the following is correct?

a. Sears can collect the $100 from Davidson because Mathews contracted outside the scope of his express or implied authority.
b. Sears can **not** collect the $100 from Davidson because Mathews as an agent with express authority to solicit orders had implied authority to give discounts and collect.
c. Sears can **not** collect the $100 from Davidson as Sears has ratified the discount granted and payment made to Mathews.
d. Sears can **not** collect the $100 from Davidson because although Mathews had **no** express or implied authority to grant a discount and collect, Mathews had apparent authority to do so.

12. Moderne Fabrics, Inc., hired Franklin as an assistant vice president of sales at $2,000 a month. The employment had no fixed duration. In light of their relationship to each other, which of the following is correct?

a. Franklin has a legal duty to reveal any interest adverse to that of Moderne in matters concerning his employment.
b. If Franklin voluntarily terminates his employment with Moderne after working for it for several years, he can **not** work for a competitor for a reasonable period after termination.
c. Moderne can dismiss Franklin only for cause.
d. The employment contract between the parties must be in writing.

13. Smith has been engaged as a general sales agent for the Victory Medical Supply Company. Victory, as Smith's principal, owes Smith several duties which are implied as a matter of law. Which of the following duties is owed by Victory to Smith?

a. Not to compete.
b. To reimburse Smith for all expenditures as long as they are remotely related to Smith's employment and not specifically prohibited.
c. Not to dismiss Smith without cause for one year from the making of the contract if the duration of the contract is indefinite.
d. To indemnify Smith for liability for acts done in good faith upon Victory's orders.

14. Dill is an agent for Mint, Inc. As such, Dill made a contract for and on behalf of Mint with Sky Co. which was not authorized and upon which Mint has disclaimed liability. Sky has sued Mint on the contract asserting that Dill had the apparent authority to make it. In considering the factors which will determine the

scope of Dill's apparent authority, which of the following would **not** be important?

a. The express limitations placed upon Dill's authority which were **not** known by Sky.
b. The custom and usages of the business.
c. The status of Dill's position in Mint.
d. Previous acquiescence by the principal in similar contracts made by Dill.

15. Futterman operated a cotton factory and employed Marra as a general purchasing agent to travel through the southern states to purchase cotton. Futterman telegraphed Marra instructions from day to day as to the price to be paid for cotton. Marra entered a cotton district in which she had not previously done business and represented that she was purchasing cotton for Futterman. Although directed by Futterman to pay no more than 25 cents a pound, Marra bought cotton from Anderson at 30 cents a pound, which was the prevailing offering price at that time. Futterman refused to take the cotton. Under these circumstances, which of the following is correct?

a. The negation of actual authority to make the purchase effectively eliminates any liability for Futterman.
b. Futterman is not liable on the contract.
c. Marra has no potential liability.
d. Futterman is liable on the contract.

16. Farley Farms, Inc., shipped 100 bales of hops to Burton Brewing Corporation. The agreement specified that the hops were to be of a certain grade. Upon examining the hops, Burton claimed that they were not of that grade. Farley's general sales agent who made the sale to Burton agreed to relieve Burton of liability and to have the hops shipped elsewhere. This was done, and the hops were sold at a price less than Burton was to have paid. Farley refused to accede to the agent's acts and sued Burton for the amount of its loss. Under these circumstances

a. Farley will prevail only if the action by its agent was expressly authorized.
b. Even if Farley's agent had authority to make such an adjustment, it would not be enforceable against Farley unless ratified in writing by Farley.
c. Because the hops were sold at a loss in respect to the price Burton had agreed to pay, Burton would be liable for the loss involved.
d. Farley is bound because its agent expressly, impliedly, or apparently had the authority to make such an adjustment.

17. Ivy Corp. engaged Jones as a sales representative and assigned him to a route in southern Florida. Jones worked out of Ivy's main office and his duties, hours, and routes were carefully controlled. The employment contract contained a provision which stated: "I, *Jones,* do hereby promise to hold the corporation harmless from any and all tort liability to third parties which may arise in carrying out my duties as an employee." On a sales call, Jones negligently dropped a case of hammers on the foot of Devlin, the owner of Devlin's Hardware. Which of the following statements is correct?

a. Ivy has **no** liability to Devlin.
b. Although the exculpatory clause may be valid between Ivy and Jones, it does **not** affect Devlin's rights.
c. Ivy is **not** liable to Devlin in any event, since Jones is an independent contractor.
d. The exculpatory clause is totally invalid since it is against public policy.

18. Brian purchased an automobile from Robinson Auto Sales under a written contract by which Robinson obtained a security interest to secure payment of the purchase price. Robinson reserved the right to repossess the automobile if Brian failed to make any of the required ten payments. Ambrose, an employee of Robinson, was instructed to repossess the automobile on the ground that Brian had defaulted in making the third payment. Ambrose took possession of the automobile and delivered it to Robinson. It was then discovered that Brian was not in default. Which of the following is **incorrect**?

a. Brian has the right to regain possession of the automobile and to collect damages.
b. Brian may sue and collect from either Robinson or Ambrose.
c. If Ambrose must pay in damages, he will be entitled to indemnification from Robinson.
d. Ambrose is **not** liable for the wrongful repossession of the automobile since he was obeying the direct order of Robinson.

19. Wall & Co. hired Carr to work as an agent in its collection department, reporting to the credit manager. Which of the following is correct?

a. Carr does **not** owe a fiduciary duty to Wall since he does not compete with the company.
b. Carr will be personally liable for any torts he commits even though they are committed in the course of his employment and pursuant to Wall's directions.
c. Carr has the implied authority to engage

counsel and commence legal action against Wall's debtors.

d. Carr may commingle funds collected by him if this is convenient as long as he keeps proper records.

20. Agents sometimes have liability to third parties for their actions taken for and on behalf of the principal. An agent will **not** be personally liable in which of the following circumstances?

a. If he makes a contract which he had no authority to make but which the principal ratifies.
b. If he commits a tort while engaged in the principal's business.
c. If he acts for a principal which he knows is nonexistent and the third party is unaware of this.
d. If he acts for an undisclosed principal as long as the principal is subsequently disclosed.

21. Wanamaker, Inc., engaged Anderson as its agent to purchase original oil paintings for resale by Wanamaker. Anderson's express authority was specifically limited to a maximum purchase price of $25,000 for any collection provided it contained a minimum of five oil paintings. Anderson purchased a seven picture collection on Wanamaker's behalf for $30,000. Based upon these facts, which of the following is a correct legal conclusion?

a. The express limitation on Anderson's authority negates any apparent authority.
b. Wanamaker cannot ratify the contract since Anderson's actions were clearly in violation of his contract.
c. If Wanamaker rightfully disaffirms the unauthorized contract, Anderson is personally liable to the seller.
d. Neither Wanamaker nor Anderson is liable on the contract since the seller was obligated to ascertain Anderson's authority.

22. Wilkinson is a car salesman employed by Fantastic Motors, Inc. Fantastic instructed Wilkinson not to sell a specially equipped and modified car owned by the company. Fantastic had decided to use this car as a "super" demonstrator to impress potential purchasers. The car had just arrived from Detroit, had been serviced, and was parked alongside other similar models. Barkus "fell in love" with the car and, after some negotiation with Wilkinson, signed a contract to purchase the car. Barkus gave Wilkinson a check for 20% of the purchase price and executed a note and a purchase money security agreement. Wilkinson forged Fantastic's name on the check and disappeared. Fantastic seeks to repossess the car from Barkus. What is the probable outcome of the above facts?

a. Fantastic will be permitted to repossess the car but must compensate Barkus for any inconvenience.
b. Barkus will be permitted to keep the car if Barkus assumes the loss on the check given to Wilkinson.
c. Fantastic will be permitted to repossess the car because there was an express prohibition against the sale of this car.
d. Barkus will be permitted to keep the car because Wilkinson has the apparent authority to bind Fantastic to the contract of sale.

23. Dent is an agent for Wein pursuant to a written agreement with a three-year term. After two years of the term, Wein decides that he would like to terminate the relationship with Dent. Wein may terminate the relationship

a. Without cause, but may be held liable for breach of contract.
b. Even if Dent is an agent coupled with an interest.
c. Without cause, but may be held liable for the intentional interference with an existing contract.
d. Only if Dent breaches the fiduciary duties owed to Wein.

24. Notice to third parties is **not** required to terminate a disclosed general agent's apparent authority when the

a. Principal has died.
b. Principal revokes the agent's authority.
c. Agent renounces the agency relationship.
d. Agency relationship terminates as a result of the fulfillment of its purpose.

25. Dixon Sales, Inc., dismissed Crow as its general sales agent. Dixon notified all of Crow's known customers by letter. Hale Stores, a retail outlet located outside of Crow's previously assigned sales territory, had never dealt with Crow. However, Hale knew of Crow as a result of various business contacts. After his dismissal, Crow sold Hale goods, to be delivered by Dixon, and received from Hale a cash deposit for 20% of the purchase price. It was not unusual for an agent in Crow's previous position to receive cash deposits. In an action by Hale against Dixon on the sales contract, Hale will

a. Lose, because Crow lacked any express or implied authority to make the contract.

b. Lose, because Crow's conduct constituted a fraud for which Dixon is not liable.
c. Win, because Dixon's notice was inadequate to terminate Crow's apparent authority.
d. Win, because a principal is an insurer of an agent's acts.

May 1985 Questions

26. Wok Corp. has decided to expand the scope of its business. In this connection, it contemplates engaging several agents. Which of the following agency relationships is within the Statute of Frauds and thus should be contained in a signed writing?
a. A sales agency where the agent normally will sell goods which have a value in excess of $500.
b. An irrevocable agency.
c. An agency which is of indefinite duration but which is terminable upon one month's notice.
d. An agency for the forthcoming calendar year which is entered into in mid-December of the prior year.

27. Red entered into a contract with Maple on behalf of Gem, a disclosed principal. Red exceeded his authority in entering into the contract. In order for Gem to successfully ratify the contract with Maple,
a. Gem must expressly communicate his intention to be bound.
b. Gem must have knowledge of the relevant material facts concerning the transaction.
c. Red must **not** have been a minor.
d. Red must have acted reasonably and in Gem's best interest.

28. An agency coupled with an interest will be created by a written agreement which provides that a(an)
a. Borrower shall pledge securities to a lender which authorizes the lender to sell the securities and apply the proceeds to the loan in the event of default.
b. Employee is hired for a period of two years at $40,000 per annum plus 2% of net sales.
c. Broker is to receive a 5% sales commission out of the proceeds of the sale of a parcel of land.
d. Attorney is to receive 25% of a plaintiff's recovery for personal injuries.

29. Ritz hired West for six months as an assistant sales manager at $4,000 a month plus 3% of sales. Which of the following is correct?
a. The employment agreement must be in writing and signed by the party to be charged.
b. The agreement between Ritz and West formed an agency coupled with an interest.
c. West must disclose any interests he has which are adverse to Ritz in matters concerning Ritz's business.
d. West can be dismissed by Ritz during the six months only for cause.

Repeat Question

(585,L1,4) Identical to item 25 above

Problems

Problem 1 (580,L5a&b)

(10 to 15 minutes)

Part a. Vogel, an assistant buyer for the Granite City Department Store, purchased metal art objects from Duval Reproductions. Vogel was totally without express or apparent authority to do so, but believed that his purchase was a brilliant move likely to get him a promotion. The head buyer of Granite was livid when he learned of Vogel's activities. However, after examining the merchandise and listening to Vogel's pitch, he reluctantly placed the merchandise in the storeroom and put a couple of pieces on display for a few days to see whether it was a "hot item" and a "sure thing" as Vogel claimed. The item was neither "hot" nor "sure" and when it didn't move at all, the head buyer ordered the display merchandise repacked and the entire order returned to Duval with a letter that stated the merchandise had been ordered by an assistant buyer who had absolutely no authority to make the purchase. Duval countered with a lawsuit for breach of contract.

Required:

Answer the following, setting forth reasons for any conclusions stated.

Will Duval prevail?

Part b. Foremost Realty, Inc., is a real estate broker that also buys and sells real property for its own account. Hobson purchased a ranch from Foremost. The terms were 10% down with the balance payable over a 25 year period. After several years of profitable operation of the ranch, Hobson had two successive bad years. As a result, he defaulted on the mortgage. Foremost did not want to foreclose, but instead offered to allow Hobson to remain on the ranch and suspend the payment schedule until Foremost could sell the property at a reasonable price. However, Foremost insisted that it be appointed as the irrevocable and exclusive agent for the sale of the property. Although Hobson agreed, he subsequently became dissatisfied with Foremost's efforts to sell the ranch and gave Foremost notice in writing terminating the agency. Foremost has indicated to Hobson that he does not have the legal power to do so.

Required:

Answer the following, setting forth reasons for any conclusions stated.

Can Hobson terminate the agency?

Problem 2 (1178,L3a&b)

(10 to 15 minutes)

Part a. Rapid Delivery Service, Inc., hired Dolson as one of its truck drivers. Dolson was carefully selected and trained by Rapid. He was specifically instructed to obey all traffic and parking rules and regulations. One day while making a local delivery, Dolson double parked and went into a nearby customer's store. In doing so, he prevented a car legally parked at the curb from leaving. The owner of the parked car, Charles, proceeded to blow the horn of the truck repeatedly. Charles was doing this when Dolson returned from his delivery. As a result of a combination of several factors, particularly Charles' telling him to "move it" and that he was "acting very selfishly and in an unreasonable manner," Dolson punched Charles in the nose, severely fracturing it. When Charles sought to restrain him, Dolson punched Charles again, this time fracturing his jaw. Charles has commenced legal action against Rapid.

Required:

Answer the following, setting forth reasons for any conclusions stated.

1. Will Charles prevail?
2. What liability, if any, would Dolson have?

Part b. Harold Watts was employed by Superior Sporting Goods as a route salesman. His territory, route, and customers were determined by Superior. He was expected to work from 9:00 a.m. to 5:00 p.m., Monday through Friday. He received a weekly salary plus time and one-half for anything over 40 hours. He also received a small commission on sales which exceeded a stated volume. The customers consisted of sporting goods stores, department stores, athletic clubs, and large companies which had athletic programs or sponsored athletic teams. Watts used his personal car in making calls or, upon occasion, making a delivery where the customer was in a rush and the order was not large. Watts was reimbursed for the use of the car for company purposes. His instructions were to assume the customer is always right and to accommodate the customer where to do so would cost little and would build goodwill for the company and himself.

One afternoon while making a sales call and dropping off a case of softballs at the Valid Clock Company, the personnel director told Watts he was planning to watch the company's team play a game at a softball field located on the other side of town, but that his car would not start. Watts said, "Don't worry, it will be my pleasure to give you a lift and I would like to take in a few innings myself." Time was short and while on the way to the ballpark, Watts ran a light and collided with another car. The other care required $800 of repairs and the owner suffered serious bodily injury.

Required:

Answer the following, setting forth reasons for any conclusions stated.

1. What is Superior's potential liability, if any, to the owner of the other car?

2. What is Valid's potential liability, if any, to the owner of the other car?

Multiple Choice Answers

1.	a	7.	c	13.	d	19.	b	25.	c
2.	c	8.	a	14.	a	20.	a	26.	d
3.	b	9.	a	15.	d	21.	c	27.	b
4.	a	10.	a	16.	d	22.	d	28.	a
5.	a	11.	c	17.	b	23.	a	29.	c
6.	c	12.	a	18.	d	24.	a		

Multiple Choice Answer Explanations

A. Characteristics

1. (1181,L1,15) (a) A servant is an employee whose physical conduct is controlled or subject to the right of control by the employer. In contrast, an agent is subject to a lesser and more general control, but not necessarily control of the agent's physical conduct. Answer (b) is incorrect because the manner in which a person is compensated does not distinguish between a servant and an agent. Answer (c) is incorrect because although an agent has greater authority to contract on behalf of the principal than a servant would have concerning the master, a servant is not entirely precluded from contracting on behalf of the master. Answer (d) is incorrect because a servant could have apparent authority to bind his employer, if the employer manifests such intent to another and this third party has a reasonable belief of servant's authority based upon the employer's representation.

2. (578,L1,4) (c) An agent who sells on credit and guarantees the accounts to his principal is known as a del credere agent. Answer (a) is incorrect because a del credere agent's guarantee is not a suretyship agreement and is not required to be in writing. Answer (b) is incorrect because Winter promised to indemnify Magnum if the customers failed to pay; the agreement did not require Magnum to try to collect from the customers. Answer (d) is incorrect because as an agent, Winter is a fiduciary and owes the duty of loyalty, good faith, obedience, duty to account, not to commingle, etc.

A.6. Types of Principals

3. (584,L1,4) (b) Once the third party learns the identity of an undisclosed principal, the third party may elect to hold either the agent or the principal liable on the contract. Since Sam did not know that Rick was acting as an agent at the time the contract was entered into, Rick is liable as a party to the contract. The mere disclosure of the existence and identity of the principal after the parties have entered into the contract does not relieve the agent of his contractual obligations. Answer (a) is, therefore, incorrect. Answer (c) is also incorrect because an agent acting on behalf of an undisclosed principal is a party to the contract. Rick may, therefore, enforce the contract against Sam. Answer (d) is incorrect because specific performance is not an appropriate remedy when money damages will adequately compensate the plaintiff. Plain white paper is not unique; consequently, specific performance is not available.

4. (1183,L1,14) (a) Classification of a principal as disclosed, undisclosed, or partially disclosed affects the contractual liability of the agent toward third parties. The authority given the agent, however, is not affected. An agent representing an undisclosed principal has the same implied authority as an agent representing a disclosed principal. Answer (b) is incorrect because a principal's liability for his agent's torts is the same regardless of whether the principal is disclosed, undisclosed, or partially disclosed. Answer (c) is incorrect because once the identity of a previously undisclosed principal is known, the third party may elect to hold either the principal or the agent liable on the contract. Answer (d) is incorrect because a fictitious business name statute requires a party conducting business under an assumed name to receive the state's permission to use that name. Such a statute has no applicability to the Lux—Steel agency relationship.

B. Methods of Creation

5. (1181,L1,12) (a) A contract is not required to create an agency relationship. Such relationships can be created in numerous ways, including by agreement, operation of law, ratification and estoppel. Answer (b) is incorrect because an agent is subject to the continuous general control of the principal. Answer (c) is incorrect because an agent is a fiduciary; he owes the principal the obligation of faithful service. Answer (d) is incorrect because an agent must act for the benefit of the principal; an agent acts for and in place of the principal to effect legal relations with third persons.

6. (581,L1,33) (c) The Statute of Frauds provides that contracts not performable within one year must be in writing to be enforceable. Since the Duval-Harris contract cannot be performed within one year (18 month duration), it is required to be in writing to be enforceable. Answer (a) is incorrect since Harris' past performance would allow him to recover any amount owed him from services rendered before termination. However, it will not enable him to enforce the executory portion (unperformed part) of the oral contract. Answer (b) is incorrect since the economic factors cited by Duval would not be proper grounds for avoidance of the contract. Economic

factors do not qualify as an objective impossibility which would excuse Duval's duty to perform. Answer (d) is incorrect since the Statute of Frauds does apply.

7. (1180,L1,26) (c) A power of attorney is a written document authorizing another to act as one's agent. The written authorization must only be signed by the principal. Besides the express authority granted in the power of attorney, the agent can also have implied and apparent powers by which to bind the principal. Thus, answer (c) is correct.

8. (578,L1,5) (a) Generally an agency relationship involves trust and confidence and therefore cannot be delegated without consent. However, an agent would have implied authority to delegate duties in an emergency where the delegation is necessary to meet the emergency. Answer (b) is incorrect because convenience is not an adequate excuse to delegate an agent's duties. Answer (c) is incorrect because express consent is not always necessary to make a delegation, as the authority to delegate can arise from implications such as the type of business, usage, prior conduct, and the emergency doctrine as explained above. Answer (d) is incorrect because if a principal sells his business, the agency is likely to terminate rather than authorize a sales agent to delegate his duties to another.

B.5. Ratification

9. (584,L1,3) (a) Although the agent's act was outside the scope of his authority, the principal may, nevertheless, ratify the contract. Retention of the benefits of the contract constitutes implied ratification. Answer (b) is incorrect because ratification must occur before the third party withdraws from the contract. Answer (c) is incorrect because when the contract is unauthorized, the third party does not have the option of electing to hold the principal liable. The third party's awareness of the limitation on the agent's authority does not change the fact that the contract is unauthorized. Answer (d) is, therefore, also incorrect.

10. (1182,L1,7) (a) Before a person can ratify the acts of another, the supposed agent must purport to act in the name and on behalf of the ratifying party (principal). Since Myers is an undisclosed principal, he would be unable to ratify the unauthorized acts of Davidson in that Davidson never represented to Wallop that he was acting on behalf of Myers. Answer (b) is incorrect because Wallop will be bound to Myers regardless of whether or not Davidson acts outside the scope of his authority. If Davidson acts within the scope of his authority, Wallop is bound to Myers. If Davidson acts outside the scope of his authority, Wallop will be bound to Davidson. Answer (c) is incorrect because since Davidson acted for an undisclosed principal, Wallop can hold Davidson personally liable on the contract. However, upon learning of the existence of the undisclosed principal (Myers), Wallop can elect to hold Myers liable. Answer (d) is incorrect because the concept of agency by substitution does not exist.

11. (582,L1,7) (c) Ratification occurs when the principal, after the fact, approves an unauthorized act performed on his behalf by another individual. The essence of ratification is that the prior unauthorized act is treated as if it had been authorized by the "principal" at the outset. Ratification requires some conduct by the principal which manifests his intent to affirm the agreement. Voluntary acceptance or retention by the principal of the benefits of a transaction purportedly entered into on his behalf will generally establish ratification by the principal. Therefore, since Sears shipped the order and cashed Davidson's check, this was sufficient evidence of its intent to affirm the discount agreement, and Sears becomes bound on the contract. Answer (a) is incorrect because even though Mathews contracted outside the scope of his authority, Sears ratified the sales agreement, thereby becoming bound on the contract. Answer (b) is incorrect because Mathews' express authority consists of the duties which the principal, Sears, specifically instructed him to do, which was only to solicit orders. Implied authority normally arises to do acts reasonably necessary to accomplish an authorized act; therefore, Mathews had no implied authority to grant discounts or collect payment since this was not necessitated in Mathews carrying out his function of soliciting orders for Sears. Answer (d) is incorrect because apparent authority arises when the principal's manifestations or conduct lead a third party to believe that the agent has authority beyond that to which the principal actually consented. Therefore, Mathews would not have apparent authority to grant discounts or collect payment, since Sears made no such manifestations or representations which would cause Davidson, the third party, to reasonably believe so.

E. Obligations and Rights

12. (581,L1,30) (a) An agency relationship is a fiduciary relationship which means that the agent owes great trust and loyalty to the principal while acting as an agent. An agent with interests adverse to his principal must disclose these facts to the principal. Answer (b) is incorrect since the employment contract di[illegible] not contain a restrictive covenant prohibiting competition. The agent may work for a competitor, but has a

duty not to disclose confidential information if detrimental to his old principal. Answer (c) is incorrect because a principal can normally dismiss the agent without cause even though the principal may be liable for breach. Answer (d) is incorrect since the contract is capable of being performed in one year; the oral contract is enforceable.

13. (578,L1,3) (d) A principal (employer) owes a duty to its agent (employee) to indemnify the agent for acts carried out in good faith upon the principal's (employer's) behalf. Answer (a) is incorrect because a principal owes no duty not to compete with its agent. It is the agent who has a duty not to compete with its principal. Answer (b) is incorrect because a principal has the duty to reimburse an agent only for expenditures directly related to employment. Answer (c) is incorrect because agency agreements of an indefinite duration are generally implied to continue from pay period to pay period and may be terminated by notice of either party.

E.3. Principal's Liability to Third Parties

14. (584,L1,1) (a) Since the limitations on Dill's authority were not known by Sky, they are not relevant to the issue of apparent authority. A third party such as Sky ordinarily has no way of learning of such limitations. The doctrine of apparent authority allows a third party to make reasonable assumptions concerning an agent's authority. Custom and useage in the business is, therefore, relevant. Likewise, the status of the agent's position with the principal is relevant. The agent's status might lead a third party to reasonably believe that the agent has a certain scope of authority. If the principal has acquiesced in similar acts by the agent and this acquiescence is known to the third party, it may also provide a basis for apparent authority. Therefore, answers (b), (c), and (d) are incorrect.

15. (578,L1,10) (d) The principal, Futterman, is liable for the acts of his general agent, even though the agent violated rules which were unknown to the third party. Answer (a) is incorrect because even though Marra did not have actual authority to buy at 30 cents a pound, she had apparent authority to do so (because she was a general purchasing agent). Answer (b) is incorrect because Futterman is liable on this contract. Answer (c) is incorrect because Marra has potential liability both to third parties for violating her warranty of authority and to her principal for disregarding proper instructions.

16. (1175,L1,15) (d) A general sales agent such as Farley's would have implied or apparent authority, if not express authority, to make such an adjustment and this would bind the principal, Farley. Farley will prevail only if his agent did not have any authority. Ratification is only used where the agent did not have authority in the first place, i.e., for an authorized act, and it need not be in writing. Burton would be liable for the loss only if he had breached. Since Farley arguably breached by shipping the wrong grade, and also because the parties have negotiated a modification, accord, or rescission, Burton is not liable.

E.3.g. Principal's Liability for Servant's Torts

17. (1183,L1,12) (b) Jones' activity is subject to the extensive control of Ivy Corp. Consequently, Jones must be considered Ivy Corp.'s employee and not an independent contractor. Although the exculpatory clause contained in the employment contract is valid and not against public policy, the clause only affects the rights and liabilities which Jones and Ivy Corp. owe each other. Devlin's rights are not affected by the clause and he may sue Ivy Corp., the employer, which remains liable for Jones' torts committed within the agent's scope of employment, under the doctrine of respondeat superior. Accordingly, answers (a), (c), and (d) are incorrect.

18. (1181,L1,16) (d) Ambrose's act of repossessing the car constituted the tort of conversion. An agent or employee is always liable for his own torts, even if committed in the course of discharging his duties. Answer (a) is incorrect because the injured party, Brian, has the right to regain possession of his automobile and collect money damages for the tortious act of conversion committed upon him. Answer (b) is incorrect because any third person injured by the agent's or employee's tortious act, when committed within the course of employment, can proceed against either the employee or employer—Ambrose being directly liable for his wrongful act, and Robinson being vicariously liable therefor. Brian can sue either, but can take judgment against only one. Answer (c) is incorrect because when the employee is held liable for a tortious act, which was committed upon direct instructions from the employer, he has a right of indemnification against the employer for any damages he must pay a third person.

E.4. Agent's Liability to Third Parties

19. (1183,L1,13) (b) An agent is personally liable for the torts he commits, whether inside or outside the scope of his employment, and regardless of whether or

not the principal is also liable for the tort. The principal's authorization of the tort is no defense to the agent's liability. Answer (d) is incorrect because an agent has the duty to keep the funds and property of his principal separate from his own. Maintaining proper records is no defense to the breach of this duty. Answer (a) is incorrect because every agent owes his principal a fiduciary duty of loyalty and trust. The fact that the agent does not compete with his principal does not relieve the agent of this duty. Answer (c) is incorrect because the circumstances indicate Carr's implied authority is limited. The fact that Carr must report directly to his superior, the credit manager, infers that Carr's authority does not extend to such managerial decisions as instituting legal action.

20. (1180,L1,27) (a) The correct answer is (a) since an agent, after the principal ratifies an unauthorized act, is acting within his authority and is free of any liability on the contract. An agent is personally liable for all torts he commits; therefore, answer (b) is incorrect. An agent is liable if he acts for a principal which he knows is non-existent and knows the third party is unaware of this. Thus, answer (c) is incorrect. If an agent contracts for an undisclosed principal, the agent remains liable to the third party even though he is acting within the scope of his authority. The agent, however, has recourse against the principal. The third party can sue either the principal or agent. As a result, answer (d) is incorrect.

21. (1179,L1,33) (c) If the principal, Wanamaker, rightfully disaffirms the unauthorized contract by Anderson, the agent, Wanamaker, is personally liable to the seller on the theory of the implied warranty of authority. Anderson warranted to the seller that he had authority to bind Wanamaker to the sale contract. Answer (a) is incorrect because an express limitation on an agent's authority does not negate any apparent authority. Apparent authority is based on prior action and on what is customary in the general business community. Answer (b) is incorrect because Wanamaker, the principal, could ratify the contract made by Anderson since Anderson was purporting to act for Wanamaker. Answer (d) is incorrect because the agent is always liable on a contract that he makes on behalf of his principal on the theory that he warrants to the third party that he has authority. The seller should have ascertained Anderson's authority in order to assure that he had an enforceable contract against Wanamaker.

22. (577,L2,27) (d) Whether a contract made by an agent is binding on the principal depends on authority. While the agent, Wilkinson, lacked express or implied authority (and in fact had specific instructions not to sell this car), he nevertheless had apparent authority insofar as third persons without knowledge were concerned. A contract based on apparent authority is enforceable if it is the type usually or customarily made by similar agents in the performance of their employment relationships. In general, established business customs permit a new car salesman to bind his principal to a contract for the sale of an automobile from inventory, accept a down payment by check, and make the usual warranties and financing arrangements. The buyer can keep the car and the principal, Fantastic Motors, is deemed to have received the check when it was delivered to an agent with apparent authority.

F. Termination of Principal-Agent Relationship

23. (1184,L1,14) (a) Generally, a principal always has the power, but not necessarily the right, to terminate the agency relationship. Therefore, Wein may release Dent without cause, but Dent may seek compensatory damages for breach of contract. Answer (d) is thus incorrect. An exception to this general rule exists in the case of an agency coupled with an interest. When the agent has either a property interest or a security interest in the subject matter of the agency, the principal has neither the power nor the right to terminate the relationship. Therefore, answer (b) is incorrect. Answer (c) is incorrect because the appropriate action on Dent's part would be to bring a suit against Wein for breach of contract, not for interference with an existing contract.

24. (584,L1,2) (a) Upon the death of either the principal or agent, the agency relationship terminates by operation of law, and there is generally no requirement that third parties be notified. If, however, the agency terminates by act of the parties, it is necessary that notice be given to third parties in order to terminate the agent's apparent authority. Answers (b), (c), and (d) state circumstances that constitute termination by act of the parties. Notice, therefore, would be required.

25. (1183,L1,11) (c) When the agency relationship is terminated by an act of the principal and/or agent, third parties are entitled to notice of the termination from the principal. Failure of the principal to give the required notice gives the agent apparent authority to act on behalf of the principal. Specifically, the principal must give actual notice to all parties who had prior dealings with the agent or principal. Constructive or public notice must be given to parties who knew of the existence of the agency relationship, but did not actually have business dealings with the agent or principal. Since Dixon Sales, Inc. did not give proper constructive notice to Hale Stores, Crow had apparent

authority to bind the principal and, therefore, Hale Stores will win. Accordingly, answer (a) is incorrect. Answer (b) is incorrect because Dixon is liable for the torts of its authorized agent under the doctrine of respondeat superior. Answer (d) is incorrect because a principal is not an absolute insurer of his agent's acts. A principal is liable for his agent's torts only if the principal expressly authorizes the conduct or the tort is committed within the scope of the agent's employment.

May 1985 Answers

26. (585,L1,1) (d) Under the Statute of Frauds, certain contracts must be contained in a signed writing to be enforceable. Among these is a contract that can not be performed within one year. In a personal service contract, the one-year period begins running at the time that the contract is formed, not at the time the service is to commence. A contract creating an agency relationship for the forthcoming year which is entered into in mid-December of the prior year could not possibly be performed within one year and, therefore, must be contained in a signed writing in order to be in compliance with the Statute of Frauds. Answer (a) is incorrect because an agreement creating an agency relationship authorizing the agent to sell goods that have a value in excess of $500 need not be in writing, although any such contracts entered into by that agent must be in writing in order to be enforceable under the Statute of Frauds. Answer (b) is incorrect because an irrevocable agency need not be contained in a signed writing. Answer (c) is incorrect since it describes an agency relationship which is capable of being performed within one year.

27. (585,L1,2) (b) Ratification takes place when there is a subsequent approval by the principal of an agent's unauthorized action. In order for ratification to occur, the principal must have knowledge of all material facts regarding the contract. Answer (a) is incorrect because it is not necessary that the principal expressly communicate an intent to be bound. If the principal acts in a manner so as to imply ratification (e.g., by taking advantage of the benefits of the contract), then the principal's actions will be construed as ratification. Answer (c) is incorrect because even though minors have limited contractual capacity, the minor is capable of ratifying an unauthorized contract entered into by an agent. Answer (d) is incorrect since it makes no difference whether or not the agent acts reasonably and in the best interest of the principal. The principal may ratify any contract as long as the requirements for ratification are satisfied.

28. (585,L1,3) (a) An agency coupled with an interest will be created any time the agent has either a property interest or a security interest in the subject matter of the agency. If a lender obtains authorization to sell pledged securities and applies the proceeds to the loan in the event of the borrower's default, that lender becomes an agent with a security interest in the subject matter of the agency relationship and the agency is irrevocable. Answers (b), (c), and (d) are all incorrect because they describe situations in which the agent merely has rights to a percentage of proceeds to be received, but has no interest in the subject matter of the agency relationship.

29. (585,L1,5) (c) As a fiduciary to the principal, an agent must act in the best interest of the principal. Therefore, the agent has an obligation to refrain from competing with or acting adversely to the principal, unless the principal knows and approves of such activity. Answer (a) is incorrect because the Statute of Frauds would not require that the described agency relationship be contained in a signed writing since it is possible for the contract to be performed within 1 year. Answer (b) is incorrect because the mere right of the agent to receive a percentage of proceeds is not sufficient to constitute an agency coupled with an interest. In order to have an agency coupled with an interest, the agent must have either a property interest or a security interest in the subject matter of the agency relationship. Answer (d) is incorrect because in all agency relationships, except agencies coupled with an interest, the principal always has the power to dismiss the agent. However, the principal does not necessarily have the right to terminate the relationship. In certain situations the dismissed agent could sue for breach of contract.

Answer Outline

Problem 1 Ratification; Agency Coupled With an Interest (580,L5a&b)

a. Yes, Duval will prevail in breach of contract action
- Initially Vogel (agent) had no express or apparent authority; however, principal ratified unauthorized contract by
  - Retaining and displaying goods
  - Lack of timely notification of refusal of goods
- Granite would not be liable if immediate notification had occurred

b. May Hobson terminate agency unilaterally
- No, most agency-principal relationships terminable by either party
- However, agency coupled with an interest is irrevocable
  - As mortgagee of defaulting mortgagor, creditor has interest in property

Unofficial Answer

Problem 1 Ratification; Agency Coupled With an Interest (580,L5a&b)

a. Yes. Despite the stated lack of express or apparent initial authority of Vogel, Granite City Department Store's agent, there would appear to be a ratification by the principal.

It is clear from the facts stated that Granite would not have been liable on the Vogel contract if the head buyer had immediately notified Duval and returned the goods. Instead the head buyer retained the goods and placed some on display in an attempt to sell them. Had they proved to be a "hot" item, undoubtedly the art objects would have been gratefully kept by Granite. Granite wants to reject the goods if they don't sell. Such conduct is inconsistent with a repudiation based upon the agent's lack of express or apparent authority. The retention of the goods for the time indicated, the attempted sale of the goods, and a failure to notify Duval in a timely way, when taken together, constitute a ratification of the unauthorized contract.

b. No. The facts reveal an agency coupled with an interest and therefore an irrevocable agency. Most agency-principal relationships are terminable by either party. However, one clearly recognized exception to this generally prevailing rule is that the agency may not be terminated when the agent has an interest in property that is the subject of the agency. This agency, coupled with an interest rule, applies here since the creditor (Foremost Realty, Inc.) has the requisite interest in the property because it is the mortgagee-creditor of the defaulting mortgagor-debtor. Thus, the appointment by Hobson of Foremost as the irrevocable agent for the sale of the mortgaged property cannot be terminated unilaterally by Hobson.

Answer Outline

Problem 2 Vicarious Liability (1178,L3a&b)

a1. Yes, Rapid is probably liable for Dolson's action
- Master is liable for servants' tortious conduct
- Employee's conduct must be within scope of employment
- Employer's lack of fault does not relieve liability

a2. Dolson is liable to Charles
- For tortious injury inflicted
- Rapid's liability does not relieve Dolson from liability

b1. Superior is liable to the owner of the other car
- Watt's automobile trip was within scope of employment with Superior

b2. Valid has no liability to the owner of the other car
- Valid's personnel director was not negligent re accident
- Valid had no control or responsibility over Watts

Unofficial Answer

Problem 2 Vicarious Liability (1178,L3a&b)

Part a.

1. Probably yes. A master is liable for his servant's unauthorized tortious conduct within the scope of employment. This is true despite the fact that the master is in no way personally at fault or has forbidden the type of conduct engaged in by the servant. A servant is normally an employee who renders personal service to his employer and whose activities are subject to the control of the employer. A truck driver such as Dolson would clearly fall within such a description. Once this has been established, the question is whether the assaults committed upon Charles by Dolson were within the scope of his em-

ployment. When the intentional use of force is involved, the courts have taken an expansive view insofar as imposition of liability upon the employer. If the servant's actions are predictable, there is likelihood that liability will be imposed upon the master. Where the servant deals with third persons in carrying out his job, the courts ask whether the wrongful act which occurred was likely to arise out of the performance of his job. Additionally, consideration is given to whether any part of his motive was the performance of his job, or if not, whether it was a normal reaction to a situation created by the job. Truck drivers using force in situations involving parking space or after a collision resulting in a dispute are not uncommon. The courts have usually imposed liability in cases such as this unless the assault was unrelated to the job, was solely personal, or was outrageous.

2. Dolson is liable to Charles for the tortious injury inflicted. The fact that Dolson may have been acting as a servant of Rapid and may impose liability upon his employer does not relieve him from liability.

Part b.

1. Superior Sporting Goods is liable for the negligence of its servant-agent Watts. The requisite control of his activities is apparent from the facts. Furthermore, based upon the instructions Watts received, it would appear that he was acting within the scope of his employment. In fact, one could conclude from the facts that Watts had express authority to make a trip such as the one he made when the accident occurred. He specifically was told to generally accommodate the customer where to do so would cost little and would build goodwill for the company and himself. This appears to be exactly what he did. Superior will undoubtedly attempt to assert the "independent frolic" doctrine and claim that Watts had abandoned his employment in order to pursue his own interest, or pleasures. However, the deviation was not great, it took place during normal working hours, and, most importantly, was at the request of a customer and was a type of conduct Superior specifically encouraged.

2. Valid Clock Company has no liability. Its agent was not at fault, nor can it be reasonably argued that an agency relationship was created between itself and Watts because its personnel director accepted the ride offered by Watts. The requisite control of Watts' physical activities by Valid is not present.

PARTNERSHIP LAW

Overview

The Uniform Partnership Act is the uniform statute adopted by most states and is the basis for partnership questions on the exam. A partnership is an association of two or more persons to carry on a business as co-owners for profit. For most purposes, the partnership is not considered a separate entity, but a specialized form of agency. The major areas tested on partnerships are the characteristics of a partnership, comparisons with corporations, the rights and liabilities of the partnership itself, the rights, duties, and liabilities of the partners among themselves and to third parties, the allocation of profits and losses, and the rights of various parties, including creditors, upon dissolution.

The law of joint ventures is similar to that of partnerships with some exceptions. Note that the joint venture is more limited in scope than the partnership form of business. The former is typically organized to carry out one single business undertaking; whereas, the latter is formed to conduct ongoing business.

A. Nature of Partnerships

1. A partnership is an association of two or more persons to carry on a business as co-owners for profit
    a. To carry on a business includes almost every trade, occupation, or profession
        1) It does not include passive co-ownership of property, e.g., joint tenants of a piece of land
    b. Co-ownership of the "business" (and not merely of assets used in a business) is an important element in determining whether a partnership exists. Each partner has a proprietary interest in the business.
        1) Co-ownership of property (including capital) is one element
        2) The most important and necessary element of co-ownership (and thereby partnership) is profit sharing
            a) Need not be equal and need not include loss sharing, although it usually does and is so presumed
            b) Receipt of a share of profits is prima facie evidence (raises a presumption) of a partnership
                1] Presumption rebutted by establishing that profit sharing was only for payment of debt, interest on loan, services performed, rent, etc.
        3) Another important element of co-ownership is joint control
            a) Each partner has an equal right to participate in management. May be contracted away to a managing partner.

2. The partnership relationship creates a fiduciary relationship between partners
    a. Partnership relationship is based on contract but arrangements may be quite informal
    b. Nevertheless, agreement can be inferred from conduct, e.g., allowing someone to share in management and profits may result in partnership even though actual intent to become partner is missing
    c. Fiduciary relationship arises because each partner is an agent for partnership and for each other in partnership business
3. In general, partnerships are governed by the Uniform Partnership Act (UPA) and by agency law
    a. UPA is a codification of the old common law and enunciates formation, rights, duties, liability, etc.
        1) Most aspects may be changed by agreement; e.g., rights and duties between partners by agreement among them, liability to third parties by agreement with them
        2) Also helps determine when a partnership exists
    b. Agency law also governs because partners are agents. Much of this is incorporated in the UPA.
4. Generally, any person (entity) who has the capacity to contract (see CONTRACTS) may become a partner
    a. Corporations can, but see CORPORATIONS for problems with excessive delegation of management
    b. Minors can, but contract of partnership is voidable (see CONTRACTS). Nevertheless, a minor's investment in the partnership is subject to creditor's claims.
    c. Partnerships can become partners
    d. Trustees can, if acting prudently (see TRUSTS AND ESTATES)
5. Common characteristics of partnerships
    a. Limited duration; when partner dies, partnership terminates
    b. Transfer of ownership requires agreement
    c. Not a distinct separate entity for many purposes, e.g., liability and taxation
        1) However, is a separate legal entity for purposes of ownership of property
    d. Unlimited liability of partners for partnership debts
    e. Ease of formation, can be very informal
        1) Thereby freedom from much government regulation
    f. Since partners are personally liable for debts, partnership may obtain credit more easily than a corporation given same financial condition
        1) A theoretical distinction. Practically, a corporation will either be:
            a) Large or sound enough to warrant availability of credit, or
            b) One or more stockholders or directors will be asked to assume personal liability

B. Types of Partnerships and Partners

1. Limited partnership is a special statutory relationship consisting of general partners and limited partners. The limited partners only contribute capital and are only liable to that extent, analogous to shareholder.

   a. See "G. Limited Partnership" for detailed Limited Partnership rules

2. General partner is one who shares in the management of the business and has unlimited liability

3. Limited partner is one who does not take part in the management process and whose liability is limited to his capital contribution

4. Silent partners have no voice in management, but share unlimited liability and are disclosed

5. Dormant partner is an inactive partner with right to management participation (although seldom used), but who is undisclosed; once disclosed has same liability as general partner

6. Ostensible partner is one who holds self out as a partner or other partners represent him/her as a partner to third persons. If not actually a partner, s/he becomes a partner by estoppel.

C. Formation of Partnership

1. By agreement, express or implied

   a. Partnership relationship can be implied by the acts of the parties
   b. Partnership may be used to hold "partners" liable if third parties are led to believe a partnership exists

2. Creation of a partnership may be very informal, either oral or written

   a. Written partnership agreement not required unless within Statute of Frauds, e.g., partnership that cannot be completed within one year

      1) Usually wise to have in writing

3. Under the Uniform Partnership Act, anyone who receives a share of profits is presumed to be a partner. This is, however, a rebuttable presumption.

4. Articles of copartnership (Partnership Agreement). Not legally necessary, but a good idea to have. Following are some typical provisions:

   a. Parties involved (partners)
   b. Name of partnership
   c. Duration
   d. Purposes
   e. Rights and duties, including profit and loss sharing, property management, etc.
   f. Dissolution procedures and rights

5. Fictitious name statutes require partners to register fictitious or assumed names

   a. Failure to comply does not invalidate partnership but may result in fine
   b. Purpose -- to allow third parties to know who is in partnership

D. Partner's Rights

1. Partnership agreement, whether formal or informal, would be controlling
   a. Secondly, partner's intent inferred from conduct is controlling
   b. Lastly, the following rules are determinative of partner's rights
2. Partnership interest
   a. Refers to partner's right to share in profits and return of contribution on dissolution
   b. Is considered personal property
      1) Even if partnership property is real estate
   c. Does not include specific partnership property, merely right to use it for partnership purposes
   d. Freely assignable without other partner's consent
      1) Assignee is not substituted as a partner without consent of all other partners
      2) Assignee does not receive right to interfere in management, to have an accounting, to inspect books, etc.; simply receives assigning partner's share of profits
      3) Assignor remains liable as a partner
      4) Does not cause dissolution unless assignor also retires (withdraws)
   e. If partner withdraws, selling his/her interest back to the partnership:
      1) Loses all partner's rights and interests in the partnership
      2) If sold on time (installments), is merely a creditor of partnership
      3) May subsequently be partner by estoppel if s/he fails to give notice to third parties
3. Partnership property
   a. Includes:
      1) Property acquired with partnership funds unless different intent is shown
      2) Capital contributed by partners, e.g., cash, land, building, fixtures, securities. Contribution is determined by objective intent.
      3) Partnership profits before the profits are distributed
      4) Goodwill, partnership name, etc.
   b. All partners have equal rights to the partnership property
      1) Even if title is in name of one partner
   c. Not assignable nor subject to attachment individually, only by a claim on the partnership
      1) All partners can agree and assign property
      2) Any partner can assign or sell if for apparently carrying on the business of the partnership in the usual way
   d. Each partner has an insurable interest in partnership property
   e. Upon partner's death, his/her estate is only entitled to the deceased partner's interest in partnership, not specific property

1) Partnership may have to be liquidated to settle his/her estate
2) Life insurance often carried to avoid liquidation
3) Heirs not automatically partners

f. May not be conveyed to point of making partnership insolvent. Such would be a fraudulent conveyance.

1) Insolvency is determined by adding net assets of all general partners to net assets of partnership
2) Includes a conveyance to a partner even if he promises to pay partnership debts

4. Participate in management

a. Right to participate equally in management

1) Ordinary business decisions by a majority vote
2) Unanimous consent needed to make fundamental changes

b. Power to act as an agent for partnership in partnership business
c. Also has right to inspect books and have full knowledge of partnership affairs

5. Share in profits and losses

a. Profits and losses are shared equally unless agreement specifies otherwise

1) Even if contributed capital is not equal
2) E.g., agreement may specify in proportion to contributed capital
3) E.g., agreement may specify one partner to receive greater share of profits for doing more work, while losses still shared equally

b. If partners agree on unequal profit sharing but are silent on loss sharing, losses are shared per the profit sharing proportions

1) May choose to share losses in a different proportion from profits if specific agreement

6. Other monetary rights

a. Indemnification for expenses incurred on behalf of the partnership
b. Interest on loans and extra advances to partnership

1) No interest on capital contributions unless in partnership agreement

c. Indemnification by partnership for partnership expenses paid by a partner or contribution (by other partners) for expenses paid in excess of one's share

EXAMPLE: Partner A pays the taxes on the land owned by the partnership. Partner A should be indemnified from the partnership cash account or one-third each from Partners B and C if the partnership is unable to pay.

d. No right to salary for work performed because this is a duty

1) Common for partners to agree to pay salaries, especially if only one or two do most of the work

7. Nonmonetary rights between partners

a. Based on fiduciary duty
   1) Partners cannot gain personally from partnership transactions without agreement by other partners
   2) Any wrongly derived profits must be held by partner as trustee for others
   3) Must not compete with partnership
   4) May participate in other business as long as it is not competition
   5) Must abide by partnership agreement

b. Exercise of reasonable skill

c. Formal accounting of partnership affairs
   1) A comprehensive investigation of partnership transactions and decision on rights of partners
   2) Available when agreement provides for, or when partner is excluded from partnership business, or when some other irregularity occurs

d. May sue partners or partnership in only limited situations
   1) Usually must petition for a formal accounting and dissolution

E. <u>Relationship to Third Parties</u>

1. Partners are agents of the partnership. See AGENCY for types of authority and how it is created.

   a. Can bind partnership to contracts with third parties
      1) Even where no actual authority, can bind partnership where there is apparent authority

   b. Partnership is liable for partner's torts committed in course and scope of business and for partner's breach of trust, i.e., misapplication of third party's funds

      EXAMPLE: A partner takes a third party's money on behalf of the partnership to invest in government bonds. Instead he uses it himself to build an addition onto his home.

   c. Partners usually have authority to buy and sell goods, receive money, and pay debts
      1) No authority to make the partnership a surety or guarantor

   d. Partnership is not liable for acts of partners outside of express, implied, or apparent authority

      EXAMPLE: A partner of a hardware store attempts to buy some real estate in the name of the partnership. Here apparent authority does not exist.

   e. Person who represents self to be a partner is liable to third parties as a partner
      1) Called partner by estoppel
      2) Same liability if consents to have another represent him/her as a partner
      3) Courts split on whether liable if only allows another to represent him/her as partner

2. Third parties should be aware that for certain acts, unanimous consent of the partners is needed

    a. Admission of a new partner
    b. Assignment of partnership property

        1) If title is only in name of one partner, innocent third party could get good title from this one partner because there is no notice that it is partnership property

    c. Disposition of partnership goodwill
    d. Make the partnership a surety or guarantor
    e. Admit to claim against partnership in court
    f. Submit a partnership claim to an arbitrator or a referee
    g. Any act making it impossible to carry on the business

3. Partner's liability is personal, i.e., extends to all his personal assets, not just investment in partnership, for all debts and liabilities of the partnership

    a. Partners are jointly liable on contracts, debt, and other obligations

        1) Joint liability means all partners must be sued together. Cannot sue only one.
        2) Partnership assets must be exhausted before partner's individual assets can be reached
        3) Release of one partner releases all
        4) Since majority vote rules, all partners are liable even if they did not vote or objected to the action

    b. Partners are jointly and severally liable for torts and breaches of trust (see "E.1.b." above)

        1) Several liability means a party may sue just one partner (any one) for the full amount
        2) Party has choice whether to sue one or all parties. If one partner has enough assets, he will be sued severally for simplicity.
        3) Partnership assets need not be exhausted first. Partnership need not even be sued.
        4) Release of one does not release others from liability

    c. Partners may split losses or liability between themselves according to any proportion agreed upon; however, third parties can still hold each partner personally liable despite agreement

        EXAMPLE: A, B and C are partners who agree to split losses 10%, 10% and 80%, respectively. Y sues the partners for a tort based on the partnership business. C takes out bankruptcy. Y can recover from A and B and is not bound by the agreement between A, B and C.

    d. New partners coming into a partnership are liable for existing debts only to the extent of their capital contributions

        1) Unless new partners assume personal liability for old debts

    e. Partners withdrawing or dead (then their estates) are liable for subsequent liabilities unless notice of withdrawal or death is given to third parties

1) Actual notice to creditors who previously dealt with partnership
2) Constructive, e.g., published, notice is sufficient for others

f. Partners are not criminally liable unless they personally participate in some way or statute prescribes liability to all members of management, e.g., antitrust laws, environment regulation or sale of alcohol to a minor

g. Liability of withdrawing partner may be limited by agreement between partners but agreement is not binding on third parties (unless they join in on agreement)

F. <u>Termination of a Partnership</u>

1. Termination occurs when the winding up (often called liquidation) of partnership affairs is complete

   a. First, dissolution must occur--when the partners stop carrying on a business together
   b. Second, winding up takes place--the process of settling of partnership
   c. Lastly, termination occurs--winding up completed, i.e., partnership no longer exists

2. Voluntary dissolution can occur by agreement of the partners

   a. Prior agreement, e.g., partnership agreement

      1) Specified term of existence may have been reached
      2) Particular undertaking may have been accomplished
      3) Expulsion of a partner from business if so provided for in agreement

         a) If not provided for in agreement, partnership can be voluntarily dissolved and a new one formed without unwanted partner

   b. Present agreement of <u>all</u> partners

      1) Admittance of a new partner. But for all practical purposes nothing happens, e.g., no liquidation.
      2) All may agree to dissolution and to end the business

3. Involuntary dissolution

   a. Withdrawal of a partner

      1) If agreement specifies a term of existence or a particular undertaking, withdrawing partner will be in breach of contract if his withdrawal is prior to agreed time
      2) If no agreed length of partnership, any partner can terminate at any time

   b. Death of a partner

      1) Executor may require an accounting and payment to estate of decedent's interest

   c. Bankruptcy of a partner or partnership
   d. Subject matter of partnership business becomes illegal
   e. By decree of court in such cases as:

1) Partner is declared insane
2) Partner continually or seriously breaches partnership agreement

f. Assignment, selling, or pledging of partnership interest does <u>not</u> cause dissolution. See "D.2.d."

1) Even if no consent of other partners

4. Rights of partners in dissolution

a. Where the cause of dissolution is not a violation of the partnership agreement (e.g., a dissolution upon expiration of specified partnership term)

1) No partner has a claim or cause of action against any other partner for any loss sustained in the dissolution
2) Each partner has right to have partnership assets applied to discharge of his/her liabilities, and balance distributed to partners in accordance with their respective interests

b. Where the dissolution is caused by an act in violation of the partnership agreement (e.g., a partner's electing to dissolve a partnership for a fixed term prior to the expiration thereof; consequently, this would not be relevant to a partnership at will)

1) The other ("innocent") partners are accorded certain rights in addition to those listed above; the right to damages, the right to purchase business (continue partnership business in firm name), and the right to wind up partnership affairs and arrange for distribution of assets
2) The partnership interest of the partner that caused wrongful dissolution will be valued without taking goodwill into consideration

5. At dissolution, and during winding up

a. Partners have no actual authority to act for partnership except as is necessary to wind up
b. Partners are still liable to creditors
c. Partners are responsible for distributing assets and satisfying creditors

6. Distribution priority (different from limited partnerships; see "G.10.")

a. Creditors
b. To partners for liabilities other than capital
c. To partners for capital contributions
d. To partners as to profits

EXAMPLE: The partnership of Herb, Ike, and Bucky was dissolved. The partnership had liquid assets of $260,000 and liabilities of $240,000, of which $210,000 is owed to outside creditors and $30,000 is owed to Herb for a loan Herb made to the partnership. The capital contributions were: Herb, $20,000 and Ike, $15,000. Profits and losses are to be shared according to the following ratio: Herb, 50%; Ike, 30%; and Bucky, 20%. The order of distribution of firm assets of a general partnership would be as follows: First, the outside creditors are satisfied, $210,000. Second, Herb receives $30,000 representing his loan to the firm. Third, capital contributions are returned to Herb ($20,000) and Ike ($15,000). This results in a $15,000 deficit [$260,000 - ($210,000 + $30,000 + $20,000 + $15,000)]. The partners must contribute toward this deficiency according *to the loss sharing ratio. Therefore, Herb must contribute $7,500 (50% x $15,000), Ike must contribute $4,500 (30% x $15,000), and Bucky must contribute $3,000 (20% x $15,000). Thus, in the final result, Herb receives a net distribution of $42,500 [($30,000 + $20,000) - $7,500], Ike receives a net distribution of $10,500 ($15,000 - $4,500), and Bucky must contribute $3,000.*

If Bucky is personally insolvent, the other partners (Herb and Ike) are liable in the relative proportion in which they share in the profits: Herb, $1,875 ($3,000 x 50%/80%) and Ike, $1,125 ($3,000 x 30%/80%). Therefore, Herb and Ike must reduce their net distributions by these respective amounts.

7. Partners are personally liable to partnership for any deficits in their capital accounts and to creditors for insufficiency of partnership assets
   a. Partners must contribute toward this deficiency according to loss sharing ratio, always same as profit sharing ratio unless agreed otherwise
   b. Priority between partnership creditors and partner's personal creditors (called marshalling of assets rule)
      1) Partnership creditors have first priority to partnership assets, any excess goes to personal creditors
      2) Usually, personal creditors have first priority to personal assets, any excess goes to partnership creditors. However, the Bankruptcy Reform Act of 1979 revised this so that the Trustee in bankruptcy of a partnership is entitled to share pro rata with unsecured creditors of a partner.
8. Partnership agreement may provide for partnership to continue without winding up
9. If business is continued after dissolution, a new partnership is formed and old creditors become creditors of the new partnership
   a. No name change is required, e.g., a retired partner's name may be used in the partnership name
10. Partners can bind the other partners and the partnership on contracts until third parties who have known of the partnership are given notice of the dissolution
    a. Actual notice must be given to third parties who have dealt with the partnership prior to dissolution
    b. Constructive notice, e.g., notice in newspaper, is adequate for third parties who have only known of the partnership

G. Limited Partnerships

1. Regulated by state statutes based on Uniform Limited Partnership Act - ULPA
   a. These statutes must be complied with for limited partner status, otherwise partners are general partners

1) Without statutes, no limited partnership can exist
2) Limited partnerships must file (with state) a certificate of limited partnership
    a. Public information
    b. A formal proceeding is required for formation and amendments
    c. Contains information about the partnership, partners, contributions, profit sharing, rights, etc.
3) A person who erroneously believes he is a limited partner, e.g., error in filing certificate, may avoid liability as a general partner by
    a. Renouncing his interest in the profits or other compensation immediately upon learning of the mistake

b. In certain cases state "blue sky" laws (anti-fraud laws for sale of securities) must be complied with because limited partnership interests are considered securities
    1) E.g., where large number of limited partnership interests are offered to the public
c. If limited partnership interests are offered for sale in more than one state, the Securities Act of 1933 will have to be complied with (see FEDERAL SECURITIES LAW)

2. Must have at least one general partner
    a. Manage and conduct partnership business
    b. General partnership rules apply to them
    c. Liability cannot be limited
3. Limited partner (one or more are required to have a limited partnership)
    a. Contributes capital only
        1) May be cash or property
        2) Cannot consist of services if involves management of partnership
        3) May not withdraw capital so as to impair any creditor's status
            a) Need sufficient partnership property to pay all creditors before partner can withdraw capital
    b. Liability is limited to capital contributed
        1) Personal assets cannot be reached
    c. Has creditor status for loans to partnership
        1) See distribution of assets (see "G.7." below)
    d. Cannot take part in any management or control of the partnership
        1) Limited partner status lost if s/he becomes active in management
            a) Becomes liable as if general partner and is personally liable for partnership debts

2) Can lend money and transact business with the partnership

a) May not hold partnership property as collateral

3) Has no apparent authority (as defined in AGENCY)

e. Liable as general partner if limited partner allows name to be put in firm name
f. Can inspect books and require an accounting
g. Owes no fiduciary duty to partnership

1) May own interest in competing business

h. Can be a limited partner and a general partner at the same time

1) Has rights and powers, and is subject to all restrictions of a general partner
2) Has rights against other partners with respect to contributions as a limited partner

4. Additional limited partners may be admitted if requirements for amendment are met

a. To admit any new partner, there must be unanimous written consent by present partners

1) Can be in original agreement

b. Substitution of limited partners must meet same requirements
c. Certificate must be amended

5. Death, insanity, bankruptcy, or retirement of a general partner dissolves the partnership unless the other general partners continue it

a. Death, insanity, bankruptcy, or retirement of a limited partner does not dissolve the partnership unless there are no more partners

6. Limited partner's interest

a. As in general partnership, refers to limited partner's right to share of profits and return of contribution on dissolution
b. It is personal property
c. Freely assignable without consent of other partners

1) Assignee is not substituted as a limited partner unless all others agree to the substitution

a) And certificate is amended

2) Assignee has no right to inspect books, obtain an accounting, etc.

7. Distribution (priority, order) of assets on dissolution

a. Creditors, including limited partners who are creditors
b. Limited partners' profits and compensation by way of income on contributions
c. Limited partners' capital contributions
d. General partners' claims such as loans
e. General partners' profits
f. General partners' capital contributions

H. Joint Ventures

1. Definition of joint venture--association of two or more persons (or entities) organized to carry out single business undertaking (or series of related undertakings) for profit
   a. Distinguished from partnership because purpose is not to conduct ongoing business involving various transactions
      1) Joint venture is more limited
      2) Partnership is formed for indefinite period of time
   b. Also called joint enterprise or joint adventure
   c. Purpose is to combine skill, knowledge, property, money
      1) Sharing risks of investment is often main motive

         EXAMPLE: A and B agree to combine their resources to buy an old car, fix it up, and sell it while splitting expenses and profits.
   d. Generally, corporations may engage in joint ventures

      EXAMPLE: X corporation, O corporation, and N corporation decide to form a joint venture to bring oil from the north to the south of Alaska.
      1) In some states, corporations may not be partners in a partnership
2. Law of joint ventures is similar to that of partnerships with some exceptions
   a. Each joint venturer is not necessarily an agent of other joint venturers--limited power to bind others
      1) Can be express agent by agreement
      2) Apparent authority possible in individual cases
         a) Increasing reluctance to find apparent authority
   b. Death of joint venturer does not automatically dissolve joint venture
   c. Joint venture is interpreted as special form of partnership
      1) Uniform Partnership Act generally applies
      2) Most court interpretations on partnership law apply
      3) Fiduciary duties of partners in partnership law apply
         a) Duty to provide full disclosure to each other
         b) Possible conflict of interest in disclosing trade secrets between members
      4) No formalities necessary for creation
         a) Usually written contract anyway
      5) No name is required for joint venture
      6) Each member has right to participate in management
         a) Management of joint venture is often placed on one member by agreement
      7) Liability is unlimited and each joint venturer is personally liable for debts
      8) Each is liable for own negligence as well as negligence of other joint venturers
      9) Each member is entitled to an accounting
      10) In general, treated as partnership for tax purposes
         a) Profits taxable when earned whether or not distributed

Multiple Choice Questions (1–32)

1. Darla, Jack, and Sam have formed a partnership with each agreeing to contribute $100,000. Jack and Sam each contributed $100,000 cash. Darla contributed $75,000 cash and agreed to pay an additional $25,000 two years later. After one year of operations the partnership is insolvent. The liabilities and fair market value of the assets of the partnership are as follows:

Assets:	
Cash	$ 40,000
Trade accounts receivable	35,000
Receivable from Darla	25,000
Equipment	100,000
	$200,000
Liabilities:	
Trade accounts payable	$410,000

Both Jack and Sam are personally insolvent. Darla has a net worth of $750,000.

If Darla is a general partner, what is her maximum potential liability?

a. $ 95,000
b. $185,000
c. $210,000
d. $235,000

2. Lamay Associates, a general partnership, and Delray Corporation are contemplating entering into a joint venture. Such a joint venture

a. Will be treated as an association for federal income tax purposes and taxed at the prevailing corporate rates.
b. Must incorporate in the state in which the joint venture has its principal place of business.
c. Will be treated as a partnership in most important legal respects.
d. Must be dissolved upon completion of a single undertaking.

3. For which of the following purposes is a general partnership recognized as an entity by the Uniform Partnership Act?

a. Recognition of the partnership as the employer of its partners.
b. Insulation of the partners from personal liability.
c. Taking of title and ownership of property.
d. Continuity of existence.

4. Many states require partnerships to file the partnership name under laws which are generally known as fictitious name statutes. These statutes

a. Require a proper filing as a condition precedent to the valid creation of a partnership.
b. Are designed primarily to provide registration for tax purposes.
c. Are designed to clarify the rights and duties of the members of the partnership.
d. Have little effect on the creation or operation of a partnership other than the imposition of a fine for noncompliance.

5. Three independent sole proprietors decided to pool their resources and form a partnership. The business assets and liabilities of each were transferred to the partnership. The partnership commenced business on September 1, 1981, but the parties did not execute a formal partnership agreement until October 15, 1981. Which of the following is correct?

a. The existing creditors must consent to the transfer of the individual business assets to the partnership.
b. The partnership began its existence on September 1, 1981.
c. If the partnership's duration is indefinite, the partnership agreement must be in writing and signed.
d. In the absence of a partnership agreement specifically covering division of losses among the partners, they will be deemed to share them in accordance with their capital contributions.

6. Daniels, Beal, and Wade agreed to form the DBW Partnership to engage in the import-export business. They had been life-long friends and had engaged in numerous business dealings with each other. It was orally agreed that Daniels would contribute $20,000, Beal $15,000 and Wade $5,000. It was also orally agreed that in the event the venture proved to be a financial disaster all losses above the amounts of capital contributed would be assumed by Daniels and that he would hold his fellow partners harmless from any additional amounts lost. The partnership was consummated with a handshake and the contribution of the agreed upon capital by the partners. There were no other express agreements.

Under these circumstances, which of the following is correct?

a. Profits are to be divided in accordance with the relative capital contributions of each partner.
b. Profits are to be divided equally.

c. The partnership is a nullity because the agreement is **not** contained in a signed writing.

d. Profits are to be shared in accordance with the relative time each devotes to partnership business during the year.

7. One of your audit clients, Major Supply, Inc., is seeking a judgment against Danforth on the basis of a representation made by one Coleman, in Danforth's presence, that they were in partnership together doing business as the D & C Trading Partnership. Major Supply received an order from Coleman on behalf of D & C and shipped $800 worth of goods to Coleman. Coleman has defaulted on payment of the bill and is insolvent. Danforth denies he is Coleman's partner and that he has any liability for the goods. Insofar as Danforth's liability is concerned, which of the following is correct?

a. Danforth is **not** liable if he is **not** in fact Coleman's partner.

b. Since Danforth did **not** make the statement about being Coleman's partner, he is **not** liable.

c. If Major Supply gave credit in reliance upon the misrepresentation made by Coleman, Danforth is a partner by estoppel.

d. Since the "partnership" is operating under a fictitious name (the D & C Partnership) a filing is required and Major Supply's failure to ascertain whether there was in fact such a partnership precludes it from recovering.

8. In the course of your audit of James Fine, doing business as Fine's Apparels, a sole proprietorship, you discovered that in the past year Fine had regularly joined with Charles Walters in the marketing of bathing suits and beach accessories. You are concerned whether Fine and Walters have created a partnership relationship. Which of the following factors is the **most** important in ascertaining this status?

a. The fact that a partnership agreement is **not** in existence.

b. The fact that each has a separate business of his own which he operates independently.

c. The fact that Fine and Walters divide the net profits equally on a quarterly basis.

d. The fact that Fine and Walters did **not** intend to be partners.

9. A general partner of a mercantile partnership

a. Can by virtue of his acts, impose tort liability upon the other partners.

b. Has **no** implied authority if the partnership agreement is contained in a formal and detailed signed writing.

c. Can have his apparent authority effectively negated by the express limitations in the partnership agreement.

d. Can **not** be sued individually for a tort he has committed in carrying on partnership business until the partnership has been sued and a judgment returned unsatisfied.

10. Which of the following is a correct statement concerning a partner's power to bind the partnership?

a. A partner has **no** authority to bind the partnership after dissolution.

b. A partner can **not** bind the partnership based upon apparent authority when the other party to the contract knows that the partner lacks actual authority.

c. A partner has **no** authority in carrying on the regular business of the partnership to convey real property held in the partnership name.

d. A partner, acting outside the scope of the partner's apparent authority, but with the express authority to act, can **not** bind the partnership unless the third party knows of the express authority.

11. In determining the liability of a partnership for the acts of a partner purporting to act for the partnership without the authorization of fellow partners, which of the following actions will bind the partnership?

a. The renewal of an existing supply contract which the other partners had decided to terminate and which they had specifically voted against.

b. An assignment of the partnership assets in trust for the benefit of creditors.

c. A written admission of liability in a lawsuit brought against the partnership.

d. Signing the partnership name as a surety on a note for the purchase of that partner's summer home.

12. A question has arisen in determining the partnership's liability for actions taken for and on behalf of a partnership, but which were in fact without express or implied authority. Which of the following actions taken by a general partner will bind the partnership?

a. Renewing an existing supply contract which had previously been negotiated, but which the partners had specifically voted **not** to renew.

b. Submitting a claim against the partnership to binding arbitration.

c. Taking an action which was known by the party with whom he dealt to be in contravention of a restriction on his authority.

d. Signing the firm name as an accommodation comaker on a promissory note not in furtherance of firm business.

13. Donaldson reached the mandatory retirement age as a partner of the Malcomb and Black partnership. Edwards was chosen by the remaining partners to succeed Donaldson. The remaining partners agreed to assume all of Donaldson's partnership liability and released Donaldson from such liability. Additionally, Edwards expressly assumed full liability for Donaldson's partnership liability incurred prior to retirement. Which of the following is correct?

a. Edward's assumption of Donaldson's liability was a matter of form since as an incoming partner he was liable as a matter of law.

b. Firm creditors are **not** precluded from asserting rights against Donaldson for debts incurred while she was a partner, the agreements of Donaldson and the remaining partners notwithstanding.

c. Donaldson has **no** continuing potential liability to firm creditors as a result of the agreements contained in the retirement plan.

d. Since Donaldson obtained a release from firm debts she has **no** liability for debts incurred while she was a partner.

14. Perone was a member of Cass, Hack & Perone, a general trading partnership. He died on August 2, 1980. The partnership is insolvent, but Perone's estate is substantial. The creditors of the partnership are seeking to collect on their claims from Perone's estate. Which of the following statements is correct insofar as their claims are concerned?

a. The death of Perone caused a dissolution of the firm, thereby freeing his estate from personal liability.

b. If the existing obligations to Perone's personal creditors are all satisfied, then the remaining estate assets are available to satisfy partnership debts.

c. The creditors must first proceed against the remaining partners before Perone's estate can be held liable for the partnership's debts.

d. The liability of Perone's estate can **not** exceed his capital contribution plus that percentage of the deficit attributable to his capital contribution.

15. A general partner will not be personally liable for which of the following acts or transactions committed or engaged in by one of the other partners or by one of the partnership's employees?

a. The gross negligence of one of the partnership's employees while carrying out the partnership business.

b. A contract entered into by the majority of the other partners but to which the general partner objects.

c. A personal mortgage loan obtained by one of the other partners on his residence to which that partner, without authority, signed the partnership name on the note.

d. A contract entered into by the partnership in which the other partners agree among themselves to hold the general partner harmless.

16. Donovan, a partner of Monroe, Lincoln, and Washington, is considering selling or pledging all or part of his interest in the partnership. The partnership agreement is silent on the matter. Donovan can

a. Sell part but not all of his partnership interest.

b. Sell or pledge his entire partnership interest without causing a dissolution.

c. Pledge his partnership interest, but only with the consent of his fellow partners.

d. Sell his entire partnership interest and confer partner status upon the purchaser.

17. The partnership agreement of one of your clients provides that upon death or withdrawal, a partner shall be entitled to the book value of his or her partnership interest as of the close of the year preceding such death or withdrawal and nothing more. It also provides that the partnership shall continue. Regarding this partnership provision, which of the following is a correct statement?

a. It is unconscionable on its face.

b. It has the legal effect of preventing a dissolution upon the death or withdrawal of a partner.

c. It effectively eliminates the legal necessity of a winding up of the partnership upon the death or withdrawal of a partner.

d. It is **not** binding upon the spouse of a deceased partner if the book value figure is less than the fair market value at the date of death.

18. King, Kline and Fox were partners in a wholesale business. Kline died and left to his wife his share of the business. Kline's wife is entitled to

a. The value of Kline's interest in the partnership.
b. Kline's share of specific property of the partnership.
c. Continue the partnership as a partner with King and Fox.
d. Kline's share of the partnership profits until her death.

19. Which of the following will not result in a dissolution of a partnership?

a. The bankruptcy of a partner as long as the partnership itself remains solvent.
b. The death of a partner as long as his will provides that his executor shall become a partner in his place.
c. The wrongful withdrawal of a partner in contravention of the agreement between the partners.
d. The assignment by a partner of his entire partnership interest.

20. Unless otherwise provided in the limited partnership agreement, which of the following statements is correct?

a. A general partner's capital contribution may **not** consist of services rendered to the partnership.
b. Upon the death of a limited partner the partnership will be dissolved.
c. A person may own a limited partnership interest in the same partnership in which he is a general partner.
d. Upon the assignment of a limited partner's interest, the assignee will become a substituted limited partner if the consent of two-thirds of all partners is obtained.

21. Darla, Jack, and Sam have formed a partnership with each agreeing to contribute $100,000. Jack and Sam each contributed $100,000 cash. Darla contributed $75,000 cash and agreed to pay an additional $25,000 two years later. After one year of operations the partnership is insolvent. The liabilities and fair market value of the assets of the partnership are as follows:

Assets:	
Cash	$ 40,000
Trade accounts receivable	35,000
Receivable from Darla	25,000
Equipment	100,000
	$200,000
Liabilities:	
Trade accounts payable	$410,000

Both Jack and Sam are personally insolvent. Darla has a net worth of $750,000.

If Darla is a limited partner, what is her maximum potential liability?

a. $0
b. $ 25,000
c. $210,000
d. $235,000

22. Vast Ventures is a limited partnership. The partnership agreement does not contain provisions dealing with the assignment of a partnership interest. The rights of the general and limited partners regarding the assignment of their partnership interests are

a. Determined according to the common law of partnerships as articulated by the courts.
b. Basically the same with respect to both types of partners.
c. Basically the same with the exception that the limited partner must give ten days notice prior to the assignment.
d. Different in that the assignee of the general partnership interest does not become a substituted partner, whereas the assignee of a limited partnership interest automatically becomes a substituted limited partner.

23. Stanley is a well known retired movie personality who purchased a limited partnership interest in Terrific Movie Productions upon its initial syndication. Terrific has three general partners, who also purchased limited partnership interests, and 1,000 additional limited partners located throughout the United States. Which of the following is correct?

a. If Stanley permits his name to be used in connection with the business and is held out as a participant in the management of the venture, he will be liable as a general partner.
b. The sale of these limited partnership interests would **not** be subject to SEC registration.

c. This limited partnership may be created with the same informality as a general partnership.
d. The general partners are prohibited from also owning limited partnership interests.

24. A limited partner
a. May not withdraw his capital contribution unless there is sufficient limited-partnership property to pay all general creditors.
b. Must not own limited-partnership interests in other competing limited partnerships.
c. Is automatically an agent for the partnership with apparent authority to bind the limited partnership in contract.
d. Has no liability to creditors even if he takes part in the control of the business as long as he is held out as being a limited partner.

25. Absent any contrary provisions in the agreement, under which of the following circumstances will a limited partnership be dissolved?
a. A limited partner dies and his estate is insolvent.
b. A personal creditor of a general partner obtains a judgment against the general partner's interest in the limited partnership.
c. A general partner retires and all the remaining general partners do not consent to continue.
d. A limited partner assigns his partnership interest to an outsider and the purchaser becomes a substituted limited partner.

26. A limited partner's capital contribution to the limited partnership
a. Creates an intangible personal property right of the limited partner in the limited partnership.
b. Can be withdrawn at the limited partner's option at any time prior to the filing of a petition in bankruptcy against the limited partnership.
c. Can only consist of cash or marketable securities.
d. Need not be indicated in the limited partnership's certificate.

May 1985 Questions

27. The apparent authority of a partner to bind the partnership in dealing with third parties
a. Must be derived from the express powers and purposes contained in the partnership agreement.
b. Would permit a partner to submit a claim against the partnership to arbitration.
c. Will be effectively limited by a formal resolution of the partners of which third parties are aware.
d. Will be effectively limited by a formal resolution of the partners of which third parties are unaware.

28. Which of the following statements is correct regarding a limited partnership?
a. The general partner must make a capital contribution.
b. It can only be created pursuant to a statute providing for the formation of limited partnerships.
c. It can be created with limited liability for all partners.
d. At least one general partner must also be a limited partner.

29. Jane White acquired Zelmo's partnership interest in ZBA Partnership. All partners agreed to admit White as a partner. Unless otherwise agreed, White's admission to the partnership will automatically
a. Release Zelmo from personal liability on partnership debts arising prior to the sale of his partnership interest.
b. Release Zelmo from any liability on partnership debts arising subsequent to the sale of his partnership interest.
c. Subject White to unlimited personal liability on partnership debts arising prior to her admission as a partner.
d. Limit White's liability on partnership debts arising prior to her admission as a partner to her interest in partnership property.

30. Unless otherwise provided for, the assignment of a partnership interest will result in the
a. Dissolution of the partnership.
b. Assignee obtaining the right to receive the share of the profits to which the assignor would have otherwise been entitled.

c. Assignee succeeding to the assignor's rights to participate in the management of the partnership.
d. Vesting of the assignor's right to inspect the partnership books in the assignee.

31. Long, Pine, and Rice originally contributed $100,000, $60,000, and $20,000, respectively, to form the LPR Partnership. Profits and losses of LPR are to be distributed 1/2 to Long, 1/3 to Pine, and 1/6 to Rice. After operating for one year, LPR's total assets on its books are $244,000, total liabilities to outside creditors are $160,000 and total capital is $84,000. The partners made no withdrawals. LPR has decided to liquidate. If all of the partners are solvent and the assets of LPR are sold for $172,000

a. Rice will personally have to contribute an additional $8,000.
b. Pine will personally have to contribute an additional $4,000.
c. Long, Pine, and Rice will receive $6,000, $4,000, and $2,000, respectively, as a return of capital.
d. Long and Pine will receive $28,000 and $4,000, respectively, and Rice will have to contribute an additional $20,000.

32. Which of the following is a correct statement concerning the similarities of a limited partnership and a corporation?

a. Both are recognized for federal income tax purposes as taxable entities.
b. Both can only be created pursuant to a statute and each must file a copy of its certificate with the proper state authorities.
c. Both provide insulation from personal liability for all of the owners of the business.
d. Shareholders and limited partners may both participate in the management of the business and retain limited liability.

Problems

Problem 1 (581,L5)

(15 to 20 minutes)

Part a. Davis and Clay are licensed real estate brokers. They entered into a contract with Wilkins, a licensed building contractor, to construct and market residential housing. Under the terms of the contract, Davis and Clay were to secure suitable building sites, furnish prospective purchasers with plans and specifications, pay for appliances and venetian blinds and drapes, obtain purchasers, and assist in arranging for financing. Wilkins was to furnish the labor, material, and supervision necessary to construct the houses. In accordance with the agreement, Davis and Clay were to be reimbursed for their expenditures. Net profits from the sale of each house were to be divided 80% to Wilkins, 10% to Davis, and 10% to Clay. The parties also agreed that each was to be free to carry on his own business simultaneously and that such action would not be considered a conflict of interest. In addition, the agreement provided that their relationship was as independent contractors, pooling their interests for the limited purposes described above.

Ace Lumber Company sold lumber to Wilkins on credit from mid-1980 until February 1981. Ace did not learn of the agreement between Davis, Clay and Wilkins until April 1981, when an involuntary bankruptcy petition was filed against Wilkins and an order for relief entered. Ace Lumber has demanded payment from Davis and Clay. The lumber was used in the construction of a house pursuant to the agreement between the parties.

Required:

Answer the following, setting forth reasons for any conclusions stated.

In the event Ace sues Davis and Clay as well as Wilkins, will Ace prevail? Discuss the legal basis upon which Ace will rely in asserting liability.

Part b. Lawler is a retired film producer. She had a reputation in the film industry for aggressiveness and shrewdness; she was also considered somewhat overbearing. Cyclone Artistic Film Productions, a growing independent producer, obtained the film rights to "Claws," a recent best seller. Cyclone has decided to syndicate the production of "Claws." Therefore, it created a limited partnership, Claws Productions, with Harper, Von Hinden and Graham, the three ranking executives of Cyclone, serving as general partners. The three general partners each contributed $50,000 to the partnership capital. One hundred limited partnership interests were offered to the public at $50,000 each. Lawler was offered the opportunity to invest in the venture. Intrigued by the book and restless in her retirement, she decided to purchase 10 limited partnership interests for $500,000. She was the largest purchaser of the limited partnership interests of Claws Productions. All went well initially for the venture, but midway through production, some major problems arose. Lawler, having nothing else to do and having invested a considerable amount of money in the venture, began to take an increasingly active interest in the film's production.

She began to appear frequently on the set and made numerous suggestions on handling the various problems that were encountered. When the production still seemed to be proceeding with difficulty, Lawler volunteered her services to the general partners who as a result of her reputation and financial commitment to "Claws" decided to invite her to join them in their executive deliberations. This she did and her personality insured an active participation.

"Claws" turned out to be a box office disaster and its production costs were considered to be somewhat extraordinary even by Hollywood standards. The limited partnership is bankrupt and the creditors have sued Claws Productions, Harper, Von Hinden, Graham, and Lawler.

Required:

Answer the following, setting forth reasons for any conclusions stated.

What are the legal implications and liabilities of **each** of the above parties as a result of the above facts?

Problem 2 (579,L4)

(20 to 25 minutes)

Part a. Strom, Lane, and Grundig formed a partnership on July 1, 1974, and selected "Big M Associates" as their partnership name. The partnership agreement specified a fixed duration of ten years for the partnership. Business went well for the partnership for several years and it established an excellent reputation in the business community. In 1978, Strom, much to his amazement, learned that Grundig was padding his expense accounts by substantial amounts each month and taking secret kick-backs from certain customers for price concessions and favored service. Strom informed Lane of these facts and they decided to seek an accounting of Grundig, a dissolution of the firm by ousting Grundig, and the subsequent continuation of the firm by themselves under the name, "Big M Associates."

Required:

Answer the following, setting forth reasons for any conclusions stated.

1. Were there any filing requirements to be satisfied upon the initial creation of the partnership?

2. What will be the basis for the accounting and dissolution and should such actions be successful?

3. Can Strom and Lane obtain the right to continue to use the firm name if they prevail?

Part b. Palmer is a member of a partnership. His personal finances are in a state of disarray, although he is not bankrupt. He recently defaulted on a personal loan from the Aggressive Finance Company. Aggressive indicated that if he did not pay within one month, it would obtain a judgment against him and levy against all his property including his share of partnership property and any interest he had in the partnership. Both Palmer and the partnership are concerned about the effects of this unfortunate situation upon Palmer and the partnership.

Required:

Answer the following, setting forth reasons for any conclusions stated.

1. Has a dissolution of the partnership occurred?

2. What rights will Aggressive have against the partnership or Palmer concerning Palmer's share of partnership property or his interest in the partnership?

3. Could Palmer legally assign his interest in the partnership as security for a loan with which to pay off Aggressive?

Problem 3 (1182,L3b)

(12 to 15 minutes)

Part b. While auditing the financial statements of Graham, Phillips, Killian, and Henderson, a real estate partnership, for the year ended December 31, 1981, a CPA uncovers a number of unrelated events which warrant closer analysis:

- Graham died and left her partnership interest to her spouse.
- Phillips owned some real estate prior to the formation of the partnership but never formally transferred legal title to the partnership. The real estate has been used for partnership business since the partnership began its existence, and the partnership has paid all taxes associated with the real estate.
- Killian owes a considerable sum of money to a creditor, Jamison. Jamison has a judgment against Killian and has begun a foreclosure action against certain land owned by the partnership in order to satisfy his claim against Killian.
- Henderson sold some of the partnership real estate for value remitted to the partnership without the approval of the other partners. This sale exceeded Henderson's actual authority but appeared to be a customary sale in the ordinary course of business.

Required:

Answer the following, setting forth reasons for any conclusions stated.

1. Graham's spouse is presently seeking to exercise his spousal rights to obtain certain specific property owned by the partnership. Discuss the likely outcome of this matter.

2. Regarding the real estate that is legally in Phillips' name, can the partnership properly reflect this as an asset in the partnership's balance sheet?

3. Will Jamison succeed in his land foreclosure action?

4. If the partnership now wishes to rescind the sale of the real estate by Henderson, can it lawfully do so?

Problem 4 (584,L5a)

(7 to 10 minutes)

Part a. Hart was a partner in the Hart, Gray & Race partnership. He entered into a contract conveying to Paul his partnership interest. The contract, which was consented to by Gray and Race, provided that Paul would become a partner. All known past and present partnership creditors were given written notice of Hart's withdrawal. Within nine months, the partnership became insolvent. The parties are concerned about their liability for the partnership obligations.

Required:

Answer the following, setting forth reasons for any conclusions stated.

1. What effect does Hart's withdrawal have upon his liability with respect to existing debts of the partnership and to debts incurred after his withdrawal?

2. Describe Paul's liability for partnership obligations entered into prior to and after his admission to the partnership.

Multiple Choice Answers

1.	d	8.	c	15.	c	21.	b	27.	c
2.	c	9.	a	16.	b	22.	b	28.	b
3.	c	10.	b	17.	c	23.	a	29.	d
4.	d	11.	a	18.	a	24.	a	30.	b
5.	b	12.	a	19.	d	25.	c	31.	a
6.	b	13.	b	20.	c	26.	a	32.	b
7.	c	14.	b						

Multiple Choice Answer Explanations

A. Nature of Partnerships

1. (1184,L1,12) (d) Darla, as a general partner, is individually liable for all obligations of the partnership which would amount to $210,000. She is also personally liable for the additional $25,000 she promised to pay; her maximum potential liability would be $235,000. Therefore, answers (a), (b), and (c) are incorrect.

2. (1183,L1,21) (c) A joint venture will be treated as a partnership in most important legal respects. Answer (a) is incorrect because a joint venture falls within the definition of a partnership by the Internal Revenue Code and, therefore, is taxed as a partnership. Answer (b) is incorrect because a joint venture is **not** a corporation and, therefore, is not required to incorporate. Answer (d) is incorrect as dissolution occurs based upon the joint venture agreement or when **all** operations cease. There is no legal requirement that a joint venture must be dissolved upon completion of a single undertaking.

3. (583,L1,3) (c) Under the Uniform Partnership Act, a partnership is recognized as a separate entity for the purposes of taking title and ownership of property. Answer (a) is incorrect because partnerships are not recognized as an entity for the purpose of being an employer of its partners. Each partner is both a principal of and an agent of the other partners. Answer (b) is incorrect because a general partnership is never formed to insulate the partners from personal liability. All general partners are personally liable to third parties for all obligations of the partnership. Answer (d) is incorrect since the partnership does not have continuity of existence. A general partnership is dissolved every time there is a change in the relationship of the partners caused by any partner ceasing to be associated with the partnership.

C. Formation of Partnership

4. (1183,L1,15) (d) The purpose of fictitious name statutes is to enable interested parties to learn the identity of the individuals who operate the business. Since the name under which the business is operating often does not include the names of the partners, these statutes provide the necessary link between the name of the business and the names of the individual partners. The typical fictitious name statute provides for the imposition of a fine in the event of noncompliance. Answer (a) is incorrect because such statutes do not affect the creation of a partnership. Answer (b) is incorrect because fictitious name statutes are not related to tax purposes. It should be kept in mind that a partnership is not a separate taxable entity. Answer (c) is incorrect because such statutes are designed for the benefit of parties outside the partnership, not for the purpose of defining the rights and duties of the partners themselves.

5. (582,L1,1) (b) The Uniform Partnership Act defines a partnership as an association of two or more persons to carry on as co-owners a business for profit. A partnership relationship can be implied by the acts of the parties, as long as it appears that the parties intended joint responsibility in the management and operation of the business, and intended to share in its profits and losses. Therefore, the partnership began its existence on September 1, 1981, when the three sole proprietors demonstrated the necessary intent to carry on a business as partners. Answer (a) is incorrect because the existing creditors do not have to consent to the transfer of the individual business assets to the partnership. However, the creditors' rights are not affected or destroyed, and the creditors can avoid the transfer of assets if proved to be a fraudulent conveyance on the part of the three sole proprietors. Answer (c) is incorrect because a written agreement is not ordinarily necessary to create a partnership, unless it falls within the provisions of the Statute of Frauds (i.e., a partnership agreement which by its terms can not be performed within a year). Therefore, this partnership agreement falls outside the Statute of Frauds, since the partnership's duration is indefinite. Answer (d) is incorrect because unless the partnership agreement provides otherwise, the law implies that profits and losses are to be shared equally by the partners.

6. (1181,L1,18) (b) Unless the partnership agreement provides otherwise, the law implies that profits are to be shared equally by the partners. The agreement to form DBW Partnership only made reference to the manner in which losses are to be handled; therefore, profits are to be divided equally. Answer (d) is incorrect because the relative time each partner devotes to the partnership business has no effect on distribution of profits. Answer (c) is incorrect because a written agreement is not ordinarily necessary to create a partnership, unless it falls within the provisions of the

Statute of Frauds. This partnership agreement falls outside the requisites of the Statute of Frauds; therefore, it does not need to be evidenced by a sufficient writing in order to be effective.

7. (1180,L1,22) (c) A partnership can be created by estoppel. This occurs when a third party changes his position in reliance upon a misrepresentation of the fact that a partnership exists. Danforth is a partner by estoppel. Danforth does not need to make a statement to become a partner by estoppel; his silence would be sufficient considering he is present at the time Coleman represents that they are partners. Answer (c) is correct.

8. (1180,L1,23) (c) Two or more persons sharing profits of a business is prima facie evidence (raises a presumption) that a partnership exists. This presumption is overcome if it can be shown that the sharing of profits are for: services rendered, interest on loans, payment of debts, rent, any other reasonable explanation. The lack of intent or lack of a partnership agreement will not necessarily determine whether a partnership exists. Answer (c) is the correct answer.

E. Relationship to Third Parties

9. (1183,L1,16) (a) Partners are jointly and severally liable for torts committed by a copartner while carrying on partnership business. The partner who commits the tort can always be sued for his own actions regardless of whether the partnership has been sued. Thus, answer (d) is incorrect. Answer (b) is incorrect because the existence of implied authority is not inconsistent with a formal, detailed partnership agreement. While such an agreement may carefully spell out a partner's express authority, the partner still retains implied authority to do those things which are reasonably necessary to the exercise of his/her express authority. Answer (c) is incorrect because apparent authority is based upon the reasonable belief of a third party that the partner with whom he dealt possessed authority to represent the partnership in that matter. Since the third party is not a party to the partnership agreement and does not ordinarily have access to it, the third party is not bound by the terms of the agreement unless he has actual knowledge of its terms. The partnership agreement is, of course, binding among the partners themselves.

10. (1183,L1,17) (b) A third party, who has no notice of the dissolution of the partnership, may reasonably believe that a partner who is conducting partnership business in the usual way has authority to do so. Under such circumstances, the partner has apparent authority. Thus, answer (a) is incorrect. Likewise, if the sale of real estate is within the regular course of a partnership's business, a partner has apparent authority to convey real property held in the partnership name. Answer (c) is, therefore, incorrect. If, however, the third party knows that the partner with whom he deals lacks actual authority, there can be no apparent authority. With such knowledge, the third party can no longer reasonably believe that the partner has authority to represent the partnership. Answer (b), therefore, is correct. Answer (d) is incorrect because express authority is not based upon the knowledge of the third party. Instead it is based upon the partnership agreement itself.

11. (583,L1,5) (a) A partner has apparent authority to renew an existing supply contract which is apparently for the purpose of carrying on the partnership business in the usual way. In the absence of knowledge by a third party, that such action was unauthorized by the other partners, the contract renewal is binding on the partnership. The matters described in answers (b), (c), and (d) are actions requiring the unanimous consent of the partners: (1) assignment of partnership assets to creditors, (2) written admission of the liability of the partnership in a lawsuit, and (3) committing partnership as surety on a partner's personal debt. Therefore, a partner does not have apparent authority to bind the partnership in these matters because third parties are supposed to be aware of the requirement of unanimity.

12. (582,L1,2) (a) Every partner is an agent of the partnership for the purpose of conducting its business, and can bind the partnership to contracts with third parties. Any contracts made by a partner on behalf of the partnership and related to its business are deemed to be within the partner's apparent authority, and hence binding on the partnership, notwithstanding a limitation or agreement between the partners of which the third party had no notice. Such limitation on the partner's normal authority will only bind the third party if known to the third party before entering into the contract with the partnership. Therefore, the renewal of the supply contract would bind the partnership, regardless of the partners' vote not to renew. Answers (b) and (d) are incorrect because the Uniform Partnership Act provides certain inherent limitations on a partner's authority. Unless the partnership business has been abandoned, or all partners have expressed unanimous assent, no partner has authority to submit a partnership claim to arbitration; and no partner has authority to bind the partnership on accomodation paper unless expressly authorized, or in furtherance of firm business. Answer (c) is incorrect because when the

partner is acting in excess of his authority and the person with whom he is dealing knows of that fact, the partnership is not bound.

13. (1181,L1,21) (b) A retiring partner is liable to creditors for existing debts of the partnership, but not for those incurred after retirement, so long as creditors had notice of the retirement before extending the credit. Partners may agree not to hold a retiring partner liable among themselves, but they cannot prevent him being held personally liable by third parties. Therefore, when Donaldson leaves the partnership, she is still individually liable on all past contracts and obligations, unless existing creditors agree to release her and look to the new incoming partner, Edwards (a novation). Therefore, answers (c) and (d) are incorrect. A withdrawing partner may protect herself/himself against liability upon contracts which are entered into by the firm subsequent to her/his withdrawal by giving notice that s/he is no longer a member of the firm. Otherwise, s/he is liable for the debts thus incurred and due and owing to a creditor who had no notice or knowledge of the partner having withdrawn from the firm. Answer (a) is incorrect because new partners coming into a partnership are liable for antecedent debts and obligations of the firm only to the extent of their capital contribution, unless the new partners assume personal liability for prior partnership debts.

14. (1180,L1,19) (b) In a partnership, a general partner has unlimited liability for the partnership debts. Upon the death of a partner, this liability continues and is assumed by the deceased partner's estate. Under the doctrine of marshalling of assets, personal creditors have first priority to Perone's personal assets, with any excess going to the partnership creditors. This makes answer (b) correct and answers (a) and (d) incorrect. Answer (c) is incorrect since each partner, including a deceased partner's estate, is individually liable for the entire amount of partnership debts. However, if a partner pays more than his share of the partnership debts, he can sue his co-partners to recover the excess.

15. (1177,L1,12) (c) A partner who signs the partnership name to his personal mortgage has attempted to make the partnership a guarantor or surety. Unanimous consent is needed or the other partners will not be personally liable since apparent authority is lacking. General partners are personally liable for the partnership's debts and liabilities. Answer (a) is incorrect because gross negligence of an employee may create such a liability. Answer (b) is incorrect because partnership business is carried out by majority rule and each partner will be personally liable whether he objected or not. Answer (d) is incorrect because the other partners can agree not to hold a partner liable among themselves but they cannot prevent his being held personally liable by third parties.

F. Termination of a Partnership

16. (583,L1,4) (b) A partner can sell or pledge his entire interest in a partnership without causing a dissolution of the partnership regardless of whether he has the consent of the other partners. Therefore, answers (a) and (c) are incorrect. Answer (d) is incorrect because the purchase of an interest in a partnership does not confer partner status upon the purchaser. The assignee (purchaser) receives only the right to the partner's share of the profits and upon dissolution to the value of the partner's interest, and does not receive partnership status nor the accompanying rights such as participation in management, right to an accounting, right to inspect the books, etc.

17. (1180,L1,20) (c) Such a partnership agreement does not prevent the dissolution of the partnership upon the death or withdrawal of a partner; it merely eliminates the necessity of the second step in the termination of the partnership which is the winding up process. Such an agreement is enforceable. Answer (c) is the correct answer.

18. (1179,L1,16) (a) When a partner dies, his heirs or those named in his will are entitled to the value of the deceased partner's interest in the partnership. The heirs do not become and are not entitled to become partners as in answer (c) and the survivors acquire no interest in specific property of the partnership as in (b). The heirs are only entitled to the deceased partner's interest in the partnership. Answer (d) is incorrect because the surviving wife of a deceased partner is only entitled to her husband's rights at the time of his death.

19. (1179,L1,17) (d) The assignment by a partner of his entire partnership interest does not dissolve a partnership. Answer (a) is incorrect because the bankruptcy of a partner or of the partnership itself results in dissolution. Answer (b) is incorrect because the death of a partner generally results in a court ordered dissolution even if there is a purported agreement which attempts to substitute an executor as a partner in place of the decedent. Answer (c) is incorrect because the wrongful withdrawal of a partner even though in contravention of the partnership agreement will result in a dissolution of the partnership.

G. Limited Partnerships

20. (1184,L1,11) (c) One person may be both a limited partner and a general partner in the same limited partnership. Answer (a) is incorrect because a general partner's capital contribution may consist of services. However, a limited partner's capital contribution may not consist of services. Answer (b) is incorrect because of death of a limited partner does not cause dissolution. Answer (d) is incorrect because upon assignment of a limited partner's interest, the assignee does not automatically become a substitute limited partner. Unless stated otherwise in the limited partnership agreement, all partners must give written consent before an assignee becomes a new limited partner.

21. (1184,L1,13) (b) Darla, as a limited partner, is not liable for debts of the partnership beyond the amount of her capital contribution. However, she is still liable for the $25,000 of her capital contribution that she has not yet paid. Therefore, answers (a), (c), and (d) are incorrect.

22. (1183,L1,18) (b) The assignment of a limited partner's interest in the partnership is treated essentially the same as the assignment of a general partner's interest. The assignee does not become a substitute partner whether the assignment is of a general or limited partnership interest. Therefore, answer (d) is incorrect. Answer (a) is incorrect because a limited partnership can only be created if a state statute exists which would permit the creation of such an entity. Limited partnerships are governed by statute, not by common law. Answer (c) is incorrect because there is no ten-day notice requirement applicable to the assignment of a limited partnership interest.

23. (582,L1,3) (a) A limited partner will be held liable as a general partner, and therefore personally liable on partnership debts, where he takes an active part in management of the business or permits his name to be used in the firm's name. Answer (b) is incorrect because the definition of securities under the Securities Act of 1933 includes limited partnership interests. Therefore, the sale of these limited partnership interests, if interstate in character and not specifically exempted, may be covered by SEC regulations and subject to SEC registration. Answer (c) is incorrect because limited partnerships are regulated by state statutes based on the Uniform Limited Partnership Act. These statutes must be complied with when creating a limited partnership, otherwise the partners are general partners. Therefore, in contrast to the formation of a general partnership, the formation of a limited partnership must be in accordance with strict statutory requirements. Answer (d) is incorrect because a person may be both a general partner and a limited partner in the same partnership at the same time.

24. (1176,L1,11) (a) Limited partners may not withdraw their capital contributions so as to impair a creditor's status. Unless there is sufficient partnership property to pay all general creditors, withdrawal of limited partner capital impairs a creditor's status. Limited partners are not restricted in owning competing interests (but general partners are), because limited partners do not participate in management, i.e., they are merely investors. Limited partners are not agents and do not have apparent authority. General partners are agents, because they participate in management. If limited partners take part in the management of a business, they become liable as general partners.

25. (1176,L1,13) (c) If a general partner retires and the others do not consent to continue, the partnership is dissolved. Such dissolution can be avoided by a provision in the partnership agreement. If a limited partner dies (whether or not his estate is insolvent) or if he assigns his partnership interest, there is no dissolution. Remember a limited partner is similar to a stockholder of a corporation. A partnership is not dissolved if a creditor obtains a judgment against a partner's partnership interest. The creditor only has the right to income from the partnership interest; the creditor is not a substituted partner and does not have the right to manage or inspect the books.

26. (1176,L1,15) (a) A limited partner's (as does a general partner's) capital contribution creates an intangible property right in the partnership. Limited partners have no right to any specific partnership property, but rather a share of the total. The capital contribution cannot be withdrawn if it will impair a creditor's status, i.e., there must be enough partnership property to satisfy all creditors. A limited partner may contribute property just as a general partner may. A limited partner cannot contribute services if they will involve managing or operating the business. Each limited partner's capital contribution is one of the required inclusions in the limited partnership certificate (generally required to be filed).

May 1985 Answers

27. (585,L1,6) (c) A partner's apparent authority is derived from the reasonable perceptions of third parties due to the manifestations or representations of the partnership concerning the authority each partner possesses to bind the partnership. However, if third parties are aware of a formal resolution which limits the partner's actual authority to bind the partnership, then that partner's apparent authority will also be limited. Answer (a) is incorrect because as stated above, the apparent authority of a partner to bind the partnership is not derived from the express powers and purposes contained in the partnership agreement. Answer (b) is incorrect because third parties should be aware that in order for a partner to submit a claim against the partnership to arbitration, unanimous consent of the partners is needed. Therefore, a partner has no apparent authority to take such an action. Answer (d) is incorrect because if third parties are unaware of such a resolution which limits the partner's actual authority, then the partner retains apparent authority to bind the partnership.

28. (585,L1,7) (b) A limited partnership is a creature of state statutes that are based on the Uniform Limited Partnership Act. In the creation of a limited partnership, these statutes must be complied with for the limited partners to maintain their limited liability status. Answer (a) is incorrect since the general partner, i.e., the one who manages and conducts partnership business, need not make a capital contribution to the partnership. Answer (c) is incorrect because general partners do not enjoy limited liability. Answer (d) is incorrect because there is no requirement that at least one general partner must also be a limited partner (however, it is possible for a general partner to be a limited partner). However, once a limited partner engages in the management of partnership business, the cloak of limited liability is automatically shed and that partner assumes the full liability of a general partner.

29. (585,L1,8) (d) When a new partner enters a partnership, s/he is liable for existing debts only to the extent of his/her capital contributions. An exception to this rule exists only when the new partner assumes personal liability for existing partnership debts. Therefore, answer (c) is incorrect. Answer (a) is incorrect because a withdrawing partner continues to be personally liable on partnership debts arising prior to the sale of his/her partnership interest. Answer (b) is incorrect because a withdrawing partner is released from liability on any partnership debts arising subsequent to the sale of his/her partnership interest only if notice of withdrawal is given to third parties. Actual notice is owed to third parties who have previously dealt with the partnership. Constructive notice, e.g., publishing in a newspaper, is sufficient for third parties who knew of the partnership but had no prior dealings with the partnership.

30. (585,L1,9) (b) Unless otherwise stipulated in the partnership agreement, an individual partner's interest in the partnership is freely assignable without the consent of the other partners. However, upon the assignment, the assignee merely obtains the right to receive the assigning partner's share of the profits and return of capital contribution. Answer (a) is incorrect because the assignment of a partnership interest will not result in the dissolution of the partnership unless the assignor also withdraws. Answers (c) and (d) are incorrect because the assignee of a partnership interest is not substituted as a partner without the consent of all the other partners. Therefore, the assignee does not necessarily succeed to the assignor's right to participate in management, nor the right to inspect the partnership books.

31. (585,L1,10) (a) Upon the liquidation of the partnership, the claims of the outside creditors must be satisfied first. This leaves the partnership with $12,000 (cash received of $172,000 minus outside claims of $160,000). Since total capital contributions are $180,000, there is a deficit of $168,000 ($12,000 – $180,000). Rice's share in this deficit is equal to $28,000 (1/6 x $168,000). Since Rice's capital contribution is $20,000, Rice will personally have to contribute $8,000 toward the elimination of the deficit ($28,000 – $20,000). Answers (b), (c), and (d) are incorrect because Long will receive $16,000, an amount equal to Long's capital contribution ($100,000) minus his share of the deficit (1/2 x $168,000 = $84,000); Pine will receive $4,000, an amount equal to Pine's capital contribution ($60,000) minus his share in the deficit (1/3 x $168,000 = $56,000).

32. (585,L1,11) (b) Both limited partnerships and corporations can only be created pursuant to statutes, and both require that a copy of its certificate be filed with the proper state authorities. Answer (a) is incorrect because a limited partnership is not recognized for federal income tax purposes as a taxable entity. Answer (c) is incorrect because there is no insulation from personal liability for the general partners of a limited partnership. Answer (d) is incorrect because a limited partner will lose his/her limited liability once that partner participates in the management of the business.

Answer Outline

Problem 1 Creation of Partnership; Limited Partnership (581,L5)

a. Ace will prevail in his suit
   - Ace will rely upon the existence of a partnership relationship
     - Sharing of profits raises presumption of partnership
     - Receipt of gross returns does not itself establish a partnership
     - Joint ownership of property not prima facie evidence of partnership, but only one factor to consider
   - Objective intent of Davis, Clay and Wilkins supercedes their subjective intent
     - Parties' agreement to maintain independent contractors relationship does not contravene manifestation of partnership existence
   - Ace's lack of knowledge of partnership existence is irrelevant
     - No requirement for third party reliance on relationship
   - Partners are agents of the partnership
     - Wilkins can bind partnership to contracts with third parties
   - Partners are jointly liable for debts and obligations of the partnership

b. The limited partnership, the general partners and Lawlor are jointly liable for debts and obligations of Claws Productions
   - Limited partnership is liable to the extent of Claws Productions' assets
   - Partnership assets must be exhausted before general partners' individual assets can be reached
     - Harper, Von Hinden and Graham, as general partners, are liable for unpaid debts of Claws Productions
   - Limited partners liable for debts of partnership to extent of capital contributed
     - Lose status of limited partner where take active part in business and management functions
       - Lawlor becomes liable as general partner
         - Personally liable for partnership debts

Unofficial Answer

Problem 1 Creation of Partnership; Limited Partnership (581,L5)

Part a.

Yes. Ace will prevail. A partnership did exist and the parties are jointly liable. The legal basis upon which Ace will seek recovery is that a partnership exists among Wilkins, Davis, and Clay. If the parties are deemed partners among themselves, then Ace can assert liability against such partnership and against the individual partners as members thereof, since they are jointly liable for such partnership obligations.

The Uniform Partnership Act, section 7, provides rules for determining the existence of a partnership. Although it is frequently stated that the intent of the parties is important in determining the existence of a partnership relationship, this statement must be significantly qualified: it is not the subjective intent of the parties that is important when they categorically state that they do not wish to be considered as partners. If much effect were given to such statements, partnership liability could easily be shed. Further, the party dealing with the partnership need not in fact rely upon the existence of a partnership. Thus, the fact that Ace did not learn of the Davis, Clay, Wilkins agreement until after he had extended credit does not preclude him from asserting partnership liability.

The bearing of section 7 of the Uniform Partnership Act on this case can be examined as follows. First, joint, common, or part ownership of property of any type does not of itself establish a partnership. It is only one factor to be considered and was present to a limited extent in this case. Second, the sharing in gross returns does not of itself establish a partnership, but its importance is rendered moot as a result of the profit-sharing arrangement between the parties. Finally, and the key factor in partnership determination, is the receipt of profits: The act states "the receipt by a person of a share of the profits of a business is prima facie evidence that he is a partner in the business . . ."

Sharing in profits is prima facie evidence of the existence of a partnership. The defendants (Davis and Clay) must affirmatively rebut this prima facie case against them or lose. There do not appear to be facts sufficient to accomplish this.

Part b.

The limited partnership, the general partners, and Lawler are all jointly liable for the debts of Claws Productions.

Claws Productions limited partnership is liable and must satisfy the judgment to the extent it has assets. Harper, Von Hinden, and Graham are liable for the unpaid debts of the limited partnership. An interesting problem posed by the fact situation is Lawler's liability. The general rule, in fact the very basis for the existence of the limited partnership, is that the limited partner is not liable beyond its capital contribution. However, a notable exception contained in section 7 of the Uniform Limited Partnership Act applies to the facts presented here:

> A limited partner shall not become liable as a general partner unless, in addition to the exercise of his rights and powers as a limited partner, he takes part in the control of the business.

The statutory language covers the facts stated. Lawler assumed a managerial role vis à vis the partnership and in the process became liable as a general partner.

Answer Outline

Problem 2 Assumed Name Statute; Fiduciary Responsibility; Dissolution; Assignment of Partnership Interest (579,L4)

a1. Yes, fictitious name statute must be complied with since partnership name is not actual name of partners
- Requires recording in public records
- Purpose is to advise public who real parties are

But no filing of the partnership agreement is required

a2. Each partner is a fiduciary for all partnership related affairs per uniform partnership act (UPA)

UPA holds breach of fiduciary duty to be grounds for accounting
- Courts grant partnership dissolution when
  - Partner breaches fiduciary duty to partnership
  - Persistent breach of partnership agreement by partner makes it impractical to carry on partnership business

Dissolution and accounting should be granted
- Grundig breached fiduciary duty by
  - Dishonesty with partners
  - Stealing from partners
  - Involved partnership in illegal price discrimination

a3. Yes, continuing partners should obtain right to use firm name

UPA provides for continuation of business in same firm name when partnership has
- Fixed duration (10 years here) and
- Dissolution is a violation of the partnership agreement
  - Here, because Grundig's conduct is wrongful

b1. No, partner default on personal debt does not cause dissolution

Only bankruptcy of partner causes dissolution
- Facts state Palmer was not bankrupt
- Threats or action against partner's interest in partnership does not cause dissolution

b2. Partner creditors have no rights against partnership property
- Only partners have rights to use partnership property for partnership purposes

Aggressive has right to obtain first a judgment against Palmer and then a charging order
- Charging order entitles creditor to obtain debtor's future distributions from the partnership

b3. Yes, partner may assign his partnership interest
- Unless prohibited by partnership agreement
- Does not cause dissolution
- Does not make assignee a partner
  - Assignee only entitled to assignor's profits and capital distributions

Unofficial Answer

Problem 2 Assumed Name Statute; Fiduciary Responsibility; Dissolution; Assignment of Partnership Interest (579,L4)

Part a.

1. Yes. Although no filing of the partnership agreement is required, virtually all states have statutes that require registration of fictitious or assumed names used in trade or business. The purpose of such statutes is to disclose the real parties in interest to creditors and those doing business with the company. This is typically accomplished by filing in the proper office of public records the names and addresses of the parties doing business under an assumed name. The statutes vary greatly in detail (e.g., some states require newspaper publication).

2. The facts indicate a clear breach of fiduciary duty by Grundig. Section 21 of the Uniform Partnership Act holds every partner accountable as a fiduciary. It provides that "every partner must account to the

partnership for any benefit, and hold as trustee for it any profits derived by him without the consent of other partners from any transactions connected with the . . . conduct . . . of the partnership or from any use by him of its property." Grundig's conduct is squarely within the act's language. Section 22 of the act gives any partner a right to a formal accounting of partnership affairs if there is a breach of fiduciary duty by a fellow partner.

Section 32 (c) and (d) of the act provides for a dissolution by court decree upon application of a partner whenever—

- A partner has been guilty of conduct that tends to prejudicially affect the business.
- A partner willfully or persistently commits a breach of the partnership agreement or otherwise so conducts himself in matters relating to the partnership business that it is not reasonably practicable to carry on the business in partnership with him.

Certainly Grundig's conduct would appear to fall within one or both of the above categories. He breached his fiduciary duty, was dishonest with his fellow partners, was in fact stealing from his partners, and may have involved the partnership in illegal price discrimination. Thus, the grant of application for dissolution would be appropriate.

3. Probably yes. Section 38(2) (b) of the Uniform Partnership Act relating to the right to continue the business in the same firm name, under the circumstances described, is narrowly drawn. This provision was designed to cover situations where partnerships have fixed durations and one of the partners has caused a dissolution wrongfully "in contravention of the partnership agreement." The facts indicate that Big M Associates did have a fixed duration (10 years); consequently, this requirement is met. While the acts by Grundig are not in contravention of any specific express language of the partnership agreement, as would be the case where a partner wrongfully withdraws, the courts treat other types of wrongful conduct to be in contravention of the partnership agreement and thus, to be the basis for dissolution. Strom and Lane could obtain the right to continue to use the firm name for the duration of the partnership agreement if Grundig's conduct was deemed both wrongful and in contravention of the agreement.

Part b.

1. No. Since the facts clearly indicate that Palmer is not bankrupt, his financial problems will not precipitate a dissolution of the partnership. However, if Palmer were bankrupt, the Uniform Partnership Act [Sec.31(5)] specifically provides that the bankruptcy of one of the partners causes a dissolution. The fact that creditors take action against a delinquent partner's interest in the partnership, although annoying and inconvenient, does not result in a dissolution.

2. Aggressive will have no rights to the partnership property either directly or indirectly by asserting Palmer's rights. In fact, Palmer only has the right to the use of partnership property for partnership purposes. Since partnership property is insulated from attack by Aggressive, Aggressive will assert its rights against Palmer's partnership interest. The method used to reach this interest is to reduce its claim against Palmer to a judgment and then obtain from the court a "charging order" to enable Aggressive to collect on the judgment. In effect, Aggressive has obtained a right comparable to a lienholder against Palmer's interest in the partnership. The "charging order" would provide Aggressive with the right to payments (earnings or capital distributions) that would ordinarily go to Palmer, the partner-debtor.

3. Yes. There is nothing in the Uniform Partnership Act that prevents a partner from assigning all or part of his interest in a partnership. The assignment may be outright or for the more common purpose of securing loan. If there is to be any such restriction on a partner's right to assign his partnership interest, the partnership agreement must so provide. Section 27 of the Uniform Partnership Act specifically provides that a partner's assignment of his partnership interest does not cause a dissolution. The act limits such an assignment to the partner's right to share in profits and capital distributions but does not make the assignee a partner.

Answer Outline

Problem 3 Partnership Property Rights of Individual Partner's Spouse and Creditors (1182,L3b)

Part b.

1. Graham's spouse will not be able to exercise spousal rights
   Partners own partnership property as tenants in partnership
      Partners have right of survivorship concerning specific pieces of property
         A partner's right in specific partnership property vests in the surviving partners
         Spouse has no rights in specific partnership property

2. Yes. The partnership can reflect this real estate as a partnership asset
   - Court will consider several factors in determination of whether partnership property or property of individual partner
     - How property is used
     - Source of funds to purchase property
     - Owner of record
     - Other indicia of ownership
   - Real estate has been used for partnership business
   - Partnership has paid all taxes
     - Property will be classified as partnership asset
3. No. Jamison will not succeed in land foreclosure action
   - Creditor of individual partner cannot attach partner's right in specific partnership property
   - Creditor can acquire charging order against a partner's interest in the partnership
4. No. The partnership cannot rescind the sale of real estate
   - Henderson had apparent authority to engage in sale of property
     - As long as in ordinary course of partnership business

Unofficial Answer
(Author Modified)

Problem 3 Partnership Property Rights of Individual Partner's Spouse and Creditors (1182,L3b)

Part b.

1. Graham's spouse will not be able to exercise his spousal rights to obtain specific property owned by the partnership. Individual partners own partnership property as tenants in partnership with the other partners. Under the tenancy in partnership concept, a partner's right in specific partnership property does not pass to his/her heirs in the event of death, but vests in the surviving partners. Consequently, a partner's right to specific partnership property is not subject to allowances to spouse, heirs, or next of kin. However, the remaining partners are under a duty to account to the deceased partner's estate for the value of the deceased partner's interest in the partnership.

2. Yes, the partnership can reflect real estate in question as a partnership asset. When deciding whether property is partnership property or the property of an individual partner, the courts will consider four factors:

1. How the property is used by the partnership;
2. The source of funds used to purchase the property;
3. The owner of record to the property; and
4. Other indicia of ownership, such as who pays the taxes on the property.

Consequently, even though the property is titled in Phillip's name, the real estate would be classified as a partnership asset because the property has been used for partnership purposes and the partnership has paid all taxes.

3. No, Jamison will not succeed in his land foreclosure action. A creditor of a partner cannot attach a partner's right in specific partnership property. However, a creditor may proceed by securing a charging order from the appropriate court against a partner's interest in the partnership, allowing the creditor to receive any distribution of profits or return of capital intended for the partner.

4. No, the partnership cannot rescind the sale of the real estate by Henderson. Every partner is considered an agent of the partnership for the purposes of conducting its business. Henderson had apparent authority to sell the real estate since the sale appeared to be a customary sale in the ordinary course of the partnership business. This sale is just as binding on the partnership as it would have been if Harrelson had been acting with express authority.

Answer Outline

Problem 4 Withdrawal and Admission of Partner (584,L5a)

Part a.

1. Hart liable for partnership debts incurred prior to his withdrawal unless released by existing creditors
   - Hart not liable for partnership debts incurred after his withdrawal if Hart gave actual notice to existing creditors, and constructive notice to other third parties knowing of partnership existence
     - Since constructive notice not given, Hart may be liable to future creditors and third parties not aware of Hart's withdrawal

2. UPA provides person admitted as partner into existing partnership (Paul) has no personal liability for partnership obligations arising prior to his admission
   However, these prior partnership obligations may be satisfied out of partnership property
   Paul has personal liability for debts incurred subsequent to admission

Unofficial Answer

Problem 4 Withdrawal and Admission of Partner (584,L5a)

Part a.

1. An outgoing partner, such as Hart, continues to have potential liability for partnership debts incurred prior to his withdrawal unless he obtains a release from the existing creditors. Hart has no liability for partnership obligations incurred subsequent to his withdrawal provided that appropriate notice is given to the partnership creditors and other third parties. In this case, actual notice was given to the partnership's creditors in existence at the time of Hart's withdrawal but constructive notice (i.e., notice by publication) was not given to those third parties who had not dealt with the partnership but may have known of its existence. By giving the appropriate type of notice, Hart would have effectively eliminated third parties' rights to rely on Hart's membership, i.e., his apparent authority in the partnership after his withdrawal. Because constructive notice was not given, creditors or other third parties who deal with the partnership after Hart's withdrawal may not be aware of his withdrawal and he may be liable to them. However, Hart will not be liable to existing creditors who, after receiving actual notice of Hart's withdrawal, dealt with the partnership.

2. The Uniform Partnership Act provides that a person admitted as a partner into an existing partnership is liable for all the obligations of the partnership arising before his admission as though he had been a partner when such obligations were incurred. However, this liability shall be satisfied only out of partnership property. Therefore, Paul has no personal liability as to partnership obligations existing at the time he became a partner but can be held personally responsible for those debts incurred after his admission as a partner.

CORPORATIONS

Overview

A corporation is an artificial being which is created by or under law and which operates under a common name through its elected management. It is a legal entity, separate and distinct from its shareholders. The corporation has the authority vested in it by statute and its corporate charter. The candidate should understand the characteristics and advantages of the corporate form over other forms of business organization.

Basic to preparation for questions on corporation law is an understanding of the following: the liabilities of a promoter who organizes a new corporation; the liability of shareholders; the liability of the corporation with respect to preincorporation contracts made by the promoter; the fiduciary relationship of the promoter to the stockholders and to the corporation; the various circumstances under which a stockholder may be liable for the debts of the corporation; the rights of shareholders particularly concerning payment of dividends; the rights and duties of officers, directors, and other agents or employees of the corporation to the corporation, to stockholders, and to third persons; subscriptions; and the procedures necessary to merge, consolidate, or otherwise change the corporate structure.

A. Characteristics and Advantages of Corporate Form

1. Limited liability

   a. Generally a shareholder in a corporation risks only a sum equal to the amount of his investment. Liability for corporate affairs does not extend to his personal assets.

2. Transferability of interest

   a. A share or interest in a corporation is represented by stock and can be freely bought, sold or assigned with little effect on the operations of the company

3. Continuous life

   a. Unlike a partnership, a corporation is not terminated by the death of a shareholder, or his incapacity. It is customary to regard a corporation as perpetual, and it continues to exist until dissolved, merged, or otherwise terminated, entirely independent of the misfortunes of its shareholders.

4. Separate entity

   a. A corporation is a legal entity in itself and is treated separately from its stockholders

1) A corporation can take, hold, and convey property
2) It can contract in its own name with its shareholders or third parties
3) It can sue and be sued

5. Financing
   a. Easy to raise capital in large amounts by issuance of stock or other securities, e.g., bonds
   b. Flexibility because it can issue a number of classes of stock and bonds to suit its needs and investor demands

6. Corporate management
   a. Corporations can employ management personnel who are experts in their fields of business
   b. Persons who manage corporations are not necessarily shareholders
   c. The management of a corporation is usually vested in a board of directors elected by the shareholders

B. Disadvantages of Form

1. Taxation (can be an advantage depending on circumstances)
   a. Tax burdens may be heavier than on individuals operating sole proprietorship because of federal "double taxation"
      1) Corporate taxation
      2) Distributed earnings taxed to shareholders
      3) Subchapter S status can alleviate
      4) Various tax breaks may partially or completely avoid double taxation
   b. Many states have a state corporate income tax
2. Costs of incorporating, because must meet formal creation requirements
3. Formal operating requirements must be complied with
   a. Procedural and administrative details to be complied with
   b. Continuing governmental supervision
   c. Some states allow less formal operating requirements for small, closely held corporations
4. Traditionally most professionals could not practice under the corporate form, but many states now allow professional corporations in which personal liability is retained for professional acts

C. Types of Corporations

1. Domestic corporation is one which operates and does business within the state in which it was incorporated
2. Foreign corporation is one doing business in any state except the one in which it was incorporated
   a. Foreign corporations are not exempt from the requirements and administrative details of domestic corporations
   b. A corporation does business in a state when there are continuous transactions, i.e., not an isolated transaction

3. Professional corporations are ones under state laws which allow professionals to incorporate, e.g., doctors, accountants, attorneys

   a. Shares may only be owned by the licensed professionals
   b. Retain personal liability for their professional acts
   c. Obtain other corporation benefits, e.g., limited liability for corporate debts, pension and profit-sharing benefits

4. Closely held corporation is one whose stock is owned by a limited number of persons usually with restrictions on the transfer of stock to keep it out of the hands of outsiders

   a. Informal administration of the corporation permitted, e.g., missing regular board of directors meeting

5. De facto corporation has been formed in fact but has not properly been formed under the law

   a. Usually defective because of some small error

      1) There must have been a good faith attempt to form
      2) There must have been at least an attempt to substantially comply with the incorporation statute

      EXAMPLE: An organization filed all the necessary papers but did not pay the filing fee.

   b. It is necessary that there has been exercise of corporate power by this group

      EXAMPLE: The organization in the example above is completely idle, holds no organizational meeting, and transacts no business in the corporate name. It is not even a de facto corporation.

   c. Shareholders in a de facto corporation still have limited liability to third parties

      1) If de facto incorporation is not achieved, the stockholders are treated as partners

   d. A de facto corporation may only be challenged by the state directly (quo warranto proceeding) and may not be challenged by third parties

6. De jure corporation has been formed correctly in compliance with the incorporation statute

7. Corporation by estoppel is a term used in equity to prevent injustice when an organization has not qualified as either a de jure or a de facto corporation but has held itself out as one or has been recognized as being a corporation

   EXAMPLE: Purchaser who makes a promissory note payable to a "corporation" cannot refuse to pay on the grounds that the "corporation" does not exist.

   EXAMPLE: "Corporation" owes a debt to a supplier. The "corporation" cannot avoid the obligation by claiming that it is not a valid corporation.

D. Formation of Corporation

1. Promoter is the person(s) who forms the corporation, arranges the capitalization, and begins the business

   a. Promoter handles the issuing of the prospectus, promoting stock subscriptions, and drawing up the charter

b. Position of promoter is a fiduciary relationship to the corporation, and the promoter is not permitted to act against the interest of the corporation in any manner

   1) Does not prevent personal profit if fully disclosed

c. Promoter is not an agent of the corporation, because the corporation is still not in existence

d. Any agreements (preincorporation contracts) made by the promoter are not binding on the future corporation until adopted after the corporation comes into existence

   1) If the corporation does not come into existence or does not adopt the contracts:

      a) Promoter is not liable if he specified he was not contracting individually, but in name of proposed corporation (actually no contract in these cases)
      b) Otherwise promoter is personally liable on contract. Adoption by corporation does not relieve promoter, novation required.

   2) The corporation may explicitly or implicitly adopt the promoter's actions

e. In the absence of a statute or charter provision the corporation is not liable to the promoter for his services unless later approved by the corporation

2. Authority to grant corporate charters is vested in the states

   a. Charters are granted by the states subject to the right of the state to repeal, amend, or alter the charter within constitutional limitations

3. Incorporation

   a. Incorporator must generally be an adult (age 18 or 21), a natural person, and a United States citizen. This, however, varies from state to state, (trend is to allow corporation to be an incorporator)

   b. Articles of incorporation (charter) are filed with the state. They contain:

      1) Proposed name which cannot be the same or closely resemble the name of another corporation so as to be misleading
      2) Purpose of corporation. The purpose is usually drafted as broadly as possible.
      3) Powers of corporation. Also drafted broadly.
      4) The amount of capital stock authorized and the types of stock to be issued
      5) Location of home offices and principal place of business
      6) Duration. In the absence of a specific statement, corporation existence is deemed to be perpetual.
      7) Temporary directors (may be incorporators) and incorporators
      8) Original stock subscribers
      9) Designation of agent for service of process

   c. First shareholder's meeting

      1) Stock certificates issued to shareholders
      2) Resignation of temporary directors and election of new
      3) Adoption of bylaws--the rules governing the operation of the corporation, e.g.

a) Duties and authority of officers
b) Notice, time, place of meetings (directors' and shareholders')
c) Rules for issuance and transfer of securities

d. At same meeting or subsequent meeting, directors

1) Elect officers
2) Adopt or reject preincorporation contracts
3) Begin business of corporation

E. Corporate Financial Structure

1. Definitions

a. Authorized stock--that permitted in articles of incorporation, e.g., amount and types
b. Unissued stock--authorized but not yet issued
c. Issued stock--authorized and delivered to shareholders
d. Outstanding stock--issued and not repurchased by the corporation, i.e., it is still owned by shareholders
e. Treasury stock--issued but not outstanding, i.e., corporation repurchased it. There are special rules for treasury stock.

1) The shares are not votable and do not receive dividends
2) Corporation does not recognize gain or loss on transactions with its own stock
3) Must be purchased with surplus, i.e., not legal capital
4) May be resold without regard to par value

f. Cancelled stock--treasury stock that is cancelled

1) No longer issued or outstanding
2) Makes room for more stock to be issued

g. Par value or stated value--amount stated on the shares

1) Stock should be issued for this amount or more
2) May subsequently be traded for any amount
3) Creditors may hold purchaser liable if purchases stock at below par

a) Contingently liable for difference between amount paid and par value
b) Subsequent purchaser also liable unless purchased in good faith without notice that sale was below par

h. Legal capital or stated capital or capital stock--number of shares issued times par value (or stated value)

1) Dividends may not be declared or paid out of it
2) Must be kept in corporation as a buffer for creditors

i. Paid-in surplus--amount paid for stock on issuance which is greater than par or stated value
j. Contributed capital--total amount paid for stock on issuance, i.e., stated capital plus paid-in surplus
k. Earned surplus (retained earnings)--total net profits retained by the corporation during its existence

1) Reduced by any dividends paid out in prior years

l. Surplus--includes earned surplus and paid-in surplus

 1) Also same as net assets less legal capital

2. Classes of stock

 a. Common stock usually gives each shareholder one vote per share and is entitled to dividends if declared by the directors

  1) Has no priority over other stock for dividends
  2) Shareholders entitled to share in final distribution of assets
  3) Votes may be apportioned to shares in other ways, e.g., 1 vote per 10 shares
  4) Nonvoting common stock may be issued if provided for in the articles of incorporation

 b. Preferred stock is given preferred status as to liquidations and dividends, but dividends are still discretionary

  1) Usually nonvoting stock
  2) Dividend rate is generally a fixed rate
  3) Cumulative preferred means that if a periodic dividend is not paid at the scheduled time, the obligation continues and accumulates; and must be satisfied before common stock may receive a dividend

   a) Noncumulative preferred means that if the dividend is passed, it will never be paid (i.e., the obligation to pay ceases)

   b) Held to be implicitly cumulative unless different intent shown

  4) Participating preferred participates further in corporate earnings left after a fixed amount is paid to preferred shares. The participation with common shares is generally on a fixed percentage basis.

 c. Callable (or redeemable) stock may be redeemed at a fixed price by the corporation. This call price is fixed in the articles of incorporation or may be subject to an agreement among the shareholders themselves.

 d. Convertible preferred gives the owner the option to convert the preferred stock to common stock at a fixed exchange rate

3. Marketing of stock

 a. May be subject to state "blue sky" laws or the Federal Securities Act. See FEDERAL SECURITIES LAW.
 b. Stock subscriptions are contracts to purchase a given number of shares in an existing corporation or one to be organized

  1) Subscription to stock is an offer to buy and is not binding until accepted by the corporation
  2) The subscriber may revoke his offer at any time prior to incorporation because the corporation cannot accept until it exists

   a) But if subscription is a contract among subscribers then it cannot be cancelled without consent of other subscribers--whether subscription is with corporation or other subscribers usually determined on basis of whether solicitation was from public or limited group
   b) Under the Model Incorporation Act, followed by many states, stock subscriptions are irrevocable for six months

3) Once accepted, the subscriber becomes liable
    a) For the purchase, and
    b) As a corporate shareholder
4) An agreement to subscribe in the future is not a subscription

c. Watered stock
1) Stock is said to be watered when the cash or property exchanged is less than par value or stated value
    a) No-par stock cannot be watered as long as issue amount is reasonable
2) Stock must be issued for consideration equal to the par or stated value
    a) No-par stock may be issued for consideration that the directors determine to be reasonable
3) Creditors of the corporation may recover from the stockholders the amount of water in their shares; i.e., the amount the stockholders would have paid to the corporation had they paid the full amount required (i.e., par value less amount paid)
    a) If the corporation becomes insolvent
    b) Subsequent purchaser of watered stock is not liable unless he had knowledge thereof

d. Consideration
1) Consists of cash, property, services performed
    a) Directors' duty to set value on property received
2) Executory promises are not good consideration, e.g.
    a) Promise to perform services is not good
    b) Promise to pay is not good
    c) Promissory note is not good (whether negotiable or not)

4. Bonds

a. Evidence of debt of the corporation. The owner of a bond is not an owner of the corporation but a creditor.
b. Interest is paid on the debt at fixed intervals, and at a designated time, the principal is repaid
c. Types
    1) Bearer--holder of the bond is entitled to the interest
    2) Convertible--convertible into common stock
    3) Debenture--unsecured
    4) Income--interest payable only if and when income is earned
    5) Registered--owner registered with corporation is entitled to the interest

F. <u>Powers of Corporation</u>

1. Types of corporate power

a. Inherent power is that power which is necessary for corporate existence, e.g., power to contract

b. Express powers are set out in the charter and bylaws at the time corporation is organized
c. Implied powers are those which are necessary to carry out the express powers and the purpose of the incorporation

EXAMPLE: Open a checking account.

d. Acts within the corporation's implied or express power are intra vires and outside are ultra vires

2. Corporations generally have the particular power to
   a. Acquire their own shares (treasury stock) out of available surplus according to state laws
   b. Acquire shares of other corporations
   c. Make charitable contributions
      1) Political contributions are usually not allowed
      2) Contributions to change laws are a valid business purpose, e.g., referendum measure
   d. Guarantee obligations of others only if in reasonable furtherance of corporations' business
      1) Does not allow indorsement for accommodation purposes only
   e. Become a partner only if expressly stated in charter or statute
      1) The problem with becoming a partner is that a corporation is to be managed by its board of directors and they cannot delegate this duty. In a partnership, all partners manage
   f. To buy, own, hold, and sell real and personal property
   g. To contract through its agents in the name of the corporation
   h. To sue and be sued in its own name
   i. To have exclusive use of its corporate name in the jurisdiction
   j. To have a corporate seal

G. Liabilities of Corporations

1. Crimes
   a. Corporations are liable for crimes they are capable of committing, i.e., antitrust, but not murder
   b. Punishment generally consists of fines or forfeiture, although recently directors have been faced with prison sentences for crimes of the corporation
2. Torts
   a. Corporations are liable for the damages resulting from torts committed by their officers, directors, agents, or employees within the course and scope of their corporate duties

   EXAMPLE: Fraudulent deceit of a customer.

   EXAMPLE: Employee assaults a complaining customer.

   b. The defense that the tort occurred in connection with ultra vires acts is not valid

3. Ultra vires acts

   a. Illegal and ultra vires acts are not the same

      1) Illegal acts are acts in violation of statute or public policy

         EXAMPLE: False advertising.

      2) Whereas ultra vires acts are merely beyond the scope of the corporate powers, i.e., a legal act may be ultra vires

         EXAMPLE: Although legal to become a surety, the articles of incorporation may not allow it.

   b. The state and stockholders have the right to object to ultra vires acts. A competitor does not.

   c. An ultra vires contract will be upheld to the extent of performance by both sides

      1) Directors or officers may be sued by shareholders on behalf of the corporation or by the corporation itself if there are damages to the corporation

   d. An ultra vires contract that is wholly executory, i.e., no performance on either side is void and neither party can enforce it

   e. If partially or fully performed on one side, then other side is estopped from raising ultra vires as a defense without being liable for damages

4. Acts of officers

   a. Corporation is liable for authorized acts

   b. Even if not authorized, if the act is of the type customarily delegated to such an officer, the corporation is liable

   c. Corporations are generally liable on contracts made by their agents within the course and scope of corporate authority

      1) Corporations are not obligated to perform illegal contracts

      2) Preincorporation contracts must be adopted before there is liability

H. Officers and Directors of Corporations

1. Directors are elected by the shareholders. Officers are retained by the board of directors.

   a. Directors elected at annual meeting

   b. Term of office is usually 1 year

2. Directors' duties and powers

   a. Generally to guide policies of company. They are generally in charge of a company's operations.

      1) Power to discharge their duties

   b. Must comply with statutes, articles of incorporation, and bylaws

   c. Select officers

   d. Declare dividends. May not abuse discretion.

   e. A director as an individual has no power to bind the corporation. Must act as a board member at a duly constituted meeting of the board.

      1) Must hold directors' meetings at times designated in the charter

2) May not vote by proxy
   a) Majority vote of those present is needed for most business decisions (a quorum)
   b) Some statutes require a majority vote of total directors to make business decisions
3) Action may be taken by the board with no meeting
   a) Unless prohibited by articles of incorporation or by corporate bylaws, and
   b) There must be unanimous written consent by the board members to the action to be taken

f. May delegate some authority, e.g., day to day or routine matters, to an executive committee
   1) Composed of members of the board of directors

g. Directors are not entitled to compensation unless so provided in articles, bylaws, or by a resolution of the board passed before the services are rendered
   1) May be reimbursed for expenses incurred on behalf of corporation
   2) Entitled to compensation if acting in role as employee

3. Director's liability

a. The general rule is that directors must exercise ordinary care and due diligence in performing the duties entrusted to them by virtue of their positions as directors. Trend is toward increased liability.
   1) Business judgment rule--As long as director is acting in good faith he will not be liable for errors of judgment unless he is negligent
   2) Directors are chargeable with knowledge of the affairs of the corporation
      a) Normally may rely on reports of officers

b. Directors only liable for negligence if their action was the proximate cause of the corporation's loss

c. Directors have a fiduciary relationship to the corporation
   1) Owe fiduciary duties of loyalty and due care to the corporation
   2) If directors engage in business transactions with the corporation, director must make full and complete disclosure to the board
      a) Transaction must be fair and equitable
      b) Cannot vote on this issue as a director

d. Directors are personally liable for ultra vires acts of the corporation unless they specifically dissented

EXAMPLE: Loans made to stockholders by a corporation.

EXAMPLE: Dividends that impair capital.

4. Officers

   a. An officer of the corporation is one of its agents and can bind the corporation by his individual acts if within the scope of his authority

      1) The corporation is not bound by the acts of an agent beyond the scope of authority
      2) President usually has authority in transactions that are part of usual and regular course of business

         a) No authority for extraordinary transactions
         b) Rules of estoppel are applicable; e.g., corporation may not claim president had no authority if he acted as if he did

      3) Acts of officers may be ratified by board

   b. Officers and directors may be the same persons
   c. Officers are selected by the directors for a fixed term under the bylaws

      1) If a term is not definite, it is governed by the directors

   d. Officers have a fiduciary relationship with the corporation and are limited in business transactions as are directors

5. Courts are recognizing a fiduciary duty owed by majority shareholders to minority shareholders based on differences in ability to control corporation

6. Indemnification of directors and employees

   a. A corporation has the power to indemnify any employee or director who is sued in a criminal or civil action if he acted in good faith and for what he reasonably believed to be the best interests of the corporation. The only exception is when it is proved the person engaged in misconduct in the performance of his/her duty to the corporation.

I. Stockholders' Rights

1. Types of stockholders

   a. Stockholder in equity is one for whose benefit stock is held by another

      EXAMPLE: Beneficiary of a trust that holds stock is a stockholder in equity.

   b. Stockholder at law is a person who holds the stock directly
   c. Stock can be acquired by original issue, by purchase from another stockholder, or by purchase of treasury stock

2. Stockholders' rights commence

   a. At the time the corporation accepts a subscription
   b. At time of payment and delivery of certificates in a contract to purchase
   c. Between corporation and new stockholder when registration is changed on corporate books

3. Right to a stock certificate

4. Right to transfer stock by indorsement and delivery or by separate assignment

   a. Stock certificates are negotiable instruments

      1) No holders in due course, but if properly indorsed, a thief may give good title

2) If indorsement is forged, corporation will bear the loss against a purchaser in good faith if it has issued a new certificate

EXAMPLE: X steals stock certificate from Y, forges Y's indorsement, submits it to the corporation for a new certificate, and transfers the new certificate to P, a purchaser in good faith. P will get to keep the certificate as a valid stockholder and the corporation will be liable to Y for the value of the shares.

b. Corporation registers the transfer and issues new shares to transferee
c. Limitations on transfer may be imposed, but they must be reasonable

1) UCC requires that any restrictions must be plainly printed on the certificate to be effective against third party

2) These limitations are most often imposed in closely held corporations

EXAMPLE: Existing shareholders of the corporation may have first option to buy.

5. Right to vote for: election of directors, amendment of bylaws and charter, decision to dissolve the corporation, and any other fundamental corporate changes

a. Governed by the charter and the class of stock owned
b. Trustee votes shares held in trust
c. Stockholders do not vote on how to manage the corporation. Management is entrusted to the board of directors.
d. Cumulative voting may be required, i.e., a person gets as many votes as he has shares times the number of directors being elected

EXAMPLE: 100 shares x 5 directors is 500 votes.

1) Gives minority shareholders an opportunity to get some representation by voting all shares for one or two directors

e. Can vote by proxy--an assignment of voting rights

1) See FEDERAL SECURITIES LAW for proxy solicitation
2) Shareholder may give up his voting power and place it irrevocably in the hands of others as in a voting trust

f. The directors have the power to amend or repeal the bylaws unless reserved to the shareholders by the articles of incorporation

g. Amendment of the articles of incorporation and approval of fundamental corporate changes such as a merger, consolidation, or sale of all assets requires only majority approval by shareholders

6. Right to dividends

a. Shareholder generally has no inherent right to dividends unless they are declared by the board of directors

1) Power to declare is discretionary based on the board's assessment of business needs
2) When there is a surplus together with available cash, the shareholders may be able to compel declaration of dividends on the grounds that board's refusal to declare a dividend is in bad faith or its refusal is unreasonable so as to constitute an abuse of director discretion

b. Dividends are normally payable to stockholders of record on a given date
c. Dividend becomes a debt to the corporation when declared
   1) Generally cannot be revoked once declared
d. Cannot be paid out of legal capital. See Director's Liability, "H.3."
   1) Some states allow payment out of paid-in surplus and some do not
   2) Earned surplus (retained earnings) is always a proper source
e. Stock dividends also cannot be paid out of legal capital
   1) They must be paid out of retained earnings
   2) They increase legal capital

7. Right of stockholders to inspect books and records exists in common law and may be provided for by statute
   a. These books and records include minute books, stock certificate books, stock ledgers, general account books
   b. Must have a purpose reasonably related to his interest as shareholder, e.g., to communicate with other shareholders
      1) Not to compete with corporation
   c. Corporation may be subject to fines for refusal
   d. Directors, as opposed to shareholders, have an absolute right of inspection
   e. May bring his accountant or attorney along

8. Preemptive right
   a. This is the right to subscribe to new issues of stock (at FMV) so that a stockholder's ownership will not be diluted without the opportunity to maintain it

      EXAMPLE: Corporation has one class of common stock. Stockholder A owns 15%. A new issue of the same class of stock is to be made. Stockholder A has the right to buy 15% of it.
   b. This is the right of first refusal and applies to issuances of new stock of the same class or series that the shareholder owns
   c. Usually only applies to common stock, not preferred
   d. Not for treasury stock
   e. There is no preemptive right to purchase stock at par value
   f. This right may be denied by the charter

9. Stockholders' right to sue
   a. Stockholder can sue in his own behalf where his interests have been directly injured, e.g.
      1) Denial of right to inspect records
      2) Denial of preemptive right
   b. Stockholders can sue on behalf of the corporation, i.e., a derivative suit
      1) In cases where a duty to the corporation is violated and corporation does not enforce, e.g.
         a) Director violates his fiduciary duty to corporation
         b) Illegal declaration of dividends
         c) Fraud by officer on corporation

2) Must first demand that directors sue in name of corporation and then may proceed if they refuse

a) Suit may be barred if directors make good faith business judgment that the suit is not in the corporation's best interests

3) Damages go to corporation
4) Plaintiff must be a shareholder of record

10. Right to a pro rata share of distribution of assets on dissolution after creditors have been paid

J. Stockholder's Liability

1. Generally stockholder's liability is limited to his paid-in capital

2. May be liable to creditors for

a. Original issue stock sold at a discount (below par value). See watered stock discussion.
b. Unpaid balance on no-par stock
c. Dividends paid which impair capital

1) If the corporation is insolvent

3. Piercing the corporate veil--courts disregard corporate entity and hold stockholders personally liable

a. Rarely happens but may occur if

1) Corporation used to perpetrate fraud
2) Owners/officers do not treat corporation as separate entity
3) Shareholders commingle assets, bank accounts, financial records with those of corporation
4) Corporate formalities not adhered to
5) In normal course of business

K. Substantial Change in Corporate Structure

1. Merger

a. This is the union of two corporations where one is absorbed into the other

1) One is dissolved and the other remains in existence
2) Survivor corporation issues its own shares to the shareholders of the other corporation

b. The remaining corporation (possessor) gets all assets but is subject to all liabilities of the merged corporation
c. Requires approval of board of directors of both companies
d. Usually requires approval of majority of shareholders of each company by state statute

1) Articles of incorporation can require a greater percentage

e. Dissenting shareholders are paid FMV for their shares

1) It is called the right of appraisal

2. Consolidation
   a. This is the joining of two (or more) corporations into a single new corporation
      1) Consolidating corporations are terminated
      2) Only the new corporation remains
   b. All assets and liabilities are acquired by the new company
   c. Consolidations, like mergers, are strictly controlled by state statutes
   d. Dissatisfied shareholders in a merger or consolidation may dissent and assert appraisal rights, thereby receiving the FMV of their stock
3. Sale of substantially all assets
   a. One corporation may buy all the assets of another corporation
   b. Requires approval of the shareholders of the selling corporation
   c. For protection of creditors
      1) Fraudulent conveyances are illegal
4. Reorganization
   a. The rearrangement and revamping of a corporation's capital and asset structure with as little effect as possible upon creditors. It is an alternative to bankruptcy and forced liquidation.
   b. Reorganization can be
      1) Voluntary
      2) Forced by Federal Bankruptcy Act

L. <u>Dissolution</u>

1. Dissolution is the termination of the corporation's status as a legal entity
   a. Liquidation is the winding up of affairs and distribution of assets
   b. Dissolution does not finally occur until liquidation is complete
2. Voluntary dissolution
   a. By expiration of time stipulated in charter
      1) Rare, usually perpetual existence
   b. Merger or consolidation
   c. Filing a certificate with the state to surrender charter
      1) By incorporators prior to issuance of shares
      2) Written consent of all stockholders
      3) Resolution at stockholders' meeting
         a) Usually by majority vote
   d. Judicial proceedings in bankruptcy by filing voluntary petition

3. Involuntary

   a. By the state because

      1) Fraud in original application for legal existence
      2) Failure to pay taxes for long period
      3) No business activity
      4) Other substantial injury to public
      5) State may only suspend corporation's right to do business

4. Creditors must be given notice of the dissolution or the corporation will remain liable on its debts

5. Shareholder may petition for judicial dissolution based on evidence that

   a. Directors are deadlocked, or
   b. Directors acted illegally or in oppressive manner, or
   c. Shareholders are deadlocked

      1) Unable to elect directors for two consecutive annual meetings

6. Dissolution does not result from

   a. Sale of all assets
   b. Appointment of receiver
   c. Assignment for benefit of creditors

Multiple Choice Questions (1–35)

1. For which of the following reasons would the corporate veil most likely be pierced and the shareholders held personally liable?
   a. The corporation is a personal holding company.
   b. The corporation was organized because the shareholders wanted to limit their personal liability.
   c. The corporation and its shareholders do **not** maintain separate bank accounts and records.
   d. The corporation's sole shareholder is another domestic corporation.

2. Golden Enterprises, Inc., entered into a contract with Hidalgo Corporation for the sale of its mineral holdings. The transaction proved to be *ultra vires.* Which of the following parties, for the reason stated, may properly assert the *ultra vires* doctrine?
   a. Golden Enterprises to avoid performance.
   b. A shareholder of Golden Enterprises to enjoin the sale.
   c. Hidalgo Corporation to avoid performance.
   d. Golden Enterprises to rescind the consummated sale.

3. Sandy McBride, president of the Cranston Corporation, inquired about the proper method of handling the expenditures incurred in connection with the recent incorporation of the business and sale of its shares to the public. In explaining the legal or tax treatment of these expenditures, which of the following is correct?
   a. The expenditures may be paid out of the consideration received in payment for the shares without rendering such shares not fully paid or assessable.
   b. The expenditures are comparable to goodwill and are treated accordingly for nontax and tax purposes.
   c. The expenditures must be capitalized and are nondeductible for federal income tax purposes since the life of the corporation is perpetual.
   d. The expenditures may be deducted for federal income tax purposes in the year incurred or amortized at the election of the corporation over a five-year period.

4. Destiny Manufacturing, Inc., is incorporated under the laws of Nevada. Its principal place of business is in California and it has permanent sales offices in several other states. Under the circumstances, which of the following is correct?
   a. California may validly demand that Destiny incorporate under the laws of the state of California.
   b. Destiny must obtain a certificate of authority to transact business in California and the other states in which it does business.
   c. Destiny is a foreign corporation in California, but not in the other states.
   d. California may prevent Destiny from operating as a corporation if the laws of California differ regarding organization and conduct of the corporation's internal affairs.

5. Hobson, Jones, Carter, and Wolff are all medical doctors who have worked together for several years. They decided to form a corporation and their attorney created a typical professional corporation for them. Which of the following is correct?
   a. Such a corporation will not be recognized for federal tax purposes if one of its goals is to save taxes.
   b. The state in which they incorporated must have enacted professional corporation stattutes permitting them to do so.
   c. Upon incorporation, the doctor-shareholder is insulated from personal liability beyond his capital contribution.
   d. The majority of states prohibit the creation of professional corporations by doctors.

6. Generally, articles of incorporation must contain all of the following **except** the
   a. Names of the incorporators.
   b. Name of the corporation.
   c. Number of shares authorized.
   d. Names of initial officers and their terms of office.

7. Phillips was the principal promoter of the Waterloo Corporation, a corporation which was to have been incorporated not later than July 31, 1981. Among the many things to be accomplished prior to incorporation were the obtaining of capital, the hiring of key executives and the securing of adequate office space. In this connection, Phillips obtained written subscriptions for $1.4 million of common stock from 17 individuals. He hired himself as the chief executive officer of Waterloo at $200,000 for five years and leased three floors of office space from Downtown Office Space, Inc. The contract with Downtown was made in the name of the corporation. Phillips had indicated orally

that the corporation would be coming into existence shortly. The corporation did not come into existence through no fault of Phillips. Which of the following is correct?

a. The subscribers have a recognized right to sue for and recover damages.
b. Phillips is personally liable on the lease with Downtown.
c. Phillips has the right to recover the fair value of his services rendered to the proposed corporation.
d. The subscribers were **not** bound by their subscriptions until the corporation came into existence.

8. Bixler obtained an option on a building he believed was suitable for use by a corporation he and two other men were organizing. After the corporation was sucessfully promoted, Bixler met with the Board of Directors who agreed to acquire the property for $200,000. Bixler deeded the building to the corporation and the corporation began business in it. Bixler's option contract called for the payment of only $155,000 for the building and he purchased it for that price. When the directors later learned that Bixler paid only $155,000, they demanded the return of Bixler's $45,000 profit. Bixler refused, claiming the building was worth far more than $200,000 both when he secured the option and when he deeded it to the corporation. Which of the following statements correctly applies to Bixler's conduct?

a. It was improper for Bixler to contract for the option without first having secured the assent of the Board of Directors.
b. If, as Bixler claimed, the building was fairly worth more than $200,000, Bixler is entitled to retain the entire price.
c. Even if, as Bixler claimed, the building was fairly worth more than $200,000, Bixler nevertheless must return the $45,000 to the corporation.
d. In order for Bixler to be obligated to return any amount to the corporation, the Board of Directors must establish that the building was worth less than $200,000.

9. Which of the following statements concerning treasury stock is correct?

a. Cash dividends paid on treasury stock are transferred to stated capital.
b. A corporation may **not** purchase its own stock unless specifically authorized by its articles of incorporation.
c. A duly appointed trustee may vote treasury stock at a properly called shareholders' meeting.
d. Treasury stock may be resold at a price less than par value.

10. Global Trucking Corporation has in its corporate treasury a substantial block of its own common stock, which it acquired several years previously. The stock had been publicly offered at $25 a share and had been reacquired at $15. The board is considering using it in the current year for various purposes. For which of the following purposes may it validly use the treasury stock?

a. To pay a stock dividend to its shareholders.
b. To sell it to the public without the necessity of a registration under the Securities Act of 1933, since it had been previously registered.
c. To vote it at the annual meeting of shareholders.
d. To acquire the shares of another publicly held company without the necessity of a registration under the Securities Act of 1933.

11. The Larkin Corporation is contemplating a two-for-one stock split of its common stock. Its $4 par value common stock will be reduced at $2 after the split. It has 2 million shares issued and outstanding out of a total of 3 million authorized. In considering the legal or tax consequences of such action, which of the following is a correct statement?

a. The transaction will require both authorization by the Board of Directors and approval by the shareholders.
b. The distribution of the additional shares to the shareholders will be taxed as a dividend to the recipients.
c. Surplus equal to the par value of the existing number of shares issued and outstanding must be transferred to the stated capital account.
d. The trustees of trust recipients of the additional shares must allocate them ratably between income and corpus.

12. Surplus of a corporation means

a. Net assets in excess of stated capital.
b. Liquid assets in excess of current needs.
c. Total assets in excess of total liabilities.
d. Contributed capital.

13. Ambrose purchased 400 shares of $100 par value original issue common stock from Minor Corporation

for $25 a share. Ambrose subsequently sold 200 of the shares to Harris at $25 a share. Harris did not have knowledge or notice that Ambrose had not paid par. Ambrose also sold 100 shares of this stock to Gable for $25 a share. At the time of this sale, Gable knew that Ambrose had not paid par for the stock. Minor Corporation became insolvent and the creditors sought to hold all the above parties liable for the $75 unpaid on each of the 400 shares. Under these circumstances

a. The creditors can hold Ambrose liable for $30,000.
b. If $25 a share was a fair value for the stock at the time of issuance, Ambrose will have no liability to the creditors.
c. Since Harris acquired the shares by purchase, he is not liable to the creditors, and his lack of knowledge or notice that Ambrose paid less than par is immaterial.
d. Since Gable acquired the shares by purchase, he is not liable to the creditors, and the fact that he knew Ambrose paid less than par is immaterial.

14. Plimpton subscribed to 1,000 shares of $1 par value common stock of the Billiard Ball Corporation at $10 a share. Plimpton paid $1,000 upon the incorporation of Billiard and paid an additional $4,000 at a later time. The corporation subsequently became insolvent and is now in bankruptcy. The creditors of the corporation are seeking to hold Plimpton personally liable. Which of the following is a correct statement?

a. Plimpton has no liability directly or indirectly to the creditors of the corporation since he paid the corporation the full par value of the shares.
b. As a result of his failure to pay the full subscription price, Plimpton has unlimited joint and several liability for corporate debts.
c. Plimpton is liable for the remainder of the unpaid subscription price.
d. Had Plimpton transferred his shares to an innocent third party, neither he nor the third party would be liable.

15. Watson entered into an agreement to purchase 1,000 shares of the Marvel Corporation, a corporation to be organized in the near future. Watson has since had second thoughts about investing in Marvel. Under the circumstances, which of the following is correct?

a. A written notice of withdrawal of his agreement to purchase the shares will be valid as long as it is received prior to incorporation.
b. A simple transfer of the agreement to another party will entirely eliminate his liability to purchase the shares of stock.
c. Watson may not revoke the agreement for a period of six months in the absence of special circumstances.
d. Watson may avoid liability on his agreement if he can obtain the consent of the majority of other individuals committed to purchase shares to release him.

16. Which of the following statements is correct regarding the fiduciary duty?

a. A majority shareholder as such may owe a fiduciary duty to fellow shareholders.
b. A director's fiduciary duty to the corporation may be discharged by merely disclosing his self-interest.
c. A director owes a fiduciary duty to the shareholders but **not** to the corporation.
d. A promoter of a corporation to be formed owes no fiduciary duty to anyone, unless the contract engaging the promoter so provides.

17. Fairwell is executive vice president and treasurer of Wonder Corporation. He was named as a party in a shareholder derivative action in connection with certain activities he engaged in as a corporate officer. In the lawsuit, it was determined that he was liable for negligence in performance of his duties. Fairwell seeks indemnity from the corporation for his liability. The board would like to indemnify him. The articles of incorporation do not contain any provisions regarding indemnification of officers and directors. Indemnification

a. Is **not** permitted since the articles of incorporation do **not** so provide.
b. Is permitted only if he is found **not** to have been grossly negligent.
c. Can **not** include attorney's fees since he was found to have been negligent.
d. May be permitted by court order despite the fact that Fairwell was found to be negligent.

18. At their annual meeting, shareholders of the Laurelton Corporation approved several proposals made by the Board of Directors. Among them was the ratification of the salaries of the executives of the corporation. In this connection, which of the following is correct?

a. The shareholders can **not** legally ratify the compensation paid to director-officers.

b. The salaries ratified are automatically valid for federal income tax purposes.
c. Such ratification by the shareholders is required as a matter of law.
d. The action by the shareholders serves the purpose of confirming the board's action.

19. Derek Corporation decided to acquire certain assets belonging to the Mongol Corporation. As consideration for the assets acquired, Derek issued 20,000 shares of its no-par common stock with a stated value of $10 per share. The value of the assets acquired subsequently turned out to be much less than the $200,000 in stock issued. Under the circumstances, which of the following is correct?
a. It is improper for the board of directors to acquire assets other than cash with no-par stock.
b. Only the shareholders can have the right to fix the value of the shares of no-par stock exchanged for assets.
c. In the absence of fraud in the transaction, the judgment of the board of directors as to the value of the consideration received for the shares shall be conclusive.
d. Unless the board obtained an independent appraisal of the acquired assets' value, it is liable to the extent of the overvaluation.

20. Donald Walker is a dissident stockholder of the Meaker Corporation which is listed on a national stock exchange. Walker is seeking to oust the existing board of directors and has notified the directors that he intends to sue them for negligence. Under the circumstances, Walker
a. Can be validly denied access to the corporate financial records.
b. Can be legally prohibited from obtaining a copy of the stockholder list because his purpose is not bona fide.
c. Must show personal gain on the part of the directors if he is to win his lawsuit.
d. Can insist that the corporation mail out his proxy materials as long as he pays the cost.

21. Which of the following statements concerning cumulative preferred stock is correct?
a. Upon the dissolution of a corporation the preferred shareholders have priority over unsecured judgment creditors.
b. Preferred stock represents a type of debt security similar to corporate debentures.
c. If dividends are **not** declared for any year, they become debts of the corporation for subsequent years.
d. Upon the declaration of a cash dividend on the preferred stock, preferred shareholders become unsecured creditors of the corporation.

22. Decanter Corporation declared a 10% stock dividend on its common stock. The dividend
a. Must be registered with the SEC pursuant to the Securities Act of 1933.
b. Requires a vote of the shareholders of Decanter.
c. Has no effect on the earnings and profits for federal income tax purposes.
d. Is includable in the gross income of the recipient taxpayers in the year of receipt.

23. The stock of Crandall Corporation is regularly traded over the counter. However, 75% is owned by the founding family and a few of the key executive officers. It has had a cash dividend record of paying out annually less than 5% of its earnings and profits over the past 10 years. It has, however, declared a 10% stock dividend during each of these years. Its accumulated earnings and profits are beyond the reasonable current and anticipated needs of the business. Which of the following is correct?
a. The shareholders can compel the declaration of a dividend only if the directors' dividend policy is fraudulent.
b. The Internal Revenue Service can **not** attack the accumulation of earnings and profits since the Code exempts publicly held corporations from the accumulations provisions.
c. The fact that the corporation was paying a 10% stock dividend, apparently in lieu of a cash distribution, is irrelevant insofar as the ability of the Internal Revenue Service to successfully attack the accumulation.
d. Either the Internal Revenue Service or the shareholders could successfully obtain a court order to compel the distribution of earnings and profits unreasonably accumulated.

24. Able and Baker are two corporations, the shares of which are publicly traded. Baker plans to merge into Able. Which of the following is a requirement of the merger?
a. The IRS must approve the merger.
b. The common stockholders of Baker must receive common stock of Able.
c. The creditors of Baker must approve the merger.

d. The boards of directors of both Able and Baker must approve the merger.

25. Universal Joint Corporation has approached Minor Enterprises, Inc., about a tax-free statutory merger of Minor into Universal. The stock of both corporations is listed on the NYSE. Which of the following requirements or procedures need **not** be complied with in order to qualify as a statutory merger pursuant to state and federal law?

a. The boards of directors of both corporations must approve the plan of merger.
b. Universal, the surviving corporation, must apply for and obtain a favorable revenue ruling from the Treasury Department.
c. The boards of both corporations must submit the plan of merger to their respective shareholders for approval.
d. The securities issued and exchanged by Universal for the shares of Minor must be registered since they are considered to be "offered" and "sold" for purposes of the Securities Act of 1933.

26. Barton Corporation and Clagg Corporation have decided to combine their separate companies pursuant to the provisions of their state corporation laws. After much discussion and negotiation, they decided that a consolidation was the appropriate procedure to be followed. Which of the following is an incorrect statement with respect to the contemplated statutory consolidation?

a. A statutory consolidation pursuant to state law is recognized by the Internal Revenue Code as a type of tax-free reorganization.
b. The larger of the two corporations will emerge as the surviving corporation.
c. Creditors of Barton and Clagg will have their claims protected despite the consolidation.
d. The shareholders of both Barton and Clagg must approve the plan of consolidation.

27. Under which of the following circumstances would a corporation's existence terminate?

a. The death of its sole owner-shareholder.
b. Its becoming insolvent.
c. Its legal consolidation with another corporation.
d. Its reorganization under the federal bankruptcy laws.

28. Which of the following would be grounds for the judicial dissolution of a corporation on the petition of a shareholder?

a. Refusal of the board of directors to declare a dividend.
b. Waste of corporate assets by the board of directors.
c. Loss operations of the corporation for three years.
d. Failure by the corporation to file its federal income tax returns.

May 1985 Questions

29. The corporate veil is most likely to be pierced and the shareholders held personally liable if

a. The corporation has elected S corporation status under the Internal Revenue Code.
b. A partnership incorporates its business solely to limit the liability of its partners.
c. An ultra vires act has been committed.
d. The shareholders have commingled their personal funds with those of the corporation.

30. Generally, officers of a corporation

a. Are elected by the shareholders.
b. Are agents and fiduciaries of the corporation, having actual and apparent authority to manage the business.
c. May be removed by the board of directors without cause only if the removal is approved by a majority vote of the shareholders.
d. May declare dividends or other distributions to shareholders as they deem appropriate.

31. The essential difference between a stock dividend and a stock split is that a

a. Stock split will increase the amount of stockholders' equity.
b. Stock split will increase a stockholder's percentage of ownership.
c. Stock dividend must be paid in the same class of stock as held by the stockholder.
d. Stock dividend of newly-issued shares will result in a decrease in retained earnings.

Repeat Question

(585,L1,12) Identical to item 16 above

November 1985 Questions

32. Which of the following is a characteristic of an unincorporated association?
    a. It may only be used for not-for-profit purposes.
    b. Members who actively manage the association may be held personally liable for contracts they enter into on behalf of the association.
    c. Certificates representing ownership in the association must be distributed to the members.
    d. Its duration must be for a limited period of time **not** to exceed 12 months.

Items 33 and 34 are based on the following information:

Jane Cox, a shareholder of Mix Corp., has properly commenced a derivative action against Mix's Board of Directors. Cox alleges that the Board breached its fiduciary duty and was negligent by failing to independently verify the financial statements prepared by management upon which Smart & Co., CPAs, issued an unqualified opinion. The financial statements contained inaccurate information which the Board relied upon in committing large sums of money to capital expansion. This resulted in Mix having to borrow money at extremely high interest rates to meet current cash needs. Within a short period of time, the price of Mix Corp. stock declined drastically.

33. Which of the following statements is correct?
    a. The Board is strictly liable, regardless of fault, since it owes a fiduciary duty to both the corporation and the shareholders.
    b. The Board is liable since any negligence of Smart is automatically imputed to the Board.
    c. The Board may avoid liability if it acted in good faith and in a reasonable manner.
    d. The Board may avoid liability in all cases where it can show that it lacked scienter.

34. If the court determines that the Board was negligent and the Board seeks indemnification for its legal fees from Mix, which of the following statements is correct?
    a. The Board may **not** be indemnified since a presumption that the Board failed to act in good faith arises from the judgment.
    b. The Board may **not** be indemnified unless Mix's shareholders approve such indemnification.
    c. The Board may be indemnified by Mix only if Mix provides liability insurance for its officers and directors.
    d. The Board may be indemnified by Mix only if the court deems it proper.

35. Rice is a promoter of a corporation to be known as Dex Corp. On January 1, 1985, Rice signed a nine-month contract with Roe, a CPA, which provided that Roe would perform certain accounting services for Dex. Rice did not disclose to Roe that Dex had not been formed. Prior to the incorporation of Dex on February 1, 1985, Roe rendered accounting services pursuant to the contract. After rendering accounting services for an additional period of six months pursuant to the contract, Roe was discharged without cause by the board of directors of Dex. In the absence of any agreements to the contrary, who will be liable to Roe for breach of contract?
    a. Both Rice and Dex.
    b. Rice only.
    c. Dex only.
    d. Neither Rice nor Dex.

Repeat Question

(1185,L1,2) Identical to item 22 above

Problems

Problem 1 (579,L3)

(25 to 30 minutes)

Part a. The Decimile Corporation is a well-established, conservatively-managed, major company. It has consistently maintained a $3 or more per share dividend since 1940 on its only class of stock, which has a $1 par value. Decimile's board of directors is determined to maintain a $3 per share annual dividend distribution to maintain the corporation's image in the financial community, to reassure its shareholders, and to prevent a decline in the price of the corporation's shares which would occur if there were a reduction in the dividend rate. Decimile's current financial position is not encouraging although the corporation is legally solvent. Its cash flow position is not good and the current year's earnings are only $0.87 per share. Retained earnings amount to $17 per share. Decimile owns a substantial block of Integrated Electronic Services stock which it purchased at $1 per share in 1950 and which has a current value of $6.50 per share. Decimile has paid dividends of $1 per share so far this year and contemplates distributing a sufficient number of shares of Integrated to provide an additional $2 per share.

Required:

Answer the following, setting forth reasons for any conclusions stated.

1. May Decimile legally pay the $2 per share dividend in the stock of Integrated?

2. As an alternative, could Decimile pay the $2 dividend in its own authorized but unissued shares of stock? What would be the **legal** effect of this action upon the corporation?

3. What are the federal income tax consequences to the noncorporate shareholders—

(a) If Decimile distributes the shares of Integrated?

(b) If Decimile distributes its own authorized but unissued stock?

Part b. Clayborn is the president and a director of Marigold Corporation. He currently owns 1,000 shares of Marigold which he purchased several years ago upon joining the company and assuming the presidency. At that time, he received a stock option for 10,000 shares of Marigold at $10 per share. The option is about to expire but Clayborn does not have the money to exercise his option. Credit is very tight at present and most of his assets have already been used to obtain loans. Clayborn spoke to the chairman of Marigold's board about his plight and told the chairman that he is going to borrow $100,000 from Marigold in order to exercise his option. The chairman was responsible for Clayborn's being hired as president of Marigold and is a close personal friend of Clayborn. Fearing that Clayborn will leave unless he is able to obtain a greater financial interest in Marigold, the chairman told Clayborn: "It is okay with me and you have a green light." Clayborn authorized the issuance of a $100,000 check payable to his order. He then negotiated the check to Marigold in payment for the shares of stock.

Required:

Answer the following, setting forth reasons for any conclusions stated.

What are the legal implications, problems, and issues raised by the above circumstances?

Part c. Towne is a prominent financier, the owner of 1% of the shares of Toy, Inc., and one of its directors. He is also the chairman of the board of Unlimited Holdings, Inc., an investment company in which he owns 80% of the stock. Toy needs land upon which to build additional warehouse facilities. Toy's president, Arthur, surveyed the land sites feasible for such a purpose. The best location in Arthur's opinion from all standpoints, including location, availability, access to transportation, and price, is an eight-acre tract of land owned by Unlimited. Neither Arthur nor Towne wish to create any legal problems in connection with the possible purchase of the land.

Required:

Answer the following, setting forth reasons for any conclusions stated.

1. What are the legal parameters within which this transaction may be safely consummated?

2. What are the legal ramifications if there were to be a $50,000 payment "on the side" to Towne in order that he use his efforts to "smooth the way" for the proposed acquisition?

Problem 2 (1184,L5)

(15 to 25 minutes)

Jim Bold is a promoter for a corporation to be formed and known as Wonda Corp. Bold entered into several supply and service agreements with Servco. These agreements were executed in Wonda's name, expressly contingent upon adoption by Wonda, when formed, and were based solely on Wonda's anticipated financial strength. Within two weeks after the signing of the agreements, Wonda was duly formed and operating. Shortly thereafter, Wonda by its board of directors rejected the preincorporation agreements entered into by Bold and Servco, stating that it could obtain more beneficial contracts elsewhere.

During the first year of Wonda's operations certain members of its board of directors were accused of negligence in the performance of their duties. In addition, there were allegations made that these same directors failed to exercise due care by paying cash dividends to shareholders that exceeded the profits and paid in capital. These directors based their decision upon negligently prepared reports issued by the Vice-President of Finance indicating that there were sufficient funds to pay cash dividends to shareholders. These incidents caused Wonda severe liquidity problems and huge losses in the following year of operation. White, a shareholder in Wonda, has properly commenced a suit against these directors.

Required:

Answer the following, setting forth reasons for any conclusions stated.

a. Discuss Wonda's and Bold's liability to Servco on the preincorporation agreements.

b. What are the necessary requirements to properly declare and pay cash dividends.

c. What defense(s) are available to the directors regarding the charges of negligence in the performance of their duties and the failure to exercise due care in declaring cash dividends?

Problem 3 (1182,L4b)

(8 to 12 minutes)

Part b. Powell Corporation, which owns 5% of the stock of Baron, Inc., approached the board of directors and several of the principal shareholders of Baron to see if they were willing to sell to Powell their effective controlling interest. Baron is listed on the American Stock Exchange and its management either owns or has the unquestioned support of approximately 37% of the shares outstanding. Baron's board and the shareholders who were contacted rejected Powell's overtures. Powell is now considering waging a proxy fight to obtain effective control of Baron.

Required:

Answer the following, setting forth reasons for any conclusions stated.

1. Can Baron lawfully refuse to give Powell access to the list of shareholders?

2. What rights does Powell have under the Securities Exchange Act of 1934 to have its proxy materials distributed to shareholders?

3. What major requirements under the Securities Exchange Act of 1934 must be met by both sides in a proxy fight?

Multiple Choice Answers

1. c	8. c	15. c	22. c	29. d
2. b	9. d	16. a	23. c	30. b
3. a	10. a	17. d	24. d	31. d
4. b	11. a	18. d	25. b	32. b
5. b	12. a	19. c	26. b	33. c
6. d	13. a	20. d	27. c	34. d
7. b	14. c	21. d	28. b	35. a

Multiple Choice Answer Explanations

A. Characteristics and Advantages of Corporate Form

1. (584,L1,8) (c) The court will disregard the corporate entity and hold the shareholders individually liable when the corporate form is used to perpetrate a fraud or is found to be merely an agent or instrument of its owners. An example of when the corporate veil is likely to be pierced is if the corporation and its shareholders commingle assets and financial records. In such a situation the shareholders lose their limited liability and will be personally liable for the corporation's obligations. Answer (a) is incorrect because personal holding companies are allowed to exist as corporate entities separate from the shareholders so long as the intention in forming the corporation was not to perpetrate a fraud and the assets and records of the corporation and its shareholders are maintained separately. Answer (b) is incorrect because the desire of shareholders to limit their personal liability is a valid reason to form a corporation. Limited personal liability is one advantage of the corporate entity. Answer (d) is incorrect because corporations are allowed to own 100% of another corporation as long as the owned corporation is not merely used as an instrumentality of the parent corporation.

2. (580,L1,12) (b) An *ultra vires* doctrine applies when a corporation enters a contract outside the scope of its express or implied authority granted by its articles of incorporation. Answer (b) is correct because since the state or shareholder has the right to object to an *ultra vires* act, a competitor could not object. A shareholder can institute a derivative action against directors and officers to recover damages for such acts. Answers (a) and (c) are incorrect because when an *ultra vires* contract has been executed on one side, most state courts hold the nonperforming party may not raise the defense of *ultra vires.* Answer (d) is incorrect because when both parties have performed, neither party may sue to rescind an *ultra vires* contract.

C. Types of Corporations

3. (582,L1,11) (a) The expenditures incurred in connection with the incorporation of the business and sale of its shares to the public may be treated as an offset against the proceeds from the stock issuance and are chargeable against the paid-in capital, as long as it does not impair the amount of legal capital. This treatment is based on the premise that issue costs are unrelated to corporate operations and thus are not properly chargeable against earnings from operations; but rather viewed as a reduction of proceeds of the financing activity. Answer (b) is incorrect because goodwill is an intangible asset, which is recorded only when an entire business is purchased. Goodwill is a "going concern" valuation and cannot be separated from a business as a whole. The amount of goodwill is capitalized and amortized over the business' useful life not to exceed a period of 40 years. Answers (c) and (d) are incorrect because expenses of issuing shares of stock, such as commissions, professional fees, printing costs, and listing the stock on the exchange are not to be capitalized and amortized over the life of the corporation, and thus would not be capitalized and amortized under the organizational expenditure provision.

4. (580,L1,14) (b) A corporation "doing business" in a state other than that of incorporation must comply with that state's license requirements. This usually requires filing a certificate of authority. The concept of doing business involves something more than isolated transactions. Answer (a) is incorrect because a corporation is not required to incorporate in a state in which it does business. Answer (c) is incorrect because Destiny is a foreign corporation in any state in which it does business other than that state in which it is incorporated. Answer (d) is incorrect because Destiny needs to comply only with the incorporation laws in its state of incorporation, in this case, Nevada.

5. (1178,L1,22) (b) Professional corporations are only allowed in states which have enacted statutes permitting their incorporation. They are not normally allowed under the general corporation statutes. Answer (a) is incorrect because such a corporation will be recognized for federal tax purposes even if its goal is to save taxes. Answer (c) is incorrect because the typical statute provides that the professional being incorporated remains personally liable for his professional acts. His liability will only be limited for ordinary business debts of the corporation. Answer (d) is incorrect because most states now permit the creation of professional corporations by doctors and similar professional persons.

D. Formation of Corporation

6. (584,L1,10) (d) The articles of incorporation are not required to contain the names of initial officers and their terms of office. This is true because the initial officers are not elected until the first board of directors' meeting which cannot be held until after the articles of incorporation have been filed. Answers (a), (b), and (c) are all incorrect since the articles of incorporation must contain each of these items.

7. (582,L1,9) (b) A corporation is not liable on pre-incorporation contracts entered into on behalf of the corporation by the promoter unless and until the corporation approves and thereby adopts the contract of the promoter upon coming into corporate existence. However, the promoter is personally bound on these contracts. Even if the corporation adopts the contract, the promoter remains personally liable unless a novation occurs (i.e., third party agrees to look to corporation for satisfaction of the contract). However, if the promoter had clearly specified that he was contracting "in the name of the proposed corporation and not individually," the third party must rely solely on the credit of the proposed corporation and has no claim against the promoter individually. Answer (a) is incorrect because when a corporation fails to come into existence, the preincorporation stock subscribers have no legal right to sue for damages. Answer (c) is incorrect because in the absence of a statute or charter provision, the corporation is not liable for promoter's preincorporation services unless the board of directors approves payment after the corporation comes into existence. Answer (d) is incorrect because the Model Business Corporation Act provides that pre-incorporation stock subscriptions are deemed to be continuing offers which are irrevocable for a period of six months. Therefore, the subscribers are bound by their subscriptions for this six month period.

8. (581,L1,23) (c) Promoters are persons who originate and organize the formation of a corporation. They have a fiduciary duty to act for the corporation and its shareholders. For Bixler to retain the profits made from the sale of property to the corporation, he must make full disclosure to and receive approval from either the board of directors or existing shareholders. Since Bixler did not comply with these procedures, the $45,000 would be considered secret profits and must be returned to the corporation even though the building might have a market value of $200,000. Thus, answers (b) and (d) are incorrect. Answer (a) is incorrect since the promoter may enter into preincorporation contracts (e.g., employment contracts, options on property) on behalf of the corporation. The corporation is not liable on these contracts until it adopts such agreements or enters a novation (a second agreement whereby corporation replaces the promoter under the same terms as the preincorporation contract). The corporation cannot ratify the agreement since the corporate entity was not in existence when the promoter entered the contract.

E. Corporate Financial Structure

9. (584,L1,9) (d) Treasury stock may be resold at a price less than par value. Answer (a) is incorrect because cash dividends are not paid on treasury stock. Answer (b) is incorrect because a corporation need not have specific authorization from its articles of incorporation to purchase its own stock; all corporations have the inherent authority to do so if not denied such right by state law. Answer (c) is incorrect because treasury stock cannot be voted.

10. (581,L1,26) (a) Treasury stock may be disposed of at the discretion of the board of directors through a sale or through the declaration of dividends to shareholders. Answer (b) is incorrect since the original public offering was sufficiently long ago to require the filing of a new registration statement before selling these treasury shares. Answer (c) is incorrect because treasury shares cannot be voted. Answer (d) is incorrect because treasury shares exchanged for the stock of another publicly held corporation are considered to be "offered" and "sold" for the purposes of the Securities Act of 1933. Therefore, a registration statement would have to be filed and approved before the transaction could be completed.

11. (581,L1,27) (a) Both the board of directors and the shareholders of a corporation must approve a fundamental change in the corporate structure. Examples of fundamental corporate changes would be: dissolution of corporation, amendment of corporate charter, increase of capital stock, etc. Larkin would need to amend its corporate charter to increase the number of authorized shares before engaging in the stock split. Answer (b) is incorrect because stock splits are normally exempt from income tax because the shareholder-recipient maintains the same proportionate interest of ownership. Answer (c) is incorrect because a stock split decreases the par value in proportion to the increase in the number of shares. Therefore, total par value is unchanged. Answer (d) is incorrect because trustees are to include shares received through a stock split or stock dividend in the principal (corpus) of the trust. Cash dividends are considered income when allocating trust items between principal (corpus) and income beneficiaries.

12. (1175,L2,22) (a) Surplus of a corporation means net assets in excess of stated capital. Liquid assets in excess of current needs are net quick assets. Total assets in excess of total liabilities is net assets. Contributed capital is capital paid into the corporation not in the conduct of business, i.e., not earned surplus (retained earnings).

E.3. Marketing of Stock

13. (1183,L1,24) (a) A corporation cannot legally reduce the price of par value stock below the established par value, without amending the articles of incorporation. Since Ambrose purchased original issue stock for less than par value, he can be held liable to the creditors for the $30,000 difference between the par value of the stock and the price he actually paid. Answer (b) is, therefore, incorrect. A transferee of shares, for which full consideration has not been paid, can be held liable to the corporation or its creditors for the unpaid portion of the consideration; unless the transferee took the shares in good faith and without knowledge or notice that full consideration has not been paid. Harris is, therefore, not liable to creditors. Answer (c), however, is incorrect because it states that Harris' lack of knowledge is immaterial. Likewise, answer (d) is incorrect. Gable is liable to the creditors because of his knowledge that full consideration for the shares had not been paid.

14. (580,L1,16) (c) Plimpton has breached his subscription contract with the Billiard Ball Corporation, and is therefore liable for the remainder of the unpaid subscription price. Shares may be purchased for money, services already rendered, and property. Promissory notes are not proper consideration for the purchase of shares. Plimpton is liable to creditors for the balance due on the subscription price. This is true even if Plimpton transfers the shares to an innocent third party. The issuing corporation has a lien on those shares that have not been paid for fully. However, this lien would not be effective against an innocent third party purchaser unless the lien was conspicuously noted on the stock certificate. Plimpton's failure to pay the full purchase price of the shares would not change his limited liability concerning corporate debts.

15. (1178,L1,15) (c) The subscriber, Watson, may not revoke the agreement to purchase stock in the Marvel Corporation for a period of six months in the absence of special circumstances. Under the Model Business Corporation Act, preincorporation stock subscriptions are deemed to be continuing offers which are irrevocable for purposes of administrative convenience for a period of six months. Answer (a) is incorrect because a notice indicating withdrawal, even if written, will not be valid until the expiration of six months. Answer (b) is incorrect because a simple transfer of an agreement does not constitute a novation and thus the assigning party remains liable. Answer (d) is incorrect also because a subscriber can only avoid liability during the six-month period by obtaining the unanimous consent of the other subscribers.

H. Officers and Directors of Corporations

16. (1183,L1,23) (a) Since a majority shareholder is able to exercise substantial control over the corporation, courts have recognized that there is a fiduciary duty owed to minority shareholders. If, for instance, a majority shareholder sells controlling interest in the corporation to a party whom he should know will plunder the company, the duty owed to fellow shareholders has been breached. A director also owes a fiduciary duty to the corporation. Answer (c) is, therefore, incorrect. The duty is not discharged by disclosure alone. The director who has a conflict of interest must refrain from voting on that matter. Thus, answer (b) is incorrect. Answer (d) is incorrect because a promoter owes a fiduciary duty to subscribers, shareholders, and the corporation itself.

17. (582,L1,10) (d) Corporations have the power to properly indemnify their directors or officers for expenses incurred in defending suits against them for conduct undertaken in their official and representative capacity on behalf of the corporation. However, in shareholder derivative suits, normally no indemnification is permitted where the director or officer has been adjudged to be liable for negligence in the performance of his duty to the corporation. However, if the court in which the action or suit was brought determines that, despite the adjudication of liability, the director or officer is fairly and reasonably entitled to indemnification under the circumstances, then indeminification may be permitted regardless of the fact that the articles of incorporation do not provide therefor. Answer (c) is incorrect because under indemnification, Fairwell is entitled to expenses, judgments, fines, and amounts actually paid and reasonably incurred by him, which include reasonable attorney's fees.

18. (581,L1,28) (d) The compensation of corporate officers is fixed by a resolution of the board of directors. If none is fixed, the law implies that the officer is paid a reasonable sum for his services. Any action by the shareholders serves merely to confirm the board's action concerning the officers' salaries. It is not needed as a matter of law, therefore, answer

(c) is incorrect. Answer (a) is incorrect because the directors can confirm the officers' salaries even though not legally needed. Answer (b) is incorrect because the IRS has the power to attack any officer's salary as unreasonable. If the compensation is deemed unreasonable, the IRS treats the excessive amount as a constructive dividend.

19. (1178,L1,19) (c) The board of directors has the power and duty to determine the value of property received for stock. In the absence of fraud, such judgment shall be conclusive. Answer (a) is incorrect because cash, property, and services performed are all good consideration for both par and no-par stock. Answer (b) is incorrect because, as stated above, it is within the power and duty of the board of directors to fix the value of property received for stock. Shareholders have no right to determine the value of no-par stock. Answer (d) is not as correct because directors are merely required to exercise ordinary care and prudence in the exercise of their duties. They are not liable for honest mistakes in judgment.

I. Stockholders' Rights

20. (1174,L3,36) (d) A stockholder has a common law right to inspect the books of the corporation including the list of stockholders. This right may not be denied unless the stockholder's purpose is hostile to the corporation or the stockholder is attempting to use the corporation's books and records for unwarranted purposes. Stockholders may readily inspect the books in attempt to uncover corporate mismanagement. A dissident stockholder must also be given a list of corporation's shareholders if he is attempting to oust the management and proposes a proxy fight. Federal securities regulation requires that the corporation supply such a list and also mail the dissident's proxy material. The dissident shareholder, however, must pay the cost of the mailing. Regarding Walker's planned negligence suit, it is unnecessary that he prove personal gain on the part of the directors. Directors are liable for damages resulting from lack of reasonable care regardless of personal gain.

I.6. Right to Dividends

21. (584,L1,5) (d) Upon declaration, a cash dividend on preferred stock becomes a legal debt of the corporation, and the preferred shareholders become unsecured creditors of the corporation. Answer (a) is incorrect because upon the dissolution of a corporation, the preferred shareholders do not have priority over unsecured creditors. Only after all debts owing to creditors are satisfied will the remaining corporate assets be distributed among the shareholders. Preferred shareholders will have priority over common shareholders. Answer (b) is incorrect because although preferred stock does assume many characteristics of a debt security, preferred stock represents a type of ownership security and is not similar to corporate debentures which are unsecured debt securities with no such ownership rights. Answer (c) is incorrect because any dividends not paid in any year concerning cumulative preferred stock must be made up before any future distributions can be made to common shareholders. These unpaid dividends are not a liability of the corporation until they are declared.

22. (1183,L1,25) (c) A stock dividend is not considered an "Ordinary" dividend and is, therefore, not paid out of the corporation's earnings and profits. Answer (a) is incorrect because a stock dividend is an exempt transaction under the Securities Act of 1933. Answer (b) is incorrect because a dividend payment is at the discretion of the board of directors, not the stockholders. Answer (d) is incorrect because a stock dividend is combined with the old stock to compute an adjusted basis and will affect gross income of the recipient tax payer in the year the stock is sold by the shareholder.

23. (581,L1,25) (c) The fact that the corporation was paying a 10% stock dividend instead of a cash distribution would not hinder the IRS from attacking the accumulation of earnings. Answer (a) is incorrect because stockholders can compel the declaration of a dividend when withholding dividends would be a clear abuse of the board of directors' discretion, even when such a dividend policy is not fraudulent. The Code does not exempt publicly held corporations from the accumulation provisions, therefore, answer (b) is incorrect. Answer (d) is incorrect because the IRS cannot compel the corporation to distribute earnings and profits that have unreasonably accumulated. However, the corporation is subject to an additional tax on earnings retained in excess of $150,000 if such retention is unreasonable.

K. Substantial Change in Corporate Structure

24. (584,L1,7) (d) The merger of two corporations requires the approval from the boards of directors of both merging corporations. Also, normally a majority of the shareholders of each corporation must approve the merger. Answer (a) is incorrect since the merger of two corporations is not subject to the approval of the IRS. Answer (b) is incorrect because a merger can be accomplished in several different ways besides the issuance of stock to the shareholders of the merged corpo-

ration. Answer (c) is incorrect because the approval of the merging corporations' creditors is not required for a valid merger to occur. The merging corporations' creditors merely become creditors of the existing corporation upon completion of the merger.

25. (581,L1,21) (b) There is no provision requiring the surviving corporation of a tax-free statutory merger to apply for and obtain a favorable revenue ruling from the Treasury Department. Answers (a) and (c) are incorrect because the board of directors and shareholders of both corporations must approve the merger. Answer (d) is incorrect since only securities issued in conjunction with a court supervised reorganization are exempt from the registration requirements of the Securities Act of 1933. For purposes of the act, the shares exchanged between Union and Universal would be "offered" and "sold."

26. (580,L1,6) (b) A consolidation is the unifying of two or more corporations into one new corporation, extinguishing both existing corporations. Therefore, answer (b) is the correct answer since neither corporation will survive the consolidation. Answer (a) is incorrect because under the Internal Revenue Code reorganizations, including statutory mergers or consolidations, receive nonrecognition treatment for tax purposes. Answer (c) is incorrect because the rights of the creditors of the consolidating corporations are in no way impaired by the consolidation. Before a corporation can engage in a consolidation or merger, shareholder approval must be obtained. Approval by a majority is normally sufficient but some states demand approval by two-thirds of the shareholders.

L. Dissolution

27. (1174,L3,35) (c) One of the attributes of a corporation is its perpetual existence irrespective of the lives of its owners. The death of a corporation's sole shareholder would not result in the termination. Ownership would change to the deceased's heirs. The insolvency or appointment of a receiver does not terminate the existence of a corporation. Reorganization under the federal bankruptcy laws may result in the termination of the corporation, and the creation of a new corporation to conduct the business of the old corporation (this is not always the case). The best answer to this question is (c). In a consolidation with another corporation, both of the consolidating corporations are terminated and a new corporation is formed. By definition, a consolidation cannot occur without the termination of a corporation's existence.

L.5. Judicial Dissolution

28. (584,L1,6) (b) A judicial dissolution may be brought by a shareholder in the event that there has been a waste of the corporate assets by the board of directors. The following reasons would also constitute proper grounds for judicial dissolution:

- Directors are deadlocked in the management of the corporate affairs.
- Acts of the directors are illegal or oppressive.
- Shareholders are deadlocked and have not been able to elect directors for two consecutive annual meetings.

Answers (a), (c), and (d) are all incorrect because none of them states sufficient grounds for the judicial dissolution of a corporation on the petition of a shareholder.

May 1985 Answers

29. (585,L1,13) (d) The court will disregard the corporate entity and hold the shareholders individually liable when the corporate form is used to perpetrate a fraud or is found to be merely an agent or instrument of its owners. An example of when the corporate veil is likely to be pierced is if the corporation and its shareholders commingle assets and financial records. In such a situation, the shareholders lose their limited liability and will be held personally liable for the corporation's legal obligations. Answer (a) is incorrect because the election of S-corporation status is allowable under the law and is not in itself, grounds for piercing the corporate veil. Answer (b) is incorrect because the desire of shareholders to limit their personal liability is a valid reason to form a corporation. Limited personal liability is one advantage of the corporate entity. Answer (c) is incorrect since the court will hold personally liable only those corporate officers responsible for the commission of an ultra vires act. The court will not pierce the corporate veil and hold the shareholders personally liable for such an act.

30. (585,L1,14) (b) Officers of a corporation are agents of that corporation having actual and apparent authority to manage the business; consequently, officers occupy a fiduciary relationship with the corporation. Answer (a) is incorrect since officers are appointed by the directors of a corporation who are in turn elected by the shareholders. Answer (c) is incorrect since officers may be removed by the board of directors without cause and without any form of approval from the shareholders whenever in the board's judgment the best interests of the corporation are served. In such a case,

the officer removed may have an action for breach of contract. Answer (d) is incorrect since the directors of a corporation, and not the officers, have the power to declare dividends or other distributions to shareholders.

31. (585,L1,15) (d) A stock dividend of newly-issued shares will result in a transfer of the market value of the shares issued in the dividend from Retained Earnings to the paid-in capital accounts. A stock split does not result in a transfer of Retained Earnings to the paid-in capital accounts, but merely results in a decrease in the par value of the stock proportionate to the number of new shares issued as compared to the number issued and outstanding prior to the split. Answer (a) is incorrect because a stock split or dividend will never result in an increase in the amount of stockholder's equity. An increase in equity may only be caused by an additional contribution of capital by the shareholders or the earning of income by the corporation. Answer (b) is incorrect because a stock split will not change a stockholder's percentage of ownership. A stock split increases the number of shares held by each shareholder proportionately. Answer (c) is incorrect because a stock dividend may be paid in a different class of stock than the class being held by the stockholder.

November 1985 Answers

32. (1185,L1,1) (b) An unincorporated association is a partnership-like entity that has characteristics very similar to a partnership. Managing members of the association may be held personally liable for the contracts they or their agents enter into on behalf of the association and for the torts they or their agents may commit during their operation of association activities. Answer (a) is incorrect because an unincorporated association is not limited to not-for-profit purposes. Answer (c) is incorrect because certificates representing ownership need not be distributed, in contrast to corporations. Answer (d) is incorrect because unincorporated associations are not limited to durations of 12 months or less.

33. (1185,L1,3) (c) The board of directors of a corporation owes the corporation a fiduciary duty. The board must exercise ordinary care and due diligence (i.e., in good faith and in a reasonable manner) in performing its duties in order to avoid liability. Mix's Board of Directors exercised good faith and acted in a reasonable manner by relying upon the audited financial statements prepared by management. Thus, the Board was not liable. Answer (a) is incorrect because the Board does not have strict liability, even though it owes a fiduciary duty to the corporation. This duty only requires the Board to act in good faith and in a reasonable manner. Answer (b) is incorrect because any negligence of the auditor (Smart) is not automatically imputed to the Board. Answer (d) is incorrect because the Board cannot avoid liability in all cases where scienter is missing. The Board cannot avoid liability where it did not act in good faith or in a reasonable manner.

34. (1185,L1,4) (d) Corporations have the power to indemnify their boards of directors for legal fees incurred in defending suits against the boards for normal or expected duties. Normally, in a suit brought by a shareholder, no indemnification is permitted where the board has been found liable for negligence in carrying out its duties, unless the court in which the suit was brought determines that the board is fairly and reasonably entitled to indemnification. Answer (a) is incorrect because a presumption of lack of good faith does not arise from the judgement. Answer (b) is incorrect because indemnification of the board does not require shareholder approval. Answer (c) is incorrect because the carrying of liability insurance is not a deciding factor in an indemnification decision.

35. (1185,L1,5) (a) When a promoter enters into contracts on behalf of a corporation yet to be formed, the promoter is personally liable on the contracts unless the promoter explicitly states that s/he is contracting for the corporation. After the corporation is formed, the promoter remains liable on the contracts until a novation occurs substituting the corporation for the promoter in the contracts. The corporation's adoption, either explicit or implicit, of the contracts does not relieve the promoter of liability. Dix implicitly adopted the contract with Roe by continuing to accept the accounting services, thus making Dix liable on the contract. Since a novation did not occur, Rice remains liable on the contract to Roe. Answers (b), (c), and (d) are incorrect because both parties (Rice and Dix) are liable on the contract.

Answer Outline

Problem 1 Dividends; Contracts with Director; Director Fiduciary Responsibility (579,L3)

a1. Yes, property dividends may be paid by corporations
 With investments in stock of other companies
 Issuing company must be solvent
 Limited to unrestricted retained earnings (earned surplus)
 Decimile has retained eranings of $17/share

a2. Yes, stock dividends may be paid by corporations
 The dividends must be charged to unrestricted retained earnings
 At not less than par value
 With the amount to be credited to stated capital

a3(a) Issuance of stock of another company is a property dividend
 Recipients must report FMV as dividend income
 Dividend income is ordinary income
 Subject to $100 dividend exclusion
 Recipient's basis in property dividend is FMV when received

a3(b) If Decimile Corporation issues its own stock as dividend
 It is a non-taxable transaction
 Recipients must reallocate original cost to total shares owned after distribution

b. Loans by corporations must be for benefit of corporation
 If for corporate benefit, board of directors may approve
 Otherwise, stockholder approval is required
 Here, loan is for corporate benefit
 But chairman lacked authority and may be personally liable
 Board of directors should ratify, or recall loan

c1. To avoid contracts with interested directors being void or voidable
 The relationship of interested directors is disclosed to those approving the contracts or
 Approval by board of directors without counting votes of interested directors, or
 Interested directors may be counted to establish quorum
 Shareholders, knowing of director interest, approve the contract, or
 The transaction must be fair and reasonable to corporation

c2. Side payments to corporate directors violate fiduciary duty
 And probably constitutes a criminal act
 Towne must return money to Toy
 Toy Corporation could treat transaction as voidable

Unofficial Answer

Problem 1 Dividends; Contract with Director; Director Fiduciary Responsibility (579,L3)

Part a.

1. Yes. The Model Business Corporation Act authorizes the declaration and payment of dividends in cash, property, or the shares of the corporation as long as the corporation is not insolvent and would not be rendered insolvent by the dividend payment. The act limits the payment of dividends in cash or property to the unreserved and unrestricted earned surplus of the corporation. Decimile meets this requirement since it has retained earnings of $17 per share. Thus, payment of the dividend in the shares of Integrated is permitted.

2. Yes. The Model Business Corporation Act permits dividends to be declared and paid in the shares of the corporation. However, where the dividend is paid in its authorized but unissued shares, the payment must be out of unreserved and unrestricted surplus. Furthermore, when the shares paid as a dividend have a par value, they must be issued at not less than par value. Concurrent with the dividend payment, an amount of surplus equal to the aggregate par value of the shares issued as a dividend must be transferred to stated capital.

3. (a) If the shares of Integrated stock are paid as a dividend to the noncorporate shareholders, the shareholders must include the fair market value of the Integrated shares as dividend income received. Such income is ordinary income subject to a $100 dividend exclusion. The recipient taxpayer will have as a tax basis for the Integrated shares an amount equal to the fair market value of the stock received.

(b) If the shares of Decimile stock are paid as a dividend, the recipient taxpayer is not subject to tax upon receipt of the shares. Internal Revenue Code Section 305 provides that such stock dividends are not taxable. However, the recipient must allocate his basis (typically his cost) for the shares he originally owned to the total number he owned after the distribution.

Part b.
The Model Business Corporation Act specifically deals with loans to employees and directors. If the loan is not for the benefit of the corporation, then such a loan must be authorized by the shareholders. However, the board of directors may authorize loans to employees when and if the board decides that such loan or assistance may benefit the corporation. It would appear that the loan was made for the benefit of the corporation so the latter rule applies. However, the chairman's individual authorization clearly does not meet these statutory requirements and could subject him to personal liability. Therefore, a meeting of the board should be called to consider the ratification or recall of the loan.

Part c.
1. The Model Business Corporation Act allows such transactions between a corporation and one or more of its directors or another corporation in which the director has a financial interest. The transaction is neither void nor voidable even though the director is present at the board meeting which authorized the transaction or because his vote is counted for such purpose if—

- The fact of such relationship or interest is disclosed or known to the board of directors or committee that authorizes, approves, or ratifies the contract or transaction by a vote or consent sufficient for the purpose without counting the votes or consents of such interested directors; or
- The fact of such relationship or interest is disclosed or known to the shareholders entitled to vote and they authorize, approve, or ratify such contract or transaction by vote or written consent; or
- The contract or transaction is fair and reasonable to the corporation. Common or interested directors may be counted in determining the presence of a quorum at a meeting of the board of directors or a committee thereof that authorizes, approves, or ratifies such contract or transaction.

2. A $50,000 payment to Towne would be a violation of his fiduciary duty to the corporation. In addition, it might be illegal depending upon the criminal law of the jurisdiction. In any case he would be obligated to return the amount to the corporation. Furthermore, the payment would constitute grounds for permitting Toy to treat the transaction as voidable.

Answer Outline

Problem 2 Promoter's Preincorporation Contracts; Cash Dividends; Director's Liability (1184,L5)

a. Wonda not liable to Servco
   Corporation is not bound on promoter's preincorporation contracts until corporation adopts agreements
   Bold not liable to Servco
   Bold clearly manifested his intent not to be bound
   Promoter is liable only if such interest is not manifested
   This preincorporation agreement is not contract but revocable offer

b. Corporation must be solvent
   Dividends must come from unrestricted retained earnings
   Total assets must be maintained at level above total liabilities

c. Charges of negligence are without merit
   Directors are usually jointly and severally liable for assenting to unlawful payment of dividends
   Exception occurs if directors act in good faith and in reliance upon information prepared by management
   No liability for honest mistakes in business judgment

Unofficial Answer

Problem 2 Promoter's Preincorporation Contracts; Cash Dividends; Director's Liability (1184,L5)

a. Wonda is not liable to Servco on the preincorporation agreements. A preincorporation agreement made by a promoter does not bind the corporation even though it is made in the corporation's name. The corporation prior to its formation lacks the capacity to enter into contracts or to employ agents since it is nonexistent. Furthermore, unless after being formed the corporation adopts or knowingly accepts the benefits under the contract, it will not be held liable. Therefore, Wonda's express rejection of the preincorporation agreement will allow it to avoid liability.

Bold's liability to Servco depends on whether Bold clearly manifested his intent not to be personally bound on the preincorporation agreements. Such manifestation of intent can be shown by the express language or acts of the parties. The facts of the case at hand clearly show that Bold did not intend to be held personally liable on the agreements with Servco, since the contracts were executed in the name of Wonda, contingent upon adoption by Wonda, and were based solely on Wonda's anticipated credit. Therefore, Bold will not be held liable on the agreements with Servco.

Furthermore, a preincorporation agreement that is entered into by a promoter on behalf of a corporation to be formed and that is intended not to bind the promoter is not a contract but is merely a revocable offer to be communicated to the proposed corporation after its formation. Thus, under the facts, neither Bold nor Wonda will enjoy rights or suffer liabilities under the agreement.

b. Cash dividends may be declared and paid if the corporation is solvent and payment of the dividends would not render the corporation insolvent. Furthermore, each state imposes additional restrictions on what funds are legally available to pay dividends. One of the more restrictive tests adopted by many states permits the payment of dividends only out of unrestricted and unreserved earned surplus (retained earnings). The Model Business Corporation Act as recently amended prohibits distributions if, after giving effect to the distribution, the corporation's total assets would be less than the sum of its total liabilities.

c. The charge of negligence will fail if the directors can establish that they acted in good faith, in a manner reasonably believed to be in the best interests of the corporation and with such care as an ordinary prudent person in a like position would use under similar circumstances. Furthermore, under the business judgment rule, the court will not substitute its judgment for that of the board of directors as long as the directors acted in good faith and with due care.

The allegation that the directors failed to exercise due care by declaring cash dividends to shareholders that exceeded Wonda's profits and paid-in capital is without merit. Generally, if a director votes for or assents to the unlawful payment of dividends, that director will be jointly and severally liable, along with all other directors so voting or assenting. However, directors will be relieved of liability if in voting or assenting to the payment of cash dividends they acted in good faith and in reliance upon information, opinions, reports or statements prepared or presented by an officer or employee of the corporation whom the directors reasonably believe to be reliable and competent in the matters presented. Thus, the directors' reliance on the reports prepared and issued by Wonda's vice-president of finance was proper so long as the directors exercised due care, acted in good faith, and acted without knowledge that would cause reliance on the reports to be unwarranted. The reason for such a rule is to allow directors to use their best business judgment without incurring liability for honest mistakes.

Answer Outline

Problem 3 Proxy Solicitation (1182,L4b)

Part b.

1. No. Baron cannot lawfully refuse to give Powell access to shareholders list
    - A shareholder has right to inspect records for any legitimate purpose
        - Obtaining stocklist in order to wage proxy fight is legitimate purpose
2. Powell has right to have Baron distribute the proxy materials
    - 1934 Act requires management to send out insurgent's proxy materials to shareholders
        - Insurgent must bear expenses
3. Proxies solicited through interstate commerce must comply with proxy solicitation provisions contained in 1934 Act
    - Proxy materials must set forth complete information
    - Proxy materials must include names and interests of all participants
        - If proxy contest involves control of management
    - Proxy materials must be filed with and approved by SEC before distribution

Unofficial Answer
(Author Modified)

Problem 3 Proxy Solicitation (1182,L4b)

Part b.

1. No, Baron cannot lawfully refuse to give Powell access to the list of shareholders. Under the Model Business Corporations Act, any person who has owned stock for at least six months immediately preceeding the demand or owns at least 5% of the outstanding shares of the corporation, upon written demand has a right to examine for any proper purpose the corporate books ,including the record of shareholders. Obtaining a list of shareholders in order to wage a proxy fight for control of the corporation is a legitimate purpose for inspecting the corporate books. Under the Model Act,

Baron will be liable to Powell for 10% of the value of shares owned by Powell, if Powell is wrongfully denied access to the books.

2. Since Baron's shares fall within the provisions of the Security Exchange Act of 1934, Baron must send out Powell's proxy materials. The 1934 Act requires the management of a corporation to mail the proxy materials of the insurgents to the shareholders if the insurgents so request and pay the expenses incurred.

3. Since Baron's shares are traded on a national stock exchange, these securities must be registered under the Securities Exchange Act of 1934. All proxies solicited through interstate commerce from the holders of securities registered under the 1934 Act must comply with the proxy solicitation provisions contained in this Act. The 1934 Act requires proxy materials to set forth complete information on the matters at issue. If the proxy contest involves the control of management, the proxy materials must include names and the interest of all participants and a complete corporate financial report. These materials must be filed with and approved by the SEC before issuance to insure compliance with the above mentioned disclosure requirements.

ANTITRUST AND GOVERNMENT REGULATION

This module was deleted because the AICPA has discontinued coverage of this topic effective May 1986.

November 1985 Questions

(1185,L1,23)*

(1185,L1,24)*

(1185,L1,25)*

Deleted by AICPA; effective 5/86

FEDERAL SECURITIES LAW

Overview

The bulk of the material tested on the exam from this area comes from the Securities Act of 1933, as amended, and the Securities Exchange Act of 1934, as amended. Topics included under the scope of the 1933 Act are registration requirements, exempt securities, and exempt transactions. The purpose of the 1933 Act is to provide investors with full disclosure of a security offering and to prevent fraud. The basic prohibition of the 1933 Act is that no sale of a security shall occur in interstate commerce without registration and without furnishing a prospectus to prospective purchasers unless the security or the transaction is exempt from registration.

The purpose of the 1934 Act is the establishment of the Securities Exchange Commission and to assure fairness in the trading of securities subsequent to issuance. The basic scope of the 1934 Act is to require periodic reports of financial and other information concerning registered securities, and prohibit manipulative and deceptive devices in both the sale and purchase of securities. The exam nearly always includes an essay question on Federal Securities Regulation; however, this is frequently combined with accountant's liability or is included within a question concerning corporation law.

A. Securities Act of 1933 (Generally applies to initial issuances of securities)

1. Purposes of Act are to provide investors with full and fair disclosure of all material information relating to issuance of securities and to prevent fraud or misrepresentation

    a. Accomplished by requiring

        1) A registration statement to be filed with Securities and Exchange Commission (SEC) before either a public sale or an offer to sell securities in interstate commerce

            a) This is the fundamental thrust of Act
            b) The SEC is government agency comprising commissioners and its staff which was created to administer and enforce the Federal Securities Laws. The Commission interprets the acts, conducts investigations, adjudicates violations, and performs a rule-making function to implement the acts.

                1] Can subpoena witnesses
                2] Cannot assess monetary penalties without court proceedings

        2) Prospectuses to be provided to investors with or before the sale or delivery of the securities to provide public with information given to SEC in registration statement

            a) For definition of prospectus, see "A.2.i." below

3) And by providing civil and criminal liabilities for failure to comply with these requirements and for misrepresentation or fraud in the sale of securities even if not required to be registered

b. SEC does not evaluate the merits or value of securities

1) SEC can only compel complete disclosure
2) In theory, public can evaluate merit of security when provided with complete disclosure

c. The major items you need to know are

1) That registration statement and prospectus are usually required
2) What transactions are exempt from registration
3) What the liability is for false or misleading registration statements
4) What securities are exempt from registration

2. Definitions

a. Security--any note, stock, bond, certificate of interest, investment contract, etc., or any interest or instrument commonly known as a security

1) A very broad term under 1933 Act
2) Includes limited partnership interests
3) Includes rights and warrants to subscribe for the above
4) Investment contract is a security when profits are to come from the efforts of others

b. Person--individual, corporation, partnership, unincorporated association, business trust, government

c. Controlling person--has power, direct/indirect, to influence the management and/or policies of an issuer, whether by stock ownership, contract, position, or otherwise

EXAMPLE: A 51% stockholder is a controlling person by virtue of a majority ownership.

EXAMPLE: A director of a corporation also owns 10% of that same corporation. By virtue of the stock ownership and position on the board of directors, he has a strong voice in the management of the corporation. Therefore, he is a controlling person.

d. Issuer--every person who issues or proposes to issue any security

1) Includes a controlling person

e. Underwriter--any person who has purchased from issuer with a view to the public distribution of any security or participates in such undertaking

1) Includes any person who offers or sells for issuer in connection with the distribution of any security
2) Does not include person who sells or distributes on commission for underwriter (i.e., dealers)
3) Remember, an issuer includes a controlling person

f. Dealer--agent, broker, or principal who spends either full or part time in the business of dealing or trading securities issued by another person

g. Sale--every contract for sale or disposition of security for value (consideration)

1) Offer to sell--every attempt to dispose of security for value
2) Includes neither preliminary negotiations nor agreements between an issuer and an underwriter
3) Under Rule 145, the issuance of securities as part of business reorganization (e.g., merger or consolidation) constitutes a sale and must be registered unless the issue qualifies as an exemption to the 1933 Act

h. Registration statement--the statement required to be filed with SEC before initial sale of securities in interstate commerce

1) Includes financial statements and all other relevant information about the registrant's property, business, directors, principal officers, together with prospectus
2) Also, includes any amendment, report, or document filed as part of the statement or incorporated therein by reference

i. Prospectus--any notice, circular, advertisement, letter, or communication offering any security for sale

1) May be a written, radio, or television communication
2) After the effective date of registration statement, communication (written or oral) will not be considered a prospectus if

a) Prior to or at same time, a written prospectus was also sent, or
b) If it only states from whom written prospectus is available, identifies security, states price, and who will execute orders for it (i.e., tombstone ad)

3) Preliminary prospectus may be sent during the waiting period (i.e., time interval between time of first filing with SEC and effective date), if so identified and states that it is subject to completion and amendment

a) These statements must be made in red ink ("red herring" prospectus)

3. Registration requirements

a. Registration is required under the Act if

1) The securities are to be offered, sold, or delivered in interstate commerce or through the mails

a) Interstate commerce means trade, commerce, transportation, or communication (e.g., telephone call) of securities among several states or territories of U.S.

2) Unless it is an exempted security or exempted transaction

b. Issuer has primary duty of registration

1) Any person who sells unregistered securities that should have been registered may be liable to a purchaser, unless transaction is exempt

c. Registration statements are public information
d. Information required, in general

1) Names of issuer, directors, officers, general partners, underwriters, large stockholders, counsel, etc.
2) Description of property, business, and capitalization of issuer
3) Description of security to be sold and use to be made by issuer of proceeds

4) Information about management of issuer
5) Financial statements certified by independent accountant
6) Risks associated with the securities

e. Prospectus is also filed as part of registration statement

1) Generally must contain same information as registration statement, but it may be condensed or summarized

f. The registration statement and prospectus are examined by SEC

1) Amendments are almost always required by SEC
2) SEC may issue stop-order suspending effectiveness of registration if statement appears misleading
3) Otherwise registration becomes effective on 20th day after filing (or on 20th day after filing of amendment)

a) 20 days is called the waiting period

4) It is unlawful for company to offer or sell the securities prior to approval (effective registration date)

a) Except for preliminary prospectuses

g. Applies to both corporate and noncorporate issuers
h. Registration covers a single distribution, so second distribution must also be registered
i. State "Blue Sky" laws must also be complied with (see "C." below)

4. Exempt securities (need never be registered but still subject to antifraud provisions under the Act)

a. Securities of governments, banks, quasi-governmental authorities (e.g., local hospital authorities), building and loan associations, farmers' co-ops, and railroads

1) Public utilities are not exempt

b. Commercial paper, e.g., note, draft, check, etc., with a maturity of nine months or less

1) Must be for commercial purpose and not investment

c. Securities of nonprofit religious, educational, or charitable organizations
d. Certificates issued by receiver or trustee in bankruptcy
e. Insurance and annuity contracts
f. Security exchanged by issuer exclusively with its existing shareholders

1) No commission is paid
2) Both sets of securities must have been issued by the same person

EXAMPLE: A stock split is an exempt transaction under the 1933 Act and thus, the securities need not be registered at time of split.

g. Intrastate issues--securities offered and sold only within one state

1) Issuer must be resident of state and doing 80% of business in the state and must use at least 80% of sale proceeds in connection with business operations in the state
2) All offerees and purchasers must be residents of state
3) For 9 months after last sale by issuer, resales can only be made to residents of state

4) Either all of particular issue must qualify under this rule or this exemption cannot be used for any

EXAMPLE: A regional corporation in need of additional capital makes an offer to the residents of the state in which it is incorporated to purchase a new issue of its stock. The offer expressly restricts sales to only residents of the state and all purchasers are residents of the state.

h. Small issues (Regulation A)--issuances up to $1,500,000 may be exempt if

1) There is a notice filing with SEC
2) An offering circular (containing financial information about the corporation and descriptive information about offered securities) must be provided to offeree. Financial statements in offering circular need not be audited.
3) Note that the offering circular is required under Regulation A instead of the more costly and time-consuming prospectus

5. Exempt transactions (still subject, however, to antifraud provisions of the Act)

a. Casual sales--transaction by any person other than an issuer, underwriter, or dealer

1) Generally covers sales by individual investors on their own account
2) May be transaction by broker on customer's order

a) Does not include the solicitation of these orders

3) Does not apply to sales by controlling persons (see "2.c." above)

b. Regulation D establishes three exemptions in Rules 504, 505, and 506

1) Rule 504 exempts an issuance of securities up to $500,000 sold in 12-month period to any number of investors

a) No general offering or solicitation is permitted
b) The securities are restricted as to resale
c) No specific disclosure is required

2) Rule 505 exempts issuance of up to $5,000,000 in 12-month period

a) No general offering or solicitation is permitted
b) Permits sales to 35 unaccredited investors and to unlimited number of accredited investors

1] Accredited investors are banks, insurance companies, persons with net worth exceeding $1,000,000 or having annual income of $200,000 for two most recent years or make purchases of more than $150,000 of securities where purchaser's total purchase price does not exceed 20% of purchaser's net worth at time of sale

c) Resale is restricted; in general must be held for two years
d) These securities typically state that they have not been registered and that they have resale restrictions

e) If purchased solely by accredited investors, no specific disclosure needed
f) Unlike under Rule 504, if nonaccredited investor purchases these securities, audited statements and other information must be supplied

3) Rule 506 allows private placement of unlimited amount of securities

a) In general, same rules apply here as outlined under Rule 505

b) However, an additional requirement is that the unaccredited investors (up to 35) must be sophisticated investors (individuals with knowledge and experience in financial matters) or be represented by individual with such knowledge and experience

EXAMPLE: A growing corporation is in need of additional capital and decides to make a new issuance of its stock. The stock is only offered to 10 of the president's friends who regularly make financial investments of this sort. They are interested in purchasing the stock for an investment and each of them is provided with the type of information that is regularly included in a registration statement.

4) A controlling person who sells restricted securities may be held to be an underwriter unless requirements of Rule 144 are met when controlling person is selling through a broker

a) Broker performs no services beyond those of typical broker who executes orders and receives customary fee

b) Ownership (including beneficial ownership) for at least two years

c) Only limited amounts of stock may be sold--the lesser of

1] 1% of outstanding stock, or

2] If traded on an exchange, the average weekly volume of previous four weeks

d) Public must have available adequate disclosure of issuer corporation

e) Notice of sale must be filed with SEC

f) If "a)" through "e)" are met, the security can be sold without registration

c. Post-registration transactions by dealer, i.e., dealer is not required to deliver prospectus

1) If transaction is made at least 40 days after first date security was offered to public, or

2) After 90 days if it is issuer's first public issue

3) Does not apply to sales of securities that are leftover part of an allotment from the public issue

B. Securities Exchange Act of 1934 (Generally applies to subsequent trading of securities)

1. Purposes of the Act

a. Federally regulate securities exchanges and securities traded thereon

b. Require adequate information be provided in various transactions

c. Regulate the use of credit in securities transactions

d. Prevent unfair use of information by insiders

e. Prevent fraud and deceptive practices

2. Each of following are required to register with SEC if they use interstate commerce or the mails

a. National securities exchanges

b. Brokers and dealers (must register whether or not members of an exchange)

c. Dealers in municipal securities

d. Securities that are traded on any national securities exchange must be registered
   1) Securities exempted under 1933 Act may still be regulated under 1934 Act
e. Over-the-counter and other equity securities traded in interstate commerce and having assets of more than $3 million and 500 or more holders of record (stockholders) as of the last day of the issuer's fiscal year
   1) Equity securities--stock, rights to subscribe to, or securities convertible into stock. Not ordinary bonds.
f. Exempt securities
   1) Obligations of U.S. government, guaranteed by, or in which U.S. government has interest
   2) Obligations of state or political subdivision, or guaranteed thereby
      a) Municipal securities traded by broker or dealer are not exempt
   3) Industrial development bonds

3. Issuers of registered securities must file the following reports with SEC
   a. Current reports (Form 8-K) of certain material events such as change in corporate control, revaluation of assets, or change in amount of issued securities
      1) Filed within 10 days of the close of month in which events took place
   b. Quarterly reports (Form 10-Q) must be filed for each of first three fiscal quarters of each fiscal year of issuer
      1) Not required to be certified
   c. Annual reports (Form 10-K) must be certified by independent public accountant
   d. These reports are not to be confused with reports to shareholders

4. Credit rules for brokers, dealers, banks, and members of exchanges
   a. The Federal Reserve Board regulates the maximum amount of credit (margin) that brokers, dealers, and banks may extend to purchasers of securities
      1) Guidelines vary from 50% to 100%
      2) Does not apply to exempt securities
   b. May borrow for business only through
      1) A bank that is member of Federal Reserve System, or
      2) A bank agreeing to follow same procedures as members of Federal Reserve System
   c. May not lend customer's securities without written consent
   d. May not hypothecate any customer's securities
      1) I.e., pledge without giving up possession or subject to lien
      2) May do so to extent customer is indebted on security

      EXAMPLE: Broker holds customer's securities for him. In order to make an investment of his own, broker needs collateral for a loan. He pledges his customer's securities as collateral. This is hypothecation and a violation of the Act unless the customer is indebted to the broker on these securities.

e. Member of exchange may not transact for his/her own account, except

1) Odd-lot dealers--those who deal with lots less than units traded on exchange

EXAMPLE: Certain shares are traded in 100-share units. An odd-lot dealer might execute a customer's order for 80 shares and he will have to take the other 20 shares himself.

2) Specialist--one who deals with limited price orders and also deals for himself

EXAMPLE: A specialist receives an order to buy 80 shares at price X. Only if the price is down to X will he buy 100 shares: 80 shares for his customer at price X, and 20 shares for himself.

5. Proxy solicitations

a. Proxy--grant of authority by shareholder to someone else to vote his shares at meeting
b. Proxy solicitation provisions apply to solicitation (by any means of interstate commerce or the mails) of holders of securities required to be registered under the 1934 Act
c. Proxy statement must be sent with proxy solicitation

1) Must contain disclosure of all material facts concerning matters to be voted upon
2) Purpose is for fairness in corporate action and election of directors

d. Requirements of proxy itself

1) Shall indicate on whose behalf solicitation is made
2) Provide space to date it
3) Identify clearly and impartially each matter to be acted on
4) Means to choose approval or disapproval of each matter, e.g., yes or no

e. Other inclusions in proxy material

1) Proposals by shareholders which are a proper subject for shareholders to vote on
2) Financial statements for last two years, certified by independent accountant, if

a) Solicitation is on behalf of management, and
b) It is for annual meeting at which directors are to be elected

f. The proxy statement, proxy itself, and any other soliciting material must be filed with SEC
g. Brokers are required to forward proxies for customers' shares held by broker
h. Incumbent management is required to mail proxy materials of insurgents to shareholders if requested and expenses are paid by the insurgents

C. State "Blue Sky" Laws

1. These are state statutes regulating the issuance and sale of securities. They contain anti-fraud and registration provisions as in the Federal Acts.
   a. They are called "Blue Sky" laws because they were first enacted to prevent investors from being sold "a piece of the sky", i.e., a worthless security
2. Must be complied with in addition to federal laws
3. If registered under 1933 Act, frequently all that is needed is to file same documents with state
   a. Exemptions from federal laws are not exemptions from state laws
4. If privately placed without registration, filings may be subject to "merit" review by state commissions

Multiple Choice Questions (1–24)

1. Under the Securities Act of 1933, an accountant may be held liable for any materially false or misleading financial statements, including an omission of a material fact therefrom, provided the purchaser
   a. Proves reliance on the registration statement or prospectus.
   b. Proves negligence or fraud on the part of the accountant.
   c. Brings suit within four years after the security is offered to the public.
   d. Proves a false statement or omission existed and the specific securities were the ones offered through the registration statement.

2. Under the Securities Act of 1933, subject to some exceptions and limitations, it is unlawful to use the mails or instruments of interstate commerce to sell or offer to sell a security to the public unless
   a. A surety bond sufficient to cover potential liability to investors is obtained and filed with the Securities and Exchange Commission.
   b. The offer is made through underwriters qualified to offer the securities on a nationwide basis.
   c. A registration statement has been properly filed with the Securities and Exchange Commission, has been found to be acceptable, and is in effect.
   d. The Securities and Exchange Commission approves of the financial merit of the offering.

3. Mr. Jackson owns approximately 40% of the shares of common stock of Triad Corporation. The rest of the shares are widely distributed among 2,000 shareholders. Jackson needs funds for other business ventures and would like to raise about $2,000,000 through the sale of some of his Triad shares. He accordingly approached Underwood & Sons, an investment banking house in which he knew one of the principals, to purchase his Triad shares and distribute the shares to the public at a reasonable price through its offices in the United States. Any profit on the sales could be retained by Underwood pursuant to an agreement reached between Jackson and Underwood. In this situation
   a. The securities to be sold probably do not need to be registered with the Securities and Exchange Commission.
   b. Underwood & Sons probably is not an underwriter as defined in the federal securities law.
   c. Jackson probably is considered an issuer under federal securities law.
   d. Under federal securities law, no prospectus is required to be filed in connection with this contemplated transaction.

4. Tweed Manufacturing, Inc., plans to issue $5 million of common stock to the public in interstate commerce after its registration statement with the SEC becomes effective. What, if anything, must Tweed do in respect to those states in which the securities are to be sold?
   a. Nothing, since approval by the SEC automatically constitutes satisfaction of any state requirements.
   b. Make a filing in those states which have laws governing such offerings and obtain their approval.
   c. Simultaneously apply to the SEC for permission to market the securities in the various states without further clearance.
   d. File in the appropriate state office of the state in which it maintains its principal office of business, obtain clearance, and forward a certified copy of that state's clearance to all other states.

5. Harvey Wilson is a senior vice president, 15% shareholder and a member of the Board of Directors of Winslow, Inc. Wilson has decided to sell 10% of his stock in the company. Which of the following methods of disposition would subject him to SEC registration requirements?
   a. A redemption of the stock by the corporation.
   b. The sale by several brokerage houses of the stock in the ordinary course of business.
   c. The sale of the stock to an insurance company which will hold the stock for long-term investment purposes.
   d. The sale to a corporate officer who currently owns 5% of the stock of Winslow and who will hold the purchased stock for long-term investment.

6. Which of the following is subject to the registration requirements of the Securities Act of 1933?
   a. Public sale of its bonds by a municipality.
   b. Public sale by a corporation of its negotiable five-year notes.

c. Public sale of stock issued by a common carrier regulated by the Interstate Commerce Commission.
d. Issuance of stock by a corporation to its existing stockholders pursuant to a stock split.

7. Which of the following financing methods will be exempt from the registration requirements of the Securities Act of 1933?
a. Direct public offering of stock to potential investors without the use of an underwriter.
b. Interstate marketing of securites by a subsidiary which is engaged in intra-state commerce.
c. Sale of long-term notes to a consortium of local banks.
d. Public sale of nonconvertible bonds to investors.

8. The Securities Act of 1933 specifically exempts from registration, securities offered by any person
a. Other than an issuer, underwriter, or dealer.
b. Who is an issuer of a public offering.
c. If the securities in question have previously been registered.
d. In a small company.

9.–13. *Deleted by AICPA; effective 5/86*

14. Which of the following is required under the Securities Exchange Act of 1934 or the SEC's reporting requirements issued pursuant thereto?
a. Current reporting by issuers of registered securities of certain specified corporate and financial events within ten days after the close of the month in which they occur.
b. Quarterly audited financial reports and statements by those corporations listed on a national exchange.
c. Reporting by issuers of securities which are traded over-the-counter, but only if the securities are actively traded.
d. Annual filing of audited financial reports by all corporations engaged in interstate commerce.

15. The Securities Exchange Act of 1934 requires that certain persons register and that the securities of certain issuers be registered. In respect to such registration under the 1934 Act, which of the following statements is **incorrect?**
a. All securities offered under the Securities Act of 1933 also must be registered under the 1934 Act.
b. National securities exchanges must register.
c. The equity securities of issuers, which are traded on a national securities exchange, must be registered.
d. The equity securities of issuers having in excess of $1 million in assets and 500 or more stockholders which are traded in interstate commerce must be registered.

16.–22. *Deleted by AICPA; effective 5/86*

May 1985 Questions

23. Securities available under a private placement made pursuant to Regulation D of the Securities Act of 1933
a. Must be sold to accredited institutional investors.
b. Must be sold to less than 25 nonaccredited investors.
c. Can **not** be the subject of an immediate reoffering to the public.
d. Can **not** be subject to the payment of commissions.

24. Wells Corp., an established manufacturer, has decided to make an offering of $4.5 million of its securities pursuant to Regulation D of the Securities Act of 1933. The sale will be made to accredited and nonaccredited investors. Which of the following is a correct statement with regard to such an offering?
a. No more than 35 accredited investors may purchase securities.
b. Since there are nonaccredited investors who are purchasing securities, at least an audited balance sheet must be provided.
c. A general solicitation of potential investors is permitted.
d. The offering limit is $10 million within a two-year period.

Problems

Problem 1 (1181,L2)

(15 to 20 minutes)

Part a. Diversified Enterprises, Inc., and Cardinal Manufacturing Corporation have each appointed a committee to discuss Diversified's proposed acquisition of Cardinal. After protracted bargaining, the two committees have agreed to the following terms: Diversified would acquire Cardinal in exchange for 500,000 shares of Diversified's voting common stock and 250,000 shares of its 11% noncumulative, nonvoting preferred. The committees have submitted a proposal incorporating the above to their respective boards of directors. Both corporations are incorporated in the same state and this state has adopted the Model Business Corporation Act. Cardinal has only one class of stock outstanding, 250,000 shares of common. Diversified has 2,000,000 shares of $1 par value common stock authorized of which 700,000 shares are outstanding. The preferred stock would be a new class of stock with a $5 par value. Diversified is in the lower 20th percentile of the Fortune 500 companies and is listed on the New York Stock Exchange. Cardinal is considerably smaller with assets of $11 million and sales of $4 million. It is traded in the over-the-counter market. Diversified does not compete with, nor does it buy from or sell to, Cardinal. The form of the acquisition is to be a statutory merger.

You have been assigned to an accounting team to provide assistance to Diversified in this undertaking.

Required:

Answer the following, setting forth reasons for any conclusions stated.

1. In separate paragraphs, discuss the requirements of the Securities Act of 1933 arising out of the above facts as well as federal antitrust implications. *

2. From a corporate law standpoint, what must be done to validly consummate the proposed merger?

Part b. During the initial audit of Haskell Corporation, a medium-sized company engaged in interstate commerce, the CPA discovers that Haskell has recently instituted a generous and broadly-based employees' stock purchase plan. Haskell's philosophy is based upon maximum participation by all employees. This philosophy is generally stated in Haskell's employment brochures and has been fully implemented.

Antitrust will not be tested effective 5/86.

Haskell employs approximately 13,000 people in plants located in several states. Approximately 95% of the employees are participating in the plan.

Required:

Answer the following, setting forth reasons for any conclusions stated.

Does the Securities Act of 1933 pose any problems to Haskell in connection with its employees' stock purchase plan or can it claim an exemption as a private placement?

Problem 2 (582,L2)

(15 to 20 minutes)

Various Enterprises Corporation is a medium sized conglomerate listed on the American Stock Exchange. It is constantly in the process of acquiring smaller corporations and is invariably in need of additional money. Among its diversified holdings is a citrus grove which it purchased eight years ago as an investment. The grove's current fair market value is in excess of $2 million. Various also owns 800,000 shares of Resistance Corporation which it acquired in the open market over a period of years. These shares represent a 17% minority interest in Resistance and are worth approximately $2½ million. Various does its short-term financing with a consortium of banking institutions. Several of these loans are maturing; in addition to renewing these loans, it wishes to increase its short-term debt from $3 to $4 million.

In light of the above, Various is considering resorting to one or all of the following alternatives in order to raise additional working capital.

- An offering of 500 citrus grove units at $5,000 per unit. Each unit would give the purchaser a 0.2% ownership interest in the citrus grove development. Various would furnish management and operation services for a fee under a management contract and net proceeds would be paid to the unit purchasers. The offering would be confined almost exclusively to the state in which the groves are located or in the adjacent state in which Various is incorporated.
- An increase in the short-term borrowing by $1 million from the banking institution which currently provides short-term funds. The existing debt would be consolidated, extended, and increased to $4 million and would mature over a nine-month period. This would be evidenced by a short-term note.

- Sale of the 17% minority interest in Resistance Corporation in the open market through its brokers over a period of time and in such a way as to minimize decreasing the value of the stock. The stock is to be sold in an orderly manner in the ordinary course of the broker's business.

Required:

Answer the following, setting forth reasons for any conclusions stated.

In separate paragraphs discuss the impact of the registration requirements of the Securities Act of 1933 on each of the above proposed alternatives.

Multiple Choice Answers

1. d	6. b	11. *	16. *	21. *
2. c	7. c	12. *	17. *	22. *
3. c	8. a	13. *	18. *	23. c
4. b	9. *	14. a	19. *	24. b
5. b	10. *	15. a	20 *	

**Deleted by AICPA; effective 5/86*

Multiple Choice Answer Explanations

A. Securities Act of 1933

1. (1179,L1,29) (d) Under the Securities Act of 1933, an accountant is liable to a purchaser of securities if the purchaser proves a false financial statement (including statements with a material omission), and the specific securities were ones offered through a registration statement. Answer (a) is incorrect because the purchaser need not prove reliance on the registration statement or prospectus. Instead, the burden is shifted from the plaintiff to the defendant accountant to show that he is not responsible for the investment loss by the purchaser, i.e., accountant must prove due diligence. Answer (b) is incorrect because the purchaser need not prove negligence or fraud on the part of the accountant. Again, all that need be proven is the misstatement or omission. Answer (c) is incorrect because the maximum time limitation for bringing such an action is 3 years after the security is offered to the public.

2. (577,L1,3) (c) Unless a registration statement has been filed with the SEC and accepted, it is generally unlawful under the 1933 Act to offer or sell securities to the public using instruments of interstate commerce. There is no exception to registration by obtaining a surety bond. Nor does it matter who makes the offer; qualified underwriters are subject to the same rules. The SEC never evaluates the financial merit of an offering. Instead, the SEC requires full and fair disclosure so that investors can make their own determination. Registration statements are the vehicles of full and fair disclosures.

3. (578,L1,6) (c) Jackson is considered to be an issuer under the Securities Act of 1933. The definition of issuer includes a controlling person. Jackson is a controlling person because as substantial holder (40%), he has the power to influence the management and policies of the corporation. This transaction does not come within any exception and, therefore, is required to be registered with the SEC. Thus, answer (a) is incorrect since a registration is required. Answer (b) is incorrect because Underwood & Sons is an underwriter. It has purchased securities from an issuer for public distribution. Answer (d) is incorrect since this is a public sale of securities under the provisions of the Securities Act of 1933, i.e., all registration requirements including the filing of a prospectus are necessary.

4. (579,L1,43) (b) Anyone planning to issue common stock must make a filing in those states that have laws governing such offerings and obtain their approval in addition to meeting the registration requirements of the SEC. Answer (a) is incorrect since approval by the SEC does not automatically constitute satisfaction of state "blue-sky" laws. Answer (c) is incorrect because the issuer must apply to each state for permission to market the securities in addition to the SEC. Answer (d) is incorrect because each state makes its own approval of the stock issue; it cannot be done by one state for the other states.

5. (579,L1,48) (b) Wilson, the officer and stockholder of Winslow, Inc., will be required to comply with SEC registration requirements if he chooses to dispose of his 15% stock in the corporation by having it sold by several brokerage houses in the ordinary course of business. Wilson is deemed to be a controlling person, i.e., one who has the power to influence management and policies of the issuer, and thus his stock would be considered to be restricted stock. Sale by a controlling person through a broker is not exempted from SEC registration if more than 1% of the outstanding stock is sold. Answer (a) is incorrect because a redemption of stock is not an offering to the public and therefore not covered by the 1933 Act. Answers (c) and (d) are not subject to the SEC registration requirements because they are private placements of securities to sophisticated investors.

A.5. Exempt Transactions

6. (1184,L1,42) (b) Section 5 of the Securities Act of 1933 provides that if a security fails to qualify for one of the exemptions, the security must be registered before it is offered or sold in interstate commerce. The sale of commercial paper is only an exemption from the registration requirements when the paper has a maturity not exceeding nine months. Thus, a public sale by a corporation of its negotiable five-year notes is subject to the registration requirements. Answers (a) and (c) are exempt from registration under the 1933 Act. Sales of securities by a federal, state, or municipal government are exempt, as are securities sold by a common carrier subject to regulation by the Interstate Commerce Commission. Answer (d) is incorrect because in order for the registration requirements to become operative there must be a "sale" or "offer" of a security for value. Any security exchanged by the issuer with its existing shareholders exclusively

does not constitute a sale or offer to sell. Thus, the issuance of stock pursuant to a stock split is not a sale of a security. The 1933 Act does not require registration for stock splits or stock dividends.

7. (584,L1,30) (c) A nonpublic offering to sophisticated investors who have access to the type of information required in a registration statement is exempt under the 1933 Act. Answer (a) is incorrect because a direct public offering by the issuer is not exempt. Answer (b) is incorrect because to qualify for the intrastate exemption the offering must be completely intrastate. Answer (d) is incorrect because nonconvertible bonds are considered securities. A public sale of such bonds is not exempt.

8. (576,L2,30) (a) There is a broad specific exemption for securities offered by any person other than an issuer, underwriter, or dealer. Thus under the Act public offerings of securities are regulated, but private offerings are exempted. This exemption permits most investors to sell their own securities without registration, prospectus, or other regulations except the antifraud provisions. To avoid circumvention of the Act, the SEC has promulgated a number of complicated provisions dealing with this exemption when the security sold is "restricted" or the seller is a "controlling person."

A.6.c. Criminal Liability

9. *Deleted by AICPA; effective 5/86*

B. Securities Exchange Act of 1934

10.–13. *Deleted by AICPA; effective 5/86*

14. (1182,L1,32) (a) Under the Securities Exchange Act of 1934, current reports of certain specified corporate and financial items such as a change in corporate control, revaluation of assets, or a change in the amount of issued securities must be filed within ten days of the close of the month in which the events took place. Answer (b) is incorrect because although quarterly financial reports must be filed, they are not required to be audited. Answer (c) is incorrect because issuers of securities which are traded over-the-counter must report only when they have in excess of $3 million in total assets and more than 500 holders of record (stockholders) as of the last day of the issuer's fiscal year. Answer (d) is incorrect because only those issuers registered under the Securities Exchange Act of 1934 must file annual audited financial reports; and not all corporations engaged in interstate commerce fall within the jurisdiction and scope of the registration requirements under the 1934 Act.

15. (1180,L1,39) (a) The correct answer is (a). The Securities Act of 1933 applies to the initial issuance of securities and has the purpose of providing investors with full and fair disclosure concerning these securities. The Securities Exchange Act of 1934 generally applies to the subsequent trading of securities but not necessarily all securities required to register under the 1933 Act. Each of the following are required to register under the 1934 Act: (1) national securities exchange; (2) brokers and dealers, (3) dealers in municipal securities, (4) securities that are traded on any national exchange, (5) equity securities traded in interstate commerce having in excess of $1 million in assets and 500 or more shareholders.

16.–18. *Deleted by AICPA; effective 5/86*

B.6. Regulation of Insiders and Insiders' Profits

19.–20. *Deleted by AICPA; effective 5/86*

D. Foreign Corrupt Practices Act of 1977

21.–22. *Deleted by AICPA; effective 5/86*

May 1985 Answers

23. (585,L1,28) (c) Regulation D established three exemptions to the full registration requirements of the Securities Act of 1933. These three exemptions are Rules 504, 505, and 506. Each of these rules contains a restriction on the resale of qualifying issues. In general, the initial purchasers must hold the issues for a two-year period. Answer (a) is incorrect because none of the rules require **all** of the investor purchasers to be accredited institutional purchasers. Answer (b) is incorrect because only Rules 505 and 506 place a limit on the number of nonaccredited investors and the limit is 35, not 25. Answer (d) is incorrect because Regulation D exempt issues may be subject to commission costs.

24. (585,L1,29) (b) Regulation D, Rule 505, exempts issues of $5,000,000 in securities over a twelve-month period from the full registration requirements of the Securities Act of 1933. Pursuant to Rule 505, if nonaccredited investor purchasers are involved, then they must be furnished with at least an audited balance sheet. Other audited financial statements and information should also be provided if readily available. Answer (a) is incorrect because Rule 505 permits sales to an unlimited number of accredited investors plus 35 purchasers that are not accredited investors. Answer (c) is incorrect because a general offer or solicitation is prohibited. Answer (d) is incorrect because a maximum of $5,000,000 of securities sold in a twelve-month period is exempted under Rule 505.

Answer Outline

Problem 1 Legal Implications of Merger; Securities Implications in Employee Stock Purchase Plan (1181,L2)

Part a1.

SEC ruled that merger constitutes a sale
The securities must be registered pursuant to Securities Act of 1933
- A registration statement must be filed with the SEC
- A prospectus must be distributed to Cardinal's shareholders

Congress has required all mergers to be scrutinized under the provisions of Section 7 of the Clayton Act
- Applies to vertical, horizontal, and conglomerate mergers
- Violation of Clayton Act if merger substantially lessens competition or tends to create a monopoly
  - Must apply judicial standards
  - Department of Justice Merger Guidelines should be examined

Part a2.

Form of acquisition is a statutory merger
- Must comply with applicable state laws and Model Business Corporation Act

Diversified's and Cardinal's boards must approve formal plan of merger
Majority of shareholders of each corporation must approve the proposed merger
Articles of merger are executed and filed with Secretary of State
Diversified need not amend its corporate charter to reflect new class of preferred stock
- Model Business Corporation Act provides articles of surviving corporation (Diversified) are automatically amended
  - So as to reflect the formal plan of merger

Part b.

Employees' stock purchase plan is subject to provisions of Securities Act of 1933
- Haskell engaged in the offering and sale of its securities in interstate commerce
  - A registration statement must be filed with the SEC
  - A prospectus must be distributed to the employees

Stock purchase plan does not qualify for a private placement exemption
- Employees are neither sophisticated nor sufficiently informed about the issuer
- Number of employees involved is too large

Haskell subject to sanctions for noncompliance with registration requirements
- SEC could obtain injunction prohibiting sale of stock
- Damages could be awarded
- Employees could seek legal remedy of rescission

Unofficial Answer

Problem 1 Legal Implications of Merger; Securities Implications in Employee Stock Purchase Plan (1181,L2)

Part a.

1. The Securities and Exchange Commission has ruled that a merger such as this one constitutes a "sale." Therefore, this merger must satisfy the requirements of the Securities Act of 1933. Accordingly, absent some possible exemption or exclusion, the securities must be registered and a prospectus must be distributed by Diversified to the Cardinal shareholders.

Also a possible danger, albeit a remote one, is that the merger may violate the provisions of section 7 of the Clayton Act. Although the two corporations do not compete and Cardinal is not a customer of Diversified's, the act applies not only to vertical or horizontal mergers but also to conglomerate mergers such as this one. The Justice Department's guidelines should be examined, and if there is any doubt about the validity of the acquisition from an antitrust standpoint, a ruling from the Justice Department should be sought.

2. Since this is to be a statutory merger pursuant to state law, the provisions of the appropriate statute, the Model Business Corporation Act, must be strictly complied with as well as any additional state law requirements. The steps to be followed by Diversified and Cardinal are as follows:

- The representatives of the two corporations must agree on a formal plan of merger. The plan containing the details of the merger must then be submitted to the board of directors in the form of a resolution and be approved by both boards.
- After approval of the plan of merger, the board, by resolution, directs that the plan be submitted to a vote at a meeting of shareholders.
- Due notice of the meeting, including a copy or summary of the plan, should be given to the shareholders. At each corporation's meeting, a vote of

the shareholders must be taken on the proposed plan. The plan or merger must be approved upon the affirmative vote of a majority of the shareholders of each corporation.

• Upon such approval by the respective shareholders, articles of merger are executed by the president or a vice president and the secretary of each corporation and then verified by one of the officers signing. The articles, along with the appropriate fees and taxes, must then be filed with the secretary of state, who will then issue a certificate of merger if the articles conform to law.

• Diversified need not amend its corporate charter to reflect the new class of preferred stock to be used in the merger. The act provides that, "In the case of a merger, the articles of the surviving corporation shall be deemed to be amended to the extent, if any, that changes in the articles of incorporation are stated in the plan of merger."

Part b.

Yes. Problems are posed for Haskell Corporation because it is engaged in the offering and sale of its securities in interstate commerce. Therefore, under the Securities Act of 1933, it must file a registration statement, have it become effective, and supply a prospectus to the employees to whom stock is offered.

A claim of exemption as a private placement would fail for several reasons. First, among a great number of the employees, the quality of the investor's financial knowledge would undoubtedly be quite low, and their employee relationship to Haskell would likely be such that they would not have access to the kind of information a registration would disclose. These are the very individuals that the act seeks to protect. Second, the number of individuals involved is so large that the offering cannot be considered nonpublic.

If Haskell does not comply with the registration and prospectus requirements, the SEC could obtain an injunction prohibiting such offers and sales. The possibility of damages is also present. In addition, purchasers of the Haskell stock could later seek rescission or damages based on noncompliance with the act's requirements.

Answer Outline

Problem 2 Registration Requirements Under 1933 Act (582,L2)

Since sale of interest in citrus groves meets definition of security, must comply with registration requirement of 1933 Act
- Unless one of the three exemptions are present
  - Small offering exemption
  - Intrastate offering exemption
  - Private offering exemption
- None met; therefore, Various must comply

Short-term note qualifies as exempt security under 1933 Act
- Since it is commercial paper with maturity of nine months or less
  - And proceeds to be used for current operations
- Also qualifies as exempt transaction as private offering

Issue is whether Various is a controlling person of Resistance Corporation
- If not controlling person, sale of these shares exempted from registration requirements
  - Under casual sales exemption
- If controlling person, Various must meet registration requirements of 1933 Act
  - Unless sale of shares meets requirements of Rule 144

Unofficial Answer

(Author Modified)

Problem 2 Registration Requirements Under 1933 Act (582,L2)

• The sale of the ownership interests in the citrus groves qualifies as a security under the 1933 Act. A security is the sale of any interest in a scheme where a person invests money in a common enterprise and is led to expect profits solely from the endeavors of others. The purchasers of the citrus grove units would be expecting profits from the operation and management of these units by Various. Consequently, unless an exemption can be found under the 1933 Act, Various must file a registration statement with the SEC, and such statement must be approved before the issuance of these interests. The only possible exemptions would be an intrastate offering, a small offering and a private offering. The sale of citrus grove interests would not constitute an intrastate offering because interests are offered to persons residing in more than one state. This offering would not qualify as a small offering in that the aggregate value would exceed $1,500,000. Also, it does not appear that it is a private offering, since the offering is not limited to a small number of sophisticated investors.

• The issuance of a short-term note by Various would not require the filing of a registration statement with the SEC. Commercial paper having a maturity date not exceeding nine months is exempt from the registration requirements of the 1933 Act. This is only true if the proceeds gained from the issuance of this paper have been or are to be used for current operations. However, if the proceeds are to be used for long-term capital investments, this exemption would not apply. Since the problem states the instrument would be used to finance current operations, it appears that the note would qualify as an exemption to the 1933 Securities Act requirement for filing. It appears that the requirements for a private placement would be met in this situation. The offering is limited to one sophisticated investor, since institutional investors such as banks and insurance companies are considered to be sophisticated in nature.

• Concerning Various' sale of the Resistance shares, the important fact is to determine whether Various qualifies as a controlling person of Resistance Corporation. If Various does not qualify as a controlling person, the sale of these shares would be exempted from the registration requirements of the 1933 Act under the casual sales exemption. The casual sales exemption states that a transaction by any person other than an issuer, underwriter or dealer is exempt from registration. A controlling person in a corporation has been construed to mean anyone with direct or indirect power to determine the policies of the business. Obviously, ownership of a majority share of existing stock in a company would constitute control. However, in past court decisions, as little as 10% ownership of outstanding shares has been determined to constitute control when combined with such other factors as being a member of the board of directors; an officer of the corporation; or the fact that the remaining shares are distributed over a large number of shareholders. Thus, the fact that Various only owns 17% would not keep it from being a controlling person. If held to be a controlling person, Various' sale of shares would not fall within the casual sales exemption of the 1933 Act. Since this exemption is not met, Various would have to file a registration statement when selling these shares even though the sale is accomplished through a broker. However, the SEC does permit controlling persons to sell limited quantities of their securities without registration of their security if their sale complies with requirements of Rule 144. Rule 144 requires: adequate information concerning the company be publicly available; sale of no more than 1% of all outstanding shares of that class during any three month period; that all sales take place in broker's transactions, with the broker receiving only the ordinary brokerage commission and the broker not engaging in any solicitations of offers to buy from prospective purchasers. Thus, even if Various was considered to be a controlling person, upon compliance with the above requirements, Various would still be able to sell a limited number of its shares without registration.

ACCOUNTANT'S LEGAL LIABILITY

Overview

Accountant's legal liability is often tested on the CPA exam by use of essay questions that require the candidate to apply the legal principles contained in this module to hypothetical fact patterns. Multiple choice questions are used on some exams which also require application as well as knowledge of this material.

Accountant's civil liability arises primarily from contract law, the law of negligence, fraud, the Securities Act of 1933, and the Securities Exchange Act of 1934. The first three are common law and largely judge-made law; whereas, the latter two are federal statutory law.

The agreement between an accountant and his/her client is generally set out in a carefully drafted engagement letter. Additionally, the accountant has a duty to conduct his/her work with the same reasonable care as an average accountant. This duty defines the standard used in a negligence case. It is important to understand:

1. When an accountant can be liable to his/her client.
2. When an accountant can be liable to third parties; the courts are not in agreement on this issue when ordinary negligence is involved as discussed herein.
3. That an accountant is liable to the client and to all third parties that relied on the financial statements when the accountant committed fraud, constructive fraud, or was grossly negligent; furthermore in these cases, the accountant can be assessed punitive damages.
4. The extent of liability under the Securities Act of 1933 and the Securities Exchange Act of 1934 as well as how they differ from each other and from common law.

The CPA examination also tests the dual nature of the ownership of the accountant's working papers. Although the accountant owns the working papers and retains them as evidence of his/her work, confidentiality must be maintained. Therefore, the CPA cannot allow this information to reach another without the client's consent. In general, privileged communications between a CPA and the client are not sanctioned under federal statutory law or common law, but the privilege is in existence in states that have passed statutes granting such a right.

A. Common Law Liability to Clients

1. Liability to clients for breach of contract
   a. Occurs if accountant fails to perform substantially as agreed under contract
      1) Duties under contract may be
         a) Implied--accountant owes duty in contract to perform in nonnegligent manner
         b) Express--accountant owes duty to perform under terms of the contract
            1] This duty can extend liability beyond that which is standard under a normal audit
            2] Typically terms are expressed in engagement letter
      2) Accountant is not an insurer of financial statements and thus does not guarantee against losses from irregularities. "Normal" audit is not intended to uncover fraud, shortages, defalcations, or irregularities in general but is meant to provide audit evidence needed to express opinion on fairness of financial statements.
      3) Accountant is not normally liable for failure to detect fraud, irregularities, etc. unless

a) "Normal" audit would have detected it, or
b) Accountant by agreement has undertaken greater responsibility such as defalcation audit, or
c) Wording of audit report indicates greater responsibility

EXAMPLE: A CPA has been hired by a client to perform an audit. A standard engagement letter is used. During the course of the audit, the CPA fails to uncover a clever embezzlement scheme by one of the client's employees. The CPA is not liable for the losses unless a typical, reasonable audit should have resulted in discovery of the scheme.

4) Accountant is in privity of contract with client based on contractual relationship

b. Client must not interfere or prevent accountant from performing
c. When breach of contract occurs

1) Accountant is not entitled to compensation if breach is major

EXAMPLE: M failed to complete the audit by the agreed date. If time is of the essence so that the client receives no benefit from the audit, M is not entitled to compensation.

2) Accountant is entitled to compensation if there are only minor errors but client may deduct from fees paid any damages caused by breach

3) In general, punitive damages are not awarded for breach of contract

2. Liability to clients based on negligence

a. Accountants are required to perform professionally with same degree of skill and judgment possessed by average accountant

1) This is standard used in case involving ordinary negligence (or simply called negligence)
2) Standard is similar to that imposed on other professions
3) Standard for accountants is guided by

a) State and federal statutes
b) Court decisions
c) Contract with client
d) GAAP and GAAS (persuasive but not conclusive)
e) Customs of the profession (persuasive but not conclusive)

EXAMPLE: W, a CPA, issued an unqualified opinion on the financial statements of X Company. Included in the assets was inventory stated at cost when the market was materially below cost. This violation of GAAP can be used to establish that W was negligent.

4) Accountant's liability is not based on honest errors of judgment. Liability requires at least negligence.

b. For accountant to be liable, damages must be proximate result of the negligence

EXAMPLE: A CPA negligently fails to discover during an audit that several expensive watches are missing from the client's inventory. Subsequently, an employee is caught stealing some watches. He confesses to stealing several before the audit and more after the audit when he found out he did not get caught. Only five of the watches can be recovered from the employee who is unable to pay for those stolen. The CPA may be liable for those losses sustained after the audit if discovery could have prevented them. However, the CPA normally would not be liable for the watches taken before the audit when the loss is not the proximate result of the negligent audit.

c. Damages

1) Limited to losses that use of reasonable care would have avoided
2) Punitive damages not normally allowed for ordinary negligence
3) Contributory negligence may be a defense in many states if client's own negligence substantially contributed to accountant's failure to perform audit adequately

3. Liability to client for fraud

a. Intentional act of deceit or misrepresentation. This is the scienter requirement under fraud. See CONTRACTS, Fraud.

b. Gross negligence or constructive fraud based on reckless disregard of truth or willful blindness to suspicious circumstances (used to satisfy the scienter requirement)

EXAMPLE: During the course of an audit, a CPA fails to verify the existence of the company's investments which amount to a substantial portion of the assets. Many of these, it is subsequently found, were nonexistent. Even in the absence of intent to defraud, the CPA is liable for constructive fraud based on reckless disregard of the truth.

B. Common Law Liability to Third Parties (Nonclients)

1. Client is in privity of contract with accountant based on contractual relationship. Traditionally, accountants could use defense of no privity against suing third parties.

2. More recently, many courts have expanded liability to some third parties. The following distinctions should be understood:

a. Third-party beneficiary -- client and accountant intended this party to be primary beneficiary under contract

1) Accountant liable for negligence, gross negligence, or fraud

b. Foreseen party -- nonprivity third party who accountant knew would rely on financial statements, or member of limited class that accountant knew would rely on financial statements for specified transaction

1) Accountant liable for gross negligence or fraud
2) Courts split on whether accountant is liable to foreseen party based on negligence

EXAMPLE: A CPA agrees to perform an audit for ABC Client knowing that the financial statements will be used to obtain a loan from XYZ Bank. Relying on the financial statements, XYZ Bank loans ABC $100,000. ABC goes bankrupt. If XYZ can establish that the financial statements were not fairly stated thus causing the bank to give the loan and if negligence can be established, some courts will allow XYZ Bank to recover from the CPA.

EXAMPLE: Facts are the same as in the example above except that XYZ Bank was not specified. Since the CPA knew that some bank would rely on these financial statements, the actual bank is a foreseen party since it is a member of a limited class.

3) Recovery not allowed by an indeterminate class for an indefinite period of time
4) Liability not extended to investors in general
5) Liability not extended to all persons foreseeably injured

c. Other third parties

1) Accountant liable for gross negligence or fraud

EXAMPLE: A CPA is informed that financial statements after being audited will be used to obtain a bank loan. The audited financial statements are also shown to trade creditors and potential investors. These third parties are not actually foreseen parties and thus cannot recover from the CPA for ordinary negligence.

3. To recover, plaintiff must also prove

a. Material misstatement or omission on financial statements
b. Accountant's fault caused damages to third party
   1) Actual damages if based on negligence
   2) Punitive damages may be added if based on gross negligence or fraud

C. Statutory Liability to Third Parties--Securities Act of 1933

1. General Information on Securities Act of 1933

a. Covers regulation of sales of securities registered under 1933 Act

1) Act requires registration of initial issuances of securities with SEC
2) Section 11 makes it unlawful for registration statement to contain untrue material fact or to omit material fact

   a) Material fact--one about which average prudent investor should be informed
   b) Most potential accountant liability occurs because registration statement (and prospectus) includes audited financial statements
   c) Accountant's legal liability arises for untrue material fact or omission of material fact in registration statement (or prospectus)
   d) Act does not include periodic reports to SEC or annual reports to stockholders

3) Plaintiff need not be initial purchaser of security

2. Parties that may sue

   a. Any purchaser of registered securities

      1) Purchaser generally must prove that specific security was offered through registration statement

   b. Third parties can sue without having privity of contract with accountant

3. Proof Requirements

   a. Plaintiff (purchaser) must prove damages were incurred
   b. Plaintiff must prove there was material misstatement or omission in financial statements included in registration statement
   c. Plaintiff <u>need not</u> prove reliance on financial statements

      1) Exception--Plaintiff must prove reliance if s/he purchased security after firm issued an earnings statement covering at least 12 months subsequent to effective date of registration statement

   d. If "a." and "b." above are proven, it is a <u>prima facie</u> case (sufficient to win against the CPA unless rebutted) and shifts burden of proof to accountant who may escape liability by proving:

      1) "Due Diligence," that is, after reasonable investigation, accountant had reasonable grounds to believe that statements were true and there was no material misstatement

         NOTE: Although the basis of liability is not negligence under Section 11, an accountant who was at least negligent will probably not be able to establish "due diligence"

      2) Plaintiff knew financial statements were incorrect when investment was made, or
      3) Lack of causation--loss was due to factors other than the misstatement or omission

4. Damages

   a. Difference between amount paid and market value at time of suit
   b. If sold, difference between amount paid and sale price
   c. Damages cannot exceed price at which security was offered to public
   d. Plaintiff cannot recover decrease in value after suit is brought

      1) Accountant is given benefit of any increase in market value during suit

5. Statute of limitations

   a. Action must be brought against accountant within one year from discovery (or when discovery should have been made) of false statement or omission

   b. Action must be brought within three years after security is offered to public even if formula in "a." would be longer

D. <u>Statutory Liability to Third Parties--Securities Exchange Act of 1934</u>

1. General Information on Securities Exchange Act of 1934

   a. Regulates securities sold on national stock exchanges

      1) Includes securities traded over-the-counter and other equity securities having more than $3 million in total assets and held by 500 or more persons at the end of a fiscal year

   b. Requires each company to furnish to SEC an annual report (Form 10-K)

      1) Includes financial statements (not necessarily the same as an annual report to shareholders) attested to by an accountant

      2) Accountant civil liability comes from 2 sections--10 (and Rule 10b-5) and 18

         a) Section 10 (and Rule 10b-5)--Makes it unlawful to:

            1] Employ any device, scheme, or artifice to defraud
            2] Make untrue statement of material fact or omit material fact
            3] Engage in act, practice, or course of business to commit fraud or deceit in connection with purchase or sale of security

         b) Section 18--Makes it unlawful to make false or misleading statement with respect to a material statement unless done in "good faith"

2. Parties who may sue

   a. Purchasers <u>and</u> sellers of registered securities

3. Proof requirements--Section 10 (and Rule 10b-5)

   a. Plaintiff (purchaser or seller) must prove damages were incurred
   b. Plaintiff must prove there was a material misstatement or omission in information released by firm

      1) Information may, for example, be in form of audited financial statements in report to stockholders or in Form 10-K

   c. Plaintiff must prove reliance on financial information

   d. Plaintiff must prove existence of <u>scienter</u>

      1) Includes reckless disregard of truth as well as knowledge of falsity
      2) E.g., accountant guilty of "only" ordinary negligence would not be liable

   e. Plaintiff cannot recover if reckless or fraudulent. Negligence will not bar recovery.

4. Proof requirements--Section 18

   a. Plaintiff (purchaser or seller) must prove damages were incurred
   b. Plaintiff must prove there was a material misstatement or omission on a report (usually Form 10-K) filed with SEC
   c. Plaintiff must prove reliance on Form 10-K (this, in past, has limited the number of cases under Section 18)
   d. If "a.", "b.", and "c." are proven, burden of proof is shifted to accountant who may escape liability by proving s/he acted in "good faith"

1) Although basis of liability here is not in negligence, an accountant who has been grossly negligent typically will not be able to establish "good faith"
2) An accountant who has been only negligent will probably be able to establish "good faith"

5. Damages

a. Generally, difference between amount paid and market value at time of suit
b. If sold, difference between amount paid and sale price
c. Damages may not exceed investor's actual damages

6. Statute of Limitations

a. Section 10 (Rule 10b-5)--Varies by state (because all liability is implied in this section)
b. Section 18--Action must be brought within 1 year after discovery of facts and within 3 years after cause of action

E. Summary of Accountant's Civil Liability[1]

THE INDEPENDENT AUDITOR'S CIVIL LIABILITY—AN OVERVIEW

	Law						
	Common				1933 Act	1934 Act	
		Third Parties			Section 11	Section 10	Section 18
Elements of Proof	*Client*	*Primary Beneficiary*	*Foreseen*	*Ordinary*	*Stock Purchasers*	*Stock Purchasers and Sellers*	*Stock Purchasers and Sellers*
Resultant Damages	P	P	P	P	P	P	P
Material Misstatement or Omission	P	P	P	P	P	P	P
Justifiable Reliance	P	P	P	P	D[a]	P	P
Minimum Degree of Auditor Deficiency or Behavior	P(N)	P(N)	P(N or GN)	P(GN)	D(DD)	P(GN)	D(GF)

P = Burden of proof rests with plaintiff.
D = Burden of proof rests with defendant.
N = Ordinary negligence.
GN = Gross negligence.
DD = Due diligence. This term includes the auditor's ability to show good faith in the conduct of the audit and no knowledge of the material misstatement.
GF = Good faith. Auditor must prove s/he had not acted with scienter.
a = Defendent may escape liability by proving plaintiff knew of error (omission) before purchase. Plaintiff must prove reliance if an earnings statement covering at least 12 months subsequent to registration was available when security was purchased.

[1]Schultz, J. J., Jr., and K. Pany, "The Independent Auditor's Civil Liability--an Overview," The Accounting Review (April, 1980), p. 320 (adapted).

F. Legal Considerations Affecting the Accountant's Responsibility

1. Accountant's working papers
   a. Consist of notes, computations, etc. that accountant accumulates when doing professional work for client
   b. Owned by accountant unless there is agreement to the contrary
   c. Ownership is essentially custodial in nature (to serve dual purpose)
      1) To preserve confidentiality
         a) Absent client consent, cannot allow transmission of information in working papers to another
      2) Retention by accountant as evidence of nature and extent of work performed
   d. Accountant must produce, upon being given an enforceable subpoena, workpapers requested by court of law or government agency
      1) Subpoenas should be limited in scope and specific in purpose
      2) Accountant may challenge a subpoena as being too broad and unreasonably burdensome
2. Privileged communications between accountant and client
   a. Do not exist at common law so must be created by statute
      1) Only a few states have privileged communications
      2) Federal law does not recognize privileged communications
   b. To be considered privileged, accountant-client communication must
      1) Be located in a jurisdiction where recognized
      2) Have been intended to be confidential at time of communication
      3) Not be waived by client
   c. If considered privileged, valid grounds exist for accountant to refuse to testify in court concerning these matters
      1) This privilege is for benefit of client
      2) Can be waived by client
      3) If part of privileged communication is allowed, all of privilege is lost
   d. Code of Professional Ethics prohibits disclosure of confidential client data unless
      1) Client consents
      2) To comply with GAAS and GAAP
      3) To comply with enforceable subpoena (e.g., courts where privilege not recognized)
      4) Quality review under AICPA authorization
      5) Responding to AICPA or state trial board
3. Acts of employees
   a. Accountant is liable for acts of employees in the course of employment (see AGENCY)

      EXAMPLE: XYZ, a partnership of CPAs, hires Y to help perform an audit. Y is negligent in the audit causing the client damage. The partners cannot escape liability by showing they did not perform the negligent act.

   b. Insurance used to avoid loss

4. Duty to perform audit is not delegable because it is contract for personal services. See CONTRACTS, Assignment and Delegation.

5. Generally, basis of relationship of accountant to his/her client is that of independent contractor (see AGENCY)

6. Insurance

   a. Accountants' malpractice insurance covers their negligence
   b. Fidelity bond protects client from accountant's fraud
   c. Client's insurance company is subrogated to client's rights (i.e., has same rights of recovery of loss against accountant that client had)

7. Reliance by auditor on other auditor's work

   a. Principle auditor still liable for all work unless audit report clearly indicates divided responsibility
   b. Cannot rely on unaudited data; must disclaim or qualify opinion

8. Subsequent events and subsequent discovery

   a. Generally not liable on audit report for effect of events subsequent to last day of fieldwork

      1) Unless report is dated as of the subsequent event
      2) Liability extends to effective date of registration for reports filed with SEC

   b. Liable if subsequently discovered facts that existed at report date indicate statements were misleading unless

      1) Immediate investigation is conducted, and
      2) Prompt revision of statements is possible, or
      3) SEC and persons known to be relying on statements are notified by client or CPA

9. Liability from preparation of unaudited financial statements

   a. Financial statements are unaudited if

      1) No auditing procedures have been applied
      2) Insufficient audit procedures have been applied to express an opinion

   b. Failure to mark each page, "unaudited"
   c. Failure to issue a disclaimer of opinion
   d. Failure to inform client of any discovery of something amiss

      1) E.g., circumstances indicating presence of fraud

G. Criminal Liability

1. Sources of Liability

   a. Securities Act of 1933 (Section 24)
   b. Securities Exchange Act of 1934 (Section 32)
   c. Various other federal statutes (e.g., Federal Mail Fraud Statute, Federal Wire Fraud Statute, Federal False Statement Statute)
   d. Various state laws

2. General Proof Requirements
   a. Prosecution must prove that defendent realized s/he was performing a wrongful act or
   b. Defendent deliberately closed his/her eyes to facts s/he had a duty to see
3. Examples of Possible Criminal Actions
   a. CPA aids management in a fraudulent scheme
   b. CPA covers up prior year financial statement misstatements
4. Criminal Violations of Internal Revenue Code
   a. For willfully preparing false return (perjury)
   b. For willfully assisting others to evade taxes (tax evasion)

H. Liability of Income Tax Return Preparers (1976 and 1978 Revenue Acts, 1982 Tax Equity and Fiscal Responsibility Act)

1. Definitions
   a. Preparer - an individual who prepares for compensation, or who employs one or more persons to prepare for compensation, a return, or a substantial portion of a return, under Subtitle A of the Internal Revenue Code, or a claim for refund. Subtitle A of the Internal Revenue Code covers income tax returns; as such, the preparer of an excise tax return, a gift tax return, or an estate tax return is not considered a preparer subject to the requirements and penalties described below.
      1) A preparer need not be enrolled to practice before the Internal Revenue Service. Preparation of tax returns is not included under the concept of "practice before the IRS."
   b. Compensation - must be received and can be implied or explicit [e.g., a person who does his neighbor's return and receives a gift has not been compensated. An accountant who prepares the individual return of the president of a company, for which he performs the audit, for no additional fee as part of a prior agreement has been compensated (implied)].
2. Requirements
   a. Preparer must sign returns done for compensation
      1) Must be a manual signature
      2) Include preparer's identification number and address
   b. Returns and claims for refund must contain the identification number of the preparer and the identification number of that preparer's employer or partnership, if any
   c. Preparer must provide a finished copy of the return or refund claim to the taxpayer before or at the time when s/he presents a copy to her/him for signing
   d. Employers of income tax preparers must retain information on all preparers employed by them as follows:
      1) Name
      2) Taxpayer identification number
      3) Principal place of work
   e. Preparer must either keep a list of those for whom returns were filed with the following information, or copies of the actual returns, for a minimum of three years

1) Name
2) Taxpayer identification number
3) Taxable year
4) Type of return or claim for refund filed

3. Preparer penalties

a. The general period for assessing preparer penalties is three years; however, there is no statutory limitation for preparer fraud

b. Negligent or intentional disregard for the "rules and regulations" which results in an understatement of the taxpayer's liability is subject to a $100 penalty

1) The rules and regulations include the Internal Revenue Code, the Treasury Regulations, and Revenue Rulings
2) A reasonable position that is disclosed in the return and is taken contrary to the existing rules and regulations in good faith is <u>not</u> considered to be negligence or intentional disregard
3) The preparer bears the burden of proof

c. Willful disregard for the "rules and regulations" resulting in an understatement of the taxpayer's liability is subject to a $500 penalty

1) There is no limitation for assessing the penalty for willful disregard of the "rules and regulations"

d. Additional penalties related to the requirements imposed upon a tax return preparer

1) Failure to furnish the taxpayer with a copy of the return or claim for refund. A $25 penalty per failure.
2) Failure to retain copies of the returns for at least three years, or a list of clients. A $50 penalty per failure subject to a maximum of $25,000.
3) Failure to sign a return. A $25 penalty per failure.
4) Failure to include social security number or employer identification number. A $25 penalty per failure.
5) Failure by an employer to prepare and make available a list of preparers. Subject to a penalty of $100 or $5 per item missing from the list.
6) The preparer indorsing or negotiating a refund check issued to the taxpayer is subject to a $500 penalty per occurrence

e. Promoting abusive tax shelters, etc.

1) Any person who

a) Organizes and/or participates in the sale of any interest
b) Makes a statement with respect to the allowability of deduction or credit, or
c) Makes a gross valuation overstatement as to any material matter

2) Such person shall pay a penalty equal to the greater of $1,000 or 10% of the income to be derived by such person from the activity

f. Penalties for aiding and abetting understatement of tax liability

   1) Any person who assists in the preparation of a document under the internal revenue laws knowing that such information will be used in connection with a material matter and that the information will result in an understatement of the tax liability will be subject to a $1,000 penalty unless the understatement applies to the liability of a corporation where the penalty is $10,000

g. Fraud and false statements

   1) Any person who

      a) Willfully subscribes to a return, statement, or other document which is verified by a written declaration that is made under the penalties of perjury, and which s/he does not believe to be true and correct as to every material matter; or

      b) Willfully aids, counsels, advises, etc. in the fraudulent preparation of such documents

   2) Such person is guilty of a felony and upon conviction shall be fined not more than $100,000 ($500,000 in the case of a corporation) or imprisoned not more than 3 years, or both, together with the costs of prosecution

h. Disclosure or use of information by preparers of returns

   1) Any preparer who discloses any information furnished to him/her for the preparation of a return or uses the information for any purposes other than to prepare such a return is guilty of a misdemeanor

   2) Such preparer shall be fined no more than $1,000, or imprisoned not more than one year, or both, plus payment of the costs of prosecution

4. An injunction can be sought by the IRS to prohibit an income tax preparer from engaging in the following practices

   a. Actions subject to disclosure requirement penalties and understatement of liability penalties
   b. Actions subject to criminal penalties under the Code
   c. Misrepresentation of the preparer's eligibility to practice, experience, or education as an income tax preparer
   d. Guaranteeing the payment of a tax refund or allowance of a tax credit
   e. Other actions of a fraudulent or deceptive nature that substantially interfere with proper administration of the Internal Revenue Law

Multiple Choice Questions (1–20)

1. In a common law action against an accountant, the lack of privity is a viable defense if the plaintiff
   a. Bases his action upon fraud.
   b. Is the accountant's client.
   c. Is a creditor of the client who sues the accountant for negligence.
   d. Can prove the presence of gross negligence which amounts to a reckless disregard for the truth.

2. Rhodes Corp. desired to acquire the common stock of Harris Corp. and engaged Johnson & Co., CPAs, to audit the financial statements of Harris Corp. Johnson failed to discover a significant liability in performing the audit. In a common law action against Johnson, Rhodes at a minimum must prove
   a. Gross negligence on the part of Johnson.
   b. Negligence on the part of Johnson.
   c. Fraud on the part of Johnson.
   d. Johnson knew that the liability existed.

3. Dexter and Co., CPAs, issued an unqualified opinion on the 1983 financial statements of Bart Corp. Late in 1984, Bart determined that its treasurer had embezzled over $1,000,000. Dexter was unaware of the embezzlement. Bart has decided to sue Dexter to recover the $1,000,000. Bart's suit is based upon Dexter's failure to discover the missing money while performing the audit. Which of the following is Dexter's best defense?
   a. That the audit was performed in accordance with GAAS.
   b. Dexter had **no** knowledge of the embezzlement.
   c. The financial statements were presented in conformity with GAAP.
   d. The treasurer was Bart's agent and as such had designed the internal controls which facilitated the embezzlement.

4. In an action for negligence against a CPA, "the custom of the profession" standard is used at least to some extent in determining whether the CPA is negligent. Which of the following statements describes how this standard is applied?
   a. If the CPA proves he literally followed GAAP and GAAS, it will be conclusively presumed that the CPA was **not** negligent.
   b. The custom of the profession argument may only be raised by the defendant.
   c. Despite a CPA's adherence to the custom of the profession, negligence may nevertheless be present.
   d. Failure to satisfy the custom of the profession is equivalent to gross negligence.

5. Locke, CPA, was engaged by Hall, Inc., to audit Willow Company. Hall purchased Willow after receiving Willow's audited financial statements, which included Locke's unqualified auditor's opinion. Locke was negligent in the performance of the Willow audit engagement. As a result of Locke's negligence, Hall suffered damages of $75,000. Hall appears to have grounds to sue Locke for

	Breach of contract	*Negligence*
a.	Yes	Yes
b.	Yes	No
c.	No	Yes
d.	No	No

6. A CPA was engaged by Jackson & Wilcox, a small retail partnership, to examine its financial statements. The CPA discovered that due to other commitments, the engagement could not be completed on time. The CPA, therefore, unilaterally delegated the duty to Vincent, an equally competent CPA. Under these circumstances, which of the following is true?
   a. The duty to perform the audit engagement is delegable in that it is determined by an objective standard.
   b. If Jackson & Wilcox refuses to accept Vincent because of a personal dislike of Vincent by one of the partners, Jackson & Wilcox will be liable for breach of contract.
   c. Jackson & Wilcox must accept the delegation in that Vincent is equally competent.
   d. The duty to perform the audit engagement is nondelegable and Jackson & Wilcox need not accept Vincent as a substitute if they do not wish to do so.

7. To recover in a common law action based upon fraud against a CPA with regard to an audit of financial statements, the plaintiff must prove among other things
   a. Privity of contract.
   b. Unavailability of any other cause of action.
   c. That there was a sale or purchase of securities within a six-month period that resulted in a loss.
   d. Reliance on the financial statements.

8. If a stockholder sues a CPA for common law fraud based upon false statements contained in the financial statements audited by the CPA, which of the following is the CPA's best defense?

a. The stockholder lacks privity to sue.
b. The CPA disclaimed liability to all third parties in the engagement letter.
c. The contributory negligence of the client.
d. The false statements were immaterial.

9. Lewis & Clark, CPAs, rendered an unqualified opinion on the financial statements of a company that sold common stock in a public offering subject to the Securities Act of 1933. Based on a false statement in the financial statements, Lewis & Clark are being sued by an investor who purchased shares of this public offering. Which of the following represents a viable defense?

a. The investor has **not** met the burden of proving fraud or negligence by Lewis & Clark.
b. The investor did **not** actually rely upon the false statement.
c. Detection of the false statement by Lewis & Clark occurred after their examination date.
d. The false statement is immaterial in the overall context of the financial statements.

10. Major, Major & Sharpe, CPAs, are the auditors of MacLain Industries. In connection with the public offering of $10 million of MacLain securities, Major expressed an unqualified opinion as to the financial statements. Subsequent to the offering, certain misstatements and omissions were revealed. Major has been sued by the purchasers of the stock offered pursuant to the registration statement which included the financial statements audited by Major. In the ensuing lawsuit by the MacLain investors, Major will be able to avoid liability if

a. The errors and omissions were caused primarily by MacLain.
b. It can be shown that at least some of the investors did **not** actually read the audited financial statements.
c. It can prove due diligence in the audit of the financial statements of MacLain.
d. MacLain had expressly assumed any liability in connection with the public offering.

11. A CPA is subject to criminal liability if the CPA

a. Refuses to turn over the working papers to the client.
b. Performs an audit in a negligent manner.
c. Willfully omits a material fact required to be stated in a registration statement.
d. Willfully breaches the contract with the client.

12. Josephs & Paul is a growing medium-sized partnership of CPAs. One of the firm's major clients is considering offering its stock to the public. This will be the firm's first client to go public. Which of the following is true with respect to this engagement?

a. If the client is a service corporation, the Securities Act of 1933 will not apply.
b. If the client is not going to be listed on an organized exchange, the Securities Exchange Act of 1934 will not apply.
c. The Securities Act of 1933 imposes important additional potential liability on Josephs & Paul.
d. As long as Josephs & Paul engages exclusively in intrastate business, the federal securities laws will not apply.

13. A CPA firm is being sued by a third-party purchaser of securities sold in interstate commerce to the public. The third party is relying upon the Securities Act of 1933. The CPA firm had issued an unqualified opinion on incorrect financial statements. Which of the following represents the best defense available to the CPA firm?

a. The securities sold had not been registered with the SEC.
b. The CPA firm had returned the entire fee it charged for the engagement to the corporation.
c. The third party was not in privity of contract with the CPA firm.
d. The action had not been commenced within one year after the discovery of the material misrepresentation.

14. Doe and Co., CPAs, issued an unqualified opinion on the 1983 financial statements of Marx Corp. These financial statements were included in Marx's annual report and form 10K filed with the SEC. Doe did not detect material misstatements in the financial statements as a result of negligence in the performance of the audit. Based upon the financial statements, Fitch purchased stock in Marx. Shortly thereafter, Marx became insolvent, causing the price of the stock to decline drastically. Fitch has commenced legal action against Doe for damages based upon section 10(b) and

rule 10b-5 of the Securities Exchange Act of 1934. Doe's best defense to such an action would be that

a. Fitch lacks privity to sue.
b. The engagement letter specifically disclaimed all liability to third parties.
c. There is **no** proof of scienter.
d. There has been **no** subsequent sale for which a loss can be computed.

15. The accountant-client privilege

a. May **not** be waived by either the accountant or the client.
b. Is intended to protect full and honest disclosure between accountant and client.
c. Is as widely recognized as the attorney-client privilege.
d. Only applies to written documents.

16. Working papers prepared by a CPA in connection with an audit engagement are owned by the CPA, subject to certain limitations. The rationale for this rule is to

a. Protect the working papers from being subpoenaed.
b. Provide the basis for excluding admission of the working papers as evidence because of the privileged communication rule.
c. Provide the CPA with evidence and documentation which may be helpful in the event of a lawsuit.
d. Establish a continuity of relationship with the client whereby indiscriminate replacement of CPAs is discouraged.

17. Gaspard & Devlin, a medium-sized CPA firm, employed Marshall as a staff accountant. Marshall was negligent in auditing several of the firm's clients. Under these circumstances which of the following statements is true?

a. Gaspard & Devlin is not liable for Marshall's negligence because CPAs are generally considered to be independent contractors.
b. Gaspard & Devlin would not be liable for Marshall's negligence if Marshall disobeyed specific instructions in the performance of the audits.
c. Gaspard & Devlin can recover against its insurer on its malpractice policy even if one of the partners was also negligent in reviewing Marshall's work.
d. Marshall would have no personal liability for negligence.

18. A preparer of a tax return may incur penalties under the Internal Revenue Code in all of the following cases **except** where the taxpayer

a. Substantially overvalues property donated to a charitable organization.
b. Claims a substantial deduction for unpaid expenses incurred by the cash basis taxpayer.
c. Claims a substantial deduction for a loss resulting from an accidental fire.
d. Takes a position at variance with the Internal Revenue Code and a U.S. Supreme Court decision on the specific point.

19. Alex Stone, CPA, prepared Ray Pym's 1983 federal income tax return. Pym advised Stone that he had paid doctors' bills of $15,000 during 1983, when in fact Pym had paid only $3,000 of bills. Based on Pym's representations, Stone properly computed the medical expense deduction, with consequent understatement of tax liability of more than $5,000. Pym's total tax liability shown on the return was $40,000. Stone had no reason to doubt the accuracy of Pym's figures, although Stone did not request documentation for the expenses claimed; but he was assured by Pym that sufficient corroborative evidence of these expenses existed. In connection with Stone's preparation of Pym's 1983 return, Stone is

a. Not subject to any IRS penalty or interest.
b. Not subject to any IRS penalty, but is liable for interest on the underpayment of tax.
c. Subject to the negligence penalty.
d. Subject to the penalty for willful understatement of tax liability.

20. The Internal Revenue Code provisions dealing with tax return preparation

a. Require tax return preparers who are neither attorneys nor CPAs to pass a basic qualifying examination.
b. Apply to all tax return preparers whether they are compensated or uncompensated.
c. Apply to a CPA who prepares the tax returns of the president of a corporation the CPA audits, without charging the president.
d. Only apply to preparers of individual tax returns.

Problems

Problem 1 (1180,L4)

(15 to 20 minutes)

Part a. Whitlow & Company is a brokerage firm registered under the Securities Exchange Act of 1934. The Act requires such a brokerage firm to file audited financial statements with the SEC annually. Mitchell & Moss, Whitlow's CPAs, performed the annual audit for the year ended December 31, 1979, and rendered an unqualified opinion, which was filed with the SEC along with Whitlow's financial statements. During 1979 Charles, the president of Whitlow & Company, engaged in a huge embezzlement scheme that eventually bankrupted the firm. As a result substantial losses were suffered by customers and shareholders of Whitlow & Company, including Thaxton who had recently purchased several shares of stock of Whitlow & Company after reviewing the company's 1979 audit report. Mitchell & Moss' audit was deficient; if they had complied with generally accepted auditing standards, the embezzlement would have been discovered. However, Mitchell & Moss had no knowledge of the embezzlement nor could their conduct be categorized as reckless.

Required:

Answer the following, setting forth reasons for any conclusions stated.

1. What liability to Thaxton, if any, does Mitchell & Moss have under the Securities Exchange Act of 1934?

2. What theory or theories of liability, if any, are available to Whitlow & Company's customers and shareholders under the common law?

Part b. Jackson is a sophisticated investor. As such, she was initially a member of a small group who was going to participate in a private placement of $1 million of common stock of Clarion Corporation. Numerous meetings were held among management and the investor group. Detailed financial and other information was supplied to the participants. Upon the eve of completion of the placement, it was aborted when one major investor withdrew. Clarion then decided to offer $2.5 million of Clarion common stock to the public pursuant to the registration requirements of the Securities Act of 1933. Jackson subscribed to $300,000 of the Clarion public stock offering. Nine months later, Clarion's earnings dropped significantly and as a result the stock dropped 20% beneath the offering price. In addition, the Dow Jones Industrial Average was down 10% from the time of the offering.

Jackson has sold her shares at a loss of $60,000 and seeks to hold all parties liable who participated in the public offering including Allen, Dunn, and Rose, Clarion's CPA firm. Although the audit was performed in conformity with generally accepted auditing standards, there were some relatively minor irregularities. The financial statements of Clarion Corporation, which were part of the registration statement, contained minor misleading facts. It is believed by Clarion and Allen, Dunn, and Rose that Jackson's asserted claim is without merit.

Required:

Answer the following, setting forth reasons for any conclusions stated.

1. Assuming Jackson sues under the Securities Act of 1933, what will be the basis of her claim?

2. What are the probable defenses which might be asserted by Allen, Dunn, and Rose in light of these facts?

Problem 2 (582,L3)

(15 to 20 minutes)

Part a. Ralph Sharp, CPA, has audited the Fargo Corporation for the last ten years. It was recently discovered that Fargo's top management has been engaged in some questionable financial activities since the last audited financial statements were issued.

Subsequently, Fargo was sued in state court by its major competitor, Nuggett, Inc. In addition, the SEC commenced an investigation against Fargo for possible violations of the federal securities laws.

Both Nuggett and the SEC have subpoenaed all of Sharp's workpapers relating to his audits of Fargo for the last ten years. There is no evidence either that Sharp did anything improper or that any questionable financial activities by Fargo occurred prior to this year.

Sharp estimates that the cost for his duplicate photocopying of all of the workpapers would be $25,000 (approximately one year's audit fee). Fargo has instructed Sharp not to turn over the workpapers to anyone.

Required:

Answer the following, setting forth reasons for any conclusions stated.

1. If Sharp practices in a state which has a statutory accountant–client privilege, may the state's accountant—client privilege be successfully asserted to avoid turning over the workpapers to the SEC?

2. Assuming Sharp, with Fargo's permission, turns over to Nuggett workpapers for the last two audit years, may the state's accountant—client privilege be successfully asserted to avoid producing the workpapers for the first eight years?

3. Other than asserting an accountant—client privilege, what major defenses might Sharp raise against the SEC and Nuggett in order to resist turning over the subpoenaed workpapers?

Part b. Pelham & James, CPAs, were retained by Tom Stone, sole proprietor of Stone Housebuilders, to compile Stone's financial statements. Stone advised Pelham & James that the financial statements would be used in connection with a possible incorporation of the business and sale of stock to friends. Prior to undertaking the engagement, Pelham & James were also advised to pay particular attention to the trade accounts payable. They agreed to use every reasonable means to determine the correct amount.

At the time Pelham & James were engaged, the books and records were in total disarray. Pelham & James proceeded with the engagement applying all applicable procedures for compiling financial statements. They failed, however, to detect and disclose in the financial statements Stone's liability for certain unpaid bills. Documentation concerning those bills was available for Pelham & James' inspection had they looked. This omission led to a material understatement ($60,000) of the trade accounts payable.

Pelham & James delivered the compiled financial statements to Tom Stone with their compilation report which indicated that they did not express an opinion or any other assurance regarding the financial statements. Tom Stone met with two prospective investors, Dickerson and Nichols. At the meeting, Pelham & James stated that they were confident that the trade accounts payable balance was accurate to within $8,000.

Stone Housebuilders was incorporated. Dickerson and Nichols, relying on the financial statements, became stockholders along with Tom Stone. Shortly thereafter, the understatement of trade accounts payable was detected. As a result, Dickerson and Nichols discovered that they had paid substantially more for the stock than it was worth at the time of purchase.

Required:

Answer the following, setting forth reasons for any conclusions stated.

Will Pelham & James be found liable to Dickerson and Nichols in a common law action for their damages?

Problem 3 (584,L2)

(15 to 20 minutes)

Perfect Products Co. applied for a substantial bank loan from Capitol City Bank. In connection with its application, Perfect engaged William & Co., CPAs, to audit its financial statements. William completed the audit and rendered an unqualified opinion. On the basis of the financial statements and William's opinion, Capitol granted Perfect a loan of $500,000.

Within three months after the loan was granted, Perfect filed for bankruptcy. Capitol promptly brought suit against William for damages, claiming that it had relied to its detriment on misleading financial statements and the unqualified opinion of William.

William's audit workpapers reveal negligence and possible other misconduct in the performance of the audit. Nevertheless, William believes it can defend against liability to Capitol based on the privity defense.

Required:

Answer the following, setting forth reasons for any conclusions stated.

1. Explain the privity defense and evaluate its application to William.

2. What exceptions to the privity defense might Capitol argue?

Problem 4 (585,L4)

(15 to 20 minutes)

Arthur & Doyle, CPAs, served as auditors for Dunbar Corp. and Wolfe Corp., publicly held corporations listed on the American Stock Exchange. Dunbar recently acquired Wolfe Corp. pursuant to a statutory merger by issuing its shares in exchange for shares of Wolfe. In connection with that merger, Arthur & Doyle rendered an unqualified opinion on the financial statements and participated in the preparation of the pro forma unaudited financial statements contained in the combined prospectus and proxy statement circulated to obtain shareholder approval of the merger and to register the shares to be issued in connection with the merger. Dunbar prepared a form 8-K (the current report with unaudited financial statements) and form 10-K (the annual report with audited financial statements) in connection with the merger. Shortly thereafter, financial disaster beset the merged company which resulted in large losses to the shareholders and creditors. A class action suit on behalf of the shareholders and creditors has been filed against Dunbar and its management. In addition, it names Arthur & Doyle as co-defendants, challenging the fairness, accuracy, and truthfulness of the financial statements.

Required:

Answer the following, setting forth reasons for any conclusions stated.

As a result of the CPAs having expressed an unqualified opinion on the audited financial statements of Dunbar and Wolfe and as a result of having participated in the preparation of the unaudited financial statements required in connection with the merger, indicate and briefly discuss the various bases of the CPAs' potential civil liability to the shareholders and creditors of Dunbar under:

a. The federal securities acts.

b. State common law.

Multiple Choice Answers

1.	c	5.	a	9.	d	13.	d	17.	c
2.	b	6.	d	10.	c	14.	c	18.	c
3.	a	7.	d	11.	c	15.	b	19.	a
4.	c	8.	d	12.	c	16.	c	20.	c

Multiple Choice Answer Explanations

A. Common Law Liability to Clients

1. (1184,L1,1) (c) Privity of contract between an accountant and others denotes a mutual legal relationship to each other by virtue of being parties to the same contract. Where privity with the accountant is present, a suit may be brought against the accountant for breach of contract if it can be proved that the accountant was negligent in the performance of his/her duties. Clients and third-party primary beneficiaries are considered to have privity of contract with the accountant, and thus may sue in the case of negligence. Therefore, answer (b) is incorrect. However, other third parties, for whose express purpose the audit was not undertaken, are not considered to have privity of contract with the accountant. Therefore, in a common law action against an accountant, the lack of privity is a viable defense if the plaintiff is a creditor of the client who sues the accountant, for negligence. In the case of fraud or gross negligence which amounts to a reckless disregard for the truth (i.e., constructive fraud), the accountant is liable not only to those parties considered to have privity, but to other third parties who relied on the misrepresentation. Therefore, answers (a) and (d) are incorrect.

2. (1184,L1,2) (b) In this case, it is important first to note that the client is not the firm being audited. In other words, Rhodes Corp., not Harris Corp., is the client. Under common law the accountant can be held liable to the client for negligence, which is the failure to exercise due care. Therefore, Rhodes Corp. must prove at a minimum that Johnson & Co. failed to do that which an ordinary, reasonable, prudent accountant would do under the same or similar circumstances. Answers (a), (c) and (d) are incorrect since they describe situations in which Johnson could only be held liable for something greater than ordinary negligence.

3. (1184,L1,6) (a) The final objective of an external financial audit is to express an opinion as to the fairness of the financial statements in accordance with GAAP. In meeting this objective, the CPA must adhere to GAAS. At no time during the audit does the CPA assure that all material errors or irregularities will be detected. Therefore, if Dexter and Co. prove that the audit was performed in accordance with GAAS, they will not be held liable to Bart for their failure to detect the treasurer's embezzlement. Note, however, that if Bart could establish a lack of reasonable care on the part of Dexter in performance of the audit, Dexter would be held responsible if the irregularity would have been discovered in an audit performed with average professional care and skill. Answer (b) is incorrect because proof of knowledge of the embezzlement is not necessary when suing the CPA for negligence. Answer (c) is incorrect because proof that the financial statements were presented in conformity with GAAP would prove only that management had fulfilled its responsibility in the preparation of those statements and would say nothing about the level of skill and care exercised by the CPA in the performance of the audit. Answer (d) is incorrect because it, too, implies nothing as to the level of skill and care exercised in the performance of the audit.

4. (1183,L1,4) (c) Despite a CPA's adherence to custom of the profession, negligence may nevertheless be present. In certain cases the SEC and the courts have held that even though the CPA adhered to GAAP and GAAS, negligence was present when misleading financial statements resulted. Answer (a) is incorrect because literal adherence to GAAP and GAAS will be persuasive, but not conclusive, in proving that the CPA was not negligent. Answer (b) is incorrect because the custom of the profession argument may be raised by the plaintiff—client to prove that the CPA's deviation from that standard constituted negligence. Answer (d) is incorrect because failure to satisfy the custom of the profession constitutes negligence, but not gross negligence. To prove gross negligence, the client would have to show a reckless disregard for the truth by the CPA.

5. (1183,L1,1) (a) Breach of contract and negligence are two potential common law grounds upon which Hall, Inc. may sue Locke. Hall may sue for negligence if Locke fails to exercise due care in the performance of the audit. Due care, in this case, means that degree of care which the reasonable CPA would exercise in this circumstance. Also, Hall may sue for breach of contract if Locke contracts to perform an audit and issues a standard report, but does not make an examination of the financials in accordance with GAAS. Locke did not discharge his contractual obligation. Since the facts indicate that Locke was negligent in his/her performance of the audit, it appears that Hall, Inc. has grounds to sue Locke under both breach of contract and negligence.

6. (1177,L1,3) (d) The duty to perform the audit is not delegable, because the audit is a contract for personal services based on personal trust or character. Only in certain cases, i.e., where services are mechanical and only the end result is desired, can personal services be delegated, e.g., moving goods, but never an audit. Jackson and Wilcox need not accept Vincent as a substitute, but they may if they wish. Thus answers (a) and (c) are incorrect. Answer (b) is incorrect because since Jackson and Wilcox have no duty to accept Vincent, they may refuse him for any reason, even personal dislike.

B. Common Law Liability to Third Parties (Nonclients)

7. (1184,L1,3) (d) To recover in a common law action based upon fraud against a CPA with regard to the audit of financial statements, the plaintiff must prove that damages were incurred, that there was a material misstatement or omission of a material fact on the financial statements, and that he justifiably relied on the financial statements which led to the damages. Answer (d) is correct since it describes the latter of these requirements. Answer (a) is incorrect because proof of privity of contract between the plaintiff and the CPA is not needed when attempting to recover in a common law action based upon fraud. To recover in an action based upon the negligence of the CPA, proof of privity of contract is usually required. Answers (b) and (c) are incorrect because the plaintiff is neither required to prove the unavailability of another course of action nor that there was a sale or purchase of securities within a six-month period that resulted in a loss.

8. (1184,L1,7) (d) Under common law, a third party (e.g., a stockholder) attempting to sue a CPA for fraud must prove that damages were incurred, there was a material misstatement or omission of a material fact in the financial statements, and that there was justifiable reliance on the financial statements which led to the damages. Of the defenses listed, answer (d) is the best defense because it relates directly to the second requirement stated above. Answer (a) is incorrect because common law does not require privity to be established in a suit for fraud against a CPA based on false statements contained in the financial statements audited by the CPA. Answer (b) is incorrect because CPAs cannot release themselves from liabilities to third parties by specifically disclaiming such liability in the engagement letter. Answer (c) is incorrect because proof of the client's contributory negligence will not relieve the CPA of liability to third parties.

C. Statutory Liability to Third Parties — Securities Act of 1933

9. (1183,L1,5) (d) Section II of the Securities Act of 1933 makes it unlawful for a registration statement to contain an untrue material fact or to omit a material fact. Under the 1933 Act, the plaintiff must prove damages were incurred and that there was a **material** misstatement or omission in the financials included in the registration statement. Thus, proving that the false statement is **immaterial** is a viable defense. Other viable defenses are the due diligence defense, proving that the plaintiff knew the financials were incorrect when the investment was made, and proving the loss was caused by factors other than the misstatement or omission. Answer (a) is incorrect because the plaintiff need not prove fraud or negligence. Answer (b) is incorrect because the plaintiff need not prove reliance on the financials (unless the securities were purchased after the CPA firm issued an income statement covering at least 12 months subsequent to the effective date of the registration statement). Answer (c) is incorrect because Lewis & Clark's unqualified opinion, included in the registration statement, is a certification of the financials as of the time the registration statement becomes effective. Thus, it extends Lewis & Clark's legal liability from the examination date to the effective date. They would have a duty to disclose the detection of the false statement.

10. (581,L1,3) (c) The SEC Act of 1933 concerns the regulation of initial public offerings of stock. The Act requires the filing of a registration statement including a certified financial statement. Any person acquiring a security covered by the registration can sue the accountant, if the certified financial statements contained false statements or omitted material facts. The presence of such misstatements and omissions is prima facie evidence that the accountant is liable. This means that plaintiff-purchaser does not have the burden of proving the accountant's negligence; the accountant must prove he was not negligent and that he acted with due diligence (skill and care of the average accountant). Answer (a) is incorrect since the auditor's certification of the financial statements covers management's representations. The fact that the errors were caused by MacLain's actions will not relieve the auditor of liability. Answer (b) is also incorrect since the plaintiff does not have to prove reliance on the financial statements or that the loss was suffered from the misstatement. Answer (d) is incorrect since MacLain's express assumption of liability will not relieve the auditor.

11. (1177,L1,1) (c) Criminal liability is only incurred by violating a statute. A CPA who willfully omits a material fact required to be stated in a registration statement is in violation of the Securities Acts and is subject to criminal liability. Civil liability is incurred by violating a legal duty owed to another. Answers (b) and (d) are incorrect because performing an audit in a negligent manner and willfully breaching a contract are violations of a legal duty owed to another and give rise to civil liability. Answer (a) is incorrect because a CPA owns his workpapers and has no duty to turn them over to a client.

12. (1177,L1,9) (c) Before the client goes public, Josephs & Paul is only liable to the client and known intended third-party beneficiaries (i.e., users) of the financial statements, absent fraud or constructive fraud. After the client "goes public" and becomes subject to the 1933 Act, Josephs & Paul may be held liable by any purchaser of the securities for any misleading statement in addition to incurring criminal liability. Answer (a) is incorrect because the Securities Act of 1933 covers the initial sales of securities regardless of the seller's form of organization. Answer (b) is incorrect because the Securities Exchange Act of 1934 applies to over-the-counter stocks in addition to securities listed on organized exchanges. Answer (d) is incorrect because the securities acts apply to securities sold in interstate commerce or through the mails even if the seller or its CPAs conduct business wholly intrastate.

13. (1178,L1,11) (d) The best defense for the CPA firm is that the third-party purchaser failed to commence his action within one year after discovery of the untrue statement or omission, or after such discovery should have been made by the exercise of reasonable diligence. This is the statute of limitations under the Securities Act of 1933. Answer (a) is not the best defense, because these securities should have been registered with the SEC and therefore the CPA firm can be held liable under the 1933 Act whether or not the securities were registered. Answer (b) is not the best defense because an accountant can be held liable whether or not he was paid. Answer (c) is not the best defense because the Securities Act of 1933 eliminates the necessity for privity of contract.

D. Statutory Liability to Third Parties – Securities Exchange Act of 1934

14. (1184,L1,4) (c) In any legal action brought against a CPA based on Section 10(b) and Rule 10b-5 of the Securities Exchange Act of 1934, the plaintiff must prove that damages were incurred, that there was a material misstatement or omission of a material fact in the information released by the firm, that there was justifiable reliance on the information which led to the damages, and the existence of **scienter** on the part of the CPA. Scienter means that the defendant had knowledge of false information or that the information was prepared with a reckless disregard for the truth. Answer (c) is correct since it describes a situation in which the plaintiff has been unable to fulfill the scienter proof requirement under Section 10b. Answer (a) is incorrect since Section 10b and Rule 10b-5 of the Securities Exchange Act of 1934 deal with the CPA's civil liability to third-party purchasers and sellers of securities. In other words, the plaintiff need not prove privity of contract. Answer (b) is incorrect because CPAs cannot release themselves from liability to third parties by specifically disclaiming such liability in the engagement letter. Answer (d) is incorrect since a sale of the securities is not required for computation of a loss.

F.2. Privileged Communications Between Accountant and Client

15. (1184,L1,8) (b) Under common law, confidential communications between accountant and client are not recognized as privileged. Privileged accountant-client communications are strictly a creature of statute. In the minority of jurisdictions which have adopted such statutes, the purpose has been to promote and protect full and honest disclosure between accountant and client. Answer (a) is incorrect since the client, not the accountant, may waive the privilege. Answer (c) is incorrect because the attorney-client privilege is granted by common law and, consequently, is recognized in all jurisdictions. Answer (d) is incorrect because where privileged communication statutes have been adopted, they extend to both written and oral communications.

16. (1183,L1,10) (c) The rationale behind granting ownership of the working papers to the CPA who prepared them is twofold. First, the working papers are documentation of the nature and extent of the services rendered by the CPA. They are also the evidence to support the conclusions reached by the CPA. As such, they are invaluable evidence when preparing a defense in the event of a lawsuit against the CPA. Answer (a) is incorrect because even though working papers are owned by the CPA, they may be subpoenaed by a court or government agency. Answer (b) is incorrect because ownership of the working papers by the accountant is not a valid ground for refusing to produce them in evidence when required by legal process. Answer (d) is incorrect because preventing the indiscriminate replacement of CPAs is not a rationale behind granting ownership to the CPA.

F.3. Acts of Employees

17. (1177, L1,4) (c) Gaspard & Devlin can recover on its malpractice insurance no matter who in the firm was negligent, i.e., a malpractice policy insures negligence. Although CPA firms and individual practitioners are independent contractors, the firm independently contracted with the client. Answer (a) is incorrect because the firm as employer is liable for the negligence of its employees acting within the course and scope of their employment. Answer (b) is incorrect because Marshall's disobeyance of instructions would not matter because the firm is responsible for the actions of its employees. Answer (d) is incorrect because Marshall may be held personally liable either by the client, or by the firm if it is held liable by the client.

H. Liability of Income Tax Return Preparers

18. (1184,L1,9) (c) A preparer of a tax return would not incur penalties under the Internal Revenue Code where the taxpayer reduces his/her tax liability by justifiably claiming a deduction for a substantial loss, e.g., a loss resulting from an accidental fire. Answer (a) is incorrect because the preparer of a tax return will incur penalties under the Internal Revenue Code if the taxpayer's tax liability is substantially understated due to the preparer's negligence or intentional disregard of rules and regulations. Answer (b) is incorrect since a cash basis taxpayer is not allowed to deduct unpaid expenses. Answer (d) is incorrect because U.S. Supreme Court decisions constitute the law in the area of taxes. Therefore, a preparer of a tax return will incur penalties if s/he takes a position at variance with these decisions.

19. (1184,L1,10) (a) As long as the preparer of a tax return exercises due professional care in the performance of his duties, he will not incur penalties for an understatement of the taxpayer's tax liability. In this situation, the facts specify that "Stone had no reason to doubt the accuracy of Pym's figures." Since there is no evidence of negligence or willful misconduct on Stone's part, he is not subject to any IRS penalty or interest. Therefore, answers (c) and (d) are incorrect. Answer (b) is incorrect because the taxpayer, not the tax preparer, is liable for the interest on the underpayment of tax.

20. (1183,L1,6) (c) The Internal Revenue Code provisions dealing with tax return preparation apply to preparers. A preparer is defined as an individual or firm who prepares returns for compensation. The compensation can be implied or explicit. This is an example of implied compensation. Answer (a) is incorrect because anyone may prepare a return; passage of an exam is only necessary to practice before the IRS. Answer (b) is incorrect as the Code applies to compensated preparers. Answer (d) is incorrect as the Code applies to preparers of all returns or claims for refund.

Answer Outline

Problem 1 Anti-fraud Section of Security Act of 1934; Liability and Defenses Under Sec. 11(A) of 1933 Act (1180,L4)

a1. Under antifraud provision in section 10(b) of SEC Act of 1934, Thaxton is required to show
 Misstatement or omission of material fact in financials utilized in purchasing Whitlow & Co. stock
 Loss resulted from purchase of stock
 Loss resulted from reliance on misleading financials
 Auditors acted with knowledge (scienter)
 Facts indicated that proof of first three requirements by Thaxton is probable; however, facts show that auditors did not have knowledge

a2. Negligence as evidenced by failure to comply with GAAS; if auditors were negligent, customers and shareholders must show
 They had third party beneficiary status relative to auditor's contract to audit Whitlow & Co., or
 A legal duty to act without negligence was due to them

b1. Basis of claim is that loss was sustained from using misleading statements; section 11(a) of 1933 SEC Act applies
 Potential liability arises if minor irregularities result in certification of materially false or misleading financials
 Jackson's case asserts that financials contain false statement and that damages were sustained
 Jackson does not have to prove reliance of negligence (company or auditor)
 To avoid liability defendant must supply acceptable defenses

b2. Probable defenses which Allen, Dunn and Rose might assert are
 Jackson knew of false statement or omission in audited financials included in registration statement
  Jackson (plaintiff) may not recover if proof exists that she had knowledge of "untruth or omission"
  Facts indicate Jackson may have had adequate knowledge
 False statement or omission was not material; test is whether investor would have been influenced not to purchase stock if right information had been disclosed
 Loss did not result from false statement or omission
  Portion of loss probably resulted from stock market decline
  Lack of evidence linking earnings decline to false statement or omission would give auditors defense
 Departure from GAAS did not represent noncompliance with due diligence standard

Unofficial Answer

Problem 1 Anti-fraud Section of Security Act of 1934; Liability and Defenses Under Sec. 11(A) of 1933 Act (1180,L4)

Part a.

1. In order for Thaxton to hold Mitchell & Moss liable for his losses under the Securities Exchange Act of 1934, he must rely upon the antifraud provisions of section 10(b) of the act. In order to prevail Thaxton must establish that

- There was an omission or misstatement of a material fact in the financial statements used in connection with his purchase of the Whitlow & Company shares of stock.
- He sustained a loss as a result of his purchase of the shares of stock.
- His loss was caused by reliance on the misleading financial statements.
- Mitchell & Moss acted with scienter.

Based on the stated facts, Thaxton can probably prove the first three requirements cited above. To prove the fourth requirement, Thaxton must show that Mitchell & Moss had knowledge (scienter) of the fraud or recklessly disregarded the truth. The facts clearly indicate that Mitchell & Moss did not have knowledge of the fraud and did not recklessly disregard the truth.

2. The customers and shareholders of Whitlow & Company would attempt to recover on a negligence theory based on Mitchell & Moss' failure to comply with GAAS. Even if Mitchell & Moss were negligent, Whitlow & Company's customers and shareholders must also establish either that —

- They were third party beneficiaries of Mitchell & Moss' contract to audit Whitlow & Company, *or*
- Mitchell & Moss owed the customers and shareholders a legal duty to act without negligence.

Although recent cases have expanded a CPA's legal responsibilities to a third party for negligence, the facts of this case may fall within the traditional rationale limiting a CPA's liability for negligence; that is, the unfairness of imputing an indeterminate amount of liability to unknown or unforeseen parties as a result of mere negligence on the auditor's part. Accordingly, Whitlow & Company's customers and shareholders will prevail only if (1) the courts rule that they are either third-party beneficiaries or are owed a legal duty and (2) they establish that Mitchell & Moss was negligent in failing to comply with generally accepted auditing standards.

Part b.

1. The basis of Jackson's claim will be that she sustained a loss based upon misleading financial statements. Specifically, she will rely upon section 11(a) of the Securities Act of 1933, which provides the following:

> In case any part of the registration statement, when such part became effective, contained an untrue statement of a material fact or omitted to state a material fact required to be stated therein or necessary to make the statements therein not misleading, any person acquiring such security (unless it is proved that at the time of such acquisition he knew of such untruth or omission) may, either at law or in equity, in any court of competent jurisdiction, sue . . . every accountant . . . who has with his consent been named as having prepared or certified any part of the registration statement . . .

To the extent that the relatively minor irregularities resulted in the certification of materially false or misleading financial statements, there is potential liability. Jackson's case is based on the assertion of such an untrue statement or omission coupled with an allegation of damages. Jackson does not have to prove reliance on the statements nor the company's or auditor's negligence in order to recover the damages. The burden is placed on the defendant to provide defenses that will enable it to avoid liability.

2. The first defense that could be asserted is that Jackson knew of the untruth or omission in audited financial statements included in the registration statement. The act provides that the plaintiff may not recover if it can be proved that at the time of such acquisition she knew of such "untruth or omission."

Since Jackson was a member of the private placement group and presumably privy to the type of information that would be contained in a registration statement, plus any other information requested by the group, she may have had sufficient knowledge of the facts claimed to be untrue or omitted. If this be the case, then she would not be relying on the certified financial statements but upon her own knowledge.

The next defense assertable would be that the untrue statement or omission was not material. The SEC has defined the term as meaning matters about which an average prudent investor ought to be reasonably informed before purchasing the registered security. For section 11 purposes, this has been construed as meaning a fact that, had it been correctly stated or disclosed, would have deterred or tended to deter the average prudent investor from purchasing the security in question.

Allen, Dunn, and Rose would also assert that the loss in question was not due to the false statement or omission; this is, that the false statement was not the cause of the price drop. It would appear that the general decline in the stock market would account for at least a part of the loss. Additionally, if the decline in earnings was not factually connected with the false statement or omission, the defendants have another basis for refuting the causal connection between their wrongdoing and the resultant drop in the stock's price.

Finally, the accountants will claim that their departure from generally accepted auditing standards was too minor to be considered a violation of the standard of due diligence required by the act.

Answer Outline

Problem 2 Accountant—Client Privilege; Accountants' Liability for Compilation of Financial Statements (582,L3)

Part a.

1. Common law does not recognize accountant-client privilege
   - Privilege can be created by statute to be adopted by state
     - No such privilege exists under federal law
   - Subpoena issued by SEC falls within federal law
     - State statute creating privilege is not applicable
       - Sharp must produce workpapers
2. Accountant-client privilege preserves confidentiality of communications between client and accountant
   - Privilege can only be claimed by the client
     - Client may waive the statutory privilege
   - Fargo's waiver for two years of workpapers constitutes waiver of privilege for remaining years
3. SEC has power to subpoena relevant material
   - Subpoena must be limited in scope
   - Subpoena must be relevant in purpose
     - Such that compliance will not be unreasonably burdensome
   - Sharp could contend subpoena unreasonably burdensome
     - Sharp did nothing improper
     - Cost of duplicating workpapers is excessive

Part b.

Compilation of financial statements is representation of management's information
Accountants must still exercise ordinary and reasonable care
In accordance with professional standards of competence
Failure to meet these standards is negligence
Accountant liable to third party for negligence
If accountant knows services are primarily for third party
Accountant liable for constructive fraud
If shows reckless disregard for truth
Accountant had duty to all third parties to prepare reports without fraud
Third party can recover if reasonably relied on accountant's work
Pelham & James oral representation was reckless disregard for truth
Pelham & James foresaw Dickerson's and Nichols' reliance on financial representations

Unofficial Answer
(Author Modified)

Problem 2 Accountant–Client Privilege; Accountants' Liability for Compilation of Financial Statements (582,L3)

Part a.

1. No. In the absence of statute or agreement to the contrary, workpapers are generally owned by the accountant. But ownership of the workpapers is not a valid ground for refusing to produce them in evidence when such production is required by legal process. The common law recognizes no accountant–client privilege, but such privilege can be created by statute. Several states have adopted such statutes, but Congress has not. Due to the fact that the federal government has not yet granted such privilege, and this case applies federal law (i.e., federal securities laws), the accountant must produce the workpapers for the federal government or for a federal agency (i.e., SEC, IRS) if served with an enforceable subpoena. Since the matters before these agencies are based on federal law, state statutes creating the accountant–client privilege are not applicable, and no privilege exists on behalf of accountants in these proceedings. Therefore, since Sharp was served with an enforceable subpoena by the SEC, a federal agency, he must turn over the workpapers.

Also, Rule 301 of the AICPA Professional Code of Ethics, dealing with the accountant's duty not to disclose any confidential information obtained in the course of a professional audit, states that such Rule is not to be construed to affect the accountant's compliance with a validly issued subpoena.

2. No. To properly perform an audit, the accountant should have access to the details of his client's operations, many of which the client may consider confidential. The accountant–client privilege enables the accountant to obtain more complete information, by preserving the confidentiality of communications between the client and the accountant, thus promoting increased financial disclosure and greater accuracy. But where this privilege does exist, it can only be claimed by the client. This privilege belonging to the client is consistent with the AICPA Code of Professional Ethics provisions which prohibit disclosure of confidential information attained in the course of a professional engagement except with the consent of the client. Therefore, the client may waive this privilege, resulting in the accountant being required to comply with Nuggett's request. By Fargo giving permission for the introduction of two years of workpapers, this constitutes waiver of the accountant–client privilege and Sharp must comply by producing the previous eight years as well as the last two audit years.

3. Congress has endowed the SEC with power to conduct investigations. This power allows the SEC to issue subpoenaes for the production of relevant documents concerning a matter under investigation. However, this investigatory power does not provide the SEC with a "blank check." The investigation must not be of such a sweeping and broad nature and so unrelated to matters properly under inquiry as to exceed this granted investigatory power. Therefore, the subpoena issued by the SEC is required to be sufficiently limited in scope, relevant in purpose and specific so that compliance will not be unreasonably burdensome.

Because there is no evidence that Sharp did anything improper during the last ten years, Sharp could contend that a subpoena calling for the production of all his workpapers would be unreasonably burdensome and too broad in nature, thereby exceeding the SEC's investigatory power.

Although a subpoenaed party can legitimately be required to absorb reasonable expenses of compliance with administrative subpoenas, Sharp could assert that the subpoena is unduly burdensome due to the fact that the cost of producing (i.e., photocopying) all the workpapers exceeds that which a party ought reasonably be expected to bear.

Part b.

Yes. A compilation of statements is the presentation in the form of financial statements consisting of information that is the representation of management (owners), without the accountants undertaking to express any assurances on the statements. The accountants engaged for such a procedure are normally not required to make inquiries or to perform any procedures to validate or verify the information provided to them. However, Pelham & James must still exercise ordinary and reasonable care in accordance with the special skills and training of reasonably prudent auditors.

The law imposes upon the accountants the profession's generally accepted standards of competence and due care. Failure to meet these professional standards constitutes negligence. In order to have an action for negligence, the injured party does not have to be in privity of contract with the accountants, but must be a person whose reliance on the financial representations was actually foreseen by the accountant. An accountant may be held liable by third parties for ordinary negligence when the accountant knows that the services for a client are primarily for a third party. Pelham & James knew that Dickerson and Nichols were intended beneficiaries of both the compilation report and the oral statements concerning the accuracy of payables. Therefore, Pelham & James had a duty to perform with due care which appears to have been breached.

In addition, Pelham & James may be found liable for constructive fraud. The court will find constructive fraud where the performing party, based on gross negligence or willful indifference, shows a reckless disregard for the truth. Accountants owe a duty to all third parties to prepare their reports without fraud. This third party liability for fraud exists regardless of whether the accountant's services were intended primarily for the benefit of the client or primarily for the benefit of third parties. Therefore, in constructive fraud there need not be actual intent to deceive. In order for a third party to recover damages from an accountant for constructive fraud, the third party must show that s/he reasonably relied on the accountant's work.

Pelham & James were advised to pay particular attention to the trade accounts payable. They did not engage in audit verification procedures to determine the accuracy of these payables. Yet, they informed Dickerson and Nichols that the accounts payable balance was accurate to within $8,000, when in fact it was materially understated by $60,000. Such an understatement could have been discovered had the compilation been made with average professional skill and related reasonable care by inspecting Stone's unpaid bills. This indicates a reckless disregard for the truth and gross negligence. Dickerson and Nichols reasonably relied on both the financial statements and Pelham & James' oral representations. Therefore, regardless of Pelham & James' disclaimer of opinion in the compilation report concerning the financial statements, they will be found liable to Dickerson and Nichols in a common law action for damages.

Answer Outline

Problem 3 Privity Defense of the Accountant (584,L2)

1. Privity is common law concept
   - Prevents third parties from bringing legal action based upon contract on which they were not directly involved

   William was in privity with audit client, Perfect
   - But William had no contractual relationship with Capitol

   Under strict application of privity rule,
   - Capitol lacks basis for valid suit

   Privity has been subject to much reevaluation
   - Courts have frequently narrowed or rejected its application
   - But in Ultramares case privity requirement was partially retained in negligence action against CPA firm
2. First exception to privity requirement is fraud
   - Injured party has basis to sue whether privity exists or not
     - Third party must prove scienter on part of CPA

   Second exception is constructive fraud
   - Constructive fraud is false representation of material fact with lack of reasonable ground for belief and with expectation of reliance by another
   - Constructive fraud also inferred from evidence of gross negligence or recklessness

   Third exception is gross negligence
   - Gross negligence is flagrant or reckless departure from standards of due care
     - Failing to follow GAAS on material matters

   Privity will not bar third party from recovery if third party was party contract intended to benefit
   - Recovery under this theory has greatly expanded

Unofficial Answer

Problem 3 Privity Defense of the Accountant (584,L2)

1. Privity is an early common law concept which was adopted by the courts to prevent third parties from bringing a legal action based upon a contract to which they were not parties. William was in privity of contract with Perfect, its audit client, but William had no contractual relationship with Capitol despite Capitol's reliance upon the statements audited by William. Moreover, Capitol gave no consideration to William. Therefore, under strict application of the privity rule, Capitol lacks the standing to sue for breach of contract or negligence since Capitol is not in a direct contractual relationship with William.

Privity has been the subject of much critical reevaluation, and the courts have frequently narrowed or rejected it. However, in a landmark opinion (Ultramares), privity was retained to some extent in an action against a CPA firm based partially upon negligence. Some court decisions, however, have directly overruled the privity defense in actions against CPAs, particularly when the third party was contemplated as a user of the financial statements, as in this case.

2. The first major exception to the privity requirement is fraud. Although a CPA may generally avoid liability for ordinary negligence based upon privity, where the action is for fraud, an injured party has the requisite standing to sue. However, in order to recover based on fraud, the third party (Capitol) must prove scienter or guilty knowledge on the part of the CPA.

The second exception to the privity defense is constructive fraud. Constructive fraud is generally defined as a false representation of a material fact with lack of reasonable ground for belief and with an expectation of reliance by another, and, in fact, there is reasonable reliance resulting in damage. Constructive fraud may also be inferred from evidence of gross negligence or recklessness, although they are not necessarily constructive fraud in and of themselves. The dividing line between what actions will meet the scienter requirement for actual fraud and what is necessary to evoke the constructive fraud doctrine is not clear.

The third exception to the privity defense is gross negligence. Gross negligence represents an extreme, flagrant, or reckless departure from standards of due care. For example, a knowing failure to follow GAAS on a material matter might be held by a jury to be gross negligence. The jury might then find that the defendant's conduct was so gross as to satisfy the scienter requirement.

In addition to fraud and its various offshoots, one may avoid the privity barrier if it can be established by the third party that it was the party that the contract was intended to benefit. Thus, if a third party plaintiff suing a CPA can establish that the audit was for his benefit, then the injured third party may have standing to sue. He is a third party beneficiary of the contract and privity will not bar him from recovery. Recovery under this theory has been significantly expanded. It has recently been held that liability extends to those in a fixed, definable, and contemplated group whose conduct is to be governed by the contract's performance.

Answer Outline

Problem 4 CPA's Federal Statutory Liability; CPA's State Common Law Liability (585,L4)

a. Bases for third party suits under federal securities acts:
   - Misstatements or omissions in the registration statement in violation of 1933 Act
   - Fraudulent misstatements or omissions in violation of antifraud provisions of 1933 and 1934 Acts and Rule 10b-5
   - Misstatements or omissions included in forms 8-K and 10-K in violation of reporting provisions of 1934 Act
   - Misstatements or omissions included in proxy statement circulated to gain approval of merger in violation of proxy solicitation rules of 1934 Act

b. Bases for third party suits under state common law:
   - Breach of contract; shareholders and creditors, as third party beneficiaries, are in privity of contract with CPAs and therefore may claim breach of contract
   - Negligence is present when CPAs fail to exercise reasonable care; shareholders and creditors, if considered reasonably foreseen third parties, can assert negligence
   - Actual or constructive fraud; actual fraud if CPAs intentionally deceived third parties, constructive fraud if CPA's work was so deficient that it constituted gross negligence

Unofficial Answer

Problem 4 CPA's Federal Statutory Liability; CPA's State Common Law Liability (585,L4)

a. The bases for shareholders' and creditors' suits against Arthur & Doyle under federal securities acts include

- That a violation of the 1933 act has occurred as a result of misstatements or omissions in the prospectus or elsewhere in the registration statement required in order to "sell' the securities. The Securities and Exchange Commission has ruled that the issuance and exchange of stock pursuant to a merger constitutes a "sale" within the meaning of the Securities Act of 1933.
- That a violation of the anti-fraud provisions of the 1934 act and of Rule 10b-5 issued pursuant thereto has occurred since misstatements and omissions of material facts may be fraudulent. Additionally, the anti-fraud provision (Sec. 17) of the 1933 act could be asserted.
- That a violation of the reporting requirements of the Securities Exchange Act of 1934 has occurred to the extent that false or misleading statements were included or material facts were omitted in the reports or other documents relating to the merger and which were filed with the SEC.
- That a violation of the proxy rules of the Securities Exchange Act of 1934 resulted from misstatements in or omissions from the merger proxy statement used in soliciting shareholder approval.

b. The bases for shareholders' and creditors' suits against Arthur & Doyle under state common law include

- Breach of contract. The relationship between Arthur & Doyle, and Dunbar is contractual and requires that the CPAs performance be rendered in a competent manner. The shareholders and creditors may claim breach of contract as third-party beneficiaries of the contract between the CPAs and Dunbar, since it could be held that the contract was entered into for their benefit and therefore they are in privity with the CPAs.
- Negligence. The shareholders and creditors could assert an independent claim of negligence in addition to the action for breach of contract. Negligence will be established when the CPAs fail to exercise reasonable care, taking into account such superior skill and knowledge the CPAs have or hold themselves out as having. Despite their lack of contractual privity, the shareholders and creditors will probably be able to successfully assert this action if they can show that they are members of a class of persons intended to benefit from the services performed by the CPAs and that this was reasonably foreseen by the CPAs.
- Actual fraud or constructive fraud. Recent court decisions have substantially eroded the privity barrier faced by third parties. Arthur & Doyle may be held liable for actual fraud if it can be shown that they intentionally deceived the shareholders and creditors. Arthur & Doyle may be held liable for constructive fraud if there are deficiencies or lapses in their professional work of such a magnitude that they constitute gross negligence or a reckless disregard for the truth.

EMPLOYER – EMPLOYEE RELATIONSHIPS

Overview

Issues on this topic are based on the Worker's Compensation Laws and Federal Social Security Rules including the Federal Insurance Contributions Act (FICA) and the Federal Unemployment Tax Act (FUTA). These laws supplement the law of agency. In this area, emphasis is placed on the impact that state and federal laws have on the regulation of employment.

To adequately understand these materials, you should emphasize the theory and purpose underlying the Worker's Compensation laws. You should also focus on the effect that these laws have on employers and employees. Notice the changes these laws have made on common law.

Upon looking at the Federal Social Security Laws, emphasize the coverage and benefits of the respective programs.

A. Federal Social Security Act

1. Main purpose of Act is as name implies, i.e., attainment of the social security of people in our society
   a. Basic programs include
      1) Old age insurance
      2) Survivor's and disability insurance
      3) Hospital insurance (Medicare)
      4) Unemployment insurance
   b. Sources of financing for these programs
      1) Old-age, survivor's, disability, and hospital insurance programs are financed out of taxes paid by employers, employees, and self-employed under provisions of Federal Insurance Contributions Act and Self-Employment Contributions Act
      2) Unemployment insurance programs are financed out of taxes paid by employers under the Federal Unemployment Tax Act and various state unemployment insurance laws
2. Federal Insurance Contributions Act (FICA)
   a. Imposes social security tax on employees, self-employed, and employers
   b. Social security tax applies to compensation received which is considered to be wages (see "A.6.")
   c. In general, tax rates are same for both employer and employee
      1) Rates changed frequently

d. Taxes are paid only up to base amount which is also changed frequently

1) If employee pays FICA tax on more than base amount, s/he has right to refund for excess

a) May happen when employee works for two or more employers

1] These two or more employers do not get refunds

e. It is employer's duty to withhold employee's share of FICA from employee's wages and remit both employee's amount and employer's equal share to government

1) Employer is required to match FICA contributions of employees on dollar-for-dollar basis
2) If employer neglects to withhold, employer may be liable for both employee's and employer's share of taxes, i.e., to pay double tax (100% penalty)
3) Employer is required to furnish employee with written statement of wages paid and FICA contributions withheld during calendar year

f. Taxes paid by employer are deducted on tax return of employer

1) Employee may not deduct taxes paid on his/her tax return

g. Neither pension plans nor any other programs may be substituted for FICA coverage

1) Individuals receiving payments from private pension plans may also receive social security payments

3. Self-Employment Contributions Act

a. Self-employed persons are required to report their own taxable earnings and pay required social security tax
b. Self-employment income is net earnings from self-employment
c. Tax rates paid on self-employment income up to base rate

1) Since self-employed does not have employer to match the rate, tax rate is set to be less than amount paid by employer and employee together but more than amount paid by employee alone
2) Rate is amended frequently
3) Base rate is reduced by any wages earned during year because wages are subject to FICA

4. Unemployment Insurance (Federal Unemployment Tax Act - FUTA)

a. Tax is used to provide unemployment compensation benefits to workers who lose jobs and cannot find replacement work
b. Federal unemployment tax must be paid by employer if employer employs one or more persons covered by act

1) Deductible as business expense on employer's federal income tax return
2) Not deductible by employee because not paid by employee
3) Even though federal government does not tax employees, states not prohibited from doing so

c. Employer must also pay a state unemployment tax

1) An employer is entitled to credit against his/her federal unemployment tax for state unemployment taxes paid

2) State unemployment tax may be raised or lowered according to number of claims against employer
3) If employer pays a low state unemployment tax because of good employment record, then employer is entitled to additional credit against federal unemployment tax

5. Coverage under Social Security Act is mandatory for qualifying employees

   a. Person may not elect to avoid coverage
   b. Nor may person give up his/her rights in exchange for money or other benefits
   c. Must be an "employee"
   d. Services rendered must be "employment"
   e. Part-time and full-time employees are covered
   f. Compensation received must be "wages"
   g. Employees in private businesses and nonprofit organizations are covered
   h. New federal employees hired after 1983 are covered
   i. State employees under the federal act are covered
   j. Non-federal employees not permitted to withdraw

6. Definitions

   a. Wages--all compensation for employment

      1) Include

         a) Money wages
         b) Compensation in general even though not in cash
         c) Servicemen's base pay
         d) Bonuses and commissions
         e) Vacation and dismissal allowances
         f) Tips if greater than $20

      2) Exclude

         a) Wages greater than base amount (see "A.2.d.")
         b) Travel expenses
         c) Employee medical and hospital expenses paid by employer
         d) Employee insurance premiums paid by employer
         e) Payment to employee retirement plan by employer

   b. Employee--person whose performance is subject to physical control by employer not only as to results but also as to methods of accomplishing those results

      1) Partners, self-employed persons, and independent contractors are not covered by unemployment compensation provisions since they are not "employees."

         a) Are covered as self-employed persons for old-age, survivor's, and disability insurance program purposes.

      2) Independent contractor distinguished from an employee

         a) Independent contractor not subject to control of employer or regular supervision as employee
         b) Employer seeks results only and contractor controls method

         EXAMPLE: A builder of homes has only to produce the results.

      3) Officers and directors of corporations are "employees" if they perform services and receive remuneration for these services from corporation

c. Employment--all service performed by employee for person employing him

   1) Must be continuing or recurring work

   2) Services from following are exempt from coverage

      a) Student nurses
      b) Certain public employees
      c) Non-resident aliens
      d) Ministers

   3) Services covered if performed by employee for employer without regard to residence or citizenship

      a) Unless employer not connected with U.S.

   4) Domestic workers, agricultural workers, government employees, and casual workers are governed by special rules

d. Self-employment--carrying on trade or business either as individual or in partnership

   1) Wages greater than base amount are excluded (see "A.2.d.")
   2) Can be both employed (in one job) and self-employed (another business), but must meet requirements of trade or business, i.e., not a hobby, occasional investment, etc.

e. Employer

   1) For Federal Unemployment Tax Act (FUTA) need only employ one person or more for specified short period of time

   2) In general, may be individual, corporation, partnership, trust, or other entity

7. Old-age, survivor's, and disability insurance benefits

   a. Availability of benefits depends upon attainment by individual of "insured status"

      1) A certain length of working time ("quarters of coverage") is required to obtain insured status
      2) A person is "fully insured" when s/he has been credited with either

         a) Forty quarters of coverage, or
         b) One quarter of coverage each year from age 21 until death or retirement

      3) A person is "currently insured" when s/he has been credited with at least six quarters of coverage during 13-quarter period ending with his/her death, disability, or retirement

   b. An individual who is "fully insured" is eligible for following benefits

      1) Survivor benefits for widow or widower and dependents
      2) Benefits for disabled worker and his/her dependents
      3) Old-age retirement benefits payable to retired worker and dependents

         a) Retirement age to receive full benefits is 65
         b) Increased benefits for delaying retirement until after age 65
         c) Reduced benefits for retirement at age 62

      4) Lump-sum death benefits

c. Individual who is "currently insured" is eligible for following benefits

1) Limited survivor benefits

a) In general, limited to dependent minors (18 years) or those caring for dependent minors

2) Benefits for disabled worker and his/her dependents
3) Lump-sum death benefits
4) Survivors or dependents need not have paid in program to receive benefits

d. Amount of benefits defined by statute which changes from time to time and depends upon

1) Average monthly earnings, and
2) Relationship of beneficiary to retired, deceased, or disabled worker

a) E.g., husband, wife, child, grandchild--may be entitled to different benefits

3) Benefits increased based on cost of living
4) Benefits increased for delayed retirement

8. Reduction of social security benefits

a. Early retirement (results in reduced benefits)

1) Retirement age is increasing in steps

b. Returning to work after retirement can affect social security benefits

1) Earned income, after retirement, which exceeds an annual limitation results in reduced benefits of $1 in benefits for each $2 of earnings above a specified amount of annual earned income

a) A person age 70 or older will not suffer a reduction in retirement benefits
b) Earned income in general means income from work (wages or self employment)

2) Income from private pension plans, savings, investments, or insurance do not affect benefits because not earned income
3) Income from limited partnership is considered investment income rather than self-employment income

9. Federal income tax treatment

a. Formerly benefits were not taxable
b. Now portion of benefits are taxable when certain conditions are met

1) Up to 1/2 of benefits taxable above specified amount

c. Employer's portion of social security tax payments is deductible from his/her gross income
d. Employee's portion not deductible

10. Unemployment benefits

a. Eligibility for and amount of unemployment benefits are governed by state laws
b. Does not include self-employed

c. Generally available only to persons unemployed through no fault of their own; however, not available to seasonal workers if paid on yearly basis, e.g., professional sports player in off-season

d. One must have worked for specified period of time and/or earned specified amount of wages

B. <u>Worker's Compensation Acts</u>

1. Worker's compensation is a form of strict liability whereby employer is liable to employee for injuries or diseases sustained by employee which arise out of and in course (scope) of employment

   a. Employee is worker subject to control and supervision of employer

   b. Distinguish independent contractor

      1) Details of work not supervised
      2) Final result can of course be monitored (based on contract law)

2. Purpose

   a. To give employees and their dependents benefits for job-related injuries or diseases with little difficulty

      1) Previously, employee had to sue employer for negligence to receive any benefits in form of damages
      2) Employee usually cannot waive his/her right to benefits

   b. Puts burden where it can be afforded, i.e., cost is passed on as an expense of production to be borne by employers (industry)

   c. No fault need be shown. Payment is automatic upon satisfaction of requirements.

      1) Removes employer's common law defenses of

         a) Assumption of risk--employee assumed risk of injury upon consenting to do work
         b) Negligence of a fellow employee (fellow servant doctrine)--employer formerly could avoid liability by proving it was another employee's fault
         c) Contributory negligence--injured employee was also negligent

3. Regulated by states

   a. Except that federal government employees are covered by federal statute
   b. Each state has its own statute
   c. Interstate commerce not necessary

4. Generally, there are two types of statutes

   a. Elective statutes (rapidly disappearing under threat of federal intervention)

      1) Employer may accept or reject provisions of statute
      2) If employer rejects, s/he loses three common law defenses [see "3.2.c.1)" above] against an employee's common law suit for damages

      3) Most employers accept worker's compensation provisions, since loss of these common law defenses seriously impairs employer's overall legal defense when employee sues for damages

b. Compulsory statutes

  1) Require that all employers within coverage of statute provide benefits
  2) Majority of states has compulsory coverage
  3) Strong trend to compulsory statutes

5. Insurance required to provide benefits

  a. Employer may obtain an insurance policy

    1) Either with state fund or private company

  b. In lieu of insurance policy, employer may assume liability for worker's compensation claims but must show proof of financial responsibility to carry own risk, i.e., self-insurance

6. Legislative scope

  a. Worker's compensation coverage extends to all employees who are injured on job or in course (scope) of employment

    1) During authorized time;
    2) In authorized geographical location; and
    3) While acting in furtherance of employer's business purpose

  b. Coverage does not extend to employee while traveling to or from work
  c. Out of state work may be covered if it meets above mentioned criteria
  d. Although all states have worker's compensation law, not all employees are covered

    1) Typical exemptions

      a) Agricultural workers
      b) Domestic workers
      c) Casual employees, i.e., employment not in usual course of business or not regular
      d) Public employees (less frequently exempted than others)
      e) Employers who employ below a fixed number of people, e.g., four or five (half the states--no exemption)

  e. Must be employee; coverage does not extend to independent contractors
  f. Most worker's compensation laws extend coverage to minors
  g. Public employees are often covered
  h. In general, charitable institutions are excluded from provisions
  i. To avoid requiring most recent employer to pay all compensation, funds have been set up to pay for previous injuries

7. Legal action for damages

  a. Employers covered by worker's compensation insurance are generally exempt from lawsuits by employees
  b. Acceptance of benefits under worker's compensation laws by employee is in lieu of action for damages against employer and such a suit is barred

    1) Employer assumes definite liability (strict liability) in exchange for employee giving up his/her common law rights to sue employer for damages caused by the job
    2) When employee is covered by worker's compensation law, his/her sole remedy against employer is that which is provided for under appropriate worker's compensation act (exclusivity of remedy)
    3) However, if employer intentionally injures employee, employee may proceed against employer based on intentional tort

c. Employee is entitled to worker's compensation benefits without regard to fault

1) Negligence or even gross negligence of injured employee is not a bar to recovery
2) Failure of employee to follow employer's rules is not a bar to recovery
3) Employee's negligence plays no role in determination of amount of benefits awarded
4) However, injuries caused by intentional self-infliction, participation in mutual altercation, or intoxication of employee do constitute a bar to recovery

d. When employer fails to provide worker's compensation insurance or when employer's coverage is inadequate, injured employee may sue in common law for damages, and employer cannot resort to usual common law defenses. [See "B.2.c.1)" above.]

1) When employer uninsured, many states have a fund to pay employee for job-related injuries

a) State then proceeds against uninsured company
b) Penalties imposed

8. Actions against third parties

a. Employee's acceptance of worker's compensation benefits does not bar suit against third party whose negligence caused injury

1) If employee sues and recovers from third party, employer (or its insurance carrier) is entitled to compensation for worker's compensation benefits paid to employee

a) Any recovery in excess of worker's compensation benefits received belongs to injured employee
b) To the extent that recovery duplicates benefits already obtained from employer (or carrier), that employer (or carrier) is entitled to reimbursement from employee

EXAMPLE: Kraig, an employee of Badger Corporation, was injured in an auto accident while on the job. The accident was due to the negligence of Todd. Kraig can recover under workers' compensation and also fully recover from Todd in a civil court case. However, Kraig must reimburse the workers' compensation carrier to the extent the recovery duplicates benefits already obtained under workers' compensation laws.

b. If employee accepts worker's compensation benefits, employer (or its insurance carrier) is subrogated to right of employee against third party whose negligence caused injury

1) Therefore, if employee elects not to sue third party, employer (or its insurance carrier) obtains employee's right of action against third person

9. Claims

   a. Normally administered by state compensation board or commission
   b. Employers are required to report all injuries
   c. Employees are required to give prompt notice of injury
   d. Employees are also required to file claim forms on timely basis

      1) In some states, failure to file claim on time may bar employee's recovery
      2) In other states, failure to file claim on time will bar recovery only if delay has been prejudicial to employer.

10. Benefits

   a. Medical

      1) Provides for medical care to injured or diseased employee

         a) Normally unlimited with regard to time and dollar amount limitations

   b. Disability

      1) This is partial wage continuation plan whereby employee is paid percentage of his/her regular weekly wage subject to maximum amount and maximum number of payments

   c. Death

      1) Various plans and schedules provide payments to widow and minor children

         a) May be discontinued upon remarriage of widow or children reaching age of majority (usually 18)

   d. Special provisions

      1) Normally, statutes call for specific scheduled payments for loss of limb or eye
      2) Also, if employee's injury is of a nature which prevents his returning to his occupation, plan may pay cost of retraining to prepare him for another occupation (rehabilitation)

   e. Normally not subject to waiver by employee

Multiple Choice Questions (1–25)

1.–7. *Deleted by AICPA; effective 5/86*

8. Federal unemployment taxes
   a. Are deductible by an employee on his individual tax return.
   b. Are deductible as a business expense on the federal income tax return of a corporate employer.
   c. May be offset by a credit equal to the amount of the federal tax liability if the employer contributes to an approved state unemployment fund.
   d. Are imposed on the employer and employee.

9. Social security benefits are available
   a. To a qualifying individual or his family only upon such individual's death or retirement.
   b. Only to those who have taxable income under a maximum limitation.
   c. To an otherwise qualifying individual who is also receiving payments under a private pension plan.
   d. To children of a deceased worker who was covered under social security, until such children reach age 25 or complete their education, whichever occurs first.

10. Which of the following statements is correct regarding social security benefits?
   a. Retirement benefits are fully includable in the determination of the recipient's federal taxable income if his gross income exceeds certain maximum limitations.
   b. Retirement benefits paid in excess of the recipient's contributions will be included in the determination of the recipient's federal taxable income regardless of his gross income.
   c. Individuals who have made **no** contributions may be eligible for some benefits.
   d. Upon the death of the recipient, immediate family members within certain age limits are entitled to a death benefit equal to the unpaid portion of the deceased recipient's contributions.

11. Hicks is employed as executive sales manager by Foster Fabrics. She received a salary of $30,000 in 1982. In addition, she earned $15,000 net in 1982 as a free lance photographer. As a result of the above earnings for 1982 and the application of the provisions of the Federal Insurance Contributions Act, Hicks
   a. Owed nothing since her salary was fully subjected to withholding of FICA tax by Foster.
   b. Was required to pay a self-employment tax on the difference between the FICA tax base amount and $30,000.
   c. Was required to pay both an employer and employee FICA tax on the $15,000.
   d. Was required to ascertain the gross amount of income from the free lance photography and compute the FICA tax owed on that amount.

12. The social security tax does **not** apply to which of the following?
   a. Payments on account of sickness including medical and hospital expenses paid by the employer.
   b. Compensation paid in forms other than cash.
   c. Self-employment income of $1,000.
   d. Bonuses and vacation time pay.

13. The Social Security Act provides for the imposition of taxes and the disbursement of benefits. Which of the following is a correct statement regarding these taxes and disbursements?
   a. Only those who have contributed to Social Security are eligible for benefits.
   b. As between an employer and its employee, the tax rates are the same.
   c. A deduction for federal income tax purposes is allowed the employee for Social Security taxes paid.
   d. Social Security payments are includable in gross income for federal income tax purposes unless they are paid for disability.

14. During the 1976 examination of the financial statements of Viscount Manufacturing Corporation, the CPAs noted that although Viscount had 860 full-time and part-time employees, it had completely overlooked its responsibilities under the Federal Insurance Contributions Act (FICA). Under these circumstances, which of the following is true?
   a. No liability under the act will attach if the employees voluntarily relinquish their rights under the act in exchange for a cash equivalent paid directly to them.
   b. If the union which represents the employees has a vested pension plan covering the employees which is equal to or

exceeds the benefits available under the act, Viscount has no liability.

c. Since employers and employees owe FICA taxes at the same rate and since the employer must withhold the employees' tax from their wages as paid, Viscount must remit to the government a tax double the amount assessed directly against the employer.

d. The act does not apply to the part-time employees.

15. Jane Sabine was doing business as Sabine Fashions, a sole proprietorship. Sabine suffered financial reverses and began to use social security and income taxes withheld from her employees to finance the business. Sabine finally filed a voluntary petition in bankruptcy. Which of the following would not apply to her as a result of her actions?

a. She would remain liable for the taxes due.

b. She is personally liable for fines and imprisonment.

c. She could justify her actions by showing that the use of the tax money was vital to continuation of the business.

d. She may be assessed penalties up to the amount of taxes due.

16. Which of the following is required in order for an employee to recover under a compulsory state worker's compensation statute?

a. The employee must be free from any wrongdoing.

b. The injury must arise out of the negligence of the employer or fellow employee.

c. The injury must arise out of and in the course of employment.

d. The injury must occur while the employee is engaged in interstate commerce.

17. Wilk, an employee of Young Corp., was injured by the negligence of Quick, an independent contractor. The accident occurred during regular working hours and in the course of employment. If Young has complied with the state's workers' compensation laws, which of the following is correct?

a. Wilk is barred from suing Young or Quick for negligence.

b. Wilk will be denied workers' compensation if he was negligent in failing to adhere to the written safety procedures.

c. The amount of damages Wilk will be allowed to recover from Young will be based on comparative fault.

d. Wilk may obtain workers' compensation benefits and also properly maintain an action against Quick.

18. Which of the following would be the employer's best defense to a claim for workers' compensation by an injured route salesman?

a. A route salesman is automatically deemed to be an independent contractor, and therefore excluded from workers' compensation coverage.

b. The salesman was grossly negligent in carrying out the employment.

c. The salesman's injury was caused primarily by the negligence of an employee.

d. The salesman's injury did **not** arise out of and in the course of employment.

19. Musgrove Manufacturing Enterprises is subject to compulsory worker's compensation laws in the state in which it does business. It has complied with the state's worker's compensation provisions. State law provides that where there has been compliance, worker's compensation is normally an exclusive remedy. However, the remedy will **not** be exclusive if

a. The employee has been intentionally injured by the employer personally.

b. The employee dies as a result of his injuries.

c. The accident was entirely the fault of a fellow-servant of the employee.

d. The employer was only slightly negligent and the employee's conduct was grossly negligent.

20. Yeats Manufacturing is engaged in the manufacture and sale of convertible furniture in interstate commerce. Yeats' manufacturing facilities are located in a jurisdiction which has a compulsory worker's compensation act. Hardwood, Yeats' president, decided that the company should, in light of its safety record, choose to ignore the requirement of providing worker's compensation insurance. Instead, Hardwood indicated that a special account should be created to provide for such contingencies. Basset was severely injured as a result of his negligent operation of a lathe which accelerated and cut off his right arm. In assessing the potential liability of Yeats, which of the following is a correct answer?

a. Federal law applies since Yeats is engaged in interstate commerce.
b. Yeats has no liability, since Basset negligently operated the lathe.
c. Since Yeats did not provide worker's compensation insurance, it can be sued by Basset and cannot resort to the usual common law defenses.
d. Yeats is a self-insurer, hence it has no liability beyond the amount of the money in the insurance fund.

21. *Deleted by AICPA; effective 5/86*

May 1985 Questions

22. Silk was employed at Rosco Corp. as a chauffeur. While in the course of employment, Silk was involved in an automobile accident with Lake who was employed by Stone Corp. as a truck driver. While making a delivery for Stone, Lake negligently drove through a red light causing the accident with Silk. Both Silk and Lake have received workers' compensation benefits as a result of the accident. Silk

a. Is precluded from suing Lake since both are covered under workers' compensation laws.
b. Is precluded from suing Stone if Stone complied fully with the state's workers' compensation laws.
c. Can recover in full against Lake only, but must reimburse the workers' compensation carrier to the extent the recovery duplicates benefits already obtained under workers' compensation laws.
d. Can recover in full against Lake or Stone, but must reimburse the workers' compensation carrier to the extent the recovery duplicates benefits already obtained under workers' compensation laws.

23. Which of the following statements is correct regarding social security taxes?

a. The annual contributions made by a self-employed person with net earnings of $30,000 in 1985 will be the same as the combined contributions made by an employee and employer on that same amount.
b. A self-employed person is subject to social security taxes based on that person's gross earnings from self-employment.
c. An employer who fails to withhold and pay the employee's portion of social security taxes remains primarily liable for the employee's share.
d. An individual who receives net earnings from self-employment of $30,000 and wages of $30,000 in 1985 will be subject to social security taxes on $60,000.

24. The Federal Unemployment Tax Act

a. Imposes a tax on all employers doing business in the U.S.
b. Requires contributions to be made by the employer and employee equally.
c. Permits the employer to take a credit against the federal tax if contributions are made to a state unemployment fund.
d. Permits an employee to receive unemployment benefits which are limited to the contributions made to that employee's account.

November 1985 Questions

25. Jay White, an engineer, entered into a contract with Sky, Inc., agreeing to provide Sky with certain specified consulting services. After performing the services, White was paid pursuant to the contract but social security taxes were not withheld from his check since Sky considered White an independent contractor. The IRS has asserted that White was an employee and claims that a deficiency exists due to Sky's failure to withhold and pay social security taxes. Which of the following factors is most likely to support the IRS's position that White is an employee?

a. White was paid in one lump sum after all the services were performed.
b. White provided his own office and supplies.
c. Sky supervised and controlled the manner in which White performed the services.
d. Sky reserved the right to inspect White's work.

Repeat Question

(1185,L1,21) Identical to item 18 above

Problem

Problem 1 (1178,L3c)

(5 to 10 minutes)

Part c. Eureka Enterprises, Inc., started doing business in July 1977. It manufactures electronic components and currently employs 35 individuals. In anticipation of future financing needs, Eureka has engaged a CPA firm to audit its financial statements. During the course of the examination, the CPA firm discovers that Eureka has no worker's compensation insurance, which is in violation of state law, and so informs the president of Eureka.

Required:

Answer the following, setting forth reasons for any conclusion stated.

1. What is the purpose of a state worker's compensation law?
2. What are the legal implications of not having worker's compensation insurance?

Multiple Choice Answers

1.	*	6.	*	11.	b	16.	c	21.	*
2.	*	7.	*	12.	a	17.	d	22.	d
3.	*	8.	b	13.	b	18.	d	23.	c
4.	*	9.	c	14.	c	19.	a	24.	c
5.	*	10.	c	15.	c	20.	c	25.	c

**Deleted by AICPA; effective 5/86*

Multiple Choice Answer Explanations

Fair Labor Standards Act

1.—7. *Deleted by AICPA; effective 5/86*

A. Federal Social Security Act

8. (1184,L1,37) (b) Federal unemployment tax must be paid if an employer employs one or more persons covered by the Federal Social Security Act **or** pays wages of $1,500 or more during any calendar quarter. Federal income taxes are deductible as a business expense on the federal income tax return of a corporate employer. Answer (a) is incorrect because an employee may not deduct federal unemployment taxes on his individual return since employees do not pay federal unemployment tax. Answer (c) is incorrect because federal unemployment taxes may be offset by a credit equal to the greater of the amount of contributions paid to an approved state unemployment fund or, as of 1983, 2.7% of the federal unemployment tax but not an amount equal to the federal tax liability. Answer (d) is incorrect because federal unemployment taxes are imposed only on the employer, not on the employee.

9. (1184,L1,40) (c) The fact that an individual is receiving payments under a private pension plan will not deny social security benefits to a qualifying individual. Answer (a) is incorrect because full benefits are available to a qualifying individual at age 65. Answer (b) is incorrect because excess earnings after retirement results in reduced benefits of $1 in benefits for each $2 of earnings above a specified annual amount, but do not completely deny benefits. Prior to retirement there is no maximum limitation on the taxable income of a qualifying individual. Answer (d) is incorrect because social security benefits are available to the children of the deceased worker until such children reach age 18, not age 25.

10. (584,L1,27) (c) Since children may receive death benefits because of the death of a parent, it is possible for some individuals who have made no contributions to be eligible to receive social security benefits. Answers (a) and (b) are incorrect because the amount of Social Security benefits included in Gross Income is computed on the following basis: if modified AGI plus one half of the Social Security benefits received exceeds a base amount ($32,000 for married filing jointly; $25,000 for all others), the amount of benefits included in Gross Income is the lesser of (1) one half of that excess or (2) one half of the benefits received. However, if modified AGI plus the benefits does not exceed the base amount, none of the benefits are included in Gross Income and are thus not taxable. Answer (d) is incorrect because upon the death of a recipient, immediate family members within certain age limits are not entitled to a death benefit equal to the unpaid portion of the deceased recipient's contributions. The amount of survivor's benefits is not dependent upon the amount of contributions made by the deceased. Rather, the amount received by the beneficiary is dependent on both the average monthly earnings and the relationship of the beneficiary to the deceased worker.

11. (1183,L1,39) (b) In 1982 only the first $32,400 of wages were taxable under FICA. Thus, Hicks was required to pay the self-employment FICA tax rate on $2,400 of her earnings as a free-lance photographer which is the difference between the FICA tax base amount and $30,000 (her salary from Foster). Answer (a) is incorrect because a self-employed individual must pay FICA tax if s/he has not already paid such taxes on a salary equal to the base amount. Answer (c) is incorrect because Hicks would only pay the self-employment tax rate (9.35%) on her self-employed income, which is less than the sum of the employer's and employee's tax rates (13.4%). Answer (d) is incorrect because the FICA tax would not be computed on Hicks' gross income from the photography, but the net income.

12. (1181,L1,30) (a) The social security tax within the Federal Social Security Act applies to compensation received which is considered to be "wages." Answers (b), (c), and (d) are incorrect because under the Act wages include compensation paid in forms other than cash, such as bonuses and vacation time, and self-employment income. But hospitalization and medical expenses paid by the employer are not considered wages.

13. (581,L1,59) (b) An employer is required to match contributions of employees to the Social Security System on a dollar-for-dollar basis. Answer (a) is incorrect since benefits may be paid to the surviving

spouse or other dependents of a deceased individual who was covered under the Social Security System. Answer (c) is incorrect since the amount of Social Security taxes paid is not an allowable deduction on an individual's tax return. Payments to the system are taxed in full when made, and are recovered on a tax-free basis when received by the individual in the form of benefits. Answer (d) is incorrect because Social Security payments are not included in the gross income of a taxpayer.

14. (1177,L1,13) (c) It is the employer's duty to withhold FICA taxes from the employee and remit both these and the employer's share to the government. If the employer neglects to withhold, the employer is liable for both the employer and employee taxes, i.e., to pay double. Answer (a) is incorrect because FICA is mandatory and employees may not relinquish their rights. Answer (b) is incorrect because pension plans and other benefits are no substitute for FICA. Answer (d) is incorrect because FICA applies to all employees whether part-time or full-time.

15. (579,L1,50) (c) The requirement is the statement that would not apply to Jane Sabine's actions. An employer who withholds social security and income taxes from employees may not justify using such funds to finance her business even if such action were vital to continuation of the business. Such action is a criminal act and would subject the perpetrator to absolute liability. Even should she be adjudicated a bankrupt, she would, as in answer (a), remain personally liable for taxes due. As in answer (b), she would be personally liable for fines and imprisonment. Also in answer (d), she may be assessed penalties up to the amount of the taxes due (100%).

B. Worker's Compensation Acts

16. (1184,L1,39) (c) Under the various states' compulsory Worker's Compensation Acts, any employee injured within the scope of employment is entitled to receive medical or disability benefits. There is no need, as there is under the common law, to prove negligence on the part of the employer. Therefore, the employer's common law defenses, such as contributory negligence on the part of the employee and negligence of a fellow employee, are destroyed. Thus, answers (a) and (b) are incorrect. Answer (d) is incorrect because there is no requirement that the worker be engaged in interstate commerce to recover since most Worker's Compensation Acts are state statutes.

17. (584,L1,28) (d) Wilk may obtain worker's compensation benefits and also maintain an action against Quick (third party that caused injury). If Wilk recovers against third party (Quick) after obtaining worker's compensation benefits, a part of the recovery equal to the benefits received belong to the employer (Young Corp.). Answer (a) is incorrect because although Wilk is barred from suing the employer for negligence, he can sue Quick. Answer (b) is incorrect because worker's compensation laws eliminate the employer's defense of contributory negligence. Consequently, Wilk will recover because the injury occurred in the course of employment. Answer (c) is incorrect because the amount of damages Wilk will be allowed is not based on comparative fault but on a scheme proscribed by state statute, usually a percentage of the injured employee's wages.

18. (1182,L1,27) (d) Worker's compensation laws provide coverage for employees' injuries which occur on the job or in the course of employment. Answer (a) is incorrect because although an independent contractor is not entitled to worker's compensation coverage, a route salesman would be considered an employee, since his work is subject to the control and supervision of the employer, and thus be extended worker's compensation coverage. Answers (b) and (c) are incorrect because the liability of an employer is a form of strict liability, whereby an employee is entitled to worker's compensation for an injury related to employment without regard to fault. Negligence, or even gross negligence, on the part of the employee is not a bar to such recovery. The only injuries which are generally not covered are those which are intentionally self-inflicted, and those which result from the employee's intoxication.

19. (581,L1,60) (a) If the employer intentionally injures the employee, the employee would not only have a right to proceed under worker's compensation, but could sue the employer in a civil court of law on the basis of an intentional tort. Answers (b), (c) and (d) are incorrect because they do not state grounds that would allow the injured employee to sue in a civil court of law if covered by a proper worker's compensation plan. Even though the injury was caused by contributory negligence of the employee or the act of a fellow servant, the injured employee could still recover, but recovery under worker's compensation would be the exclusive remedy.

20. (1179,L1,48) (c) The usual result when the employer fails to provide worker's compensation insurance is that the injured employee may sue in a common law action, and the employer cannot resort to the usual common law defenses (such as contributory negligence, assumption of risk, or fellow servant rule). Answer (a) is incorrect because there is no feder-

al law applying to worker's compensation. Worker's compensation is regulated by state statutes, which are only affected by federal guidelines. Answer (b) is incorrect because the employer does have liability for job-related injuries even if the injured employee was negligent. Answer (d) is incorrect in that Yeats is not a self-insurer because the problem indicates that he is doing business in a state that has a compulsory worker's compensation act, i.e., does not recognize self-insurance plans.

Equal Employment Opportunity Laws

21. *Deleted by AICPA; effective 5/86*

May 1985 Answers

22. (585,L1,30) (d) Silk may recover damages from either Lake or Stone since it appears that Lake negligently struck Silk while s/he was acting within the scope of his/her employment. Consequently, both the principal and the agent would be liable for the agent's negligence. However in the event that Silk recovers damages from Lake or Stone, Silk must reimburse the workers' compensation carrier to the extent the recovery duplicates benefits already received under workers' compensation. Answer (a) is incorrect since Silk has the right to sue Lake regardless of whether both of them are covered under workers' compensation laws. Answer (b) is incorrect because compliance with the state's workers' compensation laws will not protect an employer from suits brought against him/her for negligent acts of his/her employees. Answer (c) is incorrect since under agency laws a party who is injured by an employee's negligent act, which occurs within the scope of his/her employment, may sue the employer, the employee, or both for recovery.

23. (585,L1,31) (c) It is the employer's duty to withhold the employee's share of FICA and remit both the employee's and the employer's shares to the government. If the employer fails to withhold, then the employer is liable to the government for both the employee's and employer's taxes. Answer (a) is incorrect because the FICA tax rate for a self-employed person is greater than the tax rate applicable to the employee individually, but less than the combined rate applicable to the employee and employer together. Thus, a self-employed individual with net earnings of $30,000 makes a smaller FICA contribution than that made by an employer and employee collectively for an employee making the same amount. Answer (b) is incorrect because a self-employed individual's FICA contribution is based on net earnings from self-employment, not gross income. Answer (d) is incorrect because a self-employed individual may reduce his/her net earnings from self-employment by the amount of earned wages subject to FICA. The net effect is that the individual will only pay social security taxes on the portion of his self-employment income equal to the amount left after his $30,000 of wages have been subtracted from the base amount.

24. (585,L1,32) (c) Under the Federal Unemployment Tax Act, an employer is entitled to a credit against his/her federal unemployment tax for contributions paid under state unemployment compensation laws. Answer (a) is incorrect because the tax is imposed only if an employer has one or more employees which are covered by the Federal Unemployment Tax Act. Coverage under the Act is based on a wage service requirement. Basically, one or more employees must work more than a specified number of weeks during the year or the employer's quarterly payroll must exceed a certain minimum amount. Answer (b) is incorrect because the employer and employee make equal payments under the Federal Insurance Contributions Act, not the Federal Unemployment Tax Act. Answer (d) is incorrect because the benefits an employee is entitled to recover depend upon the attainment of "insured status." An employee must work a certain length of time, measured by quarters of coverage, to obtain insured status. Employees receive one-quarter of coverage for each specified increment in earnings in a year, up to a maximum of four quarters per year. The benefits an employee may be entitled to receive can exceed the amount contributed to his/her account.

November 1985 Answer

25. (1185,L1,22) (c) When deciding whether a person is an employee or an independent contractor for the purposes of social security legislation, the most important factor is whether the person's performance is subject to the physical control of the employer. If Sky supervised and controlled the manner in which White performed the services, this factor would support the IRS's position that White is an employee. The fact that White was paid in one lump sum and provided his own office and supplies would support Sky's position that White was an independent contractor. Thus answers (a) and (b) are incorrect. Answer (d) is incorrect because the fact that Sky reserved the right to inspect White's work would not necessarily mean that Sky was supervising and controlling the manner in which White performed the services. An employer of an independent contractor would always have the right to inspect the independent contractor's work when finished. Thus this factor would not support the IRS's position that White is an employee.

Answer Outline

Problem 1 Worker's Compensation (1178,L3c)

c1. Worker's comp compensates employees injured at work
   - Benefits available to injured, survivors, or dependents

c2. Worker's comp is generally mandatory by statute
   - Employers with no worker's comp have liability
   - Also precludes common-law defenses of
     - Fellow-servant
     - Assumption of risk
     - Contributory negligence
   - Employer may also be liable for worker's comp benefits, also fines and possibly imprisonment

Unofficial Answer

Problem 1 Worker's Compensation (1178,L3c)

Part c.

1. Worker's compensation laws provide a system of compensation for employees who are injured, disabled, or killed as a result of accidents or occupational diseases in the course of their employment. Benefits also extend to survivors or dependents of these employees.

2. In all but a distinct minority of jurisdictions, worker's compensation coverage is mandatory. In those few jurisdictions that have elective worker's compensation, employers who reject worker's compensation coverage are subject to common law actions by injured employees and are precluded from asserting the defenses of fellow-servant, assumption of risk, and contributory negligence. The number of such jurisdictions having elective compensation coverage has been constantly diminishing. The penalty in these jurisdictions is the loss of the foregoing defenses.

The more common problem occurs in connection with the failure of an employer to secure compensation coverage even though he is obligated to do so in the majority of jurisdictions. The one uniform effect of such unwise conduct on the part of the employer is to deny him the use of the common law defenses mentioned above.

In addition to the foregoing, an increasing number of states have provided for the payment of worker's compensation by the state to the injured employee of the uninsured employer. The state in turn proceeds against the employer to recover the compensation cost and to impose penalties that include fines and imprisonment. Other jurisdictions provide for a penalty in the form of additional compensation payments over and above the basic amounts, or they require an immediate lump-sum payment.

PROPERTY

Overview

Property entails items capable of being owned, i.e., the rights related to the ownership of things that society will recognize and enforce. Property is classified as real or personal, and as tangible or intangible. Protection of property and settlement of disputes concerning property is a major function of the legal system.

The candidate should be able to distinguish between personal and real property and between tenancies in common, joint tenancies, and tenancies by the entirety. The candidate also should understand that an instrument given primarily as security for real property is a mortgage and be able to distinguish between the legal results arising from "assumption" of a mortgage and taking "subject to" a mortgage. Other questions concerning mortgages require basic knowledge of the concepts of novation, suretyship, subrogation, redemption, and purchase money mortgages.

Questions on deeds usually distinguish between the legal implication of warranty deeds, quitclaim deeds, and special warranty deeds. Both mortgages and deeds should be publicly recorded, and the questions frequently require the candidate to identify a priority and explain constructive notice. The most important topics under lessor-lessee law are the Statute of Frauds, the effect of a sale of leased property, assignment, and subleasing.

A. Distinctions Between Real and Personal Property

1. Real property (realty)--includes land and things attached to land in a relatively permanent manner

   EXAMPLE: A building is erected on a parcel of land. Both the land and the building are real property.

2. Personal property (personalty)--property not classified as real property or a fixture (see Fixture "A.3.")

   a. May be either

      1) Tangible--subject to physical possession

         EXAMPLE: Automobiles and books are tangible personal property.

      2) Intangible--not subject to physical possession but subject to legal ownership

         EXAMPLE: Contractual rights to receive payment for automobiles sold are intangible personal property.

3. Fixture--item that was originally personal property but which is affixed to real property in relatively permanent fashion such that it is considered to be part of real property

   a. Several factors are applied in determining whether personal property that has been attached to real property is a fixture

      1) Affixer's objective intent as to whether property is to be regarded as personalty or realty

         a) In general, item is a fixture if it was intention of parties that it become part of real property
         b) If intent is clear, then this becomes controlling factor in determination of whether an item is fixture or not

      2) Method and permanence to which item is physically attached (annexed to the real property)

         a) If item cannot be removed without material injury to real property, it is generally held that item has become part of realty (i.e., a fixture)

      3) Adaptability of use of personal property for purpose for which real property is used

         a) If personal property is necessary or beneficial to use of real property, more likely that item is fixture

         b) But if use or purpose of item is unusual for type of realty involved, it might be reasonable to conclude that it is personalty, and affixer intends to remove item when s/he leaves

      4) Property interest of that person in real property at time of attachment of item

   b. Trade fixture is a fixture installed (affixed) by tenant in connection with business on leased premises

      EXAMPLE: A tenant who is leasing premises for use as grocery store installs refrigeration unit on property. Refrigeration unit is integral to conducting of business for which tenant occupies premises and therefore qualifies as trade fixture.

      1) Trade fixtures remain personal property, giving tenant right to remove these items upon expiration of lease

         a) If item is so affixed to real property that removing it would cause substantial damage, then it is considered part of realty

B. Interests in Real Property

1. Present interests

   a. Fee simple absolute

      1) Highest estate in law (has the most ownership rights)
      2) May be transferred inter vivos (while living), by intestate succession (without will), or by will (testate at death)

      3) May be subject to mortgages, state laws, etc.

         EXAMPLE: Most private residences are fee simple absolute estates although they are commonly subject to mortgage.

b. Fee simple defeasible

1) Fee simple determinable--upon the happening of the stated event the estate automatically reverts to the grantor

EXAMPLE: Conveyance to the holder of an interest was, "to A as long as A uses it for church purposes." The interest will revert back to the grantor or his heirs if the property is not used for church purposes.

2) Fee simple subject to condition subsequent--upon the happening of the stated event the grantor must take affirmative action to divest the grantee of the estate

EXAMPLE: Conveyance to the holder of the interest was "to A, but if liquor is ever served on the premises, the grantor has right to re-enter the premises." The grantor has power of termination so as to repossess the premises.

c. Life interest--an interest whose duration is usually measured by the life of the holder but may be measured by lives of others

EXAMPLE: Conveyance of land, "to A so long as she shall live."

1) Upon termination (death), the property reverts to grantor or grantor's heirs, or to a named remainderman (see "B.2.b.")

2) Usual life interest can be transferred by deed only, i.e., not by a will because it ends on death

3) Holder of a life interest (life tenant) is entitled to ordinary use and profits of land but may not commit waste (injure interests of remainder-man)

a) Must maintain property (in reasonable state of repair)
b) May not misuse property

d. Leaseholds--see Lessor-Lessee at end of PROPERTY module

2. Future interest (holder of this interest has right to or possibility of possession in the future)

a. Reversion--future interest reverts back to transferor (or his/her heirs) at end of transferee's estate

1) Usually kept when conveying a life interest or an interest for a definite period of time

EXAMPLE: X conveys, "to Y for life" or "to Y for 10 years." X has a reversion.

b. Remainder--future interest is in a third party at the end of transferee's estate

EXAMPLE: X conveys, "to Y for life, remainder to Z and her heirs."

3. Concurrent interest--two or more persons (co-tenants) have undivided interests and concurrent possessory rights in real or personal property--each has a non-exclusive right to possess whole property

a. Tenancy in common

1) A concurrent interest with no right of survivorship (interest passes to heirs, donee, or purchaser)

2) Unless stated otherwise, multiple grantees are presumed to be tenants in common
3) Tenant in common may convey individual interest in the whole but cannot convey a specific portion of the property
   a) Unless there is a judicial partition to split up ownership
      1] Creditors may sue to compel a partition to satisfy individual's debts

b. Joint tenancy
   1) A concurrent interest with all rights of ownership going to the surviving joint tenants (i.e., rights of survivorship)
      a) Cannot be transferred by will because upon death, other co-tenants own it
   2) If conveys rights in property without consent of others, new owner becomes a tenant in common rather than joint tenant; remaining co-tenants are still joint tenants

   EXAMPLE: A, B, and C are joint tenants of Greenacre. A sells his interest to D without the consent of B and C. D is a tenant in common with a one-third interest in the whole. B and C are still joint tenants (with the right of survivorship) each having a one-third undivided interest.

c. Tenancy by the entirety
   1) Joint interest held by husband and wife
   2) It is presumed when both spouses' names appear on title document
   3) To transfer, both must convey
   4) Each spouse has a right of survivorship
   5) Divorce creates a tenancy in common

C. Contracts for Sale of Land

1. Generally precede transfers of land. Often includes escrows. (See "E.1.c.")

   EXAMPLE: An earnest money agreement. The purchaser puts the money down to show his seriousness while he investigates the title and arranges for a mortgage.

   a. Generally, agreement must
      1) Be in writing and signed by the party to be bound
         a) To satisfy Statute of Frauds under contract law
      2) Identify land and parties
      3) Identify purpose
      4) Contain terms or promises
      5) Contain purchase price
   b. Assignable unless prohibited in contract

2. If not expressed, there is an implied promise that seller will provide a marketable title (implied warranty of marketability)

   a. A marketable title is one reasonably free from doubt. Does not contain such defects as breaks in the chain of title, outstanding liens, or defective instruments in the past (chain of title).

      1) Zoning restrictions do not make a title unmarketable

   b. Agreement may provide for marketable or "insurable" title

      1) Insurable title is one which a title insurance company will insure against defects, liens, and invalidity

   c. If title is not marketable, purchaser may

      1) Rescind and recover any down payment
      2) Sue for damages
      3) Sue for specific performance with a reduction in price

3. Risk of loss before deed is conveyed, e.g., if house burns who bears the burden?

   a. General rule is purchaser bears the risk of loss, subject to terms of the contract
   b. Courts may look to who has the most ownership rights and benefits (normally the buyer)
   c. Either party can insure against a risk of loss

D. <u>Types of Deeds</u>

1. Warranty deeds contain the following covenants (unconditional promises) by grantor

   a. Grantor has title and right to convey it
   b. Free from encumbrances except as disclosed in the deed

      EXAMPLE: O conveys by warranty deed Blackacre to P. There is a mortgage still unpaid on Blackacre. Unless O discloses this mortgage to P, O has violated the covenant that the deed be free from encumbrances.

   c. Quiet enjoyment--neither grantor nor third party with rightful claim will disturb grantee's possession
   d. Further assurance--grantor will procure any further documents to perfect title
   e. General warranty--grantor will defend title against claims by other parties

2. Bargain and sale deed

   a. Generally, only covenants that grantor has done nothing to impair title, e.g., he has not created any encumbrances

   b. Does not warrant against prior (before grantor's ownership) impairments

3. Quitclaim deed conveys only whatever interest in land the grantor has. No warranty of title is made by grantor.

   a. It is insurable, recordable, and mortgagable as with any other deed

E. Executing a Deed

1. There must be delivery for the deed to be effective; there must be an intent on the part of the grantor to pass title (convey) to the grantee
   a. Possession of the deed by grantee raises a presumption (rebuttable) of delivery
   b. A recorded deed raises a presumption (rebuttable) of delivery
   c. A deed given to a third party to give to the grantee upon performance of a condition is a delivery in escrow
      1) Escrow agent--intermediary between the two parties who holds deed until grantee pays, then gives deed to grantee and money to grantor

F. Recording a Deed

1. Gives constructive notice to the world of grantee's ownership (this is important)
   a. Protects grantee (new owner) against subsequent purchasers

      EXAMPLE: X sells land to Y. Y records his deed. Later X sells land to Z. Z loses as against Y because Y recorded the deed giving constructive notice of the prior sale.

      1) However, deed is valid between immediate parties without recording
   b. Most recording statutes provide that a subsequent purchaser (bona fide) who takes without notice of the first sale has priority
      1) I.e., if a grantee does not record immediately, he may lose his priority
   c. Notice refers to actual knowledge of prior sale and constructive knowledge, i.e., one is deemed to be aware of what is filed in the records
   d. To be a purchaser, one must give value which does not include antecedent debts (as it does in SECURED TRANSACTIONS and NEGOTIABLE INSTRUMENTS)

G. Title Insurance

1. Generally used to insure that title is good and to cover the warranties by seller
2. Without title insurance purchaser's only recourse is against grantor and he may not be able to satisfy the damages
   a. Standard insurance policies generally insure against all defects of record and defects grantee may be aware of, but not defects disclosed by survey and physical inspection of premises
   b. Title insurance company is liable for any damages or expenses if there is a title defect or encumbrance that is insured against
      1) Certain defects are not insured by the title policy
         a) These exceptions must be shown on face of policy

H. Adverse Possession

1. Possessor of land who was not owner may acquire title if he holds it for the statutory period

   a. The statutory period is the running of the Statute of Limitations. Varies by state from 5 to 20 years.
   b. The statute begins to run upon the taking of possession
   c. True owner must commence legal action before the statute runs or the adverse possessor obtains title
   d. Successive possessors may tack (cumulate the required time together)

      1) Each possessor must transfer to the other. One cannot abandon or the statute begins over again for the next possessor.

   e. True owner of a future interest, e.g., a remainder, is not effected by adverse possession

      EXAMPLE: X dies and leaves his property to A for life, remainder to B. A pays little attention to the property and a third party acquires it by adverse possession. When A dies, B is entitled to the property regardless of the adverse possession.

2. Necessary elements

   a. Open and notorious possession

      1) Means type of possession that would give reasonable notice to owner

   b. Hostile possession

      1) Must indicate intentions of ownership

         a) Does not occur when possession started permissively or as co-tenants
         b) Not satisfied if possessor acknowledges other's ownership

      2) Color of title satisfies this requirement. When possession is taken under good faith belief in a defective instrument or deed purporting to convey the land.

   c. Actual possession

      1) Possession of land consistent with its normal use, e.g., farm land is being farmed

   d. Continuous possession

      1) Need not be constant, but possession as normally used

   e. Exclusive possession

      1) Possession to the exclusion of all others

I. Mortgages

1. Definition--nonpossessory lien on real property to secure the performance of an obligation (usually a debt)

   a. Under law of majority of states, debtor has title
   b. Obligation or debt is usually evidenced by a promissory note which is incorporated into the mortgage
   c. Purchase-money mortgage is created when the seller takes a mortgage from the buyer at the time of sale

      1) Or the lender furnishes the money with which the property is purchased

d. A mortgage may be given to secure future advances
e. A mortgage is an interest in real property and must be in writing, signed, etc. (must satisfy Statute of Frauds)

2. Mortgage may be recorded and receives the same benefits as recording a deed or recording an assignment of contract

a. Gives constructive notice of the mortgage

1) But mortgage is effective between mortgagor and mortgagee and third parties, who have actual notice, even without recording

b. Protects against subsequent mortgagees (priority of mortgage), purchasers, or other takers
c. Recording statutes are generally similar to (or the same ones) those used in recording deeds (see "F.1.b.")

1) First mortgagee to obtain a mortgage and to record it will have priority over all subsequent mortgagees subject to special rights of purchase money security interests and certain statutory liens (i.e., mechanic's or construction lien)

EXAMPLE: M loans money to X on some property and becomes the first mortgagee in time. M does not record the mortgage. N loans money on the same property. N is unaware of the prior mortgage and records the second mortgage. N has priority over M.

EXAMPLE: Same as above except N is aware of the first mortgage. M wins because N had actual notice despite the lack of recordation.

2) The first mortgage to have priority is satisfied in full (upon default) before the next mortgage to have priority is satisfied

a) Second mortgagee can require first mortgagee to resort to other property for payment if first mortgagee has other property available as security

d. If the first mortgagee does not record, a subsequent mortgagee who records will have priority if he did not have notice of the first mortgage

1) If he had notice, he cannot get priority in most jurisdictions

3. When mortgaged property is sold the buyer may

a. Assume the mortgage

1) If "assumed," the buyer becomes personally liable (mortgage holder is third-party beneficiary)
2) Seller remains liable (unless released by mortgage holder by a novation)

a) But between the seller and buyer, the buyer has primary responsibility and the seller has the rights and responsibilities of a surety

3) Normally the mortgage holder's consent is needed due to "due on sale clauses"

a) Terms of mortgage may permit acceleration of principal or renegotiation of interest rate upon transfer of the property

b. Take subject to the mortgage

1) If buyer takes "subject to" then buyer accepts no liability for the mortgage and the seller is still primarily liable

a) Buyer may pay the mortgage and the mortgage holder must accept

2) Mortgage holder may still foreclose on the property even in the hands of the buyer

a) Buyer has no right against seller concerning the mortgage subject to terms of contract or conveyance

3) Mortgage holder's consent not needed unless stipulated in mortgage and in no event can consent be unreasonably withheld, unless a "due on sale clause" is present

c. Novation--occurs when purchaser assumes mortgage and mortgagee (lender) releases in writing the seller from the mortgage

EXAMPLE: O has a mortgage on Redacre. He sells Redacre to T. T agrees to assume the mortgage and the mortgagee bank agrees in writing to substitute T as the only liable party in place of O. Because of this novation, O is no longer liable on the mortgage.

4. Rights of parties

a. Mortgagor (owner, debtor) retains possession and the right to use the land

1) May transfer the land encumbered by the mortgage

b. Mortgagee (creditor) has a lien on the land and may assign the mortgage to third parties or foreclose on the land to satisfy the debt upon default

1) Even if mortgagor transfers the land, it is still subject to the mortgage if it has been properly recorded

c. If the mortgagor defaults on payment of the note, the mortgagee may resort to the land for payment by foreclosure

1) Requires judicial action that directs a foreclosure sale

a) Court will refuse to confirm sale if price is so low as to raise a presumption of unfairness

b) However, court will not refuse to confirm sale merely because higher price might have been received at a later time

2) Mortgagor usually can save real estate (redeem the property) by use of equity of redemption

a) Pays interest, debt, and expenses

b) Exists until foreclosure sale

c) Cannot be curtailed by prior agreement

3) After foreclosure sale debtor has right of redemption

a) Affords mortgagor one last chance to redeem the property

b) Pays off loan within statutory period

4) If mortgagee forecloses and sells the property and mortgagor does not use equity of redemption or right of redemption

a) Mortgagee must return any excess proceeds from the sale to the mortgagor

b) If proceeds from the sale are insufficient to pay note, the mortgagor is still indebted to the mortgagee for the deficiency

1] Grantee of the mortgagor who assumed the mortgage would also be liable for the deficiency but one who took subject to the mortgage would not be personally liable

5. Deed of Trust--also a nonpossessory lien on real property to secure a debt
   a. Like a mortgage, debtor retains possession of the land and creditor has a lien on it
   b. Legal title is given to a trustee to hold
      1) Upon default, trustee may sell the land for the benefit of the creditor
6. Sale on Contract
   a. Unlike a mortgage or a deed of trust, the seller retains title to the property
   b. Purchaser takes possession and makes payments on the contract
   c. Purchaser gets title when debt fully paid

J. <u>Lessor-Lessee</u>

1. Relationship which arises from contracting for the possession of real property for some period of time
   a. A lease is a contract and a conveyance
      1) Contract is the primary source of rights and duties
      2) May be oral if less than one year
      3) Lease is actually personal property
   b. Landlord is the lessor and has the ownership interest called reversion
   c. Tenant is the lessee and has a possessory interest
2. Types of leaseholds
   a. Period-to-period
      1) Lease is for a fixed time such as a month or year but it continues from period-to-period until proper notice of termination
      2) Notice of termination must be given in the same amount of time as the rent or tenancy period (i.e., if tenancy is from month-to-month then the landlord or tenant must give at least one month's notice)
   b. Definite period of time (called lease for years)
      1) Lease is for a fixed amount of time, e.g., lease of two years or six months
      2) Ends automatically at date of termination
   c. Holdover by tenant after definite term with express or implied approval of landlord creates a period-to-period lease
3. Lessor covenants (promises) and tenant's rights
   a. Generally, lessor's covenants are independent of lessee's rights; therefore, lessor's breach does not give lessee the right to breach
   b. Right to possession--lessor makes premises available to lessee
   c. Quiet enjoyment--neither lessor nor a third party with a valid claim will evict the lessee unless there has been a breach of the lease
   d. Fitness for use--premises are fit for human occupation, i.e., warranty of habitability
   e. Lessee may assign or sublease unless prohibited or restricted in lease
      1) Assignment is the transfer by lessee of his/her entire interest reserving no rights
         a) Assignee is in privity of contract with lessor and lessor may proceed against him for rent and breaches

b) Assignor (lessee) is still liable to lessor unless there is a novation or release
c) Clause prohibiting sublease does not prohibit assignment

2) A sublease is the transfer by lessee of less than his/her entire interest; e.g., for three months during summer, then lessee returns to it in the fall

a) Lessee (sublessor) is still liable on the lease
b) Lessor has no privity with sublessee and can take no action against him for rent, but certain restrictions of original lease run with the land and are enforceable against sublessee

c) Sublessee can assume obligations in the sublease and be liable to pay the landlord
d) Clause prohibiting assignment does not prohibit sublease

f. Subject to lease terms, trade fixtures attached by lessee may be removed if can be removed without substantial damage to premises

g. Tenant can use premises for any legal purpose unless lease restricts

4. Lessee's duties and lessor's rights

a. Rent--due at end of term or period of tenancy unless otherwise agreed in lease

1) No right to withhold rent even if lessor is in breach (unless so provided by lease or by statute)
2) Nonpayment gives lessor right to sue for it or to bring an eviction suit or both

b. Lessee has obligation to make ordinary repairs. Lease or statute may make lessor liable.

1) Structural repairs are lessor's duty

c. If tenant wrongfully retains possession after termination, lessor may

1) Evict lessee, or
2) Treat as holdover tenant and charge with fair rental value, or
3) Tenancy becomes one of period-to-period, and lessee is liable for rent the same as in the expired lease

5. Termination

a. Expiration of lease
b. Proper notice in a tenancy from period-to-period
c. Surrender by lessee and acceptance by lessor
d. Death of lessee terminates lease except for a lease for a period of years

1) Death of lessor generally does not terminate the lease

e. Eviction

1) Actual eviction--ousting directly
2) Constructive eviction--allowing conditions which make the property unusable if lessor is liable for the condition of the premises

f. Transfer of property does not affect tenancy

1) New owner cannot rightfully terminate lease unless old owner could have, e.g., breach by tenant

Multiple Choice Questions (1–34)

1. Wilmont owned a tract of waterfront property on Big Lake. During Wilmont's ownership of the land, several frame bungalows were placed on the land by tenants who rented the land from Wilmont. In addition to paying rent, the tenants paid for the maintenance and insurance of the bungalows, repaired, altered and sold them, without permission or hindrance from Wilmont. The bungalows rested on surface cinderblock and were not bolted to the ground. The buildings could be removed without injury to either the buildings or the land. Wilmont sold the land to Marsh. The deed to Marsh recited that Wilmont sold the land, with buildings thereon, "subject to the rights of tenants, if any, . . ." When the tenants attempted to remove the bungalows, Marsh claimed ownership of them. In deciding who owns the bungalows, which of the following is **least** significant?

a. The leasehold agreement itself, to the extent it manifested the intent of the parties.
b. The mode and degree of annexation of the buildings to the land.
c. The degree to which removal would cause injury to the buildings or the land.
d. The fact that the deed included a general clause relating to the buildings.

2. Franklin's will left his ranch "to his wife, Joan, for her life, and upon her death to his sons, George and Harry, as joint tenants." Because of the provisions in Franklin's will

a. Joan cannot convey her interest in the ranch except to George and Harry.
b. The ranch must be included in Joan's estate for federal estate tax purposes upon her death.
c. If George predeceases Harry, Harry will obtain all right, title, and interest in the ranch.
d. Joan holds the ranch in trust for the benefit of George and Harry.

3. Dombres is considering purchasing Blackacre. The title search revealed that the property was willed by Adams jointly to his children, Donald and Martha. The language contained in the will is unclear as to whether a joint tenancy or a tenancy in common was intended. Donald is dead and Martha has agreed to convey her entire interest by quitclaim deed to Dombres. The purchase price is equal to the full fair market price of the property. Dombres is not interested in anything less than the entire title to the tract. Under the circumstances, which of the following is correct?

a. There is a statutory preference which favors the finding of a joint tenancy.
b. Whether the will created a joint tenancy or a tenancy in common is irrelevant since Martha is the only survivor.
c. Dombres will not obtain title to the entire tract of land by Martha's conveyance.
d. There is no way or means whereby Dombres may obtain a clear title under the circumstances.

4. Marcross and two business associates own real property as tenants in common that they have invested in as a speculation. The speculation proved to be highly successful, and the land is now worth substantially more than their investment. Which of the following is a correct legal incident of ownership of the property?

a. Upon the death of any of the other tenants, the deceased's interest passes to the survivor(s) unless there is a will.
b. Each of the co-tenants owns an undivided interest in the whole.
c. A co-tenant cannot sell his interest in the property without the consent of the other tenants.
d. Upon the death of a co-tenant, his estate is entitled to the amount of the original investment, but not the appreciation.

5–6. *Deleted by AICPA; effective 5/86*

7. A condition in a contract for the purchase of real property which makes the purchaser's obligation dependent upon his obtaining a given dollar amount of conventional mortgage financing

a. Can be satisfied by the seller if the seller offers the buyer a demand loan for the amount.
b. Is a condition subsequent.
c. Is implied as a matter of law.
d. Requires the purchaser to use reasonable efforts to obtain the financing.

8. Fulcrum Enterprises, Inc., contracted to purchase a four acre tract of land from Devlin as a site for its proposed factory. The contract of sale is silent on the type of deed to be received by Fulcrum and does not contain any title exceptions. The title search revealed that there are 51 zoning laws which affect Fulcrum's use of the land and that back taxes are due. A survey revealed a stone wall encroaching upon a portion of th land Devlin is purporting to convey. A survey made 23

years ago also had revealed the wall. Regarding the rights and duties of Fulcrum, which of the following is correct?

a. Fulcrum is entitled to a warranty deed with full covenants from Devlin at the closing.
b. The existence of the zoning laws above will permit Fulcrum to avoid the contract.
c. Fulcrum must take the land subject to the back taxes.
d. The wall results in a potential breach of the implied warranty of marketability.

9. Purdy purchased real property from Hart and received a warranty deed with full covenants. Recordation of this deed is

a. Not necessary if the deed provides that recordation is **not** required.
b. Necessary to vest the purchaser's legal title to the property conveyed.
c. Required primarily for the purpose of providing the local taxing authorities with the information necessary to assess taxes.
d. Irrelevant if the subsequent party claiming superior title had actual notice of the unrecorded deed.

10. Your client, Albert Fall, purchased a prominent industrial park from Josh Barton. At the closing, Barton offered a quitclaim deed. The contract of sale called for a warranty deed with full covenants.

a. Fall should accept the quitclaim deed since there is no important difference between a quitclaim deed and a warranty deed.
b. An undisclosed mortgage which was subsequently discovered would violate one of the covenants of a warranty deed.
c. Fall cannot validly refuse to accept Barton's quitclaim deed.
d. The only difference between a warranty deed with full covenants and a quitclaim deed is that the grantor of a quitclaim does not warrant against defects past his assumption of title.

11. Smith purchased a tract of land. To protect himself, he ordered title insurance from Valor Title Insurance Company. The policy was the usual one issued by title companies. Accordingly

a. Valor will **not** be permitted to take exceptions to its coverage if it agreed to insure and prepared the title abstract.
b. The title policy is assignable in the event Smith subsequently sells the property.
c. The title policy provides protection against defects in record title only.
d. Valor will be liable for any title defect which arises, even though the defect could **not** have been discovered through the exercise of reasonable care.

12. Dunbar Dairy Farms, Inc., pursuant to an expansion of its operations in Tuberville, purchased from Moncrief a 140-acre farm strategically located in the general area in which Dunbar wishes to expand. Unknown to Dunbar, Cranston, an adjoining landowner, had fenced off approximately five acres of the land in question. Cranston installed a well, constructed a storage shed and garage on the fenced-off land, and continuously farmed and occupied the five acres for approximately 22 years prior to Dunbar's purchase. Cranston did this under the mistaken belief that the five acres of land belonged to him. Which of the following is a correct answer in regard to the five acres occupied by Cranston?

a. Under the circumstances Cranston has title to the five acres.
b. As long as Moncrief had properly recorded a deed which includes the five acres in dispute, Moncrief had good title to the five acres.
c. At best, the only right that Cranston could obtain is an easement.
d. If Dunbar is unaware of Cranston's presence and Cranston has failed to record, Dunbar can oust him as a trespasser.

13. Which of the following is an **incorrect** statement regarding a real property mortgage?

a. It transfers title to the real property to the mortgagee.
b. It is invariably accompanied by a negotiable promissory note which refers to the mortgage.
c. It creates an interest in real property and is therefore subject to the Statute of Frauds.
d. It creates a nonpossessory security interest in the mortgagee.

14. Moch sold her farm to Watkins and took back a purchase money mortgage on the farm. Moch failed to record the mortgage. Moch's mortgage will be valid against all of the following parties **except**

a. The heirs or estate of Watkins.
b. A subsequent mortgagee who took a second mortgage since he had heard there was a prior mortgage.

c. A subsequent bona fide purchaser from Watkins.
d. A friend of Watkins to whom the farm was given as a gift and who took without knowledge of the mortgage.

15. Peters defaulted on a purchase money mortgage held by Fairmont Realty. Fairmont's attempts to obtain payment have been futile and the mortgage payments are several months in arrears. Consequently, Fairmont decided to resort to its rights against the property. Fairmont foreclosed on the mortgage. Peters has all of the following rights **except**

a. To remain in possession as long as his equity in the property exceeds the amount of debt.
b. An equity of redemption.
c. To refinance the mortgage with another lender and repay the original mortgage.
d. A statutory right of redemption.

16. Golden sold his moving and warehouse business, including all the personal and real property used therein, to Clark Van Lines, Inc. The real property was encumbered by a duly-recorded $300,000 first mortgage upon which Golden was personally liable. Clark acquired the property subject to the mortgage but did not assume the mortgage. Two years later, when the outstanding mortgage was $260,000, Clark decided to abandon the business location because it had become unprofitable and the value of the real property was less than the outstanding mortgage. Clark moved to another location and refused to pay the installments due on the mortgage. What is the legal status of the parties in regard to the mortgage?

a. Clark took the real property free of the mortgage.
b. Clark breached its contract with Golden when it abandoned the location and defaulted on the mortgage.
c. Golden must satisfy the mortgage debt in the event that foreclosure yields an amount less than the unpaid balance.
d. If Golden pays off the mortgage, he will be able to successfully sue Clark because Golden is subrogated to the mortgagee's rights against Clark.

17. Tremont Enterprises, Inc., needed some additional working capital to develop a new product line. It decided to obtain intermediate term financing by giving a second mortgage on its plant and warehouse. Which of the following is true with respect to the mortgages?

a. If Tremont defaults on both mortgages and a bankruptcy proceeding is initiated, the second mortgagee has the status of general creditor.
b. If the second mortgagee proceeds to foreclose on its mortgage, the first mortgagee must be satisfied completely before the second mortgagee is entitled to repayment.
c. Default on payment to the second mortgagee will constitute default on the first mortgage.
d. Tremont can **not** prepay the second mortgage prior to its maturity without the consent of the first mortgagee.

18. Farber sold his house to Ronald. Ronald agreed among other things to pay the existing mortgage on the house. The Safety Bank, which held the mortgage, released Farber from liability on the debt. The above described transaction (relating to the mortgage debt) is

a. Invalid in that the bank did not receive any additional consideration from Farber.
b. Not a release of Farber if Ronald defaults, and the proceeds from the sale of the mortgaged house are insufficient to satisfy the debt.
c. A novation.
d. A delegation.

19. Marks is a commercial tenant of Tudor Buildings, Inc. The term of the lease is five years and two years have elapsed. The lease prohibits subletting, but does **not** contain any provision relating to assignment. Marks approached Tudor and asked whether Tudor could release him from the balance of the term of the lease for $500. Tudor refused unless Marks would agree to pay $2,000. Marks located Flint who was interested in renting in Tudor's building and transferred the entire balance of the lease to Flint in consideration of his promise to pay Tudor the monthly rental and otherwise perform Marks' obligations under the lease. Tudor objects. Which of the following statements is correct?

a. A prohibition of the right to sublet contained in the lease completely prohibits an assignment.
b. The assignment need **not** be in writing.
c. The assignment does **not** extinguish Marks' obligation to pay the rent if Flint defaults.
d. The assignment is invalid without Tudor's consent.

20. Vance obtained a 25-year leasehold interest in an office building from the owner, Stanfield.

a. Vance's interest is nonassignable.
b. The conveyance of the ownership of the building by Stanfield to Wax will terminate Vance's leasehold interest.
c. Stanfield's death will not terminate Vance's leasehold interest.
d. Vance's death will terminate the leasehold interest.

May 1985 Questions

21. Which of the following factors is **least** significant in determining whether an item of personal property has become a fixture?

a. The value of the item.
b. The manner of attachment.
c. The adaptability of the item to the real estate.
d. The extent of injury which would be caused to the real property by the removal of the item.

Items 22 and 23 are based on the following information:

On July 1, Bean deeded her home to Park. The deed was never recorded. On July 5, Bean deeded the same home to Noll. On July 9, Noll executed a deed, conveying his title to the same home to Baxter. On July 10, Noll and Baxter duly recorded their respective deeds.

22. In order for Noll's deed from Bean to be effective it must

a. Contain the actual purchase price paid by Noll.
b. Be signed by Noll.
c. Include a satisfactory description of the property.
d. Be recorded with Bean's seal affixed to the deed.

23. If Noll and Baxter are bona fide purchasers for value, which of the following statements is correct?

a. Baxter's interest is superior to Park's.
b. Bean's deed to Park was void as between Bean and Park because it was **not** recorded.
c. Bean's deed to Noll was void because she had **no** interest to convey.
d. Baxter can recover the purchase price from Noll.

24. In order to create an easement by prescription a person must, in addition to fulfilling other requirements, have

a. Recorded the easement immediately upon its creation.
b. Received the express or implied consent of the true owner.
c. Used the land of another out of necessity.
d. Used the land of another in a manner that is open and notorious.

25. Lake purchased a home from Walsh for $95,000. Lake obtained a $60,000 loan from Safe Bank to finance the purchase, executing a promissory note and mortgage. The recording of the mortgage by Safe

a. Gives the world actual notice of Safe's interest.
b. Protects Safe's interest against the claims of subsequent bona fide purchasers for value.
c. Is necessary in order that Safe have rights against Lake under the promissory note.
d. Is necessary in order to protect Safe's interest against the claim of a subsequent transferee who does **not** give value.

26. Gray owned a warehouse free and clear of any encumbrances. Gray borrowed $30,000 from Harp Finance and executed a promissory note secured by a mortgage on the warehouse. The state within which the warehouse was located had a notice-race recording statute applicable to real property. Harp did not record its mortgage. Thereafter, Gray applied for a loan with King Bank, supplying King with certified financial statements which disclosed Harp's mortgage. After review of the financial statements, King approved Gray's loan for $25,000, taking an executed promissory note secured by a mortgage on the warehouse. King promptly recorded its mortgage. Which party's mortgage will be superior?

a. Harp's, since King had notice of Harp's interest.
b. Harp's, since it obtained a purchase money security interest.
c. King's, since it was the first to file.
d. King's, since a title search would fail to reveal Harp's interest.

27. A mortgagor who defaults on his mortgage payments will **not** be successful if he attempts to

a. Assert the equitable right to redeem.
b. Redeem the property after a judicial foreclosure sale has taken place.

c. Obtain any excess resulting from a judicial foreclosure sale.
d. Contest the validity of the price received at a judicial foreclosure sale by asserting that a higher price could have been received at a later date.

November 1985 Questions

Items 28 and 29 are based on the following information:

Mini, Inc., entered into a five-year lease with Rein Realtors. The lease was signed by both parties and immediately recorded. The leased building was to be used by Mini in connection with its business operations. To make it suitable for that purpose, Mini attached a piece of equipment to the wall of the building.

28. Which of the following is most important in determining whether the equipment became a fixture?
    a. Whether the equipment can be removed without material damage to the building.
    b. Whether the attachment is customary for the type of building.
    c. The fair market value of the equipment at the time the lease expires.
    d. The fact that the equipment was subject to depreciation.

29. Which of the following statements is correct regarding Mini's rights and liabilities?
    a. Mini is prohibited from assigning the lease if it is silent in this regard.
    b. Mini has a possessory interest in the building.
    c. Mini is strictly liable for all injuries sustained by any person in the building during the term of the lease.
    d. Mini's rights under the lease are automatically terminated by Rein's sale of the building to a third party.

30. Jane and her brother each own a ½ interest in certain real property as tenants in common. Jane's interest
    a. Is considered personal property.
    b. Will pass to her brother by operation of law upon Jane's death.
    c. Will pass upon her death to the person Jane designates in her will.
    d. May **not** be transferred during Jane's lifetime without her brother's consent.

31. Real estate title insurance
    a. May be transferred to a subsequent bona fide purchaser for value.
    b. Assures that the purchaser will take title free and clear of all defects.
    c. Assures that the purchaser will take title free and clear of all record defects since all exceptions to title must be cleared prior to the purchaser taking possession of the realty.
    d. Is generally **not** required where the contract is silent on this point.

Items 32 and 33 are based on the following information:

On June 1, 1985, Byrd Corp. purchased a high-rise building from Slade Corp. for $375,000. The building was encumbered by a mortgage and note dated May 1, 1980, executed by Slade. The mortgage had been duly recorded by the mortgagee, Fale Bank. The outstanding balance on the mortgage at the time of Byrd's purchase was $300,000. Byrd acquired the property subject to the mortgage held by Fale and, in addition, gave a mortgage on the building to Foxx Finance to secure a nonpurchase money promissory note in the sum of $50,000. Prior to any payments being made on either loan, Byrd defaulted. As a result, the building was properly sold at a foreclosure sale for $280,000.

32. Which of the following statements is correct regarding Byrd's and Slade's liability to Fale?
    a. Byrd is liable to Fale for any deficiency.
    b. Byrd is secondarily liable to Fale as a surety.
    c. Slade was automatically released from all liability to Fale upon Byrd's acquisition of the building subject to the mortgage.
    d. Slade is liable to Fale for any resulting deficiency.

33. As a result of the foreclosure sale
    a. Fale is entitled to receive the full $280,000 out of the proceeds.
    b. Fale is entitled to receive $240,000 out of the proceeds.
    c. Foxx is entitled to receive its full $50,000 from either Byrd or Slade.
    d. Foxx is entitled to receive $50,000 out of the proceeds.

34. Farr obtained a $45,000 loan from State Bank, executing a promissory note and mortgage. The loan was secured by a factory which Farr purchased from Datz for $79,000. State's recording of the mortgage

a. Cuts off the rights of all prior and subsequent lessees of the factory.
b. Transfers legal title to the factory to State.
c. Generally creates a possessory security interest in State.
d. Generally does **not** affect the rights of Farr and State against each other under the promissory note.

Problems

Problem 1 (1184,L2)

(15 to 25 minutes)

Joe Fine, a clothing manufacturer for the past 30 years, owns a plant on which Muni Bank holds a mortgage. He also leases a warehouse from Jay Co. in which he stores the clothing manufactured in the plant. There are 10 years remaining on the lease term. Fine plans to move his operations to another location and has decided to sell to Bean his interests in the plant and lease.

Fine is contemplating selling the plant to Bean under one of the following conditions:

- Bean taking the plant subject to the mortgage.
- Bean assuming the mortgage on the plant.
- Fine obtaining a duly executed novation from Muni and Bean.

The lease contains a clause prohibiting assignment to third parties. Fine is concerned with this clause as well as his continuing liability to Jay upon the transfer of his interests in the lease to Bean. In this regard, Fine asserts that:

- The clause prohibiting the assignment of the lease is void.
- The prohibition against assignment will not affect his right to sublease.
- He will be released from liability to pay rent upon obtaining Jay's consent either to sublet or to assign.

Required:

Answer the following, setting forth reasons for any conclusions stated.

a. In separate paragraphs, discuss Fine's and Bean's liability to Muni under each of the three aforementioned conditions relating to the mortgage, if Bean after purchasing the plant defaults on the mortgage payments, thereby creating a deficiency after a foreclosure sale.

b. In separate paragraphs, comment on Fine's assertions regarding the lease, indicating whether such assertions are correct and the reasons therefore.

Problem 2 (1182,L5b)

(7 to 10 minutes)

Part b. Darby Corporation, a manufacturer of power tools, leased a building for 20 years from Grayson Corporation commencing January 1, 1981. During January 1981, Darby affixed to the building a central air conditioning system and certain heavy manufacturing machinery, each with an estimated useful life of 30 years.

While auditing Darby's financial statements for the year ended December 31, 1981, the auditor noted that Darby was depreciating the air conditioning equipment and machinery, for financial accounting purposes, over their estimated useful lives of 30 years. In reading the lease, the auditor further noted that there was no provision with respect to the removal by the lessee of the central air conditioning system or machinery upon expiration of the lease. To verify that the appropriate estimated useful lives are being utilized for recording depreciation, the auditor is interested in establishing the rightful ownership of these assets upon the expiration of the lease. The auditor knows that in order to determine ownership of the assets at the expiration of the lease, one must first determine whether the assets would be considered personalty or realty.

Required:

Answer the following, setting forth reasons for any conclusions stated.

What major factors would likely be considered by a court in determining whether the air conditioning system and the machinery are to be regarded as personalty or realty, and what would be the likely determination with respect to each?

Multiple Choice Answers

1. d	8. d	15. a	22. c	29. b
2. c	9. d	16. c	23. a	30. c
3. c	10. b	17. b	24. d	31. d
4. b	11. d	18. c	25. b	32. d
5. *	12. a	19. c	26. a	33. a
6. *	13. a	20. c	27. d	34. d
7. d	14. c	21. a	28. a	

**Deleted by AICPA; effective 5/86*

Multiple Choice Answer Explanations

A.3. Fixture

1. (583,L1,53) (d) In order to establish the rightful ownership of the bungalows, it must be determined whether these bungalows would be considered personalty or realty. If these assets are considered personalty, then upon expiration of the lease, the tenants retain ownership and the right of removal. But if these assets are considered realty, then they remain with the land and Marsh retains ownership of the bungalows. Therefore, the issue is whether the bungalows become realty, as a result of being fixtures. A fixture is an item that was originally personal property, but which is affixed in a relatively permanent fashion such that it is considered to be part of the real property. There are several factors which must be applied in determining whether personal property (bungalows) which has been attached to real property is a fixture (realty).

1. The leasehold agreement itself, to the extent it manifested the intent of the parties (i.e., objective intent as to whether property is to be regarded as personalty or realty).
2. The mode and degree of annexation of the buildings to the land (i.e., the method and permanence to which the bungalow is physically attached to the real property).
3. The degree to which removal of the bungalows would cause injury to the buildings or the land.

The fact that the deed included a general clause relating to the bungalows is the least significant factor with regard to the determination of rightful ownership.

B. Interests in Real Property

2. (575,L1,8) (c) Joan has a life estate and may convey it to anyone. Upon Joan's death the ranch becomes the estate of George and Harry and will not be included in Joan's estate. George and Harry have joint tenancy so if George dies first, Harry obtains all rights, title, and interest in the ranch. The holder of a life estate does not hold it in trust for the future interests.

B.3. Concurrent Interest

3. (580,L1,26) (c) When the deed is unclear as to whether a joint tenancy or tenancy in common was intended, there is a statutory presumption in favor of tenancy in common. Thus, Donald and Martha were tenants in common and when Donald died his interest passed to his heirs. Thus, if Dombres wanted to obtain the entire title, he would have to purchase the interest of Donald's heirs, as well as Martha's interest.

4. (1179,L1,10) (b) The correct legal incident of ownership of property as tenants in common is that each of the co-tenants owns an undivided interest in the whole. Answer (a) is incorrect because upon the death of any of the other tenants in common, the deceased tenant's interest will pass to his heirs and not to the surviving co-tenants. Answer (c) is incorrect because a co-tenant in common can sell his interest in the property without the consent of the other co-tenants. Answer (d) is incorrect because upon the death of a co-tenant, his estate owns the same interest as the decedent.

B.4. Easement

5–6. *Deleted by AICPA; effective 5/86*

C. Contracts for Sale of Land

7. (582,L1,51) (d) When a "subject to financing" clause is in a contract for the purchase of real property, there must be good faith on the part of the buyer to use reasonable efforts to search out and obtain the requisite financing amount. Answer (a) is incorrect because a demand loan offered by the seller is inconsistent with the parties' intent of obtaining conventional mortgage financing and therefore does not satisfy the financing condition of the sales contract. Answer (b) is incorrect because a "subject to financing" clause is a condition precedent to the buyer's performance of the contract. Answer (c) is incorrect because a "subject to financing" clause is not implied as a matter of law, but must appear as part of the contract for purchase of real property. The rule in construing a "subject to financing" clause is that the court will infer the intent of the parties in light of the contract and all the circumstances surrounding the making of the contract, including customary community practices in financing of similar transactions. Unless the "subject to financing" clause is definite enough so as to determine the necessary financing requirements, the contract may become illusory in nature and not be enforceable.

8. (582,L1,53) (d) Unless there is a provision in the contract to the contrary, it is implied in a contract of sale that the seller must furnish the buyer with good and marketable title at closing (implied warranty of marketability). Marketable title is title which is reasonably free from doubt, one which a prudent purchaser would accept. The title should be free from all encumbrances, encroachments and other such defects. Therefore, the stone wall encroaching upon the land results in a potential breach of the implied warranty of marketability. Answer (a) is incorrect because when the contract is silent on the type of deed to be given, the buyer is not entitled to a warranty deed with full covenants, but rather a special warranty deed which does not contain full covenants. Answer (b) is incorrect because zoning law restrictions will not render a title unmarketable. Therefore, Fulcrum would not be permitted to avoid the contract. Answer (c) is incorrect because Fulcrum does not have to take the land subject to back taxes unless it appears as a reservation on the face of the deed.

D. Types of Deeds

9. (583,L1,56) (d) Recordation of a deed gives constructive notice "to the world" that title to the property has been conveyed. Therefore, the primary purpose of recording is to protect the grantee against subsequent purchasers, by putting subsequent purchasers "on notice." If the subsequent party claiming superior title had actual notice of the unrecorded deed, then the recordation objective has been met and recordation of the deed is irrelevant with regard to this particular party. An unrecorded deed is binding upon all persons having actual notice of its existence. Answer (a) is incorrect because recording of a deed is necessary to protect the grantee against subsequent purchasers even though the deed provides that recordation is not required. Answer (b) is incorrect because recordation is not essential to the validity of the deed, as between the grantor (Hart) and grantee (Purdy). A deed is effective when delivered and vests the purchaser's legal title to the property conveyed without recording. Answer (c) is incorrect because the primary purpose of recording a deed is to protect grantee against subsequent purchasers, not to provide local taxing authorities with information necessary to assess taxes.

F. Recording a Deed

10. (1173,L3,40) (b) There is an important difference between a quitclaim deed and a warranty deed in that the quitclaim deed does not contain any of the warranties of a warranty deed. An undisclosed mortgage violates a covenant that the deed is free from encumbrances. If the deed does not comply with the contract of sale, Fall does not have to accept it.

G. Title Insurance

11. (583,L1,55) (d) Title insurance is insurance against loss or damage resulting from defects in the title for a particular parcel of realty. Standard title insurance policies insure the buyer against title defects, such that the title insurance company is liable for any damages or expenses for a defect which is later discovered that is insured against. The maximum liability of the insurance company is the amount set in the policy. The company is generally liable for the difference in value of the property with and without the defect, up to the maximum set by the policy. The title insurance company (Valor) will be liable for title defects which arise, even though the defect could not have been discovered through the exercise of reasonable care. Therefore, answer (c) is incorrect because the title policy also provides protection against defects which are not shown on the public record. Answer (a) is incorrect because the title insurance company (Valor) is permitted to take exceptions to its insurance coverage, even if it agreed to insure and prepare the title abstract. Certain defects may not be insured against (i.e., "excepted") by the title policy. But such exceptions must be present on the face of the policy. A standard title insurance policy normally does not insure against losses arising from the following defects (i.e., exceptions which are stated on face of policy): liens imposed by law but not shown on the public record; claims of parties in possession not shown on the public record; zoning and building ordinances. Answer (b) is incorrect because Smith, the purchaser of a title insurance policy, is insured, but the policy does not run with the land. A subsequent purchaser of the land must procure his/her own title policy.

H. Adverse Possession

12. (1179,L1,41) (a) Cranston has acquired title to the 5 acres by adverse possession. Even though by mistake, Cranston did occupy the property under the claim of right doctrine, hostile to the actual owner in an open, notorious, and exclusive manner for a continuous period which would be sufficient under common law and most jurisdictions. Answer (b) is incorrect because an actual owner of rural property can lose title by adverse possession as described above. Answer (c) is incorrect because at best, Cranston could and apparently did, obtain full ownership of the property by adverse possession. Note that "at worst,"

Cranston could only obtain an easement but answer (c) said "at best." Answer (d) is incorrect because a purchaser of real property is deemed to have constructive notice of the presence of all persons located on the property that he is buying. Thus, in law, Dunbar is on notice of Cranston's presence.

I. Mortgages

13. (583,L1,57) (a) Answer (a) is an incorrect statement because under the "lien theory," a mortgage does not transfer title to the real property to the mortgagee. The mortgagor (borrower) gives the mortgagee (lender) a nonpossessory lien to secure the debt, and therefore, legal title remains with the mortgagor. Answer (b) is a true statement because a mortgage is usually accompanied by a negotiable promissory note which is incorporated in or refers to the mortgage. Answer (c) is a true statement because since a mortgage is an interest in real property, it is subject to the Statute of Frauds and, therefore, must be in writing and signed by the party to be charged (mortgagor). Answer (d) is a true statement because a mortgage provides a nonpossessory security interest in the mortgagee, with the mortgagor retaining possession of the real property used as the collateral.

14. (583,L1,59) (c) A purchase money mortgage is created when a mortgage is given concurrently with a sale of property by the buyer to the seller to secure the unpaid balance of the purchase price. A purchase money mortgage creates a nonpossessory lien that attaches to the land purchased. The purpose for recordation of a real property mortgage is to give constructive notice of the mortgage, such that all persons who subsequently acquire an interest in the mortgaged property will take subject to it. Therefore, if a mortgage is not duly recorded, a subsequent purchaser from Watkins will take property free of mortgage as long as purchaser had no knowledge of prior, unrecorded mortgage (i.e., a subsequent bona fide purchaser). Answer (a) is incorrect because an unrecorded mortgage is binding and valid against the mortgagor (Watkins) and his heirs or estate. Answer (b) is incorrect because an unrecorded mortgage is binding upon all persons having actual notice of its existence. For a subsequent mortgagee to have priority, or take free of the mortgage, s/he must have no knowledge of the prior, unrecorded mortgage. Therefore, Moch's mortgage will be valid against a subsequent mortgagee who had actual notice of the prior mortgage. Answer (d) is incorrect because donees do not come within the protection of the recording system since they do not give valuable consideration and therefore do not qualify as a bona fide purchaser for value. Thusly, Moch's mortgage will be valid against Watkin's friend who was given the farm as a gift, regardless if the friend took without notice of the mortgage.

15. (583,L1,60) (a) If the mortgagor (Peters) defaults on payment of the note which refers to the mortgage, the mortgagee (Fairmont) may resort to the land for payment. Fairmont may foreclose his mortgage upon Peters' default. If the foreclosure is successful, the court will direct that the property be sold at a foreclosure sale. The mortgagor, Peters, has several rights upon the foreclosure on the mortgage. The mortgagor has an equity of redemption. This right entitles the mortgagor to redeem the property even after foreclosure, but before the foreclosure sale, by paying the amount due plus interest and any other costs. When a mortgage foreclosure sale is held the equity of redemption ends. But the mortgagor has a statutory right of redemption which commences when the equity of redemption ends. The right of redemption affords the mortgagor one last chance to redeem the property. This right is strictly statutory in nature and the period of redemption after foreclosure sale varies from state to state. The mortgagor also has the right to refinance the loan with another lender and repay the original mortgage to Fairmont. The fact that the mortgagor's (Peters') equity in the property exceeds the amount of debt does not give Peters the right to remain in possession upon the mortgage foreclosure. However, Peters does have a right to the proceeds of the foreclosure sale to the extent the proceeds exceed the outstanding balance plus interest and any other costs the mortgagee has incurred.

16. (581,L1,53) (c) Golden, the original debtor, must satisfy the mortgage debt in the event that the foreclosure yields an amount less than the unpaid balance. Golden was originally liable on the mortgage, and no novation or release was granted by the mortgagor when Golden sold the warehouse to Clark. Answer (a) is incorrect because Clark did not take the property free of the mortgage. The property was subject to the mortgage at all times, but Clark was not personally liable as he did not **assume** the mortgage. Answer (b) is incorrect because Clark bought the property only **subject** to the mortgage and therefore, did not breach his agreement with Golden when he abandoned the location and stopped making the mortgage payments. Answer (d) is incorrect because Golden will not be able to sue Clark because Clark did not contract to be liable on the mortgage debt. Thus, there is no one for Golden to be subrogated to.

17. (581,L1,54) (b) Upon foreclosure, the first mortgagee has priority and must be paid in full before any payment is made to a subsequent mortgagee (second or third mortgagees). Answer (a) is incorrect because a second mortgagee remains a secured creditor in the bankruptcy proceedings although his interest is inferior to a first mortgagee. The doctrine of marshalling of assets may help a second mortgagee since it allows him to compel a first mortgagee to foreclose on other property available to the first mortgagee as security before foreclosing on property which a second mortgagee has a claim on. Answer (c) is incorrect because default of the second mortgage does not constitute a default of the first mortgage. Answer (d) is incorrect since second mortgages are sometimes obtained for a short period of time and can be paid off before maturity without consent of first mortgagee.

18. (1176,L3,40) (c) A novation (a substituted contract) in a mortgage transaction occurs when the purchaser agrees to assume the mortgage and the mortgagee agrees to release the original mortgagor with the purchaser as replacement. It is not invalid. In consideration for releasing Farber, the bank got Ronald to be personally liable on the debt. After the novation Farber has no liability even if Ronald defaults and the proceeds from the sale of the house are insufficient to satisfy the debt. A delegation is when a party to a contract turns over his duties to another party. Duties are delegated and rights are assigned. A delegant is still liable if the delegatee defaults, but Farber (as delegant) had no liability because of the novation.

J. Lessor-Lessee

19. (1180,L1,48) (c) A tenant may engage in an assignment or a sublease unless expressly prohibited by the lease. An assignment of the lease is the transfer by the lessee of his entire interest without reserving any right of re-entry. The assignor remains liable on the lease despite the assignment. Answer (c) is correct. Answer (a) is incorrect because a clause in the lease prohibiting a sublease does not prohibit an assignment. Since there were 3 years left on the lease when assigned, it was not capable of being performed within one year and consequently the agreement to transfer such an interest must be in writing [answer (b)]. There is no need for the landlord to consent to the assignment unless the lease expressly prohibited assignment.

20. (1176,L3,41) (c) A lease is not terminated by the death of either the lessor or the lessee. Thus, neither Stanfield's death nor Vance's death will terminate the lease. Transfer of ownership of leased property also does not terminate a lease. Therefore, if Stanfield conveys to Wax, Wax will take subject to the lease. As a general rule a lessee may assign or sublet a leasehold interest in accordance with reasonable restrictions in the lease; thus, Vance's interest is assignable.

May 1985 Answers

21. (585,L1,51) (a) A fixture is an item that was originally personal property but which is affixed to real property in a relatively permanent fashion such that it is considered to be part of the real property. Many factors must be considered when determining whether an item of personal property has become a fixture. Of the listed factors, the value of the item is the least significant. Answers (b), (c) and (d) are all significant factors used to determine whether an item of personal property has become a fixture, thus, they are all incorrect answers.

22. (585,L1,52) (c) The necessary requirements for a valid deed are (1) the names of the buyer (grantee) and the seller (grantor), (2) words evidencing an intent to convey, (3) a legally sufficient description of the land, (4) the grantor's (and usually the spouse's) signature, and (5) delivery of the deed. Answer (a) is incorrect since the purchase price need not be stated on the deed in order for it to be valid. Answer (b) is incorrect since a deed need not be signed by the buyer (grantee), but only by the seller (grantor) in order to be valid. Answer (d) is incorrect since the seller's (grantor's) seal need not be affixed to a deed in order for it to be effective, nor does it have to be recorded to be effective between the buyer and seller. Recordation of the deed merely protects the buyer from third parties claiming an interest in the property.

23. (585,L1,53) (a) Ordinarily, priorities as to titles are governed by a first in time, first in right rule. In this case, this would mean that Park would be the legal owner of the property since the property was deeded to him/her first. However, if a subsequent bona fide purchaser for value (i.e., a person who pays valuable consideration for the land, who acts in good faith and without knowledge of any previous conveyance or sale) records his/her deed before the party to whom the property was first deeded (Park), this subsequent bona fide purchaser will have legal title which will prevail over that of the party originally granted the deed. Thus in this case since Noll and Baxter were bona fide purchasers and, since they recorded their deeds before Park recorded his/hers, Baxter's interest in the property is superior to Park's. Answer (b) is incorrect since recordation of a deed is not necessary for it to be effective between the buyer and seller; recordation merely protects the deed holder from third parties claiming an

interest in the property. Answer (c) is incorrect since as discussed above, Noll and Baxter had legal title to the property. Answer (d) is incorrect because Baxter has received legal title to the property, thus Noll did not breach the contract.

24. (585,L1,54) (d) An easement is a nonpossessory interest in land consisting of the right to use someone else's property. In order to create an easement by prescription, a person must have used the land (1) in an open and notorious manner, (2) over a continuous and uninterrupted statutory period of time, and (3) under an adverse claim or right. The use must be "hostile," that is, without permission or consent from the owner. Answer (a) is incorrect because the recording statutes and the satisfaction thereof have no relevance or application to an easement created by prescription. Answer (b) is incorrect because, as discussed above, the use of the land must be "hostile." Answer (c) is incorrect because the use of the land need not arise out of necessity for creation of an easement by prescription.

25. (585,L1,55) (b) A mortgage is effective between the mortgagor, mortgagee and third parties who have actual or constructive notice of the mortgagee's interest. By Safe Bank's recording of the mortgage, the world receives constructive notice of the Bank's outstanding interest in the land. Since Safe Bank was the first to record a mortgage, it will have priority over all subsequent mortgagees subject to only purchase money security interests and statutory liens. Answer (a) is incorrect because recording a mortgage does not give actual notice to the world but merely constructive notice. Answer (c) is incorrect because recording is not necessary to have rights under a promissory note. Answer (d) is incorrect because only a good faith purchaser, for value, without notice of the mortgage, will be able to defeat a prior unrecorded mortgage in Lake's property.

26. (585,L1,56) (a) A bona fide purchaser, that is, one who has paid the purchase price in good faith and without knowledge of a prior unrecorded mortgage, will have superior rights if such purchaser records first. Since King Bank had actual knowledge of Harp's mortgage, it is not a bona fide purchaser. Harp's mortgage will have priority over King Bank's claim. Answer (b) is incorrect because Harp had a purchase money mortgage but failed to record. A purchase money mortgage takes priority over other recorded interests only if it is recorded. Answers (c) and (d) are incorrect because King had actual knowledge of Harp's interest.

27. (585,L1,57) (d) A judicial foreclosure sale of the debtor's real property is conducted generally at the direction of a court official (county sheriff) and confirmed by the court. A court will not refuse to confirm a sale merely because a higher price might have been received at a later time. The court will refuse to confirm a sale if the price is so low as to raise a presumption of unfairness or lack of protection for the mortgagor. Answer (a) is incorrect because a mortgagor has an equitable right to redeem the property up until foreclosure on the property. Answer (b) is incorrect because in a majority of states, a mortgagor has a statutory right of redemption following a foreclosure sale for a stipulated period of time. Under both an equity and a statutory redemption, the mortgagor must pay the sales price plus reasonable costs and expenses to redeem the property. Answer (c) is incorrect because a mortgagor is entitled to any excess resulting from a judicial foreclosure sale after all costs and expenses have been paid along with the amount outstanding on the mortgage note.

November 1985 Answers

28. (1185,L1,51) (a) There are several factors which must be considered in determining whether personal property attached to real property is a fixture. The most important consideration is the method and permanence with which the item is physically attached to the real property. If the item cannot be removed without material damage to the real property, then it is generally held that the item has become part of the real property. Therefore, answers (b), (c), and (d) are incorrect.

29. (1185,L1,52) (b) A lease creates a possessory interest in real property. Mini has the right to occupy the building for the term of the lease regardless of whether the owner, Rein, sells the property to a third party. Answer (a) is incorrect because lessee may engage in an assignment unless expressly prohibited by the lease; thus Mini may engage in an assignment if the lease is silent in this regard. Answer (c) is incorrect because Mini is only liable for those injuries that arise out of Mini's negligence. Answer (d) is incorrect because Mini's rights under the lease are not affected by a sale of the building.

30. (1185,L1,53) (c) Under tenancy in common, a deceased tenant's interest in real property will pass to the individual named in a will if the deceased died testate, that is, with a valid will. Therefore, if Jane executed a valid will before her death, the interest in the property will pass to the person she designated in the will. Answer (a) is incorrect because Jane has an interest in real property, not personal property. Answer (b) is incorrect because tenancy in common, unlike joint tenancy, does not have the right of survivorship. If

Jane and her brother had owned the property as joint tenants, upon Jane's death the property would have passed to her brother by operation of law. Answer (d) is incorrect because Jane, as a co-tenant in common, may convey her individual interest in her lifetime.

31. (1185,L1,54) (d) Real estate title insurance, while often present, is not required if the contract is silent on this point. Answer (a) is incorrect because even though the property may be transferred to a subsequent bona fide purchaser, the title insurance does not run with the property and cannot be transferred to the purchaser. Answer (b) is incorrect because title insurance insures against all defects of record; however, it does not insure against those defects which would be disclosed by physical inspection of the property or those defects listed as exceptions on the face of the policy. Answer (c) is incorrect because the face of the title insurance policy will often state existing exceptions (taxes, easements, etc.) that are not cleared prior to the purchaser taking possession and which the policy will not insure against.

32. (1185,L1,55) (d) When a buyer purchases property "subject to" a mortgage the buyer has **no** personal liability on the seller's mortgage. The seller remains personally liable on the mortgage. In a "subject to sale" the mortgagee may foreclose on the property in the hands of the purchaser. In the event the foreclosure sale yields an amount less than the unpaid balance, the original mortgagor is personally liable for the unpaid balance. Since Fale, the mortgagee, only received $280,000 from the foreclosure sale, Slade, the original mortgagor, is liable to Fale for the $20,000 unpaid balance. Answers (a) and (b) are incorrect because a buyer assumes **no** personal liability for a seller's mortgage when property is taken "subject to" a mortgage. Answer (c) is incorrect because in a "subject to" sale the seller remains personally liable to the mortgagee.

33. (1185,L1,56) (a) A mortgage provides the mortgagee with a nonpossessory security interest in real property. The purpose of recording the mortgage is to give constructive notice to third parties acquiring an interest in the property that the property is subject to an existing mortgage. When there are multiple mortgages on a single parcel of real property, the first mortgagee to duly record the mortgage will have priority over all subsequent mortgagees. Therefore, Fale's claim of $300,000 has priority over Foxx's $50,000 claim. Since the foreclosure sale only netted $280,000, Fale is entitled to receive the entire amount.

34. (1185,L1,57) (d) The recording of a mortgage has no effect on the rights of mortgagor or mortgagee. The purpose of recording a mortgage is to give constructive notice to third parties acquiring interest in the property that the property is subject to an existing mortgage. Answer (a) is incorrect because a mortgage has no effect on prior or subsequent lessees of property; rather, the mortgage only protects against subsequent purchasers. Answer (b) is incorrect because a mortgage does not transfer title to the mortgagee (State). The mortgagor (Farr) gives the mortgagee a nonpossessory lien to secure the debt, and therefore title remains with the mortgagor. Answer (c) is incorrect because a mortgage provides the mortgagor with a nonpossessory security interest in the collateral; the mortgagor retains the possession of the collateral for personal use.

Answer Outline

Problem 1 Purchase of Property with Existing Mortgage; Assignment and Sublease of Lease (1184,L2)

a. If Bean takes plant subject to mortgage
 Fine remains liable to Muni for any deficiency after foreclosure sale
 Bean avoids liability for any deficiency
  Bean's liability limited to his equity in plant
 If Bean assumes mortgage
 Fine remains liable to Muni for any deficiency after foreclosure sale
 Bean also liable to Muni for any deficiency
 If parties execute novation
 Fine completely released from liability to Muni
 Bean liable to Muni for any deficiency after foreclosure sale
 This novation must be in writing

b. Incorrect assertion
 Clause prohibiting assignment is valid since Fine consented to it
 Correct assertion
 Prohibition against assignment does not constitute prohibition against subletting premises
 Incorrect assertion
 Original tenant remains fully liable for stipulated rent under sublease or assignment unless specifically released by landlord

Unofficial Answer

Problem 1 Purchase of Property with Existing Mortgage; Assignment and Sublease of Lease (1184,L2)

a. If Bean purchases the plant subject to the mortgage, Fine will remain liable to Muni on the note and the underlying mortgage. Thus, Fine will be liable to Muni for any deficiency which may exist after a foreclosure sale. By taking the plant subject to the mortgage, Bean avoids liability for any deficiency. Therefore, Bean's potential liability is limited to any equity he may have built up in the plant.

If Bean assumes the mortgage, Fine will continue to be liable to Muni despite the agreement permitting Bean to assume the mortgage. Therefore, any resulting deficiency from a foreclosure sale will be Fine's responsibility. In addition, since Bean assumed the mortgage, he would also be held liable to Muni.

The execution of a novation would release Fine from his liability to Muni on the mortgage and would substitute Bean in his place. In order to have a valid novation involving real property, Muni must agree to it in writing.

b. Fine is incorrect in his assertion that the clause prohibiting the assignment of the lease is void. A clause prohibiting the assignment of a lease will not constitute a disabling restraint sufficient to prevent the free alienation of property and is therefore valid. Fine is bound by the restrictive clause since he consented to it when entering into the lease.

Fine's assertion that the prohibition against assignment will not affect his right to sublease is correct. In the absence of a provision in the lease to the contrary, a tenant has the right to assign the lease or sublet the premises. A prohibition against either will not be a prohibition against both. Therefore, Fine may sublease the warehouse to Bean despite the clause forbidding the assignment of the lease.

Fine's assertion that he will be released from liability under the lease upon obtaining Jay's consent to either sublet or assign is incorrect. Under a sublease or assignment, the original tenant will remain fully liable for the stipulated rent unless the landlord releases the original tenant from that obligation. The fact that the landlord consents to the sublease or assignment will not automatically relieve the original tenant from his obligation to pay rent. Therefore, any rent due pursuant to the lease will continue to be Fine's legal responsibility.

Answer Outline

Problem 2 Trade Fixtures (1182,L5b)

Part b.

To establish rightful ownership of air conditioning and machinery
 Auditor must determine whether these items are personalty or realty
  If personalty, then Darby has ownership rights
  If realty, then Grayson has ownership rights
Issue is whether these items have become realty by virtue of being fixtures
 Several factors must be considered in determining whether personal property attached to real property is a fixture
  Affixer's objective intent as to whether property is to be regarded as personalty or realty
  Method and permanence of physical attachment
  Adaptability of personal property use for the purpose for which real property is used
Personal property affixed by tenant for purpose of conducting business is a trade fixture
 Trade fixtures remain personal property
  Tenant has right to remove upon expiration of lease
Manufacturing machinery is a trade fixture
 Since integral part of Darby's business
Darby has right to remove upon expiration of lease
 Therefore, should be depreciated over machinery's useful life, i.e., 30 years

Air conditioning system is a fixture
  Does not appear to be used by Darby for conducting business
  Would result in material damage to realty if removed
Darby does not have right to remove upon expiration of lease
  Therefore, should be depreciated over life of lease, i.e., 20 years

Unofficial Answer

(Author Modified)

Problem 2 Trade Fixtures (1182,L5b)

Part b.

In order for the auditor to establish the rightful ownership of the central air conditioning system and the manufacturing machinery upon the expiration of the lease, s/he must determine whether these items would be considered personalty or realty. If these assets are considered **personalty,** then upon expiration of the lease Darby Corporation retains ownership. But if these assets are considered **realty**, then upon expiration of the lease they remain with the leased building (real property) and Grayson Corporation has ownership rights. Therefore, the issue is whether the air conditioning system and the machinery have become realty, as a result of being fixtures.

A fixture is an item that was originally personal property, but which is affixed to real property in a relatively permanent fashion such that it is considered to be part of the real property. There are several factors which must be applied in determining whether personal property which has been attached to real property is a fixture (realty).

1. **Affixer's objective intent as to whether property is to be regarded as personalty or realty.** In general, a court will hold that an item is a fixture if it were the intention of the parties that it becomes part of the real property. If the intent is clear, then this becomes the controlling factor in the determination of whether an item is a fixture or not.

This intent can be determined from various factors:

- The intention of the parties as expressed in the agreement.
- The nature of the article affixed.
- The relationship of the parties (i.e., the affixer and the owner of the real property).

2. **The method and permanence with which the item is physically attached (annexed) to the real property.** If the item cannot be removed without material injury to the real property, it is generally held that the item has become part of the realty (i.e., a fixture).

3. **Adaptability of use of the personal property for the purpose for which the real property is used.** If the personal property is necessary or beneficial to the use of the real property, the more likely the item is a fixture. But if the use or purpose of the item is unusual for the type of realty involved, it might be reasonable to conclude that it is personalty, and the affixer intends to remove the item when s/he leaves.

4. **The property interest of that person in the real property at the time of the attachment of the item.**

An item installed (affixed) by a tenant in connection with a business s/he is conducting on the leased premises is called a trade fixture. The personal property must be brought onto the leased business premises for the purpose of conducting and engaging in the trade or business for which the tenant occupies the premises.

Trade fixtures remain personal property, giving the tenant the right to remove these items upon expiration of the lease. But the tenant's right is limited to the extent that his/her action of removing the fixture may not materially damage the realty. If the item is so affixed onto the real property that removing it would cause substantial damage, then it is considered part of the realty.

Based upon the aforementioned analysis, the manufacturing machinery qualifies as a trade fixture. Since Darby Corporation is a manufacturer, this asset is integral to the conduct of business for which Darby occupies the premises. As a trade fixture, Darby retains rightful ownership of the machinery, giving Darby the right to remove the machinery upon expiration of the lease. However, Darby would be required to compensate Grayson for any damage caused by removal of the machinery. Therefore, Darby was correct to depreciate the machinery over its estimated useful life (i.e., 30 years).

However, the air conditioning system would not appear to qualify as a trade fixture. It does not appear to be employed by Darby in the furtherance of business operations for which the premises are leased. The air conditioning system would also be considered part of the realty, since it is probably so attached to the building that it would result in permanent structural damage to the building upon removal. Therefore, the air conditioning system would be considered a fixture (realty). As such, Darby would not have the right to remove it upon expiration of the lease. Thus, Darby should depreciate the air conditioning system over the life of the lease, (i.e. 20 years).

INSURANCE

Overview

Insurance is a contract whereby the insurer (insurance company) indemnifies the insured (policyholder) against loss on designated property due to specified risks such as fire, storm, etc. The obligation of the insured under the insurance contract is the payment of the stipulated premium. Before an insured can recover under a property insurance policy, the policyholder must have an insurable interest in the property at the time it was damaged or destroyed. Basically, insurance is limited to providing protection against the risk of loss arising from a happening of events caused by the negligence of insured and negligence and intentional acts of third parties. Insurance does not protect against loss due to intentional acts of insured. Insurance contracts like others, require agreement, consideration, capacity, legality, compliance with the Statute of Frauds, and delivery.

Primary emphasis on the exam is placed upon knowledge of fire and casualty insurance. The exam has emphasized insurable interest, co-insurance and pro rata clauses, risks protected against, subrogation, and assignment of insurance contracts.

A. General Considerations

1. Insurance is the distribution of the cost of risk over a large number of individuals subject to the same risk, in order to reimburse the few who actually suffer from the risk
2. Insurance is designed to protect against the large unexpected losses, not small everyday losses
   a. This is one reason for the $50 or $100 deductible clause in auto-collision insurance
3. Rates are based on past losses. There must be a large number of risks to provide an accurate average loss.
4. Insurance is not supposed to be gambling. Therefore, only those who may suffer loss from the risk may insure and only to the extent that loss may occur. (See Insurable interest below.)
   a. Indemnity is the purpose of insurance
5. Intentional acts of the insured usually are not insurable, e.g., fire by arson, liability for assault and battery
   a. Negligence or carelessness is insurable and is generally not a defense of the insurer
   b. Negligence of an insured's employees is also covered
6. Self-insurance is the periodic setting aside of money into a fund to provide for possible losses
   a. Not true insurance, because it is not a distribution of risk; it is preparation to meet possible losses
   b. Advantage is the saving if losses are small or nonexistent

c. Disadvantages are the possibility of loss before a sufficient reserve is created and the possibility of losses greater than the cost of regular insurance premiums

7. Insurers

a. Most insurers have incorporated due to conditions of the business
b. Stock companies--typical corporation with capital stock and shareholders
c. Mutual companies--no capital stock. Policyholders are the capital contributors and are actually the shareholders.

d. Mixed companies--issue capital stock and ordinary policies of stock companies. Also issue participating policies (entitled to share in surplus).

B. <u>Insurance Contract</u>

1. Similar to a common law contract. Must contain all the essential elements, i.e., agreement, legality, capacity, and consideration

a. Minors are often allowed, by statute, to take out insurance policies

2. Generally a unilateral contract where the insured prepays the premiums and the insurer promises to indemnify the insured against loss

3. Insurance is generally binding at the time of unconditional acceptance of the application and communication of this to the insured

a. The application is the offer, and issuance of the policy is acceptance
b. A company agent (as opposed to an independent agent) usually has power to issue a temporarily binding slip which obligates the insurer during the interim before issuance of the policy
c. Physical delivery of the written policy is not necessary
d. Insurer may require conditions to be met before the policy becomes effective, e.g., pay a premium

1) A general agent may accept a policy for the insured

4. Policy is voidable at option of insurer (because assent was not real in law) if there is

a. Concealment--the insured failed to inform the insurer at the time of application of a fact material to the insurer's risk

EXAMPLE: An applicant for auto insurance is unable to drive and does not so inform the insurer.

1) Any matter specifically asked by insurer is by law material and failure to disclose or a misleading answer is concealment

2) Need not disclose facts learned after making the contract

b. Material misrepresentation by insured, e.g., nonexistent subject matter

1) Representation acceptable if substantially true, e.g., value of subject matter does not have to be exact

c. Breach of warranty. A warranty is a representation incorporated in the policy. It constitutes a condition precedent to the liability of the insurer and generally is presumed to be material (therefore, does not have to be proved material as do misrepresentations and concealments).

EXAMPLE: An applicant for fire insurance warrants that a night watchman will be on duty at night at all times to check for fire. If he is not and a loss occurs, this may release the insurer.

5. Statute of Frauds does not require the insurance contract to be in writing because it may fall within the one-year rule (but usually is required by state statutes)
6. Insurable interest
   a. There must be a relationship between the insured and the insured event so that if the event occurs the insured will suffer substantial loss
   b. In property, there must be both a legal interest and a possibility of pecuniary loss
      1) Legal interest may be ownership or a secured interest, e.g., general creditors do not have an insurable interest but judgment lien creditors and mortgagees do
      2) The insurable interest need not necessarily be present at the inception of the policy so long as it is present at the time of the loss
      3) One can insure only to the extent one has an insurable interest, e.g., mortgagee can insure only the amount still due
      4) Contract to purchase or possession of property can give an insurable interest, e.g., bailee has insurable interest
      5) UCC expands the instances when an insurable interest exists. See Overview.

         EXAMPLE: Owners, partners, lessees, mortgagees, bailees, and judgment lien creditors.

C. <u>Subrogation</u>

1. This is the right of the insurer to step into the shoes of the insured as to any cause of action relating to a third party whose conduct caused the loss

   EXAMPLE: While driving his car, X is hit by Y. If X's insurance company pays X, the insurance company is subrogated to X's claim against Y.

   a. Applies to accident, automobile collision, and fire policies
2. A general release of a third party, who caused the loss, by the insured will release the insurer from his obligation

   EXAMPLE: While driving his car, X is hit by Y. Y talks X into signing a statement that X releases Y from all liability. X will not be able to recover on his insurance. X's insurance company is released when Y is released.

   a. Because the insurer's right of subrogation has been cut off
   b. A partial release will release the insurer to that extent

D. Liability Insurance

1. Insurer agrees to protect insured against liability for accidental damage to persons or property

   a. Usually includes duty to defend in a law suit brought by third parties
   b. Intentional wrongs not covered, e.g., fraud
   c. Insurer has not rights against the insured for causing the loss because this is what the insurance is to protect against

2. Malpractice--a form of personal liability

   a. Used by accountants, doctors, lawyers
   b. Protects against liability for harm caused by errors or negligence in work
   c. Does not protect against intentional wrongs, e.g., fraud

E. Fire Insurance (see also Theory and Practice Module 26, Fixed Assets)

1. Generally covers direct fire damage and also damage as a result of fire such as smoke, water, or chemicals

   a. Does not cover damage from a friendly fire, e.g., smoke from a fire in a fireplace
   b. Covers hostile fires, i.e., those not intended or those that have left the intended burning spot

2. Blanket policy applies to a class of property which may be changing (inventory) rather than a specific piece of property (specific policy)

3. Valued policy predetermines value of property which becomes the face value of the policy

   a. Unvalued policy (open) is one wherein the value of the property is determined at time of loss but there is a maximum amount of the policy

4. Recovery

   a. Under an open policy (unvalued) the insured recovers the FMV (determined at date of loss) of the property destroyed
   b. A valued policy pays the face of the policy for a total loss
   c. Always limited, at maximum, to face value of the policy
   d. For partial destruction, the actual damage is recovered

5. Coinsurance clause

   a. The insured agrees to maintain insurance equal to a specified percentage of the value of his property. Then when a loss occurs, the insurer only pays a proportionate share if the insured has not carried the specified percentage.

      EXAMPLE: Insured owns a building valued at $100,000. He obtains 2 insurance policies for $20,000 each and they both contain 80% coinsurance clauses. There is a fire and his loss is $40,000. He will only collect $20,000 on his insurance. See formula below.

   b. Formula

$$\text{Recovery} = \text{Actual Loss} \times \frac{\text{Amount of Insurance}}{\text{Coinsurance \% X FMV of Property*}}$$

* At time of loss

c. Does not apply when insured property is totally destroyed

EXAMPLE: On October 10, Harry's warehouse was totally destroyed by fire. At the time of the fire, the warehouse had a value of $500,000 and was insured against fire for $300,000. The policy contained an 80% coinsurance clause. Harry will recover $300,000, the face value of the policy, because total destruction occurred and the coinsurance clause would not apply. If the warehouse had been only partially destroyed, with damages amounting to $300,000, Harry would only recover $225,000 (based on the formula above), because the coinsurance clause would apply.

d. When multiple policies exist, they share responsibility in proportion to their face amounts.

EXAMPLE: Market value $200,000, loss $60,000.

Policy	Coins	Face	Loss Proration	Coins Limitation	Lower of last 3 col.
1	---	10,000	6,000	---	6,000
2	70%	40,000	24,000	17,143*	17,143
3	80%	30,000	18,000	11,250**	11,250
4	90%	20,000	12,000	6,667***	6,667
		100,000	60,000		41,060

* $\frac{40,000}{140,000}$ X 60,000   ** $\frac{30,000}{160,000}$ X 60,000   *** $\frac{20,000}{180,000}$ x 60,000

In the case of multiple policies, the formula to remember for computing the coinsurance limitation for cash policy is:

$$\frac{\text{Face of Policy}}{\text{Greater of Aggregate Insurance Coverage of All Companies } \underline{\text{or}} \text{ Coinsurance Requirement}} \times \text{Loss}$$

6. Pro rata clause

a. Someone who is insured with multiple policies can only collect, from each insurer, the proportionate amount of the loss

1) Proportion is the amount insured by each insurer to the total amount of insurance

EXAMPLE: Insured incurs a loss due to fire on property and is entitled to a $10,000 recovery. The property is covered by two insurance policies, one for $8,000 from Company A and one for $12,000 from Company B. Consequently, total insurance coverage on the property was $20,000. Company A will be liable for 40% ($8,000/$20,000) of fire loss, i.e., $4,000 (40% x $10,000). Company B will be liable for 60% ($12,000/$20,000) of fire loss, i.e., $6,000 (60% x $10,000).

7. Proof of loss

   a. Insured must give insurer a statement of the amount of loss, cause of loss, etc.
   b. Must be done within a time period, e.g., 60 days

      1) Failure to comply will excuse the insurer's liability unless performance is made impracticable, e.g., death of insured

8. After destruction of property, creditors may treat the insurance proceeds as any other asset of the insured. Secured creditors have an interest in the proceeds without a special agreement to that effect.

9. Mortgagor and mortgagee have insurable interests, and mortgagees usually require insurance for their protection

10. Fire policies are usually not assignable because of the risk

    a. I.e., danger that new owner would not be reliable, e.g., record of arson
    b. Even if property is sold, there can be no assignment of insurance without insurer's consent
    c. A claim against an insurer may be assigned, e.g., house burns and insurance company has not yet paid

Multiple Choice Questions (1–17)

1. Fuller Corporation insured its factory and warehouse against fire with the Safety First Insurance Company. As a part of the bargaining process, in connection with obtaining the policy Fuller was required by Safety First to give in writing certain warranties regarding the insured risk. Fuller did so and they were incorporated into the policy. Which of the following correctly describes the law applicable to such warranties?
   a. The warranties given by Fuller will be treated as representations.
   b. It was **not** necessary that the warranties given by Fuller be in writing to be effective.
   c. In the event that Fuller does **not** strictly comply with the warranties it has given, it will be denied recovery in a substantial number of states.
   d. In deciding whether the language contained in a policy constitutes a warranty, the courts usually construe ambiguous language in a way which favors the insurance company.

2. The insurable interest in property
   a. Can be waived by consent of the parties.
   b. Is subject to the incontestability clause.
   c. Must be present at the time the loss occurs.
   d. Is only available to owners, occupiers, or users of the property.

3. A fire insurance policy is one common type of contract. As such it must meet the general requirements necessary to establish a binding contract. In a dispute between the insured and the insurance company, which of the following is correct?
   a. The contract is always unilateral.
   b. Insurance contracts are specifically included within the general Statute of Frauds.
   c. The insured must satisfy the insurable interest requirement.
   d. The actual delivery of the policy to the insured is a prerequisite to the creation of the insurance contract.

4. Burt owns an office building which is leased to Hansen Corporation under the terms of a long-term lease. Both Burt and Hansen have procured fire insurance covering the building. Which of the following is correct?
   a. Both Burt and Hansen have separate insurable interests.
   b. Burt's insurable interest is limited to the book value of the property.
   c. Hansen has an insurable interest in the building, but only to the extent of the value of any additions or modifications it has made.
   d. Since Burt has legal title to the building, he is the only party who can insure the building.

5. Peters leased a restaurant from Brady with all furnishings and fixtures for a period of five years with an option to renew for two additional years. Peters made several structural improvements and modifications to the interior of the building. He obtained a fire insurance policy for his own benefit insuring his interest in the property for $25,000. The restaurant was totally destroyed by an accidental fire. Peters seeks recovery from his insurer. Subject to policy limits, which of the following is correct?
   a. Peters is entitled to recover damages to the extent of the value of his leasehold interest.
   b. Peters is entitled to recover for lost profits due to the fire even though the policy is silent on the point.
   c. Peters must first seek redress from the owner before he is entitled to recover.
   d. Peters will not recover because he lacks the requisite insurable interest in the property.

6. Bernard Manufacturing, Inc., owns a three-story building which it recently purchased. The purchase price was $200,000 of which $160,000 was financed by the proceeds of a mortgage loan from the Cattleman Savings and Loan Association. Bernard immediately procured a standard fire insurance policy on the premises for $200,000 from the Magnificent Insurance Company. Cattleman also took out fire insurance of $160,000 on the property from the Reliable Insurance Company of America. The property was subsequently totally destroyed as a result of a fire which started in an adjacent loft and spread to Bernard's building. Insofar as the rights and duties of Bernard, Cattleman, and the insurers are concerned, which of the following is a correct statement?
   a. Cattleman Savings and Loan lacks the requisite insurable interest to collect on its policy.
   b. Bernard Manufacturing can only collect $40,000.

c. Reliable Insurance Company is subrogated to Cattleman's rights against Bernard upon payment of Cattleman's insurance claim.
d. The maximum amount that Bernard Manufacturing can collect from Magnificent is $40,000, the value of its insurable interest.

7. Alphonse, a sole CPA practitioner, obtained a malpractice insurance policy from the Friendly Casualty Company. In regard to this coverage
a. Issuance of an unqualified opinion by Alphonse when he knows the statements are false does not give Friendly a defense.
b. The policy would automatically cover the work of a new partnership formed by Alphonse and Borne.
c. Friendly will not be subrogated to rights against Alphonse for his negligent conduct of an audit.
d. Coverage includes injury to a client resulting from a slip on a rug negligently left loose in Alphonse's office.

8. *Deleted by AICPA; effective 5/86*

9. Adams Company purchased a factory and warehouse from Martinson for $150,000. Adams obtained a $100,000 real estate mortgage loan from a local bank and was required by the lender to pay for the cost of title insurance covering the bank's interest in the property. In addition, Adams was required to obtain fire insurance sufficient to protect the bank against loss due to fire. The co-insurance factor has been satisfied. Under these circumstances, which of the following is correct?
a. Adams can purchase only $50,000 of title insurance since it already obtained a $100,000 title policy for the bank equal to the bank loan.
b. The bank could not have independently obtained a fire insurance policy on the property because Adams has legal title.
c. If Adams obtained a $150,000 fire insurance policy which covered its interest and the bank's interest in the property and there is an estimated $50,000 of fire loss, the insurer will typically be obligated to pay the owner and the bank the amounts equal to their respective interests as they may appear.
d. If Adams obtained a $100,000 fire insurance policy covering the bank's interest and $150,000 covering his own interest, each would obtain these amounts upon total destruction of the property.

10. Margo, Inc., insured its property against fire with two separate insurance companies, Excelsior and Wilberforce. Each carrier insured the property for its full value, and neither insurer was aware that the other had also insured the property. The policies were the standard fire insurance policies used throughout the United States. If the property is totally destroyed by fire, how much will Margo recover?
a. Nothing because Margo has engaged in an illegal gambling venture.
b. The full amount from both insurers.
c. A ratable or pro rata share from each insurer, not to exceed the value of the property insured.
d. Only 80% of the value of the property from each insurer because of the standard coinsurance clause.

11. The underlying rationale which justifies the use of the coinsurance clause in fire insurance is
a. It provides an insurable interest in the insured if this is **not** already present.
b. To require certain minimum coverage in order to obtain full recovery on losses.
c. It prevents arson by the owner.
d. It makes the insured more careful in preventing fires since the insured is partially at risk in the event of loss.

12. Carter, Wallace, and Jones are partners. Title to the partnership's office building was in Carter's name. The Carter, Wallace, and Jones partnership procured a $150,000 fire insurance policy on the building from the Amalgamated Insurance Company. The policy contained an 80% coinsurance clause. Subsequently, the building was totally destroyed by fire. The value of the building was $200,000 at the time the policy was issued, and $160,000 at the time of the fire. Under the fire insurance policy, how much can the partnership recover?
a. Nothing, since it did **not** have legal title to the building.
b. The face value of the policy ($150,000).
c. Eighty percent of the loss ($128,000).
d. The value at the time of the loss ($160,000).

13. Hazard & Company was the owner of a building valued at $100,000. Since Hazard did not believe that a fire would result in a total loss, it procured two standard fire insurance policies on the property. One was for $24,000 with the Asbestos Fire Insurance Company and the other was for $16,000 with the Safety Fire Insurance Company. Both policies contained standard pro rata and 80% coinsurance clauses. Six months later, at which time the building was still valued at $100,000, a fire occurred which resulted in a loss of $40,000. What is the total amount Hazard can recover on both policies and the respective amount to be paid by Asbestos?

a. $0 and $0.
b. $20,000 and $10,000.
c. $20,000 and $12,000.
d. $40,000 and $20,000.

May 1985 Questions

14. The coinsurance clause with regard to property insurance

a. Prohibits the insured from obtaining an amount of insurance which would be less than the coinsurance percentage multiplied by the fair market value of the property.
b. Encourages the insured to be more careful in preventing losses since the insured is always at least partially at risk when a loss occurs.
c. Permits the insured to receive an amount in excess of the policy amount when there has been a total loss and the insured carried the required coverage under the coinsurance clause.
d. Will result in the insured sharing in partial losses when the insured has failed to carry the required coverage under the coinsurance clause.

15. The insurable interest requirement with regard to property insurance

a. May be waived by a writing signed by the insured and insurer.
b. May be satisfied by a person other than the legal owner of the property.
c. Must be satisfied at the time the policy is issued.
d. Must be satisfied by the insured's legal title to the property at the time of loss.

November 1985 Questions

16. The coinsurance feature of property insurance

a. Prevents the insured from insuring for a minimal amount and recovering in full for such losses.
b. Precludes the insured from insuring for less than the coinsurance percentage.
c. Is an additional refinement of the insurable interest requirement.
d. Is fixed at a minimum of 80% by law.

17. West is seeking to collect on a property insurance policy covering certain described property which was destroyed. The insurer has denied recovery based upon West's alleged lack of an insurable interest in the property. In which of the situations described below will the insurance company prevail?

a. West is **not** the owner of the insured property but a mere long-term lessee.
b. The insured property belongs to a general trade debtor of West and the debt is unsecured.
c. The insured property does **not** belong to West, but instead to a corporation which he controls.
d. The property has been willed to West's father for life and, upon his father's death, to West as the remainderman.

Problems

Problem 1 (1182,L5a)

(10 to 15 minutes)

Part a. While auditing the financial statements of Jackson Corporation for the year ended December 31, 1981, Harvey Draper, CPA, desired to verify the balance in the insurance claims receivable account. Draper obtained the following information:

- On November 4, 1981, Jackson's Parksdale plant was damaged by fire. The fire caused $200,000 damage to the plant, which was purchased in 1970 for $600,000. When the plant was purchased, Jackson obtained a loan secured by a mortgage from Second National Bank of Parksdale. At the time of the fire the loan balance, including accrued interest, was $106,000. The plant was insured against fire with Eagle Insurance Company. The policy contained a "standard mortgagee" clause and an 80% coinsurance clause. The face value of the policy was $600,000 and the value of the plant was $1,000,000 at the time of the fire.
- On December 10, 1981, Jackson's Yuma warehouse was totally destroyed by fire. The warehouse was acquired in 1960 for $300,000. At the time of the fire, the warehouse was unencumbered by any mortgage; it was insured against fire with Eagle for $300,000; and it had a value of $500,000. The policy contained an 80% coinsurance clause.
- On December 26, 1981, Jackson's Rye City garage was damaged by fire. At the time of the fire, the garage had a value of $250,000 and was unencumbered by any mortgage. The fire caused $60,000 damage to the garage, which was constructed in 1965 at a cost of $50,000. In 1975 Jackson expanded the capacity of the garage at an additional cost of $50,000. When the garage was constructed in 1965, Jackson insured the garage against fire for $50,000 with Eagle, and this policy was still in force on the date of the fire. When the garage was expanded in 1975, Jackson obtained $100,000 of additional fire insurance coverage from Queen Insurance Company. Each policy contains an 80% coinsurance clause and a standard pro-rata clause.

Required:

Answer the following, setting forth reasons for any conclusions stated.

1. How much of the fire loss relating to the Parksdale plant will be recovered from Eagle?
2. How will such recovery be distributed between Second National and Jackson?
3. How much of the fire loss relating to the Yuma warehouse will be recovered from Eagle?
4. How much of the fire loss relating to the Rye City garage will be recovered from the insurance companies?
5. What portion of the amount recoverable in connection with the Rye City garage loss will Queen be obligated to pay?

Problem 2 (1176,L6b&c)

(15 to 20 minutes)

Part b. Balsam was a partner in the firm Wilkenson, Potter & Parker. The firm had a buy-out arrangement whereby the partnership funded the buy-out agreement with insurance on the lives of the partners payable to the partnership. When the insurance policies were obtained by the partnership, Balsam understated his age by three years. Eight years later, Balsam decided to sell his partnership interest to Gideon. The sale was consummated and the other partners admitted Gideon as a partner in Balsam's place. The partnership nevertheless retained ownership in the policy on the life of Balsam and continued to pay the premiums thereon. Balsam died one year later. The insurance company refuses to pay the face value of the policy claiming that the partnership is only entitled to the amount of the premiums paid. As a basis for this position, the insurance company asserts lack of an insurable interest and material misrepresentation.

Required:

Answer the following, setting forth reasons for any conclusions stated.

Will Wilkenson, Potter & Parker prevail in an action against the insurance company? Give specific attention to the assertions of the insurance company.

Part c. Anderson loaned the Drum Corporation $60,000. The loan was secured by a first mortgage on Drum's land and the plant thereon. Anderson independently procured a fire insurance policy for $60,000 on the mortgaged property from the Victory Insurance Company. Six years later when the mortgage had been amortized down to $52,000, the plant was totally destroyed by a fire caused by faulty electrical wiring in the rear storage area.

Required:

Answer the following, setting forth reasons for any conclusions stated.

1. Anderson seeks recovery of $60,000 from the Victory Insurance Company. How much will it collect?
2. Upon payment by Victory Insurance Company, what rights does Victory have?

Multiple Choice Answers

1. c	5. a	9. c	12. b	15. b
2. c	6. c	10. c	13. c	16. a
3. c	7. c	11. b	14. d	17. b
4. a	8. *			

**Deleted by AICPA; effective 5/86*

Multiple Choice Answer Explanations

B. Insurance Contract

1. (1181,L1,60) (c) A warranty is a statement of fact by the insured which materially relates to the insurer's risk and must be incorporated into the policy to qualify as a warranty. The warranties given by Fuller constitute condition precedents to the liability of the insurer. Therefore, if Fuller fails to comply with these warranties, the policy is voidable at the option of the insurer and Fuller will be denied recovery. Answer (a) is incorrect because representations are statements not inserted in the policy. By statute, most warranties in life insurance policies are representations but this is not true of warranties in property insurance policies. Answer (b) is incorrect because a warranty must appear on the face of, be embodied in, or be attached to the policy itself to be effective. Therefore, the warranties given by Fuller must be in writing. Answer (d) is incorrect because the courts will construe ambiguous language based upon the mutual intent of the parties.

B.6. Insurable Interest

2. (583,L1,36) (c) The essence of the insurable interest concept is to prevent recovery by those who have no economic interest in the property. Therefore, there must be a relationship (i.e., an insurable interest) between the insured and the insured event such that the occurrence of the event will cause the insured to suffer substantial loss. The insurable interest in property need not necessarily be present at the inception of the policy but it must be present at the time of the loss. Answer (a) is incorrect because the insurable interest requirement cannot be waived by the parties to an insurance contract. Answer (b) is incorrect because an incontestability clause relates to life insurance, whereby upon expiration of a certain time period (usually 2 years), the insurer is estopped from contesting the insurance policy based on misstatements or concealments. Answer (d) is incorrect because an insurable interest is also available to others who have a legal or economic interest and a possibility of pecuniary loss in property such as: a secured creditor who has an insurable interest in specific property that secures the debtor against which the judgment attaches; a stockholder who has an insurable interest in property owned by corporation; a bailee who has insurable interest in property held in his possession.

3. (1181,L1,59) (c) An essential element of an insurance contract is the existence of an insurable interest. There must be a relationship between the insured and the insured event such that, if the event occurs, the insured will suffer substantial loss. An insurable interest in property exists when there is both a legal interest in the property and a possibility of pecuniary loss if the property is destroyed. Answer (a) is incorrect because an insurance contract often is unilateral in nature, but there is no requirement that it must be. Answer (b) is incorrect because the Statute of Frauds does not require a written contract because the event insured against may occur within one year from the issuance of the insurance policy. Answer (d) is incorrect because physical delivery of the policy is not a requisite for validity. An act or words by the insurer that clearly manifests an intent to be bound will constitute constructive delivery. The insurance contract is generally binding at the time of unconditional acceptance of the application by the insurer and communication of such acceptance to the insured.

4. (581,L1,48) (a) A person has an insurable interest in property if he will benefit by its continued existence or suffer from its destruction and has a legal or equitable interest in the property (e.g., a mortgagee, mortgagor, tenant in rented property, or partner in partnership property). Both Burt (owner of legal title) and Hansen (tenant in leased property) have an insurable interest; therefore, answer (a) is true. Answer (b) is incorrect because Burt has an insurable interest to the extent of any economic loss he might suffer. Such a loss would normally be measured by market value of the property, not book value. Answer (c) is also false because the tenant has an insurable interest for the amount of economic loss he will suffer in the event the property is destroyed. This amount may be greater or less than the value of the additions or modifications. The tenants would measure their economic loss in reference to items such as the expense of finding a new office building or new business space.

5. (578,L1,20) (a) A lessee has an insurable interest to the extent of the value of his leasehold interest. Therefore Peters is entitled to recover damages to the extent of the value of his leasehold interest, not to exceed the $25,000 policy limit. Answer (b) is incorrect because lost profits are not recoverable unless specifically included in the policy. Answer (c) is incorrect because an insured party may recover upon loss and need not seek redress from any other party first. Peters' insurance carrier would obtain by right of subrogation, how-

ever, any potential claim he has against the owner. Answer (d) is incorrect because a lessee has an insurable interest in leased property.

C. Subrogation

6. (1180,L1,53) (c) Answer (c) is correct because under a fire insurance policy, an insurer who pays a claim is subrogated (succeeds to the rights of the insured) to any rights that the insured had against a third party. Answer (a) is incorrect since Cattleman, as mortgagee, has an insurable interest to the extent of the outstanding debt ($160,000). If the policy is a valued policy, then Bernard will collect $200,000. If it is an open policy, then Bernard will collect the market value of the building at the time of destruction up to a maximum of $200,000. Thus, answers (b) and (d) are incorrect.

7. (574,L3,53) (c) The insurance company would not be subrogated to the rights against its insured who holds a malpractice policy for negligence. The reason for a malpractice insurance policy is to protect the insured against this type of action. Malpractice insurance would not cover intentional wrongs such as fraud. A malpractice policy would not automatically cover the new partnership, because the character of the new partner is crucial to the risk that the insurance company takes. Injuries such as a slip on a rug are not covered under malpractice insurance, but under personal liability.

Automobile Insurance

8. *Deleted by AICPA; effective 5/86*

E. Fire Insurance

9. (578,L1,17) (c) Where both the owner and a mortgagee are insured under a policy, typically a loss payable clause will allow the mortgagee to collect to the extent of his loss. Answer (d) is incorrect because the policy is probably open or unvalued rather than a stated value policy. Unless it is a stated value policy, the insurance company will only be liable for the smaller of the policy face value or the FMV of the loss at the time of the loss. Answer (b) is incorrect because a mortgagee has an insurable interest and can independently obtain a fire insurance policy on mortgaged property. Answer (a) is incorrect because an owner of property can purchase any amount of title insurance that the insurance company agrees to sell.

10 (1175,L3,38) (c) A person who insures with multiple policies can only collect the proportionate amount of the loss from each insurer. The limit of recovery is the value of the loss. There is nothing illegal about insuring with more than one policy or to insure for more than the value of the property. A coinsurance clause must be stated in the policy and does not affect recovery if insurance is carried for full value.

E.5. Coinsurance Clause

11. (583,L1,37) (b) The coinsurance requirement provides that if the property is insured for less than a certain percent (usually 80%) of its fair market value at the time of the loss, the insurance company will be liable for only a portion of any loss, i.e., the owner becomes a coinsurer with the insurance company and must proportionately bear the loss. Therefore, if the owner insures his/her property at this stated minimum percentage, s/he will recover any loss in full up to the face amount of the policy. Answer (a) is incorrect because the insurable interest requirement is distinct and separate from the coinsurance feature of property insurance. Answers (c) and (d) are incorrect because the underlying rationale of the coinsurance clause is not to prevent arson by the owner nor to increase the care of the insured; the coinsurance provision only relates to the amount of insurance recovery in the event of loss.

12. (1181,L1,56) (b) The coinsurance clause would only apply if there had been partial destruction of the property insured. Since there was total destruction with the property being valued at $160,000 ($10,000 above the face value of the policy), the partnership would recover the face value ($150,000). Thus, answers (c) and (d) are incorrect. Answer (a) is incorrect because for the partnership to recover, it must have an insurable interest in the property which is satisfied by both a legal interest in the property and a possibility of pecuniary loss if the property is destroyed. The Carter, Wallace, and Jones partnership meets the requisite criteria for possessing an insurable interest in the office building without the necessity of having legal title in the partnership's name.

13. (580,L1,48) (c) When there is a partial loss for property covered under a policy with a co-insurance clause, the following formula is applied to determine the recovery:

$$\frac{\text{Face value of policy}}{\text{Fair value of property x co-insurance \%}} \text{ x Loss} = \text{Recovery}$$

$$\frac{\$16{,}000}{\$100{,}000 \times 80\%} \times \$40{,}000 = \$8{,}000$$

$$\frac{\$24{,}000}{\$100{,}000 \times 80\%} \times \$40{,}000 = \frac{\$12{,}000}{\$20{,}000}$$

Thus answer (c) is the correct answer.

May 1985 Answers

14. (585,L1,59) (d) Under a coinsurance clause, the insured agrees to maintain insurance equal to a specified percentage (usually 80%) of the value of his/her property. If the property is insured for less than the specified percentage, then the owner becomes a coinsurer with the insurance company and must bear a proportionate amount of a partial loss. Answer (a) is incorrect because a coinsurance clause does not prohibit the insured from obtaining an amount of insurance which is less than the coinsurance percentage multiplied by the fair market value of the property. Rather, a coinsurance clause provides that if the insured doesn't maintain the specified amount of insurance, then he/she will have to bear a proportionate amount of a loss resulting from a partial destruction of the property. Answer (b) is incorrect because the insured is partially at risk only when the amount of insurance maintained is less than the specified percentage times the fair market value of the property. Answer (c) is incorrect because even though the coinsurance clause does not apply when there has been a total loss, the recovery is still limited to the face amount of the policy.

15. (585,L1,60) (b) The insurable interest requirement with regard to property insurance is met when a person can show that damage to or destruction of the property will cause that person substantial economic loss. For example, a tenant in leased property has legal interest in the property during his/her lease term and would have an insurable interest to the extent of economic loss s/he might suffer. Answer (a) is incorrect because the insurable interest requirement cannot be waived by the parties to an insurance contract. Answer (c) is incorrect because the insurable interest in property need not be present at the inception of the policy, but it must be present at the time of the loss. Answer (d) is incorrect because the insurable interest requirement may be met by a person who has an economic interest, but not legal title, in the property. For example, a secured creditor has an insurable interest in the property acting as collateral.

November 1985 Answers

16. (1185,L1,59) (a) In most property insurance claims, the claim is for less than the face value of the policy. The coinsurance feature of property insurance requires the insured to "self-insure" part of property when partial destruction occurs. Coinsurance prevents the insured from carrying only a minimal amount of coverage and recovering the full amount of damages each time a partial destruction occurs. Answer (b) is incorrect because the insured can insure for less than the coinsurance percentage. If a lesser amount of insurance is carried, the insured will receive less than the full amount of damages. Answer (c) is incorrect because the coinsurance feature has no bearing on the insurable interest requirement. Answer (d) is incorrect because the rate of coinsurance is not fixed by law at 80%. However 80% is the normal stated percentage in a coinsurance clause.

17. (1185,L1,60) (b) An order to collect on property insurance, the insured must have the insurable interest at the time the property was destroyed. If the insured does not have a legal interest in the property at the time of destruction, the insured will not collect on the property insurance. In the case of an unsecured creditor (where the destroyed property was not provided as security by the debtor), an insurance claim by the creditor is not valid as the unsecured creditor does not have an insurable interest in the property of the debtor. A secured creditor would have an insurable interest in the property. Answer (a) is incorrect because a lessee does have an insurable interest in the property. Answer (c) is incorrect because West, who had legal control over the corporation owning the property, has an insurable interest in the property. Answer (d) is incorrect because any future interest in the property qualifies as an insurable interest in the property. Thus, West, as the remainderman, has an insurable interest in the property.

Answer Outline

Problem 1 Coinsurance, Standard Mortgagee, and Pro Rata Clauses (1182,L5a)

Part a.

1. Jackson will recover $150,000 from Eagle
   Fire insurance policy contains 80% coinsurance clause
      Jackson must carry an amount of insurance equal to 80% of FMV of Parksdale plant
         In order to recover full amount of loss
      Jackson did not insure property to required 80% of its value
         Becomes a coinsurer and must proportionally share with Eagle the loss suffered

$$\left(\frac{\text{Amount of insurance}}{\text{Coinsurance percentage x FMV of property}}\right) \times \text{Amount of loss} = \text{Recovery}$$

2. Second National Bank will receive $106,000 and Jackson will receive $44,000
   Insurance policy contains "standard mortgagee clause"
      Proceeds applied first to mortgagee
         In satisfaction of mortgage debt
      Any surplus paid to mortgagor
3. Jackson will recover $300,000 from Eagle
   Yuma warehouse was totally destroyed
      Coinsurance provision only applies to partial destruction of insured property
   Amount of recovery limited to face value of insurance policy
4. Jackson will recover $45,000 from the insurance companies
   Fire insurance policies contain 80% coinsurance clause
      Jackson must carry an amount of insurance equal to 80% of FMV of Rye City garage
         In order to recover full amount of loss
      Jackson did not insure property to required 80% of its value
         Becomes coinsurer and must proportionally share with the insurance companies the loss suffered

$$\left(\frac{\text{Amount of insurance policies}}{\text{Coinsurance percentage x FMV of property}}\right) \times \text{Amount of loss} = \text{Recovery}$$

5. Queen will be obligated to pay $30,000
   Insurance policies contain a pro rata clause
      If insured has multiple insurance policies covering same property
         Loss must be apportioned among the insurers
      Each insurer is liable for its pro rata share of loss

$$\frac{\text{Amount of insurance coverage from Queen}}{\text{Total amount of insurance coverage}} \times \text{Liability due to fire} = \text{Pro rata share}$$

Unofficial Answer

(Author Modified)

Problem 1 Coinsurance, Standard Mortgagee, and Pro Rata Clauses (1182,L5a)

Part a.

1. Under a fire insurance policy that contains an 80% coinsurance clause, the insured must carry an amount of insurance equal to 80% of the value of the property insured in order to recover any loss in full up to the face amount of the policy, but if the insured carries an amount of insurance less than the 80%, s/he becomes a coinsurer and must proportionally bear with the insurance company any loss suffered due to partial destruction of the property.

Jackson did not insure its property to the required 80% of its value, therefore its recovery would be computed on the following basis:

$$\left(\frac{\text{Amount of insurance}}{\text{Coinsurance percentage x FMV of property}}\right) \times \text{Amount of loss} = \textbf{Recovery}$$

$$\frac{\$600,000}{80\% \times \$1,000,000} \times \$200,000 = \mathbf{\$150,000}$$

2. The total amount of recovery from the fire loss was $150,000. Second National Bank will receive $106,000 and Jackson will receive $44,000. The insurance policy contained a "standard mortgagee clause" which provides that in the event of loss, the proceeds will be applied first to the mortgagee (Second National Bank) in satisfaction of the mortgage debt (including accrued interest) and any surplus will be paid to the owner of the property, i.e., mortgagor (Jackson).

3. Jackson will recover the face value of the insurance policy from Eagle. The application of a coinsurance provision contained in a fire insurance policy is limited to partial destruction of the insured property.

When the property is totally destroyed, as was the Yuma warehouse, the coinsurance provision has no relevance. Since the value of Jackson's Yuma warehouse, at the time of total destruction, exceeded the policy coverage, Jackson's recovery will be limited to the face value of the insurance policy ($300,000).

4. Since the insurance policy contained an 80% coinsurance clause, the insured (Jackson) must carry an amount of insurance equal to 80% of the value of the property insured in order to recover any loss in full. Jackson did not insure its property to the required 80% of its value, therefore it becomes a coinsurer and must proportionally bear with the insurance companies any loss suffered due to partial destruction of the property.

Jackson's recovery from the insurance companies would be computed on the following basis:

$$\left(\frac{\text{Amount of ins. policies}}{\text{Coinsurance percentage x FMV of property}}\right) \times \text{Amount of loss} = \textbf{Recovery}$$

$$\frac{\$50{,}000 + \$100{,}000}{80\% \times \$250{,}000} \times \$60{,}000 = \textbf{\$45,000}$$

5. A pro rata clause provides that if the insured has multiple fire insurance policies covering the same property, any loss must be apportioned among the insurers in the ratio that the amount of insurance issued by each insurer bears to the total amount of the insurance procured, and each insurer is liable to the insured for its pro rata share of such loss.

Consequently, since the total insurance coverage on the garage was $150,000, with Queen providing $100,000 of this, Queen must pay two-thirds of the liability due to the fire loss.

$$\frac{\text{Amount of insurance issued by Queen}}{\text{Total amount of insurance coverage}} \times \text{Liability due to fire} = \textbf{Queen's pro rata share}$$

$$\frac{\$100{,}000}{\$50{,}000 + \$100{,}000} \times \$45{,}000 = \textbf{\$30,000}$$

Answer Outline

Problem 2 Insurable Interests (1176,L6b&c)

b. The insurance company must pay
   An insurable interest in Balsom existed
      I.e., there was an economic interest
   Insurable interest only required at policy inception
   Age misrepresentation does not void policy
      But does reduce amount recoverable
      To the insurance purchasable with premiums paid

c1. Anderson's recovery (insurable interest) is principal plus
      Interest at time of the fire
      Limited to policy face value

c2. Victory is subrogated to Anderson's rights
      I.e., to receive mortgage payments

Unofficial Answer

Problem 2 Insurable Interests (1176,L6b&c)

b. Yes. An insurable interest in the life of another is present here since the firm has a substantial economic interest in the life of Balsam at the time the policy was procured. It is well recognized that an entity has the requisite standing to procure insurance on its key participants. Certainly a general partner qualifies as a key participant. In addition, the funding of buy-out agreements is essential in many instances, and insurance law recognizes this economic necessity. The insurable interest required for a life insurance policy need only exist at the inception of the policy. Balsam's subsequent retirement does not invalidate it.

The fact that Balsam misrepresented his age will not cause the loss of the entire insurance proceeds. The general rule provides that such a misrepresentation merely reduces the amount recoverable to that which the premiums would purchase if the correct age had been stated.

c. 1. Anderson's insurable interest equals the extent of the mortgage debt outstanding. Thus, his recovery is limited to the $52,000 debt outstanding plus accrued interest on the debt, but the total recovery cannot exceed $60,000, the maximum coverage under the policy.

2. Upon payment, Victory is subrogated to the rights of Anderson and will succeed to Anderson's rights to receive payments under the terms of the mortgage and mortgage bond. If Drum Corporation fails to continue the payments, Victory may foreclose on the mortgage.

TRUSTS AND ESTATES

Overview

This topic includes the administration of a decedent's estate and the administration of a trust.

An estate is the legal entity which comes into existence on a person's death for the purpose of succeeding to the property of the decedent, to establish liability for payment of debts of the decedent, and to distribute any remaining property. The estate is administered in accordance with the decedent's will or the intestate statutes. An executor or administrator is approved by the court and empowered to act for the estate and carry out its responsibilities. An executor or administrator may engage the necessary legal, accounting, and other services. Adequate records must be kept to show proper disposition of the assets of the estate. At the conclusion of an estate, an accounting is generally rendered and the judicial settlement is secured in probate court, thereby closing the estate.

A trust arises where one person holds legal title to certain property for the use and benefit of another. In other words, in a trust, the legal and equitable title are split so that one called a trustee holds legal title for the benefit of another person, called a beneficiary. A trust is administered by a trustee who must perform the duties imposed by law and by the trust instrument and is personally liable if he does not follow these requirements.

One of the most frequently tested topics in estates and trusts is allocation of trust principal and income. Candidates should be thoroughly familiar with this distinction, e.g., between cash dividends and stock dividends. Also tested are the rights of beneficiaries to a trust with particular emphasis on the distinction between the rights of income beneficiary and the residual beneficiary, the duties of an administrator or executor of an estate as well as the duties of a trustee. You should also understand for the CPA exam how and when a trust is created and terminated.

A. Estates

1. The execution and validity of a will is generally the province of lawyers. However, some general information regarding wills which pertains to administration of estates is useful to aid you in background knowledge for tested topics.
   a. Emphasis on CPA exam is now on administration of estates and trusts
   b. Preparation of tax returns and schedules used to render an accounting are frequently done by CPA firms
2. General information and definitions
   a. Will--legal declaration of person's intent concerning disposition of his/her property at death
      1) Will takes effect upon death--may be changed or revoked until death
   b. Estate--legal entity holding title to person's property after his/her death
      1) Pays decedent's debts
      2) Administered by executor or administrator
   c. Testate--a person is said to die testate if there is a valid will in existence
      1) Estate (decedent property) will pass to beneficiaries by terms of will
   d. Intestate--a person is said to die intestate if there is no will or if will is held invalid
      1) Estate will pass by intestate succession, i.e., state statute prescribes rules of distribution of an estate
         a) Rules are calculated to approximate probable wishes of most individuals

2) Any assets not disposed of by will are distributed by intestate succession laws

e. Testator (male) or testatrix (female)--one who makes will

f. Legacy (bequest)--gift of personal property under will

1) Specific legacy is gift of specified item

EXAMPLE: Decedent willed his car specifically to his daughter.

a) If specific item does not exist when testator dies, then beneficiary gets nothing

2) General legacy is gift payable out of general assets of estate

EXAMPLE: Decedent willed $100 to his son.

a) As long as estate is not insolvent, beneficiary will receive general legacy

g. Devise--gift of real property under will

1) Same rules apply to general and specific devises as to legacies, above

h. Residue--remainder of estate after all other gifts have been made and all debts paid

EXAMPLE: "I hereby give ...to...and the rest of my estate to A."

1) Its value is undetermined until an appraisal and inventory of estate is made and all other gifts have been made or accounted for and all debts discharged

i. Probate--process of proving validity and authenticity of a will by demonstrating that an instrument purporting to be last will and testament of person was duly executed in accordance with legal requirements

3. Validity of will

a. Testator/testatrix must be competent when s/he executes (makes) will

1) Must be of legal age (normally 18) at time of execution of will
2) Must have mental capacity to make will

a) Ability to understand nature and extent of property s/he owns and nature of will

b. Must be executed in compliance with formal requirements of state statute

1) Signature of testator/testatrix required
2) Signed by individuals who witnessed testator/testatrix signing will

a) Except where handwritten wills allowed

c. Only effective on testator's/testatrix's death ("will speaks at death")
d. Revocable and amendable during testator's/testatrix's life

B. Administration of Estates

1. Purpose of administration

   a. To carry out decedent's wishes as expressed in will
   b. To discover, collect, and conserve assets of decedent
   c. To protect creditors by paying from assets all claims and taxes against estate
   d. To identify beneficiaries and to properly distribute assets of estate according to testator's intentions or law of intestate succession

2. One who is authorized by probate court to administer the estate of decedent is called a personal representative

   a. Executor/executrix--personal representative named in will by testator to carry out provisions of will and empowered by probate court to act for estate

      1) Probate court will follow testator's wishes and appoint the person named in will to be the executor, unless person named is disqualified, unavailable, or unwilling to serve
      2) Person named as executor

         a) Can decline to serve
         b) Can be beneficiary of will

   b. Administrator--person appointed by court to administer estate when decedent dies intestate or if executor named in will cannot or will not serve

   c. Unless personal representative accepts appointment to serve gratuitously, s/he is entitled to reasonable compensation for services rendered

   d. Personal representative is required to file with the court an inventory of estate's assets for appraisal

      1) Taxes also assessed

3. Probate of will is prerequisite to administration of estate

   a. Until admitted to probate, will is ineffective and inoperative insofar as transferring title to property held by estate
   b. Will becomes effective upon probate but relates back to time of decedent's death
   c. There is basic limitation period (normally three years from date of death) within which it must be determined whether decedent left a will

      1) If no will is probated within this statutory period of time, there rises presumption that decedent died intestate

4. Petition for probate must be filed in proper court supervising distribution, usually called probate court

   a. This is necessary prior to distribution of estate
   b. Petition consists of statement of approximate value of estate and names, ages, residence, and relationship of heirs of decedent

   c. Filing generally includes a sworn statement, by original witnesses to the will, that the will being submitted is valid

   d. All executed copies of will must be presented to court before they can be admitted to probate

5. Creditors are given notice and must file their claims within statutory time period
6. Administrator or executor/executrix is fiduciary and must act accordingly to carry out wishes of testator/testatrix or statutory scheme
   a. Responsible for collecting all debts, paying all expenses, and generally carrying out distribution to those entitled
      1) May sell assets to pay debts; personal property must be sold before real property (unless otherwise directed by will)
      2) May contract and engage services, e.g., attorneys, accountants, appraisers
      3) Must post bond to ensure performance unless will provides otherwise
   b. Personally liable if s/he fails to execute his/her duties
      1) Reasonable person standard used
   c. Must not commingle estate with his/her own property
   d. Must keep an accounting of all assets and their disposition
      1) The final accounting rendered should include
         a) An inventory of all assets of estate
         b) A statement of all debts of estate
         c) A statement of disposition of all assets and income from estate
         d) A statement of expenses, costs, and commissions of administration
      2) Preparation of tax returns and financial schedules used to render an accounting in estate administration are often done by CPA firms
      3) The probate court issues a "decree of final settlement," distribution of estate assets is made pursuant to court decree, and the personal representative is discharged
7. Distribution of estate
   a. By terms of will
      1) Surviving spouse, under the concept of statutory share, has right to denounce the provision made in will for him/her and elect instead a stated share (normally 1/3) of decedent's estate
         a) Protects surviving spouse from being disinherited by will
   b. By intestate succession when there is no will or if will does not provide for entire estate
      1) Laws vary from state to state
      2) Intestate succession applies to real property as well as to personal property
   c. Property held in joint tenancy (see PROPERTY, Interests in Real Property) passes to surviving joint tenants and, therefore, does not pass through a will or intestate succession
      1) Property owned as tenants in common does pass through a will or through intestate succession

d. Abatement--process of determining distribution of estate when it is insufficient to satisfy all debts and gifts

   1) Debts and administration expenses are paid first, taking from (in order)

      a) Intestate property (property not provided for in will)
      b) Residue
      c) General devises or legacies
      d) Specific devises or legacies

   2) Any remaining assets are distributed as follows until they run out

      a) Specific devises or legacies
      b) General devises or legacies
      c) Residue
      d) Intestate property

   3) Abatement attempts to fulfill wishes of testator to best extent by protecting those bequests most important to testator, such as specific bequests

8. Ademption--when specific bequest or devise becomes impossible to perform because of circumstances or events occurring after execution of will

   a. Particular property bequeathed or devised is not part of testator's estate at time of his/her death

      1) Gift thereby fails since there is no such property in estate
      2) Only applies to specific bequests or devises

9. Lapse--a gift in a will is said to lapse if beneficiary is living when will is executed, but beneficiary subsequently predeceases the testator (i.e., when beneficiary dies between the execution of will and death of testator)

   a. Since intended beneficiary is not living at time of estate distribution, the gift to him lapses and passes to residue of estate

10. Post-mortem passing of property by means other than wills

   a. Joint tenancy--concurrent ownership of same piece of property with right of survivorship

      1) Right of survivorship means that other joint tenant(s) get property upon death of one joint tenant

         a) Heirs do not share in property by will or by intestate succession
         b) No estate administration involved

         EXAMPLE: M, N, and O own a piece of property as joint tenants. If O dies, then M and N become the two joint tenants even if O tried to pass this interest in a will.

   b. Tenancy in common--concurrent ownership with no right of survivorship

      1) This interest passes to heirs in a will, or if no will exists, by intestate succession

   c. Tenancy by entirety--concurrent interest in which the owners are husband and wife with right of survivorship
   d. Life insurance--by selection of beneficiaries who directly receive insurance proceeds
   e. Employee benefits and pensions

      1) Provisions for direct death benefits without estate administration

C. Trusts

1. Definition--a trust is fiduciary relationship wherein trustee holds legal title to property for benefit of beneficiaries

   a. Legal and equitable (beneficial) title are separated

      1) Trustee holds legal title
      2) Beneficiaries hold equitable title

   b. Trustor or settlor is the person who creates the trust

      1) Settlor can make him/herself either trustee or beneficiary (not both), but, of course, s/he does not need to be either

      2) Settlor can reserve right to revoke trust

   c. Trustee manages the property and distributes the income to the beneficiary(ies) if so provided in trust agreement

   EXAMPLE: S desires to transfer Blackacre to her son, B, who is a minor, but does not want B to control legal title until he is older and capable of managing the property. Therefore, S creates a trust by transferring title of Blackacre to a trustee, J, who will hold and manage the property until B reaches age 18 and then will convey Blackacre to B.

2. Creation of trust

   a. Elements

      1) Settlor (trustor) with legal capacity

         a) For inter vivos trusts (transfers between living persons), person must have legal capacity to transfer title of property
         b) For testamentary trusts (trusts created in wills), person must have legal capacity to make a will

      2) Settlor intends to create trust

         a) May be written or oral

            1] Note: if trust is for interest in land, then it must be in writing to satisfy Statute of Frauds
            2] If trust is in a will (i.e., testamentary trust) then will must comply with formalities

         b) No notice to or acceptance by beneficiaries required

            1] But disclaimer by beneficiary causes trust to terminate

               a] Creates "resulting trust" in which trustee holds title for settlor

         c) No notice to or acceptance by trustees required

            1] Disclaimer by trustee does not terminate trust (opposite result if beneficiary disclaims)

               a] If more than one trustee, then other trustee(s) hold legal title
               b] If sole trustee disclaims, title reverts back to settlor (constructive trust) to appoint other trustee

d) No consideration required

1] Distinguish--a contract to make a future trust does need consideration

e) Legality

1] Purpose of trust must be legal or trust is considered void

3) Trustee--one who holds legal title

a) May be minor, corporation, or other person
b) May be either settlor or beneficiary (but not both because then all three would be same person and trust would terminate)
c) Death of trustee does not destroy trust--new trustee appointed

4) Beneficiary (Cestui que trust)

a) Must be identifiable at time trust is created
b) May be minor, corporation, or other person
c) Class of persons may be beneficiaries
d) Settlor may be beneficiary

5) Trust property (also called res or corpus)

a) Must exist at time of creation of trust

b) Trust must be limited in duration so as to not violate the rule against perpetuities

1] This rule requires that trust cannot (by its terms) last longer than a life in being plus 21 years or it will fail

EXAMPLE: A forms a trust. The terms of this trust state that the income is to go to his son, B, for life unless B has a child, in which case the property will be distributed to this child at the age of 21.

2] Purpose is to prevent title to property from being tied up for an unreasonable period of time

3. Types of trusts

a. Inter vivos trust is created by settlor while living

1) Transfer in trust is the transferring of property by settlor to trustee for benefit of another
2) Declaration of trust is when settlor declares him/herself trustee for beneficiary

a) In a declaration of trust, no transfer of property is necessary

b. A testamentary trust is set up in testator's/testatrix's will to have property transferred in trust after death of settlor

1) Requires elements of valid will

c. Charitable trust--a trust that has as its object some recognized social benefit, e.g., furthering education, religion, relief to poor

1) Valid even if indefinite as to time and beneficiaries
2) Cy pres (i.e., as near as possible) doctrine is used by courts to carry out general intent when specific instructions are impossible

d. Clifford trust

1) Trust in which its creator retains right to possession of trust property after a stated period of time or upon happening of stated event
2) Based on Supreme Court's case of Helvering vs. Clifford
3) Creator of trust is taxed on trust property unless I.R.C. requirements are met because s/he is still treated as owner

a) Not treated as owner for tax purposes (i.e., not taxed on) if creator of trust will not obtain possession within 10 years from creation of trust

EXAMPLE: The Huskies decided they would like to shift some of their income to their children, Herb and Harriet. They decided to create a short-term irrecovable trust for the benefit of the children with Illini Trust Company as trustee. The duration of the trust was ten years plus one day. The trust agreement was dated August 1, 1985. The Huskies then conveyed an apartment building in trust to the trustee on October 10, 1985. The Huskies' trust was not created until October 10, 1985 when title to the building was conveyed to the trustee in writing. Consequently the duration of the trustee was less than 10 years and it would not qualify as a Clifford trust. Thus the rental income would be taxed as part of the parents' income and not as part of the children's, which was the Huskies' intent when creating the trust.

e. Spendthrift trusts

1) Trusts that prohibit beneficiary from assigning or transferring to another party any unreceived payments
2) Protects beneficiary from creditors or from his/her squandering of assets

f. Implied trusts

1) Resulting trust arises when

a) Beneficial interest(s) fail(s)

EXAMPLE: An income beneficiary is named but a remainderman is not named. At the end of the trust the beneficial interest will fail.

1] Trustee then holds for settlor or settlor's heirs, or

b) Title to property is taken (with consent) in name of one who did not furnish consideration

EXAMPLE: A prominent politician purchases some land but does not want his name associated with it. A business associate holds the land in his name for the politician.

g. Active trust is one wherein trustee has some specific duties to perform

1) Passive trust is one requiring no duties of trustee, and trustee is merely holder of legal title of trust property until ownership passes to beneficiaries

h. Totten trusts

1) Totten trust pertains to a bank savings account which depositor opens as "John Smith in trust for Sam Smith"
2) Revocable by depositor simply by withdrawing money
3) Funds may be used during depositor's life in any manner
4) Totten trusts become irrevocable at depositor's death

i. Constructive trust arises when person who takes legal interest in property cannot enjoy beneficial interest without violating some legal established principle

1) Therefore, the court converts legal owner into trustee for the party who is entitled to beneficial enjoyment
2) Arises by operation of law as remedial device
3) Imposed whenever court determines that one who acquired title to property is under duty to transfer it to another person because acquisition was by fraud, duress, mistake, etc. or because the holder of title would be unjustly enriched if he were permitted to retain it

EXAMPLE: S conveys property to A, but B fraudulently changes conveyance to his own name. Therefore, the court will impose a constructive trust whereby B is deemed to hold the property in trust for A.

D. Administration of Trusts

1. Trustee's duties

a. Fulfill terms in express trust

1) Unless illegal or impossible
2) Or unless circumstances unanticipated by settlor occur so that fulfillment of trust terms would defeat trust's original purpose
3) Or unless court decree directs otherwise

b. Trustee is fiduciary (this concept is very important)

1) Owes duty to act in best interests of beneficiary(ies) rather than his/her own
2) Duty of loyalty to beneficiary(ies)

a) Must upon request furnish all records and information on trust
b) Must keep trust property separate from own

c. Must administer trust in reasonable manner

1) Use same care as reasonable person would use in care of his/her own property
2) Must defend against actions against trust
3) Should use judgment in getting fair returns on property without unreasonable risk
4) Must collect claims owed to trust
5) Must keep reasonable records
6) Should make trust property productive

a) Unproductive property should be sold

7) May not delegate duties trustee can do him/herself

2. Trustee's powers

   a. May be express

      1) Duty to invest trust property in reasonable manner not contrary to terms of trust

   b. May be implied

      1) Only those powers that are not prohibited under trust and are reasonably necessary to fulfill purpose of trust
      2) Trustee has right to reimbursement for reasonable expenses incurred on behalf of trust
      3) May prudently sell and purchase property

         a) Diversification may be used to decrease risk of loss

      4) May lease property if reasonable
      5) If more than one trustee, unanimous consent needed

         a) Charitable trusts only need consent of majority

      6) No implied power to mortgage, pledge, or borrow on trust property

3. Liability of trustee

   a. To beneficiaries based on breach of trust or breach of fiduciary duties

      EXAMPLE: The trustee of some income property failed to make proper roof repairs resulting in extensive water damage to the trust property. Evidence shows that there was sufficient warning of needed repairs. The trustee is liable for the loss in value of the property.

      EXAMPLE: The trustee sold some shares of stock to himself from the trust property at a price below fair market value. This is a clear breach of trust.

      1) Discharged from liability if beneficiaries consent to breach before, during, or after breach

   b. To third parties

      1) Liable under contract or tort law

         a) Trustee has right of exoneration (trust property pays for liability) when in performance of trust duties

E. <u>Termination of Trust</u>

1. At end of period stated in trust
2. Revocation by settlor

   a. Can do so only if power of revocation is reserved in trust

      1) Exception: if settlor is sole beneficiary, may terminate trust when desires to

3. Achievement of trust purpose

   EXAMPLE: X creates a trust in which his daughter, C, is to receive the income (as beneficiary) to help her become a CPA. She gets her CPA license. Since the purpose of the trust has been achieved, the trust terminates.

4. Failure of trust purpose

   EXAMPLE: Same as example above, but unfortunately C dies before her goal is obtained. The trust terminates.

5. Agreement of all beneficiaries
   a. As long as trust purpose not defeated
      1) Trust purpose may be defeated if settlor joins in to terminate trust

6. By merger
   a. If trustee and beneficiary are ever the same person, legal title and equitable title are merged, thus terminating the trust

      EXAMPLE: S creates a trust which designates A and B as co-trustees and names B as beneficiary. The trust also states that after six years B has the right to remove A as trustee. If B exercises this right, the trust would terminate because the sole trustee and sole beneficiary would be the same person and legal and equitable title would merge.

      EXAMPLE: S creates a trust in which A becomes trustee for A and B as beneficiaries. This trust would not be terminated by merger because B does not hold both legal and equitable title even though A does.

   b. If sole beneficiary is co-trustee this does not terminate trust because legal and equitable title do not merge

7. Settlor may revoke (or modify) trust only if terms of trust so state or settlor has reserved that right
   a. Reason: beneficiary has rights to beneficial interest in trust

F. Allocation Between Principal and Income

1. Typically, interests are divided between an income beneficiary and a remainderman beneficiary
   a. Income beneficiary receives income from trust property (usually for specified time such as for his/her life)
   b. Remainderman gets trust property when trust terminates

      EXAMPLE: S puts income property into a trust stating that I will receive the income for life with the remainder going to R when I dies.

2. It is duty of trustee to distribute income and principal in accordance with terms of trust
   a. In absence of specific trust provisions, allocation is governed by Uniform Principal and Income Act
      1) Provisions of this uniform act are applicable to both estates and trusts

3. Principal includes
   a. Original trust property
   b. Proceeds and gains from sale of property, including insurance received on destruction of property
   c. New property purchased with principal or proceeds from principal
   d. Stock dividends and stock splits (cash dividends are income)
   e. Liquidating distributions
   f. Amortization of premium on property bought by trustee

4. Payable from principal are expenses affecting principal, e.g.,
    a. Principal payment of loans
    b. Litigation over trust property
    c. Permanent (capital) improvements
    d. Costs incurred in purchase or sale of trust property
    e. Losses on sale or exchange of trust property
5. Income includes profits from trust principal, e.g.,
    a. Rent (including prepaid rent) less costs of collection
    b. Interest
    c. Cash dividends
    d. Royalties
6. Payable from income are ordinary and operating expenses, e.g.,
    a. Ordinary administrative expenses
    b. Interest
    c. Insurance premiums
    d. Taxes
    e. Repairs and maintenance
7. Annuities are allocated between principal and income
8. Trustee is liable to income beneficiary and remainderman for confusion or commingling of assets
    a. CPA is likely to be consulted to determine the amount of money to go to income beneficiary and amount to go to remainderman

G. <u>Federal Estate Tax</u>

1. Federal estate tax is a tax imposed on the right to transfer property by death
    a. It is an excise tax levied upon value of property transferred at death
    b. Gross estate is composed of all property to extent of interest therein of decedent at time of his/her death
2. Estate tax is computed on the basis of taxable estate, which is gross estate as reduced by various allowable deductions
    a. Primary among these deductions from the gross estate is the "marital deduction"
        1) <u>Marital deduction</u>--is allowed without limitation (unlimited) for the FMV of property passing to a surviving spouse
            a) A terminable interest granted to surviving spouse will not generally qualify for marital deduction
                1] Terminable interest is one that terminates after a time or happening of an event
            b) The fair market value of <u>qualified terminal interest property</u> ("Q-tip") is eligible for the marital deduction if the executor/executrix elects. To be eligible, the income from the property must be paid at least annually to the spouse and the property is not subject to transfer during the spouse's lifetime.
3. Further explanation of federal estate tax -- see Module 44, Gift and Estate Taxes (GETX).

H. Real Estate Investment Trusts (REITs)

1. Real Estate Investment Trust Act

   a. Authorized by Congress in 1960
   b. Permits organization of unincorporated association to invest in real estate
   c. Association need not pay corporate income taxes

2. Provisions to be met

   a. 100 or more certificate holders during each year
   b. 5 or fewer holders must not own more than 50% of certificates
   c. Trustees must have centralized control
   d. Owners must have limited liability and free transferability of shares
   e. Major portion of income must be rents from real property or gains on sale of real property
   f. Must pay at least 90% of taxable income to certificate holders each year

3. Failure to meet provisions

   a. Trust taxed as if corporation

4. Tax treatment

   a. Ordinary income and capital gains pass through to investors
   b. Depreciation and other losses do not pass through

5. Trust must comply with applicable SEC securities registration laws

Multiple Choice Questions (1—23)

1. The last will and testament of Jean Bond left various specific property and sums of money to relatives and friends. She left the residue of her estate equally to her favorite niece and nephew. Which of the various properties described below will become a part of Bond's estate and be distributed in accordance with her last will and testament?
   a. A joint savings account which listed her sister, who is still living, as the joint tenant.
   b. The entire family homestead which she had owned in joint tenancy with her older brother who predeceased her and which was still recorded as jointly owned.
   c. Several substantial gifts that she made in contemplation of death to various charities.
   d. A life insurance policy which designated a former partner as the beneficiary.

2. Paul Good's will left all of his commercial real property to his wife Dorothy for life and the remainder to his two daughters, Joan and Doris, as tenants in common. All beneficiaries are alive and over 21 years of age. Regarding the rights of the parties, which of the following is a correct statement?
   a. Dorothy may **not** elect to take against the will and receive a statutory share instead.
   b. The daughters **must** survive Dorothy in order to receive any interest in the property.
   c. Either of the daughters may sell her interest in the property without the consent of their mother or the other daughter.
   d. If only one daughter is alive upon the death of Dorothy, she is entitled to the entire property.

3. The intestate succession distribution rules
   a. Do not apply to property held in joint tenancy.
   b. Do not apply to real property.
   c. Effectively prevent a decedent from totally disinheriting his wife and children.
   d. Apply to situations where the decedent failed to name an executor.

4. An executor named in the decedent's will
   a. Must consent to serve, have read the will, and be present at the execution of the will.
   b. Need **not** serve if he does **not** wish to do so.
   c. Must serve without compensation unless the will provides otherwise.
   d. Can **not** be the principal beneficiary of the will.

5. Madison died 15 years after executing a valid will. He named his son, Walker, as the executor of his will. He left two-thirds of his estate to his wife and the balance equally to his children. Which of the following is a right or duty of Walker as executor?
   a. Walker must post a surety bond even if a provision in the will attempts to exempt him from this responsibility.
   b. Walker has an affirmative duty to discover, collect, and distribute all the decedent's assets.
   c. If the will is silent on the point, Walker has complete discretion insofar as investing the estate's assets during the term of his administration.
   d. Walker can sell real property without a court order, even though he has not been expressly authorized to do so.

6. Assuming that a given trust indenture is silent on the point, the trustee has certain rights and duties as a matter of law. The trustee
   a. Has a fiduciary duty to the trust but **not** to the beneficiaries.
   b. Is **not** entitled to commissions unless so provided.
   c. Can elect to terminate the trust as long as the beneficiaries unanimously concur.
   d. Must act in a competent, nonnegligent manner, or he may face removal.

7. Martins created an irrevocable fifteen-year trust for the benefit of his minor children. At the end of the fifteen years, the principal reverts to Martins. Martins named the Bloom Trust Company as trustee and provided that Bloom would serve without the necessity of posting a bond. In understanding the trust and rules applicable to it, which of the following is correct?
   a. If Martins dies ten years after creation of the trust, it is automatically revoked and the property is distributed to the beneficiaries of his trust upon their attaining age 21.
   b. Martins may revoke the trust after eleven years, since he created it, and the principal reverts to him at the expiration of the fifteen years.

c. The facts indicate that the trust is a separate legal entity for both tax and non-tax purposes.
d. The trust is **not** a separate legal entity for federal tax purposes.

8. With respect to trusts, which of the following states an **invalid** legal conclusion?
a. The trustee must obtain the consent of the majority of the beneficiaries if a major change in the investment portfolio of the trust is to be made.
b. For federal income tax purposes, a trust is entitled to an exemption similar to that of an individual although **not** equal in amount.
c. Both the life beneficiaries of a trust and the ultimate takers have rights against the trustee, and the trustee is accountable to them.
d. A trust is a separate taxable entity for federal income tax purposes.

9. Larson is considering the creation of either a lifetime (inter vivos) or testamentary (by his will) trust. In deciding what to do, which of the following statements is correct?
a. If the trust is an inter vivos trust, the trustee must file papers in the appropriate state office roughly similar to those required to be filed by a corporation to qualify.
b. An inter vivos trust must meet the same legal requirements as one created by a will.
c. Property transferred to a testamentary trust upon the grantor's (creator's) death is **not** included in the decedent's gross estate for federal tax purposes.
d. Larson can retain the power to revoke an inter vivos trust.

10. James Gordon decided to create an inter vivos trust for the benefit of his grandchildren. He wished to bypass his own children, and to provide an independent income for his grandchildren. He did not, however, wish to completely part with the assets he would transfer to the trust. Therefore, he transferred the assets to the York Trust Company, in trust for the benefit of his grandchildren irrevocably for a period of 12 years. Which of the following is correct regarding the trust?
a. The trust will fail for want of a proper purpose.
b. The trust income will not be taxable to Gordon during its existence.
c. Gordon retains beneficial title to the property transferred to the trust.
d. If Gordon demands the return of the trust assets prior to the 12 years, York must return them to him since he created the trust and the assets will eventually be his again.

11. Wayne & Company, CPAs, was engaged by Harding, the trustee of the Timmons Testamentary Trust. The will creating the Timmons Trust gave Harding wide discretion with respect to the investment of the trust principal but was silent on the question of the allocation of receipts and charges to principal or income. Among the assets invested in by Harding is a $500,000 annuity and a $50,000 limited partnership interest in an offshore investment limited partnership. The partnership has reported a $40,000 loss for the year. Regarding the trust in general and the limited partnership loss allocation in particular, which of the following is correct?
a. It is against public policy to permit the investment by the trustee in the offshore investment limited partnership.
b. Since the trust is silent on the allocation question, Harding has wide discretion in making allocations.
c. The loss attributable to the offshore partnership is allocable equally to principal and income.
d. The receipts from the $500,000 annuity must be apportioned between principal and income.

12. The Martin Trust consisted primarily of various income-producing real estate properties. During the year, the trustee incurred various charges. Among the charges were the following: depreciation, principal payments on various mortgages, and a street assessment. Which of the following would be a proper allocation of these items?
a. All to income, except the street assessment.
b. All are to be allocated equally between principal and income.
c. All to principal.
d. All to principal, except depreciation.

13. Shepard created an inter vivos trust for the benefit of his children with the remainder to his grandchildren upon the death of his last surviving child. The trust consists of both real and personal property. One of the assets is an apartment building. In administer-

ing the trust and allocating the receipts and disbursements, which of the following would be **improper**?

a. The allocation of forfeited rental security deposits to income.

b. The allocation to principal of the annual service fee of the rental collection agency.

c. The allocation to income of the interest on the mortgage on the apartment building.

d. The allocation to income of the payment of the insurance premiums on the apartment building.

14. The Astor Bank and Trust Company is the trustee of the Wayne Trust. A significant portion of the trust principal has been invested in AAA rated public utility bonds. Some of the bonds have been purchased at face value, some at a discount, and others at a premium. Which of the following is a proper allocation of the various items to income?

a. The income beneficiary is entitled to the entire interest without dilution for the premium paid but is not entitled to the proceeds attributable to the discount upon collection.

b. The income beneficiary is entitled to the entire interest without dilution and to the proceeds attributable to the discount.

c. The income beneficiary is only entitled to the interest less the amount of the premium amortized over the life of the bond.

d. The income beneficiary is entitled to the full interest and to an allocable share of the gain resulting from the discount.

Items 15 and 16 are based on the following information:

Martin is the trustee of the Baker Trust which has assets in excess of $1 million. Martin has engaged the CPA firm of Hardy & Fox to prepare the annual accounting statement for the allocation of receipts and expenditures between income and principal. The trust indenture provides that "receipts and expenses are to be allocated to income or principal according to law."

15. Which of the following receipts should be allocated to income?

a. Rights to subscribe to shares of the distributing corporation.

b. Sale of rights to subscribe to shares of the distributing corporation.

c. A 2% stock dividend.

d. Rights to subscribe to shares of another corporation.

16. Which of the following receipts from real property should be allocated to principal?

a. An unexpected payment of nine months' arrears in rental payments.

b. A six-month prepayment of rent.

c. Insurance proceeds for the destruction of a garage on one of the properties.

d. Interest on a purchase money mortgage arising from the sale of a parcel of the trust's real property.

17. Which of the following receipts should be allocated by a trustee exclusively to income?

a. A stock dividend.

b. An extraordinary year-end cash dividend.

c. A liquidating dividend whether in complete or partial liquidation.

d. A stock split.

18. Which of the following receipts or disbursements by a trustee should be credited to or charged against income?

a. Amortization payment on real property subject to a mortgage.

b. Capital gain distributions received from a mutual fund.

c. Stock rights received from the distributing corporation.

d. The discount portion received on redemption of treasury bills.

19. Madison died 15 years after executing a valid will. In it she named her daughter, Janet, as the executrix of the will and bequeathed two-thirds of her estate to her husband after all taxes, expenses, and fees were paid, and the balance equally to her children. The approximate size of Madison's estate is $1 million. Which of the following is correct?

a. Immediately upon Madison's death, Janet has the legal right to act for and on behalf of the estate even though the will has not been admitted to probate and she has not yet been appointed as executrix.

b. All the property bequeathed to Madison's husband will be excluded from her estate for federal estate tax purposes.

c. Upon execution of her will, Madison's beneficiaries had a vested interest in her property.

d. Had Madison died without making a will, her husband would have received everything.

20. Annette's will provides for a trust upon her death. York Trust Company is named as the trustee and the trust's terms provide for the payment of income to Annette's husband for life and the remainder to her children. The Annette Trust

a Is **not** recognized as a taxable entity for income tax purposes.

b. Does qualify for the estate tax marital deduction if Annette's husband's rights represent a qualified terminable interest.

c. Is subject to an implied restriction which obligates York to obtain the beneficiaries' consent if it wishes to dispose of trust assets.

d. Vests legal and equitable title in York.

21. The Marquis Trust has been properly created and it qualifies as a real estate investment trust (REIT) for federal income tax purposes. As such, it will

a. Be taxed as any other trust for income tax purposes.

b. Have been created under the Federal Trust Indenture Act.

c. Provide limited liability for the parties investing in the trust.

d. Be exempt from the Securities Act of 1933.

May 1985 Question

22. Fine wishes to establish an inter vivos trust for the benefit of his daughter Sally, naming Sally as the sole income beneficiary for 20 years and as the sole remainder beneficiary of the corpus. The intended trust will fail if the instrument creating the trust

a. Provides for the trustee to serve without compensation, bond or other security.

b. Is **not** supported by any consideration.

c. Fails to name a trustee.

d. Names Sally as the sole trustee.

November 1985 Questions

23. A distinguishing feature between the making of an inter vivos gift and the creation of a trust is that

a. A gift may be made orally whereas a trust must be in a signed writing.

b. Generally, a gift is irrevocable whereas a trust may be revoked in certain cases.

c. In order to create a valid trust, the creator must receive some form of consideration.

d. The beneficiary of a trust must be notified of the trust's creation.

Problems

Problem 1 (1183,L5b)

(7 to 10 minutes)

Part b. Mr. & Mrs. Charles Crawford were in the 50% income tax bracket for federal income tax purposes. The Crawfords had two children, June and Virgil, ages 16 and 15. The Crawfords decided that they would like to shift some of their income to the children, but were unwilling to make outright gifts. They consulted with their CPA, banker and attorney and, after considerable discussion, decided to create a short-term irrevocable trust for the benefit of the children with Clearview Trust Company as trustee. The duration of the trust was, as stated in the trust agreement, ten years plus one day from the execution of the trust agreement. The trust agreement was dated August 1, 1982, and the intent of the parties was to convey the Sunnydale property to the trustee after the mortgage on the property had been satisfied. The mortgage was satisfied on November 15, 1982, and the property conveyed in trust to the trustee on December 1, 1982. Net rental income from the Sunnydale property for the period from December 1, 1982, to December 31, 1982, the end of the tax year chosen for the trust, was $14,000. This amount was paid to the children in 1982 and $7,000 of trust income was reported for income tax purposes by each of the children. Mr. & Mrs. Crawford excluded the $14,000 from their income tax return.

As a result of a routine audit of the Crawford family returns for 1982, the Internal Revenue Service refused to accept the income as being properly includable in the children's returns and reallocated it to Mr. & Mrs. Crawford.

Required:

Answer the following, setting forth reasons for any conclusions stated.

1. What are the basic elements for the creation of a valid trust?

2. At what point in time was the trust created in this case?

3. Is the Internal Revenue Service's denial of the shifting of the $14,000 income to the children proper?

4. Can Mr. & Mrs. Crawford, without the consent of the beneficiaries revoke the trust, assuming the Internal Revenue Service is correct?

Problem 2 (584,L4)

(15 to 20 minutes)

Ted and his wife Judy own Redacre in a tenancy by the entirety. Redacre is a lot by the seaside on which they plan someday to build a summer home. Ted also owns Bigacre in a joint tenancy with Lois, Clark, and Jeff, each owning a ¼ undivided interest. Bigacre is a large parcel of investment acreage which produces no current income. Ted and Judy have had several arguments about the raising of their son Peter, now age 18, who Judy believes has exhibited a tendency toward irresponsibility. Ted, as a result, has decided to take certain steps on his own to protect Peter's future financial security.

Ted plans to establish a trust with Guardem Trust Company and Peter as co-trustees. He plans to transfer Redacre to the trust along with $100,000 in cash. The $100,000 is to be used to purchase Ted's interest in Bigacre. Although Judy knows of the steps being taken, she has not agreed to them. Accordingly, Ted does not plan to have her participate in the establishment of the trust or in any of the transactions or paperwork involved.

The trust will provide that all income is to be paid to Peter, with final distribution of all trust assets to Peter upon his reaching age 40. The trust will also permit Peter after reaching age 21, to remove Guardem as trustee leaving himself as successor sole trustee.

Required:

Answer the following, setting forth reasons for any conclusions stated.

If Ted's plans are carried out:

1. What interest will the trust have in Redacre and Bigacre?

2. What interests will the remaining three parties have in Bigacre, if Clark dies subsequent to the transfer of Ted's interest in Bigacre to the trust?

3. Will the requirements of a valid trust be met?

4. Will the purchase of Bigacre from Ted be a proper exercise of the trustees' duties?

5. What effect would Peter's exercise of his right to remove Guardem as a trustee after he reaches 21, have on the trust and the ownership of Bigacre?

Multiple Choice Answers

1. b	6. d	11. d	16. c	20. b
2. c	7. c	12. d	17. b	21. c
3. a	8. a	13. b	18. d	22. d
4. b	9. d	14. a	19. b	23. b
5. b	10. b	15. d		

Multiple Choice Answer Explanations

A. Estates

1. (581,L1,50) (b) A joint tenancy is a form of concurrent property ownership in which the joint tenants have a right of survivorship in the property concurrently held. Thus, if a joint tenant dies, that tenant's interest in the property is divided equally among the surviving joint tenants. The deceased tenant's interest in the property will not pass to his heirs. Since Jean had full ownership of the property upon her brother's death and on her death, such property is properly included in her estate. Answer (a) is incorrect because, upon Jean's death, her sister will receive full ownership of the savings account regardless of any provision to the contrary in a will. Answer (c) is incorrect since gifts made in contemplation of death are irrevocable once made. Answer (d) is incorrect since a life insurance policy will pass to the named beneficiary without regard to the will of the deceased.

2. (1180,L1,50) (c) The will created a life estate in Dorothy, the wife, and a vested remainder in fee simple that the daughters owned as tenants in common. This means that the daughters' ownership rights to the property came into existence when Paul, the decedent, died, even though their right of possession does not occur until Dorothy dies, and her life estate terminates. One daughter could sell her interest without the consent of either of the other two parties. Answer (c) is correct. Answer (a) is incorrect because a spouse under the concept of statutory share has the right to denounce the will and elect to take stated share (normally 1/3) of the dead spouse's estate. Answer (d) is incorrect because the daughters received the remainder as tenants in common, not as joint tenants. Tenancy in common does not have the right of survivorship thus, if one of the daughters predeceased Dorothy, the interest of the dead daughter would pass by the deceased daughter's estate.

3. (1178,L1,34) (a) Property held in joint tenancy passes to the survivor whether or not there is a will. The intestate succession rules apply to persons who die intestate, i.e., without a will. Answer (b) is incorrect because intestate succession applies to all property of a decedent dying without a will. Answer (c) is incorrect because the intestate succession rules do not effectively prevent a decedent from totally disinheriting his wife and children because such effect might be accomplished by other estate planning devises such as a will. Answer (d) is incorrect because the failure to name an executor would not have the effect of converting a decedent from the status of testate to intestate. An administrator would be appointed by the court in place of an executor.

B. Administration of Estates

4. (1180,L1,52) (b) An executor is the personal representative of the decedent that is named in a will. If the decedent died intestate, then, the court would appoint an administrator as the personal representative. The person named as executor can decline to serve; in which case, the court will then appoint an executor. If the will does not provide compensation for the services of an executor, the court will order that the person serving in this capacity receive a reasonable fee for services rendered. The executor can be the principal beneficiary of the will, but need not have read the will nor be present at the signing of the will.

5. (577,L3,41) (b) As executor of his father's will, Walker has the affirmative duty to carry out the wishes of his father. He must collect all debts, pay all expenses, and carry out the distribution of the assets to those specified. The will may provide that a surety bond is not necessary for the executor but the probate court in its discretion may not comply with this provision. An executor may not sell real property without the court's approval unless the will specifically grants this power. Unless the will grants unlimited discretion, Walker must conform to various prudent investment guidelines in the management of the estate's assets during administration.

C. Trusts

6. (582,L1,55) (d) The trustee must act in a competent, nonnegligent manner. The trustee faces possible removal unless he exercises that degree of care and skill which a reasonably prudent person would in the administration of the trust. Answer (a) is incorrect because the trustee owes a fiduciary duty to the beneficiaries. A trustee holds the legal title to the trust property for the benefit of the beneficiaries. Answer (b) is incorrect because the trustee is entitled to compensation for duties performed in managing the trust property and distributing the trust income to the beneficiaries as directed by the trust instrument. Answer (c) is incorrect because the trustee does not have the

power to make such an election for termination. However, if all the parties join in a suit to terminate a trust, the trust may be terminated, with agreement of settlor, if termination would not defeat a material trust purpose.

7. (582,L1,57) (c) The trust created by Martins is a legal entity for both tax and nontax purposes even though the settlor is also the remainderman (the person who receives the trust corpus at the termination of the trust). When the grantor retains a reversionary interest in the trust property such that the corpus or income is to revert to him within ten years after the transfer into trust (this qualifies as a Grantor Trust), the trust is not considered a separate legal entity for tax purposes. The income from such trust is then taxable as personal income to the grantor. Since Martins' trust is for fifteen years, it falls outside the scope of a Grantor Trust, and consequently will be a separate legal entity for tax purposes. Answer (a) is incorrect because Martins' death does not terminate the trust since he is not the measuring life for the trust's duration. If Martins dies after ten years, the trust will continue for the remaining five years for the benefit of the children and will then pass to his heirs or devisees. Answer (b) is incorrect because the trust is irrevocable for a fifteen-year period, and Martins can revoke only if he reserved a power of revocation in the trust agreement or if all the beneficiaries agree and the termination would not defeat a material trust purpose.

8. (581,L1,49) (a) A trust is a fiduciary relationship wherein one person (trustee) holds legal title to property for the benefit of another (beneficiary). A trustee has the power to do what is necessary to fulfill the terms of the trust. A trustee cannot speculate, must diversify and can make major changes in an investment portfolio without the consent of beneficiaries. Answer (b) is not incorrect because a simple trust is entitled to a $300 per year exemption for federal tax purposes which is similar to an individual's exemption. Answer (c) is not incorrect because a trustee is a fiduciary to the beneficiaries and can take no personal advantage from his position. All beneficiaries can sue for mismanagement, conversion or waste by the trustee. A trustee must also keep trust assets separate from his personal assets and be accountable for both trust assets and his actions. Answer (d) is not an incorrect statement since a trust is a separate taxable entity for federal income tax purposes although it may not be subject to any tax.

9. (1180,L1,51) (d) A settlor may revoke a trust if the trust instrument reserves this right. Thus, answer (d) is correct. Creation of an inter vivos (living) trust only need be in writing when the trust involves real property, or where performance is not capable of being completed in one year from the date of creation. Inter vivos trusts involving personal property can be oral. Testamentary trusts must meet the same legal requirements for a valid will (i.e., in writing, signed, witnessed, etc.). Thus, answers (a) and (b) are incorrect. Answer (c) is incorrect because property in a testamentary trust is considered to have been transferred at the decedent's death and is therefore part of the decedent's gross estate for federal estate tax purposes.

10. (1179,L1,44) (b) In a properly drafted inter vivos trust, irrevocable for a period of 12 years, the trust income will not be taxable to the donor (settlor) during its existence but will be taxable to the beneficiaries. Answer (a) is incorrect because the trust as described will not fail for lack of a proper purpose. The property that has been transferred to the trust must be managed; thus the trust is an active one with a proper purpose since the trustee must actually perform these duties. Answer (c) is incorrect because the settlor, Gordon, does not retain the beneficial title to the trust since the duration of the trust is sufficiently long. The beneficiary holds the beneficial title to the property. Answer (d) is incorrect because under the facts as stated, Gordon has created an irrevocable trust. Thus, he may not demand return of the trust assets prior to the expiration of the 12 years. The only possibility of this occuring is if the settlor and all beneficiaries agree to a termination prior to the expiration of the 12 years.

F. Allocation of Principal and Income

11. (582,L1,56) (d) The allocation of principal and income is governed by the provisions of the Uniform Principal and Income Act. The receipts from the annuity are equitably apportioned between principal and income. Answer (a) is incorrect because it is not against public policy for the trustee to invest in the offshore investment limited partnership. The trustee has a duty to preserve the trust assets and to make the trust property productive. The trustee must invest the trust assets as a reasonably prudent person. The limited partnership can be construed to be a prudent investment due to its limited liability aspect, unlike investment in a general partnership where there is unlimited liability. Answer (b) is incorrect because the trustee, Harding, has no discretion in making allocations since the Uniform Principal and Income Act governs. Answer (c) is incorrect because the loss attributable to the partnership is chargeable to trust principal.

12. (1181,L1,51) (d) The Uniform Principal and Income Act governs the allocation of Principal and Income. Items allocated to income include ordinary operating expenses such as depreciation. This is further supported by Internal Revenue Code § 167 permitting a deduction of a reasonable allowance for exhaustion, or wear and tear (i.e., depreciation of property held for the production of income). On the other hand, principal paid on the mortgage and permanent improvements to the trust property (e.g., a street assessment) are expenses incurred in preserving the trust corpus (the income-producing real estate). They are, therefore, allocated to principal.

13. (581,L1,51) (b) An inter vivos trust comes into existence while the settlor (grantor) is living. The allocation of trust items to principal and income is governed by the Uniform Principal and Income Act (adopted by most states). Allocations made to trust principal include: original trust property, proceeds and gains from sale of trust property, insurance received on destruction of property, new property purchased with principal or proceeds from the principal, stock dividends and splits and a reserve for depreciation. Disbursements from trust principal are for reduction of indebtedness, litigation over trust property, permanent improvements and costs related to purchase/sale of trust property. Income includes profits from trust principal, e.g., rent, interest, cash dividends and royalties. Expenses from income include interest, insurance premiums, taxes, repairs, and depreciation. The annual service fee should be allocated to income because it is an expense associated with administration and management of trust property. It should not be allocated to principal. Answers (a), (c), and (d) are all proper allocations to income.

14. (580,L1,28) (a) Normally the income beneficiary is entitled to all interest earned by the items making up the corpus of the trust and the principal beneficiary is charged with any loss or gain relevant to the value of the corpus of the trust. Thus, answer (a) is correct.

15. (1179,L1,46) (d) Rights to subscribe to shares of another corporation should be allocated to income. Answers (a), subscription rights to the distributing corporation, (b) sale of subscription rights to the distributing corporation, and (c), a stock dividend, are examples of items that should be allocated to principal.

16. (1179,L1,47) (c) Insurance proceeds for the destruction of a garage located on the trust property should be allocated to principal since the insurance proceeds represent a change in the form of principal. The rental payments in answer (a), the prepayment of rent in answer (b), and the interest on a purchased money mortgage in answer (d) are all items that should be allocated to income.

17. (1178,L1,37) (b) Under the Uniform Principal and Income Act a year-end cash dividend, whether regular or extraordinary, should be allocated by a trustee exclusively to income. Stock dividends, liquidating dividends, and stock splits are all examples of receipts which should be allocated to principal.

18. (1178,L1,40) (d) In allocating between income and principal of a trust, the trustee should credit the discount portion received on redemption of treasury bills to income. This is essentially interest, which is an income item. The mortgage payments in answer (a), the capital gains distribution in answer (b), and the stock rights received from a distributing corporation in answer (c) are all examples of receipts or disbursements which a trustee should allocate to principal.

G. Federal Estate Tax

19. (1181,L1,52) (b) Under the Economic Recovery Tax Act of 1981 (which applies to decedents dying after December 31, 1981), there is an unlimited marital deduction for the fair market value of the property passing to a surviving spouse. Therefore, all the property bequeathed to Madison's husband will qualify for the marital deduction, and thereby be excluded from Madison's estate for federal estate tax purposes. Answer (a) is incorrect because an executrix is appointed by and under the control of the probate court. Hence, the executrix, Janet, does not have the legal right to act for and on behalf of the estate until she has been duly appointed in a probate proceeding. Answer (c) is incorrect because execution of a will does not vest ownership rights in the named beneficiaries. The testator is free to dispose of the property if he/she wishes after execution of the will. Answer (d) is incorrect because no state would allow a decedent's spouse to receive everything when there are surviving children.

20. (1181,L1,53) (b) A terminable interest granted to a surviving spouse will **not** generally qualify for the marital deduction. However, the Economic Recovery Tax Act of 1981 (which applies to decedents dying after December 31, 1981) stipulates that if certain conditions are met, a life interest granted to a surviving spouse (i.e., Annette's husband's life estate) will not be treated as a terminable interest, but rather as a **qualified terminable interest.** If decedent's executor elects, a transfer of **qualified terminable interest**

property (i.e., property placed in trust with income to surviving spouse for life and remainder to someone else at surviving spouse's death) will qualify for the unlimited marital estate deduction, provided that income from the property is paid at least annually to the surviving spouse and the property is not subject to transfer during the surviving spouse's lifetime. Therefore, Annette's husband's rights would qualify for the estate tax marital deduction, assuming it meets the aforementioned criteria for qualified terminable interest property. Answer (a) is incorrect because a trust is recognized as a taxable entity for income tax purposes. Answer (c) is incorrect because although the trustee is a fiduciary with respect to the beneficiaries and must act with their interest in mind, in the absence of an explicit restriction, there is no implied restriction which obligates the trustee, York, to obtain the beneficiaries' consent if he wishes to dispose of the trust assets. Answer (d) is incorrect because the trustee, York, holds only legal title, not equitable title. The beneficiaries of the trust hold equitable title.

H. Real Estate Investment Trusts (REITs)

21. (1180,L1,45) (c) The certificateholders (owners) of a real estate investment trust have limited liability. Their liability is limited to their investment in the trust similar to the limited liability of a shareholder in a corporation and a limited partner. Thus answer (c) is correct. Answer (d) is incorrect because the sale of an interest in a real estate investment trust is the sale of a security under the Securities Act of 1933. Consequently, the seller of these interests would have to comply with the registration requirements of this act. A real estate investment trust does not fall within the provisions of the Federal Trust Indenture Act. This makes answer (b) incorrect. The normal trust, as distinguished from a real estate investment trust, is a taxable entity for income tax purposes, while a real estate investment trust is not a taxable entity. Ordinary income passes through to the investors and each investor pays income tax on his/her share.

May 1985 Answer

22. (585,L1,58) (d) A trust, by definition, is a fiduciary relationship in which one person holds legal title to property for the benefit of another person. If Sally, the sole beneficiary, is named as sole trustee then merger of the equitable and legal titles occurs, and hence there is no trust. Answer (a) is incorrect because the trust will not fail due to the fact that the trustee is not being compensated. Answer (b) is incorrect because there is no requirement that the instrument creating the trust be supported by consideration. Answer (c) is incorrect because normally if the instrument fails to name a trustee the court will appoint one.

November 1985 Answer

23. (1185,L1,58) (b) Once the necessary elements of a gift are present, the gift may not be revoked. However, a trust may be legally revoked if the settlor has reserved the power to revoke the trust, or if the settlor and beneficiaries of an irrevocable trust mutually agree to terminate the trust. Answer (a) is incorrect because a trust need only be in writing if it involves real property; all other trusts may be created orally. Answer (c) is incorrect because a contract need not be present in order to create a valid trust. Answer (d) is incorrect since notification of the beneficiary is not a necessary element to create a trust.

Answer Outline

Problem 1 Creation of Trust; Clifford Trust (1183,L5b)

Part b.

1. Trust must have
   Creator
   Trust property
   Trustee
   Beneficiary
   If trust property is real property, there must be a writing
2. Trust was created on December 1, 1982, when Crawfords conveyed land to trustee in writing
   Inter vivos trust begins when title to real property vests in trustee
3. Yes, duration of trust is less than 10 years
   Thus, does not qualify as a Clifford trust, which would have properly shifted income to children
4. No, normally once irrevocable trust is created, state law prohibits termination until expiration of stated term

Unofficial Answer

Problem 1 Creation of Trust; Clifford Trust (1183,L5b)

Part b.

1. A trust must have a creator (settlor or grantor), trust property, (principal, corpus, or res), a trustee, and a beneficiary. There must be a writing if the subject matter of the trust is real property.

2. The Crawfords' trust was not created until December 1, 1982, when the land (the res) was conveyed to the trustee in writing. In the case of an intervivos trust of real property with an independent trustee, the settlor (here the Crawfords) must go through whatever formalities (here a conveyance) are required to vest title in the trustee.

3. Yes. Although a trust having a duration of 10 years or more will qualify as a bona fide transferee of property for the purposes of shifting income to the trust or its beneficiaries, a transfer to a trust for a lesser duration will not qualify according to the Internal Revenue Code and Regulations. This trust was intended to be what is popularly known as a "Clifford Trust."

4. No. State law precludes, except in rare circumstances, the termination of an irrevocable trust once created. Hence, the Crawfords are stuck with a useless trust for the balance of its term.

Answer Outline

Problem 2 Concurrent Ownership; Trust Requirements; Trustee's Duties; Termination of Trust (584,L4)

1. Trust has no interest in Redacre
   But has 1/4 interest in Bigacre as tenant in common
   Realty held as tenants by entirety may not be transferred without co-owner's consent
   Joint tenant may transfer interest in tenancy without consent of co-tenants
   Such transfer destroys joint tenancy of interest transferred
2. Trust acquires no further interest in Bigacre upon Clark's death
   No right of survivorship to tenant in common
   Jeff and Lois as joint tenants have right of survivorship
   They own 3/8 interest in Bigacre as joint tenants
3. Requirements of valid trust met
   Property (res) transferred to co-trustees for benefit of Peter (beneficiary)
   Intent to create for lawful purpose is evident
   Sole beneficiary may act as co-trustee
4. Trustees have fiduciary duty to manage trust for benefit of beneficiaries
   Trustees required to invest according to standards of prudent investor
   Purchase of Bigacre meets standard of prudent investor if amount paid is fair and future value expected to increase
5. Removal of Guardem as trustee terminates trust with interest in Bigacre vesting in Peter
   Trust terminates when sole beneficiary and sole trustee are same person
   Legal and equitable titles merge

Unofficial Answer

Problem 2 Concurrent Ownership; Trust Requirements; Trustee's Duties; Termination of Trust (584,L4)

1. The trust will have no interest in Redacre but would have a one-quarter interest as tenant in common in Bigacre. The attempted transfer of realty held as tenants by the entirety without the co-owner's consent does not transfer the property. Therefore, Ted is unable to transfer any portion of Redacre since Judy has not consented to the transfer. A joint tenant may transfer his interest in the tenancy without the consent of the co-tenants. However, such a transfer destroys the joint tenancy of the interest transferred. Therefore, the purchase of Ted's interest in Bigacre gives the trust a one-quarter interest in the property as tenant in common with Clark, Lois, and Jeff remaining as joint tenants as to three-quarters of the property.

2. Despite the trust's one-quarter interest in Bigacre, it acquires no additional interest due to Clark's death, since there is no right of survivorship with respect to a tenant in common. However, Jeff and Lois will acquire Clark's one-quarter interest by operation of law, due to the right of survivorship feature among joint tenants. Therefore, Jeff and Lois will each own a three-eighths interest in Bigacre as joint tenants, whereas the trust will retain its one-quarter interest as a tenant in common.

3. A valid trust has been created. Ted, as grantor or settlor, has transferred property (res) to Guardem and Peter for the benefit of Peter. Intent to create a trust is evident, and the trust is established for a lawful purpose. It is proper for the sole beneficiary to act as co-trustee.

4. The trustees have a fiduciary duty to manage the trust for the benefit of the beneficiaries. In the absence of trust provisions otherwise, the trustees are required to invest in accordance with the standard of a prudent man in the conduct of his own investments. A trustee should ordinarily invest in income-producing property. However, the purchase of Bigacre by the trustees could meet this standard even though Bigacre is not currently earning income if the amount paid is fair and the future value may be expected to increase.

5. The trust would terminate and the interest in Bigacre would vest in Peter if he exercises his right to remove Guardem as trustee. As sole trustee Peter would hold legal title, and as sole beneficiary he would hold equitable title. A trust terminates when the sole beneficiary and sole trustee are the same person as legal and equitable title will be merged.

EXAMINATION IN BUSINESS LAW

(Commercial Law)

NOTE TO CANDIDATES: Suggested time allotments are as follows:

All questions are required:	*Estimated Minutes* Minimum	Maximum
No. 1	110	130
No. 2	15	20
No. 3	15	20
No. 4	15	20
No. 5	15	20
Total	170	210

Number 1 (Estimated time — 110 to 130 minutes)

Select the **best** answer for each of the following items.

1. DMO Enterprises, Inc., engaged the accounting firm of Martin, Seals & Anderson to perform its annual audit. The firm performed the audit in a competent, nonnegligent manner and billed DMO for $16,000, the agreed fee. Shortly after delivery of the audited financial statements, Hightower, the assistant controller, disappeared, taking with him $28,000 of DMO's funds. It was then discovered that Hightower had been engaged in a highly sophisticated, novel defalcation scheme during the past year. He had previously embezzled $35,000 of DMO funds. DMO has refused to pay the accounting firm's fee and is seeking to recover the $63,000 that was stolen by Hightower. Which of the following is correct?
   a. The accountants can **not** recover their fee and are liable for $63,000.
   b. The accountants are entitled to collect their fee and are **not** liable for $63,000.
   c. DMO is entitled to rescind the audit contract and thus is **not** liable for the $16,000 fee, but it can **not** recover damages.
   d. DMO is entitled to recover the $28,000 defalcation, and is **not** liable for the $16,000 fee.

2. If a CPA firm is being sued for common law fraud by a third party based upon materially false financial statements, which of the following is the best defense which the accountants could assert?
   a. Lack of privity.
   b. Lack of reliance.
   c. A disclaimer contained in the engagement letter.
   d. Contributory negligence on the part of the client.

3. Jackson Enterprises dismissed its auditors for cause. The CPA firm failed to complete its audit within the time stipulated due to its own inefficiency. Under the circumstances
   a. The client has the right to all of the CPA's working papers relating to the engagement which are retained by the CPA.
   b. The CPA firm is entitled to recover the full fee agreed upon less a per diem diminution of 5% for each day delayed.
   c. Recovery by the CPA firm in quasi-contract will not be available if as a result of the delay the audit is worthless to Jackson.
   d. If Jackson sues the CPA firm for damages for breach of contract, recovery will be denied because it is commonly recognized that unless the contract so stipulates, time is not of the essence.

4. Gibson is suing Simpson & Sloan, CPAs, to recover losses incurred in connection with Gibson's transactions in Zebra Corporation securities. Zebra's Annual Form 10-K Report contained material false and misleading statements in the financial statements audited by Simpson & Sloan. To recover under the Securities and Exchange Act of 1934, Gibson must, among other things, establish that
   a. All of his past transactions in Zebra securities, both before and after the auditors' report date, resulted in a net loss.
   b. The transaction in Zebra securities that resulted in a loss occurred within 90 days of the auditors' report date.
   c. He relied upon the financial statements in his decision to purchase or sell Zebra securities.
   d. The market price of the stock dropped significantly after corrected financial statements were issued by Zebra.

5. The traditional common-law rules regarding accountants' liability to third parties for negligence
   - a. Remain substantially unchanged since their inception.
   - b. Were more stringent than the rules currently applicable.
   - c. Are of relatively minor importance to the accountant.
   - d. Have been substantially changed at both the federal and state levels.

6. A third-party purchaser of securities has brought suit based upon the Securities Act of 1933 against a CPA firm. The CPA firm will prevail in the suit brought by the third party even though the CPA firm issued an unqualified opinion on materially incorrect financial statements if
   - a. The CPA firm was unaware of the defects.
   - b. The third-party plaintiff had no direct dealings with the CPA firm.
   - c. The CPA firm can show that the third-party plaintiff did not rely upon the audited financial statements.
   - d. The CPA firm can establish that it was not guilty of actual fraud.

7. The 1976 Tax Reform Act substantially changed the regulation of tax return preparers by
   - a. Granting the Internal Revenue Service the power to seek injunctive relief against a wrongdoing preparer.
   - b. Providing criminal sanctions.
   - c. Imposing civil liability regardless of whether the preparer does the preparation for compensation.
   - d. Expanding the legal remedies of the client for whom the return was prepared.

8. The CPA firm of Knox & Knox has been subpoenaed to testify and produce its correspondence and workpapers in connection with a lawsuit brought by a third party against one of their clients. Knox considers the subpoenaed documents to be privileged communication and therefore seeks to avoid admission of such evidence in the lawsuit. Which of the following is correct?
   - a. Federal law recognizes such a privilege if the accountant is a Certified Public Accountant.
   - b. The privilege is available regarding the working papers since the CPA is deemed to own them.
   - c. The privileged communication rule as it applies to the CPA-client relationship is the same as that of attorney-client.
   - d. In the absence of a specific statutory provision, the law does **not** recognize the existence of the privileged communication rule between a CPA and his client.

9. Which of the following can a CPA firm legally do?
   - a. Accept a competing company in the same industry as another of its clients.
   - b. Establish an association of CPAs for the purpose of determining minimum fee schedules.
   - c. Effectively disclaim liability to third parties for any and all torts.
   - d. Effectively establish an absolute dollar limitation on its liability for a given engagement.

10. Henry Lamb worked for several years for a major CPA firm which has offices in 37 states. He resigned his position with the CPA firm, then returned to his home state where he opened his own CPA practice. Under the circumstances
    - a. Lamb will be liable for damages to his former employer if he engages in the practice of accounting in any state in which the firm has offices.
    - b. Lamb will be liable for damages to his former employer if he accepts as his client any party, solicited or unsolicited, who had been a client of his former employer immediately prior to his being retained by said client.
    - c. He must obtain permission of the state board of accountancy in the state in which he was previously employed in order to relocate.
    - d. He must be licensed to practice as a CPA in his home state.

11. To successfully invoke the doctrine of ratification
    - a. The agent must have had the legal capacity to have so acted.
    - b. The agent must in fact be the agent of the principal although the action taken was totally without authority.
    - c. The ratification must have been stated expressly.
    - d. The ratification must be made with knowledge of the material facts of the transaction.

12. Barton, a wealthy art collector, orally engaged Deiter to obtain a rare and beautiful painting from Cumbers, a third party. Cumbers did not know that Barton had engaged Deiter to obtain the painting for Barton because as Barton told Deiter "that would cause the price to skyrocket." Regarding the liability of the parties if a contract is made or purported to be made, which of the following is correct?

   a. Since the appointment of Deiter was oral, **no** agency exists, and any contract made by Deiter on Barton's behalf is invalid.
   b. Because Barton specifically told Deiter **not** to reveal for whom he (Deiter) was buying the painting, Deiter can **not** be personally liable on the contract made on Barton's behalf.
   c. If Deiter makes a contract with Cumbers which Deiter breaches, Cumbers may, after learning of the agreement between Barton and Deiter, elect to recover from either Barton or Deiter.
   d. If Deiter makes a contract to purchase the painting, without revealing he is Barton's agent, Cumbers has entered into a contract which is voidable at his election.

13. The liability of a principal to a third party for the torts of his agent

   a. Can be effectively limited by agreement with the agent.
   b. Can **not** extend to the inclusion of a criminal act committed by the agent.
   c. Is less onerous if the agent is acting for an undisclosed principal.
   d. Is an example of the imposition of liability without fault upon the principal.

14. Under which of the following circumstances will an agent acting on behalf of a disclosed principal not be liable to a third party for his actions?

   a. He signs a negotiable instrument in his own name and does not indicate his agency capacity.
   b. He commits a tort in the course of discharging his duties.
   c. He is acting for a non-existent principal which subsequently comes into existence after the time of the agent's actions on the principal's behalf.
   d. He lacks specific express authority but is acting within the scope of his implied authority.

15. Park Manufacturing hired Stone as a traveling salesman to sell goods manufactured by Park. Stone also sold a line of products manufactured by a friend. He did **not** disclose this to Park. The relationship was unsatisfactory and Park finally fired Stone after learning of Stone's sales of the other manufacturer's goods. Stone, enraged at Park for firing him, continued to make contracts on Park's behalf with both new and old customers that were almost uniformly disadvantageous to Park. Park, upon learning of this, gave written notice of Stone's discharge to all parties with whom Stone had dealt. Which of the following statements is **incorrect?**

   a. Park can bring an action against Stone to have him account for any secret profits.
   b. Prior to notification, Stone retained some continued authority to bind Park despite termination of the agency relationship.
   c. New customers who contracted with Stone for the first time could enforce the contracts against Park if they knew that Stone had been Park's salesman but were unaware that Stone was fired.
   d. If Park had promptly published a notification of termination of Stone's employment in the local newspapers and in the trade publications, he would **not** be liable for any of Stone's contracts.

16. For which of the following is a partnership recognized as a separate legal entity?

   a. The liability for and payment of taxes on partnership gains from the sale of capital assets.
   b. In respect to contributions and advances made by partners to the partnership.
   c. The recognition of net operating losses.
   d. The status of the partnership as an employer for worker's compensation purposes.

17. Grand, a general partner, retired, and the partnership held a testimonial dinner for him and invited ten of the partnership's largest customers to attend. A week later a notice was placed in various trade journals indicating that Grand had retired and was no longer associated with the partnership in any capacity. After the appropriate public notice of Grand's retirement, which of the following best describes his legal status?

   a. The release of Grand by the remaining partners and the assumption of all past and future debts of the partnership by them via a "hold harmless" clause constitutes a novation.

b. Grand has the apparent authority to bind the partnership in contracts he makes with persons who have previously dealt with the partnership and are unaware of his retirement.

c. Grand has no liability to past creditors upon his retirement from the partnership if they have all been informed of his withdrawal and his release from liability, and if they do not object within 60 days.

d. Grand has the legal status of a limited partner for the three years it takes to pay him the balance of the purchase price of his partnership interest.

18. For which of the following does a partner have joint liability as contrasted with joint and several liability?

a. The negligent injury of a third person by a partner while acting in the ordinary course of the firm's business.

b. The misapplication of funds by a partner acting within the scope of his apparent authority.

c. The intentional interference with an existing contractual relationship with the tacit approval of his fellow partners.

d. The bond and mortgage on the partnership's office building.

19. Jack Gordon, a general partner of Visions Unlimited, is retiring. He sold his partnership interest to Don Morrison for $80,000. Gordon assigned to Morrison all his rights, title, and interests in the partnership and named Morrison as his successor partner in Visions. In this situation

a. The assignment to Morrison dissolves the partnership.

b. Absent any limitation regarding the assignment of a partner's interest, Gordon is free to assign it at his will.

c. Morrison is entitled to an equal voice and vote in the management of the partnership, and he is entitled to exercise all the rights and privileges that Gordon had.

d. Morrison does not have the status of a partner, but he can, upon demand, inspect the partnership accounting records.

20. Teal and Olvera were partners of the T & O Real Estate Investment Company. They decided to seek more capital in order to expand their participation in the booming real estate business in the area. They obtained five individuals to invest $100,000 each in their venture as limited partners.

Assuming the limited partnership agreement is silent on the point, which of the following acts may Teal and Olvera engage in without the written consent of all limited partners?

a. Admit an additional person as a general partner.

b. Continue the partnership business upon the death or retirement of a general partner.

c. Invest the entire amount ($500,000) of contributions by the limited partners in a single venture.

d. Admit additional limited partners from time to time in order to obtain additional working capital.

21. Bunker's son, Michael, was seeking an account executive position with Harrison, Inc., the largest brokerage firm in the United States. Michael was very independent and wished no interference by his father. The firm, after several weeks deliberation, decided to hire Michael. They made him an offer on April 12, 1982, and Michael readily accepted. Bunker feared that his son would not be hired. Unaware of the fact that his son had been hired, Bunker mailed a letter to Harrison on April 13 in which he promised to give the brokerage firm $50,000 in commission business if the firm would hire his son. The letter was duly received by Harrison and they wish to enforce it against Bunker. Which of the following is correct?

a. Harrison will prevail since the promise is contained in a signed writing.

b. Past consideration is **no** consideration, hence there is **no** contract.

c. Harrison will prevail based upon promissory estoppel.

d. The preexisting legal duty rule applies and makes the promise unenforceable.

22. Patton is a partner in an accounting firm. His partnership contract contains a clause which states that should Patton leave the firm, he agrees not to compete with the firm for one year, either as an individual or as a member of another accounting firm, anywhere within the city limits of New York City. The accounting firm does most of its business with clients in the states of New York, Pennsylvania and New Jersey. The clause would be held

a. Legally enforceable in most states.
b. An illegal restraint of trade under federal anti-trust statutes.
c. Illegal, thereby invalidating the entire contract.
d. Unconscionable under the Uniform Commercial Code.

23. Strattford Theaters made a contract with Avon, Inc., for the purchase of $450 worth of theater supplies. Delivery was to take place in one month. One week after accepting the order, the price of materials and labor increased sharply. In fact, to break even on the contract, Avon would have to charge an additional $600. Avon phoned Strattford and informed them of the situation. Strattford was sympathetic and said they were sorry to hear about the situation but that the best they would be willing to do was split the rise in price with Avon. Avon accepted the modification on Strattford's terms. As a result of the above modification, which of the following is correct?

a. Avon's continuing to perform the contract after informing Strattford of the price difficulty constitutes consideration for the modification of the price.
b. The oral modification is not effective since there was no consideration.
c. The statute of frauds applies to the contract as modified.
d. The contract contained an implied promise that it was subject to price rises.

24. Filmore purchased a Miracle color television set from Allison Appliances, an authorized dealer, for $499. The written contract contained the usual one-year warranty as to parts and labor as long as the set was returned to the manufacturer or one of its authorized dealers. The contract also contained an effective disclaimer of any express warranty protection, other than that which was included in the contract. It further provided that the contract represented the entire agreement and understanding of the parties. Filmore claims that during the bargaining process Surry, Allison's agent, orally promised to service the set at Filmore's residence if anything went wrong within the year. Allison has offered to repair the set if it is brought to the service department, but denies any liability under the alleged oral express agreement. Which of the following would be the best defense for Allison to rely upon in the event Filmore sues?

a. The Statute of Frauds.
b. The parol evidence rule.
c. The fact that all warranty protection was disclaimed other than the express warranty contained in the contract.
d. The fact that Surry, Allison's agent, did **not** have express authority to make such a promise.

25. On August 1, 1982, Fields & Boss, CPAs, made a contract with Gil Manufacturing to audit Gil's financial statements for calendar year 1982 and to render an opinion thereon. Gil agreed to an estimated fee of $7,500 for the services. Gil changed its mind and on September 2, 1982, before any services had been performed, notified Fields & Boss that it was repudiating the contract. Which of the following is correct?

a. The CPA firm may sue for breach of contract immediately and need **not** wait until after performance is due and refused.
b. The CPA firm is no longer bound on the contract but can **not** sue until after January 1, 1983.
c. The CPA firm remains bound by the contract until January 1, 1983.
d. There has been a present breach of the contract.

26. An otherwise valid petition for involuntary bankruptcy has been filed against Mohawk Corporation. This will be sufficient to obtain an order for relief against Mohawk provided

a. Mohawk is generally not paying debts as they become due.
b. A custodian has been appointed to take charge of substantially all of Mohawk's debts within four months of filing.
c. The creditor or creditors can establish that Mohawk is bankrupt in the bankruptcy sense.
d. The majority of creditors join in the filing if there are more than two creditors involved.

27. Merchant is in serious financial difficulty and is unable to meet current unsecured obligations of $25,000 to some 15 creditors who are demanding immediate payment. Merchant owes Flintheart $5,000 and Flintheart has decided to file an involuntary petition against Merchant. Which of the following is necessary in order for Flintheart to validly file?

a. Flintheart must be joined by at least two other creditors.
b. Merchant must have committed an act of bankruptcy within 120 days of the filing.
c. Flintheart must allege and subsequently establish that Merchant's liabilities exceed Merchant's assets upon fair valuation.
d. Flintheart must be a secured creditor.

28. On January 10, 1978, Edwards gave Cantrell a mortgage on his office building to secure a past-due $40,000 obligation which he owed Cantrell. Cantrell promptly recorded the mortgage. On March 15,1978, a petition in bankruptcy was filed against Edwards. Simpson, the trustee in bankruptcy, desires to prevent Cantrell from qualifying as a secured creditor. In seeking to set aside the mortgage, which of the following statements is correct?
    a. The mortgage cannot be set aside since it is a real property mortgage and recorded.
    b. Even if the mortgage is set aside, Cantrell has a priority in respect to the office building.
    c. The mortgage can only be set aside if the mortgage conveyance was fraudulent.
    d. The mortgage can be set aside if it was taken with knowledge of the fact that Edwards was insolvent in the bankruptcy sense.

29. Chapter 11 of the Bankruptcy Reform Act of 1978 deals with reorganizations. This Chapter
    a. Is exclusively available to corporations.
    b. Permits the debtor-in-possession to continue to operate the business in the same manner as a Chapter 11 trustee.
    c. Provides for filing of voluntary petitions but prohibits the filing of involuntary petitions.
    d. Provides separate procedures for corporations with publicly-held securities.

30. Abrams owned a fee simple absolute interest in certain real property. Abrams conveyed it to Fox for Fox's lifetime with the remainder interest upon Fox's death to Charles. What are the rights of Fox and Charles in the real property?
    a. Charles may not sell his interest in the property until the death of Fox.
    b. Fox has a possessory interest in the land and Charles has a future interest.
    c. Charles must outlive Fox in order to obtain any interest in the real property.
    d. Any conveyance by either Fox or Charles must be joined in by the other party in order to be valid.

31. Which of the following can not properly be received as the consideration for the issuance of shares?
    a. Promissory notes.
    b. Services actually performed for the corporation.
    c. Shares of stock of another corporation.
    d. Intangible property rights.

32. Which of the following regarding workers' compensation is correct?
    a. A purpose of workers' compensation is for the employer to assume a definite liability in exchange for the employee giving up his common law rights.
    b. It applies to workers engaged in or affecting interstate commerce only.
    c. It is optional in most jurisdictions.
    d. Once workers' compensation has been adopted by the employer, the amount of damages recoverable is based upon comparative negligence.

33. Which of the following is a part of the social security law?
    a. A self-employed person must contribute an annual amount which is less than the combined contributions of an employee and his or her employer.
    b. Upon the death of an employee prior to his retirement, his estate is entitled to receive the amount attributable to his contributions as a death benefit.
    c. Social security benefits must be fully funded and payments, current and future, must constitutionally come only from social security taxes.
    d. Social security benefits are taxable as income when they exceed the individual's total contributions.

34. Miltown borrowed $60,000 from Strauss upon the security of a first mortgage on a business building owned by Miltown. The mortgage has been amortized down to $50,000. Sanchez is buying the building from Miltown for $80,000. Sanchez is paying only the $30,000 excess over and above the mortgage. Sanchez may buy it either "subject to" the mortgage, or he may "assume" the mortgage. Which is a correct statement under these circumstances?
    a. The financing agreement ultimately decided upon must be recorded in order to be binding upon the parties.
    b. The financing arrangement is covered by the Uniform Commercial Code if Sanchez takes "subject to" the existing first mortgage.
    c. Sanchez will acquire no interest in the property if he takes "subject to" instead of "assuming" the mortgage.
    d. Sanchez would be better adivsed to take "subject to" the mortgage rather than to "assume" the mortgage.

35. Issuer, Inc., a New York corporation engaged in retail sales within New York City, was interested in raising $1,600,000 in capital. In this connection it approached through personal letters eighty-eight people in New York, New Jersey, and Connecticut, and then followed up with face-to-face negotiations where it seemed promising to do so. After extensive efforts in which Issuer disclosed all the information that these people requested, nineteen people from these areas purchased Issuer's securities. Issuer did not limit its offers to insiders, their relatives, or wealthy or sophisticated investors. In regard to this securities issuance

a. The offering is probably exempt from registration under federal securities law as a private placement.
b. The offering is probably exempt from registration under federal securities law as a small offering.
c. The offering is probably exempt from registration under federal securities law as an intrastate offering.
d. The offering probably is not exempt from registration under federal securities law.

36. Which of the following statements is correct regarding qualification for the private placement exemption from registration under the Securities Act of 1933?

a. The instrumentalities of interstate commerce must **not** be used.
b. The securities must be offered to **not** more than 35 persons.
c. The minimum amount of securities purchased by each offeree must **not** be less than $100,000.
d. The offerees **must** have access to or be furnished with the kind of information that would be available in a registration statement.

37. Charles is a commercial tenant of Luxor Buildings, Inc. The term of the lease is five years and two years have elapsed. The lease prohibits subletting, but does not contain any provision relating to assignment. Charles approached Luxor and asked whether Luxor could release him from the balance of the term of the lease for $500. Luxor refused unless Charles would agree to pay $2,000. Charles located Whitney who was interested in renting in Luxor's building and transferred the entire balance of the lease to Whitney in consideration of his promise to pay Luxor the monthly rental and otherwise perform Charles' obligations under the lease. Luxor objects. Which of the following statements is correct?

a. The assignment is invalid without Luxor's consent.
b. The assignment does not extinguish Charles' obligation to pay the rent if Whitney defaults.
c. The assignment need not be in writing.
d. A prohibition of the right to sublet contained in the lease completely prohibits an assignment.

38. Lutz sold his moving and warehouse business, including all the personal and real property used therein, to Arlen Van Lines, Inc. The real property was encumbered by a duly-recorded $300,000 first mortgage upon which Lutz was personally liable. Arlen acquired the property subject to the mortgage but did not assume the mortgage. Two years later, when the outstanding mortgage was $260,000, Arlen decided to abandon the business location because it had become unprofitable and the value of the real property was less than the outstanding mortgage. Arlen moved to another location and refused to pay the installments due on the mortgage. What is the legal status of the parties in regard to the mortgage?

a. Lutz must satisfy the mortgage debt in the event that foreclosure yields an amount less than the unpaid balance.
b. If Lutz pays off the mortgage, he will be able to successfully sue Arlen because Lutz is subrogated to the mortgagee's rights against Arlen.
c. Arlen took the real property free of the mortgage.
d. Arlen breached its contract with Lutz when it abandoned the location and defaulted on the mortgage.

39. The Securities Act of 1933, in general, exempts certain small stock offerings from full registration. What is the maximum dollar amount which would qualify for this exemption?

a. $300,000.
b. $1,500,000
c. $750,000.
d. $1,000,000.

40. The Securities Act of 1933 applies to the

a. Sale in interstate commerce of insurance and regular annuity contracts.
b. Sale by a dealer of securities issued by a bank.
c. Sale through a broker of a controlling person's investment in a public corporation.
d. Sale in interstate commerce of bonds issued by a charitable foundation.

41. A negotiable bill of lading
    a. Is one type of commercial paper as defined by the Uniform Commercial Code.
    b. Can give certain good faith purchasers greater rights to the bill of lading or the goods than the transferor had.
    c. Can **not** result in a loss to the owner if lost or stolen, provided prompt notice is given to the carrier in possession of the goods.
    d. Does **not** give the rightful possessor the ownership of the goods.

42. A merchant's irrevocable written offer (firm offer) to sell goods
    a. Must be separately signed if the offeree supplies a form contract containing the offer.
    b. Is valid for three months unless otherwise provided.
    c. Is nonassignable.
    d. Can **not** exceed a three-month duration even if consideration is given.

43. Stand Glue Corp. offered to sell Macal, Inc., all of the glue it would need in the manufacture of its furniture for one year at the rate of $25 per barrel, F.O.B. seller's city. Macal accepted Stand's offer. Four months later, due to inflation, Stand wrote to Macal advising Macal that Stand could no longer supply the glue at $25 per barrel, but offering to fulfill the contract at $28 per barrel instead. Macal, in need of the glue, sent Stand a letter agreeing to pay the price increase. Macal is
    a. Legally obligated to pay only $25 per barrel under the contract with Stand.
    b. Legally obligated to pay $28 per barrel under the contract with Stand.
    c. **Not** legally obligated to purchase any glue henceforth from Stand since Stand has breached the contract.
    d. Legally obligated to pay $28 per barrel due to the fact inflation represents an unforeseen hardship.

44. Doral Inc., wished to obtain an adequate supply of lumber for its factory extension which was to be constructed in the spring. It contacted Ace Lumber Company and obtained a 75-day written option (firm offer) to buy its estimated needs for the building. Doral supplied a form contract which included the option. Ace Lumber signed at the physical end of the contract but did not sign elsewhere. The price of lumber has risen drastically and Ace wishes to avoid its obligation. Which of the following is Ace's best defense against Doral's assertion that Ace is legally bound by the option?
    a. Such an option is invalid if its duration is for more than two months.
    b. The option is **not** supported by any consideration on Doral's part.
    c. Doral is **not** a merchant.
    d. The promise of irrevocability was contained in a form supplied by Doral and was **not** separately signed by Ace.

45. Ace Auto Sales, Inc., sold Williams a secondhand car for $9,000. One day Williams parked the car in a shopping center parking lot. When Williams returned to the car, Montrose and several policemen were waiting. It turned out that the car had been stolen from Montrose who was rightfully claiming ownership. Subsequently, the car was returned by Williams to Montrose. Williams seeks recourse against Ace Auto Sales who had sold him the car with the usual disclaimer of warranty. Which of the following is correct?
    a. Since Ace Auto Sales' contract of sale disclaimed "any and all warranties" arising in connection with its sale to Williams, Williams must bear the loss.
    b. Since Ace Auto and Williams were both innocent of any wrongdoing in connection with the theft of the auto, the loss will rest upon the party ultimately in possession.
    c. Had Williams litigated the question of Montrose's ownership to the auto, he would have won since possession is nine-tenths of the law.
    d. Ace Auto will bear the loss since a warranty of title in Williams' favor arose upon the sale of the auto.

46. Viscount Appliances sold Conway a refrigerator. Viscount wishes to disclaim the implied warranty of fitness for a particular purpose. Which of the following will effectively disclaim this warranty?
    a. The fact that the refrigerator is widely advertised and was sold under its brand name.
    b. A conspicuous written statement which states that "any and all warranty protection is hereby disclaimed."
    c. A conspicuous written statement indicating that "there are no warranties which extend beyond the description contained in the contract of sale."
    d. An inconspicuous written statement which specifically negates the warranty.

47. Donaldson suffered an injury due to a malfunction of a power tool he had purchased from Malloy Hardware. The tool was manufactured by Superior Tool

Company. Donaldson has commenced an action against Malloy and Superior based upon strict liability. Which of the following is a correct statement?

a. Donaldson's suit against Malloy will be dismissed since Malloy was **not** at fault.
b. Privity will **not** be a valid defense against Donaldson's suit.
c. Superior will **not** be liable if it manufactured the tool in a nonnegligent manner.
d. The lawsuit will be dismissed since strict liability has **not** been applied in product liability cases in the majority of jurisdictions.

48. Pure Food Company packed and sold quality food products to wholesalers and fancy food retailers. One of its most popular items was "southern style" baked beans. Charleston purchased a large can of the beans from the Superior Quality Grocery. Charleston's mother bit into a heaping spoonful of the beans at a family outing and fractured her jaw. The evidence revealed that the beans contained a brown stone, the size of a marble. In a subsequent lawsuit by Mrs. Charleston, which of the following is correct?

a. Mrs. Charleston can collect against Superior Quality for negligence.
b. Privity will not be a bar in a lawsuit against either Pure Food or Superior Quality.
c. The various sellers involved could have effectively excluded or limited the rights of third parties to sue them.
d. Privity is a bar to recovery by Mrs. Charleston, although her son may sue Superior Quality.

49. Milgore, the vice president of Deluxe Restaurants, telephoned Specialty Restaurant Suppliers and ordered a made-to-order dishwashing unit for one of its restaurants. Due to the specifications, the machine was not adaptable for use by other restauranteurs. The agreed price was $2,500. The machine was constructed as agreed but Deluxe has refused to pay for it. Which of the following is correct?

a. Milgore obviously lacked the authority to make such a contract.
b. The statute of frauds applies and will bar recovery by Specialty.
c. Specialty can successfully maintain an action for the price.
d. Specialty must resell the machine and recover damages based upon the resale price.

50. On March 11, Vizar Sales Corporation telegraphed Watson Company:

> "Will sell 1,000 cases of coffee for $28 a case for delivery at our place of business on April 15. You may pick them up at our loading platform."

Watson telegraphed its acceptance on March 12. On March 20, coffee prices rose to $30 a case. Vizar telegraphed Watson on March 21 that it repudiated the sale and would not make delivery. The telegram was received by Watson on March 22 when the price was $32; Watson could have covered at that price but chose not to do so. On April 15 the coffee was selling at $35 a case. Watson tendered $28,000 to Vizar and indicated it was ready to take delivery. Vizar refused to deliver. What relief, if any, is Watson entitled to?

a. Specific performance, because it made a valid tender of performance.
b. Nothing, because it failed to cover.
c. Damages of $4,000 (the difference between the contract price and the fair market value at the time Watson learned of the breach).
d. Damages of $7,000 (the difference between the contract price and the fair market value at the time delivery should have been made).

51. Draper Corporation, a retail merchant, was indebted to Cramer Corporation in the amount of $25,000 arising out of the sale of goods delivered to Draper on credit. Cramer and Draper signed a security agreement creating a security interest in certain collateral of Draper. The collateral was described in the security agreement as "the inventory of Draper Corporation, presently existing and thereafter acquired." This description of Draper's collateral

a. Is insufficient because it is too broad.
b. Is sufficient.
c. Must be more specific for the security interest to be perfected.
d. Is sufficient, but the security interest is valid only insofar as it is limited to Draper's presently existing inventory.

52. A filing requirement applies to which of the following transactions under Article 9 (Secured Transactions) of the Uniform Commercial Code?

a. The factoring of accounts receivable.
b. A collateralized bank loan, with securities serving as the collateral.

c. The transfer of an interest in an insurance policy to secure a loan.
d. The retention of title by a seller of land to secure payment under the terms of a land contract.

53. Johnstone Hardware Company sold a $450 drill press to Markum for use in his home workshop. Markum paid 20% initially and promised to pay the balance in monthly installments over a period of one year. Johnstone took a purchase money security interest in the drill press to secure payment. Markum promised not to sell or otherwise transfer the drill press without Johnstone's consent. Johnstone did not file a financing statement in connection with the transaction. Markum subsequently found himself hard pressed to make the payments and defaulted. He then sold the drill press to his neighbor Harper for $250 without disclosing Johnstone's interest and without Johnstone's consent. Under the circumstances

a. The security agreement need not be in writing and signed in order to be valid since the purchase price of the drill press is less than $500.
b. No one can obtain superior rights to the drill press in that transfer of the press was prohibited without Johnstone's consent.
c. Johnstone's security interest is perfected against the other creditors of Markum, but not against Harper.
d. Harper would take the drill press free of Johnstone's security interest even if Johnstone had filed.

54. Perfection of a security interest by a creditor provides added protection against other parties in the event the debtor does not pay his debts. Which of the following is **not** affected by perfection of a security interest?

a. A buyer in the ordinary course of business.
b. A subsequent personal injury judgment creditor.
c. The trustee in a bankruptcy proceeding.
d. Other prospective creditors of the debtor.

55. The Jolly Finance Company provides the financing for Triple J Appliance Company's inventory. As a part of its sales promotion and public relations campaign, Jolly Finance placed posters in Triple J's stores indicating that Triple J is another satisfied customer of Jolly and that the goods purchased at Triple J are available through the financing by Jolly. Jolly also files a financing statement which covers the financed inventory. Victor Restaurants purchased four hi-fi sets for use in its restaurants and had read one of the Jolly posters. Triple J has defaulted on its loan and Jolly Finance is seeking to repossess the hi-fi sets. Which of the following is correct?

a. Jolly has a perfected security interest in the hi-fi sets which is good against Victor.
b. Victor's knowledge of the financing arrangement between Jolly and Triple J does **not** affect its right to the hi-fi sets.
c. Jolly's filing was unnecessary to perfect its security interest in Triple J's inventory since it was perfected upon attachment.
d. The hi-fi sets are consumer goods in Victor's hands.

56. Donaldson, Inc., loaned Watson Enterprises $50,000 secured by a real estate mortgage which included the land, buildings, and "all other property which is added to the real property or which is considered as real property as a matter of law." Wilkins also loaned Watson $25,000 and obtained a security interest in all of Watson's "inventory, accounts receivable, fixtures, and other tangible personal property." Watson defaulted and there is insufficient property to fully satisfy the two creditors. There is some doubt as to the nature of certain property and Donaldson is attempting to include all the property under the terms and scope of its real property mortgage. What is the probable outcome for Donaldson?

a. Donaldson will prevail in that real property is preferred over personal property.
b. Assuming Donaldson was the first lender and duly filed its real property mortgage, Donaldson will prevail in respect to all property necessary to satisfy its $50,000 loan.
c. If the fixtures in question are detachable trade fixtures, Donaldson will not prevail in its attempt to include them.
d. The problem will be decided by taking all of Watson's property (real and personal) subject to the two secured creditors' claims and dividing it in proportion to the respective debts.

57. Maxwell purchased real property from Plumb and received a warranty deed at the closing. Maxwell neglected to record the deed. In this situation

a. A subsequent purchaser from Plumb will obtain a better title to the real property than Maxwell even if the subsequent purchaser is aware of Maxwell's prior purchase.
b. Maxwell must record his deed in order to perfect his rights against Plumb.

c. Recordation would provide constructive notice of Maxwell's rights to subsequent purchasers of the real property even though they do not have actual notice.
d. Maxwell lacks an insurable interest in the property and any fire insurance he obtains is void.

58. Recordation of a real property mortgage
a. Is required to validate the rights of the parties to the mortgage.
b. Will **not** be effective if improperly filed even if the party claiming superior title had actual notice of its existence.
c. Perfects the interest of the mortgagee against subsequent bona fide purchasers for value.
d. Must be filed in the recordation office where the mortgagee's principal place of business is located.

59. Which of the following is an **incorrect** statement regarding the insurable interest requirement as it applies to property insurance?
a. It is used to determine the amount of recovery to be awarded the insured.
b. It need **not** necessarily be present at the inception of the policy so long as it is present at the time of the loss.
c. One of its functions is to prevent recovery by those who have **no** economic interest in the property insured.
d. It can be waived by the parties so long as both are fully competent to contract.

60. The coinsurance feature of property insurance
a. Is fixed at a minimum of 80% by law.
b. Prevents the insured from insuring for a minimal amount and recovering in full for such losses.
c. Precludes the insured from insuring for less than the coinsurance percentage.
d. Is an additional refinement of the insurable interest requirement.

Number 2 (Estimated time — 15 to 20 minutes)

Part a. Grace Dawson was actively engaged in the promotion of a new corporation to be known as Multifashion Frocks, Inc. On January 3, 1978, she obtained written commitments for the purchase of shares totaling $600,000 from a group of 15 potential investors. She was also assured orally that she would be engaged as the president of the corporation upon the commencement of business. Helen Banks was the principal investor, having subscribed to $300,000 of the shares of Multifashion. Dawson immediately began work on the incorporation of Multifashion, made several contracts for and on its behalf, and made cash expenditures of $1,000 in accomplishing these goals. On February 15, 1978, Banks died and her estate has declined to honor the commitment to purchase the Multifashion shares. At the first shareholders' meeting on April 5, 1978, the day the corporation came into existence, the shareholders elected a board of directors. With shareholder approval, the board took the following actions:

1. Adopted some but not all of the contracts made by Dawson.
2. Authorized legal action, if necessary, against the Estate of Banks to enforce Banks' $300,000 commitment.
3. Declined to engage Dawson in any capacity (Banks had been her main supporter).
4. Agreed to pay Dawson $750 for those cash outlays which were deemed to be directly beneficial to the corporation and rejected the balance.

Required: Answer the following, setting forth reasons for any conclusions stated.

Discuss the legal implications of each of the above actions taken by the board of directors of Multifashion.

Part b. Boswell Realty Corporation, whose sole business is land development, purchased a large tract of land on which it intended to construct a high-rise apartment-house complex. In order to finance the construction, Boswell offered to sell $3,000,000 worth of shares in Boswell Realty to about 1,000 prospective investors located throughout the United States.

Required:

1. Discuss the implications of the Securities Act of 1933 to Boswell's offering to sell shares in the corporation.

2. The Securities Act of 1933 is considered a disclosure statute. Briefly describe the means provided and the principal types of information required to accomplish this objective of disclosure.

3. If an investor acquires shares of stock in Boswell Realty Corporation, is his interest real or personal property? Explain.

Number 3 (Estimated time —— 15 to 20 minutes)

Part a. Fennimore owned a ranch which was encumbered by a seven percent (7%) mortgage held by the Orange County Bank. As of July 31, 1980, the outstanding mortgage amount was $83,694. Fennimore decided to sell the ranch and engage in the grain storage business. During the time that he was negotiating the sale of the ranch, the bank sent out an offer to several mortgagors indicating a five percent (5%) discount on the mortgage if the mortgagors would pay the entire mortgage in cash or by certified check by July 31, 1980. The bank was doing this in order to liquidate older unprofitable mortgages which it had on the books. Anyone seeking to avail himself of the offer was required to present his payment at the Second Street branch on July 31, 1980. Fennimore, having obtained a buyer for his property, decided to take advantage of the offer since his buyer was arranging his own financing and was not interested in assuming the mortgage. Therefore, on July 15th he wrote the bank a letter which stated: "I accept your offer on my mortgage, see you on July 31, 1980, I"ll have a certified check." Fennimore did not indicate that he was selling the ranch and would have to pay off the full amount in any event. On July 28, the bank sent Fennimore a letter by certified mail which was received by Fennimore on the 30th of July which stated: "We withdraw our offer. We are over subscribed. Furthermore, we have learned that you are selling your property and the mortgage is not being assumed." Nevertheless, on July 31 at 9:05 in the morning when Fennimore walked in the door of the bank holding his certified check, Vogelspiel, a bank mortgage officer, approached him and stated firmly and clearly that the bank's offer had been revoked and that the bank would refuse to accept tender of payment. Dumbfounded by all this, Fennimore nevertheless tendered the check, which was refused.

Required:

Answer the following, setting forth reasons for any conclusions stated.

In the eventual lawsuit that ensued, who will prevail?

Part b. Austin wrote a letter and mailed it to Hernandez offering to sell Hernandez his tuna canning business for $125,000. Hernandez promptly mailed a reply acknowledging receipt of Austin's letter and expressing an interest in purchasing the cannery. However, Hernandez offered Austin only $110,000. Later Hernandez decided that the business was in fact worth at least the $125,000 that Austin was asking. He therefore decided to accept the original offer tendered to him at $125,000 and telegraphed Austin an unconditional acceptance at $125,000. The telegram reached Austin before Hernandez' prior letter, although the letter arrived later that day. Austin upon receipt of the telegram telegraphed Hernandez that as a result of further analysis as to the worth of the business, he was not willing to sell at less than $150,000. Hernandez claims a contract at $125,000 resulted from his telegram. Austin asserts either that there is no contract or that the purchase price is $150,000.

Required:

Answer the following, setting forth reasons for any conclusions stated.

If the dispute goes to court, who will prevail?

Number 4 (Estimated time —— 15 to 20 minutes)

Part a. Glasco Machinery and Manufacturing, Inc., sells industrial machinery to various customers on credit terms of 20% down and three-month promissory notes for the balance.

Glasco was experiencing severe financial difficulty and desperately needed a loan for working capital and to stave off persistent creditors. Its bank insisted upon security for any loan it might make. Glasco agreed to pledge $25,000 of its customer's promissory notes as collateral for a $20,000 demand loan. The notes pledged included some which Glasco knew had been received on sales of defective machinery and several notes which Glasco's president forged in anticipation of future shipments to customers.

After a short time Glasco's president saw that detection was inevitable, withdrew all funds in the bank, and absconded with the cash. The bank is seeking to enforce payment of the notes against the various parties.

Required: Answer the following, setting forth reasons for any conclusions stated.

Discuss the bank's rights, if any, to collection on the various promissory notes.

Part b. Grover had an $80 check payable to the order of Parker that Parker had indorsed in blank. The check was drawn by Madison on State Bank. Grover deftly raised the amount to $800 and cashed it at Friendly Check Cashing Company. Friendly promptly presented it at State Bank where it was dishonored as an overdraft. Grover has been apprehended by the police and is awaiting trial. He has no known assets. Friendly is seeking collection on the instrument against any or all of the other parties involved.

Required: Answer the following, setting forth reasons for any conclusions stated.

Will Friendly recover against Madison, State Bank, or Parker?

Part c. Horn Audio purchased some audio components from Samuels Sounds. The high quality audio components were to be used by Horn in its expensive customized sound systems to be sold to its customers. Samuels fraudulently substituted a large number of reconditioned audio components for the new ones that Horn was shown and believed he had purchased. In payment of the purchase, Horn executed and delivered the following instrument to Samuels:

> January 8, 1979
>
> For value received, Horn Audio promises to pay Three Thousand Dollars ($3,000.00) to the order of Samuels Sounds, two weeks after their receipt and out of the proceeds from the resale of the audio components this day purchased from Samuels Sounds and used as major components in the customized sound system sold to our customers.
>
> John Horn
> Horn Audio

Samuels transferred the instrument to Wilmont for value by signing it on the back and delivering it to him. Wilmont had no knowledge of the fraudulent substitution of the audio components by Samuels. Several months later, Wilmont presented the instrument to the maker for payment. Horn refused to pay the instrument alleging fraud and breach of warranty. Furthermore, Horn stated that all the audio components were returned to Samuels immediately upon discovery of the facts. Wilmont has commenced legal action against Horn on the instrument.

Required: Answer the following, setting forth reasons for any conclusions stated.

Will Wilmont prevail in his legal action against Horn on the instrument?

Number 5 (Estimated time —– 15 to 20 minutes)

Part a. You have been assigned by a CPA firm to work with the trustees of a large trust in the preparation of the first annual accounting to the court. The income beneficiaries and the remaindermen are in dispute as to the proper allocation of the following items on which the trust indenture is silent:

(1) Costs incurred in expanding the garage facilities of an apartment house owned by the trust and held for rental income.

(2) Real estate taxes on the apartment house.

(3) Cost of casualty insurance premiums on the apartment house.

(4) A two-for-one stock split of common stock held by the trust for investment.

(5) Insurance proceeds received as the result of a partial destruction of an office building which the trust owned and held for rental income.

(6) Costs incurred by the trust in the sale of a tract of land.

(7) Costs incurred to defend title to real property held by the trust.

Required:

1. Explain briefly the nature of a trust, the underlying concepts in the allocation between principal and income, and the importance of such allocations.

2. Indicate the allocations between principal and income to be made for each of the above items.

Part b. Albert Gideon, Jr., doing business as Albert's Boutique, ordered $480 of mini-skirts from Abaco Fashions. Abaco refused to make delivery, having had previous collection problems with Gideon. Albert's father, Slade Gideon, a prominent manufacturer, called Abaco and said, "Ship the goods my son needs, and I will pay for them." Abaco delivered the mini-skirts, and they were received by Albert's Boutique. Albert's Boutique is in bankruptcy, and Slade Gideon refuses to pay. You are the accountant for Abaco Fashions.

Required:

What are Abaco's rights against Slade Gideon? Explain.

Part c. Superior Construction Company, Inc., submitted the successful bid for the construction of your client's new factory. As part of the contract, Superior was required to obtain a performance bond from an acceptable surety company. Ace Surety, Inc., wrote the bond for the proposed building.

After the project was about one-third completed, Superior suggested several major changes in the contract. These included the expansion of the floor space by 10% and construction of an additional loading platform.

Required:

1. What problem does your client face if it agrees to the proposed changes? Explain.
2. What advice would you suggest in order to avoid this problem?

ANSWERS TO SAMPLE EXAMINATION

BUSINESS LAW

Answer 1

1. b	11. d	21. b	31. a	41. b	51. b
2. b	12. c	22. a	32. a	42. a	52. a
3. c	13. d	23. c	33. a	43. b	53. c
4. c	14. d	24. b	34. d	44. d	54. a
5. d	15. d	25. a	35. d	45. d	55. b
6. c	16. d	26. a	36. d	46. c	56. c
7. a	17. b	27. a	37. b	47. b	57. c
8. d	18. d	28. d	38. a	48. b	58. c
9. a	19. b	29. b	39. b	49. c	59. d
10. d	20. c	30. b	40. c	50. c	60. b

Answer 2

Part a.

In general, pre-incorporation contracts are not binding upon a newly created corporation prior to their adoption by its board of directors. Overall, one would conclude that the board acted properly and legally with respect to the actions taken. Each item is discussed separately below.

1. The board's action was proper and within its discretion. Care, however, should be taken to avoid an implied adoption by having the corporation avail itself of some or all of the benefits of a contract while purporting to reject the contract. The corporation is not legally bound prior to adoption, because it was not in existence at the time the contract was made. Dawson, on the other hand, has liability on the contracts she made prior to incorporation. Moreover, with respect to the contracts adopted by the corporation, she assumes the status of a surety unless a novation was entered into, releasing Dawson of all liability. The nonexistent principal rule would apply to Dawson unless the contract she made was contingent upon the corporation's adopting it after coming into existence.

2. An exception is made to the general rule of pre-incorporation actions insofar as stock subscriptions are concerned. Due to necessity and practical considerations, the parties who agree to provide the capital vital to the corporation's creation are not permitted to withdraw their commitments for six months. The Model Business Corporation Act provides that "a subscription for shares of a corporation to be organized shall be irrevocable for a period of six months, unless provided by the terms of the subscription agreement or unless all of the subscribers consent to the revocation of such subscriptions." Hence, the subscription by Banks is valid and is a bona fide claim against the Estate of Banks.

3. The board of a newly created corporation is, at its inception, free to either adopt or reject pre-incorporation contracts made on behalf of the corporation. This general rule also applies to the employment contract of a promoter such as Dawson. The rationale for this rule is founded upon the belief that the corporation should not be shackled by commitments that it did not have an opportunity to adequately consider. In addition, promoters as a class have often abused their power and made what have proved to be self-serving contracts. Thus, the board acted properly, and it need not engage Dawson.

4. The only problem that arises is that Dawson was not paid in full. She might be entitled to the full $1,000 under two possible theories. The first is a contract implied in fact (an implied adoption) by the board accepting all the benefits of the $1,000 expenditure. The other theory would be a contract implied in law based upon unjust enrichment. Under this theory, if Dawson can prove that the corporation did receive benefits which were worth $1,000, she can recover the additional $250.

Part b.

a. 1. The offering is subject to registration under the Securities Act of 1933. Despite the fact that the underlying property is real property, the shares represent the ownership in the corporation which in turn owns the real property. When these shares are offered for sale in interstate commerce (or by the use of instrumentalities of interstate commerce), the registration requirements of the Securities Act of 1933 must be met. These include filing a registration statement with the Securities and Exchange Commission (SEC) and giving a copy of the prospectus to each prospective purchaser of the registered securities.

2. The means of disclosure are the registration statement and the prospectus. The registration statement is filed with the SEC. The prospectus which contains much of the information included in the registration statement, must be furnished to prospective investors of the registered securities. Both documents must contain full and accurate disclosure of all relevant information relating to such things as the company's business, its officers and directors, its securities, its financial position and earnings, and details about the underwriting. With rare exception, all information in a registration statement is part of the public record and open to public inspection. Photocopies of part or all of a registration statement may be obtained from the SEC at nominal costs.

3. His interest is personal property, because the property held is the shares in the corporation. The shares represent ownership in the corporation which owns the underlying real property. The separate entity doctrine applies.

Answer 3

Part a.

Orange County Bank will prevail. The fact situation poses a classic illustration of a withdrawl of an offer to enter into a unilateral contract. The bank's offer to Fennimore called for the performance of an act (the actual paying of the mortgage), not a promise to pay it, as the means of acceptance. The language in the offer is clear and unambiguous, providing a 5 percent discount on a mortgage if the mortgagor would pay the entire mortgage in cash or by certified check by July 31, 1980, at the Second Street branch of the bank. Thus, the bank's letter was an offer to enter into a unilateral contract that required the performance of the act as the authorized and exclusive means of acceptance. Fennimore's promise to perform the act was ineffectual in creating a contract. Contract law generally provides that offers may be revoked at any time prior to acceptance; even if the bank revoked its offer the instant before the purported acceptance, it was a timely revocation and the acceptance was too late. The tender of performance would also be of no avail since notice of revocation had been received on the 30th.

In this situation, strict common law rules would deny the creation of a contract. Some states, in recognition of the hardship of such results, have adopted what is known as the *restatement of contracts* rule. This modification of the common law rule in respect to the unilateral contract rule holds that the unilateral promise in an offer calling for an act becomes binding as soon as part of the requested performance actually has been rendered or a proper tender of performance has been made. The courts have required substantial action on the part of the offeree, which does not appear to be present here.

The fact that Fennimore was selling his property and did not disclose the fact that he would have to pay the mortgage off in any event is immaterial. There was no material misrepresentation of fact made by him, hence his action was not fradulent nor did he misrepresent. He was silent. Additionally, the fact that the bank was using the sale as a reason for terminating the offer was immaterial.

Part b.

Hernandez will prevail. An offer is not effective until communicated to the offeree. The same rule applies to counteroffers including a change in the price, as occurred here. Therefore, a counteroffer is not effective until received by Austin, the original offeror. Hernandez's counteroffer does not destroy the offer until it is received. Thus, Hernandez's telegram, which accepted Austin's offer and arrived ahead of Hernandez's letter containing the counteroffer, is effective in creating a binding contract.

This rule applies even if Hernandez had mailed a letter that unequivocably accepted Austin's offer and that would have been effective upon dispatch. The general rule that an acceptance is effective when dispatched is subject to an exception that is designed to prevent entrapment of an offeror who is misled to his disadvantage by an offeree who attempts to take two inconsistent positions. Thus, when an offeree first rejects an offer, then subsequently accepts it, the subsequent acceptance will be considered effective upon dispatch by an authorized means only if it arrives prior to the offeror's receipt of the rejection. If the rejection arrives first, the original offeror may treat the attempted acceptance as a counteroffer which he is free to accept or not. Were this not the rule, an offeror who, upon receipt of a rejection, in good faith changed his position (that is, sold the goods to another customer), could find himself having sold the same goods twice.

Answer 4

Part a.

The first issue to be decided is whether the bank is a holder in due course, which would require that the notes in question be negotiable and that the bank be a holder. When a bank is involved, these requirements usually would be met. The next question is whether the bank took for value and, if so, to what extent. Section 3-303 of the Uniform Commercial Code provides that a holder takes for value to the extent that he acquires a security interest in or a lien on the instrument. A lender taking one or several negotiable instruments as security for a loan becomes a holder in due course to the extent of the amount loaned (and not the face amount as would a holder in due course who purchased notes at a discount). Thus, the bank will not be entitled to recover more than the amounts it advanced. However, this creates a problem based upon the facts in this situation—Does the bank qualify as a holder in due course collectively against all of the notes or is it limited to a collection of the amount loaned attributable to each note individually?

There are two assertable defenses—forgery and breach of contract and/or warranty. Additionally, there are a number of notes against which no defense is applicable. Forgery is a real defense and is valid even against a holder in due course. As to the forged notes, the bank will not be able to collect anything from the purported makers. Breach of contract, or breach of warranty is only a personal defense and not assertable against a holder in due course. Thus, the bank will recover against the makers of those notes, but the question is to what extent? If each note is considered individually, then the bank can only collect 80 percent on each. If, however, the notes are considered to secure the loan collectively, then the bank will obtain a recovery of the overall amount loaned. This could increase the percentage payable due to the uncollectibility of the forged notes.

Part b.

Grover materially altered the instrument within the meaning of Uniform Commercial Code Section 3-407, which provides that a holder in due course, such as Friendly, in all cases may enforce the instrument according to its original tenor. Thus, Friendly would be entitled to recover $80, the original tenor of the instrument, from Madison.

Friendly is entitled to nothing from State Bank. The bank rightfully dishonored the instrument, but even had it done so wrongfully, Friendly has no relationship to the bank and hence no right to recover from it.

Parker, as a transferor of the instrument by indorsement, gave certain implied warranties, including that the instrument had not been materially altered. This warranty is at the time of transfer and is not a warranty that the instrument will not be subsequently altered, as it was in this case. Although there would appear to be no recourse against Parker under the alteration warranty, in the event of dishonor by the maker, Parker is liable on the instrument according to its tenor ($80) at the time of indorsement.

There is one possibility for full recovery against Madison; Friendly must assert and prove that Madison was negligent in the way he drafted the instrument and thereby contributed to the alteration.

Part c.

No. The instrument is not negotiable. First, it is not payable at a definite time, and second, it is payable only out of the proceeds from the resale of the audio components. This is referred to as the "particular fund doctrine." Once there has been an initial determination that the instrument is non-negotiable, it does not matter that the remaining steps for qualification as a holder in due course have been met. The defense is clearly a personal defense, but because Wilmont is a mere transferee (assignee), he has no better rights than Samuels. In light of the facts, Wilmont has no right to recovery because the goods were properly returned by Horn, and thus Wilmont will not prevail against Horn.

Answer 5

a. 1. A trust generally involves a transfer of income-producing property (principal) by will, deed, or indenture to a trustee who takes legal title to the property subject to a fiduciary obligation to manage and conserve the property for the benefit of others who are described as beneficiaries. A trust generally provides that the trustee shall invest the trust principal and pay the income therefrom to the income beneficiary and at the termination of the trust transfer the trust principal to the remainderman. The property that composes the principal of the trust may change from time to time as the trustee sells and reinvests the proceeds.

The will or trust agreement can provide the rules for allocation of items between principal and income. In the absence of specific trust provisions, the law of the jurisdiction in which the trust is located will govern. For this purpose, most jurisdictions have adopted the Uniform Principal and Income Act or some variation thereof. Income produced by the investment and management of the trust principal is kept separate for distribution to the income beneficiary. However, ordinary operating expenses incurred by the trust in generating earnings are charged against income. Similarly, expenses incurred in acquiring or protecting the trustee's title to principal are charged against principal. Thus, the allocation between principal and income of a trust is of great importance because it affects the respective benefits derived from the trust by the income beneficiary and the remainderman.

2. (1) Principal
(2) Income
(3) Income
(4) Principal
(5) Principal
(6) Principal
(7) Principal

Part b.

Abaco can proceed successfully against Slade Gideon to collect the debt. Slade Gideon created a direct obligation to Abaco (a third-party beneficiary contract) by his statement, "Ship the goods my son needs and I will pay for them." The Statute of Frauds is not at issue because the debt is for less than $500. Were the Statute of Frauds at issue, it would have been satisfied by the shipment of the merchandise by Abaco and its receipt by Albert's Boutique.

Part c.

1. The suggested changes represent material alterations of the original construction contract. If the client agrees to the proposed changes, it faces the loss of the surety company's protection. Material alteration of the contract affords the surety a defense against recovery on its undertaking.

2. The client should either obtain a consent to the changes from the surety company in writing or reject the proposed changes.

MINI OUTLINES

To assist candidates in testing their memory of essential legal principles, we have developed a set of **Mini Outlines.** These can be used after studying each module in depth and as a final review immediately prior to the CPA exam. **In no way are these outlines intended to be a complete coverage of the subject matter.** Candidates should use them to jog their minds by recalling as much information as possible and constructing legal examples to test their comprehension of the subject matter. Using the outlines in this fashion will serve as a barometer (or self-diagnostic tool) of your knowledge. Finally, because the outlines contain only the essential legal principles, **the lettering and numbering of the several levels in the Mini Outlines do not correspond to that found in module outlines.** For those points in the Mini Outlines which you have forgotten, use the index to find the page(s) where that principle is discussed. However, if you are confused about a number of the principles, go back to the module and work through it again.

CONTRACTS (7) *

A. **Essential elements of contract****
   1. Offer and acceptance
      a. Offer
         1) Newspaper advertisement
         2) Termination of offer
            a) Death
            b) Insanity
            c) Illegality
            d) Destruction of subject matter
            e) Rejection
            f) Revocation
      b. Acceptance
         1) Mirror image
         2) Silence
         3) Time of acceptance
            a) Reasonable means rule
         4) Offeree must intend to accept
         5) Only offeree may accept
   2. Reality of consent
      a. Duress
      b. Fraud
      c. Undue influence
      d. Mistake
   3. Consideration
      a. Legal detriment
         1) Preexisting legal duty
         2) Illusory promise
      b. Bargained for element
      c. Past consideration
      d. Moral consideration
      e. Exceptions
         1) Promissory estoppel
         2) Promise to pay debt barred by Statute of Limitations
         3) UCC–modification of contract for sale of goods
   4. Capacity
      a. Minors
         1) Necessaries
         2) Contracts for personal property
         3) Contracts for real property
         4) Ratification may only occur after reaching majority age
      b. Incompetent persons
      c. Intoxicated persons
   5. Legality
      a. Illegal if contract violates public policy
      b. Illegal if contract violates a statute
   6. Compliance with Statute of Frauds
      a. Promise to pay debt of another
         1) Leading object exception
      b. An agreement made upon consideration of marriage
         1) Exception–mutual promises of marriage
      c. Sale of any interest in land
         1) Exception–part performance
      d. An agreement not capable of being performed within one year
      e. Sale of goods $500 or more
         1) Exceptions
            a) Written confirmation between merchants
            b) Substantial start on specially manufactured goods
            c) Admission in court
            d) Part or full performance
      f. The writing must be signed by the party to be charged
         1) Can combine two documents together to create sufficient writing

**Numbers in parentheses refer to Modules.*

***The mnemonic "COLLARS" may be useful in remembering the essential elements of a contract (Consideration, Offer, Legality, Legal capacity, Acceptance, Reality of consent, and Statute of Frauds).*

B. **Parol evidence rule**

C. **Assignment and delegation**
   1. Assignee receives no better rights than the assignor had

D. **Third-party beneficiary contracts**
   1. Creditor beneficiary
   2. Donee beneficiary
   3. Incidental beneficiary

E. **Discharge of contractual obligation**
   1. By performance
      a. Doctrine of substantial performance
   2. Objective impossibility
      a. Subjective impossibility
   3. Frustration of purpose
   4. Novation
   5. Accord and satisfaction
   6. Breach of contract by other party
      a. Anticipatory breach (repudiation)
   7. Occurrence or nonoccurrence of contractual condition
      a. Condition precedent
      b. Condition subsequent
      c. Condition concurrent
   8. Tender of performance
      a. Tender of payment of money merely stops interest running

F. **Remedies**
   1. Damages
      a. Compensatory
         1) Must be foreseeable
         2) Mitigation of damages
      b. Punitive
      c. Liquidated
   2. Specific performance
      a. Only available when item is unique
   3. Recision and restitution

SALES (8)

A. **Sale vs. bailment**

B. **Formation of sales contract**
   1. Firm offer rule
   2. Battle of forms
   3. Modification of preexisting contract for the sale of goods
   4. Sale of goods $500 or more must be in writing

C. **Identification of goods**
   1. Buyer's special property interest

D. **Risk of loss rules**
   1. Party with title does not necessarily have risk of loss
   2. Parties can allocate through provision in contract
   3. Breaching party has risk of loss
   4. Carriage contracts
      a. FOB point of shipment
      b. FOB point of destination
   5. Merchant seller transfers risk when goods are delivered to buyer
   6. Nonmerchant seller transfers risk when seller tenders goods
   7. Concerning goods evidence by negotiable document of title risk transfers upon proper negotiation of document
   8. In sale on approval (goods purchased for use) risk transfers when buyer approves goods
   9. In sale or return (goods purchased for resale) risk transfers when buyer takes possession

E. **Sale of goods by nonowner**
   1. Thief
   2. Entrusting situation (deceptive bailment)
   3. Seller has voidable title
   4. Seller has void title

F. **Product liability**
   1. Negligence
   2. Warranty liability
      a. Warranty of title
         1) Merchant seller warns against infringement of patent or trademark
      b. Express warranties
      c. Implied warranties
         1) Merchantability—granted by merchant seller
            a) Fit for ordinary purposes
            b) Properly packaged
         2) Fit for particular purpose
         3) Disclaimers
            a) Merchantability—can be oral or written but must contain some form of the word "merchantability"
            b) Fit for particular purpose—must be in writing but no need for specific language
            c) Goods sold "as is" or "with all faults" excludes both implied warranties but not the warranty of title

d) Offer of inspection by seller disclaims implied warranties concerning all patent defects
d. Magnuson–Moss Warranty Act
3. Strict liability
a. Defense—product was not used for intended purpose

G. Seller's rights and remedies for breach of contract

1. Seller's right to cure
2. Seller's monetary damages
a. Difference between market value at the time of tender and contract price plus incidental expenses
b. Lost profits plus incidental expenses
c. Full contract price
3. Seller may refuse to deliver goods unless insolvent buyer is willing to pay cash
4. Seller may stop goods in transit if buyer is insolvent
5. Seller may demand return of goods received by insolvent buyer if done within 10 days of delivery
6. Both buyer and seller have right to demand written assurances of performance

H. Buyer's rights and remedies for breach of contract

1. Right of cover
2. Right to reject nonconforming goods
a. Merchant must follow seller's reasonable instructions concerning rejected goods
3. Buyer may accept nonconforming goods
a. Buyer may revoke acceptance when
1) Defect was hidden
2) Guaranteed defect was to be cured and is not
4. Recover damages
a. Difference between market value at time buyer should have learned of breach and contract price plus incidental expenses plus consequential damages

I. Statute of Limitations is 4 years

1. Parties may reduce to 1 year by agreement

NEGOTIABLE INSTRUMENTS (9)

A. Types

1. Notes
2. Drafts
a. Checks—drawn on a bank and payable on demand
3. Certificates of deposit
4. Trade acceptances

B. Requirements of negotiability

1. Written and signed
2. Unconditional promise or order to pay sum certain
a. "Subject to" vs. "in accordance with" another agreement
b. Limiting payment to particular fund
c. Cost of collection does not destroy sum certain
d. Foreign currency okay
3. Payment at a definite time or on demand
a. Payable on death of someone not payable at definite time
4. Words of negotiability
5. Contain no other promise except a promise granting security for the instrument

C. Negotiation

1. Indorsement
a. Blank vs. special
b. Qualified
1. Destroys secondary (contractual) liability and alters warranty liability
c. Restrictive
2. Order paper—delivery and indorsement
3. Bearer paper—delivery only

D. Holder in due course

1. Must be a holder
2. Gives executed value
a. Discharge of prior debt
b. Taking as security for existing debt
3. Takes in good faith
4. Takes through proper negotiation prior to knowledge that instrument is overdue or that a defense exists concerning it

E. Shelter provision

F. Defenses

1. Real
a. Forgery
1) Fictitious payee
2) Imposter
b. Material alteration
c. Fraud in the execution
d. Minority
e. Illegality
f. Discharge in bankruptcy

g. Extreme duress
h. Mistake

2. Personal
   a. Misdelivery
   b. Unauthorized completion of an incomplete instrument
   c. Fraud and the inducement
   d. Duress
   e. Undue influence
   f. Breach of contract
   g. Lack of consideration

G. Liability of parties

1. Primary
   a. Acceptance by drawee
   b. Certification by bank
2. Secondary
   a. Presentment
   b. Dishonor
   c. Notice of dishonor
3. Warranties on transfer
4. Warranties on presentment

H. Banks

1. Relationship between banks and payee-holder
2. Stop payment orders

I. Negotiable document of title

1. Holder by due negotiation
   a. Value does not include discharge of existing debt

J. Investment securities

1. Article 8 of UCC
2. Bona fide purchase

SECURED TRANSACTIONS (10)

A. Types of collateral

1. Tangible personal property
   a. Consumer goods
   b. Equipment
   c. Inventory
   d. Farm products
2. Intangible personal property
   a. Accounts
3. Documentary collateral
   a. Instruments
   b. Documents of title
4. The use debtor makes of the property determines the type of collateral

B. Attachment of security interest

1. Three requirements necessary
   a. There is a security agreement
      1) When collateral possessed by debtor, security agreement must be in writing, signed by debtor, and contain reasonable description of collateral
      2) When possessed by secured party, security agreement may be oral
   b. Secured party gives value
   c. Debtor has rights in collateral

C. Perfection of security interest (3 methods)

1. Filing a financing statement
   a. Valid for all collateral except money and negotiable instruments
   b. Must be signed by debtor
2. Possession
   a. The only method available concerning perfection in money and negotiable instruments
3. By attachment only (automatic perfection)
   a. Only available for purchase money security interest in consumer goods
   b. Not available against good faith purchaser for value who purchases from consumer for consumer use

D. Other issues

1. After acquired property
2. Field warehousing
   a. Perfection by possession
3. Consignments
   a. True consignments
      1) File a financing statement
   b. Other consignments
      1) Look for secured transaction

E. Priorities

1. If both parties perfect by filing, then first to file has priority
2. If both do not perfect by filing, then first to perfect has priority
3. Perfected over unperfected
4. If both unperfected, first to attach
5. Purchase money security interest has priority over all other security interests if perfected within ten days of delivery except when collateral is inventory
6. Purchaser in ordinary course of business defeats prior perfected security interest

F. Remedies upon default

1. Secured party has right to take possession of collateral
   a. By self-help
   b. By judicial process

2. Secured party may sell collateral
   a. Sale may be public or private
   b. Must be handled in commercially reasonable manner
   c. Debtor can require sale under some conditions
3. If secured party retains collateral, entire obligation is discharged

BANKRUPTCY (11)

A. Alternatives to bankruptcy relief are sometimes available
1. Legal proceedings, judgment, levy, attachment, execution
   a. Recover fraudulently conveyed property
2. Assignment for the benefit of creditors—nonconsenting creditor unaffected
3. Receiverships
4. Creditors' composition agreements

B. Voluntary bankruptcy petition
1. Order of relief automatically given upon filing of voluntary petition
2. Exempt entities

C. Involuntary petition
1. Less than 12 creditors—one can file if owed $5,000 in excess of any security
2. 12 or more creditors—three must sign that are owed $5,000 in excess of security
3. Exempt entities
4. Order of relief automatically granted if debtor does not contest petition
5. If debtor contests, then creditors must show
   a. Debtor not paying debts as they become due, or
   b. During the 120 days preceding the filing a custodian was appointed or took possession of substantially all of the property of the debtor

D. Proceedings and parties
1. Always a federal proceeding
2. All actions by creditors against debtor are stayed by filing petition, at least temporarily
3. First creditors' meeting, notice, time, voting, election of trustee
4. Debtor's exempt property
   a. Federal exemptions
      1) State may prohibit selection of federal exemptions

E. Powers of trustee
1. Contest improper claims by creditors
2. Set aside improper transfers by debtor
   a. Preferences
      1) General
         a) Occurred within 90 days of filing petition
         b) Debtor's insolvency presumed
         c) Payment or granting of security interest concerning antecedent debt
      2) Insider preference
         a) Within one year of filing petition
         b) Debtor's insolvency is not presumed
   b. Fraudulent conveyances
      1) Transfer with intent to delay, hinder, or defraud creditors
      2) Transfer of property by debtor for less than reasonable value
      3) Occurred within one year of filing petition

F. Priority of claims

G. Nondischargeable debts

H. Acts that bar discharge of any debts

I. Reorganizations—Chapter 11
1. Can be voluntary or involuntary proceedings
2. Creditors' committee

J. Debt adjustment plans—Chapter 13
1. Only a voluntary proceeding is available

SURETYSHIP (12)

A. Surety is party who promises to be answerable for debt or default of another
1. Surety is primarily liable to creditor upon default of debtor
   a. Notice of debtor's default not necessary

B. Formation of surety contract
1. Must meet essential elements of a contract
   a. Consideration
      1) If surety's promise is contemporaneous with primary contract, separat[e] consideration not needed

b. Compliance with Statute of Frauds since promise to answer for debt of another
    1) Exception for "main purpose" rule
        a) When surety's promise is made for own benefit

C. Creditor's rights

1. Against debtor
    a. Where debtor owes more than one debt, to apply payment to debt of creditor's choice
        1) Unless debtor identifies the debt to which payment should apply
2. Against surety
    a. To proceed immediately against surety upon debtor's default
3. Against collateral
    a. If debtor pays, collateral must be returned
    b. Creditor may resort to collateral (held by surety or creditor) to satisfy debt
        1) If insufficient, may proceed against debtor or surety for deficiency
        2) If in excess of debt, excess amount must be returned to debtor
    c. Not required to resort to collateral
        1) May instead proceed immediately against surety

D. Surety's rights

1. Before surety pays creditor
    a. Exoneration
2. After surety pays creditor
    a. Right of reimbursement
    b. Subrogation to creditor's rights

E. Surety's defenses

1. Contractual defenses derived from debtor against creditor
    a. Except debtor's personal defenses
        1) Death or insolvency of debtor
        2) Lack of capacity of debtor
2. Surety's own contractual defenses such as fraud, duress, set-offs, etc.
3. Acts of creditor materially affecting surety's performance
    a. Release of debtor
    b. Release of surety
    c. Release or impairment of collateral held by creditor
        1) Surety's liability reduced only to extent of collateral released or impaired
    d. Tender of performance and refusal by creditor
    e. Binding material alteration or variance of suretyship agreement without consent of surety
        1) Substitution of debtors
        2) Changes in debtor's duties
        3) Variance in amount, place, or time of debtor's payment

F. Following are not defenses of surety

1. Death of debtor
2. Insolvency of debtor
3. Lack of notice given to surety
    a. Unless conditional guarantor
4. Creditor does not resort to collateral

G. Co-sureties

1. When more than one surety promises to answer for the debt of another, each surety
    a. Bound to answer for same debt
    b. Shares in burden upon debtor's default
2. Co-sureties are jointly and severally liable
3. Each surety is liable for its proportionate share
4. Co-sureties entitled to share in collateral pledged
    a. In proportion to each's liability
5. Right of contribution exists among co-sureties
6. Discharge or release of one co-surety
    a. Releases remaining co-sureties to extent of the released surety's pro rata share of liability

H. Surety bonds

1. Acknowledgement of obligation to make good a duty or performance of another

AGENCY (13)

A. Agent vs. independent contractor

1. Employee (servant)
2. Subagent

B. Types of agent

1. General
2. Special
3. Del credere

C. Creation

1. By agreement
2. Estoppel
3. Ratification

D. Contractual liability

1. Principal is liable for contracts agent enters into within agent's scope of authority

a. Express authority
b. Implied authority
c. Apparent authority
2. Agent's liability on contracts entered into on behalf of principal
a. If within scope of authority and
1) Representing disclosed principal, agent is not liable on contract
2) Representing undisclosed principal, agent is liable
b. If acting outside scope of authority, then agent is only party liable on contract

E. Tort liability
1. Principal is liable if agent commits tort within agent's scope of employment
2. Agent is also liable for commission of torts

F. Termination of relationship
1. The power vs. the right to terminate
a. Agency coupled with an interest
2. By operation of law
a. Death or insanity of either party
b. Bankruptcy of principal
c. Subject of agreement becomes illegal
3. By acts of the parties
a. Unilateral action by either agent or principal
b. By mutual consent
c. Expiration of agreement
d. Principal must give notice of the termination
1) Notice by publication to all who knew of the relationship but had not dealt with agent
2) Actual notice to all who had previously dealt with agent

PARTNERSHIP LAW (14)

A. General partnership
1. Characteristics
a. Normally not a separate entity from general partners
b. Common law allows formation; no need for statutory authorization
c. Easy to create
d. Partners have unlimited liability
2. Creation
a. By agreement
b. By estoppel
c. Is presumed if parties are sharing net profits
3. Partnership property
a. Owned by partners as tenants in partnership
1) Surviving partners have right to specific partnership property
2) Heirs of deceased partner have no claim to specific partnership property
4. Partner's partnership interest
a. Is considered personal property
b. Can be assigned without consent of other partners
1) Does not cause dissolution
2) Assignee is not a substitute partner
3) Assignee receives assigning partner's share of profits
5. Partner's rights
a. To share in profits
b. To equal voice in management
1) Ordinary decisions by majority vote
2) Unanimous consent needed for certain acts
c. To inspect books
d. To return of capital contribution
e. No right to salary
f. No right to interest on capital contribution
6. Liability to third parties
a. Partners are agents of copartners
1) Partners are jointly and severally liable for torts committed by copartners within scope of partnership business
2) Partners are jointly liable for contracts entered into within copartners' authority
7. Termination
a. Dissolution occurs every time makeup of partnership changes
1) Admission of new partners
a) New partner only liable to extent of capital contribution concerning existing partnership debts
2) Withdrawal of partner
a) Withdrawing partner must give notice of withdrawal to terminate further liability
b) Priorities upon winding up
1) Creditors
2) To partners for loans

3) To partners for capital contribution
4) To partners for share of profits

b. Marshalling of assets

B. Limited partnerships
1. Need state statutory authority to create
2. Must have at least one general partner
3. Limited partner's liability is limited to capital contribution
4. Limited partner cannot take part in management
5. Limited partner's name may not be used in name of firm
6. Limited partner has right to an accounting
7. Limited partner has right to inspect books
8. Priorities on dissolution

C. Joint ventures
1. Characteristics
   a. Association of two or more persons for single business undertaking
   b. Unlike partnership which is formed to conduct ongoing business
   c. Corporations can be joint venturers
2. Each joint venturer has limited power to bind others
3. Rights, duties, and liabilities
   a. Fiduciary duty
   b. Right to participate in management
   c. Unlimited liability
   d. Liability for negligence
   e. Tax treatment similar to partnership

CORPORATIONS (15)

A. Types
1. De jure
2. De facto
3. Domestic
4. Foreign
   a. Doing business outside state of incorporation requires permission from foreign state

B. Characteristics
1. Separate entity
   a. Shareholders have limited liability
   b. Piercing corporate veil
2. Must have state statutory authorization to create
3. Duration may be perpetual
4. Expensive to create

C. Creation
1. Promoters
   a. Corporations must adopt promoter's contracts before being liable
   b. Promoter remains liable even after adoption of contracts by corporation
2. Preincorporation stock subscriptions
   a. Subscribers unable to revoke for six months
3. Articles of incorporation

D. Types of shares
1. Treasury stock—may be sold at less than par value
2. Watered stock

E. Directors
1. Must act as a board
2. Unable to vote by proxy
3. No right to salary for services
4. Individual director is not agent of corporation
5. Declaration of dividends within directors' discretion
   a. Declaration of dividends is illegal if impairs capital
      1) Payable out of surplus only
6. Liable for negligence but not for bad business judgment
7. Directors may contract with corporation

F. Officers
1. Agents of corporation
2. Indemnification of officers for expenses incurred in legal actions arising from officers' representation of corporation

G. Shareholders
1. Right to transfer shares
2. Preemptive rights
3. Right to vote
   a. By proxy
   b. On amendments of articles of incorporation but not necessarily amendments of the bylaws
   c. For election of directors
   d. On fundamental changes (mergers, consolidations)
   e. Voting trusts

4. Engage in derivative lawsuit
5. Right to inspect corporate books
6. Right to fair market value of shares from corporation if fundamental change is proposed

H. Corporate powers

1. Corporation may become partner
2. Corporation may lend money to employees but not to directors without shareholder approval
3. Corporation may not act as accommodating endorser
4. Corporation may only act as a surety if engaged in such business
5. Ultra vires contracts

I. Fundamental changes

1. Mergers
2. Consolidations
3. Must have majority shareholder approval

J. Dissolution

ANTITRUST AND GOVERNMENT REGULATION (16)

(This module was deleted because the AICPA has discontinued coverage effective May 1986.)

FEDERAL SECURITIES REGULATIONS (17)

(See note at Module 17 for material herein not tested after November 1985 Examination.)

A. Blue Sky Laws—State Security Laws

B. 1933 Act

1. Registration statement and prospectus must be approved by SEC before offer to sell or sale of a security in interstate commerce
   a. Security includes:
      1) Stocks
      2) Bonds
      3) Limited partnership interest
      4) Investment contracts where profits are to come from the efforts of others
         a) Shares in a citrus growing farm
         b) Shares in a cattle raising ranch
   b. Applies primarily to original issues of securities
   c. Purpose of Act
      1) To allow investor to make informed investment decision
      2) Not to tell investor that security is a good buy
   d. Exempt securities
      1) Banks
      2) Railroads
      3) Commercial paper—with a maturity of nine months or less
      4) Charitable organizations
      5) Insurance contracts
      6) Intrastate issues
      7) Small issuances up to 1,500,000
         a) Notification of filing is requir
   e. Exempt transactions
      1) Stock split
      2) Stock dividend
      3) Sales by person other than issuer, underwriter, or dealer
         a) Controlling person must register sale, e.g., director owning 10% of stock
      4) Regulation D—private placement of stock
         a) Purchasers must buy for investment purposes
   f. Registration statement
      1) Signers, directors of issuer, underwriters, and experts are liable for omission or misrepresentation
         a) Investor does not have to prove reliance on misrepresentation
         b) CPA has burden of proving due diligence defense
   g. Sanctions
      1) Civil
      2) Criminal
      3) Administrative
      4) Treble damages not available

h. Statute of limitations—one year from the time the misrepresentation should have been discovered but never longer than three years from the sale of the security

C. 1934 Act

1. Reporting requirements
2. Short-swing profits by insiders
3. Proxy solicitations
4. Tender offers for more than 5% of the shares
5. Anti-fraud provisions
6. Remedies
   a. Civil
   b. Criminal
   c. Administrative
   d. Treble damages not available

D. Foreign Corrupt Practices Act

1. Prohibits offers to bribe foreign officials
   a. Applies to all U.S. companies involved in interstate commerce
2. Accounting requirements
   a. Applies only to companies required to register under 1934 Act
3. Sanctions—fines and imprisonment

ACCOUNTANT'S LEGAL LIABILITY (18)

A. Common law liability to clients

1. Liability for breach of contract
   a. Based on accountant's failure to carry out contract terms
      1) Accountant's duty to perform cannot be delegated
      2) Client must not interfere with accountant's performance
      3) If major breach, accountant not entitled to compensation
   b. Accountant not under duty to discover fraud or irregularities
      1) Unless accountant's negligence prevents discovery
      2) Unless engaged in special purpose defalcation audit and lack of reasonable professional care prevents discovery
2. Liability for negligence
   a. Based on accountant's failure to exercise due professional care
      1) Following GAAS and GAAP does not conclusively prove absence of negligence
   b. Client is contributorily negligent if client restricted accountant's investigation
      1) May limit accountant's liability
3. Liability for fraud
   a. Actual fraud
      1) Intentional act or omission designed to deceive
   b. Constructive fraud
      1) Gross negligence with reckless disregard for truth

B. Common law liability to third parties

1. Accountant is liable to
   a. Third-party primary beneficiary for ordinary negligence
   b. Foreseen third party-courts are split
   c. All third parties for fraud or gross negligence
2. Third party must prove
   a. Material misstatement or omission on financial statements
   b. Reliance on financial statements
   c. Damages resulted from such reliance

C. Statutory liability to third parties—Securities Act of 1933

1. Act requires filing of certified financial statements with SEC
2. Any purchaser of security may sue accountant
3. Purchaser establishes prima facie case if s/he proves
   a. Material misstatement or omission on financial statements
   b. Damages were incurred
      1) Measured by difference between purchase price and market value at time of suit
   c. Need not prove reliance on financial statements
4. Accountant may avoid liability by proving
   a. Due diligence
      1) After reasonable investigation accountant had reasonable grounds to believe statements were true
   b. Purchaser knew financial statements were incorrect when s/he bought stock
   c. Loss caused by factor other than misstatement or omission on financial statements

D. Statutory liability to third parties—Securities Exchange Act of 1934
1. Accountant's liability arises from annual report containing certified financial statements
2. Any purchaser or seller of registered security may sue accountant
3. Third party must prove
   a. Material misstatement or omission on financial statements
   b. Accountant's intent to deceive (scienter)
   c. Reliance on financial statements
   d. Damages resulted from such reliance
4. Accountant may avoid liability if s/he acted in good faith

E. Criminal liability
1. Guilty of "willful and knowing" violation
   a. Federal statutes
      1) Securities Act of 1933
      2) Securities Exchange Act of 1934
      3) Internal Revenue Code
   b. State statutes

F. Other potential liability of accountant from
1. Discovery of subsequent events

G. Privileged communications
1. Preserves confidentiality of communications between accountant and client
2. Does not exist at common law
   a. Must be created by statute
3. Privilege protects accountant from being required to testify in court

H. Working papers
1. Owned by accountant
2. Must be kept confidential
3. Must relinquish on an enforceable subpoena

I. Preparation of income tax returns
1. Federal law applies to all compensated preparers

EMPLOYER—EMPLOYEE RELATIONSHIPS (19)

A. Federal Social Security Act
1. Provides financing for several social insurance programs
   a. Old-age, survivor's, and disability coverage
   b. Hospital insurance coverage (Medicare)
   c. Unemployment insurance coverage
2. Coverage under the Act is mandatory
   a. Must be an employee
   b. Compensation received must be wages
3. Federal Insurance Contributions Act
   a. Imposes social security tax on wages
   b. Imposes an equal tax rate on both employee and employer
4. Self-Employment Contributions Act
   a. Imposes social security tax on self-employment income
   b. A higher tax rate is imposed than under FICA
5. Unemployment insurance
   a. Employer must pay both federal and state unemployment tax
   b. Employer entitled to credit against federal tax for state tax paid
6. Benefits under the Act
   a. Availability depends upon attainment of insured status
      1) Determined by "quarters of coverage" obtained
   b. Amount depends upon
      1) Average monthly earnings
      2) Relationship of beneficiary to employee
7. Income tax considerations
   a. Benefits received are tax-free
      1) Excludable from gross income
   b. Employee's portion of social security tax is nondeductible from gross income
   c. Employer's portion of social security tax is deductible from gross income

B. Worker's Compensation Acts
1. Employer liable for injuries sustained by employee which arise in the course of employment
2. Employer assumes liability in exchange for employee's forfeiture of right to sue employer for damages
3. Removes employer's common law defenses
   a. Assumption of risk
   b. Fellow servant doctrine
   c. Contributory negligence
4. Employee is entitled to benefits without regard to fault
   a. Employee's negligence or gross negligence does not bar recovery

PROPERTY (20)

A. **Fixtures**
   1. Trade fixtures

B. **Present interest in real property**
   1. Fee simple
   2. Life estate

C. **Future interest**
   1. Remainder
   2. Reversion

D. **Concurrent ownership interest**
   1. Joint tenancy—right of survivorship
   2. Tenancy in common—deceased tenant's share passes by his/her estate

E. **Sale of land**
   1. Contract
      a. Must be in writing
      b. Buyer is entitled to marketable title.
      c. Buyer has risk of loss before deed is transferred
      d. Does not transfer title to buyer
      e. Specific performance is possible remedy for breach
   2. Deeds
      a. Warranty—make various guarantees, e.g., title, quiet enjoyment, etc.
      b. Bargain and sale
      c. Quitclaim
      d. Must be delivered before title passes to buyer
      e. Recording protects buyer against subsequent good faith purchasers
   3. Mortgages
      a. Must be in writing
      b. Recording protects mortgagee against subsequent purchasers
      c. Mortgagee's foreclosure rights upon default
      d. Equity of redemption
      e. Buyer who "assumes" mortgage has personal liability
      f. Buyer who purchases "subject to" mortgage has no personal liability
   4. Deeds of trust
      a. Like mortgages, but a judicial proceeding can be avoided upon default
      b. No redemption by mortgagor
   5. Land installment contract sales
      a. Allows seller to keep money paid and property upon default unless inequitable

F. **Title Insurance**
   1. Insures against loss due to defect of good title
   2. Title insurance company liable for damages due to title defects

G. **Adverse possession**
   1. Requirements
      a. Open
      b. Notorious
      c. Hostile
      d. Actual

H. **Lessor-lessee**
   1. Lease may be oral if less than one year
   2. Various types of leaseholds, e.g., period to period, lease for years
   3. Lessor's rights and duties
   4. Lessee's right to assign sublease

INSURANCE (21)

A. **Insurance contract**
   1. Offer and acceptance
   2. Representations
      a. Statements of fact not included as part of policy
      b. Only affect policy when material misrepresentation occurs
   3. Warranties
      a. Statements of fact included in the policy
      b. Even immaterial breaches of warranty release insurer from liability
   4. Statute of Frauds does not require writing

B. **Property insurance**
   1. Insurable interest
      a. Must be present at time of loss
      b. Following have insurable interest in property:
         1) Owners
         2) Partners
         3) Secured creditors
         4) Lessees
         5) Mortgagees
         6) Bailees
         7) Identification of goods gives buyer insurable interest

2. Valued or unvalued policy
3. Can insure against
   a. Own negligence
   b. Other party's negligence
   c. Other party's intentional acts
   d. But not against own intentional acts
   e. Hostile fires
   f. But not friendly fires
4. Coinsurance clause
   a. Know—usually tested
   b. Does not apply when there is total destruction of property
5. Pro rata clause
6. Loss payable clause
7. Insurer's right of subrogation

TRUSTS AND ESTATES (22)

A. Administration of an estate
1. Testate—will is present
2. Intestate—property passes by intestate succession statutes
3. Executor and administrator
   a. Right to compensation
   b. Duties and liabilities
4. Spouse's rights under dower and statutory share
5. Creditors' rights concerning decedent's estate
6. Tax considerations—particularly marital deduction

B. Trust
1. Creation
   a. By implication
      1) Resulting trust
      2) Constructive trust
   b. By express intent
2. Parties
   a. Trustee
      1) Occupies fiduciary relationship
      2) Has legal title to property
      3) Duties and liabilities
         a) Reasonable prudent investor standard applied to performance of the trustee
   b. Beneficiary—has beneficial title
      1) Income
      2) Principal
3. Types of trust
   a. Inter vivos
   b. Testamentary
   c. Charitable
   d. Constructive trust
4. Allocation of expenses and receipts to income and principal beneficiaries—very important—know
5. Tax considerations

C. Real Estate Investment Trusts
1. Must comply with SEC securities registration laws
2. Tax considerations

ABBREVIATIONS

AICPA	American Institute of CPAs
BFP	Bona Fide Purchaser
CIF	Cost, Insurance, and Freight
CPA	Certified Public Accountant
FAS	Free Along Side
FICA	Federal Insurance Contribution Act
FMV	Fair Market Value
FOB	Free on Board
FUTA	Federal Unemployment Tax Act
GAAP	Generally Accepted Accounting Principles
GAAS	Generally Accepted Auditing Standards
HDC	Holder in Due Course
REITs	Real Estate Investment Trusts
SEC	Securities and Exchange Commission
UCC	Uniform Commercial Code
ULPA	Uniform Limited Partnership Act
UPA	Uniform Partnership Act

A

B

C

Q

R

S

OTHER ACCOUNTING TEXTBOOKS FROM JOHN WILEY & SONS

Arpan and Radebaugh: INTERNATIONAL ACCOUNTING AND MULTINATIONAL ENTERPRISES, 2nd edition
Burch and Sardinas: COMPUTER CONTROL AND AUDIT
Burch and Grudnitski: INFORMATION SYSTEMS: THEORY AND PRACTICE, 4th edition
DeCoster and Schafer: MANAGEMENT ACCOUNTING: A DECISION EMPHASIS, 3rd edition
Defliese, Jaenicke, Sullivan, and Gnospelius: MONTGOMERY'S AUDITING, 10th edition; college version
Gaffney, Skadden, Wheeler, Laverty, Outslay, and Gaffney: WILEY'S FEDERAL INCOME TAXATION, annual edition
Guy and Carmichael: AN INTRODUCTION TO STATISTICAL SAMPLING IN AUDITING, 2nd edition
Haried, Imdieke, and Smith: ADVANCED ACCOUNTING, 3rd edition
Helmkamp, Imdieke, and Smith: PRINCIPLES OF ACCOUNTING, 2nd edition
Kell, Boynton, and Ziegler: MODERN AUDITING, 3rd edition
Kieso and Weygandt: INTERMEDIATE ACCOUNTING, 5th edition
Laughlin: FINANCIAL ACCOUNTING
McCullers and Schroeder: ACCOUNTING THEORY, 2nd edition
Moscove and Simkin: ACCOUNTING INFORMATION SYSTEMS, 2nd edition
Ramanathan: MANAGEMENT AND CONTROL IN NONPROFIT ORGANIZATIONS: TEXT AND CASES
Ramanathan and Hegstad: READINGS IN MANAGEMENT CONTROL IN NONPROFIT ORGANIZATIONS
Romney, Cherrington, and Hansen: CASEBOOK IN ACCOUNTING INFORMATION SYSTEMS
Sardinas, Burch, and Asebrook: EDP AUDITING: A PRIMER
Taylor and Glezen: AUDITING: Integrated Concepts and Procedures, 3rd edition
Taylor and Glezen: CASE STUDY IN AUDITING, 3rd edition
Tricker and Boland: MANAGEMENT INFORMATION AND CONTROL SYSTEMS, 2nd edition
Wilkinson: ACCOUNTING AND INFORMATION SYSTEMS, 2nd edition

BUSINESS LAW TEXTBOOKS FROM JOHN WILEY AND SONS

Atteberry, Pearson, and Litka: REAL ESTATE LAW, 3rd edition
Cataldo, Kempin, Stockton, and Weber: INTRODUCTION TO LAW AND THE LEGAL PROCESS, 3rd edition
Collins, Cihon, Donnelly, Hartzler, Karp, Naffziger, and Wolfe: BUSINESS LAW – TEXT AND CASES
Deaver: THE COMPLETE LAW SCHOOL COMPANION
Delaney and Gleim: CPA REVIEW: BUSINESS LAW
Dunfee and Gibson: AN INTRODUCTION TO GOVERNMENT AND BUSINESS, 3rd edition
Dunfee and Gibson: AN INTRODUCTION TO CONTRACTS, 2nd edition
Dunfee and Gibson: ANTITRUST AND TRADE REGULATION: CASES AND MATERIALS, 2nd edition
Gleim and Delaney: CPA EXAMINATION REVIEW: VOLUME I OUTLINES AND STUDY GUIDES
Gleim and Delaney: CPA EXAMINATION REVIEW: VOLUME II PROBLEMS AND SOLUTIONS
Griffith: THE LEGAL ENVIRONMENT OF BUSINESS
Henszey and Friedman: REAL ESTATE LAW, 2nd edition
Inman: THE REGULATORY ENVIRONMENT OF BUSINESS
Litka and Inman: THE LEGAL ENVIRONMENT OF BUSINESS, 3rd edition
Litka and Jennings: BUSINESS LAW, 3rd edition
Rothenberg and Blumenkrantz: PERSONAL LAW
Wolfe and Naffziger: THE LAW OF AMERICAN BUSINESS ASSOCIATIONS: AN ENVIRONMENTAL APPROACH

ORDER INFORMATION FOR ACCOUNTING RELATED TITLES

☐ INTERMEDIATE ACCOUNTING, 5th edition by Donald E. Kieso and Jerry J. Weygandt
(0 471 88716 1) 1986 1297 pp. $34.95

☐ ADVANCED ACCOUNTING, 3rd edition by Andrew A. Haried, Leroy F. Imdieke, and Ralph E. Smith
(0 471 88009 4) 1985 912 pp. $36.95

☐ MODERN AUDITING, 3rd edition by Walter G. Kell, William C. Boynton, and Richard E. Ziegler
(0 471 81919 0) 1986 706 pp. $30.95

☐ AUDITING, 3rd edition by Donald H. Taylor and G. William Glezen
(0 471 88721 8) 1985 931 pp. $34.95

☐ MONTGOMERY'S AUDITING, 10th edition, College Version, by Philip L. Defliese, Henry R. Jaenicke, Jerry D. Sullivan, and Richard A. Gnospelius
(0 471 07756 9) 1984 1275 pp. $36.95

☐ AN INTRODUCTION TO STATISTICAL SAMPLING IN AUDITING, 2nd edition by Dan M. Guy and Douglas R. Carmichael
(0 471 81540 3) 1986 229 pp. $21.95

☐ INFORMATION SYSTEMS: THEORY AND PRACTICE, 4th edition by John G. Burch and Gary Grudnitski
(0 471 83758 X) 1986 656 pp. $31.95

☐ ACCOUNTING INFORMATION SYSTEMS: CONCEPTS AND PRACTICE FOR EFFECTIVE DECISION MAKING, 2nd edition by Stephen A. Moscove and Mark G. Simkin
(0 471 88354 9) 1984 800 pp. $35.45

☐ ACCOUNTING AND INFORMATION SYSTEMS, 2nd edition by Joseph W. Wilkinson
(0 471 81292 7) 1986 845 pp. $33.95

☐ BUSINESS LAW: TEXT AND CASES by Collins, Cihon, Donnelly, Hartzler, Karp, Naffziger, and Wolfe
(0 471 04075 4) 1986 1040 pp. $29.95

For prompt service check with your local bookstore, or remove and complete this form and return it to John Wiley and Sons, Inc., One Wiley Drive, Somerset, NJ 08873, or call our hotline at (815)756-8486.

Full credit is guaranteed, if not satisfied, when books are returned within 30 days in saleable condition. We normally ship within ten days. If payment accompanies order and shipment cannot be made within 90 days, full payment will be refunded. Complete the following information and mail it (**by envelope if sending check**) to the address above.

☐ Check Enclosed ☐ Bill Me ☐ Charge to my Credit Card

Charge Card Expiration Date

Credit Card No. (All Digits Please)

Mastercard ☐ Visa ☐ American Express ☐

signature

Note:

1. If ordering by credit card, list complete card number, expiration date and sign order with full signature. Mastercard, Visa, and American Express honored.
2. If your order totals $126.00 or more, please attach a company purchase order or enclose 25% partial payment.
3. **Proprietary Schools Note:** To expedite orders at time of need, if you do not already have an account established at Wiley, contact in advance, **Marvin Willig, Credit Manager, John Wiley and Sons, Inc., One Wiley Drive, Somerset, NJ 08873.** Provide bank name and three credit references.

BILL TO ______	SHIP TO ______
ADDRESS ______	ADDRESS ______
CITY ______	CITY ______
STATE ______ ZIP ______	STATE ______ ZIP ______

For details regarding future issues and advance purchase plans write or call CPA Examination Review, P.O. Box 886, DeKalb, Illinois 60115, (815) 756-8486.

PRICES SUBJECT TO CHANGE WITHOUT NOTICE

081-5-1107

Fold here

Cut Here

BUSINESS REPLY MAIL

FIRST CLASS PERMIT NO. 2277 NEW YORK, N.Y.

POSTAGE WILL BE PAID BY

JOHN WILEY & SONS, INC.
1 Wiley Drive
Somerset, N.J. 08873

Staple or tape closed

Feedback to Authors

We invite your suggestions, corrections, typographical errors, etc. Please send these to Patrick R. Delaney, c/o CPA Examination Review, P.O. Box 886, DeKalb, Illinois 60115 before August 1, 1986 for inclusion in the 1987 Edition.

1.

2.

3.

4.

5.

6.

7.

8.

9.

10.

11.

12.

13.

14.

15.

FORMAT OPTIONS AND FEATURES OF CPA EXAMINATION REVIEW

FORMAT OPTIONS

Publication date and format / *Contents*	*June* *Volumes* *I*	*II*	*December* *Auditing*	*Business Law*	*Theory and Practice*
Outlines and Study Guides	X		X	X	X
Problems and Solutions		X	X	X	X

FEATURES

OUTLINES AND STUDY GUIDES

- Coverage of all four sections of the CPA examination.
- Structured point-by-point coverage of all accounting, auditing, and business law material tested on the exam.
- Comprehensive guidance on establishing and following a self-study preparation program.
- Study programs for each of the 44 modules (self-contained, manageable study units).
- Outline format, type styles and spacing designed to facilitate readability.
- Outlines supplemented by brief examples and illustrations.
- Clear and concise phraseology to help candidates understand and remember the material.
- Detailed outlines of AICPA and FASB pronouncements.
- Frequency analysis of the content of the last nine exams using the *AICPA's Content Specification Outlines for the Uniform Certified Public Accountant Examination* as the basis for our classification.
- An in-depth analysis of the AICPA examination grading and "grader orientation."
- Explanation and step-by-step examples of the "solutions approach."
- Up-to-date coverage (including authoritative pronouncements and changes in law through date indicated below).

Volume I	*Three Part Set*
May 15	November 15

PROBLEMS AND SOLUTIONS

- Carefully selected problem material from all four sections of the examination plus several problems from the CIA and CMA exams.
- Over 1,950 multiple choice questions (including all 300 from the latest exam as indicated below).

Volume II	*Three Part Set*
May exam	November exam

- Over 180 essay questions and practice problems (majority from most recent exams).
- AICPA Unofficial Answers for all questions and problems.
- One-paragraph explanations (stating why the alternative answers are right or wrong) for each of the multiple choice answers.
- Outlines of the Unofficial Answer for each essay question.
- Explanations of how to solve each of the practice problems, i.e., the "solutions approach."
- Unofficial Answers updated to reflect current tax laws, FASB pronouncements, etc. (in explanations of unofficial answers and solutions guides).
- Multiple choice questions are grouped into topical categories within each module in the same sequence as the topics appear in the outlines/text. In the answer explanations to the multiple choice questions, headings appear which can be used as cross-references to the corresponding topic in the outlines/text.
- A complete "Sample Examination" for each of the four parts of the exam.